It's a Crime

It's a Crime
Women and Justice

Third Edition

❖

ROSLYN MURASKIN
Long Island University

Prentice Hall

Upper Saddle River, NJ 07458

Library of Congress Cataloging-in-Publication Data

It's a crime : women and justice / [edited by] Roslyn Muraskin.--3rd ed.
   p. cm.
  Includes bibliographical references and index.
  ISBN 0-13-048200-5
   1. Female offenders. 2. Women criminal justice personnel. I. Muraskin, Roslyn.

HV6046.I86 2002
364.3'74'0973--dc21   2002021130

Publisher: Jeff Johnston
Executive Editor: Kim Davies
Assistant Editor: Sarah Holle
Production Editor: Naomi Sysak
Production Liaison: Barbara Marttine Cappuccio
Director of Production and Manufacturing: Bruce Johnson
Managing Editor: Mary Carnis
Manufacturing Buyer: Cathleen Petersen
Creative Director: Cheryl Asherman
Cover Design Coordinator: Miguel Ortiz
Marketing Manager: Jessica Pfaff
Editorial Assistant: Korrine Dorsey
Cover Designer: Amy Rosen
Cover Image: Linda Bleck, SIS/Images.com
Composition: Naomi Sysak
Printing and Binding: R.R. Donnelley & Sons

Pearson Education LTD, *London*
Pearson Education Australia Pty, Limited, *Sydney*
Pearson Education Singapore, Pte. Ltd.
Pearson Education North Asia Ltd., *Hong Kong*
Pearson Education Canada, Ltd., *Toronto*
Pearson Educación de Mexico, S.A. de C.V.
Pearson Education—Japan, *Tokyo*
Pearson Education Malaysia, Pte. Ltd.

10 9 8 7 6 5 4 3
ISBN: 0-13-048200-5

Dedication

Dedicated to all those women and men who gave of their time
and energy so that all women could be free!

And dedicated to my family, who has tolerated my giving of my
time to the cause of all women everywhere.

May my daughter, Tracy, my daughters-in-law, Stacy and Savet,
and my granddaughters, Linday and Nickia, and my grandson,
Benjamin, always know what it is to enjoy all the advantages
that life has to offer.

—Roslyn Muraskin

Contents

Foreword

--- ❖ ---

Although relatively neglected until the 1980s, the study of women employees in the justice system, of women who break the law, and of women who suffer criminal victimization has received growing attention from theorists, researchers, and policymakers. The literature has made its way into both mainstream and specialized journals, specifically *Women and Criminal Justice* and *Violence Against Women*. There are numerous examples of concepts that had previously not been considered as central in criminological theory, but that once named and explored, allowed for the development of considerable research and policy agendas.

The War on Drugs and related invasive, aggressive, and punitive justice practices—which have been supported by local, state, and national criminal justice agencies—have been referred to as the War on Women, which has resulted in a tremendous influx of women into the courts and both jails and prisons. Large numbers of children have been separated from their primary caregiver, and large numbers of incarcerated women experience the stress of worry that their children do not have adequate care or just that of not knowing what is happening to their children.

Intimate partner violence is one of a number of offense types that damage women disproportionately. Others are sexual and gender harassment and sexual assault. Since the victimization of women has been highlighted by research in the last few decades, there has been a continuous discovery of previously unrecognized forms of abuse and previously unknown groups of women who are affected. For instance, women are controlled not only through physical battering but by economic deprivation that they can ameliorate only by obeying an oppressive husband or partner; and immigrant groups thought to be relatively untouched by wife abuse are found to be unknown to criminal justice system agencies, but to suffer both physically and emotionally.

Although theories relevant to gender and crime have been set forth and elaborated increasingly in publications and at conferences, there are still areas that are relatively unexplored or that are neglected in typical collections of readings and textbooks. One of these is the intertwining of gender with race, class, and ethnicity. Research designs that omit subgroups or ignore them in analysis, theories that focus on gender but ignore the multiple statuses that people hold, and a continuing tendency to view gender as a variable at the individual level and ignore the different opportunities and experiences afforded due to gender on a societal level perpetuate the deficits in existing knowledge.

Roslyn Muraskin's third edition of *It's a Crime: Women and Justice* contains articles written by people who approach their topics with passion and concern. Each chapter meets a need for further exploration of the reality of justice for women, and several provide information about previously unstudied or understudied groups. The content places what we know about women and justice within the broader area of women's issues, and extends to medical concerns of offenders and workforce dilemmas of women who work as judges, police, and lawyers. The book accomplishes its task by providing a critical examination of justice for women, and exposing the reader to a wide variety of viewpoints, analyses, and examples.

Merry Morash
School of Criminal Justice
Michigan State University
East Lansing, MI 48824

Preface

---------------------------- ❖ ----------------------------

It's a Crime: Women and Justice (third edition) is probably the most comprehensive text with readings on the subject of women and the criminal justice system. "Never doubt that a small group of thoughtful, committed citizens can change the world. Indeed, it's the only thing that ever has" (Margaret Mead). Over these many generations, dramatic social and legal changes have been accomplished on behalf of women's equality. Women have made these changes happen. They have not been passive, but rather, have worked together to make changes, to create a better world where there are few constrictions. During the times of the American Revolution when America gained a new democracy, women had yet to gain the freedom they deserved as human beings. There have always been women who have worked throughout history for the betterment of society.

At the Seneca Falls Conference in 1848, women gathered together to declare that "we hold these truths to be self evident that all *men and women* [emphasis mine] are created equal." In the *Declaration of Sentiments*, Elizabeth Stanton pointed out that "the history of mankind is a history of repeated injuries and usurpations on the part of man toward woman, having in direct object the establishment of an absolute tyranny over her. To prove this, let facts be submitted to a candid world." It went into specifics:

- Married women were legally dead in the eyes of the law.
- Women were not allowed to vote.
- Women had to submit to laws when they had no voice in their formation.
- Married women had no property rights.
- Husbands had legal power over and responsibility for their wives to the extent that they could imprison or beat them with impunity.

- Divorce and child custody laws favored men.
- Women had to pay property taxes although they had no representation in the levying of these taxes.
- Most occupations were closed to women and when women did gain entry, they were paid only a fraction of what men earned.
- Women were not allowed to enter professions such as medicine or law.
- Women had no means to gain an education since no college or university would accept women students.
- With only a few exceptions, women were not allowed to participate in the affairs of the church.
- Women were robbed of their self-confidence and self-respect, and were made totally dependent on men.

These were strong words. This was the status quo for women in the United States in 1848. In the words of Elizabeth Stanton: "Now in view of this entire disenfranchisement of one-half the people of this country, their social and religious degradation—in view of the unjust laws . . . and because women feel themselves aggrieved, oppressed, and fraudulently deprived of their most sacred rights, we insist that they have immediate admission to all the rights and privileges which belong to them as citizens of these United States." That was then. The movement produced few results. Women did not receive the right to vote until the passage of the Nineteenth Amendment to the Constitution early in the twentieth century.

In the words of Supreme Court Justice Ruth Bader Ginsburg: "I think about how much we owe to the women who went before us—legions of women, some known but many unknown. I applaud the bravery and resilience of those who helped all of us—you and me—to be here today" (1998).

The potential for progress in the realm of women's issues and the criminal justice system is possible because of the continuous battles that women have continued to fight in striving for something called *equality* or *parity of treatment*. The history of women indicates that gender should not be a factor in determining the legal rights of women and men, but it has been. Dating back to 1776, when this country was being formed and the laws were being written by men, it was Abigail Adams, in a letter to her husband, John, who insisted that if in the new American Constitution, "care and attention are not paid to the ladies," they will foment a rebellion. Women have been fomenting that rebellion ever since. The reader will find that the struggle is not over, even though women may have a voice and are being heard.

In this work we talk about women as slaves; witchcraft; affirmative action; disparate treatment of women; sexual harassment; crimes of violence; rights of privacy; women, drugs, and AIDS; women in prison; women as victims of crime; women in criminal justice professions; women and crime; and girls and delinquency.

The chapters that follow are written primarily by scholars and researchers in the field. This third edition, as the previous two, deals with the most up to-date-issues and policies that pertain to women as they are affected and treated by the criminal justice system as well as those basic rights believed to be most fundamental by all. The material and topics provide the best there is as they concern the gender-based problems we face in society today.

In the words of the late Ted Alleman (with whom I worked on the first edition): "Those who see the world entirely from a man's perspective and are simply blind to the existence and influence of women are said to be androcentric in their thinking." Traditional literature ignores the role of women. There are those who will deprecate and/or ignore a woman's point of view entirely. For women, public denigration is not socially acceptable. Personal attacks should be a thing of the past.

Today, women and girls live the legacy of women's rights. It is my passionate hope that this work will result in more meaningful and thought-provoking dialogue concerning the important problems women face in the criminal justice system. *It's a crime*, if we do not realize the importance of the role that women play. Basic human rights are fundamental to all, women and men alike. The raw material is presented in this text—hopefully, you will make it come alive.

Roslyn Muraskin
Long Island University

About the Author and Contributors

Roslyn Muraskin, Ph.D., is Professor of Criminal Justice at the C.W. Post Campus of Long Island University. Her published works include *Visions for Change: Crime and Justice in the Twenty-First Century* (2002) (with A. Roberts), 3rd edition, Prentice Hall; *Morality and the Law* (2001) (with M. Muraskin), Prentice Hall; *Women and Justice: Development of International Policy* (1999), Gordon & Breach Publishers; "Police Work and Juveniles," in *Juvenile Justice Policies, Programs and Services* (1997), Nelson-Hall; "Mothers and Fetuses: Enter the Fetal Police," "Directions for the Future," and "Measuring Disparity in the Correctional Institutions." Dr. Muraskin serves as the editor of the *Women's Series* for Prentice Hall. The first volume is titled *Women Incarcerated: The Next Step*, and the second volume, *With Justice for All: Minorities and Women in Criminal Justice*. Dr. Muraskin serves on the Editorial Board of the *Encyclopedia of Criminology* and has written an article entitled "The Issue Is Abortion" for the next issue. Currently, she is working on a major text in the field of corrections for Prentice Hall.

Dr. Muraskin served in the capacity of Associate Dean of the College of Management (1990–1996) as well as the Director of the School of Public Service. She currently serves as the Director of the Long Island Women's Institute as well as Executive Director of the Alumni Chapter, both for the College of Management. She is Trustee of the Northeast Region for the Academy of Criminal Justice Sciences, and served as President of the Northeastern Association of the Academy of Criminal Justice Sciences.

She received her doctorate in criminal justice from the Graduate Center at the City University of New York, and her master's degree at New York University. She received her bachelor's degree from Queens College.

Dr. Muraskin's main interests are those of gender disparities within the criminal justice system. She is a frequent lecturer on issues of gender.

CONTRIBUTORS

Spencer R. Baker, Ph.D., is Assistant Professor of Education at Hampton University, Hampton, Virginia.

Cyndi Banks, Ph.D., is assistant professor in the Department of Criminal Justice at Northern Arizona University.

Barbara Bloom, Ph.D., is a faculty member of the Department of Criminal Justice at the California State University–Sonoma, Rohnert Park, California.

Hoan N. Bui, Ph.D., is a faculty member at the School of Criminal Justice at Michigan State University.

Jody Clay-Warner, Ph.D., is Assistant Professor of Sociology at the University of Georgia.

Meda Chesney-Lind, Ph.D., is Professor of Women's Studies at the University of Hawaii at Manoa.

Mona J. E. Danner, Ph.D., is Associate Professor of Sociology and Criminal Justice at Old Dominion University.

Elizabeth Piper Deschenes, Ph.D., is with the Department of Criminal Justice at California State University, Long Beach, California.

Lynette Feder, Ph.D., is an Associate Professor of Criminology and Criminal Justice at the University of Memphis.

Laura L. Finley is a doctoral student in criminology at Western Michigan University.

Peter S. Finley is a master's degree student in educational leadership.

Laura T. Fishman, Ph.D., is Associate Professor of Sociology at the University of Vermont.

Kimberly L. Freiberger is employed as an investigator in the Enforcement Division of the Department of Professional Occupational Regulation in Virginia.

Evelyn Gilbert, Ph.D., is a visiting professor in the Criminal Justice Program at the University of North Florida.

Thomas E. Guild, J.D., is Professor of Business Law at the University of Central Oklahoma.

Zelma Weston Henriques, Ph.D., is a professor in the Department of Law and Police Science at the John Jay College of Criminal Justice, City University of New York.

Drew Humphries, Ph.D., is Professor of Sociology as well as Director of the Criminal Justice Program at Rutgers University, Camden Campus.

Ida M. Johnson, Ph.D., is an associate professor in the Department of Criminal Justice at the University of Alabama.

Ciuinal Jones serves on the staff of Illinois Treatment Alternatives for Safe Communities.

Janice Joseph, Ph.D., is Professor of Criminal Justice at the Richard Stockton College of Criminal Justice.

Kimberly Kempf-Leonard, Ph.D., is Professor of Criminology, Sociology, and Political Economy, and Director of the Center for Crime and Justice Policy in the School of Social Sciences at the University of Texas at Dallas.

Arthur J. Lurigio, Ph.D., a social psychologist, is Professor of Criminal Justice and a member of the graduate faculty at Loyola University, where he serves as department chair.

Joan Luxenburg, Ed.D., L.C.S.W., is a professor and Chair of the Sociology, Criminal Justice, and Substance Abuse Studies Department at the University of Central Oklahoma.

Sue Mahan, Ph.D., is Coordinator of the Criminal Justice Program at the University of Central Florida–Daytona Beach.

Zina T. McGee, Ph.D., is Endowed University Professor of Sociology at Hampton University, Hampton, Virginia, where she also serves as codirector of the Behavioral Science Research Center.

Michelle L. Meloy, Ph.D., is Assistant Professor of Criminology at Widener University.

Cheryl L. Meyer, Ph.D., J.D., is a faculty member at Wright State University in the School of Professional Psychology.

Susan L. Miller, Ph.D., is Professor of Sociology and Criminal Justice at the University of Delaware.

Etta F. Morgan, Ph.D., is Assistant Professor of Criminal Justice at Pennsylvania State University–Harrisburg.

Laura J. Moriarty, Ph.D., is associate professor in the Department of Criminal Justice and Assistant Dean of the College of Humanities and Sciences at Virginia Commonwealth University.

Martin L. O'Connor, J.D., is Associate Professor of Criminal Justice at the C.W. Post Campus of Long Island University.

Barbara Owen, Ph.D., is in the Department of Criminology at California State University, Fresno, California.

Tara C. Proano-Raps has earned her doctorate in clinical psychology at Wright State University, School of Professional Psychology.

Christine E. Rasche, Ph.D., is Associate Professor of Criminal Justice and Sociology at the University of North Florida, Jacksonville, Florida, where she also serves as the Director of the Graduate Program.

Jill Rosenbaum, Ph.D., is with the Department of Criminal Justice at California State Univrsity, Fullerton, California.

Inger Sagatun-Edwards, Ph.D., is a professor in the Administration of Justice Department at San Jose State University, where she has been department chair since 1992.

David E. Schulberg, J.D., is a part-time instructor at the Long Beach Community College in California.

Robert T. Sigler, Ph.D., is a professor in the Department of Criminal Justice at the University of Alabama.

Alisa Smith, Ph.D., is an assistant professor at Ramapo College of New Jersey.

James A. Swartz, Ph.D., is Director of Research and Information Services at Illinois Treatment Alternatives for Safe Communities.

Paul E. Tracy, Ph.D., is Professor of Criminology, Sociology, and Political Economy, as well as Director of the Crime and Justice Studies Program in the School of Social Sciences at the University of Texas at Dallas.

Cindy E. Weisbart is currently completing her doctoral degree from Wright State University's School of Professional Psychology in Dayton, Ohio.

Nanci Koser Wilson, Ph.D., is Professor of Criminology at Indiana University of Pennsylvania, where she is also a member of the Women's Studies Faculty.

Acknowledgments

❖

Tremendous thanks to all the contributors to the third edition of *It's a Crime: Women and Justice*. Their contribution has made this the largest volume ever and the best yet to be produced with regard to women and justice. All of the contributors have written in their areas of expertise, lending their research, knowledge, and love of the topic. They are all to be commended for their outstanding contributions.

A big "hug" and "thank you" to my editor, Kim Davies, who is one of the best in the field. She is a delight to work with and I look forward to many more projects. Thanks also to her assistant, Sarah Holle, who works hard to put together a finished project that all of us can be proud of. Special thanks to Naomi Sysak, an editor with whom it has been my pleasure to work, who knows how to lend an ear when needed.

My appreciation goes to Long Island University for their continued support and encouragement, especially for giving me the time to work on a project of love.

I would also like to thank the following reviewers: William E. Kelly, Auburn University, Auburn, Alabama, and Carol Bohmer, Ohio State University, Columbus, Ohio.

And once again a BIG THANK YOU to my husband, Matthew, who stood by me continuously while I devoted so much of my time to my "second love," that of writing.

Roslyn Muraskin

It's a Crime

SECTION I

Historical Development of Women's Issues

1
"Ain't I a Woman?"

Roslyn Muraskin

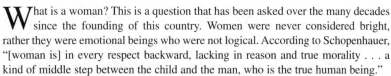

What is a woman? This is a question that has been asked over the many decades since the founding of this country. Women were never considered bright, rather they were emotional beings who were not logical. According to Schopenhauer, "[woman is] in every respect backward, lacking in reason and true morality . . . a kind of middle step between the child and the man, who is the true human being."

Controversy still abounds even in the twenty-first century. Although women are involved in professions where once they were not allowed, the classification by gender, although slowly eroding, still does not give equality where equality is due. The women's movement has been the most integrated and populist force in this country. More than 200 years has passed since the Declaration of Independence declared that *all men are equal* (my emphasis). We still wait for the day when both women and men will be defined as persons; then equality will abound for all.

Sojourner Truth gave her famous "Ain't I a Woman" speech at the Women's Rights Convention in 1815 in Akron, Ohio. Sojourner Truth, a Negro slave, stood at the podium and began to talk: "Well, children, where there is so much racket, there must be something out of kilter, I think between the Negroes of the South and the women of the North—all talking about rights—the white men will be in a fix pretty soon. But what's all this talking about?"

At this point Sojourner pointed to one of the ministers and stated: "That man over there says that women need to be helped into carriages, and lifted over ditches, and to have the best place everywhere. Nobody helps *me* any best place. *And ain't I a woman?*" She then raises her self to her full height, about six feet tall, and states: "Look at me! Look at my arm. I have plowed, I have planted and I have gathered into barns. And no man could head me. *And ain't I a woman? I* could work as much, and eat as much as a man—when I could get it—and bear the lashes as well! *And ain't I a woman?* I have borne children and seen most of them sold into slavery, and when I cried out with a mother's grief, none but Jesus heard me. *And ain't I a woman?"*

The women in the audience cheered. Sojourner then points to another minister: "He talks about this thing in his head. What's that they call it?" "Intellect," some woman whispers. "That's it, honey. What's intellect got to do with a woman's rights or black folks' rights? If my cup won't hold but a pint and yours holds a quart, wouldn't you be mean not to let me have my little half-measure full? That little man in black there! He says women can't have as much rights as men. 'Cause Christ wasn't a woman.'"

At this point she stands with outstretched arms and with eyes lit like fire: "Where did your Christ come from? From God and a Woman! Man had nothing to do with him!" There is alleged to be deafening applause at this moment. "If the first woman God ever made was strong enough to turn the world upside down all alone, these women together ought to be able to turn it back and get it right-side up again. And now that they are asking to do it men better let them."

HISTORICAL OVERVIEW

The search by women for equality is not a recent phenomenon. Earlier in 1776, Abigail Adams admonished her husband, John, to "remember the ladies" in the drafting of the Constitution. She insisted that

> . . . in the new code of laws which I suppose it will be necessary for you to make, I desire you would remember the ladies and be more generous and favorable to them than your ancestors. Do not put such unlimited power into the hands of the husbands. Remember, all men would be tyrants, if they could. If particular care and attention is not paid to the ladies, we are determined to foment a rebellion, and will not hold ourselves bound by any laws in which we have no voice or representation.

Adams replied back to his wife:

> As to your extraordinary code of laws, I cannot but laugh. We have been told that our struggle has loosened the bonds of government everywhere; that children and apprentices were disobedient; that schools and colleges were grown turbulent; that Indians slighted their guardians and Negroes grew insolent to their masters. But your letter was the first intimation that another tribe, more numerous and powerful than all the rest, were grown discontented.

The wife, Abigail, responded:

> I cannot say that I think you are very generous to the ladies; for, whilst you are proclaiming power and good-will to men, emancipating all nations, you insist upon retaining an absolute power over wives. But you must remember that arbitrary power is like most other things which are very hard, very liable to be broken; and not withstanding all your wise laws and maxims, we have it in our power, not only to free ourselves, but to subdue our masters, and, without violence, throw both your natural and legal authority at our feet.

Nowhere in the Constitution of the United States is the word *woman* used. The battle had begun.

The Declaration of Independence as signed in 1776 stated that *all men are created equal* and that the *government derive their power from the consent of the governed*. Women were not included in either concept. The only time the word *sex* is referred to is in the Nineteenth Amendment to the Constitution, signed in 1920, giving women the right to vote.

The original American Constitution of 1787 was founded on English law and did not recognize women as citizens or as individuals with legal rights. A woman was expected to obey her husband or nearest male kin—the power of the ballot having been denied to her. Women were not considered persons under the Fourteenth Amendment to the Constitution, which guaranteed that no state shall deny to "any person within its jurisdiction the equal protection of the laws." Women have historically been victimized by policies designed to protect them (Muraskin & Alleman, 1993).

SENECA FALLS

Constitutionally, no obligation exists for the government to provide any benefits beyond basic requirements. In 1848, a convention was held in Seneca Falls, New York to mark the beginnings of the first organized feminist movement of the nineteenth century. The convention, attended by some 300 women, demonstrated a collective effort to achieve equal rights for women. Their focus was property and suffrage. They went so far as to adopt their own Declaration of Independence:

> We hold these truths to be self-evident; that all men and women are created equal; that they are endowed by their creator with certain inalienable rights; that among these are life, liberty and the pursuit of happiness; that to secure these rights governments are instituted, deriving their just powers from the consent of the governed.
>
> Whenever any form of government becomes destructive of these ends, it is the right of those who suffer from it to refuse allegiance to it, and to insist upon the institution of new government. . . . The history of mankind is a history of repeated injuries and usurpation on the part of men toward women, having in direct object the establishment of an absolute tyranny over her. To prove this let the facts be submitted to a candid world.
>
> He has never permitted her to exercise her inalienable right to the elective franchise.
>
> He has compelled her to submit to laws in the formation of which she has no voice.
>
> He has withheld from her rights which are given to the most ignorant and degraded men—both natives and foreigners.
>
> Having deprived her of this first right of a citizen, the elective franchise, thereby leaving her without representation in the halls of legislation, he has oppressed her on all sides.
>
> He has made her, if married, in the eyes of the law civilly dead.
>
> He has taken from her all rights in property, even to the wages she earns.
>
> He has made her, morally, an irresponsible being, as she can commit crimes with impunity, provided they be done in the presence of her husband, he becoming to all intents and purposes, her master—the law giving him power to deprive her of her liberty, and to administer chastisement.
>
> After depriving her of all rights as a married woman, if single, and the owner of property, he has taxed her to support a government which recognizes her only when her property can be made profitable to it.

He has denied her the facilities for obtaining a thorough education, all colleges being closed against her.

He allows her in church, as well as State, but in a subordinate position.

He has endeavored, in every way that he could, to destroy her confidence in her own powers to lessen her self-respect, and make her willing to lead a dependent and abject life. (Schneir, 1972, pp. 77–82)

So 300 women declared. They therefore resolved the following at Seneca Falls:

That all laws which prevent women from occupying such a station in society as her conscience shall dictate, or which place her in a position to that of men, are contrary to the great precept of nature, and therefore of no force or authority.

That the women of this country ought to be enlightened in regard to laws under which they live, that they may no longer publish their degradation by declaring themselves satisfied with their present position. . . .

That the same amount of virtue, delicacy, and refinement of behavior that is required of women in the social state, should be required of men, and the same transgression should be visited with equal severity on both man and woman.

And that it be further resolved "[t]hat the speedy success of our cause depends upon the zealous and untiring efforts of both men and women, for the overthrow of the monopoly of the pulpit, and for the security to women an equal participation with men in the various trades, professions, and commerce" (Schneir, 1972).

THE LEGAL SYSTEM

According to Catherine MacKinnon (2001), "[e]quality in human societies is commonly affirmed but rarely practiced. As a principle, it can be fiercely loved, passionately sought, highly vaunted, sentimentally assumed, complacently taken for granted, and legally guaranteed. Its open detractors are few. Yet despite general consensus on equality as a value, no society is organized on equality principles. Few lives are lived in equality, even in democracies" (p. 2).

Seneca Falls took place in 1848. The property rights of U.S. women in the nineteenth century as truly reflected in the declaration at Seneca Falls was set forth earlier by the legal scholar Blackstone, who wrote that by marriage, the husband and wife are one person in law. The very being of all women at this time was suspended during marriage. Laws were passed that gave the husband the right to give his wife "moderate correction"; he could hit her to *restrain her* but with nothing wider than his thumb.

A federal equal rights amendment was first introduced to Congress in 1923 and was submitted to the states continuously over a period of time for ratification until it finally failed in 1972. Stated simply:

- *Section 1.* Equality of rights under the law shall not be denied or abridged by the United States or by any other State on account of sex.
- *Section 2.* The Congress shall have the power to enforce, by appropriate legislation, the provisions of this Article.
- *Section 3.* This Amendment shall take effect two years after the date of ratification.

It never happened.

Jean-Jacques Rousseau, an eighteenth-century French philosopher, wrote in his work, *Emile*:

> Men and women are made for each other then, but their mutual dependence is not equal. . . . We could survive without them better then they could without us. . . . Thus women's entire education should be planned in relation to men. To please men, to be useful to them, to win their love and respect, to raise them as children, care for them as adults, counsel and console them, make their lives sweet and pleasant; these are women's duties in all ages and these are what they should be taught from childhood. (Deckard, 1979, p. 217)

Oberlin College was the first college to admit women, in 1833. Until 1841, women could only take a shortened literary course, on the theory that the education of women had a different purpose than that of men. For many years women were not permitted to speak in class and were required to wait on male students. It was believed that women's highest calling was to be the mothers of the race and that they should stay within that special sphere in order that future generations should not suffer from want of devoted and undistracted mother care. If women were to enter the areas of law, religion, medicine, academics, government, or any sort of public character, the home would suffer from neglect. Washing men's clothes, caring for their rooms, serving the men at dining tables, remaining respectfully silent in public assemblages, the Oberlin coeds were being prepared for motherhood and to serve their men.

Elizabeth Blackwell was the first woman in the United States to get a medical degree, in 1849. She applied to 29 medical schools until one finally accepted her. She had to fight for the right to be present at the dissection of human organs, part of the training for any doctor.

In 1873, the U.S. Supreme Court upheld an Illinois state law prohibiting female lawyers from practicing in state courts (*Bradwell* v. *Illinois*, 1872). The Court *in its wisdom* (emphasis mine) noted that

> the civil war as well as nature herself, has always recognized a wide difference in the respective spheres and destinies of man and woman. Man is or should be women's protector and defender. The natural and proper timidity and delicacy which belong to the female sex evidently unfits it for many of the occupations of civil life. The constitution of the family organization, which is founded in the divine ordinance, as well as in the nature of things indicates the domestic sphere as that which belongs to the domain and functions of womanhood. The harmony of interests and views which belong or should belong to the family institutions, is repugnant to the idea of a woman adopting a distinct and independent career from that of her husband.

The Court continued by declaring that "[t]he paramount destiny and mission of woman are to fulfill the noble and benign offices of wife and mother. This is the law of the Creator. And the rules of civil society must be adopted to the general constitution of things, and cannot be based upon exception cases."

Justice Miller summed it up when he stated: "I am not prepared to say that it is one of her fundamental rights and privileges to be admitted into every office and position, including those which require highly special qualifications and demanding social responsibilities. In the nature of things it is not every citizen of every age, sex, and condition that is qualified for every calling and position." This decision demonstrated that law reflected society as it was meant to be since the founding of this country.

It took until 1860 in New York to pass the Married Women's Property Act, an attempt to give to women property that she owned as her sole and private property. Until this time a married woman was not entitled to own or keep property after marriage. This act stated "that which a woman married in this state owns at the time of her marriage, and the rents, issues and proceeds of all such property, shall not withstanding marriage, be and remain her sole and separate property."

The right to vote, which was not won until 1920, with the passage of the Nineteenth Amendment to the Constitution, was a struggle for women. In the case of *Minor* v. *Happersett* (1874), the U.S. Supreme Court denied women the right to vote. The argument then was "that as a woman born or naturalized in the United States is a citizen of the United States and of the State in which she resides, she has therefore the right to vote." The Court stated further that there is no doubt that women may be citizens. The direct question as presented was whether all citizens are necessarily qualified to be voters. "The Constitution has not added the right of suffrage to the privileges and immunities of citizenship as they existed at the time it was adopted" (*Minor*). In no state constitution was suffrage conferred upon women. It took the Nineteenth Amendment to the Constitution to grant women the right to vote. Neither John Adams nor those following him were willing to "remember the ladies." "Federal and state legislation prohibiting sex discrimination in selected areas does not fill the absence of a constitutional prohibition of discrimination on the basis of sex. Under the federal constitution and most state constitutions, women have not yet been raised to the status of constitutional protections enjoyed by males" (Thomas, 1991, p. 95). The Nineteenth Amendment did not automatically mean an end to women's oppression. It did not "negate the term 'male' in Section 2 of the Fourteenth Amendment. The lack of an explicit guarantee of sex equality has limited the U.S. Constitution as a vehicle for securing women's rights and social advancement" (MacKinnon, 2001, p. 16).

Even the language of the law referred to such terms as a *reasonable man, he*, and *his*. When a question about this is raised, the answer given is usually that the male terms used generally include females. As Justice Scalia has stated: "The word 'gender' has acquired the new and useful connotation of cultural or attitudinal characteristics (as opposed to physical characteristics) distinct to the sexes. That is to say, gender is to sex as feminine is to female and masculine is to male" (MacKinnon, 2001, p. 210).

Gender-neutral language does not solve the problem. Such gender-neutral language "serves only to reward the employers ingenious enough to cloak their acts of discrimination in a facially neutral guise, identical though the effects of [a facially neutral seniority] system may be to those of a facially discriminatory one" (Thomas, 1991).

RIGHT TO WORK

During the nineteenth century, differential treatment of women and men was challenged. A most striking incident was that of the protective state labor laws. In the early twentieth century, protective labor laws were allegedly enacted to protect both men and women from inhuman conditions. However, it was women who suffered. In the case of *Muller* v. *Oregon* (1908), a challenge was made to the Oregon statute prohibiting the employment of women in mechanical establishments, factories, or laundries for more than 10 hours a day. This law was upheld by the U.S. Supreme Court using a reasoning that was to haunt the advocates of women's rights for years to come.

Justice Brenner delivered the majority opinion of the Court:

[W]omen's physical structure and the performance of maternal functions places her at a disadvantage in the struggle for subsistence. . . . This is especially true when the burdens of motherhood are upon her. [And] even when they are not, by abundant testimony of the medical fraternity continuance for a long time on her feet at work, repeating this from day to day, tends to injurious effects upon the body . . . the physical well-being of woman becomes an object of public interest and care in order to preserve the strength and vigor of the race. [As dictated by history] woman has always been dependent upon man. He established his control at the outset by *superior physical strength* [emphasis mine], and this control in various forms, with diminishing intensity has continued to the present. . . . She is properly placed in a class by herself, and legislation designed for her protection may be sustained, even when legislation is not necessary for men, and could be sustained.

THE RIGHT TO SERVE ON JURIES

And so it continued. Struggles ensued, with women bringing to court their case to serve on juries. In the case of *Hoyt* v. *Florida* (1961), Justice Harlan delivered the opinion of the Supreme Court. The issues was whether exclusion of women from jury service discriminated against a defendant's right to a fair trial. Justice Harlan stated:

Manifestly, Florida's [law] does not purport to exclude women from state jury service. Rather the statute "gives to women the privilege to serve but does not impose service as a duty." It accords women an absolute exemption from jury service unless they expressly waive that privilege.

It has given women an absolute exemption from jury based solely on their sex, no similar exemption obtaining as to men.

Despite the enlightened emancipation of women from the restrictions and protections of bygone years, and their entry into many parts of community life formerly considered to be reserved to men, *woman is still regarded as the center of home and family life*" [italics added].

In 1975, in *Taylor* v. *Louisiana* (1975), a male criminal defendant challenged his conviction on the ground that his jury had not been drawn from a fair cross section of the community. Women had systematically been excluded from jury lists. Using statistics to demonstrate that 54.2 percent of all women between 18 and 64 years of age were in the labor force, that 45.7 percent of women with children under the age of 18 were working, that 67.3 percent of mothers who were either widowed, divorced, or separated were in the workforce, and that 51.2 percent of the mothers whose husbands were gainfully employed were also working, the Court declared: "[I]f it was ever the case that women were unqualified to sit on juries or were so situated that none of them should be required to perform jury services that time has long past." A victory had been won.

GENDER AS A SUSPECT CLASSIFICATION

What has not been declared is that gender is a suspect classification. It was not until 1971 that the U.S. Supreme Court considered that many of the laws and official practices at all levels of government as practiced were in violation of the equal protection clause. The Fourteenth Amendment states that "[n]o state shall deny equal protection of the laws to any person." But what does that mean?

A rational relationship test was developed indicating that any classification "must be reasonable, not arbitrary, and must rest upon some ground of difference having a fair and substantial relation to the object of the legislation, so that all persons similarly situated shall be treated alike" (*Reed* v. *Reed*, 1971). There can exist no discrimination against women unless it is demonstrated that reasonable grounds exist for such discrimination.

Throughout the history of the courts, several classifications, including gender, religion, and national origin, have been labeled "suspect" classifications. What this means is that any time a law is passed that discriminates in its language or is found to have a discriminatory effect on a suspect class of persons, the state has the burden not simply of showing that the law is rational, but must prove additionally that such a law serves a compelling governmental interest and that no other discriminatory law could accomplish the same or similar purpose. This is the principle referred to as a *compelling state interest*. We came close with the case of *Frontiero* v. *Richardson* (1973), but because there was a 4–4 plurality vote of the justices of the Supreme Court, such a decision of gender as a suspect classification never came about. With gender not being labeled a suspect classification, the government has the power to justify any type of discrimination as not being arbitrary and irrational. In the words of Justice Brennan: "There can be doubt that our Nation has had a long and unfortunate history of sex discrimination. Traditionally, such discrimination was rationalized by an attitude of 'romantic paternalism' which in practical effect, put women, not on a pedestal, but in a cage."

If there had been just one more vote, the courts would have been obliged to treat gender classifications as they do race classifications. It was not to be. The rational basis for classifications is still based on the factor of women being dependent on their spouses, girls being dependent on parents for support, and men having more and better business experience than women. If the courts can determine that discrimination serves the purpose of the rational relationship test, it can and will stand. To this day there remains confusion regarding the standard of review in cases of gender discrimination. The issue remains whether gender and race classifications are ever constitutionally permissible. Are there instances in which it is proper to afford preferential treatment to one group above another? Clear answers do not exist. Each case is considered on an individual basis and on individual merit.

Even the Equal Rights Amendment (ERA) could not be passed. Concerns about family law, protective labor laws, the military, and the establishment of unisex bathrooms were enough to vote down the ERA. If ever there were stereotypical attitudes about women, one is found in the *wisdom* of many of the justices of the Supreme Court.

GENDER NEUTRAL

Admittedly, progress has been demonstrated, as, for example, in the changing roles of women and men that have led to gender-neutral, functional family laws. Today, the obligation of supporting a spouse is predicated on who can afford it, not simply on who needs it.

Women are not inferior to men. Nevertheless, in the twenty-first century, there remains evidence of sexual discrimination, even with all the history and struggles to gain equality and similarly of treatment under the law. According to MacKinnon (2001), "[u]nless something is done, even if recent rates of measurable progress for elite women continue, no American now alive will live in a society of sex equality, nor will their children or their children's children" (p. 2).

We have yet to reach the day when we can say honestly that women have been raised to the status of full constitutional protections as has always been enjoyed by the male sex. We must remember the words of Sojourner Truth: "Ain't I a woman?" We are constantly reminded of her statement and that of Abigail Adams, "remember the ladies," yet we are constantly reminded of the statement in the case of *Glover* v. *Johnson* (1975): "Keep it simple, they are only women."

REFERENCES

DECKARD, B. S. (1979). *The women's movement: Political, socioeconomic, and psychological issues.* New York: Harper & Row.

MACKINNON, C. (2001). *Sex equality.* New York: Foundation Press.

MURASKIN, R., & ALLEMAN, T. (1993). *It's a crime: Women and justice.* Englewood Cliffs, NJ: Regents/Prentice Hall.

SCHNEIR, M. (ED.). (1972). *Feminism: The essential historical writings.* New York: Vintage Press.

THOMAS, C. S. (1991). *Sex discrimination.* St. Paul, MN: West Publishing.

CASES

Bradwell v. *Illinois*, 83 U.S. 130 (1872).

Frontiero v. *Richardson*, 411 U.S. 677 (1973).

Glover v. *Johnson*, 478 F. Supp. 1075 (1975).

Hoyt v. *Florida*, 368 U.S. 57 (1961).

Minor v. *Happersett*, 88 U.S. 162 (1874).

Muller v. *Oregon*, 208 U.S. 412 (1908).

Reed v. *Reed*, 404 U.S. 71 (1971).

Taylor v. *Louisiana*, 419 U.S. 522 (1975).

2

Taming Women and Nature

The Criminal Justice System
and the Creation of Crime in Salem Village

Nanci Koser Wilson

Female-on-female violent crime is a rarity. Yet in 1692, in Puritan Salem Village, Massachusetts, hundreds of women were accused, and fourteen executed, for violent crimes, many of whose victims were female. Contemporary Americans view witchcraft as an imaginary offense, so this episode has been seen by most scholars as an aberration, atypical of U.S. criminal justice. But a careful examination of charges against these women reveals an offense that was not so imaginary after all—one for which women are still being brought to account. The Salem witches were persecuted because they were seen as wild women, in need of taming, just as was the rest of "nature." For the patriarchal mind, wild women and wild nature still pose a significant threat to orderly male-controlled production and reproduction, and are still sometimes met with a criminal justice response.

American women, like most women, are infrequent criminal offenders, especially as against one another and especially in violent crime. The rarest criminal event is female-on-female violent crime. Yet in 1692, in Puritan Salem Village, Massachusetts, hundreds of women were accused, and fourteen executed, for violent crimes, many of whose victims were female.

The Salem witch hysteria has been seen by most historians as an aberration, a bump in our history, completely atypical of U.S. criminal justice. No longer believers in witchcraft, modern Americans are horrified that such an injustice could have occurred in relatively modern times. It is assumed that the witches were innocent of any crime, and [(with the exception of Chadwick Hansen (1968)] scholars have sought explanations outside the phenomenon of witchcraft itself to account for the persecutions.

Yet if we examine carefully the charges against these women, we discover an offense that was not so imaginary after all, and one for which women are still being brought to account. The witches of Salem Village were thought to be disruptive of a natural hierarchy established by men at the behest of a male god. The image of divinely ordained masculine control of nature was captured for Puritans in the metaphor of the Great Chain of Being. This metaphor is still powerful today, with the exception that contemporary Americans have replaced the top rung in the hierarchy. Now, scientific technology reigns as God, and the only telos, or design, in nature is the continued unfolding of evolutionary process. The new divinity is as thoroughly masculinist as Yahweh and is capable of directing evolution by itself. A masculinist science embodies, as complete as did the old God, the American Dream of conquering wilderness, in its vision of total control over nature. In this vision, what counts is not so much more and more productivity (although this is certainly important) but *human control* of natural productivity.

This is well illustrated in modern agricultural practices. Bovine growth hormone does not produce more milk per cow over the entire span of a cow's life. Similarly, chemical fertilizers do not make the soil more fertile in the long run. Nor do dams create water, nor does experimentally induced laboratory growth replicate natural growth. At the core of all these ways of growing and knowing is the farmer's and the scientist's total control over (what are deemed to be) relevant conditions. It is apparent that this control is desired more than fertility itself. In the 1990s, this could be seen clearly in plans to "develop" wetlands as farms and shopping malls. Although the necessity to the hydrological cycle of these wetlands is now recognized, legislators and environmental agencies in state after state are permitting the development of wetlands upon the agreement by developers to create man-made substitute wetlands as "replacement parts."

But as Lewis (1943/1988, p. 449) has noted, control over nature is really "a power exercised by some men over other men with nature as its instrument." Many feminist scholars believe that control over women was exerted to exploit their labor and was the first form of exploitation man invented, upon which he then modeled other forms of exploitation. Ecofeminists hold that the exploitation of nature and of women developed coterminously, nourishing one another. And many scholars have noted the centrality of conquest, especially the conquest of wilderness, to the development of the American character (Turner, 1920).

In the Salem witchcraft hysteria we see the convergence of all of these themes, as the Puritan criminal justice system created in the Bay Colony a frightful specter to contain their fears of wild nature—both in human females and in the nonhuman nature around them. In tracing witch-beliefs within the context of Puritan technology and examining the evidence brought against witches, we see a strong device for social control of natural forces—as Lewis stated, the control of some men over other men (and all women), using nature as the tool. The relevance of Puritan cosmology and its use of criminal justice to achieve the ends of control and domination to contemporary gendered criminal justice can be seen as evidence for a consistent theme running through Western and American history.

PURITAN METAPHYSICS

According to a contemporary witch (Starhawk, 1989, p. 18), "witchcraft takes its teaching from nature." Further, witches understand nature as cyclical, spiral. "There is nothing to be saved *from*, no struggle of life *against* the universe, no God outside the world to be feared and obeyed; only the Goddess, the Mother, the turning spiral that whirls us in and out of existence, whose winking eye is the pulse of being" (p. 29).

Whether any Salem women understood themselves to be practicing an ancient religion centered on the immanence of divinity in the natural world [as Murray (1921) asserted of the European witches], or whether any of the accused believed themselves to be malefic witches [as Hansen (1968) maintains], it is clear that at one time such religions were strong competitors for Christianity. In Europe, that part of earlier nature-centered religion that could not be absorbed effectively into Christianity was vigorously suppressed. The struggle with these heretics left a legacy of witch-beliefs among European Christians, which, imported to the American continent with the Puritans, formed the basis for the Salem female crime wave of 1692.

Puritan metaphysics (like all such patriarchal systems) presented a markedly different view of nature to that embodied in nature-centered religions. Puritan cosmology was strongly hierarchical, and within its metaphysics, the ultimate source of life existed beyond it. Puritans saw the cosmos as a

> Vast chain of being! which from God began,
> Natures aethereal, human, angel, man,
> Beast, bird, fish, insect, what no eye can see,
> No glass can reach; from Infinite to thee,
> From thee to nothing—On Superior pow'rs
> Were we to press, inferior might on ours;
> Or in the full creation leave a void,
> Where, one step broken the great scale's destroy'd;
> From Nature's chain whatever link you strike,
> Tenth, or thousandth, breaks the chain alike.

(Pope, 1733)

These lines from Pope, although written in the eighteenth century, reflect a "conception of the plan and structure of the world which, through the Middle Ages and down to the late 18th century, many philosophers, most men of science, and indeed, most educated men, were to accept without question" (Lovejoy, 1936/1953, p. 59). The universe was seen as a Great Chain of Being, "composed of an immense . . . number of links ranging in hierarchical order from the meagerest kind of existence, which barely escape non-existence, through 'every possible' grade up to . . . the Absolute Being."

For Puritans, each link in the chain fulfilled its nature and purpose partly by obeying the next highest link in the chain. Among human beings, a similar hierarchy had been ordained with "husbands superior to wives, parents to children, masters to servants, ministers to congregants, and magistrates to subjects. . . . In each of these relations, inferiors served God by serving their superiors. Men promised to ensure obedience in all their dependents, in return for God's promise of prosperity" (Karlsen, 1987, p. 164).

Although the Puritan God existed prior to his creation, and Puritan theology embraced a deity whose transcendence outshone his immanence, their theology was also strongly incarnational. Elements of the natural world reflected and sometimes revealed to humans a supernatural plan, and, on occasion, a struggle between super-natural forces. Both God and Satan, his fallen angel, took an intense interest in the created world.

Created below God in the hierarchy, but above all other things, angels were required to fulfill their place in the chain through obedience. Satan's obedience consisted precisely in his rebellion against his place. His desire to be "as God" included a struggle with the deity *within nature itself*. Satan not only attempted to seduce humans but also caused various natural disasters lower on the chain.

Long before Puritanism arose, European Christians had begun to understand Genesis 1:28[1] as a mandate to exploit all of nature below humans in the hierarchical chain (White, 1967); and this exploitation, of course, required the taming of wild nature—both human and nonhuman. Puritan theology thus fit neatly with the colonization of an uncivilized territory. The new immigrants found a land peopled by hunting and gathering groups who, for the most part, did not have established cities, agriculture, or a settled existence. Puritans viewed this land as a wilderness in need of taming, which would order it to God.

Part of this impulse was surely secular; but it had a sacred stamp and warrant. Strong strains in Judeo-Christian mythology emphasize the wilderness experience. The wilderness is a setting for man's struggle with his lower nature, a place of suffering and purification, from which he emerges dedicated completely to God and to His divine plan.

> [T]he desert wilderness . . . where the very existence of man is constantly threatened, is also the place specially chosen by God to manifest Himself as His "mighty acts" of mercy and salvation. Obedience to a divine call brings into this dreadful wilderness those whom God has chosen to form as His own people. . . . Failure to trust Yahweh in the wilderness is not simply an act of weakness: it is disobedience and idolatry. (Merton, 1978, p. 190)

This theme of wilderness was "taken over in the theology of radical Protestantism in the seventeenth century and hence entered into the formation of the Christian ideal of North American culture that grew up out of the Puritan colonies of New England" (Merton, 1978, p. 195).

The wilderness, once tamed, would become the orderly paradise the Puritan God commanded man to create. Importantly, a failure to conquer the wilderness was also a failure at individual salvation. If the Bay Colonists failed to establish the paradise of the "City on the Hill," this might be a sign that each Puritan was damned. Fearful for their own souls, frightened of wild nature both on its own terms and for the damnation that failure to tame it portended, Puritans attempted to contain their fears by sacrificing some of their middle-aged women. These women became the very emblem of their fears—of wilderness, of failure, and ultimately, of eternal damnation.

THE WITCHES AS WILD WOMEN

Although it has been suggested that "a genuine coven was meeting in the woods of Salem before the trials" (Starhawk, 1989, p. 21), evidence from the Salem trials does not support such a conclusion. What is more important are the witch-beliefs Puritans held which allowed for the persecutions.

Nature-focused religions had been of concern to the Judeo-Christian tradition since its inception. In the fifth century B.C., tempted to desert his patriarchal God during a time of great personal suffering, Job had proclaimed: "If I beheld the sun when it shined, or the moon walking in brightness; and my heart hath seen secretly enticed . . . this also were an iniquity to be punished by the judge; for I should have denied the God that is above" (Job 31:27–28).

Steeped in a tradition that had shaped its theology in direct contrast to animistic, nature-centered rival religions, the Puritans inherited a linear, hierarchical monotheism. While ancient religions had long since ceased to pose a genuine threat to the newer, patriarchal religion, during time of stress, the fear of heresy arose with new vigor.

Christianity met the challenge in two ways. It absorbed prior religions by building churches on the old sacred sites and by changing names of festivals while keeping their dates. It directly challenged such religions by turning its gods and goddesses into the Christian devil (Adler, 1986, p. 45). The witch persecutions were part of that transformation. What came to be called witchcraft included some elements of pagan belief systems, but "these survivals only became an organized system when the Church took the older beliefs and fragments and created an organized, systematic demonology, complete with new elements including the pact with the devil, the coven and the sabat" (Adler, 1986, p. 53; Trevor-Roper, 1970).

But witch persecutions were useful beyond the purposes of the Church in validating the new patriarchal religion. As Trevor-Roper (1970) notes, in the sixteenth and seventeenth centuries this new demonology acquired momentum. These were the centuries during which modern science was born and the Western world-view became more and more human-control oriented. The massive witch persecutions of the period also validated an increasingly centralized secular and male hierarchy in medicine, politics, and agriculture. The specter of possible resistance to this project of taming all of nature produced intense witch fears, culminating in the deaths of perhaps nine million persons (Daly, 1978, p. 183).

The struggle against wild nature as seen in untamed women produced important tracts whose dissemination was abided by the invention of printing. In *Malleus Malificarum* of Institoris (Kramer and Sprenger, 1948; o.d. 1486), readers would learn precisely what to fear from women presumed to be in league with the devil. In books such as this and in the teachings of the clergy, witchcraft was invented.

The *Malleus Maleficarum* "explained and justified the Church's view that most witches were women" (Karlsen, 1987, p. 155). Women, the authors instructed, were more evil than men by nature, and because they were created inferior to men, were more susceptible to deception. Witches were also seen as dissatisfied with their place in the natural hierarchy. This made them angry and vengeful. Specific sorts of crimes were likely to be performed by witches, according to this tract. They were responsible for generative problems—they could cause men to be impotent, they could prevent conceptions and procure abortions in women. They also might kill newborns. They frequently attempted to dominate their husbands, which was a "natural vice" in women (Karlsen 1987).

The witch-beliefs that the Puritans imported thus were strongly marked by fears of disruption of the Chain of Being, particularly of rebellion among women and damage caused to domesticated nature. The fear was that of tamed nature "going wild." Theologically and legally, the crime of witchcraft consisted in making a pact with the devil, whose supernatural power he lent to humans. With this power, a person could perform *maleficium*, that is, harm various parts of the natural order. She could cause disease, injury, or even death among humans and other animals. She could interfere with domestic processes such as dairying, brewing beer, and making cloth. Witches were also thought capable of causing disturbances in weather patterns—they could create droughts and storms at sea, for instance. Maleficium could be performed by look, by touch, and specifically, by *curse*.

Although invested with supernatural power, witches apparently refrained from certain kinds of harm, and specialized in others. They were not suspected of financial offenses such as theft, fraud, or embezzlement. In fact, they appeared unable to bring about good outcomes for themselves. It was not said that they increased the productivity of their own fields or domestic stocks; that they could weave superior fabrics or make finer butter, produce more food, or enhance the health of children, adults, or stock.

Rather, witches specifically engaged in actions that threatened to upset a natural hierarchy, to wreak havoc in domesticated nature—to unleash wild forces. The New England witch "was frequently suspected of causing illnesses or death, particularly to spouses or infants and young children." She also was likely to direct her malice toward domesticated animals—she could bewitch cows, horses, and swine—they would sicken and die, or simply wander off. She was often accused of "obstructing reproductive processes, either by preventing conceptions or by causing miscarriages, childbirth fatalities or 'monstrous' (deformed) births." She could procure abortions and cause impotence among men. She harmed domestic processes by spoiling beer in the brewing or making it disappear altogether. She could cause cows to stop giving milk and hens to lay fewer eggs. She could make spinning and weaving impossible (Karlsen, 1987).

If the Salem hysteria can be explained by Puritan uneasiness and fears during a period of political upheaval, as some have suggested (see, e.g., Erikson, 1966), it is clear from the nature of the accusations that these fears were of a specific sort. And if the high concentration of women among the accused can be explained in terms of misogyny and the desire to control women, as most feminist students of witchcraft have maintained (Daly, 1978; Ehrenreich & English, 1973; Karlsen, 1987), it is similarly clear from the nature of the accusations that women were thought to pose a particular kind of danger.

The Puritans had reserved an important and specific role for their women; and it is likely that female failure to fulfill their function was seen as extremely dangerous, in that one link in the Chain of Being broken, all else would disintegrate. Women were a part of wild nature that needed taming; once tamed, their role was to nurture. Men apparently realized that the creation of an inherently unfair and exploitative system carried within it the seeds of dissatisfaction and rebellion among the tamed. They expected women to rebel, and in their cosmology created an explanation for female dissatisfaction. Just as Eve had succumbed to the devil's wiles, so might other women. But Puritans did not fear self-aggrandizement on the part of the witches. Rather, they feared the vengeance of dissatisfied women. Insufficiently tamed women, it would appear, were the cause of fear. Untamed themselves, in league with the disruptive forces of wild nature, witches might unhook the carefully constructed Chain of Being.

ACCUSATIONS AGAINST THE SALEM WITCHES[2]

The Salem hysteria began in the early months of 1692 when a number of young women were stricken with fits. Reverend Samuel Parris' household contained a prepubescent daughter and a household servant, Tituba, from the West Indies. Elizabeth Parris, age 9, a number of preteen and teenage friends, and often, three older women gossiped and chatted in the Parris kitchen. Tituba, who knew the witchcraft of her native island, helped the girls to forecast their futures, focusing on the occupations of their future husbands. Later, Jonathan Hale was to blame the entire event on these seemingly innocent actions. He maintained that the girls in their "vain curiosity" had "tampered with the devil's tools" (cited in Boyer & Nissenbaum, 1974, p. 23).

The most immediate result of this tampering was that the young girls became possessed. Their symptoms ranged from feelings of being pinched, pricked, and choked, to full-scale seizures. Two of the "circle girls" were epileptics (Gemmill, 1924, p. 48); the fits of the other girls were perhaps caused by ergot poisoning (Caporael, 1976) or the power of suggestion (Caulfield, 1943). Taken to the local doctor, they could neither be diagnosed nor cured by his arts, and he then declared that the cause was outside his profession. The appropriate jurisdiction was theological and legal.

Witchcraft was more than crime, although it was that—it was treason and heresy as well. And it was the most threatening offense in the Puritan world, because it was contagious. The authorities reacted promptly and predictably—they asked the girls to indicate who was bewitching them. Guided perhaps by the mother of one of the girls (Ann Putnam), who held grudges against some of her neighbors (Boyer & Nissenbaum, 1974; Gemmill, 1924), and by their own beliefs about just who a witch might be, the girls identified several local women—including, of course, Tituba, who confessed immediately. The hunt began.

In the pattern of the accusations, in the kinds of victims and offenders, and in the nature of the harm done, we begin to see what the Puritans feared. The power of maleficium was given by Satan himself, so Puritan officials were at pains to ascertain if the accused had actually made a pact with the devil. They looked for evidence of such a pact in confessions and in the testimony of witnesses that an accused had "signed the devil's book," had attended a witches' sabbath, or taken the devil's communion. Further, if a witness testified that an accused witch had urged her to engage in any of these actions, this testimony was evidence that the accused had attempted to seduce another human, drawing her, too, into the devil's snare, and therefore had obviously made a pact herself. Such evidence was produced for 77 percent of the accused women in our sample (see Table 1).

Entering in such a pact with the devil meant that a Puritan was in league with profane forces, unsanctioned authority. As a being who himself had rebelled against established authority, Satan was wild. Satan's fight with God was a rebellion against authority which was carried out in the world—that is, within created nature. Thus, at the heart of the witches' crime was rebellion against hierarchical order and allegiance to an alternative force whose main purpose and power appeared to be the creation of chaos.

Maleficium directed at human beings was the most common charge in Salem, as it had been in England (Macfarlane, 1970, p. 154; Thomas, 1971, p. 539, who estimates that 70 to 80 percent of the victims were other humans). In our sample, 97 percent of the women accused were charged with assaulting or murdering humans (see Table 2).

Evidence for human harm began with and most usually involved evidence that the circle girls had been tortured by the accused. These girls were present in court and frequently went into fits when an accused entered the room. Eighty-nine percent of the accused women were charged with tormenting these girls. Since the medical profession had not been able to find a natural cause, these fits were continually attributed to supernatural actions by witches. Obviously, for Salem Villagers, unexplained events were also uncontrollable events—and

TABLE 1   Evidence of Pact

	Number	Percent
Confession	7	20
Signing the devil's book	2	6
Attending the witch's sabbath	13	37
Taking the devil's communion	2	6
Seducing others	17	49
Total[a]	27	77

[a]In this and the following tables, totals will add to more than 100% because more than one form of evidence was brought for several of the witches.

it was this lack of control which they feared. The first, and always the central, victims were the circle girls. They were the reliable indicators that an accused was actually a witch. In this regard, the age and gender of the victims and offenders is important.

There were ten circle girls; their ages ranged from 9 to 20, with a mean of 15.9 years (see Table 3). One of the oldest, Mary Warren, who was 20, was later accused of witchcraft herself, as were two of the older women present (Sarah Biber and Goody Pope). The accused were, for the most part, middle-aged women who were unmarried. Although the girls themselves could logically be accused, except for Warren (who confessed

TABLE 2   Evidence of Maleficium

	Number	Percent
Harming human beings	34	97
Assault upon circle girls	31	89
Assault upon others	20	57
Murder	8	23
Harming domesticated nature	9	26
Damaging domestic production	1	3
Stopping domestic production	3	8.5
Damaging domesticated stock	9	26
Possessing supernatural powers	18	51
Flying through the air	6	17
Performing "impossible" physical feats	1	3
Predicting the future	2	6
Possessing poppets	7	20
Possessing familiars	10	29
Suckling familiars, having witch's teats	5	14

TABLE 3   The Circle Girls[a]

	Age
Elizabeth Parris	9
Abigail Williams	11
Ann Putnam	12
Mercy Lewis	17
Mary Walcott	17
Elizabeth Hubbard	17
Elizabeth Booth	18
Susan Sheldon	18
Mary Warren	20
Sarah Churchill	20

[a]In addition, three older women were often present: Sarah Bibber, Goodwife Pope, and Mrs. Ann Putnam (Gemmill, 1924).

spontaneously, then later retracted her statements) they were not. Thus the pattern is that young, fertile, nulliparous women were assaulted by postfertile and/or unmarried women. Women who were past the stage when their tamed fertility could be useful, apparently deliberately made fertile young women useless by making them wild.

The witches were thought to harm other humans as well, and 57 percent of them were accused of doing so, some (23 percent) to the point of death (see Table 2). These middle-aged women were also accused of harming domesticated nature. They were thought to be able to damage domestic processes. As Table 2 shows, 3 percent of our sample were accused of doing so. Mary Bradbury, for example, caused butter to go bad. They were also thought to stop production altogether, as when Elizabeth How caused the Perley's cow to stop giving milk. Altogether, 8.5 percent of the samples were so accused. They could damage or bewitch domestic stock, as 26 percent of them did. Sometimes the cattle, pigs, or draft animals sickened or died, and sometimes they went wild. One witch in our sample was accused of damaging an artifact—but, tellingly, one which kept tamed nature "inside": she was accused of using supernatural means to break a fence.

Evidence of maleficium also frequently took the form of testimony that the accused possessed superhuman powers. As can be seen from Table 2, such evidence was brought for 51 percent of the accused women. These women were thought to raise storms at sea, thus casting away vessels, as was thought of Mary Bradbury. They were believed to make hogs chase men, as Mary Parker was accused of doing. They were thought to create a light in a field that caused human accidents. Some of them, it was thought, could perform seemingly impossible feats, such as walking through the rain without becoming wet. Or, they could fly through the air or ride airborne on a broom. They could predict the future.

Some of the witches were believed to have worked their evil through a medium. They were accused of possessing "poppets"—small rag dolls in the image of an enemy, which when pricked with pins would cause the victim himself to suffer pain. Thirty-five percent of the women were accused of possessing "familiars," or suckling them. Familiars were small animals (dogs, cats, birds) which the devil sent to witches to aid them in doing their evil work. The familiar was believed to suckle the witch from a prenatural teat located somewhere on her body. Thus, when a witch was accused, a jury of same-gender townspeople was appointed to conduct a physical examination to determine if the witch possessed such a teat. The Salem villager who had a wart, mole, or hemorrhoid was in grave danger.

The role of the familiar was somewhat different from that of the poppet. Poppets were inert—the supernatural force somehow transferred itself from this image of the victim's body to the victim. Familiars had the added advantage that they could be sent on malefic missions—a small blue bird, a black puppy, or usually, a cat—would suddenly appear in the victim's home to torment him.

The witch's possession and use of natural and supernatural forces was threatening because it was assumed to be evil. Puritans were able to conceive of nature as saturated with supernatural forces only when such forces were evil. Why was this so?

The Puritan God was not within nature. He had made it, and existed outside and above it. As created, it was chaos and could only fulfill its telos when ordered into a Great Chain of Being, tamed and controlled from above, by man. In this manner all being was ordered to the Supreme Being in hierarchical fashion, through many layers of command and obedience. For the Puritans, there was thus only one appropriate relation to nature— to tame wild nature, order it to God, and nurture it in its tamed state. They could not conceive of working with nature, respecting its boundaries and limits, its right to be *for* itself. A careful observation of wild nature might allow one to predict its course. A respect for nature's own nature, for her limits and necessities, a capacity to "let grow and to make grow" (Meis 1986) might yield human good by creating a harmonious relationship. Instead, for the Puritans, all of nature was first, wild: uncontrollable, unpredictable, unyielding, profane. Unless it was controlled and tamed, it was not only unfruitful, it was dangerous.

In possessing supernatural powers, it was thought that the witch used life forces to pervert the Chain of Being. She did not work against nature to control it. Rather than working to tame animals, she worked with wild animals to do evil. Rather than staying in her place, she flew through the air. Rather than contending herself to whatever fate God ordained for her, calmly waiting for it to unfold, she attempted to discern the future.

Susanna Martin's case[3] is quite typical. This 72-year-old widow was accused by the circle girls, who ratified their accusations by falling into fits at her preliminary hearing. She did not help her case by laughing at their antics and declaring a lack of sympathy for them.

Martin was charged with assaulting the circle girls, and she was accused of harming others as well. Bernard Peach testified that she (or her spectral shape) entered his bedroom one Sunday night, took hold of his feet, and "drew my body into a whoope and lay upon me about an hour and one-half or two hours all of which time I could not stir or speak." He finally managed to bite three of her fingers. The next day he found her footprints and blood outside in the snow. She also apparently assaulted Elizabeth Brown, who when in her presence experienced a sensation "like birds pecking her leggs or picking her with the motion of their wings and . . . it would rise up into her stomach like a pricking payne as nayls and pinns . . . and it would rise up in her throat like a pullet's egg." She appeared in Jarvis Ring's bedchamber, lay upon him and bit his finger so hard that the mark "is still to be seen on the little finger on my right hand."

She was thought not only to have harmed humans, but to have harmed domesticated nature as well. In testimony against her, John Pressey claimed that she had bewitched his milk cattle and was capable of directing supernatural forces against him. On one occasion, he had become lost after dark and kept sighting a strange light. Frightened, he tried to strike the light with his stick, but after he gave it about "forty smart blows," he fell into a deep pit, yet "I do not know any such pit to be in the place where I was sliding into." Shortly thereafter, Susanna Martin appeared in exactly the place where the light had been. A few years later, she reviled him and his wife and claimed that he should never prosper. Specifically, she told them they would "never have but two cows" and "from that day to this we have never exceeded that number for something or other has prevented it."

John Kimball testified that he and the Martins had had a quibble about appropriate payment for a piece of land Kimball had bought from him. Kimball had offered them their choice of two cows and some other cattle but "did reserve two cows which I was not desirous to part with they being the first I ever had." Susanna threatened him in this way: "You had better [pay with those particular cows] for those will never do you no good." Kimball testified, "and so it came to pass that the next April following that very cow lay in the fair dry yard with her head to her side but stark dead; and a little while after another cow died and then an ox and then other cattle to the value of thirty pounds." In the same year Kimball desired to buy a puppy from her, but she would not let him have his choice from the litter, so he didn't agree to buy any. Upon hearing this, she said, "If I live, I'll give him puppies enough." A few days later he stumbled unaccountably upon some stumps in the woods. But soon he perceived the source of his difficulty—he was being attacked by several dark puppies, who were not hurt even when he cut them with his ax.

John Atkinson testified that Martin was angry with him because her son had traded one of their cows to him. When he went to the Martin place to receive the cow, she muttered and was unwilling that he should have the cow. When he took possession of it "notwithstanding the hamstringing and halting of her she was so mad that we could scarce get her but she broke all ropes fastened to her and we put the rope two or three times around a tree but she broke it and ran away and when she came down to the ferry we were forced to run up to our arms in water she was so fierce but after much ado we got her into the boat and she was so tame as any creature whatever."

On another occasion, William Osgood turned down the Martins when they asked him for a gift of beef. The next day one of his best cows went wild. And when Joseph Knight encountered her in the woods, his horses suddenly refused to cross a causeway—instead, they simply ran wild.

Other testimony suggested that she was a woman who could fly, walk in the rain without getting wet, and could change herself into the shape of a hog or a cat. And clearly she had made a pact with the devil because otherwise she would not possess such supernatural powers, nor would she have urged Mercy Lewis to sign the devil's book.

What did Puritans believe was the motive for such damage? The witches were asked repeatedly why they had bewitched the girls, but no satisfactory answer ever emerged. For other harms, a motive was sought and found. Usually, a witch who had harmed someone or someone's domestic production was seen to be displeased with that person. Just as Puritans believed that Satan was dissatisfied with his place, they believed some of their middle-aged women were similarly dissatisfied. Apparently, they were really frightened of this rebellion against authority and of the disruption in the Great Chain it signified.

This may explain why the officials were also interested in eliciting two other types of evidence. Table 4 shows that 34 percent of the women were accused of muttering after being refused some item for which they had begged, and 23 percent of possessing bad language or manners. Altogether, 43 percent of the women in the sample were accused of "unseemly behavior." Why were the Puritans interested in this type of evidence?

Muttering after begging might mean that the woman had actually placed a curse on the one who gave her offense. Some scholars have suggested that the real offense was not malefic witchcraft but abrasive behavior to the one who had refused, following on the heels of the refusal of neighborly aid. Thomas (1971) argues that in the most common situation, "the victim had been guilty of a breach of charity or neighborliness, by turning away an old woman who had come to the door to beg or borrow some food or drink, or the loan of some household utensil." Witch-beliefs implied that a neighborly obligation left unfulfilled might result in malefic witchcraft directed against the unneighborly person. Thomas suggests that the high percentage of women is most "plausibly explained by economic and social considerations, for it was the women who were the most dependent members of the community, and thus the most vulnerable to accusation" (Thomas, 1971, p. 553). Macfarlane's argument is similar, although he maintains that women predominated in the accusations because they were the most resistant to change, and their social position and power led to mounting hatred against them (Macfarlane, 1970).

These scholars refer to English witchcraft, but Boyer and Nissenbaum (1974) have made the same argument for Salem. They believe the accused were "on the move, socially and economically"; they were independent of the old social order. In their lack of willingness to accept their given station in life, they were typical of the emergent personality of citizens in a capitalist economy. The accusers represented the old order. "The social order was being profoundly shaken by a superhuman force which had lured all too many into active complicity with it. We have chosen to construe this force as emergent mercantile capitalism. Mather and Salem Village called it witchcraft" (Boyer & Nissenbaum, 1974, p. 209).

But this theory fails to explain why none of the men in our sample were accused of unseemly behavior and yet were accused of witchcraft. Nor does it explain why fewer than half of the accused female witches were accused of possessing bad manners, or why they were also accused of other depredations.

Rather, it seems the explanation may lie in the *meaning* of such behavior. Bad language or manners was evidence for rebellion against authority, the sign of a possible break in the Great Chain of Being. Six of the eight women accused of unmannerly behavior had been rude to a direct superior—a husband or a parent. The others were simply generally rude—but such testimony was always brought by a man.

TABLE 4   Evidence of Unseemly Behavior

	Number	Percent
Muttering after begging	12	34
Bad language/ill manners	8	23
Total	15	43

The centrality of bad manners is demonstrated also by the evidence offered in *defense* of accused women. Testimony for Elizabeth How thus indicated that she was "neighborly," that she "carried it very well," that she never reviled anyone, that she had a courteous and peaceable disposition (Woodward, 1864/1969, p. 78). Wild women were dangerous. Just by looking, touching, or cursing, just by being in the same room with domesticated pubescents, they were thought to be able to make tamed nature go wild.

The males in this sample are quite different from the women who were accused. For all thirteen, evidence was brought that they had afflicted the circle girls, and five of them were accused of harming other humans. But only one of them harmed domestic nature in any way, and none was accused of unseemly, unmannerly, or unruly behavior. The most striking thing about the male witches is their atypicality. Apart from George Burroughs, a former Puritan minister who was believed to be the Satanic priest officiating at the sabbaths (where, of course, a priest was necessary) and a deputy sheriff (John Willard), who was probably accused because he was publicly sympathetic to those he was forced to jail, 72 percent (eight of eleven) of the accused men were relatives of accused female witches. Thus, as John Demos has suggested (1970, p. 1311), they "belonged to a kind of derivative category."

The only truly typical witch among the men was Samuel Wardwell. About 55 years of age at the time of the hysteria, Wardwell owned a little farm and "for many years had been a fortune teller, strolling about, reading palms and solving life's mysteries from the broken tea leaves in the bottom of the cup" (Gemmill, 1924, p. 185). His rather high success rate at this enterprise was part of his undoing. Accused and jailed, he promptly confessed. He claimed that he was able to control animal nature—he could banish wild creatures from his fields by "bidding the devil to take" them, and he could make domesticated stock "come round about and follow me." Wardwell later retracted his confession, whereupon he was tried, convicted, and hanged (Gemmill, 1924; Woodward, 1969).

Reflection on the patterns formed by the evidence brought against witches and by their age and gender leads us to select as symbol and metaphor of witch fears the unfortunate Sarah Biber. A middle-aged woman who gossiped in the Parris kitchen with the circle girls, perhaps participating in their fortune telling, Biber was never accused of maleficium, or indeed of having made a pact with the devil. She *was* accused of "often quarreling with her husband," during which quarrels she "would call him very bad names," and of behaving in an unnurturing manner toward her children. "She wished that when her child fell into the river she had never pulled it out." Three of the four men who testified against her cited her "unruly, turbulent spirit" (Woodward, 1864/1969, pp. 203–205). Apparently, Sarah Biber's sole crime was her wildness.

WILDERNESS AND CRIMINAL JUSTICE

At its birth, philosophers justified the modern criminal justice system as a device to tame the naturally wild instincts of human beings. Its necessity was recognized when men became "weary of living in a continual state of war," as Beccaria wrote (1963, p. 11), following Hobbes's (1651/1947, p. 31) assumption that all mankind possessed "a perpetual and restless desire for power after power, that ceaseth only in death."

Contemporary criminologists often retain this frightening vision of nature as wildly dangerous. Travis Hirschi (1969, p. 31) finds no need to search for motivations to crime because "we are all animals and thus all naturally capable of committing criminal acts."

Our modern criminal justice system is permeated with this view—that only when nature is controlled is it safe. Erickson (1966) says of it that we have inherited from the Puritans an assumption that "the convict's soul is permanently depraved and that sin is an inevitable part of his personal endowment." In light of this model of the convicted criminal as inherently wild, it "makes very little sense to . . . reform him . . . The best one can do for him is to contain his reprobate spirit, in much the same way that one tames the wilder instincts of animals . . . The object [of criminal justice] is not to improve his nature but to harness it so completely that it cannot assert itself" (p. 203).

What legacy then, did the witch hysteria of 1692 and the Puritan criminal justice system's handling of it bequeath to us? What did Puritans think their purpose was? How successful were they in achieving it? How successful is the contemporary criminal justice system in achieving this same purpose?

Puritans were intensely frightened by two kinds of wilderness—that in the forests surrounding them at the edges of their carefully cultivated fields and neat towns, and that which was within human nature (and especially female human nature). Both kinds of wilderness were evil precisely because they were wild.

"Seventeenth century writing is permeated with the idea of wild country as the environment of evil," Nash (1982, p. 36) tells us. "The new world wilderness was linked with a host of monsters, witches and similar supernatural beings" (p. 29). The wilderness was evil because it had not been ordered to the patriarchal God; it was seen not only as uncontrolled, but as the location of rival religion. A "dark wilderness cave" was believed to be the site of pagan rites, and the native Americans were "not merely heathens but active disciples of the devil" (pp. 33–36). For Puritans, "the untamed forests and the Indians that lurked in their shadows represented fallen nature inhabited by the powers of darkness" (Ruether 1983, p. 81). The wild evil of nature outside the village and farm was echoed in human nature as well. The Puritan mission thus involved both "an inner battle over that 'desolate and outgrowne wildernesse of humain nature' and on the New England frontier it also meant conquering wild nature" (Nash, 1982, p. 36). In the crime of witchcraft, these two wildernesses came together in wild women who used their evil power to make tamed nature wild, too. The Puritan "errand into the wilderness" (Miller, 1956) was a mission that would bring Godly order out of a natural chaotic fecundity. Only through a project of taming could they bring fertility under control.

The criminal justice response to witchcraft focused on women apparently because it was precisely among women that the relationship to nature was wrong. Fearful of the wild in nature and in human beings, knowing no way to deal with these fears other than by creating an orderliness based upon hierarchical control, Puritan justice announced in the witch trials that which it absolutely would not tolerate. The idea of women embodied, and some of their own middle-aged widows exemplified, what Puritans feared most. Where in the natural world there is harmony based upon each creature's capacity to be for-itself and simultaneously for-the-whole, the Puritan mind saw chaos. They sought to replace the "for-itself" and "for-the-whole" of nature with a system of nature-for-man and man-for-God, ordered in hierarchical neatness through a Great Chain of (Patriarchal) Being.

In the witches, Puritans saw wild creatures independent of the Great Chain, immersed in untamed natural processes: pure chaos, pure evil. What they tried to kill in Puritan women, all Puritan women, when they hanged the witches, was a particular relationship to the created world and its fertility—a metaphysic and an epistemology diametrically opposed to their own. Were they successful?

As a boundary maintenance device (Erikson, 1966), the witch trials were certainly successful. The Puritans sacrificed a few middle-aged widows, who were not particularly useful to them in any case. But the effect of trying, imprisoning, and hanging the witches was to send a message to all the Puritans, especially to the women. Henceforward, gossiping in a group of women, having a close or familiar relationship with animals, and observing nature's ways in a respectful manner that would allow prediction of the future would be dangerous. Henceforth, fertility in women and in nature would be subjected to strict masculine design and control—and where it went wild, it would be criminally punished. Were the Puritans successful in bequeathing to their descendants a metaphysic, or epistemology, and a criminal justice system that would continue to control unruly feminine nature?

CONTEMPORARY WITCHCRAFT: THE CRIMINAL JUSTICE SYSTEM RESPONSE

> The . . . Great Chain of Being has been converted into a Becoming . . . [and] God himself is . . . identified with this Becoming. But the inversion . . . while it converts the Scale of Being into an abstract ideal schema, does not alter its essential character. (Lovejoy, 1936, p. 326)

Americans no longer hunt witches in the fashion of their Puritan ancestors. But the fear of wild nature and the intense desire to tame it for human benefit (the source of the hysteria in Salem) is still strong. Having lopped off the top of the Great Chain of Being, postmoderns have neither God nor telos to guide and restrain their interactions with nature. Instead, a "neutral," scientific technology informs our actions. Nature now tends toward no other end than to be molded by men in power to their current benefit. For while the notion of the Great Chain of Being is now identified with evolution itself and inverted so that the tendency toward diversity and fullness is seen to arise from the bottom of the hierarchy, spontaneously rather than as a deliberate plan from the top, its danger to women and nature is not lessened, but perhaps increased. If there is a God in these first years of the third millennium, He is science: now seen as capable of altering evolution itself, to the special benefit of those men currently in power.

For the patriarchal mind, wild women and wild nature still pose a significant threat to orderly, male-controlled production and reproduction. Sometimes this threat is met with a criminal justice system response, as it was in Salem Village.

Human reproduction was a significant concern of the Puritan witch hunters, who blamed female witches for abortions (both spontaneous and induced), "monstrous births," and untimely deaths from disease in young children. Exertion of male control over human reproduction is still a vital concern, as evidenced in the following recent developments: the debate over the fate of frozen embryos and their possible use for stem cell research, proposed legislation to prohibit "partial birth" abortions and to protect the "unborn victims of violence," and the first homicide conviction of a crack-using mother.

While criminal charges of various sorts have for some time been brought against crack-using pregnant women whose fetuses are harmed, the May 2001 conviction of Regina McKnight was the first conviction for homicide (Firestone, 2001). The prosecutor noted that he wanted to send a message "not to use crack cocaine" (Gaston, 2001), but the message he appeared to send was that all women have a legal duty to maintain their health during pregnancy *according to government standards*. Consider, for example, whether use of a physician-prescribed Food and Drug Administration–approved drug, which killed a fetus, would result in a homicide charge against either the doctor or the drug company. The issue here is not drug use, but control of drug use.

The debate over partial birth abortions and that surrounding the use of embryos for stem cell research share a commonality. They reveal the extent to which, consciously or unconsciously, patriarchy denies woman's bodily integrity in its willingness to use her for male-controlled reproduction. Many proponents of stem cell research are antiabortion. Their justification for the seeming inconsistency is illuminating. They make the argument that stem cell research on frozen embryos that "will be discarded anyway" is appropriate because the embryos cannot be brought to viability. The inescapable conclusion is that a pregnant woman has an obligation to carry the child to term (and perhaps to rear it). But frozen embryos are deemed fair game even to experiment with. It is judged morally appropriate to use them for the benefit of other humans, *even if* they are "human life" (Wilson, 1996).

Here the issue clearly is not the status of the embryo as a "human being from conception." Rather, the issue is who gets to control its fate. If inside a woman, it is deemed "capable of viability." If in a petri dish where no woman can be used to bring it to term, it not only can be destroyed but can be used to make cells for other humans' health needs. The inconsistency becomes a consistency. One can use women as incubators; one can use embryos to harvest stem cells. These are both under patriarchal control. Like the Salem witches, postmodern women are not allowed to be free and in control of their own bodies.

Similarly, the proposed Unborn Victims of Violence Act of 2001 criminalizes "killing or injuring an 'unborn child' during the commission of a separate federal crime. The language of the bill defines 'unborn children' as members of the human species who reside in their mothers' wombs, regardless of their developmental stage" (Colb, 2001). It finds criminal wrong not just in violation of a woman's bodily integrity and security, which an assault charge would accommodate; rather, it focuses on the life she might possibly be carrying and makes criminally liable an assailant who may have no knowledge of his "victim's" existence.

In all of these instances an embryo inside a woman is controlled by other than the woman herself; its effect on her is deemed immaterial. Similar to the homicide prosecution of a crack user, the woman is not allowed to determine what to do. Clearly, the issue is as much control of her body as it is the fate of the fetus. And it is similar in regard to non-human nature—women are still told how to interact with nonhuman nature. As well (and consistent with patriarchy's general plan), senior men may tell junior men how to interact with nonhuman nature. Thus, Vice-President Cheney's views on the environment trump those of both deep and shallow ecologists.

Domestic production is still done by women under male control. Rather than working with nature to protect humans from food poisoning, our system features farmers who raise and sell dangerous food produced unnaturally and food experts who advise housewives to overcook meat and eggs. Corporate experts prescribe antibiotic soap for "safe" kitchens, ignoring the lessons Rachel Carson taught us regarding evolution of the microbe (see Wilson, 1998). Carson's vilification by patriarchal experts (Hynes, 1989) put her in the company of the Salem witches.

Patriarchy still does not allow women to work with nature, but instead, prescribes after-the-fact control of a nature spoiled by patriarchal uses. Even environmental law is "after-the-fact" control (Wilson, 2001). As in Salem, neither nature nor woman can be wild. As with stem cells, if there is a "need," a patriarchally controlled use for nature, it trumps any prior "right" of nature to bodily integrity and its own "purposes." Currently proposed uses include oil in ANWAR and the cloning of nonhuman animals. World trade also trumps ecoprotection.

As in Salem, the desire is total control, an orderly hierarchical arrangement of fecundity. The Puritans sacrificed some of their middle-aged women to further their project of taming. In 2002, it is still powerless women who suffer, although they may not be executed as witches.

Perhaps twenty-first-century Americans have no more need than did our seventeenth-century ancestors to punish wild women for its immediate effect. Perhaps, now as then, the crucial effect of the criminal justice process is a boundary maintenance that tames all women, bringing their fertility under control, ordering it into a neat hierarchical Great Chain of (patriarchal) Being.

NOTES

1. "And God said [to man], Be fruitful, and multiply, and replenish the earth, and subdue it: and have dominion over every living thing that moveth upon the earth."
2. Information on the specific charges leveled at the witches comes from Woodward's (1864/1969) *Records of Salem Witchcraft*. Woodward collected and compiled material from preliminary hearings which includes testimony of witnesses, victims, and the accused. Woodward's records are incomplete but provide us with a sample of forty-eight accused persons, thirteen men and thirty-five women. The tables in this section are based only on the women. Later, there is a separate discussion of the accused men.
3. Evidence on Susanna Martin's case comes from Woodward (1864/1969, pp. 193ff.) and Gemmill (1924, pp. 114ff.).

REFERENCES

ADLER, M. (1986). *Drawing down the moon*. Boston: Beacon Press.

BECCARIA, C. (1963). *On crimes and punishment*. New York: Macmillan.

BOYER, P., & NISSENBAUM, S. (1974). *Salem possessed*. Cambridge, MA: Harvard University Press.

CAPORAEL, L. R. (1976, April 2). Ergotism: The satan loosed in Salem? *Science, 192*.

CAULFIELD, E. (1943, May). Pediatric aspects of the Salem witchcraft tragedy. *American Journal of Diseases of Children, 65*.

COLB, S. F. (2001). Why the Senate should refuse even to consider the Unborn Victims of Violence Act of 2001.
    Findlaw.com/colb/20010606.html

DALY, M. (1978). *Gyn/ecoolgy*. Boston: Beacon Press.

DEMOS, J. (1970, June). Underlying themes in the witchcraft of 17th century New England. *American Historical Review, 75*.

EHRENREICH, B., & ENGLISH D. (1973). *Witches, midwives and nurses: A history of women healers*. New York: Feminist Press.

ERIKSON, K. (1966). *Wayward Puritans*. Wiley.

FIRESTONE, D. (2001). Woman is convicted of killing her fetus by smoking cocaine.
    nytimes.com/2001/01/18/national/18FETU.html

GASTON, E. (2001). Drug user convicted of abuse in fetal death.
    thesunnews.com/content/myrtlebeach/2001/05/17/localA01-2092156.htm

GEMMILL, W. N. (1924). *The Salem witch trials*. Chicago, IL: A.C. McClurg.

HANSEN, C. (1968, April). Salem witches and DeForest's *Witching Times*. *Essex Institute Historical Collections, 104.*

HIRSCHI, T. (1969). *Causes of delinquency*. Berkeley, CA: University of California Press.

HOBBES, T. (1947). *Leviathan*. New York: Macmillan. (Original work published 1651)

HYNES, H. P. (1989). *The recurring silent spring*. New York: Pergamon Press.

KARLSEN, C. F. (1987). *The devil in the shape of a woman: Witchcraft in colonial New England*. New York: W.W. Norton.

KRAMER, H., & SPRENGER J. (1948). *Malleus maleficarum* (Montague Summers, Trans.). Magnolia, MA: Peter Smith Publishing. (Original work published 1486)

LEWIS, C. S. (1988). The abolition of man. In L. W. Dorset (Ed.), *The essential C. S. Lewis*. New York: Collier. (Original work published 1943)

LOVEJOY, A. O. (1953). *The great chain of being*. Cambridge, MA: Harvard University Press. (Original work published 1936)

MACFARLANE, A. (1970). *Witchcraft in Tudor and Stuart England*. London: Routledge & Kegan Paul.

MERTON, T. (1978). Wilderness and paradise. In *The Monastic Journey*. New York: Image Books.

MIES, M. (1986). *Patriarchy and accumulation on a world scale*. London: Zed Books.

MILLER, P. (1956). *Errand into the wilderness*. Cambridge, MA: Harvard University Press.

MURRAY, M. A. (1921). *The witch cult in western Europe*. New York: Oxford University Press.

NASH, R. (1982). *Wilderness and the American mind*. New Haven, CT: Yale University Press.

POPE, A. (1733). *Essay on man*.

RUETHER, R. R. (1983). Woman, body and nature. In *Sexism and God talk: Toward a feminist theology*. Boston: Beacon Press.

STARHAWK (1989). *The spiral dance: A rebirth of the ancient religion of the great goddess*. San Francisco: Harper & Row.

THOMAS, K. (1971). *Religion and the decline of magic*. London: Weidenfield and Nicoesen.

TREVOR-ROPER, H. R. (1970). The European witchcraze and social change. In M. Marwick (Ed.), *Witchcraft and sorcery*. New York: Penguin.

TURNER, F. J. (1920). *The frontier in American history*. New York: Krieger.

WHITE, L. JR. (1967, March 10). The historical roots of our ecological crisis. *Science, 155*, 1203–1207.

WILSON, N. K. (1996). An ecofeminist critique of environmental criminal law. In S. M. Edwards, T. D. Edwards, & C. B. Fields (Eds.), *Environmental crime and criminality: Theoretical and practical issues*. New York: Garland Publishing.

WILSON, N. K. (1998, November). Food fights: Libeling, labeling and the social construction of food poisoning. Paper prepared for presentation to the American Society for Criminology, Washington, DC.

WILSON, N. K. (2001). Environmental crime and justice. In M. A. DuPont-Morales, M. K. Hooper, & J. H. Schmidt (Eds.), *Handbook of criminal justice administration*. New York: Marcel Dekker.

WOODWARD, W. E. (1969). *Records of Salem witchcraft*. New York: DeCapo Press. (Original work published 1864)

3

"Mule-Headed Slave Women Refusing to Take Foolishness from Anybody"

A Prelude to Future Accommodation, Resistance, and Criminality[1]

Laura T. Fishman

The system of slavery, a reflection of a patriarchal and racist social order, legitimized and facilitated not only the economic and racist oppression but the sexual exploitation of black slave women. An extensive review of the literature on slavery was used to address how slave women accommodated and resisted these multiple forms of oppression. The findings presented here indicated that as blacks, both sexes experienced the harsh and inhuman consequences of racism and economic exploitation. In response, there was a significant convergence in male and female involvement in such forms of "criminal" resistance as murder, assault, theft, and arson. These actions were employed to improve the slaves' lot in life and to express opposition to the slave system. Criminal resistance therefore set the stage for black women's participation in the criminal activities characteristic of today. Findings also suggested that in response to sexual exploitation, gender-specific forms of accommodation (e.g., acting as breeders and sex workers) were utilized to make slave women's lives bearable. It is concluded that these forms of accommodation served as a preface to black women's vulnerability to sex-oriented crimes within the context of twentieth-century American society.

The slave system in the United States involved the forcible importation of black Africans for the express purpose of economic exploitation of their labor and bodies. Slavery was a form of involuntary servitude in which slaves were owned by others and were legal chattel. Thus slaves were a privately owned commodity to be bought and sold and disposed of at the slave owner's will. As property, slaves were deprived of most human rights and freedom, while slave owners established for themselves the rights to the services of the slaves. Given this, black slave women were obliged to submit to their masters' orders and prohibitions and therefore to submit to whatever economic and sexual exploitation was imposed upon them. Not all women reacted to the events and demands that they encountered as stoic women who accepted their life conditions passively and helplessly. Instead, slave narratives documented how black slave women actively manipulated their environment while continuously attempting to survive the inhumane conditions of slavery. In this chapter I examine how the slave system, patriarchal in its culture and structure, by legitimizing and facilitating economic and sexual exploitation, shaped some of the black women's accommodations and resistance to the institution and, in turn, set the stage for black women's participation in criminal activities characteristic of today.

Within recent years, the literature on African-American women had begun to look at the intersection of multiple structures of domination. A consistent theme in this literature (see, e.g., Dill, 1979, 1990; Lewis, 1990) suggested that the term *double jeopardy* described the dual discrimination of racism and sexism that subjugates black women. Beale (1979) contended that as blacks, they suffer all the burdens of prejudice and mistreatment that fall on anyone with dark skin. However, as women, they carry the extra burden of coping with both white and black men. King (1988, 1990) elaborated on this observation by suggesting that the reality of dual discrimination often entailed economic disadvantage. She contended that black women encountered multiple jeopardy: the simultaneous oppression of race, gender, and class. Under a system of slavery, therefore, black women were exposed simultaneously to the multiple oppressions of race, gender, and caste.

As a *total institution*[2] (Goffman, 1961), the slave system regulated every aspect of the slaves' lives from sunup to sundown (e.g., the types of work they performed; the quality and amount of food, shelter and clothing which they received; the reproductive rights of slave women). In her examination of the Auschwitz concentration camp, Pawelcznska (1979) offered some important insights into the resistance of prisoners. She observed that the formal norms and goals of the concentration camp were rendered dysfunctional to the survival of prisoners. For instance, she reported that if the prisoners abided by the rule "Thou shalt not steal" within the Ten Commandments, survival was questionable. In the face of scarce food and inadequate clothing and shelter, prisoners who did not steal would be most vulnerable to death by starvation and/or by exposure to harsh weather conditions. To steal, therefore, meant to survive. She also noted that a deeply internalized value system enabled many prisoners to survive biologically and morally, that is, to resist surrender and total submission.

Several recent research findings on the mechanisms of individual slave resistance to coercion complemented her findings. From the existing literature on slave narratives, we learned that resistance was made within the context of the slave women's particular social milieu.[3] Slave women were not only responding to their masters' values and norms, which were not, in many instances, suited to black survival, but also to stresses and strains that stemmed from their status as slaves, blacks, and women.

A number of studies reported that since black slave women shared in all aspects of the oppression of slaves in general, they participated in forms of resistance similar to those of black men. Knowing that they could not make themselves free, many investigators (e.g., Blassingame, 1972; Escott, 1979; Fox-Genovese, 1988, 1990; Genovese, 1974) reported that the vast majority of slaves struggled instead to lessen the extent of their enslavement by attempting to restrict abuses and improve their treatment. Resistance was expressed in many ways. For instance, these works indicated that such resistance was carried off both overtly in the form of slave rebellions and covertly in indirect attacks on the system, through resistance to the whip, feigning illness, conscious laziness, and other means of avoiding work and impeding production. The slave narratives also suggested that there were more extreme forms of resistance, such as murder, infanticide, assault, arson, theft, and abortion.

Within this context, then, Pawelcznska (1979) observed that not every situation in the concentration camps afforded prisoners the chance to give open battle or even to make a passive protest. Under the circumstances of the concentration camp, accommodations had to be achieved to make life more bearable and to survive. Recent research on the slave narratives (Beale, 1981; Blassingame, 1972; Rawick, 1972) has reported that slave women and slave men both accommodated to most aspects of the slave system. But as women, black slaves made some gender-specific forms of adaptation in order to improve their lot and/or to survive. Slave women outwardly accommodated to such forms of sexual oppression as breeding and prostitution. I will elaborate on these findings by describing how these forms of accommodation, functional for the perpetuation of slavery, served as a preface to black women's participation in sex-oriented crimes within the context of twentieth-century American society.

Almost no work has dealt explicitly with the more extreme forms of resistance as a precursor of current black female criminality. In the present study I examine these extreme forms of resistance as forms of "criminal resistance" that were utilized by black slave women as a means to express opposition to the slave system as well as to undermine the system that oppressed and exploited the slaves. I therefore use the concept *crimes of resistance* to broaden our analysis of crime, and I posit that crime itself can be a form of resistance insofar as it can be committed to improve one's social condition or to protest the existing social order.

However, it remains difficult to draw conclusions about the full range of patterns of accommodation and resistance employed by slave women. The literature can only provide a window on some of the kinds of accommodations and resistance strategies described by a unique population of black women and men. Information gathered here is derived primarily from the narratives of slaves who escaped to freedom through the underground railroad or by other means and from the oral history of slaves emancipated by the Civil War and whose testimonies were recorded at the end of the last century and the beginning of the twentieth century. There was consensus that these were the richest sources as to the very significant ways in which black female slaves accommodated to and resisted their condition (see, e.g., Escott, 1979; Hine, 1990; Lerner, 1972; Obitko, 1990; White, 1985). The reportings on these narratives provided an in-depth picture of the mechanisms of black slave women's accommodation and resistance, which laid the foundation for the criminal behavior of black women today.

THE SLAVE SYSTEM AND MULTIPLE OPPRESSION

As mentioned earlier, as a total institution, the slave system oppressed black women on the basis of their status as members of a degraded caste and on the basis of their race and gender. The slave and plantation system were patriarchal in structure and in culture. These systems were created by white men to benefit their monetary and personal needs. To a considerable extent, the types of jobs slaves did and the amount and regularity of labor they were forced to devote to such jobs—whether in the fields or in the masters' homes—were all dictated by the slaveholders. Given this, Fox-Genovese (1988) observed that black slave women, as workers in the fields or the Big House, were able to assume independent roles as working members of their households. As a consequence of their independence, they were able to obtain a modicum of freedom from domination of their men. It should be noted here, however, that slave women belonged to households that were not governed by their own husbands, brothers, and fathers but by their masters, and as the property of their masters, they belonged to a lower caste in which the members had no relational rights.

The treatment of slaves in terms of food, clothing, and housing was oppressive for men and women equally. Slave narratives were quite explicit about the poor quality of food, clothing, and housing that slaves were given. According to Burnham (1990), a slave woman's heavy workload, inadequate diet, and poor housing conditions constituted a serious threat to her health and life expectancy. Nevertheless, some slaves described the necessities of life as simple but supplied in adequate quantity. Others reported that food from the plantation was basically the same: cornmeal, fat pork, molasses, sometimes coffee, and depending on the master, greens and vegetables from a garden or animals hunted in the woods. As one woman said, "It warn't nothin' fine, but it was good plain eatin' what filled you up" (Blassingame, 1972). Several investigators (e.g., Blassingame, 1972; Burnham, 1990; Genovese, 1974) found that slaves resided in cramped and crowded living quarters. Shacks given to the slaves were likely to be 10 or 12 feet square with mud chimneys and no floors, doors, or windows. Because the majority of the huts contained no furniture, slaves had to sit on boxes or planks and slept on straw or dirty blankets. In addition, only enough clothing was issued for the barest level of survival. Women generally received one garment for summer and one for winter and a single pair of shoes.

Another aspect of slavery that made life onerous for male and female slaves were the harsh rules that constricted the bounds of daily life and the punishments meted out for any deviations from the rules. Most masters enforced the law strictly, rarely taking gender differences into consideration. A variety of punishments were inaugurated by slave owners, ranging from mutilation and extreme physical cruelty, to removing the slave from a work position, to selling the slave. Both Escott (1979) and Stevenson (1996) reported that the whipping of slaves was common practice, used almost universally for punishment of both female and male slaves. Punishment was meted to female slaves regardless of motherhood, pregnancy, or physical injury.

Physical coercion was not the primary territory of the male slaveholder. Jones (1985) and Fox-Genovese (1988) both observed that mistresses, in their role as labor managers, lashed out at slave women not only to punish them but also to vent their anger on slave women, who were even more oppressed than themselves. When punishing black women for minor offenses, mistresses were likely to use any readily available weapon: for example, forks, knives, or knitting needles (see, e.g., Blassingame, 1972; Burnham, 1990; Fox-Genovese, 1988; Genovese, 1974; White, 1985). According to Jones (1990): "Some of the most barbaric forms of punishment resulting in the mutilation and permanent scarring of female servants were devised by white mistresses in the heat of passion. As a group they received well-deserved notoriety for the 'veritable terror' they unleashed upon black women in the Big House" (p. 750). The slave narratives led to the conclusion that the poverty of living conditions and white violence aimed at slaves simply because of caste and race cut across gender differences.

Economic Exploitation as One Form of Oppression

> They worked, in a manner of speaking, from can to can't, from the time they could see until the time they couldn't. [Abbie Lindsay, ex-slave from Louisiana (Lerner, 1972, p. 15)]

From the earliest moments of African slavery in the United States, the economic exploitation of black women became a permanent feature of the white patriarchal and capitalist society. A brutal kind of equality was thrust upon both sexes, a process dictated by the conditions of production. The plantation system did not differentiate between the sexes in exploiting slave labor. As noted by Higgenbotham (1990), slave women were first considered to be full-time laborers and then only incidentally, wives, mothers, and homemakers. As was the case with their male counterparts, slave women labored from sunup to sundown and sometimes beyond. Unremitting toil was the cultural birth right of slave women. Jones (1985) recorded an interview by a Federal Writers Project (FWP) worker in 1937 with Hanna Davidson, who spoke of her experiences as a slave in Kentucky: "'Work, work, work,' she said; it had consumed all her days (from dawn until midnight) and all her years (she was only eight when she began minding her master's children and helping the older women with their spinning). 'I been so exhausted working, I was like an inchworm crawling along a roof. I worked till I thought another lick would kill me'" (p. 13).

Slave women generally performed the same types of labor performed by men. Fox-Genovese 1988) observed that masters commonly assigned slave women to perform labor that was considered to be inappropriate work for white women. Slaveholders did not refrain, out of respect for female delicacy, from letting a slave woman exercise her full strength. The notion of a distinctive "women's work" disappeared as slaveholders realized that "women can do the plowing very well"; slave narratives reported that a great many women did plow. To harness a double team of mules or oxen and steer a heavy wooden plow was no easy feat, yet a substantial minority of slave women endured these rigorous activities.

Although black women generally worked "like men" in the fields, researchers (Fox-Genovese, 1988; Genovese, 1974; Higginbotham, 1992; Jones, 1985, 1990) contended that masters commonly differentiated the kinds and quantities of work that slave men and women were expected to perform. Some slave narratives reported that out in the field the men each had to pick 300 pounds of cotton, while the women were each responsible for picking 250 pounds per day. Work assignments for women and men also differed according to the size of the plantation and its degree of specialization. Often, the tasks that demanded sheer muscle power were reserved exclusively for men (clearing the land of trees, rolling logs, and chopping and hauling wood). However, plantation exigencies sometimes mandated women's labor in this area, too; in general, the smaller the farm, the more arduous and varied was women's fieldwork. For instance, Jones (1990) noted: "Lizzie Atkins, who lived on a twenty-five acre Texas plantation with only three other slaves, remembered working 'until slam dark every day'; she helped to clear land, cut wood, and tend the livestock in addition to her other duties of hoeing corn, spinning thread, sewing clothes, cooking, washing dishes, and grinding corn" (p. 743).

Black women also worked under the close supervision of whites (the master, overseer, or mistress) at a forced pace in the Big House. A division of labor based on gender and age was more apparent, reflecting slave owners' attitudes about the nature of domestic service. Women predominated as household workers and were assigned to such tasks as cleaning, laundering, caring for the master's children, cooking, ironing, spinning wool, sewing, and other numerous tasks. Although the household servants may have eaten better food and worn better clothes than the field slaves, their labor was an unbearable load. It was unending toil and trouble. They were at the constant beck and call of the owner or his wife, who demanded service from the time the slaves were awakened early in the morning until the household was ready for retirement. The master's house offered no shelter from the brutality of slavery, so it is not surprising that many black women preferred fieldwork to housework.

A consistent theme in the literature suggested that the sexual division of labor under slavery actually assumed two forms: one system of work forced upon slaves by masters who valued women only as work-oxen and brood-sows, and the other initiated by the slaves themselves in the quarters. But as Jones (1985) pointed out:

> However, slave women also worked on behalf of their own families, and herein lies a central irony in the history of their labor. Under slavery, blacks' attempts to sustain their family life amounted to a political act of protest against the callousness of owners, mistresses, and overseers. In defiance of the slaveholders' tendencies to ignore gender differences in making assignments in the fields, the slaves whenever possible adhered to a strict division of labor within their own households and communities. (p. 14)

According to some researchers (see Davis, 1971, 1981; Farnham, 1990; Fox-Genovese, 1988; White, 1985), after working in the field or in the master's house all day, black women returned to their cabins to care for their children, cook, wash, sew, knit, weave, or do other kinds of work before retiring for the evening. Thus Jones (1985) and Farnham (1990) contended that the slave narratives were at odds with some historians' observations that relations between the sexes approximated domestic sexual equality. Instead, slave narratives showed that the reverse situation occurred (i.e., men working in the home was but a "sometime" activity). For example, there was no evidence that men engaged in spinning, a job that occupied much of the women's time in the evenings, nor were husbands "equally" willing to wash clothes. Men were more likely to be involved in what has been termed "traditional men's work," collecting firewood, hunting, gardening, and constructing beds, tables, and chairs. In the absence of their men, women also performed male duties, such as gathering firewood.

Sexual Oppression as Gender-Specific Oppression

In addition to economic exploitation, women under slavery were oppressed sexually. As stated by Marable (1990): "Sexual oppression and exploitation refer not only to the obvious and well-documented fact of forced sexual intercourse with white masters, but also to those forms of exploitation resulting from the very fact of her female biological system" (p. 408). Controlling black women's reproduction was essential to the perpetuation of the slave system (see, e.g., Clinton, 1990; Collins, 1990; Davis, 1971, 1981; Hine, 1990; Marable, 1990). During the decades preceding the Civil War, black women came to be valued increasingly for their fertility. Those who conceived 10 or more children became a coveted treasure. Davis (1971, 1981) noted that the ideological exaltation of motherhood did not apply to slave women. In fact, in the eyes of slaveholders, slave women were not mothers at all. Instead, as "breeders," they were simply instruments ensuring the growth of the slave labor force. They were considered animals whose monetary value could be accurately calculated in terms of their ability to bear children. Finally, as "breeders" as opposed to "mothers," their children could be sold away from them like calves from cows.

Thus it was expected that slave women would bear children as frequently as possible and if they failed to give birth, they would be sold. Barren women were avoided by their communities and punished by their owners. Some slave owners voided blacks' marriages if they suspected that the men or women were sterile. Many masters did not wait for the slaves themselves to reproduce in sufficient numbers and took matters into their own hands (Clinton, 1990; Escott, 1979). Slaves reported that one way forced breeding occurred was by masters attempting to control mating by matching up couples. In addition to manipulating pair bonding, some masters rented or borrowed men for stud service, subjecting their female slaves to forced breeding or rape. These men were referred to in slave narratives as "stock men," "travelin' niggers," or "breedin' niggers." According to Sterling (1984): "On the Blackshear place, they took all the fine looking boys and girls that was thirteen years old or older and put them in a big barn. They used to strip them naked and put them in a big barn every Sunday and leave them there until Monday morning. Out of that came sixty babies" (pp. 31–32). And Escott (1979) noted that for a much smaller number of planters, intervention took more direct forms. Some masters supervised the pairing among their slaves and encouraged or even required a "fine and stout" man to marry a similarly built woman.

Many slaveholders also took control of reproduction by constantly subjecting black slave women to violent rape. As Angela Davis (1971, 1981) observed, the slave owner, like a feudal lord, manifested and reinforced his authority to have intercourse with all the females. Many women were severely punished or threatened with being sold South if they resisted this particular terrorization. White (1985) and Farnham (1990) reported that recourse to punitive measures was not the only method employed to encourage women to reproduce. As part of their manipulation of reproduction, some slave owners adopted the practice of rewarding prolific women. For example, each time a baby was born, the slave owners might reward the mother with bonuses. Sterling (1984) further elaborated: "The majority of planters utilized the carrot rather than the stick to increase their stock. A 'good breeder' was given a pig, a calico dress, or better rations. One planter ruled that 'women with six children alive are allowed Saturday to themselves'; another promised his house servant her freedom after she bore five children, one for each of his sons and daughters. Lulu Wilson was persuaded by a white dress" (p. 32). Other subtle, or perhaps not-so-subtle, inducements were to ensure that pregnant women did less work and received more attention and rations than did nonpregnant women. This technique was employed not only to ensure the good health of mother and fetus alike, but also served as a reward for overworked slave women to have children. On plantations where the workload was exhausting and backbreaking, a lighter work assignment could be enough of an incentive to get pregnant as often as possible.

Another form that sexual exploitation assumed with the institution of slavery was prostitution. Most frequently, prostitution assumed such forms as (1) regularly providing sexual services to enhance the profit of a master, (2) concubinage, and (3) acceptance of a trinket upon acquiescing to forced sex with white overseers and planters.

However, although brothels abounded in southern cities, most of the prostitutes were not black. White (1985) provided some evidence that there existed the "fancy trade," the sale of light-skinned black women for the exclusive purpose of prostitution and concubinage. Slaves selected for their grace, beauty, and light skin were shipped to the "fancy-girl markets" of New Orleans and other cities. Thus, whereas some women worked in bordellos, the majority became the mistresses of wealthy planters, gamblers, or businessmen. Generally speaking, reported Blassingame (1972), black slave women were literally forced to offer themselves "willingly" and sometimes received a trinket for their compliance rather than a flogging for their refusal and resistance.

Expediency governed the slaveholders' posture toward female slaves. When it was profitable for the masters to exploit them as if they were men, black women were regarded in effect as genderless, but when they could be exploited and punished in ways suited only for women, they were locked into their exclusively female roles (Davis, 1971, 1981). Slave women, therefore, could hardly shape their ways of acting according to the normative structure inherent in the model of white womanhood.

ACCOMMODATIONS AND BLACK FEMALE CRIMINALITY

The findings presented here remind us about the cruelty of bondage for slave women. Like their black brothers, black women were abused physically, exploited economically, denied physical comforts and rewards, separated at times from their loved ones, denied education, and deprived of basic freedoms. But black women suffered from the anguish of sexual subjection as well. They were used as sexual objects by their masters and became victims of forced "breeding." In the face of these difficult circumstances, black slave women engaged in overt compliance to their masters' demands and conformed to the norms imposed on them in order to mollify whites, avoid trouble, or gain some benefit.

Such accommodations helped to ease the pains of their existence and to make their lives bearable. Of particular interest is that these women not only accommodated to their economic exploitation (by complying with their masters' work ethics, by working long hours in the field or in the Big House, and then returned to their homes to do domestic chores), they also coped with their sexual exploitation by becoming what their masters desired ("breeders," sexual objects to be sexually abused, prostitutes, and concubines). However, there were rewards for their compliance. Thus many slave women did not resist these exploitations because it was futile, could offer them prestige and protection, or provide them with material advantages. Clinton (1990) reported that "'[a] woman's being a slave, don't stop her from having genteel ideas; that is, according to their way, and as far as they can. They know they must submit to their masters; besides, their masters, maybe, dress 'em up, and make 'em little presents, and give 'em more privileges, while the whim lasts.' The divorce records and wills of slaveowners provide testimony of the power and influence many black concubines possessed" (p. 233).

Many slave women, especially concubines and "yeller gals," who otherwise had limited opportunities within the severely circumscribed sphere of slavery, improved their status and that of their offspring through liaisons with their owners (see Blassingame, 1972; Clinton, 1990; Frazier, 1968; White, 1985). Within this context, subjecting slave women to sexual exploitation was "naturally" done by slaveholders and overseers. This form of exploitation was justified by the common belief that unlike the sexually virtuous white woman, black women were promiscuous Jezebels. On the other hand, any kind of sexual exploitation of mistresses, who were perceived as the embodiment of various other-wordly virtues, would be sacreligious.

An important component of black womanhood is a strong work orientation and independence. Fox-Genovese (1988) contended that black women acted autonomously and self-reliantly in response to the circumstances of slavery, in order to effectively survive the system of slavery; black women took care of themselves because the circumstances of slavery forced them to do so. She argued further that the strongest case for the autonomy of slave women lay in their freedom from the domestic domination of their black men. However, slave women were not completely free of male domination. They were under the political and economic domination of their white owners. The power of the master constituted the fundamental condition of slave women's lives, however much it was hedged in by the direct and subtle resistance of the women themselves.

CRIMINAL RESISTANCE

Although black slave women accommodated to the harsh conditions of slavery, they did not passively accept the treatment dictated by their masters. Several investigators noted the significant role played by black female slaves in obstructing and thwarting the wishes and plans of their slave holders as well as the role they played resisting the slave system. This section is concerned with uncovering the more extreme forms of "criminal resistance"—murder, infanticide, theft, arson, assault—which female slaves employed to express their opposition to the slave system.

Within the more recent literature on slave women, there is consensus that since black women were equal to their men in the oppression they suffered, in some instances they asserted their equality aggressively by challenging the inhumane slave system (see Davis, 1971, 1981). Some researchers (Fox-Genovese, 1988; Genovese, 1974; White, 1985) contended that their forms of individual resistance differed somewhat from those of men, in part because of their childbearing and child care responsibilities. These responsibilities affected the female slaves' patterns of resistance. Differences in these forms of resistance also occurred as a consequence of slave owners' attitudes and beliefs about the significance of gender roles. For instance, slave narratives revealed that many slaveholders' notions of womanhood led them to reserve domestic tasks exclusively for women and specialized crafts—such as blacksmiths and carpenters—for slave men. Since these specialized crafts frequently required the men to move around the countryside, they were afforded greater opportunities to escape. In turn, as house servants, female slaves' proper "place" was in their masters' houses. Under these circumstances, they enjoyed far fewer opportunities for successful escape. Thus female and male slaves experienced some gender-specific opportunities for various forms of resistance which will be examined.

Characteristics of Female Slaves Who Resisted

In his extensive examination of slave narratives, Escott (1979) provided some important insights into characteristics of slaves who utilized some form of resistance. Escott noted that although field slaves engaged in more frequent forms of resistance, house servants also performed resistance activities. The differing roles of the sexes may account for a greater frequency of resistance performed by males. Escott's (1979) evidence showed that men were more likely to participate in those areas of resistance that required strength and endurance, such as joining in fatal confrontations with a white man. Women, on the other hand, were less likely to take part in this kind of action and approached parity with men in the area of theft. However, in two categories—verbal confrontations and striking the master—the women's resistance activities outnumbered that of the men. Most of the women who dared to strike the master were fieldhands and not house servants.

Theft: Emergence of Hustling as a Way of Life

The literature on slavery reported that stealing was commonplace among field and house slaves. Escott (1979) contended that theft was the most widespread practice of resistance and might better be called the appropriation or reappropriation of forbidden goods. Genovese (1974) reported that masters perceived theft as a normal feature of plantation life. To the slaveholders and whites generally, all blacks stole by nature. They convinced themselves that because slaves steal, they, as good fathers and mothers, merely had to take this in stride. They defined "a thieving Negro" simply as one who stole more than the average. He further stated: "Even on the best-managed plantations, which boasted well-fed slaves, the plundering of the hogpen, the smokehouse, the chicken coop, and the corncrib constituted a normal feature of plantation life" (p. 599). Acts of thievery generally were tolerated among masters and mistresses as long as the thief consumed her loot, but they were less tolerant when goods were used for trading purposes.

It was widely documented that cooks and house servants—mainly women—benefited from their position to supplement the diets of their families and friends from the storerooms of their masters (see, e.g., Burnham, 1990; Genovese, 1974). For instance, many female cooks smuggled extra rolls or meat to their homes in the slave quarters. This stolen food generally fed their families, runaways, or short-term fugitives hiding in nearby forests or swamps (Holt, 1994). Many former slaves described the pleasures of eating almost every kind of plantation produce: watermelons, eggs, chickens, sweet potatoes, hams, pig, cattle, and corn (Escott, 1979).

According to Genovese (1974), the main excuse given for stealing rested on the charge of underfeeding. Some, in fact, did not get enough to eat. Others said that even when they had no complaint about the amount of food issued, they resented the lack of variety and the assumption that they did not care about anything other than a full dinner pail of pork and cornmeal. "We had some good eats," remarked Walter Rimm of Texas "but had to steal de best things from de white folks."

Some slaves justified thievery by arguing that they stole from each other but merely took from their masters. As reported by Genovese (1974), slave women figured that if they belonged to their masters, they could not steal from him. The act of "theft" in their view only transferred the masters' property from one form to another and the slave owner lost nothing in the process. In addition, they reasoned that if it was so wrong to steal, then why had their masters stolen the black people from their homeland in the first place? There was satisfaction to be gained from outwitting and outfoxing "Old Massa" in this fashion. Other slave narratives documented another satisfaction to be gained from theft. According to Lichtenstein (1988), some slaves perceived theft as the expression of the rights of parents to provide extra food for their children. Theft then functioned not only to feed the slave children but to undermine the control of slave diets as dictated by their slave owners. Finally, a few slaves explained that theft occurred at the instigation of their masters, who encouraged them to steal from neighboring farms and plantations (see Genovese, 1974).

For the many female slaves, stealing became a science and an art employed as much for the satisfaction of outwitting the slave owner as anything else (see Lichtenstein, 1988). To prevent detection, female slaves devised many strategies from putting pepper in the dog's eyes, to striking a single blow to silence their prey, to burying all the chicken feathers in the ground (Escott, 1979; Genovese, 1974). Genovese (1974) noted that:

> Lewis Clarke told a particularly adept woman whose overseer once almost caught her boiling a pig. Upon hearing his approach, she placed the pot on the floor, covered it with a board, and sat her young daughter upon it. It seemed the poor child had a terrible cold that just had to be sweated out of her. Quick thinking, but not so quick. Like many other slaves this woman had done her thinking in advance and tried to have a contingency plan for every emergency. (p. 606)

It is clear from slave accounts that one component of the hustling strategy emerged during slavery as a response to the harsh physical deprivations as well as the inhumane treatment of masters. For example, a female ex-slave's account revealed that the slaves' food allowance was not considered a gift to them from their masters and mistresses. Instead, she argued that this food allowance was given in exchange for the slaves' labor. Upon making this observation, she then came to the conclusion that, "if a slave did steal, he never take nothin' but what been belong to him" (see Lictenstein, 1988, p. 259). Theft therefore became part of a slave's survival package, as income from theft had become an integral part of lower-income blacks' females' survival package within twentieth-century American society. Several authors who studied the more current black lower-class community (Brooks, 1980; Fields & Walters, 1985; Glasgow, 1981; Valentine, 1978) suggested that most black males and females, being offered little from the community in the way of resources or controls, developed some knowledge of hustling in order to survive. They needed to combine income from intermittent employment, welfare, and hustling to maintain even a low standard of living. According to Fields and Walters (1985) and Valentine (1978), hustling referred to a wide variety of conventional, sometimes extralegal or illegal activities, designed to produce economic gain and was widely accepted and practiced in the slums and ghettos of larger cities. The findings presented here indicated that slavery was a precursor to hustling, which not only ensured survival but served as an active form of resistance to the slave system.

Homicide and Assault as Criminal Resistance

> "Fight, and if you can't fight, kick; if you can't kick, then bite," one slave advised her daughter. A sizable minority of "fighting, mule-headed" women refused to "take foolishness" from anybody. (Sterling, 1984, p. 56)

Insolence to the masters and overseers comprised only one aspect of slave resistance to slavery. Overt resistance in the form of assaultive and homicidal behavior made up another form of slaves' reactions to the system. This form of resistance strongly suggested that female slaves took their multiple oppression personally.

Frequently, violent confrontations that led to assault and homicide were spontaneous and unplanned when they occurred in the fields and in the Big House. The most common types of violent confrontations occurred as an outcome of vigorous altercations with the slave owners or overseers. Fights were often vigorous. Disagreements could escalate into physical battles. Any spark could set off the reaction (e.g., criticism for work the slave women knew had been done). A slave woman might submit to any and all abuse for years, then, suddenly fed up, fight any owner or overseer who attempted to criticize her. The slave women who struck back did not suffer a paralysis of fear; it was not unthinkable to stand up and fight (Escott, 1979; Jones, 1985; Lerner, 1972; Sterling, 1984).

Violence also frequently grew out of confrontations in the field over the amount and pace of work. According to Fox-Genovese (1988) and Stevenson (1996), field women fiercely defended their sense of acceptable workloads and violently resisted abuse of power, which for many meant any discipline at all. In some instances, reported Fox-Genovese (1988), some overseers rashly sought confrontations:

> Irene Coates remembered that one day when a group of women were hoeing, the overseer rode by and struck one of them across the back with a whip. A woman nearby said "that if he ever struck her like that, it would be the day he or she would die." The overseer overheard her and took the first opportunity to strike her with his whip. As he started to ride off, the woman whirled around, struck him on the head with her hoe, knocking him from his horse, and then "pounced upon him and chopped his head off." Then, going temporarily mad, she "proceeded to chop and mutilate his body; that done to her satisfaction, she then killed his horse." Her work completed, she "calmly went to tell the master of the murder." (p. 317)

Some women resorted to assault and/or murder in response to threats of whippings and actual brutal assaults perpetuated by masters, mistresses, and overseers. The following account revealed several incidents in which black women reacted violently (Obitko, 1990):

> There was Crecie, for example, who pulled up a stump and whipped an overseer with it when he tried to lash her; or Aunt Susie Ann, who pretended to faint while she was being whipped and then tripped the overseer so that he couldn't stand up; or Lucy, who knocked an overseer over and tore his face up so that the doctor had to tend to him; or the mammy who nursed a child but later, when he tormented her, did not hesitate to beat him until he wasn't able to walk; or Aunt Adeline, who committed suicide rather than submit to another whipping; or Cousin Sally, who hit her master over the head with a poker and put his head in the fireplace. (p. 988)

Not only did women attempt to protect themselves but also resisted their slaveholders' meting out lashings to their children. These mothers considered protection of their children as an important obligation, and occasionally they were willing to risk death by trying to terminate these whippings by physically attacking the slaveholders (Holt, 1994). Slave women also sometimes violently resisted sexual exploitation. Since southern law did not recognize the rape of black women as a crime, often the only recourse slave women had was to fight off their assailants (Weiner, 1998). The following incident is from the life of Bishop Loguen's mother, who was the mistress of a white man near Nashville, Tennessee (Frazier, 1968):

> When she was about the age of twenty-four or five, a neighboring planter finding her alone at the distillery, and presuming upon privileges of his position, made insulting advances, which she promptly repelled. He pursued her with gentle force, and was still repelled. He then resorted to a slaveholder's violence and threats. These stirred all the tiger's blood in her veins. She broke from his embrace, and stood before him in bold defiance. He attempted again to lay hold of her—and careless of caste and slave laws, she grasped the heavy stick used to stir the malt, and dealt him a blow which made him reel and retire. But he retired only to recover and

return with the fatal knife, and threats of vengeance and death. Again she aimed the club with unmeasured force at him, and hit the hand which held the weapon, and dashed it to a distance from him. Again he rushed upon her with the fury of a madman, and she then plied a blow upon his temple, which laid him, as was supposed, dead at her feet. (p. 56)

Fox-Genovese (1988) noted that some women reacted in a violent manner when they believed their masters had overstepped the limits of their authority that they could accept as legitimate. Finding themselves in an untenable situation, they frequently turned to violent resistance. Fox-Genovese (1988) recorded how one of Nancy Bean's aunts "was a mean, fighting woman": "Her master, presumably because he could not master her, determined to sell her. 'When the bidding started she grabbed a hatchet, laid her hand on a log and chopped it off. Then she throwed the bleeding right hand in her master's face'" (p. 329).

Specialization of skills according to gender offered female slaves some gender-specific opportunities to engage in homicide. For instance, gender conventions that assigned slave women to kitchens, to child care, and to nursing resulted in poisoning becoming an increasingly female activity. In the case of cooks and house servants, they had the greatest accessibility to the necessary ingredients for poisoning. Arsenic and other similar compounds were most frequently used. When they were not accessible, slaves were known to have resorted to mixing ground glass in the gravy for their master's table. Black slave women proved especially skilled at poisoning their masters, a skill that must have been transmitted down through the generations. Generally, these acts were calculated and initiated on an individual basis (Fox-Genovese, 1988, 1990; Genovese, 1974; White, 1985).

Periodically, the slaves on a plantation conspired to murder a master or overseer; such a murder reflected the collective judgment of the quarters. According to Genovese (1974), these actions struck at especially brutal whites, but in some cases slaves claimed the lives of reputedly kind masters and thereby suggested intense hostility toward slavery itself. In the face of the kinds of physical and sexual abuse that slaves encountered, it was not surprising to find that throughout slavery there was a persistence in the hostility of slaves and violence against slave owners and overseers as immediate oppressors.

Men and women conspiring together to kill overseers and their masters was not out of the ordinary. The literature on slave revolts occasionally mentioned that a woman was part of a conspiracy, but no documentation of the specific contribution of black women in these plots had been made. Obitko (1990) contended that if more males than females participated in rebellions, perhaps such a form of resistance presented the only successful manner in which the males could resist the forces of slavery. Black women, on the other hand, were constantly in a day-to-day manner resisting the conditions of slavery. Therefore, it could not be said that females did not participate in slave insurrections but that they simply found other means of resistance more effective.

Brutal resistance therefore was not the sole preserve of slave men. As documented here, slave women also physically fought their masters, mistresses, and overseers as well as rebelled and ran away. In many instances, these women refused to be broken no matter how many floggings they received. Instead, they continued to fight back in an uncompromising manner. Black slave women earned reputations as fighters. According to Obitko (1990), they were tough, powerful, and spirited. As pointed out, the black female directed most of her resistance against physical cruelty; some women would not submit to the whip, while others endured it until they reached a point when they would no longer tolerate their oppression.

Fox-Genovese (1988) contended that black women had to rely on themselves for protection against the attacks of masters and overseers. It was they who most likely had to defend themselves and their families since their men—brothers, fathers, and husbands—could offer them neither protection nor security. It therefore was expected that slave women would learn to defend themselves against abusive masters or mistresses, against attacks on their integrity or work ethics, and finally, against sexual violation of their bodies. In addition, women who knew that they were their masters' children had special reason to resent the orders of his overseers and drivers and to test the limits of their enslavement.

Arson as a Form of Criminal Resistance

Arson was another favored form of violent resistance. For the slaves, arson had much to recommend it as a way of settling scores. Arson required no great physical strength or financial resources and could easily be concealed. Genovese (1974) noted that next to theft, arson was the most common slave "crime," one that slaveholders dreaded almost constantly. All too frequently, slaveholders saw their gin houses, barns, or homes burned down, and in some cases, slaveholders saw the better part of a year's harvest go up in smoke.

From the literature we gleaned that women, to a lesser extent than men, did participate in arson (Escott, 197; Giddings, 1984). As arsonists, women usually worked alone or at most in groups of two or three (Giddings, 1984): "In 1766 a slave woman in Maryland was executed for setting fire to her master's home, tobacco house, and outhouse, burning them all to the ground. The prosecutor in the case noted that there had been two other houses full of tobacco burnt 'in the country this winter'" (p. 39). As reported by Genovese (1974), an arsonist's display of resistance did not always win support or encouragement in the slave quarters. If the slave, for instance, burned down the master's house, the carriage-house, or some other building with little economic significance, the slaves might protect the arsonist. However, when a corncrib, smokehouse, or gin house was burned down, other slaves were not likely to feel any sympathy for the arsonist. Destruction of food stores meant that they would have less to eat. Destruction of cotton meant severe losses to their master and the potential sale of one or more members of the slave community, or even worse, bankruptcy and the breakup of the community together.

GENDER-SPECIFIC FORMS OF CRIMINAL RESISTANCE

As mentioned earlier, slave women performed a reproductive function vital to slave owners' financial interests and to the growth of the slave system in general. Yet slave women resisted slaveholders and overseers' attempts to exploit them sexually. As women, female slaves engaged in such forms of resistance associated with their sexuality and reproductive capacities as infanticide and abortion.

Possibly the most devastating means for undermining the slave system that slave women had at their disposal was infanticide. The frequency with which this occurred is by no means clear. Several historians contended that infanticide was quite rare and did not become a major problem for the slaveholders. It is important to note that the relatively small number of documented cases is not as significant as the fact that infanticide occurred at all (Genovese, 1974; Hine, 1990; White, 1985).

There was some consensus in the literature that the major motivation behind infanticide was that slave women preferred to end their children's lives rather than allow the children to grow up enslaved. Fox-Genovese (1988, pp. 315–316) observed that some women who could live with their own situation but could not accept what was done to their children, took some drastic measures. For instance:

> Lou Smith's mother told her of a woman who had borne several children, only to see her master sell them when they were one or two years old. "It would break her heart. She never got to keep them." After the birth of her fourth baby, "she just studied all the time about how she would have to give it up," and one day she decided that she just was not going to let her master sell that baby. "She got up and give it something out of a bottle and purty soon it was dead. 'Course didn't nobody tell on her or he'd of beat her nearly to death."

Hine (1990) contended that slave women did not perceive infanticide as murder but as an act that expressed a higher form of love and a clear understanding of the "living death" that awaited children under slavery. These acts also occurred in response to the slave owners abusing their children. Thus, reported White (1985): "An Alabama woman killed her child because her mistress continually abused it. In confessing her guilt, she claimed that her master was the father of the child, and that her mistress knew it and treated it so cruelly that she had to kill it to save it from further suffering" (p. 88).

Another motivation behind infanticide was that it was a response to the slave owners' threats to sell slave children. Many times, owners used the sale or the threat of sale of slave children as a means of manipulating their troublesome slaves. In turn, many slave women used their children to manipulate their masters. According to White (1985, p. 88), there was one documented instance in which a female slave was told that she must be sold following an incident in which she physically attacked her mistress. To maximize the harshness of the punishment, she was informed by her master that her infant would remain on the plantation. One of her older daughters recalled her mother's response: "At this, Ma took the baby by its feet, a foot in each hand, and with the Baby's head swinging downward, she vowed to smash its brains out before she'd leave it. Tears were streaming down her face. . . . It was seldom that Ma cried and everyone knew that she meant every word. Ma took her baby with her. . . ." And finally, infanticide occurred as a response to rape or forced pregnancy.

A second method of female resistance to slavery in general and to sexual exploitation in particular took the form of abortion. It was, however, almost impossible to determine whether slave women practiced abortion. These matters were exclusive to the female world of the slave quarters, and when the women needed abortions performed, they were attended to in secret. In a recent study of the black family, Gutman (1976) observed that the slave woman's decision to terminate her pregnancy was one act that was totally beyond the control of the master of the plantation. Gutman offered evidence of several southern physicians who commented upon abortion and the use of contraceptive methods among the slave population:

> The Hancock County, Georgia, physician E. M. Pendleton reported in 1849 that among his patients "abortion and miscarriage" occurred more frequently among slave than white free women. The cause was either "slave labor" (exposure, violent exercise, etc.) or "as the planters believe, that the Blacks are possessed of a secret by which they destroy the

fetus at an early stage of gestation." All county practitioners, he added, "are aware of the frequent complaints of planters about the unnatural tendency in the African female population to destroy her offspring. Whole families of women . . . fail to have any children. (pp. 80–81)

Gutman also recounted a situation in which a planter had kept between four and six slave women "of the proper age to breed" for 25 years and that "only two children had been born on the place." When the slave owner brought new slaves, every pregnancy miscarried by the fourth month. Finally, it was discovered that the women were taking "medicine" supplied by an old slave woman to induce abortions. Hine (1990) suggested that if those women did not resist slavery by actually having an abortion, they resisted even more covertly by aiding those who desired them. It was possible that a sort of female conspiracy existed on the southern plantation.

White (1985) indicated some reasons why slave women might have practiced abortion. Certainly, they had reason not to want to bear and nurture children who could be sold from them at a slave master's whim. They had ample cause to deny whites the satisfaction of realizing a profit on the birth of their children. They may also have sought, as might any white or free black women, to avoid pregnancy and childbirth. Since obstetrics had not yet evolved into a science, childbirth was dangerous.

In these instances, contended Hine (1990), infanticide and abortion provided slave women with an effective means for gaining power over their masters and control over at least part of their lives. Slave women knew that if their infanticide and abortions were discovered, it was a crime against their masters' property. According to Giddings (1984), as documented in a slave narrative, the women understood the significance of their act. "If all bond women had been of the same mind," wrote the slave Jane Blake, "how soon the institution could have vanished from the earth" (p. 46).

In conclusion, slave narratives indicated that mothers cared dearly for their children and that infanticide and abortion constituted costly forms of resistance. Those who employed these forms of resistance did so at considerable pain to themselves, resisting from the very core of their experiences as women. Moreover, noted Giddings (1984), they were implicitly challenging their masters, who protected the sexuality and revered the motherhood of white women while denying these attributes of black women.

DISCUSSION

The findings presented here tell us that slave women were not sheltered from life's ugliness or dependent on their men for subsistence goods and service. Their society did not discourage them from taking initiatives in their quest for survival. The dehumanizing forces and the conditions of the slave system, as a total institution, warranted the rebelliousness and resistance that black women displayed. Coupled with the deplorable conditions created by the system was the unique position of women among the slaves—that is, they were valued as economic assets and exploited as sexual objects. By virtue of their participation in the slave economy and in reproduction, these women would not act the part of the passive female but could experience the need to challenge the conditions of their subjugation. They came to be active in such criminal forms of resistance as theft, murder, assault, and arson because of their social position, a position that encouraged women to be as assertive, independent, and risk taking as men. Within this context, the findings pointed out that slave women employed such forms of resistance as hustling and fighting in order to survive within the slave system as well as to undermine the system.

The findings presented here strongly suggested that some female offending could be interpreted as challenging patriarchal control and asserting independence, but much could be attributed to both economic necessity and rebellion. As suggested by King's (1988, 1990) observations, female participation in violent crimes as well as theft may stem from the frustration, alienation, and anger that was associated with gender and race. But it was through looking at the broader issues of multiple structures—in this case, caste, race, and gender as forms of oppression—that the resistance of black women had a more complex meaning.

It is important to note here that slave women's employment of resistance strategies was effective insofar as these strategies undermined the authority of slaveholders, gained the respect of their fellow slaves, and empowered the women themselves. In turn, these acts of resistance served as a mirror image of the slave system itself. Violence was a major dimension of slavery. Most white violence, directed at slaves, assumed the form of homicide, beatings, tortures, and rape. In turn, it was not surprising that black women responded to the pervasive violence by committing violent acts themselves. Theft was another major dimension of slavery. The form it assumed was the forcible kidnapping of African women and men in order to enslave them for the purposes of slaveholders. In turn, the findings indicated that slave women's reactions to the theft of their bodies included extended participation in theft from the masters' property.

From slave narratives, we also learned that black slave women had to perform socially and biologically determined gender-role-stereotyped work. Not only did they constitute an important and necessary part of the workforce but through their childbearing function, they became the one group responsible for the perpetuation of slavery. In turn, they were also utilized to satisfy the sexual needs of slaveholders and wealthy planters (i.e., they were sexually violated and forced into prostitution and concubinage). These accounts also revealed that in many instances, the accommodations women made to sexual exploitation could also be considered acts of resistance. To survive was to resist; and in order to survive, slave women complied to their masters' sexual violations. To participate in prostitution and rape meant nothing more than to survive, to try to adapt to conditions as they were. In this sense they may well have a great deal in common with inmates in concentration camps and other forms of total institutions.

Hooks (1981) broadened the analysis by pointing out that black slave women, engaged in various forms of accommodation and resistance associated with their sexuality and reproductive capacities, were reacting to the process of defeminization. She contended that slavery, a reflection of a patriarchal and racist social order, not only oppressed black men but oppressed and defeminized slave women. Black women were not permitted to conform to the dominant culture's model of "true womanhood," just as black men were unable to conform to the dominant culture's definition of "true manhood." The slave owners attempted to reestablish black women's femaleness by reducing them to the level of their biological being. Thus whites' sexual violations, enforced breeding, and other forms of sexual exploitation established black women as female animals. Slave women's resistance to the various forms of sexual exploitation posed an undermined threat to accept their defeminized status. They attacked the very assumption upon which the slave system was constructed and maintained.

Finally, the literature on slave narratives led to the conclusion that black women historically exhibited criminal behavior in response to the multiple oppressions they encountered. And in response to being black, women, and lower class, the kinds of crimes they engaged in during slavery and the twentieth century were both similar, yet different from black men's crimes. They might participate in aggressive crime, grand larceny, and sex crimes, but they tended to bring to these activities their gender identities as women. It is this identity that created a divergence from the kinds and manner in which black men committed crimes. Thus the findings here provide some important insights into how the "criminal" response of black women to slavery had persisted through the twentieth century.

NOTES

1. This chapter is adapted from the author's article, "Slave women, resistance and criminality: A prelude to future accommodations," *Women and Criminal Justice,* 7, 35–65 (1995).
2. A total institution is one that completely absorbs and structures the identities and behavior of actors within it (see Goffman, 1961).
3. Fredrickson and Lasch (1989) corroborated the contention presented here that the social milieu in which slave resistance occurred typically was the plantation system, a total institution which for the most part resembled the prison system.

REFERENCES

BEALE, F. M. (1979). Double jeopardy: To be black and female. In T. Cade (Ed.), *The black woman: An anthology* (pp. 90–100). New York: New American Library.

BLASSINGAME, J. W. (1972). *The slave community: Plantation life in the antebellum South.* New York: Oxford University Press.

BROOKS, A. B. (1980). The black woman within the program and service delivery systems for battered women: A cultural response. In *Battered women: An effective response* (Chapter 2). St. Paul, MN: Minnesota Department of Corrections.

BURNHAM, D. (1990). The life of the Afro-African woman in slavery. In D. C. Hine (Ed.), *Black women in American history: From colonial times through the nineteenth century* (Vol. 1, pp. 197–211). Brooklyn, NY: Carlson Publishing.

CLINTON, C. (1990). Caught in the web of the Big House: Women and slavery. In D. C. Hine (Ed.), *Black women in American history: From colonial times through the nineteenth century* (Vol. 1, pp. 225–239). Brooklyn, NY: Carlson Publishing.

COLLINS, P. H. (1990). *Black feminist thought: Knowledge, consciousness, and the politics of empowerment.* Boston: Unwin Hyman.

DAVIS, A. Y. (1971). Reflections on the black women's role in the community of slaves. *Black Scholar,* 3, 2–15.

DAVIS, A. Y. (1981). *Women, race and class.* New York: Random House.

DILL, B. T. (1979). The dialectics of black womanhood. *Signs: Journal of Women in Culture and Society,* 4, 543–555.

DILL, B. T. (1990). Race, class, and gender: Prospects for an all-inclusive sisterhood. In D. C. Hine (Ed.), *Black women's history: Theory and practice* (Vol. 1, pp. 121–140). Brooklyn, NY: Carlson Publishing.

ESCOTT, P. D. (1979). *Slavery remembered: A record of twentieth-century slave narratives.* Chapel Hill, NC: University of North Carolina Press.

FARNHAM, C. (1990). Sapphire? The issue of dominance in the slave family, 1830–1865. In D. C. Hine (Ed.), *Black women in American history: From colonial times through the nineteenth century* (Vol. 2, pp. 369–384). Brooklyn, NY: Carlson Publishing.

FIELDS, A., & WALTERS, J. M. (1985). Hustling: Supporting a heroin habit. In B. Hanson, G. Beschner, J. M. Walters, & E. Bouvelle (Eds.), *Life with heroin: Voices from the inner city* (pp. 49–73). Lexington, MA: Lexington Books.

FOX-GENOVESE, E. (1988). *Within the plantation household: Black and white women in the old South.* Chapel Hill, NC: University of North Carolina Press.

FOX-GENOVESE, E. (1990). Strategies and forms of resistance: Focus on slave women in the United States. In D. C. Hine (Ed.), *Black women in American history: From colonial times through the nineteenth century* (Vol. 2, pp. 409–431). Brooklyn, NY: Carlson Publishing.

FRAZIER, E. F. (1968). *The Negro family in the United States.* New York: Macmillan.

FREDRICKSON, G. M., & LASCH, C. (1989). Resistance to slavery. In P. Finkelman (Ed.), *Rebellions, resistance, and runaways within the slave South* (pp. 141–156). New York: Garland Publishing.

GENOVESE, E. D. (1974). *Roll, Jordan, roll: The world the slaves made.* New York: Pantheon Books.

GIDDINGS, P. (1984). *When and where I enter: The impact of black women on race and sex in America.* New York: William C. Morrow.

GLASGOW, D. G. (1981). *The black underclass: Poverty, unemployment and entrapment of ghetto youth.* New York: Vintage Books.

GOFFMAN, E. (1961). *Asylums: Essays on the social situation of mental patients and other inmates.* Garden City, NY: Doubleday.

GUTMAN, H. (1976). *The black family in slavery and freedom, 1750–1925.* New York: Pantheon Books.

HIGGINBOTHAM, E. B. (1990). Beyond the sound of silence: Afro-American women in history. In D. C. Hine (Ed.), *Black women's history: Theory and practice* (Vol. 1, pp. 175–191). Brooklyn, NY: Carlson Publishing.

HIGGINBOTHAM, E. (1992). We were never on a pedestal: Women of color continue to struggle with poverty, racism, and sexism. In M. L. Andersen & P. H. Collins (Eds.), *Race, class, and gender* (pp. 183–191). Belmont, CA: Wadsworth Publishing.

HINE, D. C. (1990). Female slave resistance: The economics of sex. In D. C. Hine (Ed.), *Black women in American history: From colonial times through the nineteenth century* (Vol. 2, pp. 657–666). Brooklyn, NY: Carlson Publishing.

HOLT, S. A. (1994). Symbols, memory, and service: Resistance and family formation in nineteenth century African America. In L. E. Hudson, Jr. (Ed.), *Working toward freedom: Slave society and domestic economy in the American South* (pp. 192–210). Rochester, NY: University of Rochester Press.

HOOKS, B. (1981). *Ain't I a woman: Black women and feminism.* Boston: South End Press.

JONES, J. (1985). *Labor of love, labor of sorrow: Black women, work, and the family from slavery to the present.* New York: Basic Books.

JONES, J. (1990). "My mother was much of a woman": Black women, work, and the family under slavery. In D. C. Hine (Ed.), *Black women in American history: From colonial times through the nineteenth century* (Vol. 3, pp. 737–772). Brooklyn, NY: Carlson Publishing.

KING, D. K. (1988). Multiple jeopardy, multiple consciousness: The context of a black feminist ideology. *Signs: Journal of Women in Culture and Society, 14,* 43–72.

KING, D. K. (1990). Multiple jeopardy, multiple consciousness: The context of a black feminist ideology. In D. C. Hine (Ed.), *Black women's history: Theory and practice* (Vol. 1, pp. 331–361). Brooklyn, NY: Carlson Publishing.

LERNER, G. (Ed.). (1972). *Black women in white America: A documentary history.* New York: Pantheon Books.

LEWIS, D. K. (1990). A response to inequality: Black women, racism and sexism. In D. C. Hine (Ed.), *Black women's history: Theory and practice* (Vol. 2, pp. 383–405). Brooklyn, NY: Carlson Publishing.

Lichtenstein, A. (1988). "That disposition to theft, with which they have been branded": Moral economy, slave management and the law. *Journal of Social History*, 21, pp. 413–440.

Marable, M. (1990). Groundings with my sisters: Patriarchy and the exploitation of black women. In D. C. Hine (Ed.), *Black women's history: Theory and practice* (Vol. 2, pp. 407–445). Brooklyn, NY: Carlson Publishing.

Obitko, M. E. (1990). "Custodians of a house of resistance": Black women respond to slavery. In D. C. Hine (Ed.), *Black women in American history: From colonial times through the nineteenth century* (Vol. 3, pp. 985–998). Brooklyn, NY: Carlson Publishing.

Pawelcznska, A. (1979). *Values and violence in Auschwitz: A sociological analysis.* Berkeley, CA: University of California Press.

Rawick, G. P. (1972). *From sundown to sunup: The making of the black community.* Westport, CT: Greenwood Publishing.

Sterling, D. (1984). *We are your sisters: Black women in the nineteenth century.* New York: W.W. Norton.

Stevenson, B. E. (1996). *Life in black and white: Family and community in the slave south.* New York: Oxford University Press.

Valentine, B. L. (1978). *Hustling and other hard work: Life styles in the ghetto.* New York: Free Press.

Weiner, M. F. (1998). *Mistresses and slaves: Plantation women in South Carolina, 1830–80.* Urbana, IL: University of Illinois Press.

White, D. G. (1985). *Arn't I a woman? Female slaves in the plantation South.* New York: W.W. Norton.

SECTION II

Women and the Law

4

Postpartum Syndrome and the Legal System

Tara C. Proano-Raps and Cheryl L. Meyer

Postpartum syndromes are inconsistently acknowledged by the psychological and medical communities, resulting in a lack of definitive criteria for diagnosis. This lack of clarity can affect legal processes, particularly in criminal courts. In this chapter the current and historical status of postpartum diagnoses is examined, particularly as it relates to the admission of postpartum syndromes into evidence in criminal and civil courts. The authors of this chapter assert that gender inequality and cultural expectations of "good" women and mothers affect reactions to the use of postpartum syndromes in court processes. The politics of gender are addressed and solutions are offered for assisting, rather than pathologizing, women with postpartum syndromes.

On November 22, 1965 in Hawaii, Maggie Young drowned her five children, ages 8 months to 8 years, one by one in the bathtub. She then laid the bodies out on twin beds, four girls on one bed and the only boy on the other bed. Young was reportedly despondent over her perceived inability to care for her children. Earlier that year, she had been hospitalized for two months as the result of a "mental breakdown." Young immediately confessed to the killings and was committed to a state hospital. Approximately six months later, she escaped while on a pass and hung herself (Shapiro, 2001). During that same year, Andrea Yates was born.

Thirty-six years later, on June 20, 2001, Andrea Yates drowned her five children ages 6 months to 7 years, in their home in a Houston, Texas suburb. Like Young, she reportedly held them under the bath water, one by one, first Luke, 2, then Paul, 3, and John, 5. Noah, age 7, walked in while his mother was drowning 6-month-old Mary. He asked his mother, "What's wrong with Mary?" According to Ms. Yates, she told Noah to get into the bathtub. He ran but she caught him and forced him under the water. She then called 911 and her husband Rusty, a NASA computer engineer, who had left for work just an hour earlier. When police arrived, they found the four youngest children wrapped in sheets on a bed and the oldest child still in the bathtub. All were dead. Ms. Yates reportedly told police that she had thought about killing the children for months because she believed that they had been permanently damaged as a result of her bad mothering (Thomas, 2001).

By all accounts, Ms. Yates was a compassionate, generous person and a loving mother. She was valedictorian of her high school class and was described as a "perfect" child. As both a child and an adult, she was eager to please. Previously a nurse, Ms. Yates quit her job to stay home with her children. She took care of her father when he was ill with Alzheimer's and home-schooled the children. However, at the time of the murders, Ms. Yates was suffering from severe postpartum depression, her second episode. She experienced her first episode in 1999, after the birth of her fourth child. She attempted suicide and was subsequently hospitalized. Through the use of psychotropic medications, Ms. Yates recovered, but in November 2001 the Yates had a fifth child and the postpartum depression appeared to return. In March, Ms. Yates's father died and she became even more withdrawn and robotic. The psychotropic medications were not as successful this time. Just prior to the killings, Ms. Yates's medications were changed and she was taken off her antipsychotic medication (suggesting that she may have had postpartum psychosis). A private person, she had been reluctant to seek counseling, although told a friend that she was considering it (Thomas, 2001).

James Young, Maggie Young's husband, had the following to say about the Yates tragedy: "Medical science needs to recognize this condition earlier and help the mother before it develops into paranoid schizophrenia, as it did in the case of Maggie. . . . This ill woman [Yates] does not need to be sentenced to prison; certainly not charged with first-degree murder. . . . My wife was charged with first-degree murder. But Hawaii justice recognized her illness and gave her the medical help she needed. Unfortunately, she did not survive the cure" (Shapiro, 2001).

Like James Young, some people responded to Andrea Yates with compassion. Others reacted with anger. Most felt shocked and confused and asked themselves: "How could a mother do this to her children?" For many, the diagnosis of postpartum depression does not sufficiently explain the behavior of Andrea Yates. They want more details, a clearer understanding of how an apparently loving family could experience such tragedy.

In this chapter, we seek to discuss why postpartum syndromes are regarded with such suspicion by both professionals and laypersons and, in particular, how this can result in unjust legal outcomes for women with a postpartum syndrome. Initially, a brief history and description of postpartum syndromes is presented. Then we focus on the level of recognition and acceptance of postpartum syndromes by scientific communities and the resulting difficulty this can create in admitting postpartum syndromes into evidence in criminal courts. This is contrasted with the relative ease with which postpartum syndromes can be admitted into evidence in civil courts. An additional focus of this chapter is the politics of gender and the social construction of motherhood, which is used to explain why disparities in the legal system can continue to exist.

HISTORY OF POSTPARTUM SYNDROMES

Despite the heightened attention recently given to postpartum syndromes, they are not a new phenomenon. Hippocrates recorded the first known reports of postpartum syndromes over 2000 years ago (Baran, 1989). In describing postpartum psychosis, he wrote that it was "a kind of 'madness,' caused by excessive blood flow to the brain" (Lynch-Fraser, 1983). Since that time, physicians have struggled with the etiology of the syndromes. For example, an eleventh-century gynecologist, Trotula of Salerno, provided an interesting explanation for postpartum syndromes, suggesting that postpartum blues resulted from the womb being too moist, causing the brain to fill with water, which was then involuntarily shed as tears (Steiner, 1990). However, it was not until the nineteenth century that physicians described the symptoms of postpartum syndromes in detail and formally began to theorize about a connection between physiological events and the mind (Hamilton, 1989). Marce termed this connection *morbid sympathy* and provided the first clear description of the syndromes (Hamilton, 1989). However, physicians were unable to agree upon a classification system or even a pattern of symptoms.

Once psychologists began to study postpartum syndromes, they too struggled with developing a classification system. Similar to physicians, psychologists found that postpartum syndromes defied easy definition and were too elusive, diverse, and inconsistent to classify (Hamilton, 1989). Therefore, in the early twentieth century, when it was suggested that there was not a connection between psychiatric disorders and childbirth, the argument persuaded the medical and psychological communities. When physicians began the task of creating a comprehensive list of all medical disorders, now known as the *International Classification of Diseases* (ICD), they excluded the postpartum syndromes. Similarly, when professionals in the mental health field created their own comprehensive list, now called the *Diagnostic and Statistical Manual of Mental Disorders* (DSM), they too excluded the postpartum syndromes. These exclusions were particularly damaging since these manuals are a means by which professionals within the two fields communicate, produce research, and develop treatments.

Subsequent revisions of both the *ICD* and *DSM* ultimately began to mention postpartum syndromes. The *ICD-10*, the latest version of the *ICD*, lists three specific levels of mental and behavioral disorders associated with the puerperium, or childbirth, ranging from mild to severe: *postnatal depression, postpartum depression*, and *puerperal psychosis*. However, physicians may use these diagnoses only for patients whose symptoms do not meet criteria for other disorders, such as depression (World Health Organization, 1992).

The *DSM-IV*, the latest version of the *DSM*, has increased the recognition of postpartum syndromes slightly. With regard to postpartum depression, the *DSM-IV* indicates that the onset of a mood disorder can be triggered by a birth, but postpartum depression is not a separate diagnosis. It can only be used to specify what triggered the onset of a mood disorder. This postpartum onset specifier in the *DSM-IV* can be applied *if the onset of the depression is within four weeks after the birth of a child*. This is perplexing given evidence suggesting that a postpartum depression may begin as late as several months after the birth of a child. The description of the postpartum onset specifier consists of approximately one page in the *DSM-IV* (pp. 386–387).

Postpartum psychosis is listed under the catchall category "Psychotic Disorder Not Otherwise Specified" but not described or explained (American Psychiatric Association, 1994, p. 315). The "category includes psychotic symptomatology (i.e., delusions, hallucinations, disorganized speech, grossly disorganized or catatonic behavior) about which there is inadequate information to make a specific diagnosis or about which there is contradictory information, or disorders with psychotic symptoms that do not meet the criteria for any specific Psychotic Disorder." Neither postpartum disorder is a specific diagnosis, but they are relegated to a more general status. This lack of *DSM-IV* categorization fosters the idea that postpartum syndromes are elusive and difficult to define, despite research which suggests that postpartum syndromes are discrete entities.

Popular literature also reflects this lack of clarity. In a content analysis of popular press articles about postpartum affective disturbance from 1980 to 1998, Martinez, Johnston-Robledo, Ulsh, and Chrisler (2000) found a surprising shortage of articles on postpartum depression or "baby blues." Moreover, the information in those articles was "often confusing and contradictory, and that the dominance of medical etiologies and treatments suggests that the postpartum period, like menstruation, menopause and childbirth, is another example of the medicalization of women's experience" (p. 49). Perhaps most disconcerting were their observations regarding the content of the articles.

> The popular press pathologizes and sensationalizes women's postpartum affective disturbances. The purpose of 32% of the PPD articles appeared to be to warn or scare readers, and three of the articles were written in reaction to recent cases of infanticide for which PPD was named as the defense . . . Stories of women who have killed their children are attention grabbing and newsworthy, but infanticide is more likely a consequence of postpartum psychosis than of PPD. Articles that build stories around images of postpartum women as murderers may lead readers to believe that only "crazy" women experience postpartum blues and irritability or cause readers to link PPD and the baby blues to infanticide rather than to feelings of loss and anger. Furthermore, the stories about infanticide would not be problematic if the authors of the articles were careful to define and differentiate postpartum psychosis from PPD and the baby blues. Instead, the three are often discussed together in a way that blurs their definitions. This makes it difficult for readers to see the difference between feelings and experiences that are normal and common and those that are abnormal and infrequent. (pp. 51–52)

The case of Andrea Yates certainly reflects this confusion and inconsistency frequently seen in the media. Unfortunately, although the Yates case presents an opportunity to help educate the public about postpartum syndromes, many from the popular press have attempted to sensationalize the situation, which has not helped the public to distinguish between different types of postpartum syndromes or to develop empathy for women who suffer from postpartum syndromes.

Not surprisingly, this lack of clarity is also responsible for conflicting research findings (Thurtle, 1995). Additionally, the tendency of the *DSM* series to understate the importance and distinction of postpartum syndromes has probably been a significant cause of the lack of research because resources and funding are generally not available for onset specifiers. Since research provides a foundation for recognition, the paucity of research relating to postpartum syndromes has also probably contributed to their lack of recognition. This vicious cycle is especially problematic because treatment and prognosis for postpartum depression and psychosis may vary from other mood or psychotic disorders, so it is particularly important that research be conducted.

The use of *DSM* diagnoses in trials involving other reproductive health issues of women, such as menopause, illustrates the importance of clarity within the *DSM* (Bookspan & Kline, 1999). Although there was no *DSM* diagnosis of menopause, symptoms of menopause became associated with the *DSM* diagnosis *involutional melancholia*, agitated depression in a person of climacteric age. From this, a "menopause defense" was created. The first reported case citing the menopause defense occurred in 1900. In that case, a San Antonio gas company was unsuccessful in claiming that injuries a woman received when she fell into an uncovered trench were due to menstrual difficulties, not her physical injuries from the fall.

The menopause defense was used to persuade juries that menopausal plaintiffs were damaged people entitled to little or no recovery. In one case an insurer denied life insurance benefits to a common law wife since, they argued, a menopausal woman could not be a wife. In another case, a woman injured in an auto accident spent 31 days in a hospital, yet when she sued the driver for negligence, the defendant attempted to deny liability, claiming her injuries were due to menopause. Interestingly, some of the women were not even menopausal. The defense was used primarily in civil cases such as divorce, workers' compensation, and negligence/personal injury cases. Bookspan and Kline indicate that the menopause defense was "a creation of a civil defense bar that seized upon a cultural stereotype of aging women and prevailing sexist norms. The defense predominantly was asserted by men, in male dominated courtrooms, to devalue female plaintiffs, cast blame upon them, and attempt to deny women compensation or other remedies . . . The essential premise of this defense was that a woman approaching mid-life was either mentally ill, physically ill or both."

Between 1900 and the 1980s, Bookspan and Kline found over 50 reported appellate decisions using the menopause defense (an underestimate of the frequency of use, since most cases are not appealed). Some defendants were successful in reducing damages, others were not. Use of the defense waxed and waned until it finally disappeared in the 1980s. Bookspan and Kline indicate that the success of the defense was largely dependent on experts who applied the *DSM* diagnosis of involutional melancholia to plaintiffs. Coincidentally, involutional melancholia was dropped from the *DSM* in 1980, about the same time that the menopause defense disappeared from court records. The authors discuss how *DSM* recognition and social influences affected the use and success of the defense. Although there was no diagnosis of menopause, it was admitted into evidence at trials, generally at the expense of women. The lack of *DSM* clarity allowed for broad judicial discretion in the use of the menopause defense. The same lack of *DSM* clarity also allows for broad judicial discretion in the use of postpartum syndromes. Like postpartum syndromes, "even today, some doctors, therapists, and healthcare givers are woefully uninformed about menopause and are neither interested in nor motivated in researching this area" (Bookspan & Kline, 1999).

DESCRIPTION OF POSTPARTUM SYNDROMES

Despite the problems with classifying postpartum syndromes, three separate syndromes have reached some consensus in professional communities. From the mild to the moderate to the severe end of the continuum, the syndromes are termed postpartum or baby blues, postpartum depression, and postpartum psychosis, respectively (Lee, 1997).

Postpartum or baby blues is the least severe of the syndromes and occurs quite commonly, in from 50 to 80 percent of all mothers (Mauthner, 1998). Baby blues is described as a transient condition that typically occurs within the first week postpartum and usually lasts no more than 10 days. Symptoms include tearfulness, irritability, and mood swings (Lee, 1997). This condition could be the result of changing hormonal levels, medical procedures, or a reaction to the physical strains of childbirth (Lee, 1997).

Postpartum depression is often used as a catchall term for all three syndromes. In actuality, postpartum depression is a more severe form of postpartum blues, resembling the *DSM-IV* diagnosis criteria for a major depressive episode. Symptoms may include depression, insomnia, crying, irritability, subtle changes of personality, diminished initiative, and difficulty coping, especially with the baby (Baran, 1989; Hamilton, 1989; Jebali, 1993). Anxiety regarding how to cope with the baby is often present in postpartum depression. The depression may be related to medical issues or to sociocultural issues such as the conflict between women's expectations of motherhood and their actual experiences of motherhood. These women are often discouraged by their perceived weaknesses as a mother, with regard to issues such as childbirth, caregiving, and bonding with the child (Mauthner, 1998).

Postpartum depression develops slowly throughout the weeks following delivery (Hamilton, 1989), with the highest frequency of new cases occurring between the third and ninth months postpartum (Steiner, 1990). Most investigators estimate that the syndrome affects 10 to 20 percent of new mothers (Hamilton, 1989; Harding, 1989; Stern & Kruckman, 1983).

The most serious of all the syndromes is *postpartum psychosis*. In one such case, Angela Thompson went from being an honor society member, her school's first female senior class president, and an athletic and sociable person to a mother who drowned her second child, a 9-month-old son, in a bathtub after hearing voices telling her that her child was the devil (Japenga, 1987). After Thompson gave birth to her first child, she also suffered hallucinations, panic, and obsessions. She even attempted suicide by jumping out of a moving vehicle and then jumping from a bridge 30 feet high, which led to psychiatric hospitalization. Unfortunately, when she became pregnant with her second child, her doctors told her to forget about her previous psychosis, saying that it would not happen again (Brusca, 1990). Like Thompson, Sharon Comitz suffered a similar psychosis following the birth of her first child, but no one took notice of the repeated symptomatology with her second child until it was too late. Comitz had reported her fears of reoccurrence and of being left alone with the baby, but she was ignored.

In another case, Bethe Feltman, a Sunday school teacher and former grade-school teacher, murdered her two young children. She drugged both children then strangled 3-year-old Ben and suffocated 3-month-old Moriah. When her husband arrived home that day, both children were dead and Mrs. Feltman was "incoherent." Mrs. Feltman had suffered from postpartum depression since the birth of her second child and had been hospitalized three times. She was released from the hospital on the last occasion just three days prior to the killings. She was scheduled to see a doctor the day after her children's deaths. In July 1998, Mrs. Feltman was declared insane and sent to a state psychiatric hospital. A psychiatrist testified that she was having auditory hallucinations and was almost catatonic at times. She is currently still in the hospital but is allowed home visitations every weekend (Blevins, 1998; "Colorado Man," 2001; Oulton, 1998).

Postpartum psychosis symptoms usually begin to appear within three weeks after delivery (Baran, 1989). Symptoms of postpartum psychosis include hallucinations, delusions, confusion, irritability, emotional liability, mania, obsessional thinking, feelings of hopelessness, insomnia, headache, agitation, violence, and early signs of depressive illness. Hamilton calls postpartum psychosis mercurial because of the rapidity with which moods and symptoms change (Hamilton, 1989). However, "the principal hazard of puerperal psychosis is violent, impulsive self-destruction. Infanticide is also a hazard, when the syndrome is unrecognized or disregarded and the [mother] is left alone with her child" (Hamilton, 1989, p. 94). However, instances of infanticide are rare in proportion to the number of women who suffer symptoms of postpartum psychosis.

PROPOSED CAUSES OF POSTPARTUM SYNDROMES

The cause of postpartum syndromes is unknown. There are, however, several theories as to why a woman develops postpartum syndromes. The medical model focuses on hormonal shifts that occur during and around the birthing process and on a woman's predisposition for mental illness. Certain hormonal levels, such as those of estrogen and progesterone, may drop by a factor well over 100 in the days after birth (Gitlin & Pasnau, 1989).

Although all women normally experience these severe changes in body chemistry, women who have previously experienced a mental illness or have a history of mental illness in their family may be at greater risk of developing a postpartum disorder. Harding (1989) indicates that "[t]he risk of developing a psychotic mental illness in the first 3 months after delivery is approximately 15 times as great as in nonpuerperal women, with nearly two of every 1000 women delivered requiring hospitalization for such a postpartum psychosis" (p. 110).

The goal of the medical model is to eliminate bias and subjectivity and to produce "value-free" findings; thus, when studying postpartum syndromes, women's accounts and subjective perspectives are virtually ignored (Mauthner, 1998). Mauthner argues that the devaluing of women's experiences accounts for part of the "mixed" and "inconclusive" results produced by postpartum syndrome studies. Since mothers' viewpoints are often excluded, and since most medical diagnoses, descriptions and explanations have been developed by men, it is likely that the medical model of postpartum syndromes has largely been constructed by men. This is problematic since important issues for women may be neglected. For example, medications are the treatment of choice according to the medical model. However, medications would not cure postpartum symptoms but rather, control the symptoms. This could create dependence issues, with women reluctant to discontinue medications lest the symptoms return. If the woman is breastfeeding, medications could actually increase her anxiety, as she may be concerned about the quality of her breastmilk. Most important, the issue of social support is ignored with a purely medical treatment.

Another limitation of the medical model is that it views postpartum syndromes as an illness, or, more specifically, a pathological condition relating to the individual mother's personality or inherent characteristics. Although having a medical label attached to their condition is comforting for some women, who believe that it relieves them of blame (i.e., the postpartum condition is something happening *to* them), other women feel helpless, as though their condition is beyond their control (Mauthner, 1998).

In contrast, feminist explanations for postpartum syndromes focus on sociological factors (Thurtle, 1995). Rather than identifying individual or personality factors related to the development of postpartum syndromes, feminist perspectives believe that postpartum syndromes are related to social and cultural issues. Feminists believe that the medical model, which views postpartum syndromes as an individual pathology, is limited because "it obscures the sociopolitical nature and context of women's distress" (Mauthner, 1998, p. 328). They believe that postpartum syndromes are related to women's inferior status in society and to "structural conditions and constraints such as the medicalization of childbirth, poor provision of state-funded child care, current labour market structures and policies, inadequate parental leave options, the loss of occupational status and identity, isolation and gendered divisions of household labor" (p. 329). Based on these conditions, feminists argue that it is normal for mothers to become depressed.

Also in contrast to the medical model, feminist sociologists and social psychologists have put much emphasis on mothers' accounts and experiences of postpartum syndromes. They have found that certain sociocultural factors, such as single motherhood, lack of social support, and other stressful life events appear to increase women's risk for developing a postpartum syndrome (Harding, 1989; Lee, 1997; Thurtle, 1995). Fox and Worts (1999) conducted interviews with 40 women who had just given birth for the first time and report that women with strong support from their partners were less likely to develop a postpartum syndrome. Further, for women in their study, the development of baby blues was related to a lack of social support and feeling overwhelmed by the responsibilities of motherhood. Sociological factors are given greater examination in a later section of this chapter. It is shortsighted to consider either approach independently, when it may be the unique interaction of medical and sociocultural factors that contribute to or precipitate postpartum syndromes.

THE LEGAL SYSTEM AND POSTPARTUM SYNDROMES

Postpartum syndromes have been admitted into evidence in both criminal and civil courts. Clearly, the use of postpartum syndromes in criminal cases has become more infamous. This could be due to the nature of the crime, usually infanticide (killing a child during the first year of life), or to the media frenzy that surrounds criminal cases involving the mental health of the defendant. The fact patterns of these cases are chillingly similar (see, e.g., Gardner, 1990). Generally, the defendant had no prior history of criminal activity and often went to great lengths, including using reproductive technologies, to become pregnant. In other words, often these were planned pregnancies and/or wanted children. In many cases, the women became psychotic, often perceiving the child as a source of evil, such as the devil. The murders are particularly gruesome, including running over the child with the car, throwing the child in an icy river, and strangulation. Afterward, the mother either purportedly has no recollection of the event and reports the child missing or kidnapped or, like Andrea Yates, may call the police and report the murders.

It is difficult to estimate the frequency of infanticide in the United States. However, " . . . in the United States and throughout the world, the population under one year of age is at great risk of death from homicide. Their killers are more likely to be their own mothers than anyone else" (Oberman, 1996, p. 3). Still, very few infanticide cases are tried, as many defendants plea bargain. Of those tried, few raise postpartum syndromes as a defense. Relatively speaking, only a small percentage of women who kill their children seem to involve postpartum syndromes (less than 5 percent; Meyer & Oberman, 2001).

In colonial times, women who killed their infants were often executed (Gardner, 1990). In the eighteenth century, juries became reluctant to impose such a harsh penalty, especially if women had committed infanticide due to social and economic hardship. This resulted in an increasing number of acquittals. In the twentieth century, postpartum syndromes became formally linked to infanticide under British law. The Infanticide Act of 1922 provided for a reduction in charge from murder to manslaughter for mothers who killed their newborns while suffering from the effects of childbirth. This act was amended in 1938 to include children up to 12 months of age and the effect of lactation. The English Infanticide Act served as a model for similar codes in numerous other countries, such as the Canadian Criminal Code provision that was enacted in 1948. There is no similar statute in the United States.

In the United States, postpartum syndromes can enter into the criminal proceedings at a variety of phases, including competency issues, pleading, or sentencing. At the outset, the competency of the woman to stand trial could be at issue. *Competency* refers to a defendant's ability to assist in her defense, including the ability to understand the charges against her and the rules of the court. Competency to stand trial is not an issue in most instances of postpartum syndromes since the majority of women are not continuing to experience postpartum effects at the trial. Moreover, this would probably be an ineffective defense strategy. Since the statute on murder never runs out, the defendant would simply remain in a treatment facility until competency could be achieved in order for a trial to take place. A treatment facility would be an inappropriate place for most defendants who previously had a postpartum syndrome, as postpartum syndromes are often transitory conditions.

More commonly, postpartum syndromes are used to attempt to exculpate a defendant. At issue is whether the defendant could have had the requisite mental state (mens rea) to commit murder. One way to challenge the mental state requirement would be through use of an insanity defense. Since most of these cases are not federal cases, the jurisdictional or state definitional test for legal insanity would be used. However, state definitions are incredibly inconsistent regarding insanity. In fact, three states do not have insanity statutes. The remaining states have adopted tests (criteria) to determine insanity. There are numerous tests used in the United States, but at least half of the states use a variation of the M'Naghten test (Melton, Petrila, Poythress, & Slobogin, 1997).

The *M'Naghten test* is a cognitive test which primarily addresses the question of whether the defendant knew that her actions were wrong at the time that she committed the crime. This is a relatively strict test of insanity, as even very debilitated persons generally know that their actions are wrong. Under the M'Naghten test, it is difficult to prove insanity for mothers suffering postpartum syndromes. For example, in *People* v. *Massip* (1990), the defendant threw her colicky baby into the path of an oncoming car after voices told her to do so. When the car swerved and missed the infant, the defendant put the infant under the front tire of her own car and ran over him, disposing of his body in the trash. Under M'Naghten, the jury found her guilty of second-degree murder.[1]

Other states have an additional component to their insanity test. This component can take various forms (Melton et al., 1997), but generally is a volitional component that focuses on whether a defendant could appreciate the wrongfulness of her conduct or could control her conduct. Such tests have a tendency to be more liberal than M'Naghten. For example, Angela Thompson, a nurse, claimed that voices told her to drown her 9-month-old son, and subsequently, she did so. The defendant was found not guilty of voluntary manslaughter and felony child abuse by reason of insanity but would probably have been deemed guilty by the M'Naghten test. A not guilty by reason of insanity (NGRI) verdict means that the defendant is not guilty of the crime but may be sentenced to a treatment facility until she is deemed safe to be released. Thompson was committed to an inpatient facility for 90 days. She was also required to meet other conditions placed on her by the court, such as receive outpatient follow-up with a psychiatrist for six years (Japenga, 1987).

As an alternative to the insanity defense, postpartum syndromes can assert diminished capacity, diminished responsibility, or automatism. These are used to attempt to mitigate or exculpate a defendant's responsibility for a crime. Evidence is admitted regarding whether the defendant had the capacity to form the required mental state necessary to be found guilty of the charge. However, only about half the states recognize diminished capacity defenses, and they are not generally successful.

Alternatively, the defendant may be found guilty but mentally ill (GBMI). In general, a GBMI verdict holds the defendant responsible for the murder but the mitigating role of illness is usually recognized in sentencing. The defendant may serve the same sentence length as if she were found guilty but may stay in a treatment facility until she has recovered enough to be transferred to a prison. In *Commonwealth* v. *Comitz* (1987), Sharon Comitz, who was discussed previously, pled GBMI to dropping her 1-month-old into the icy waters of a stream and then reporting the child's disappearance to police as a kidnapping. Only under hypnosis did she recall the killing. Under M'Naghten she would have been found guilty of murder, especially given the fabricated kidnapping. Comitz received an eight- to 20-year sentence. Less than half of the states has GBMI provisions, and support is dwindling. In any case, this may not be a very functional strategy for women suffering from postpartum syndromes, as they are generally recovered by the time of the trial.

As these verdicts indicate, the criminal cases involving postpartum syndromes as a defense are very similar, but the outcomes are quite disparate (see Brusca, 1990). Brusca indicates that these defendants must overcome skepticism about the diagnosis, which may stem from the public's lack of clear and consistent information (Martinez et al., 2000). In addition, "another obstacle faced by defendants who plead the postpartum psychosis defense is that the illness lacks the full acceptance of the medical and psychiatric communities. Postpartum psychosis is not accepted as a distinct and separate form of mental illness, and therefore is not listed in the psychiatric community's bible of disorders, the *DSM III-R*" (p. 1167). Brusca discussed these obstacles in 1990, before the most recent revision of the *DSM*, which provides more recognition of postpartum syndromes than the *DSM III-R*. Still, the present lack of precise definition perpetuates such obstacles and creates a situation where experts are left to do definitional battle in the courtroom. Brusca indicates that "this problem of the lack of medical acceptance will arise when defense attorneys try to establish proof of insanity, for which they must bring in a psychiatrist. Most psychiatrists are either not familiar with the illness, or are split down the middle on its diagnosis. Prosecutors are, therefore, likely to impeach any psychiatrist offering a postpartum psychosis diagnosis on the grounds that the psychiatrist is going against the weight of the psychiatric community" (p. 1167). The reality is that if there is debate over coverage of postpartum syndromes in the *DSM*, their validity and admissibility, it will almost always occur in criminal cases, not in civil cases.

THE USE OF POSTPARTUM SYNDROMES IN CIVIL CASES

The standard of proof and rules of evidence are not the same in criminal and civil cases, as illustrated in the well-publicized criminal and civil trials of O. J. Simpson. In criminal cases the standard of proof is that the prosecution must prove each element of the crime "beyond a reasonable doubt." In contrast, in civil cases the plaintiff can be successful if the "preponderance of the evidence" is in her favor. These standards can have a significant impact on what evidence is admitted into criminal and civil trials. In addition, admissibility of scientific evidence is determined by the *Frye rule* (*Frye* v. *United States*, 1923). *Frye* held that scientific evidence should not be admitted unless it has gained general acceptance in the field to which it belongs. Therefore, the medical and/or psychological community should generally accept a disorder before it can be admitted into evidence. Recently, federal and numerous state courts have shifted from *Frye* to the *Daubert standard of admissibility* (*Daubert* v. *Merrell Dow Pharmaceuticals*, 1993). *Daubert* usually requires a pretrial hearing regarding the degree of professional acceptance and recognition of evidence, such as a disorder, before it can be admitted into evidence. The judge then determines admissibility. Given the level of *DSM* recognition and acceptance for postpartum syndromes, coupled with the strict standard of proof in criminal courts, postpartum syndromes are less likely to be admitted into evidence in criminal courts than in civil courts.

In civil courts, the rules of evidence are much less stringent, as is the standard of proof. Although *Frye* may apply, the civil court has broader discretion. Recall that the menopause defense, which was used in civil cases, was admitted into evidence despite *Frye*. In custody matters, the trial court can allow in evidence regarding the mental health of parents. Mental health can be considered and weighed in relation to other factors in custody decisions. Postpartum syndromes have been raised as a health consideration in many custody cases. It is difficult to estimate how frequently the issue is raised because undoubtedly many mothers abandon their pursuit of custody after the father indicates that he intends to make mental health an issue. In addition, it is impossible to determine how heavily postpartum syndromes weigh in the decision because trial court transcripts are often inaccessible and opinions are generally not formally written. If custody awards are appealed, the court's opinion becomes more accessible. However, custody awards are appealed infrequently.

In custody disputes involving postpartum syndromes, the father generally asserts that the mother is an unfit parent, due to her history of postpartum mental illness, even though the mother may not be currently mentally ill and may have no other history of mental illness or unfit parenting. For example, in one of the first recorded cases (*Pfeifer* v. *Pfeifer*, 1955), the father appealed an order that gave care, custody, and control of the child to the mother, based solely on her potential threat to the child due to her history of postpartum psychosis. When the couple separated, Kent, their child, went to live with Mr. Pfeifer and the paternal grandparents. Ms. Pfeifer was recently recovered from postpartum psychosis, was trying to rebuild her life, and had no home to offer Kent. The paternal grandmother became Kent's primary caretaker. Mr. Pfeifer remarried and relocated, but Kent continued to live with his paternal grandparents. Ms. Pfeifer, who had also remarried, sued and eventually won custody of Kent. Mr. Pfeifer appealed the custody award, citing the mental instability of Ms. Pfeifer. At the time of the custody hearing the mother had been asymptomatic for five years and had no intention of having more children.

On appeal, the father claimed there had been no change in circumstances warranting modification of the original custody award. The court held that " . . . the mother has remained in good mental health for more than two years without relapse; she has remarried, can offer the child a good home, and is willing to give up her profession to take care of him and her household. This change in the circumstance of the mother could in itself justify the change of custody ordered. Moreover, the father has also remarried and has moved out of the home of his parents to another neighborhood. The grandparents, with whom the child remained, have reached an age, which, notwithstanding their love and devotion, must make them less fit to educate a child of the age of Kent, and compared to them, the mother has, if she is not unfit to have custody, certainly a prior claim to the child" (*Pfeifer* v. *Pfeifer*, 1955, p. 56). Mr. Pfeifer's appeal was denied. However, several aspects of this opinion bear noting.

This case was appealed solely on the issue of postpartum psychosis. There was no other reason for Ms. Pfeifer not to be awarded custody. First, it was not Mr. Pfeifer who would have retained custody but the paternal grandparents. Had Mr. Pfeifer chosen to fight for custody, it is quite possible that the court would have reached a different opinion. Second, Mr. Pfeifer had led Kent to believe that his stepmother was his biological mother. The court felt that this posed a danger that Kent would never learn the identity of his real biological mother. This may have swayed the court's opinion. Third, Ms. Pfeifer's marriage was important to the court. It is questionable whether the court would have reached the same decision if Ms. Pfeifer had not been remarried. Fourth, the paternal grandparents were becoming too elderly to care for the child. Fifth, Ms. Pfeifer had no intention of bearing another child. Sixth, Ms. Pfeifer had been asymptomatic for five years. It would have been difficult to deny Ms. Pfeifer custody under these circumstances. In contrast, consider the following case.

Susan and Gary Grimm were married for 13 years and parented three children (*In Re the Marriage of Grimm*, 1989). Gary's occupation is unclear, but Susan was a licensed practical nurse. After the birth of each child, Susan suffered from postpartum depression and was hospitalized for treatment. During these hospitalizations, Susan phoned home daily to speak with her children and had personal visits with them. Following the last hospitalization in 1985, the Grimms separated. During the separation, the children resided with their father, while the mother lived nearby and visited daily. Susan organized, washed dishes, laundered and mended clothes, cooked for the children, and stayed with the children at night whenever Gary was working.

Eventually, the Grimms petitioned for dissolution and each sought sole custody of the children. The custody evaluation submitted to the court indicated that both Grimms were evaluated as excellent parents. Susan's treating psychiatrist testified that the depression was resolved and it had been two years since Susan's last postpartum hospitalization. However, the court placed custody with Gary. Susan appealed. The court affirmed the custody award.

It is clear that Susan Grimm's postpartum depression was an important factor in this custody award. Her treating psychiatrist was called to testify regarding her stability. Similar to *Pfeifer* v. *Pfeifer* (1955), Susan Grimm had not been hospitalized for a long period prior to the custody hearing. In addition, Susan had been and wanted to continue to be actively involved with the children's lives.

It is unclear why *Pfeifer* and *Grimm* were decided differently, especially in light of the fact that the courts have refused to allow testimony regarding postpartum depression to be persuasive in other civil matters. For example, in a 1997 adoption appeal, a biological mother who had given her child up for adoption asserted that postpartum depression rendered her incompetent to consent to the adoption. The Tennessee Appellate Court stated: "We do not dispute that [the mother] was probably depressed or emotionally distraught following this rather traumatic experience, but it is not unusual for there to be depression and distress following the birth of a child, even under the best of circumstances. If emotional distress meant that a parent was always incompetent to consent to an adoption, we would rarely have adoptions in this state" (*Croslin* v. *Croslin*, 1997, p. 10).

Similarly, the court did not find that postpartum depression nullified a woman's competency to consent to a postnuptial agreement. Kim and Anthony Latina had a 1-year-old son when Kim gave birth to a daughter, Jill, who was premature and had to be returned to the hospital daily for a short time after her birth. Kim was caring for both children and preparing to return to work while suffering from postpartum depression. Approximately three weeks after Jill was born, Kim had to be rushed to the hospital for severe hemorrhaging. Although she was not admitted to the hospital, the court acknowledged, "it was obviously a very frightening and traumatic experience" (*Latina* v. *Latina*, 1995, p. 19). A few days after Kim was rushed to the hospital, approximately one month postpartum, Anthony presented her with a postnuptial agreement to sign. Less than three months postpartum, Anthony presented Kim with a separation, child custody, and support agreement to sign. Kim signed both but later filed a motion to rescind the agreements based on a number of factors, including the impact of postpartum depression on her consent. Regarding the effect of postpartum depression on Kim's capacity to consent, the Delaware Family Court indicated:

> The break-up of a marriage never comes at a good time, and, as noted in many earlier opinions, usually separation agreements are signed in a highly charged atmosphere, thereby necessitating the precautions taken by the Delaware courts to ensure the agreements' fairness. However, if the courts could set aside agreements based upon their being signed during the emotional turmoil of a marriage splitting up, no separation agreement would ever be permitted to stand. Although the court recognizes Wife was extremely distraught and probably feeling somewhat vulnerable when she signed the agreement, the Court finds that Wife signed more because she did not understand the implications of the agreement than because she was coerced. It should be noted that the second agreement was signed by Wife approximately six weeks after the first agreement, by which time Wife's postpartum depression and concern for Jill's health should have lessened. (*Latina* v. *Latina*, 1995, p. 19)

All of these cases demonstrate a lack of a clear understanding of postpartum syndromes and are patronizing, and paternalistic. For example, the opinion in *Latina* indicates the court did not understand the etiology of postpartum depression, as it often begins weeks after a birth and can last for a year. Moreover, it is difficult to find other cases in which the court admitted in its opinion that a party was exposed to a recent trauma and yet proceeded to validate capacity to consent. Their inconsistencies simply reflect disparate treatment. How can a disorder be a key factor in one civil case but easily dismissed in another? This is particularly confusing since court cases in which postpartum syndromes were given extensive consideration involved women who had been asymptomatic for several years. Conversely, the cases in which postpartum syndromes were easily dismissed involved women who made decisions in the midst of experiencing postpartum syndromes. Even more disconcerting is the fact that these cases generally resulted in hardships for women.

THE LEGAL DILEMMA

The current status of postpartum syndromes in the medical and psychological communities affects legal decisions. However, they are compounded by legal discrepancies in insanity criteria that foster subjectivity in insanity decisions. This can even be seen in cases that involve disorders that are recognized by the psychological/medical community, such as dissociative identity disorder (formerly multiple personality disorder) or posttraumatic stress disorder (PSTD). When asserted in court, the validity of these recognized disorders, and their exculpatory capability, often become the subject of dispute between experts. This dispute may be problematic for experts whose credibility and authority in the courtroom are already under scrutiny (see, e.g., Hagen, 1997). Experts are in an even more difficult situation when disorders are ambiguous, as in the case of postpartum syndromes.

One argument against routine recognition of postpartum syndromes in criminal courts is the even greater vagaries that could be created in the already ambiguous area of mental health defenses. Courts strive for *bright lines*, or clear criteria, on which to base decisions. Bright lines are rare but are desirable because they reduce disparate treatment that results from subjectivity. Recognizing postpartum syndromes in the legal system could create relatively fine lines and slippery slopes. For example, would a woman accused of child abuse now be able to assert postpartum syndromes as an exculpatory defense? Would the defense be available for other crimes, such as assault or shoplifting?

Although at first glance it appears that recognition of postpartum syndromes could lead to such unwieldy outcomes, it is unlikely. First, this has not been the case in England, where the defense is available but rarely used. Second, and more important, perpetrators with postpartum psychosis have very specific crimes and victims—harm to themselves or to their children. Additionally, the trigger does not have multiple origins as with PTSD, but is clearly due to one cause, pregnancy, and this cause is not likely to reoccur with any frequency in a defendant's lifetime and can be monitored. Third, the dangerousness is temporary. If anything, postpartum syndromes seem to have more specificity than already recognized defenses (such as PTSD and dissociate identity disorder) and represent much less threat to the integrity of the legal system.

Overall, recognition of postpartum syndromes in criminal cases would constitute a gender defense (Denno, 1994) and, in general, the court has not been responsive to recognizing or ameliorating gender biases against women in defenses. Criminal defenses, particularly with regard to murder, have always been more applicable to crimes committed by men ("irresistible impulse") than those committed by women. More men than women murder, but the fact that women represent a minority of murder defendants should not preclude their equal treatment under the law.

Courts could facilitate preventive action and clarification by the medical community if they acknowledged the importance of postpartum syndromes in their opinions. The courts have been able to address this issue directly in cases involving insurance and disability claims for postpartum syndromes. As far back as 1964, the court was asked to determine whether postpartum syndromes represented a sickness or mental illness (*Price* v. *State Capital Insurance Company*, 1964). If postpartum syndromes represent a sickness, the level of coverage under insurance and disability is generally expanded. Conversely, if they represent a mental illness, the coverage is generally restricted. The courts have held that the cause of postpartum syndromes has not been proven to be physical and the treatment is generally psychological; therefore, postpartum syndromes are excluded from coverage (see, e.g., *Blake* v. *Unionmutual Stock Life Insurance Company*, 1990). This is reinforced in court decisions regarding pregnancy. In pregnancy discrimination, "the cases define pregnancy in terms of a biological process that begins with conception and ends with delivery" (Greenberg, 1998, p. 227). The impact on consideration of postpartum syndromes is clear, since "by using a narrow, medicalized definition of pregnancy, they [the court] have excluded the time that women take to care for young children from the statute's protection" (p. 226).[2]

The idea that legal institutions influence the medical processes, and vice versa, is discussed at length in a thought-provoking law review by Noah (1999). He suggests "just as social forces have shaped medical practice, legal institutions influence both nosology and diagnosis. Law and medicine are not autonomous domains, fully insulated from one another in spite of numerous points of intersection concerning the definition and identification of disease. Instead, at these junctures, law and medicine are mutually constitutive or perhaps co-dependent" (p. 257). Noah outlines the dangers to both professions inherent in such co-dependence. For women, the danger is reflected repeatedly in court decisions regarding reproductive issues from contraception to postpartum and beyond.

THE MEDICAL AND PSYCHOLOGICAL DILEMMA

The lack of a clear definition of postpartum syndromes and inconsistencies in the medical and psychological literature probably become self-perpetuating by leading to the inaccurate education of health professionals. Small, Epid, Johnston, and Orr (1997) found that fourth- and sixth-year medical students had inaccurate or incomplete knowledge of postpartum syndromes. Medical students had a narrower view of the factors that contribute to postpartum depression than did women who had experienced the disorder. For example, students selected hormonal or biological factors and a "tendency to depression" as most influential in the development of postpartum depression. The women, however, identified social and experiential factors, such as lack of support, as contributing the most significantly to postpartum depression. The biological focus endorsed by the students suggests a likelihood to overlook the wide range of social, physical health, and life-event factors in diagnosis and treatment (Small et al., 1997). Indeed, Mauthner (1998) indicates that "the majority of research in the area of postpartum depression has disregarded mothers as a source of knowledge or understanding about their experiences" (p. 143).

If health professionals are not aware that factors such as lack of social support are common for women with postpartum depression, they will not realize that women with these factors are at greater risk for postpartum syndromes. Moreover, they will probably prescribe treatments that are not consistent with the woman's needs: for example, medications instead of counseling. As a result, women are disadvantaged on multiple levels: health professionals *only recognize biological contributors* to postpartum syndromes, reducing treatment effectiveness, while the court *denies these biological components*, preventing women from receiving disability or insurance coverage for postpartum syndromes.

SOCIOCULTURAL CONTEXT

Fortunately, in recent years there has been an increase in the recognition of sociocultural factors that influence the development of postpartum syndromes by some professionals, such as sociologists and psychologists and by feminists. As stated previously, feminist researchers and practitioners believe that postpartum syndromes are a natural response to a patriarchal society that devalues motherhood (Lee, 1997; Mauthner, 1998).

Examining the sociocultural context of postpartum syndromes involves considering the tremendous pressures that mothers face. For instance, gender roles in the United States dictate that women understand and love everything about motherhood (Cox, 1988; Mauthner, 1993). This value can be overwhelming to new mothers, who may be feeling unsure of their caregiving abilities. Women may feel inept and inadequate if they do not instinctively know how to care for their children (Thurtle, 1995).

Further, motherhood can be a stressful time for women because it entails the adoption of new roles and perhaps the loss of others. Despite the happiness that motherhood often brings, many new mothers experience grief due to their loss of freedom (Hopkins, Marcus, & Campbell, 1984). Activities of interest and important projects may need to be put on hold or may have less time allotted to them. Lee (1997) states that women's satisfaction with their new role of mother, and the quality of their relationship with their partner, both decline with the arrival of a child. She reports that the research results have unequivocally found that this decline in satisfaction is due to the "unexpected and inequitable division of household labour" (Lee, 1997, p. 101). In fact, Lee provides strong support evidence to support the sociocultural underpinnings of postpartum syndromes.

Motherhood can also be a difficult time, as many women feel societal pressure to make motherhood their primary role (Miles, 1988). This may have been true in the case of Andrea Yates, who not only quit her nursing job to stay home with her children but also home-schooled the oldest children (Thomas, 2001). Although Ms. Yates's feelings about her role as a stay-at-home mother are unknown, for many mothers, choosing whether to work outside the home is a no-win situation. Although U.S. society gives lip service to mothers who stay at home with their children, motherhood continues to be underappreciated. We often hear the question "Do you work or do you stay at home?", as if staying at home is not work. Therefore, working outside the home is many women's only opportunity to receive respect and recognition. However, they are then faced with stress related to juggling multiple roles and finding adequate childcare and may experience guilt about not staying at home with their children (Thurtle, 1995).

Mothers who decide to stop working outside the home may experience a loss of self-esteem related to loss of roles and the lack of importance given to mother's work. Additionally, these women may experience a further decrease in self-esteem, due to isolation and work that is repetitive and frustrating (Gove, 1972). As wonderful and exciting as children are, one can only imagine the time-consuming and monotonous work required of Andrea Yates to raise five children under age 7. Multiply this by the weight of the isolation that can easily occur for stay-at-home mothers, particularly those who home-school their children.

The pressure to be a perfect mother makes many women reluctant to disclose symptoms of postpartum depression. This, in turn, makes early detection difficult and may result in the increased severity of their symptoms, especially since lack of social support has been shown to contribute to depression (Inwood, 1985; Jebali, 1993; Lee, 1997). Mauthner (1999) interviewed 40 women with postpartum syndromes and found that many of them attributed at least a part of their condition to a conflict between their expectations (i.e., the mother they wanted to be) and their perceptions of themselves as mothers. Mauthner reports that the women's unrealistic expectations for themselves appeared to stem from the cultural context in which they lived as well as their interpersonal relationships. The women generally felt that admitting their needs and feelings was an indication of weakness or failure as a mother. This hesitancy to disclose symptoms of a postpartum syndrome is particularly evident in the case of Andrea Yates, who did not want to talk with a therapist and reportedly said that she felt "OK," even when family members began to notice serious symptoms (Thomas, 2001).

One of the strongest pieces of evidence in support of the influence of sociocultural factors is the decreased incidence of postpartum syndromes in non-Western cultures (Hayes, Roberts, & Davare, 2000). Stern and Kruckman (1983) point out that "recent cross-cultural studies of childbirth have emphasized that while childbirth is universally similar physiologically, it is differentially conceptualized, structured, organized, and experienced" (p. 1027). They believe that the development of postpartum syndromes in the United States results from a lack of several practices that are present in non-Western cultures: (1) social structuring of a distinct postpartum time period; (2) protective activities and rituals resulting from the presumed vulnerability of new mothers; (3) social seclusion; (4) a mandated period of rest; (5) instrumental assistance to the new mother; and (6) social recognition of a the new social status of the mother (i.e., rituals, gifts).

There are cultural differences in the structure and organization of the family and in role expectations for the new mother and significant others. For instance, in some non-Western cultures, women are considered quite vulnerable after pregnancy and are allowed a period of rest. Relatives support this rest period by fulfilling the new mother's normal duties. Additionally, while in the United States attention is typically paid to the newborn child, in some non-Western cultures much attention and importance is also lavished on the new mother. As with other major changes in the life cycle (i.e., puberty, death), pregnancy and childbirth are considered rites of passage and are marked by special ceremonies (Stern & Kruckman, 1983). The postpartum period of rest and support and clear recognition of the important status of motherhood may make women less likely to develop a postpartum disorder.

THE IMPACT OF INCREASED RECOGNITION OF POSTPARTUM SYNDROMES

Recognition of a condition that affects women solely or primarily creates the risk of pathologizing women with that condition. This phenomenon is seen with conditions such as premenstrual syndrome (PMS). Although the aim of increased recognition of PMS has been to provide more effective prevention and treatment for women, some argue that increased recognition has pathologized a normal life event so that it is seen as a defect in a woman's character (Rome, 1986). This viewpoint may then be used to patronize or discriminate against women in situations involving education or career, since women can be seen as incapable of handling these challenging situations. Additionally, some argue that increasing the role of the medical, psychological, and legal communities with regard to PMS has taken power away from women as diagnosis and treatment of this condition has come under the control of these professions.

Beaman (1998) discusses criticisms of "women's defenses," such as battered woman's syndrome, premenstrual syndrome, and postpartum depression, which recognize, within the legal system, women's unique biology and socialization. For instance, arguments against using battered woman's syndrome as a defense include the "tendency for the experiences of the abused women to be overshadowed by expert testimony; the negative ramifications of syndromization; and the boundaries imposed by creating the 'ideal' abused women" (Beaman, 1998, p. 88). Increasing the recognition of postpartum syndromes could potentially have the same medical, psychological, and legal consequences as increased recognition of other conditions affecting women.

Thus there are significant risks associated with increased recognition of postpartum syndromes. However, deciding to keep the status quo in an effort to avoid pathologizing women has its own risks: namely, the status quo involves no opportunities for the improvement of treatment or legal options for women. Further, the status quo already involves the pathologizing and paternalization of women.

Males control the medical, psychological, and legal systems in this country. Males have the power to invent and deny disorders, and they do so based on societal standards of male health. For instance, research has shown that the concept of a healthy male differs from the concept of a healthy female. In one classic study, mental health professionals were asked to select traits characteristic of either a healthy male, healthy female, or healthy adult person. Results showed that the participants' concepts of a healthy mature adult were similar to the concepts of a healthy male, but different from concepts of a healthy female (Broverman, Broverman, Clarkson, Rosenkrantz, & Vogel, 1981). Although this study was conducted two decades ago, in many respects men continue to be the standard against which women are compared.

As the Broverman et al. (1981) study demonstrates, women are already pathologized and have little control over the treatment of their bodies. The idea that recognition of postpartum syndromes will provide an excuse for the sexist practices happening in this society seems unfounded since sexism is already occurring. With regard to postpartum syndromes, sexism is seen in the medical and psychological communities. Health professionals indoctrinated in patriarchal practice choose conditions to which they want to devote resources. Thus, certain medical or psychological states receive more funding than others for research, education, or treatment. Because postpartum syndromes are conditions affecting women, there are no male norms with which to compare them. Not surprisingly, there appears to be less interest in the male-dominated health fields for these conditions. Sexism is also found in the legal arena, where postpartum syndromes are not dealt with in any uniform fashion.

We must increase recognition of postpartum syndromes if women are to receive the medical, psychological, and legal help that they need. Beaman (1998) states that women have different biologies, psychologies, and socialization than men and thus need different or new legal strategies. Some feminist scholars hesitate to use women's legal defenses because "different" has traditionally been seen as "inferior and in need of protection" (p. 89). They worry that these defenses would be seen as evidence of women's biological inferiority to men. However, Beaman (1998) argues that women's legal defenses should be designed carefully rather than discarded because if these women's conditions are minimized, researchers will continue to ignore them and women will continue to have inadequate treatment.

Some pathologizing might actually be necessary for women to receive treatment and recognition for medical and psychological conditions. Without pathologizing, health providers minimize women's syndromes, causing women to feel "crazy" for believing that something is wrong with them and leading to further problems as women's conditions go untreated. Indeed, Mauthner (1998) explored postpartum depression from the mothers' point of view and found that many women preferred that the severity of their depression be recognized, regardless of the pathology associated with this recognition. When others took their symptoms seriously rather than minimizing or trivializing them, the women said that their experience felt less "terrifying and abnormal" (Mauthner, 1998, p. 331).

Therefore, pathologizing may help normalize the experience of women suffering from postpartum syndromes. Additionally, pathologizing some types of postpartum syndromes and not others may decrease the overall level of pathology assigned collectively to these conditions. For example, pathologizing postpartum psychosis, which is a rare and serious disorder, may increase the distinction between this condition and less severe types of postpartum syndromes, which would then be able to be normalized.

Some may argue that even pathologizing one type of postpartum syndrome does an injustice to women. In response to this argument, it is important to remember that women with postpartum syndromes are already being pathologized. One has only to consider the negative comments made toward Andrea Yates (i.e., "monster," "bad mother") to recognize this. Increased recognition may pathologize postpartum psychosis by pointing out the danger of the condition but also increases awareness of the context in which these conditions develop—biological, psychological, and societal stressors, rather than "evilness" or "bad mothering." It would also allow greater opportunity for education and awareness.

CONCLUSIONS

If the medical, psychological, and legal communities would recognize the sociocultural factors that contribute to the development of postpartum syndromes, it would be possible to increase recognition and acceptance of these conditions without pathologizing women. Women could receive the help that they need, without fear that their condition would be viewed as inherently pathological.

Sexism, along with racism and other forms of inequality, continue because people in power are rarely willing to reduce power differentials that could result in loss of their own power. Thus we cannot wait for professional communities or society as a whole to diminish sexism. It is time to empower women to take control of their bodies and the medical and psychological conditions affecting them. Women are currently relying on the paternalistic health care systems to equalize the power differential between men and women, neglecting to remember that these systems had a large role in creating inequality in the first place. If equality between men and women is to be gained, women must take an active role in defining and explaining conditions with which they are affected.

The lessons learned from the menopause defense discussed earlier in the chapter apply to postpartum syndromes and the legal system.

> The menopause defense resulted from a confluence of factors: a social climate that embraced menopause as illness; medical professionals eager to create and substantiate the perilous and evil manifestations of hormonal change; essentially unchallenged admission of expert testimony on menopausal syndrome; and unequal application of the eggshell plaintiff doctrine. The defense should have died in 1916 with the failed attempt to use it against Anna Laskowski. The stories of the women (and men) who followed Anna Laskowski reveal the misconstructions and inequalities that can result when negative social and cultural stereotypes supplant neutral decision-making. The stories also show when the intimate circumstances of women's lives become the source of public review and analysis by eager lawyers and acquiescent judges.
>
> Law develops over time in the context of theories and institutions that are controlled by the dominant political group. For the greater part of the Twentieth Century, women had little role and no power in the American judicial system. Since law is a manifestation of the socio-cultural values of dominant political groups, the development, usage, acceptance, and decline of menopause as a legal defense is an example of power and perspective as law. Thus, the menopause defense, like a mirror, reflects prevalent societal attitudes toward women. Similarly, it symbolizes how, with the strike of a gavel, law can give voice to prejudice and stereotype. It took eighty years for the gavel to crack the social mirror that reflected a mad, diseased, and useless menopausal woman. It remains for society to erase the image totally. (Bookspan & Kline, 1999, p. 1318)

Therefore, although greater recognition is needed for postpartum syndromes, this must be done with the awareness of the gender inequalities that exist in the United States. If we do not also contextualize postpartum syndromes by recognizing their sociopolitical contributors, we are at risk for further pathologizing women, as seen in the case of the menopause defense.

Encouraging women to become active with decisions affecting their bodies and their lives does not negate the influence and responsibility that men as well as medical, psychological, and legal professionals have with regard to postpartum syndromes. Women do not exist in a vacuum; therefore, a condition that affects women affects their families, friends, work, and eventually, the larger society. The impact of one woman's behavior on society and the importance of societal response to her future is illustrated by Andrea Yates. People and institutions influence the fate of women with postpartum syndromes; thus each is instrumental in helping to ameliorate the disparate treatment experienced by these women.

Simple interventions could alter tragic outcomes. After Andrea Yates killed her children, James Young, Maggie Young's husband, indicated that he hoped that increased awareness of postpartum depression would result in better screening of expectant and new mothers (Shapiro, 2001). He stated: "Why not train obstetricians to screen mothers-to-be for their potential to suffer [postpartum mood disorders]? How about a simple interview?" Young suggested that pregnant women could be asked how they felt following earlier births. Perhaps even more important, their partners should be interviewed. After all, when someone is suffering from postpartum syndromes or some mental illnesses, it is often best to solicit additional viewpoints regarding the person's health. As Young suggested, earlier intervention could lead to more effective treatment.

In fact, efforts at intervention have been successful. Zlotnick, Johnson, Miller, Pearlstein, and Howard (2001) provided four sessions of interpersonal-therapy-oriented group intervention to pregnant women receiving public assistance who had at least one risk factor for postpartum depression. Three months postpartum, 33 percent of a control group of women had developed postpartum depression, whereas none of the women receiving treatment had developed postpartum depression. The treatment consisted of four 60-minute group sessions that focused on education regarding postpartum syndromes, issues, and concerns. Despite the fact that even relatively brief cost-effective interventions, such as the four-session therapy group in the Zlotnick et al. study, have been shown to be effective, they are rarely used.

EPILOGUE

Andrea Yates has just begun to weave her way through the criminal justice system.[3] Prosecutors have already indicated that they will seek the death penalty. There is no clear motive for her crime. It is likely, although not certain, that her defense attorney will use her diagnosis of postpartum depression in her defense. If so, this case has the potential to help educate both laypersons and professionals about the nature of postpartum syndromes and to replace feelings of anger and hostility with compassion and understanding for Andrea Yates and other women suffering a postpartum syndrome. On August 27, 2001, a coalition of activist groups, including the National Organization for Women and anti–death penalty groups, formed a coalition and voiced support for Andrea Yates. Beatrice Fowler of the American Civil Liberties Union was quoted as saying: "This case has touched a nerve. Every single woman I have spoken to has had the same reaction I had: What could she have possibly been going through for her to take that kind of action? It's not real" (Parker, 2001). Andrea Yates has focused attention on postpartum syndromes and their use in the legal system.

For those fortunate enough not to have had their lives touched by postpartum syndromes, perhaps the best model for their attitudes and sentiments should be those who have lived with postpartum syndromes: either themselves or a loved one. Rusty Yates, who presumably knows his wife better than anyone, has described the changes she experienced as a result of her postpartum depression and has stated unequivocally that his wife, as he knew her, "is not the woman who killed my children . . . she wasn't in her right frame of mind" (Thomas, 2001).

Mr. Yates is not alone in his feelings. James Young is supportive of both his late wife and Andrea Yates, stating: "I feel compelled to do what I can to help this woman who is a victim of postpartum depression and the terrible feelings of inadequacy she must have felt—the same feelings my late wife must have felt. Behavioral signs we all recognized in hindsight" (Shapiro, 2001). Additionally, Jeff Thompson, Angela Thompson's husband, supported his wife after the murder and stated: "Doctors are literally ignoring mothers to death on this thing" (Japenga, 1987). Further, Glenn Comitz, husband of Sharon Comitz, said that if they had understood his wife could have a second episode of postpartum psychosis: "We would have thought twice about having a second child, or have taken precautionary measures to control the situation" (Japenga, 1987). In fact, most of the husbands whose wives killed their child or children as the result of a postpartum syndrome were extremely supportive. If these men, who have lost more than most of us can even imagine, are able to look past their shock and sadness and recognize the need to help rather than blame women with postpartum syndromes, perhaps it is time for the rest of us to do the same.

NOTES

1. However, the judge rendered a judgement notwithstanding the verdict and found Massip not guilty by reason of insanity. The prosecution then appealed this judgment, but their appeals were eventually dismissed.
2. The statute Greenberg refers to is the Pregnancy Discrimination Act.
3. Andrea Yates was found guilty of murder, and sentenced to 40 years to life in a correctional facility. The jurors did not believe her postpartum syndrome defense, nor did they understand the change of not guilty by reason of insanity.

REFERENCES

AMERICAN PSYCHIATRIC ASSOCIATION. (1994). *Diagnostic and statistical manual of mental disorders* (4th ed.). Washington, DC: APA.

BARAN, M. (1989). Postpartum illness: A psychiatric illness, a legal defense to murder, or both? *Hamlin Journal of Public Law and Policy, 10*, 121–139.

BEAMAN, L. G. (1998). Women's defenses: Contextualizing dilemmas of difference and power. *Women and Criminal Justice, 9*(3), 87–115.

BLEVINS, J. (1998, April 12). Mom not queried in deaths of kids. *Denver Post*, p. B-02.

BOOKSPAN, P. T., & KLINE, M. (1999). On mirrors and gavels: A chronicle of how menopause was used as a legal defense against women. *Indiana Law Review, 32*, 1267.

BROVERMAN, I. K., BROVERMAN, D. M., CLARKSON, F. E., ROSENKRANTZ, P. S., & VOGEL, S. R. (1981). Sex-role stereotypes and clinical judgments of mental health. In E. Howell & M. Bayes (Eds.), *Women and mental health* (pp. 86–97). New York: Basic Books.

BRUSCA, A. (1990). Postpartum psychosis: A way out for murderous moms? *Hofstra Law Review, 18*, 1133–1170.

Canadian criminal code. (1970). 2 R.S.C. 216.

Colorado man knows pain of children's death. (2001, June 21). Associated Press.

COX, J. (1988). The life event of childbirth: Sociocultural aspects of postnatal depression. In R. Kumar & I. F. Brockington (Eds.), *Motherhood and mental illness*, Vol. 2, *Causes and consequences* (pp. 64–77). London: Butterworth.

DENNO, D. W. (1994). Gender issues and criminal law: Gender crime and the criminal law defenses. *Journal of Criminal Law and Criminology, 85*, 80–173.

FOX, B., & WORTS, D. (1999). Revisiting the critique of medicalized childbirth: A contribution to the sociology of birth. *Gender and Society, 13*, 326–346.

GARDNER, C. A. (1990). Postpartum depression defense: Are mothers getting away with murder? *New England Law Review, 24*, 953–989.

GITLIN, M. J., & PASNAU, R. O. (1989). Psychiatric syndromes linked to reproductive functions in women: A review of current knowledge. *American Journal of Psychiatry, 146*, 1413–1422.

GOVE, W. R. (1972). The relationship between sex roles, marital status, and mental illness. *Social Forces, 51*, 34–44.

GREENBERG, J. G. (1998). The pregnancy discrimination act: Legitimating discrimination against pregnant women in the workplace. *Maine Law Review, 50*, 225.

HAGEN, M. A. (1997). *Whores of the court: the fraud of psychiatric testimony and the rape of American justice.* New York : Regan Books.

HAMILTON, J. A. (1989). Postpartum psychiatric syndromes. *Psychiatric Clinics of North America, 12*, 89–103.

HARDING, J. J. (1989). Postpartum psychiatric disorders: A review. *Comprehensive Psychiatry, 30*, 109–112.

HAYES, M. J., ROBERTS, S., & DAVARE, A. (2000). Transactional conflict between psychobiology and culture in the etiology of postpartum depression. *Medical Hypotheses, 55*(3), 266–276.

HOPKINS, J., MARCUS, M., & CAMPBELL, S. (1984). Postpartum depression: A critical review. *Psychological Bulletin, 95*, 498–515.

Infanticide Act of 1938. (1938). 1 & 2 Geo. 6, Ch. 26, § 1.

INWOOD, D. G. (1985). The spectrum of postpartum psychiatric disorders. In D. G. Inwood (Ed.), *Recent advances in postpartum psychiatric disorders.* Washington, DC: American Psychiatric Press.

JAPENGA, A. (1987, February 1). Ordeal of postpartum psychosis: Illness can have tragic consequences for new mothers. *Los Angeles Times*, p. 1.

JEBALI, C. (1993). A feminist perspective on postnatal depression. *Health Visitor, 66*(2), 59–60.

LEE, C. (1997). Social context, depression and the transition to motherhood. *British Journal of Health Psychology, 2*, 93–108.

LYNCH-FRASER, D. (1983). *The complete postpartum guide: Everything you need to know about taking care of yourself after you've had a baby.* New York: Harper & Row.

MARTINEZ, R., JOHNSTON-ROBLEDO, I., ULSH, H. M., & CHRISLER, J. C. (2000). Singing "the baby blues": A content analysis of popular press articles about postpartum affective disturbance. *Women and Health, 31*(2–3), 37–55.

MAUTHNER, N. (1993). Towards a feminist understanding of "postnatal depression." *Feminism and Psychology, 3*, 350–355.

MAUTHNER, N. S. (1998). "It's a woman's cry for help": A relational perspective on postnatal depression. *Feminism and Psychology, 8*(3), 325–355.

MAUTHNER, N. S. (1999). "Feeling low and feeling really bad about feeling low": Women's experiences of motherhood and postpartum depression. *Canadian Psychology, 40*(2), 143–161.

MELTON, G. B., PETRILA, J., POYTHRESS, N. G., & SLOBOGIN, C. (1997). *Psychological evaluations for the courts: A handbook for mental health professionals and lawyers.* New York: Guilford Press.

MEYER, C. L., & OBERMAN, M. (2001). *Mother who kill their children: Understanding the acts of moms from Susan Smith to the "prom mom."* New York: New York University Press.

MILES, A. (1998). *The neurotic woman.* New York: New York University Press.

NOAH, L. (1999). Pigeonholing illness: Medical diagnosis as a legal construct. *Hastings Law Journal, 50*, 241.

OBERMAN, M. (1996). Mothers who kill: Coming to terms with modern American infanticide. *American Criminal Law Review, 34*, 1–110.

OULTON, S. (1998, September 2). A tragedy is retold on Web site Internet page dedicated to wife, dead children. *Denver Post*, p. B-01.

PARKER, L. (2001, August 28). Coalition supports Houston woman. *USA Today*, p. 1A.

ROME, E. (1986). Premenstrual syndrome (PMS) examined through a feminist lens. In V. L. Olesen & N. F. Woods (Eds.), *Culture, society, and menstruation* (pp. 145–151). Washington, DC: Hemisphere Publishing.

SHAPIRO, T. (2001, June 26). Father whose wife killed their five kids in Aiea in 1965 urges compassion. *Honolulu Star-Bulletin.*

SMALL, R., EPID, G. D., JOHNSTON, V., & ORR, A. (1997). Depression after childbirth: The views of medical students and women compared. *Birth, 24*, 109–115.

STEINER, M. (1990). Postpartum psychiatric disorders. *Canadian Journal of Psychiatry, 35*, 89–95.

STERN, G. & KRUCKMAN, L. (1983). Multi-disciplinary perspectives on post-partum depression: An anthropological critique. *Social Science and Medicine, 17*(15), 1027–1041.

THOMAS, E. (2001, July 2). Motherhood and murder. *Newsweek, 138*(1), 20–25.

THURTLE, V. (1995). Post-natal depression: The relevance of sociological approaches. *Journal of Advanced Nursing, 22*, 416–424.

WORLD HEALTH ORGANIZATION. (1992). *The ICD-10 classification of mental and behavioral disor-ders: Clinical descriptions and diagnostic guidelines*. Geneva: WHO.

ZLOTNICK, C., JOHNSON, S. L., MILLER, I. W., PEARLSTEIN, T., & HOWARD, M. (2001). Postpartum depression in women receiving public assistance: Pilot study of an interpersonal-therapy-oriented group intervention. *American Journal of Psychiatry, 158*(4), 638–640.

CASES

Blake v. *Unionmutual Stock Life Insurance Company*, 906 F.2d 1525 (1990).

Commonwealth v. *Comitz*, 530 A.2d 473 (Pa. Super. 1987).

Croslin v. *Croslin*, 1997 Tenn. App. LEXIS 84.

Daubert v. *Merrell Dow Pharmaceuticals*, 509 U.S. 579 (1993).

Frye v. *United States*, 392 F. 1013 (D.C. Cir. 1923).

In re the Marriage of Grimm, 1989 Minn. App. LEXIS 143.

Latina v. *Latina*, 1995 Del. Fam. Ct. LEXIS 48.

People v. *Massip*, 271 Cal. Rptr. 868 (Cal. App. 1990).

Pfeifer v. *Pfeifer*, 280 P.2d 54 (Cal. App.1955).

Price v. *State Capital Insurance Company*, 134 S.E. 2d 171 (Super. Ct. 1964).

5

The Legal System and Sexual Harassment

Roslyn Muraskin

S exual harassment remains one of the most pervasive features of our legal system. "Sexual harassment law addresses sexual subordination as sex discrimination" (MacKinnon, 2001, p. 908). Sexual harassment is "a problem with a long past but a short history" (ibid.). There are arguments that females have more equality than ever before, and in some cases this may be true, but unfortunately, females are being victimized in more areas than ever before. As women gain more equality, they become harassed by employers in a manner that is akin to rape and cases of domestic violence. A strategy needs to be developed that provides law enforcement personnel with a better understanding of the types of crimes committed against women.

Historically, women have been discriminated against by the law, often by policies designed to protect them. During recent decades, women have found themselves in courts of law arguing for equality. The history of women's struggles has taught us that litigation becomes merely a catalyst for change. It does not guarantee results.

Sexual harassment's problem "is probably as old as sex equality. Its known past encompasses feudalism, which entitled lords to the first night of sex with vassals' new wives; American slavery, under which enslaved women of African origin or descent were routinely sexually used by white masters" (MacKinnon, 2001, p. 208).

In 1913, Rebecca West stated: "I myself have never been able to find out precisely what feminism is. I only know that people call me a feminist whenever I express sentiments that differentiate me from a doormat." Women's basic rights are inextricably linked to our treatment by and with their participation in today's political world. Due to the fact that the lives of women are reflections of what they do, what they say, and how they treat each other, women as participating members of the human race are ultimately responsible for human affairs.

Throughout this work, we note that there is no way to allow both sexes to enjoy automatically equal protection of the law unless we are committed to the elimination of all gender discrimination. The criminal justice system has slowly come to grips with the needed understanding of women and justice. Today, courts need time for discovery of evidence and the opportunity to hear expert testimony in all cases of sexual violence.

According to the Equal Employment Opportunity Commission:

> Harassment on the basis of sex is a violation of [Title VI]. Unwelcome sexual advances, request for sexual behaviors, and other verbal or physical conduct of a sexual nature constitute sexual harassment when (1) submission to such conduct is made either explicitly or implicitly a term or a condition of an individual's employment, (2) submission to or rejection of such conduct by an individual is used as the basis for employment decisions affecting such individual, or (3) such conduct has the purpose or effect of unreasonably interfering with an individual's work performance or creating an intimidating, hostile, or offensive working environment. [29 C.F.R. § 1604.11(a) (1998].

Crimes such as rape, domestic violence, and sexual harassment are all part of the continuum of violence against women. Rape is not a crime of sex; it is a crime of power. It is "an act of violence, an assault like any other, not an expression of socially organized sexuality" (MacKinnon, 1979, p. 218). The fact that rape is acted out in sex does not mean that it is an act of male sexuality. Rape is an act of violence. The act of sexual harassment has drawn parallels to the crime of rape. If sex or a sexual advance is imposed on a woman who is in no position to refuse, why is that act any different from the act of rape? Sexual harassment may be a lesser crime in the minds of many, including the courts, but nevertheless, it is an act of violence against women. Sexual harassment is gender discrimination, and laws are needed to remedy such disparities. There is a current of public discussion about the cases of women accused and sometimes convicted of assaulting and killing partners who have battered them. The actual volume of cases is small, but the attention given these cases illuminates the larger problem for which they have come to stand: the common disparity of power between men and women in familial relationships.

The laws of sexual harassment in the United States is deemed an exception. "Unlike the criminal law of rape, sexual harassment grew directly out of women's experiences of sexual violation, rather than from ruling men's notions of that experience. It sees sexual abuse as sex-based abuse: victims are understood to be violated as members of their gender group" (MacKinnon, 1979, p. 913). Further, if a crime of sex is one of power, then taken together, rape, domestic violence, and sexual harassment eroticize women's subordination. This continues the powerlessness in the criminal law of women as a gender (MacKinnon, 1979, p. 221).

From a historical point of view, there existed under the English common law the *rule of thumb*, which allowed a husband to beat his wife with a stick no wider than his thumb. The husband's prerogative was incorporated into the laws of the United States. The sad fact is that several states had laws on the book that essentially allowed a man to beat his wife with no interference from the courts. Blackstone referred to this action as the power of correction. For too many decades women have been victims of sexual assaults. Each act of "sexual assault is recognized as one of the most traumatic and debilitating crimes for adults . . . " (Roberts, 1993, p. 362). The victimization of women has been more prevalent and problematic for the criminal justice system.

As pointed out by Susan Faludi (1991): "Women's advances and retreats are generally described in military term: battles won, battles lost, points and territory gained and surrendered. In times when feminism is at a low ebb, women assume the reactive role—privately and most often covertly struggling to assert themselves against the dominant cultural tide. But when feminism becomes the tide, the opposition doesn't simply go along with the reversal, it digs in its heels, brandishes its fists, builds walls and dams."

In past decades we have seen sexual assault reform legislation, resulting "in several long-overdue improvements in the criminal justice processing of sexual assault cases for example, passage of rape shield laws, confidentiality laws to protect communications between the victims and their counselors, and laws designed to preserve medical evidence" (Roberts, 1993, p. 370). In addition, we have seen the establishment of victim assistance programs.

SEXUAL HARASSMENT

The female represents half of the U.S. population. She is deserving of the same rights and opportunities as are afforded males. There exists the rhetoric of gender equality, but it has yet to match the reality of women's experiences. Women who find themselves in the position of being sexually harassed indicate the forms that it takes:

> Wolf whistles, leering, sexual innuendo, comments about women's bodies, tales of sexual exploits, graphic descriptions of pornography, pressure for dates, hooting, sucking, lip-smacking, and animal noises, sexually explicit gestures, unwelcome touching and hugging, excluding women from meetings, sabotaging women's work, sexist and insulting graffiti, demanding "Hey, baby, give me a smile," sexist jokes and cartoons, hostile put-downs of women, exaggerated, mocking "courtesy," public humiliation, obscene phone calls, displaying pornography in the workplace, insisting that workers wear revealing clothing, inappropriate gifts (for example lingerie), inappropriate invitations (for example to go to a hot tub or nude beach), discussion of one's partner's sexual inadequacies, lewd and threatening letters, "accidentally" brushing sexual parts of the body, pressing or rubbing up against the victim, leaning over or otherwise invading a victim's space, sexual sneak attacks (such as grabbing breasts or buttocks on the run), indecent exposure, soliciting sexual services, demanding sexual services, stalking a victim, [and] sexual assault. (MacKinnon, 1979, p. 915)

Why are females forced to tolerate such action that is unwanted, in order to survive economically? The case of Anita Faye Hill, in the hearings to confirm Judge Clarence Thomas to serve as an associate justice of the U.S. Supreme Court in 1991, brought to light the terms of sexual harassment, words that gained new meaning for women. Her testimony with regard to Justice's Thomas treatment of her as sexual mistreatment while employed as his assistant helped to bring forth charges of sexual harassment from thousands of women who now understood the meaning of such actions.

Although we do not have a federal equal rights amendment, there are states that recognize its potential value. As an example, the use of male terms to indicate both sexes has been under examination for some time. There are those who choose to use gender-neutral terms. But gender discrimination is masked when gender-neutral terms are used. Words are meant to have definitive meaning. "Words are workhorses of law" (Thomas, 1991, p. 1160) Sexual harassment has become a major barrier to women's professional lives and personal development and a traumatic force that disrupts. and damages their personal lives. For ethnic-minority women who have been sexually harassed, economic vulnerability is paramount. Women feel powerless, not in control, afraid, and not flattered by sexual harassment. We need to understand that so much of the harassment that occurs is not sexual. The first case before the Supreme Court was that of *Meritor Savings Bank, FSB* v. *Vinson*, a 1986 case, in which it was decided that gender harassment is sexual discrimination and illegal under Title VII of the Civil Rights Act of 1964. Meritor (1986) recognized two types of sexual harassment: quid pro quo and hostile environment. "When sex is exchanged, or sought to be exchanged, for a workplace or educational benefit, called quid pro quo [emphasis mine] . . . and when conditions of work are damagingly sexualized or otherwise harmful, called hostile environment (*Barnes* v. *Costle*, 1977, p. 909).

Throughout this country, committees have been established to combat the charges of sexual harassment. It was almost as if the Thomas–Hill hearings brought people "out of the closet." Cases that followed include *Wagenseller* v. *Scottsdale Memorial Hospital* (1985) in Arizona, where the Arizona Supreme Court overruled earlier law and recognized a public policy exception to discharge at will in the case of an emergency room nurse who allegedly was terminated because she refused to "moon" on a rafting trip.

A worker who continually harasses female co-workers and is discharged does not have a right to reinstatement for failure of the employer to follow the notice provisions of the contract (see *Newsday, Inc.* v. *Long Island Typographical Union*, 1991). In the case of *Ellison* v. *Brady* (1991), the trial court had dismissed as trivial "love" letters that the plaintiff had received from a co-worker along with persistent requests for dates. The Ninth Circuit disagreed, however, stating that the perspectives of men and women differ. Women, as indicated by the courts, have a strong reason to be concerned about sexual behavior, as they are potential victims of rape and sexual assault.

A court in Florida ruled in the case of *Robinson* v. *Jacksonville Shipyards, Inc.* (1991) that a display of nude women can lead to the creation of a hostile environment and is therefore deemed an act of discrimination. In the case of *Continental Can Co., Inc.*, v. *Minnesota* (1980), the Minnesota Supreme Court upheld an action to stop harassment by fellow employees. In yet another case, *E.E.O.C.* v. *Sage Realty Corp.* (1981), the court held that an employer may impose reasonable dress codes for its employees, but the employer cannot require its employees to wear "revealing and sexually provocative uniforms" that would subject the employee to a form of sexual harassment. This constitutes gender discrimination.

The case of *Nichols* v. *Frank* (1994) involved Teri Nichols, who was deaf and mute. The night-shift supervisor (Francisco) with whom she worked had authority to grant employees leave as well as overtime pay. He was the only supervisor available able to communicate in sign language. At one point after asking Nichols to do some copying for him, ". . . Francisco started kissing Nichols and indicated that he wanted her to perform oral sex on him. She refused his advances, but ultimately complied because she was afraid she would lose her job if she refused. According to Nichols, 'I remember that when this first happened I was just in shock. I was nervous. I was upset. I wasn't happy doing it, and I was hoping it would never happen again. And I just kept that all to myself. But then there was repeats and repeats and repeats, and I was more upset and . . . I didn't want to do it again and again for him, and I didn't know how to say, 'Stop, just stop.'" The court concluded "that a supervisor's intertwining of a request for the performance of sexual favors with a discussion of actual or potential job benefits or detriments in a single conversation constitutes quid pro quo sexual harassment."

In the cases of *Burlington Industries* v. *Ellerth* (1998) and *Faragher* v. *Boca Raton* (1998), the court decided a chaotic body of law in the area of sexual harassment, making it easier for women whose bosses harass them to sue them under Title VII of the 1964 Civil Rights Act. Patricia Ireland, former president of the National Organization for Women (NOW), stated that "the boss who paws, propositions and warns of retaliation takes away a women's dignity . . . even if he doesn't take away her job" (1998).

In the Burlington case the claim was that the female endured a steady stream of sexual harassment from her supervisor's boss, "including pats on the buttocks, offensive sexual remarks and the threat that he could make her work life 'very hard or very easy.'" Despite the employer's argument that she suffered no tangible job loss, the U.S. Supreme Court decided that her case could go forward because it was the employer's burden to prove that reasonable steps had been taken by the company and that the complainant had failed to follow proper reporting procedures.

While in *Faragher*, the complainant, Beth Faragher, claimed that while working at a remote lifeguard station she was harassed by male supervisors, "who repeatedly touched her, called her and other women 'bitches and sluts,' made comments about her breasts and threatened 'date me or clean toilets for a year.'" It was the city's claim that she was not entitled to damages, as she failed to go over her supervisors' heads and report the harassment. The U.S. Supreme Court reinstated her damages award, deciding that the city had not taken reasonable steps to prevent and correct the harassment. In the words of Patricia Ireland, "women's rights need to be written into the Constitution. . . . [W]ithout it . . . women do not have a constitutional right to bodily integrity."

Addressing violence against women requires a national commitment. A summary of the date amassed about gender violence was included in the dissenting opinion of the Supreme Court's David Souter in *United States* v. *Morrison* (2000, pp. 1761–1763):

> Three out of four American women will be victims of violent crimes sometime during their lives.
>
> Violence is the leading cause of injuries to women ages 15–44.
>
> As many as 50% of homeless women and children are fleeing domestic violence.
>
> Since 1974, the assault rate against women has outstripped the rate for men by at least twice for some age groups, and far more for others.
>
> Battering is the largest cause of injury to women in the United States.
>
> An estimated 4 million women in the United States seek medical assistance each year for injuries sustained from their husbands or other partners.
>
> Between 2000 and 4000 women die every year from domestic abuse.
>
> Arrest rates may be as low as 1 for every 100 domestic assaults.
>
> Partial estimates show that violent crime against women costs this country at least $3 billion a year.
>
> Estimates suggest that we spend $5 to $10 billion per year on health care, criminal justice, and other social costs of domestic violence.
>
> The incidence of rape rose four times as fast as the total national crime rate over the past 10 years.
>
> According to one study, close to one-half million females now in high school will be raped before they graduate.

One hundred twenty-five thousand college women can expect to be raped before they graduate.

Three-fourths of women never go to the movies alone after dark because of the fear of rape, and nearly 50% do not use public transit alone after dark for the same reasons.

Forty-one percent of judges surveyed a Colorado study believed that juries give sexual assault victims less credibility than other victims of crime.

Less than 1% of rape victims have collected damages.

An individual who commits rape has only 4 chances in a 100 of being arrested, prosecuted and found guilty of any offense.

Almost one-fourth of convicted rapists never go to prison and another one-fourth received sentences in local jails, where the average sentence is 11 months.

Almost 50% of rape victims lose their jobs or are forced to quit because of the crime's severity.

The attorneys general from 38 states urged Congress to enact a civil rights remedy, permitting rape victims to sue their attackers because "the current system of dealing with violence is inadequate." (Muraskin & O'Connor, 2002, p. 432)

Due to these findings, Congress found it necessary to pass the Violence Against Women Act (VAWA) in 1994. This act provided for "substantial sums of money to States for education, rape crisis hotlines, training criminal justice personnel, victim services and special units in police and prosecutors' offices to deal with crimes against women. The act specifically provided incentives for the enforcement of statutory rape laws, the payment of the cost of testing for sexually transmitted diseases for victims of crime, and studies of campus sexual assaults, and the battered women's syndrome" (Muraskin & O'Connor, 2002, p. 434).

Legal scholars such as Catherine MacKinnon, a law professor at the University of Michigan Law School and visiting professor at the University of Chicago Law School, and activists such as Susan Brownmiller, are credited with initiating a view of sexual harassment that has changed radically the way that sexual harassment complaints are treated under the legal system. Shifting the focus of sexual harassment from the belief that males' sexual pursuit of a woman in the workplace or the classroom is essentially biological and that sexual harassment is therefore a "normal" consequence of attraction between the sexes, MacKinnon, Brownmiller, and others advocate a "dominance" approach. Sexual harassment is gender discrimination. It occurs in the workplace wherever women are situated in an attempt to keep them in their place (Corgin & Bennett-Haigne, 1998).

MacKinnon has asked the question as to whether "sexual harassment cases conceive gender horizontally in terms of sameness and difference, or vertically as hierarchy" (2001, p. 914). "One way women have been stigmatized as inferior is through the identification of a sometimes erroneous, usually exaggerated, always exclusive set of feminine needs. Women's sexuality has been a prime example. It has been hard to avoid branding women as inferior, long enough to balance a grasp of her dignity with an analysis of her enforced inferiority, in order to address the specificity of her situation" (MacKinnon, 1979, p. 144).

LITIGATION

Men who harass are not pathological but rather, people who exhibit behaviors that have been characteristic of the masculine gender role. The first litigation of sexual harassment claims did not occur until the mid-1970s. Title VII of the Civil Rights Act prohibiting sex discrimination in the workplace was followed eight years later by Title IX of the 1972 Higher Education Amendment, prohibiting gender discrimination in educational institutions receiving federal assistance. But in much of the early adjudication of gender discrimination, the phenomenon of sexual harassment was typically seen "as isolated and idiosyncratic, or as natural and universal and in either case, as inappropriate for legal intervention." It was in 1980 that the Equal Employment Opportunity Commission, in its guidelines on discrimination, explicitly defined sexual harassment under Title VII as a form of unlawful, gender-based discrimination.

As the law has been interpreted, prohibition against sexual harassment in the workplace technically covers any remark or behavior that is sufficiently severe and pervasive that not only the victim's but also a "reasonable person's" psychological well-being would be affected. A 1991 landmark ruling by the Court of Appeals for the Ninth Circuit in California held that the "appropriate perspective for judging a hostile environment claim [was] that of the 'reasonable woman' and recognized that a woman's perspective may differ substantially from a man's." While the 1991 Ninth Circuit Court ruling acknowledged that men and women may interpret the same behavior differently, in application this legal understanding was overshadowed by a grave misunderstanding of the nature of sexual harassment as experienced by its victims. The people doing the judging were in no position to understand the position of those being judged. The powerful were making judgments against the powerless.

But in the case of *Harris* v. *Forklift Systems, Inc.* (1993) the U.S. Supreme Court specified and refined its standards for hostile environment cases. "The U.S. Supreme Court decided in *Harris* that an environment of sexual harassment, to be actionable, had to be objectively hostile—one a 'reasonable person,' under all the circumstances, would find hostile or abusive—as well as hostile to the plaintiff herself. It also held that a hostile environment did not need to seriously affect a worker's psychological well-being to be discriminatory" (MacKinnon, 2001, p. 955).

RAPE, SEXUAL HARASSMENT, AND THE CRIMINAL JUSTICE SYSTEM

Like the crime of rape, sexual harassment is not an issue of lust; it is an issue of power. Sexual harassment does not fall within the range of personal or private relationships. It happens when a person with power abuses that power to intimidate, coerce, or humiliate someone because of gender. It is a breach of trust. In voluntary sexual relationships, freedom of choice is exercised in deciding whether to establish a close, intimate relationship. This freedom of choice is absent in sexual harassment (Paludi, 1992). Sexual harassment may be understood as an extreme acting out of qualities that are regarded as supermasculine: aggression, power dominance, and force. Men who harass are not pathological but rather, people who exhibit behaviors characteristic of the masculine gender role in U.S. culture. Most sexual harassment starts at the subtle end of the continuum and escalates over time. Each year, 1 percent of women in the U.S. labor force are sexually assaulted on the job. Yet cultural mythologies consistently blame the victim for sexual abuse and act to keep women in their place. Scholars have identified several similarities in attitudes toward rape and sexual harassment, especially revealing cultural myths that blame the victim:

1. Women ask for it.

   Rape: Victims seduce their rapists.

   Sexual harassment: Women precipitate harassment by the way they dress and talk.

2. Women say no but mean yes.

   Rape: Women secretly need and want to be forced into sex. They don't know what they want.

   Sexual harassment: Women like the attention.

3. Women lie.

   Rape: In most charges of rape, the woman is lying.

   Sexual harassment: Women lie about sexual harassment to get men they dislike into trouble.

Women who speak about being victims of sexual harassment use words such as *humiliating, intimidating, frightening, financially damaging, embarrassing, nervewracking, awful,* and *frustrating.* They are not words that are used to describe a situation that one enjoys.

Historically, the rape of a woman was considered to be an infringement of the property rights of men. Sexual harassment needs to be viewed in the same light. The message is that further changes are needed. We can no longer blame the messenger. We need to understand the message. There is no question that what is referred to as "women's hidden occupational hazard," sexual harassment, is gender victimization. The fact that sexual harassment exists demonstrates that it must be understood as part of the continuum of violence against women. In a typical sexual harassment case, the female accuser becomes the accused and the victim is twice victimized. This holds true in cases of rape and domestic violence as well as in cases of harassment. Underlying the dynamics of the situation is the profound distrust of a woman's word and a serious power differential between the accused and the accuser. As indicated, sexual harassment is the most recent form of victimization of the woman to be redefined as a social rather than a personal problem, following rape and wife abuse.

Sexual harassment continues to be a major barrier to women's professional and personal development and a traumatic force that disrupts and damages their personal lives. For ethnic-minority women who have been sexually harassed, economic vulnerability is paramount. Women feel powerless, not in control, afraid. There is nothing flattering about sexual harassment. Their emotional and physical well-being resembles that of victims of other sexual abuses (i.e., rape, incest, and battering). It must be stopped.

Women's issues infuse every aspect of social and political thought. It was Gloria Steinem who noted that cultural myths die hard, especially if they are used to empower one part of the population. The struggle of women continues under the law. There is no way to allow both sexes automatically to enjoy the equal protection of the laws unless we are committed to the elimination of all gender discrimination. Sexual harassment is gender discrimination. The criminal justice system over these many years has slowly come to grips with the need to understand women in the context of justice and fairness.

Women continue to represent half the population. They are owed the same rights and opportunities as are afforded to men. For justice to be gained, the fight for freedom and equality must continue. Prevention is the best tool that the criminal justice system has to offer as long as it takes the action mandated by legislators. Dominance takes several forms.

As stated so succinctly by Catherine MacKinnon in 1979: "Sexual harassment (and rape) has everything to do with sexuality. Gender is a power division and sexuality is one sphere of its expression" (pp. 220–221). There is no logic to inequality.

REFERENCES

CORGIN, B., & BENNETT-HAIGNE, G. (1998, August 12). Sexual harassment: Open season on working women. Available: http://www.now.org/nnt/03-97/sexual.html

FALUDI, S. (1991). *Backlash: The undeclared war against American women.* New York: Crown Publishers.

IRELAND, P. (1998). *Sexual harassment: Open season on working women. NOW Times.*

MACKINNON, C. (1979). *Sexual harassment of working women.* New Haven, CT: Yale University Press.

MACKINNON, C. (2001). *Sex equality.* New York: Foundation Press

MURASKIN, R., & O'CONNOR, M. (2002). Women and the law: An agenda for change in the twenty-first century. In R. Muraskin and A. Roberts (Eds.), *Visions for change: Crime and justice in the twenty-first century.* (3rd ed.), Upper Saddle River, NJ: Prentice Hall.

MURASKIN, R., & ROBERTS, A. (2002). *Visions for change: Crime and justice in the twenty-first century.* (3rd ed.). Upper Saddle River, NJ: Prentice Hall.

PALUDI, M. A. (1992). Working nine to five: Women, men, sex and power. In R. Muraskin (Ed.), *Women's agenda: Meeting the challenge to change.* New York: Long Island Women's Institute, College of Management, C.W. Post Campus of Long Island University.

ROBERTS, A. (1993). Women: Victims of sexual assault and violence. In R. Muraskin & T. R. Alleman (Eds.), *It's a crime: Women and justice.* Upper Saddle River, NJ: Prentice Hall.

THOMAS, C. S. (1991). *Sex discrimination.* St. Paul, MN: West Publishing.

CASES

Barnes v. *Costle,* 561 F.2d 983 (D.C. Cir. 1977).

Burlington Industries v. *Ellerth,* 123 F.3d 490 (1998).

Continental Can Co., Inc. v. *Minnesota,* 297 N.W. 2d 241 (Minn. 1980), 242.

E.E.O.C. v. *Sage Realty Corp.,* 507 F. Supp. 599 (D.C. N.Y. 1981), 243.

Ellison v. *Brady,* 924 F.2d 872 (9th Cir. 1991), 119.

Faragher v. *Boca Raton,* 111 F.3d 1530 (1998).

Harris v. *Forklift Systems, Inc.,* 510 U.S. 17 (1993).

Meritor Savings Bank, FSB v. *Vinson,* 477 U.S. 57, 106 S. Ct. 2399, 91 L. Ed. 2d 49 (1986), 239.

Newsday, Inc. v. *Long Island Typographical Union No. 915,* U.S. 111 S. Ct. 1314, 113 L. Ed. 2d 247 (1991), 195, 241.

Nichols v. *Frank,* 42 F.3d 503 (9th Cir. 1994).

Robinson v. *Jacksonville Shipyards, Inc.,* 760 F. Supp. 1486 (M.D. Fla. 1991), 241.

United States v. *Morrison,* 120 S. Ct. 1740 (2000).

Wagenseller v. *Scottsdale Memorial Hospital,* 147 Ariz. 370, 710 P.2d 1025 (Ariz. 1985), 194.

6

Abortion

Is It a Right to Privacy or Compulsory Childbearing?

Roslyn Muraskin

❖

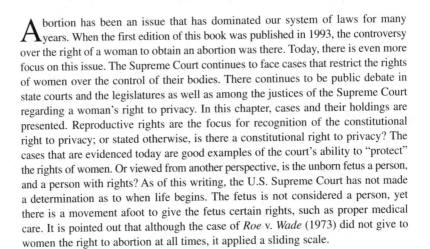

Abortion has been an issue that has dominated our system of laws for many years. When the first edition of this book was published in 1993, the controversy over the right of a woman to obtain an abortion was there. Today, there is even more focus on this issue. The Supreme Court continues to face cases that restrict the rights of women over the control of their bodies. There continues to be public debate in state courts and the legislatures as well as among the justices of the Supreme Court regarding a woman's right to privacy. In this chapter, cases and their holdings are presented. Reproductive rights are the focus for recognition of the constitutional right to privacy; or stated otherwise, is there a constitutional right to privacy? The cases that are evidenced today are good examples of the court's ability to "protect" the rights of women. Or viewed from another perspective, is the unborn fetus a person, and a person with rights? As of this writing, the U.S. Supreme Court has not made a determination as to when life begins. The fetus is not considered a person, yet there is a movement afoot to give the fetus certain rights, such as proper medical care. It is pointed out that although the case of *Roe* v. *Wade* (1973) did not give to women the right to abortion at all times, it applied a sliding scale.

It is fair to say that abortion "has dominated the landscape of procreational discourse and policy in the United States during the twentieth" century and continues into the twenty-first century (MacKinnon, 2001, p. 1212). From Alice Walker, "[a]bortion, for many women, is more than an experience of suffering beyond anything most men will ever know; it is an act of mercy and an act of self-defense. To make abortion illegal again is to sentence millions of women and children to miserable lives and even more miserable deaths" (1989, pp. 691–692). To view abortion as a crime means that many women will die.

From MacKinnon's work of 2001, she describes a young black woman who had an illegal abortion during a time prior to *Roe*:

> We were very middle class 1950s. . . . There was no spontaneous sex. . . . But on one occasion, in the fall, one of Joseph's apartment mates was away. . . . . We were kidding around and we went to [his] room, and we started fooling around. . . . We fell into his bed and had sex, and my period did not come the next time. . . . I liked the guy, but when he started talking about marriage and babies and stuff I wasn't ready. I wanted to finish my education. . . . I decided to ask my stepmother in Des Moines if she could help me. . . . We must have done it on a Friday night. . . . We went to the poor section of town. I remember not seeing anyone—just looking straight ahead.
>
> It was a kitchen table, coat hanger abortion. It took maybe six minutes. I got on the kitchen table. I think my stepmother gave me a drink of brandy or something, and she said, "Now this may hurt a little bit." She held my hand and this woman stuck a piece of coat hanger into my vagina. She stuck the coat hanger in, a piece that had been sterilized or whatever the hell she had done, and then my stepmother said, "Okay, now you get dressed." And what you were supposed to do was leave that in there until you started to abort. And then I left. I remember walking out with this coat hanger between my legs. . . . That evening I started bleeding. . . . I got up very early in the morning and went to the bathroom and there was just this passage of blood and a clot that was slightly bigger than the clots I usually passed during my menstrual period. . . . I should have been more concerned. If for no other reason than for the physical reality. I could have died. I could have become sterile. . . . When I read about people on the kitchen table I say, "I had one of those." (Messer & May, 1994, pp. 17, 19–23).

This was then. In the 1970s it was estimated that the number of deaths from illegal abortions was eight times greater than that from legal abortion. Reproductive freedom has been joined with such rights as freedom of speech or assembly. There exist those who have come to the conclusion out of simple personal concern that if women do not control their bodies from within, they can never control their lives from the skin out. There are those who feel that women's role as the most basic means of production will remain the source of their second-class status if outside forces continue either to restrict or compel that production. Remember the words of Justice Miller in *Bradwell* v. *State of Illinois* (1872), where he stated that "[t]he paramount destiny and mission of woman are to fulfill the noble and benign offices of wife and mother. This is the law of the Creator."

The freedom for women to decide when to become a mother and under what conditions is an issue of great concern. Is abortion an issue that affects women only, and is it an example of sex discrimination? Are we to think primarily of the fetus and thus conclude that abortion is murder, thereby involving the criminal courts? Is abortion to be viewed from a religious perspective, thinking of how the legal codes of Western religions treat the subject? Is abortion a question of privacy? Should states be prevented from intruding into the affairs and personal decisions of their citizens? Does there exist under *Reed* v. *Reed* (1971) a compelling state interest to interfere with a woman's right to choose? If a woman is a victim of rape or sexual abuse, is she entitled to an abortion without interference from the state? Is it an issue of discrimination against the poor, who may need the state to subsidize abortions, or even racial discrimination because of the high proportion of minorities who choose to abort? The question that comes into focus is not "how can we justify abortion?" but "can we justify compulsory childbearing?" Is there a compelling interest on the part of the state to protect what the courts have refused to define as a person?

What are the issues that the courts have faced when we discuss the issue of abortion? There are two significant constitutional issues at stake in judicial bias against women. The first issue has to do with the right to privacy, implied by our Constitution in the Fourth Amendment. The other issue concerns the Fourteenth Amendment's right to due process and equal treatment. Is the issue simply one of female autonomy over her body? The conflict continues. It is an issue that comes back repeatedly to haunt the courts, the legislators, and the executive branch of government. When can a woman have a partial abortion? Whose rights are we protecting? The U.S. Supreme Court held that laws prohibiting abortion are unconstitutional. In *Roe* v. *Wade* (1973) the Court held that "no state shall impose criminal penalties on the obtaining of a safe abortion in the first trimester of pregnancy." Women cannot be charged criminally with obtaining an abortion, but there are administrative regulations and legal penalties that prevent her from doing so.

Abortion is an emotional, legal, religious, and highly volatile issue. In December 1971, the Supreme Court heard the *Roe* v. *Wade* case, brought to it by an unmarried pregnant woman from Texas who complained that the Texas statute permitting abortions only when necessary to save the law of the mother was unconstitutional. (This person has since indicated that women should not be given the option of abortions, that all life is precious, and therefore, if pregnant, a women should not have the right to choose.)

What was held in *Roe* was that a state may not, during the first semester of pregnancy, interfere with or regulate the decision of a woman and her doctor to terminate the pregnancy by abortion; that from the end of the first trimester until the fetus becomes viable (usually about 24 to 28 weeks), a state may regulate abortions only to the extent that the regulation relates to the protection of the mother's health; and that only after the point of viability may a state prohibit abortion except when necessary to save the mother's life. The Court further permitted the state to prohibit anyone but a licensed physician from performing an abortion.

The Court did not accept the argument that a woman has a constitutional right to have an abortion whenever she wants one and that the state has no business at all interfering with her decision. Rather, the Court established a sliding scale that balanced the right of the woman against the right of the state to interfere with the decision; it would have to prove that it had a compelling interest to do so. During the first three months of pregnancy, when continuing the pregnancy is more dangerous than ending it, the Court found no such compelling state interest for overriding the private decision of a woman and her doctor. When abortion becomes a more serious procedure, the Court found that the state's interest in the matter increases enough to justify its imposition of regulations necessary to ensure that the mother's health will be safeguarded. In the last trimester of pregnancy, the Court found that the state's interest in the health and well-being of the mother as well as in the potential life of the fetus is sufficient to outweigh the mother's right of privacy except where her life is at stake.

In the language of the *Roe* Court:

> The right of privacy . . . is broad enough to encompass a woman's decision whether or not to terminate her pregnancy. The detriment that the State would impose upon the pregnant woman is apparent. Specific and direct harm medically diagnosable even in early pregnancy may be involved. Maternity, or additional offspring, may force upon the woman a distressful life and future. There is also the distress, for all concerned, associated with the unwanted child

and there is the problem of bringing a child into a family already unable psychologically and otherwise to care for it. In other cases as in this one, the additional difficulties and continuing stigma of unwed motherhood may be involved. All these are factors the woman and her responsible physician will consider in consultation.

The Court continued by indicating in *Roe* that the right to terminate the pregnancy at whatever time was not acceptable to the Court. They indicated further that the right to privacy was not absolute.

With regard to the argument presented that the fetus is a person, the Court went on to comment:

> [I]n nearly all . . . instances [in which the word "person" is used in the Constitution] the use of the word is such that it has application only postnatally. None indicates, with any assurance, that it has any possible prenatal application. All this together with our observation . . . that through the major portion of the nineteen century prevailing legal practices were far freer than they are today, persuades us that the word *person* as used in the fourteenth amendment, does *not* include the unborn. . . .

In answering the question of when life begins, the Court further stated:

> It should be sufficient to note . . . the wide divergence of thinking on this most sensitive and difficult question.
>
> In areas other than criminal abortions, the law has been reluctant to endorse any theory that life as we recognize it, begins before live birth or to accord legal rights to the unborn except in narrowly defined situations and except when the rights are contingent upon live birth. In short the unborn have never been recognized in the law as persons in the whole sense.
>
> We repeat . . . that the State does have an important and legitimate interest in preserving and protecting the health of the pregnant woman . . . [a]nd that it has still another important and legitimate interest in protecting the potentiality of human life.

The Court had decided to allow the mother to abort at the end of the first trimester and then to allow her physician to decide medically if the patient's pregnancy was to be terminated after this period. The judgment was to be effected by a decision free from the interference of the state.

At the same time that the Supreme Court decided the *Roe* case, it decided a second case, that of *Doe* v. *Bolton* (1973), which involved a Georgia abortion statute that set forth several conditions that were to be fulfilled prior to a woman obtaining an abortion. These included a statement by the attending physician that an abortion was justified, with the concurrence of at least two other Georgia-licensed physicians; the abortion was to be performed in a hospital licensed by the state board of health as well as accredited by the Joint Commission on Accreditation of Hospitals; there was to be advance approval by an abortion committee of not less than three members of the hospital staff; and the woman had to reside in the state of Georgia.

The Court then held that these provisions were overly restrictive, thereby treating abortion differently from comparable medical procedures and thus violating laws that require the husband of a pregnant woman or the parents of a single mother to give their consent prior to having an abortion. Both of these requirements were struck down by the Supreme Court (*Planned Parenthood of Central Missouri* v. *Danforth*, 1976).

What, then, is to happen when husband and wife cannot agree? Who is to prevail? The courts have argued that the woman should. Since it is the woman who bears the child physically and who is affected more directly and immediately by the pregnancy, the balance would seem to weigh in her favor.

Until this point the state did not appear to have the constitutional authority to give a third party an absolute and possibly arbitrary veto over the decision of the physician and his or her parent. There has developed the question of the authority that a parent has over a child. It has been well understood that constitutional rights do not mature and come into being magically when one attains the state-defined age of majority. Minors as well as adults are protected by the Constitution and possess constitutional rights.

There does exist a suggested interest in the safeguarding of the family unit and of parental authority. The idea of providing a parent with absolute power over a child and its veto power will enhance parental authority or control where the minor and the noncon-senting parent are so fundamentally in conflict that the very existence of the pregnancy already has fractured the family structure. The Court continues to review cases whereby the parent of the female will make the decision for her regardless of her wishes.

Two other important issues bearing on the ability of women to obtain abortions have been the right of hospitals to refuse to perform abortions and the right of Medicaid to refuse to pay for nontherapeutic abortions. In the case of *Nyberg* v. *City of Virginia* (1983), a federal court of appeals concluded that a public hospital may not refuse to perform abortions: "It would be a nonsequitur to say that the abortion decision is an election to be made by the physician and his patient without interference by the State and then allow the State, through its public hospitals, to effectively bar the physician from using State facilities to perform the operation." Theoretically, private hospitals may refuse to perform abortions, but it is not always easy to determine when a hospital is private. One needs to review whether it leases its facilities from the local government, whether it is regulated extensively by the state, whether it has received tax advantage, whether it has received public monies for hospital construction, and whether it is part of a general state plan for providing hospital services. Litigation and debate continue.

Under the decision in *Roe* v. *Norton* (1973), the Court concluded that federal Medicaid provisions prohibit federal reimbursement for abortion expenses unless a determination has been made that the abortion was medically necessary. The Court held that the government is not required by the Constitution to pay for any medical service, but once it does decide to do so, it must not unduly disadvantage those who exercise a constitutional right. Of late, laws have been passed that no birth control clinic that receives funding from the federal government may give information dealing with abortion. Of course, that has not stopped those who are against abortion from using whatever tactics are necessary to prevent such information from being disseminated, including that of bombing abortion clinics.

Those who are against abortion state that when a woman chooses to have sex, she must be willing to accept all consequences. Those who are against abortion will defend the rights of the fetus to develop, to be given life, and to grow, regardless of the wishes of the mother. Those who are against abortion state that whatever the costs, even to those who are victims of rape and incest, there is a life growing, and it is murder to do anything but carry it to full term. Better that any number of women should ruin their health or even die than one woman should get away with not having a child merely because she does not want one.

There have been cases—in the state of Idaho, for example—that have attempted to make physicians criminally liable for performing abortions rather than lay the responsibility on the mother. Under the Idaho proposal, a man who had committed *date rape*, a term describing sexual assault by an acquaintance (although rape is still defined as rape), could conceivably force the woman to carry the child.

Further decisions have been made affecting the woman's right to choose. For example, in the case of *Bellotti* v. *Baird* (1979), the Court had voted by a majority vote of 8 to 1 that a state may require a pregnant unmarried minor to obtain parental consent for an abortion if it also offers an alternative procedure. In the case of *Harris* v. *McRae* (1980), the Court upheld by a margin of 5 to 4 the Hyde amendment, which denies reimbursement for Medicaid abortions. And in the case of *City of Akron* v. *Akron Center for Reproductive Health, Inc.* (1983), the Court voted 6 to 3 that states cannot mandate what doctors will tell abortion patients or require that abortions for women more than three months pregnant be performed in a hospital. In *Thornburgh* v. *American College of Obstetricians and Gynecologists* (1986), the Court voted 5 to 4 that states may not require doctors to tell women about risks of abortion and possible alternatives or dictate procedures to third-trimester abortions.

In the case of Ohio upholding a law that required a minor to notify one parent before obtaining an abortion, Justice Kennedy wrote that "it is both rational and fair for the State to conclude that, in most instances, the family will strive to give a lonely or even terrified minor advice that is both compassionate and mature." However, Justice Blackmun, who was the senior author of *Roe*, wrote in what has been described as a stinging dissent that Kennedy and his adherents were guilty of "selective blindness" to the reality that "not all children in our country are fortunate enough to be members of loving families. For too many young pregnant women parental involvement in this intimate decision threatens harm, rather than promises of comfort." He ended by stating that ". . . a minor needs no statute to seek the support of loving parents . . . . If that compassionate support is lacking, an unwanted pregnancy is a poor way to generate it." And in *Webster* v. *Reproductive Health Services* (1989), the Court upheld 5 to 4 a Missouri law barring the use of public facilities or public employees in performing abortions and requiring physicians to test for the viability of any fetus believed to be more than 20 weeks old.

> Debate over these and other issues has spawned extensive litigation and put the Court in the position of reviewing medical and operational practices beyond its competence. We therefore believe that the time has come for the court to abandon its efforts to impose a comprehensive solution to the abortion question. Under the Constitution, legislative bodies cannot impose irrational constraints on a woman's procreative choice. But, within those broad confines, the appropriate scope of abortion regulation should be left with the people and to the political processes the people have devised to govern their affairs.

The Court stated that Missouri had placed no obstacles in the path of women seeking abortions. Rather, the state simply chose not to encourage or assist abortions in any respect.

Abortion remains as newsworthy and important a subject today. Perceptions of the abortion law differ. For the courts, it a constitutional issue. Others consider it an act of murder and believe that it should be turned over to the criminal courts. And indeed, there are those states who have at one time or other defined abortion as homicide. The focus is on the process. The issue is difficult because most people do not see it as a clear issue of law. Is the issue one that concerns a woman's right to privacy? Is it a case of sexual discrimination?

Or are we to look at the issue from the view of the fetus and view it as an issue of murder? Should abortion be viewed from a religious perspective, thinking of how the legal codes of Western religions treat the subject? Is it simply an issue of privacy and telling the states that they cannot intrude into the private affairs of its citizens? Or do we view abortion as a matter of health, of preventing injuries and death to women who undergo abortions? The answer lies in the fact that there are no easy answers and no easy solutions. Abortions is an issue that explodes in the courts, in legislators and in the minds of citizens.

In the case of *Rust* v. *Sullivan* (1991), the Court upheld 5 to 4 the federal government's ban on abortion counseling in federally funded family-planning clinics. In the case of *Planned Parenthood of Southeastern Pennsylvania* v. *Casey* (1992), the Court decided against the constitutionality of a law passed in Pennsylvania:

Informed Consent

At least 24 hours before the abortion, except in emergencies, the physician must tell the woman:

- The nature of the proposed procedure or treatment and the risks and alternatives
- The probable gestational age of the unborn child
- The medical risks associated with carrying her child to term
- That government materials are available that list agencies offering alternatives to abortions
- That medical assistance benefits may be available for prenatal care, childbirth, and neonatal care

Parental Consent

If the woman is under 18 and not supporting herself, her parents must be informed of the impending procedure. If both parents or guardians refuse to consent, judicial authorities where the applicant resides or where the abortion is sought shall . . . authorize . . . the abortion if the court determines that the pregnant woman is mature and capable of giving informed consent.

Spousal Notice

No physician shall perform an abortion of a married woman . . . without a signed statement . . . that the woman has notified her spouse.

Exceptions

- Her spouse is not the father of the child.
- Her spouse, after diligent effort, could not be located.
- The pregnancy is the result of spousal sexual assault . . . that has been reported to a law enforcement agency.
- The woman has reason to believe that notifying her spouse is likely to result in bodily injury.

Reporting

Each abortion must be reported to the state on forms that do not identify the woman but do include, among other items:

- The number of the woman's prior pregnancies and prior abortions
- Whether the abortion was performed upon a married woman and if her spouse was notified

The Constitution has been interpreted in many cases to protect the woman from arbitrary gender-based discrimination by the government, yet the struggle continues. Cases continue to be heard by the courts. In no instance is reference made to women's rights. Rather, the cases are based on the constitutional theory of the right to privacy, which is subject to interpretation, there being no exclusive right of privacy mentioned in the Constitution. Of the Supreme Court justices, Justice John Paul Stevens has supported abortion rights; Justice Antonin Scalia looks to overturn the decision in *Roe* but has yet to do so; Justice Sandra Day O'Connor has taken the *middle ground*, as articulated in her dissenting opinion in *Akron* v. *Akron* as well as in the case of *Hodgson* v. *Minnesota* (1990), where she stated that the right to an abortion is a "limited fundamental right" that may not be "unduly burdened" absent a compelling government interest, but may be burdened less severely upon a rational basis (947 F.2d, at 689–91).

What becomes noteworthy about cases dealing with the issue of abortion is that the motivation of a woman becomes entirely "irrelevant" to a determination of whether such a right is "fundamental." The Supreme Court has refused to overrule the *Roe* v. *Wade* decision, although erosion has taken place. The Court in their "wisdom" has upheld state restraints on a woman's right to choose an abortion freely, as supported in their decision in *Planned Parenthood of Southeastern Pennsylvania* v. *Casey* (1992) by a 5 to 4 decision, but the courts have yet to turn back the clocks back to 1973, a time when states could make abortion a crime and punish both a woman and her physician. The Court in the case of *Planned Parenthood* did allow states to impose conditions on women seeking an abortion—an "informed consent" provision that includes a lecture to women in an effort to "educate" them about alternative choices to abortion, as well as a 24-hour waiting period to "think it over."

The decisions of the Court have given the states considerable leeway that can make abortions costlier and more difficult to obtain. Such requirements by the state certainly continue to prove difficult for the poor woman who lives and works far from abortion clinics. Even a waiting period as short as 24 hours will force some women who cannot afford to stay overnight to make two trips to the clinic. The issue of whether such a procedure will pose an undue constitutional burden to choose remains open. Has abortion become a question of sex equality? As indicated by Reva Siegel, "[a]bortion-restrictive regulation is state action compelling pregnancy and motherhood, and this simple fact cannot be evaded by invoking nature or a woman's choices. . . . A pregnant woman seeking an abortion has the practical capacity to terminate a pregnancy, which she would exercise but for the community's decision to prevent or deter her. *If the community successfully effectuates its will, it is the state, and not nature, which is responsible for causing her to continue the pregnancy*" [emphasis mine] (MacKinnon, 2001, p. 1248).

And so the fight continues. In the case of *New Mexico Right to Choose* v. *Johnson* (1999), the court held that a "prohibition by the New Mexico Human Services Department on using state funds to pay for abortion for Medicaid-eligible women who were not covered because of the Hyde Amendment violated the state ERA." Under the right to privacy, accessibility to the use of contraceptive devices cannot be made a crime, but then insurance companies typically do not cover such devices. Is this a form of discrimination against women?

There are those that argue that abortion is counter to the interests of feminists—that abortion is sexist in nature (Bailey, 1995). The argument goes that a new movement of pro-life feminists argue that abortion is an act of desperation. The argument goes that when women "murder" their own children, society has done a great disservice to women. There arises the question of whether the act of abortion is "an offensive and sexist notion that women must deny their unique ability to conceive and bear children in order to be treated equally" (Smolin, 1990).

There is still another issue that attaches itself to the question of abortion, and that is the issue of federal funding for stem cell research, related to abortion. "Stem cell science offers a wholly new approach to intractable diseases. . . . the issue is deeply controversial. Some opponents simply argue against fiddling with Mother Nature. Others view the use of embryonic stem cells—isolated from embryos—as murder, sure that the life of an individual begins at conception. Thus it is closely tied to the abortion debate, not soon to be resolved" (Cooke, 2001, p. 1). There are those that believe that this issue of stem cell research is tied to abortion, because these embryos are defined as humans with rights and privileges attached. President George W. Bush has indicated that he will allow federally funded research on existing human embryonic stem cells to go forward, but only on cells that already exist. The debate has once again become political. Rather than allowing research to go forward that may find the cures to various diseases, the mere fact that the President has put limits on the research means that research will slow down. According to an editorial by Clymer in the *New York Times* (August 10, 2001, p. A18), "[m]ost people might have trouble seeing a tiny clump of cells in a petri dish as a human being. But some abortion opponents do, and they have argued that the thousands of excess embryos created by fertility clinics every year should be protected and 'adopted' by childless couples. They deserve respect for their beliefs. But they should not be allowed to dictate public policy, especially in an area where the health of so many people might be in the balance. As supporters of the stem cell research keep pointing out, there is more than one way to be pro-life."

According to the wording in the case of *Borowski* v. *Attorney-General of Canada* (1989), "[t]he Court must be careful not to create a time in a woman's life when, because of her unchosen biological capacities, she is outside the constitutional protection of the expansive equality rights. . . . " If we were to recognize the fetus as a person legally, and then grant legal rights over the woman's body, the woman would no longer have any legal and decision-making rights over her own body (ibid).

According to Ellen Chesler (1992), "[I]t has been seventy years since Margaret Sanger claimed that science would make women 'the owner, the mistress of her self.'" The spirit of her words lives on. The struggles of women and their right to choose and not to be punished in criminal courts continue. The final decision is not yet in. But for those who enjoy a safe bet, it is that woman in the twenty-first century will be limited in years to come to choose for themselves whether to have an abortion. That battles were fought and won in prior years does not mean that these decisions will remain. Battles won will still be fought.

REFERENCES

BAILEY, J. T. (1995). Feminism 101: A primer for prolife persons. In R. McNair (Ed.), *Profile feminism: Yesterday and today* (pp. 160, 163).

CHESLER, E. (1992, August 2). RU-486: We need prudence, not politics. *New York Times*, op. ed. page.

CLYMER, A. (1992, July 31). Lawmakers fear amendments on abortion rights. *New York Times*, p. A11.

COOKE, R. (2001, August 10). Fundamentals of stem research. *Newsday*, p. A2.

MACKINNON, C. (2001). *Sex equality*. New York: Foundation Press.

MESSER, E., & MAY, K. E. (EDS.). (1994). Lilia, in *Back rooms: Voices from the illegal abortion era*. Amherst, NY: Prometheus Books.

SMOLIN, D. (1990). The jurisprudence of privacy in a splintered Supreme Court. *Marquette Law Review, 75*, 975, 995–1001.

WALKER, A. (1989). What can the white man say to the black man? *The Nation*, pp. 691–692.

CASES

Bellotti v. *Baird*, 443 U.S. 622, 99 S. Ct. 3035, 61 L. Ed. 2d 797 (1979).

Borowski v. Attorney-General of Canada, S.C.R. 342 (1989), 1279.

Bradwell v. *State of Illinois*, 83 U.S. 130 (1872).

City of Akron v. *Akron Center for Reproductive Health, Inc.*, 462 U.S. 416, 103 S. Ct 2481, 76 L. Ed. 2d 687 (1983).

Doe v. *Bolton*, 410 U.S. 179, 93 S. Ct. 739, 35 L. Ed. 2d 201 (1973).

Harris v. *McRae*, 448 U.S. 297, 100 S. Ct. 2671, 65 L. Ed. 2d 784 (1980).

Hodgson v. *Minnesota*, 110 S. Ct. 2926 (1990).

New Mexico Right to Choose v. *Johnson*, 975 P.2d 841 (1988), *cert. denied*, 562 U.S. 1020 (1999).

Nyberg v. *City of Virginia*, 667 F.2d 754 (CA 8 1982), dsmmd 462 U.S. 1125 (1983).

Planned Parenthood of Central Missouri v. *Danforth*, 428 U.S. 52 (1976).

Planned Parenthood of Southeastern Pennsylvania v. *Casey*, 505 U.S. 833 (1992).

Reed v. *Reed*, 404 U.S. 71 (1971).

Roe v. *Norton*, 408 F. Supp. 660. (1973).

Roe v. *Wade*, 410 U.S. 113, 95 S. Ct. 705, 35 L. Ed. 2d 147 (1973).

Rust v. *Sullivan*, 114 L. Ed. 2d 233 (1991).

Thornburgh v. *American College of Obstetricians and Gynecologists*, 476 U.S. 747, 106 S. Ct. 2169, 90 L. Ed. 2d 779 (1986).

Webster v. *Reproductive Health Services*, 492 U.S. 490, 109 S. Ct. 3040, 106 L. Ed. 2d 410 (1989).

SECTION III
Women, Drugs, and AIDS

7

Revisiting "Crack Mothers at 6"

Drew Humphries

❖

In this chapter we examine ABC, CBS, and NBC evening news programs from 1983 to 1994 to understand the images associated with crack mothers, women who used crack or cocaine during pregnancy. Qualitative analysis shows that over time, news reports framed maternal crack or cocaine use in at least three ways. First, white middle-class women were presented as psychologically addicted, as guilt-ridden for having exposed their babies to cocaine, and as motivated to succeed in treatment. Second, poor black women were represented as mindlessly addicted, as knowingly having exposed their fetuses to the adversity of crack, and as unwilling to enter treatment. Third, poor black women were subsequently represented as physically and spiritually depleted, as having regretted prior drug use, and as enthusiastic drug treatment clients, if only to regain custody of their children. Findings are discussed in terms of drugs scares, racial disparity, and recent events that affect the reproductive rights of women.

Crack mothers, a media-coined phrase associated with the War on Drugs, refers to women who continued to use cocaine or crack during pregnancy. Socially constructed as black and urban, the media demonized crack mothers as the threatening symbols for everything that was wrong with the United States. Its cities, its poverty, and its welfare dependency were laid at the door of crack mothers, who by their drug use undermined the family and drove up the rates of infant mortality and morbidity. Yet crack or cocaine mothers cannot be considered innocent. Drug use during pregnancy adds avoidable risk and violates the moral duties of motherhood (i.e., pregnant women are expected to prevent risk and encourage healthy development of the fetus). The issue is not risk or violation but rather how both were constructed. The news featured significant risk and egregious violations. To prevent these, warriors in the War on Drugs invoked the law, using criminal sanctions to protect fetuses and babies from the effects of maternal drug use. More than 160 crack mothers were prosecuted in criminal courts between 1988 and 1994. Rarely, if ever, have women triggered a drug scare of this magnitude.

Past drug scares have focused on males who used cocaine, marijuana, and heroin, but the construction of the problem across different antidrug crusades shows remarkable similarities. Social historians, for instance, suggest that during drug scares, drug use is identified with an unpopular minority, individuals are held responsible for their addiction, and addiction is cast as a broader threat (Levine, 1979; Musto, 1987). Reinarman and Levine (1995) have shown that the crack scare fits this model. Crack was constructed as the cause, not the symptom, of the underlying problems. Legal liability—and mandatory prison sentences—fell to the crack addict, who epitomized a threatening underclass. As part of the larger scare, the crusade against crack mothers appealed to similar status resentments (Humphries, 1993; Humphries, Dawson, Cronin, Wisniewski, & Eichfeld, 1991). Reeves and Campbell (1994) have discussed the "crack mothers" image as a racially defined composite, a "she-devil" image that borrows both from the welfare mother and from the sexually aggressive stereotype of black women, known as "Jezebel." Reeves and Campbell contrasted the she-devil image to portraits of white mothers who used alcohol, showing racial disparities in coverage. It would have been better to compare race within the same category of drug user (e.g., black and white cocaine users), but this would have required a different approach to the problem. The longer time frame of this study permits racial comparisons among women who used cocaine or crack.

RESEARCH

The study surveys news segments shown on prime-time television during the War on Drugs (1983–1994). ABC, CBS, and NBC were the networks sampled. A review of *Television News Index and Abstracts* yielded 84 news segments that referred to women and cocaine or crack. The media center at Vanderbilt University prepared compilation tapes that included 84 news segments. The tapes provide the data for this study. They run 5½ hours, this being the amount of time the major networks devoted to the story over nine years. Taken individually, the segments have a mean running time of 2 minutes, although segment duration ranges from 20 seconds to 6 minutes.

Because news connects people to a world beyond their experience, news images have considerable power in shaping perceptions. For this reason, media images are studied, but composite images are especially important. The power of a stereotype, such as muggers, to effectuate moral panic in England depended on converging images of race, poverty, the city, violence, and social menace (see Hall, Critcher, Jefferson, Clarke, & Roberts, 1978). A similar convergence has been noted for the stereotype of crack mothers: Race, addiction, and poverty linked to sexuality and motherhood justify efforts to regulate pregnancy (Maher, 1991; Maher & Curtis, 1992).

The study focuses on news images, looking in particular for the special combination of race, class, gender (including motherhood), and addiction that created a pervasive sense of menace. To do this, the study looks at persons shown on the videotaped segments as crack or cocaine addicts. To estimate the importance of maternal themes, the study also looks at the babies represented as drug-exposed. A research assistant counted the babies and the mothers who used crack or cocaine.[1] In counting adult women, the assistant also determined race, ethnicity, and context. *Context* refers to the setting in which the addict or former addict is filmed. An ex-addict who is framed in a legitimate role (e.g., mother or spokesperson) would fall into *civil society*. Addicts who are actively involved in drug use justify the *drug life* designation. The term *treatment* applies to addicts who are shown on camera in a drug rehabilitation program. An addict who awaits trial or is receiving posttrial punishment is framed by the criminal court. The context *social services* refers to addicts who receive help in the home from social workers or support groups. *Other* is a residual category.

The news narrative is also addressed in this article. Statements made by news anchors, news correspondents, experts, and interviewees form the narrative, the ongoing discussion about maternal drug use. That discussion consists of assertions about drugs (crack or cocaine), the meaning of addiction (psychological and physical), and drug users, including motive, social class, and attitudes toward treatment or punishment.

News segments were coded for image and narrative. Coded entries have been located in a four-stage chronology of news coverage. The descriptive analysis identifies key aspects of image and narrative by stage.

FINDINGS

Drug scares and moral panics exhibit a typical pattern of news coverage: Volume increases, reaches a peak, and then trails off as other topics eclipse the story. The four-stage model of news coverage shown in Table 1 is based on the frequency distribution of news segments and is used for comparative purposes.[2] Breaks between stages reflect data shifts, including a key event, a natural break, and a context change. Because the networks' discovery of crack changed the image of an addict, this key December 1985 event divides stages 1 and 2. News segments dropped off in 1987, the natural break that separates stages 2 and 3. After 1991, the networks reduced coverage and introduced a new context, social services. Both are used to introduce stage 4.

Focusing on female crack or cocaine use, Table 1 shows a net increase in the proportion of female addicts from stages 1 to 4. That men were the majority in stage 2, however, reflects the discovery of crack and its identification as a male drug. The point at which the developing news story is clearly about maternal drug use occurs in stage 3: 63 percent of addicts shown on camera were women, and the maternal theme reached a peak with 93 babies shown on camera. Whereas white women defined the image of maternal drug use in the first two stages, black women defined it in the last two stages: 55 percent and 84 percent of the women were black in stages 3 and 4, respectively.[3] The last point concerns context. Table 1 shows that the treatment context provided a remarkable degree of continuity throughout the four-stage chronology, but as new contexts emerged, they are noted. Civil society provided a unique context for 37 percent of women who used cocaine in stage 1. As crack entered the picture in stage 2, 28 percent of the women were shown using drugs against a background of drug supermarkets. At its stage 3 peak, the news used the criminal court to frame 17 percent of the women who used crack or cocaine. Finally, social services provided a new context for 21 percent of the women in stage 4.

TABLE 1   Crack Mother Image: Descriptive Elements by Stages, 1983–1994

Descriptive Element	Stage[a] 1		Stage[a] 2		Stage[a] 3		Stage[a] 4	
	n	%	n	%	n	%	n	%
Number of news segments	10	12	16	19	43	51	15	18
Number of crack or cocaine addicts								
Women	16	42	18	34	89	63	19	76
Men	22	58	35	66	53	37	6	24
Total	38	100	5	100	142	100	25	100
Maternal theme								
Babies	3		11		93		31	
Race or ethnicity (women)								
White	12	75	13	72	28	31	3	
Black	3		2		49	55	16	84
Hispanic	1		3		3		3	
Unknown	0		0		10	11	0	
Context (women)								
Civil society[b]	6	37	1		7	8	3	
Drug life[c]	2		5	28	23	26	4	
Treatment[d]	5	31	8	44	35	39	5	26
Criminal court[e]	1		0		15	17	3	
Social services[f]	0		0		0		4	21
Other	2		4		9	10	0	
Total women	16	100	18	100	89	100	19	100

[a]The four stages encompass periods of equal intervals. The periods were divided as follows. The discovery of crack in December 1985 sets off stage 1 from stage 2. A drop in the frequency of news segments in 1987 provides a natural break between stages 2 and 3. Following peak coverage in stage 3, a dramatic decline in news segments and an increase in segments relying on social services to frame pregnant drug users identify stage 4.

[b]Domestic settings, social occasions, and workplaces that are not normally associated with drug use are settings that fall into the category *civil society*.

[c]*Drug life* refers to a lifestyle organized around drug use. It runs the gamut from cocaine parties and celebrities to crack houses, drug supermarkets, and street busts.

[d]*Treatment* refers to drug rehabilitation facilities. Facilities range from expensive private clinics to publicly financed pilot projects aimed at the poor. During the years of peak news coverage, treatment cannot easily be separated from criminal court settings because the courts often mandated treatment for pregnant substance abusers.

[e]Criminal courts were used to frame crack mothers who had been prosecuted for using drugs during pregnancy.

[f]As a context that frames crack mothers, social services signals a different approach to the problem, the provision of services (e.g., prenatal, health, and job training).

Stage 1: Women, Cocaine, and the White Middle Class

Cindy, a white middle-class housewife, was the first "cocaine mother" to appear on network news (Brinkwater, 1984). She was, however, the third woman to be interviewed on an NBC Special Segment entitled "The Cocaine Epidemic." Like the two other white middle-class women, Cindy had not sought out the drug; rather, she, like the others, had been introduced to cocaine by the men in their lives. Women used it to cope, explained Josette Mondonaro, a drug expert interviewed at a California treatment center. Women used cocaine to "pump up [their] low self-esteem," to feel better, or to gain a competitive edge. But women did not fully appreciate cocaine's addictive potential. When Cindy discovered that she was pregnant, she also discovered that she could not stop using cocaine. She sought drug treatment and succeeded in recovery. Interviewed in her home after the baby was born, Cindy was shown as a model mother, bathing a normal, healthy infant. An NBC correspondent, however, put the maternal scene in a darker context: When a woman used cocaine during pregnancy, the fetus could suffer from oxygen deprivation. Normal-looking babies such as Cindy's could still suffer long-term effects of cocaine.

Motherhood made Cindy atypical, but otherwise she resembled the other 16 women in stage 1 who admitted using cocaine. Cocaine addicts, as shown in Table 1, were still as likely to be male (58 percent) as female (42 percent). The women tended to be white (75 percent). They appear on camera as ex-addicts, but aside from this, they were represented as fulfilling legitimate roles as wives or professionals engaged in a variety of occupations. Maternal themes were not significant; instead, female cocaine use served to illustrate the dangers associated with recreational drug use. The narrative suggested that an epidemic of middle-class cocaine addiction had resulted from misinformation and errors in judgment. In May 1984, CBS aired an interview with Mark Gold, cocaine expert and director of the Cocaine Hotline in New Jersey. Gold said that cocaine produces psychological dependence, although anywhere from 25 to 50 percent of cocaine users would become addicted. The more significant risk was death (Rather, 1989a). CBS showed film footage that outlined the results of animal research: A single monkey, free to move about its cage, repeatedly pushed a button to release cocaine into its bloodstream intravenously. The monkey injected so much cocaine that it fell into a state of seizure and died. Euphoria masked the deadly effects of cocaine, explained Gold. Human beings were no different. The same CBS report introduced Kathryn, an ex-addict who recalled repetitive efforts to achieve the ultimate high. She used so much cocaine that she lost the desire to survive. She nearly died before she realized the problem.

Stage 2: The Discovery of Crack

Network news discovered crack in 1985; thereafter, the news tended to use the terms *crack, cocaine*, and *crack/cocaine* interchangeably in referring to maternal drug use. Crack as a news story, however, pushed white women to the background who used cocaine. Even though Table 1 shows that most crack or cocaine addicts were men (66 percent), women addicted still tended to be white (72 percent). Maternal themes increased: Three middle-class mothers, all of whom resembled Cindy, were featured in stage 2, but the 11 babies shown on camera were still insignificant compared with the 93 babies shown in stage 3. Less than half of the women appeared in the context of treatment, but the five women placed in the context of drug supermarkets were shown using crack.

Crack was a mystery. Relying on street users and experts, the networks frame crack as the most dangerous drug in the United States. Crack produced the most powerful high. It was so good, according to one user, that he felt he could do anything (Palmer, 1985). Michael, a crack cook and dealer, said he got hooked the first or second time he tried the drug. He lost weight, became suicidal, and almost died (Jennings, 1986a). A recovering crack addict worried about relapse, explaining that his body would take over, compelling him to use it (Jennings, 1986b). Experts offered explanations (Palmer, 1985). Mitchell Rosenthal, president of the Phoenix House Foundation, reported that crack produced a short but powerful high, followed by depression. To alleviate the depression, the user smoked more crack. Rosenthal predicted an increased rate of addiction.

The networks initially portrayed crack as everyone's drug. Crack smokers included people from all backgrounds, said Dennis Murphy, an NBC reporter (Brokaw, 1986). In the segment, a South Florida businessman claimed to have had a $1000-a-day crack habit and reported to have binged up to 30 hours at a time. The businessman appeared with two other white males before the camera cut to a litter-filled crack house in which police arrested black crack users. Film footage of a lone black man smoking cocaine ended the segment. Other segments reported that the white middle class purchased crack. The New York Police Department impounded cars of out-of-state crack buyers, according to an NBC report (Chung, 1986). Film footage showed late-model cars and white drivers. Within a year, NBC had, however, redefined crack as an inner-city minority male drug (Brokaw, 1987). Crack spread from the largest seven to the largest 40 cities in the country. But there was some good news, said Robert Stutman, spokesperson for the Drug Enforcement Administration. Crack use had leveled off in the suburbs. Stutman also said that he "did not believe it had leveled off in the inner city." Videotaped footage shown on camera included scenes of street trafficking, collection of crack vials, and black drug users. Black and Hispanic patients filled treatment centers.

Stage 3: Pregnancy, Crack, and Poor Women of Color

In October 1988, the television viewing public met its first crack mother (Brokaw, 1988a, b). NBC introduced Tracy Watson, a pregnant black woman, who sat on a narrow bed in a bare New York City apartment and smoked crack. Tracy spent $100 a day on the drug and smoked up to 20 vials. Tracy spoke. She knew crack affected her pregnancy. She knew that the baby could be born prematurely. She knew that the baby might undergo withdrawal. All the while she smoked crack. Baring her protruding belly, Tracy said, "It kicks when I smoke. It tightens up on one side. It's kicking now."

Tracy Watson typified crack mothers and, as Table 1 indicates, her profile reflects the convergence of gender, maternal themes, and race. Women accounted for 63 percent of cocaine or crack addicts. Maternal themes reached a peak. Nine times more babies were shown during stage 3 (93) than were shown during stage 2 (11). And 55 percent of the women were black. News segments placed crack mothers in three different contexts. Active crack users such as Tracy Watson were shown smoking crack or placed in the context of drug supermarkets (26 percent). Crack addicts were more frequently placed in the context of treatment (39 percent) than in the context of criminal court (17 percent), but keep in mind that the criminal court required most defendants to enroll in a drug treatment program.

Network news hardened the concept of addiction. ABC reported that crack produced a "physical addiction," a permanent change in the brain (Jennings, 1988a). Anna Rose Childress and Charles O'Brian, both of the Philadelphia Veterans Medical Center, noted that the rapid onset of euphoria, the rush, was the mechanism of change. To help the audience visualize the mechanism, the studio had supplied an outline of the human brain. The rush was represented by a moving wave of color that swept across the brain. The brain permanently encoded the rush as memory, said Childress. This fact helped Jerome Jaffee, director of the Addiction Research Center, explain the sudden relapses of people who had long since completed treatment. For women, crack was more important than their children. They did not think about pregnancy. They abandoned infants in their pursuit of crack. When irritable, they abused or neglected children (Rather, 1989d).

Crack-exposed babies dominated the news. In Florida, health workers were required to report suspected cocaine use by pregnant women to social services. From these numbers, ABC projected that 10,000 cocaine babies would be born in Florida in 1988 (Jennings, 1988b). NBC showed a Florida hospital where one in ten delivering women used cocaine within hours of childbirth, and it said, drug use had become so common among pregnant women in Chicago that routine obstetrics included drug treatment (Brokaw, 1988a, b). CBS reported the results of a 40-hospital survey conducted by Chasnoff: His conclusion was that women gave birth to 375,000 cocaine babies a year (Brokaw, 1989a; Rather, 1989a). CBS used this same figure to describe both crack and cocaine babies (Rather, 1990a, c). In New York and Kansas City, cocaine babies represented 15 percent of births (Brokaw, 1989d; Rather, 1989b). ABC reported a lower estimate: 100,000 babies had been exposed to cocaine prenatally in 1990 (Jennings, 1990b).

Prenatal cocaine exposure was linked to infant mortality. In Washington, D.C., infant mortality rates had increased by 50 percent (Brokaw, 1989c; Jennings, 1990a). ABC provided background, indicating that Washington already had the highest rates of infant mortality, which was also related to poverty, unemployment, and lack of prenatal care (Jennings, 1990a). Birth or congenital defects were reported, too. A study conducted by the Centers for Disease Control in Atlanta showed that babies exposed to cocaine were five times more likely than other babies to suffer serious birth defects (Brokaw, 1989b). Babies born to cocaine users had three times the risk of birth defects (Jennings, 1989). This was the first study, Jennings said, that linked cocaine to specific defects; previous studies had only linked cocaine to withdrawal (Jennings, 1989). In a CBS news story, Dr. Avery, a physician at Children's National Medical Center, said that he had examined hundreds of crack babies and that many were premature and underweight and some suffered brain damage (Rather, 1990a). To demonstrate, Avery held up a cross-sectional image of a child's brain, pointed to the dark spots on the film, and said that the shadows represented brain tissue that cocaine had destroyed.

Although cocaine use during pregnancy was also linked to miscarriage and premature birth, low birth weight epitomized cocaine babies. In one case, a premature baby weighing 15 ounces was described as a cocaine baby (Jennings, 1990a). The tubes taped to his body connected him to life support. He struggled in his incubator. A nurse took his minuscule hand in hers, offering comfort while he endured withdrawal. The camera panned the hospital unit showing dozens of incubators; each held a very small baby, presumably a cocaine-exposed baby. In addition, cocaine was linked to neurobehavioral problems in infants. Withdrawal made the babies irritable, and offsetting possible life-long consequences required special care, according to Dr. Chasnoff (Jennings, 1988b). ABC reported more severe difficulties: cocaine syndrome, neurological damage that created lifelong problems for the children—hyperactivity, poor concentration, and a limited attention span (Jennings, 1988b). The impact of prenatal exposure, explained an ABC correspondent, was worse in the ghetto (Jennings, 1990a). At Hale House in Harlem, a home for abused and abandoned children, six or seven crack-exposed children were shown playing games. Lorraine Hale, the director, said they were not retarded but slow learners (Brokaw, 1988b). In a Los Angeles school, teachers described drug-exposed toddlers as forgetful, unable to perform tasks they had learned the day before (Brokaw, 1988b). School-aged children were expected to have problems, too. Edward, a 7-year-old, who had been exposed to crack during his mother's pregnancy, pushed and shoved his classmates (Rather, 1990a). His foster mother described the disruptive activities that got him suspended from school: fighting, destroying property, and hitting his teacher. He had wide mood swings. He could not concentrate. His behavior was unpredictable and impulsive.

In 1990, Reed Tuckerson, the U.S. Public Health Commissioner, called for the inclusion of drug treatment in routine prenatal care; he resigned later for lack of support (Jennings, 1990a). At Harlem Hospital, more social workers were needed to track down crack mothers who had abandoned their infants (Brokaw, 1988b). Hale House was one of the few places that took the abandoned babies (Brokaw, 1988a). In Philadelphia, the Children of Light Mission ran a 24-hour-a-day emergency placement service for children whose families had been disrupted by drugs and alcohol. The welfare department in Philadelphia had certified nurses as foster care parents to provide enough placements for abandoned crack babies (Rather, 1990b). Across the country the numbers were climbing: 500,000 children were wards of the state in 1989; the figure was expected to increase to 850,000 by 1995 (Rather, 1989a). In 1990, NBC attributed the increases in children in foster care to abuse by drug- or alcohol-impaired caretakers (Brokaw, 1990). The cost required to fund treatment and foster care was staggering. Government estimates reported by ABC and CBS placed the cost at $5 billion over five years (Jennings, 1990b; Rather, 1990a).

Images of the suffering of innocent babies justified criminal prosecutions against crack mothers. In May 1989, CBS reported the case of Melanie Green (Rather, 1989c). Winnebago County (Illinois) prosecutor Paul Logli had filed manslaughter charges against Melanie Green, following the death of her 2-day-old newborn. At birth, the infant had tested positive for cocaine, so Logli, operating on the theory that the cocaine was the cause of death, charged Green. According to Logli, there was no difference between an adult giving a child cocaine and a pregnant woman ingesting the drug to the detriment of the unborn child.

In July 1989, ABC reported that the trial of Jennifer Johnson was nearing a verdict (Sawyer, 1989). The anchor, who inquired what should been done about crack mothers, provided this answer: "You should know that some law enforcement authorities think it's time to prosecute, to consider those mothers as criminals." Jeffrey Deen, Florida State attorney, had filed felony criminal charges against Jennifer Johnson after her newborn had tested positive for cocaine. The baby was Johnson's second cocaine-exposed child, a fact that led Deen to take control. Lynn Paltrow, Jennifer Johnson's defense lawyer and a staff attorney for the Reproductive Freedom Project, took issue with the prosecution's claims. "If the issue is harming the fetus, then you can arrest women for drinking alcohol, smoking cigarettes, working in places where chemicals are put into their bodies that harm fetuses, or even living with a husband who is a heavy smoker."

The last word, however, went to the babies. An ABC correspondent noted that a mother's right to privacy outweighed the right of a fetus to health but concluded: "A growing number of voices are crying out for change." The camera panned rows of incubated newborns in a neonatal intensive care unit reported to care for crack babies.

Stage 4: Women, Crack, and Community-Based Programs

Betty Collins, a 24-year-old black woman and crack mother, was interviewed in prison for an NBC segment (Chung, 1994). "Nobody," she said, "should have to go through this just to get off drugs. It doesn't take jail." Collins's 3-week-old daughter had been taken from her by the state of South Carolina after cocaine was found in the child's stool. Despite Collins's efforts to get off drugs, she was still charged with child endangerment. An angry Collins complained: "They did not consider my efforts to improve myself. They just threw me in jail. I think that is very unfair." Collins's attorney, Rauch Wise, told the CBS correspondent that his client had "abused her body in taking cocaine" but had "not abused her child." In prosecuting mothers whose babies tested positive for cocaine, Wise noted that the state of South Carolina was "playing a political and racist game." This and other statements by defense attorneys began to suggest that the prosecutions themselves might be part of the problem.

Betty Collins typified the news profile of crack mothers. As Table 1 indicates, crack mothers tended to be black (84 percent), and maternal themes continued to be important despite a precipitous reduction in the number of babies, from 93 in stage 3 to 31 in stage 4. Treatment and drug life provided a context for female addicts in stages 2, 3, and 4. What emerged as new for stage 4 were social service programs designed to manage the maternal crack or cocaine problem in the community or at a lower cost. ABC ran an American Agenda report in 1993 about an outreach program in Nashville, Tennessee (Jennings, 1993). In it, the community workers went door to door in a housing project to encourage drug-addicted black women to enter treatment programs. Even treatment had a community focus. A two-part NBC American Close-Up featured the Christian Community Youth Against Drugs (Stone, 1992a, b). This New Orleans program had been helped by a federal grant, but it ran on private donations and the profits from a car wash that employed program clients. Without additional state or federal spending, the program provided free drug treatment and long-term residential care for the poor. The Reverend Thomas Taylor, a charismatic Baptist minister, redefined addiction, taking it out of the realm of medical science and placing it in the realm of common sense and religion. Addiction represented physical problems. Drug use was hard on the body, but medical care, good food, and physical work could restore it. Addiction represented physical problems. Drug use was hard on the body, but medical care, good food, and physical work could restore it. Addiction was also constructed as a spiritual problem. The drug lifestyle tested the spirit, so prayer, human contact, and charismatic leadership were part of the program. Group therapy and recovery classes dealt with residents' drug problems. High school equivalency classes promised them a brighter future. Independent evaluators judged the program a success. Such programs suggested that the black community had effectively solved its problems

To summarize, this article surveyed television news images of maternal cocaine crack use from 1983 to 1994. It showed three different images of maternal drug use as they emerged over the four-stage chronology of news. First, white middle-class women used cocaine during pregnancy without obvious consequences to their babies. Maternal themes, however, were relatively unimportant, as the news segments addressed the cocaine epidemic among the middle class. Like other members of this class, the women were psychologically addicted and had responded to drug education by entering drug treatment. Second, poor black women used crack during pregnancy with severely damaging consequences to their babies. Active drug users appeared in the context of drug supermarkets; recovering crack addicts appeared in treatment settings. Maternal themes applied to active and recovering crack addicts. Like other members of the underclass, the women were physically addicted, indifferent to the effects of cocaine on themselves, their pregnancies, and others. They appeared as appropriate targets for punishment. Third, recovering crack mothers were also poor women of color. Maternal themes continued to be important, but by completing prison sentences or by entering treatment, mothers hoped to regain custody of their children. They suffered from a different kind of addiction, a spiritual as well as a physical problem. News coverage focused on community-based initiatives aimed at getting women into treatment, although court-mandated treatment remained an issue.

DISCUSSION

Drug Scares and Reality

Drug scares comprise a complex process that may take several years to unfold, but in the case of crack, events went quickly. The drug was immediately demonized. Addiction was promptly individualized (i.e., blamed on the addict). Within a year, crack use was associated with an urban underclass. Within four years, black women were put on trial for having used crack or cocaine during pregnancy. The War on Drugs hastened the arrival of punitive measures, but persuasive reactions are seemingly missing. The missing persuasive phase, however, reappears when crack and cocaine are treated as the same drug. Note that network news went to great lengths to differentiate the two drugs: Cocaine produced psychological addiction; crack produced physical addiction. Normally, one speaks of addiction,[4] or using an alternative approach, one refers to psychoactive substances that produce a dependence of a psychological or physical type.[5] To use the terms interchangeably is to transform a manageable "dependence" into an intractable "addiction." Thus the War on Drugs focused on cocaine, and news correspondents represented this drug as "addictive," a threatening enough term. If crack replaced cocaine as the most dangerous drug in the United States, news teams had to invent a new set of superlatives—hence, physical addiction. Admittedly, the search was on in drug research circles to find evidence that crack/cocaine caused the body to adapt permanently to the drug; and addiction research was a standard feature of news coverage. A news segment aired during stage 3 appeared to make the scientific case: With color-coded graphics, crack permanently encoded its euphoric rush on the brain. The segment had implications for how maternal crack/cocaine use was perceived. Black women who used crack during pregnancy presented a far more dangerous problem than did their white counterparts who had only used cocaine.

But to return to the missing persuasive phase in the crack mother scare, we can see that medical warnings and other persuasive strategies targeted white middle-class cocaine mothers. We can also see that punitive measures targeted poor women of color. Thus the shift from persuasive to punitive approaches reflects suspect distinctions between crack and cocaine and differential reactions to white and black user populations. Crack mother images incorporated the hyperbole associated with crack, addiction, race, and its ties to the underclass, inner-city poverty, and welfare. But the study found no evidence for the presence of a Jezebel stereotype (Reeves & Campbell, 1994). Prime-time news did not cover the sex-for-crack exchanges, nor did it allude to women's alleged hypersexuality. News images of crack mothers reviewed for this study had more to do with errant motherhood than with sexuality. Pregnant women such as Tracy Watson smoked even though they knew that crack/cocaine would adversely affect their unborn babies. They violated basic rules of motherhood, but high-profile cases selected for criminal prosecution made extreme cases appear to be the norm: Melanie Green's drug use allegedly led to the death of her baby; Jennifer Johnson gave birth to not one but two cocaine babies. The network news broadcast images based on these cases into the homes of news viewers.

In retrospect, it is possible to compare media images of crack mothers to reality. Although the rate of drug use during pregnancy for black women was higher than it was for white women, the number of white women who used illicit drugs while pregnant greatly exceeded the number of minority women who used illicit drugs (National Institute of Drug Abuse, 1996). By sheer numbers, the newscast should have focused on drug use by pregnant white women. Because the War on Drugs targeted crack, news reports amplified racial disparities already entrenched in the hospital-based system for reporting maternal drug use. A key study found that at their first prenatal examination, pregnant women of both races had comparable rates of drug use, but when admitted to the hospital for delivery, black women were more likely than white women to be tested for illicit drugs (Chasnoff, Landress, & Barrett, 1990). Because poor women go to public hospitals and because public hospitals are mandated to report drug use, poor women of color tend to be tested for drugs more frequently. When drug testing is discretionary, protocols have to be interpreted. Because hospital workers determine what constitutes incomplete prenatal care, biases about who uses drugs influence the selection of patients for testing. Public awareness of the drug problem, including awareness of maternal drug use, also affects the incidence of testing and the population tested.

We have yet to address crack mothers as freshly minted, recovering addicts. In the context of drug scares, this means asking how problems that once triggered panic are subsequently reframed as inoffensive, harmless, or resolved. In the last stage of coverage, the networks overhauled the image of the crack mother. Recovering addicts replaced women in the active phase of addiction. Recovery centers replaced street corners and hospital wards. Character traits changed as well. Hopeful, well-groomed women replaced sullen, disheveled ones. Crack mothers in recovery wanted to regain custody of their children. In that, they became a poor version of their middle-class counterparts. Both groups entered treatment: Poor black women went into publicly financed treatment programs (self-financed, community-based treatment featured in the news was atypical); affluent women entered private treatment centers financed through medical insurance. Both groups expressed regret for past conduct, seeing prior drug use as harmful. They warned others to avoid drugs. Warning, persuasive measures signaled the end of the problem, not because the problem had gone away but because menacing crack mothers had been remolded to fit middle-class stereotypes about recovering addicts.

An Equivocal Legacy

The crack epidemic is over (Egan, 1999). Research has repeatedly contradicted stereotypes of severely impaired crack babies; they have not grow up to create a chemically defined criminal class (see Humphries, 1999). Yet stereotypes associated with crack mothers and their babies have persisted. Unfortunately, they continue to influence the way in which citizens and the criminal justice system respond to women.

An organization called CRACK (Children Requiring a Caring Kommunity) gives cash incentives for addicts to undergo sterilization to prevent the birth of drug-exposed babies (CRACK, 1998–1999). Significant themes in CRACK literature are the high frequency of pregnancy among addicts, disabilities attributed to prenatal drug exposure, and the medical costs of treating such babies and their sad fate as abandoned children in foster care.

Any drug addict who voluntarily undergoes sterilization (tubal ligation) or accepts long-term contraception (e.g., Norplant) receives $200. On the surface, incentives sound like a good way to reduce the number of drug-exposed infants. But the idea raises some serious concerns, according to the Hampshire College–based Committee on Women, Population and the Environment (Committee on Women, 1999). First, incentives exploit an addict's need for cash and throw into question the ability of addicts to make informed judgments regarding medical interventions about reproductive capacity that require follow-up supervision to avoid complications. Second, sterilization and long-term birth control discourage barrier methods of contraception (e.g., condoms) that protect women from human immunodeficiency virus (HIV) and other sexually transmitted diseases. Third, like other quick fixes, sterilization detracts from the urgent need to expand the capacity of the drug treatment network to address the problem of widespread addiction.

Instead, the public receives a steady stream of media images driving home the damage inflicted on children by drug-addicted mothers. In a recent *Chicago-Sun Times* article, stereotypes of severely impaired infants, for example, were revived to document the costs of dealing with the learning disabilities experienced by maturing children who had been exposed to crack or cocaine in the womb (Rotzoll, 2000). More to the point, such images have been used to channel public hostility toward crack mothers into an assault on women's reproductive freedoms. The right to privacy protects women's decisions in reproductive matters, according to *Roe* v. *Wade* (1973). Women have the right to determine whether to carry a pregnancy to term. Underlying this decision is another principle: The fetus is not a person and is therefore not protected under the law. In South Carolina, pro-life forces have succeeded in establishing legal protection for the fetus.

In the fall 2000, the U.S. Supreme Court let stand an South Carolina ruling that reinstated an eight-year sentence for Cornelia Whitner, who had earlier pleaded guilty to endangering her child by smoking crack prior to delivery (*Whitner* v. *South Carolina*, 1996). The question in Whitner was whether a viable fetus (25 weeks or older) can be protected by South Carolina's child endangerment statute. In refusing to hear the case, the U.S. Supreme Court permitted South Carolina to define the fetus as a person. Using this precedent, South Carolina has the endangerment statute to stillborn cases. Despite conflicting testimony from doctors as to whether the crack caused the baby's death, a South Carolina jury convicted a woman of killing her unborn fetus by smoking crack/cocaine. The woman is now serving a 12-year sentence.

Attacks on reproductive rights make for bad public health policies. Punitive approaches such as those in South Carolina drive pregnant substance abusers away from services that otherwise improve outcomes for mothers and babies. Similarly, when drug and alcohol counselors have a duty to report abuse and neglect, pregnant women are less likely to stay enrolled. On the other hand, deterrent prosecution is cheaper than the provision of health, medical, and drug rehabilitation services, especially in inner cities or outlying rural areas. The public health approach is most costly, but it removes disincentives for women to access services. An approach that falls more comfortably within public health would stress education and most of all, easy access to health and related support.

In Wisconsin, a 1998 "cocaine mom law" allows judges to order alcohol and drug abuse treatment for pregnant women who chronically and severely abuse substances (Huelsman, 1998). The law is not punitive: Judges detain women in nonsecure facilities such as medical centers, not in jails or prisons. The law is not restricted to illicit substances: The abuse of alcohol, prescription drugs, or other legal substances is grounds for judicial action. However, like South Carolina's approach, the cocaine mom law restricts the mother for the purpose of protecting the fetus; hence the resulting judicial order to detain also chips away at the reproductive freedoms of women. According to news sources, Wisconsin judges have used the law only three times (Stingl, 2000). In two instances, the mothers were also charged and then sentenced on separate criminal charges. In the third, the mother asked the court for help. The constitutional challenge to this law and others like it is expected.

The single-minded focus on pregnancy presents a problem for the laws in South Carolina and Wisconsin. In both states, the laws discriminate against other addicts: men, and women who are not pregnant. In South Carolina, the biological fact of pregnancy leads to punishment; in Wisconsin, it leads to preferential access to services. A less discriminatory approach on the public health side would require a substantial buildup in the drug treatment network, state or federal subsidies to cover the costs of providing treatment on demand for uninsured addicts, and attention to the special treatment needs of different populations. Addicted women, whether they are pregnant or not, are less likely to enter treatment than are men. Once in treatment, women's ability to stay until the point of recovery is compromised by prior abuse, domestic violence, and parenting responsibilities. Some of these issues have been addressed by treatment facilities that allow women to reside with their child, but many states have not picked up the tab for the female-friendly treatment centers piloted by federal grants.

Drug courts may be an alternative (see Goldkamp, 1993). Generally speaking, drug courts place defendants on probation, a condition of which is the successful completion of a drug rehabilitation program (National Association of Drug Court Professionals, 1998). A judge and a team of probation officers, treatment providers, and ancillary service agents supervise each case, adjusting rewards and sanctions to effect long-term recovery from addiction. Conceived as alternatives to mandatory incarceration for drug violations, drug courts have moved in a number of directions. A drug court designed for women conducts business in Michigan. Family drug courts have cropped up to deal with addiction in families, more capable than regular drug court to address and support custody issues.

Drug courts have important advantages (National Association of Drug Court Professionals, 1998). First, the fact of pregnancy is not relevant to state intervention, so a woman's behavior during pregnancy is not subject to action. Any nonviolent, drug-abusing defendant may be considered for drug court. A clinically certified addiction status and a criminal record devoid of violent offenses is all that it takes to be recommended and accepted into drug court. Second, once accepted, all clients are placed in treatment, that is, inpatient or intensive outpatient treatment for an extended period of time. There are a large number of addicts in this country and a restricted number of treatment slots in rehabilitation facilities. The discrepancy makes for long waiting lists and thwarted intentions of recovery. Judicial activism characteristic of drug court and state funding help cut the red tape.

Drug courts have their critics, too (Belenko, 1998). Weighed against the provision of services are due process issues. The mix of therapy and justice that characterize drug courts runs the risk of denying due process rights to defendants. Sentence length is an issue. The longer the sentence, the more likely are violations, which may expose defendants to punishments, which exceed the underlying offense. These are significant concerns.

Even though the crack epidemic is over, its legacy remains. For women, stereotypes of crack babies and their mothers have been used to assault reproductive freedoms. The right to decide the outcome of pregnancies has been restricted, but nowhere but in South Carolina do the rights of women explicitly take second place to the rights of the fetus should the state choose to intervene. For addicts, the wars over *Roe* v. *Wade* (1973) are counterproductive in providing distractions from the shortfall in available spaces for patients in the drug treatment network. Not only this, but the wars also obscure the difficulties associated with defining effective treatments and maintaining a quality of care from one facility to another. Unfortunately, policymakers have done little to address the needs of addicted women.

CONCLUSIONS

As a window on the world, maternal drug use reveals how pregnancy and childbirth—biological potentials—can be used against women. Paternalism justified lenient treatment in cases of prenatal misconduct by middle-class women who had been misled about the recreational use of cocaine. For the poor and minority women, the biological fact of pregnancy combined with drug addiction served as a pretext to override fundamental reproductive rights. By denying public funding for abortion, the federal government eliminates the right to choose for poor women (Roberts, 1991). An affirmative step toward public financing in this area would guarantee the right to privacy and equalize access to women's health services, even though long-standing high infant mortality rates demonstrate that basic health care as well as reproductive services are sorely lacking in poor communities. On the other hand, federal and state governments have a history of terminating the parental rights of the poor, citing a number of conditions, including maternal drug use, as grounds for removing children. For Kasinsky (1994), parallels between modern crusaders who hoped to save crack babies and nineteenth-century Progressives who tried to save immigrant children boil down to this: Middle-class standards of parenthood are used to dismiss the rights of poor and working-class parents. For women labeled as crack mothers, pregnancy and childbirth trigger both kinds of infringement: the denial of reproductive and health services, on one hand, and the termination of parental rights, on the other.

NOTES

1. Multiple counts, a clear set of protocols, the inclusion of an "unknown race or ethnic" category, and conferences to resolve problems overcame any limitations arising from using only one assistant to conduct the count.

2. Unequal time intervals underpin the four-stage model of news coverage. This study is descriptive and quite properly adopts a temporal framework that captures the shifts in the data. Equal time intervals are a requirement of hypothesis testing and do not necessarily apply to case studies.

3. The finding that 11 percent of the women could not be identified racially raises some questions about this finding. However, if one assumes that 11 percent of the women who could not be identified racially were white, the data would still show a pattern of racial disparity.

4. Tolerance and withdrawal are the hallmarks of addiction. Tolerance occurs when increased doses of a drug (e.g., heroin or alcohol) are required to achieve the original euphoric effects. Withdrawal refers to physical symptoms that appear following cessation of a drug. Withdrawal from alcohol is life threatening; depression and irritation that follow the cessation of cocaine are not.

5. Cocaine produces rapid euphoria, followed by depression. Typically, it is said to produce a psychological pattern of dependence, meaning that it fosters a feeling of satisfaction that leads to continuous drug use. In contrast, physical dependence is associated with tolerance and withdrawal.

REFERENCES

BELENKO, S. (1998). Research on drug courts: A critical review. *National Drug Court Institute Review*, I (1), 3–44.

BRINKWATER, T. (Anchor). (1984, August 10). The cocaine epidemic: Part II. NBC *Evening News*. Accessed through *Media services videotape, 1983–1994* (compilation tape). Nashville, TN: Vanderbilt University (1994).

BROKAW, T. (Anchor). (1986, May 23). Cocaine/crack. *NBC Evening News*. Accessed through *Media services videotape, 1983–1994* (compilation tape). Nashville, TN: Vanderbilt University (1994).

BROKAW, T. (Anchor). (1987, February 27). Drugs/crack. *NBC Evening News*. Accessed through *Media services videotape, 1983–1994* (compilation tape). Nashville, TN: Vanderbilt University (1994).

BROKAW, T. (Anchor). (1988a, October 24). Cocaine kids: Part 1. *NBC Evening News*. Accessed through *Media services videotape, 1983–1994* (compilation tape). Nashville, TN: Vanderbilt University (1994).

BROKAW, T. (Anchor). (1988b, October 24). Cocaine kids: Part 2. *NBC Evening News*. Accessed through *Media services videotape, 1983–1994* (compilation tape). Nashville, TN: Vanderbilt University (1994).

BROKAW, T. (Anchor). (1989a, July 7). Drugs/cocaine mothers. *NBC Evening News*. Accessed through *Media services videotape, 1983–1994* (compilation tape). Nashville, TN: Vanderbilt University (1994).

BROKAW, T. (Anchor). (1989b, August 10). Medicine: Cocaine mothers. *NBC Evening News*. Accessed through *Media services videotape 1983–1994* (compilation tape). Nashville, TN: Vanderbilt University (1994).

BROKAW, T. (Anchor). (1989c, September 30). Medicine: D.C. infant mortality rate. *NBC Evening News*. Accessed through *Media services videotape, 1983–1994* (compilation tape). Nashville, TN: Vanderbilt University (1994).

BROKAW, T. (Anchor). (1989d, November 7). '89 election/drug issues. *NBC Evening News*. Accessed through *Media services videotape, 1983–1994* (compilation tape). Nashville, TN: Vanderbilt University (1994).

BROKAW, T. (Anchor). (1990, October 4). Guns and drugs. *NBC Evening News*. Accessed through *Media services videotape, 1983–1994* (compilation tape). Nashville, TN: Vanderbilt University (1994).

CHASNOFF, L. LANDRESS, H. J., & BARRETT, M. E. (1990). The prevalence of illicit drug or alcohol use during pregnancy and discrepancies in mandatory reporting in Pinellas County, Florida. *New England Journal of Medicine, 332*, 1202–1206.

CHILDREN REQUIRING A CARING KOMMUNITY. (1998–1999). Accessed January 15, 2000. www.cracksterilization.com/index.html

CHUNG, C. (Anchor). (1986, August 4). Cocaine/crack. *NBC Evening News*. Accessed through Media services videotape, 1983–1994 (compilation tape). Nashville, TN: Vanderbilt University (1994).

CHUNG, C. (Anchor). (1994, March 10). Eye on America (Medicine: crack babies). *CBS Evening News*. Accessed through *Media services videotape, 1983–1994* (compilation tape). Nashville, TN: Vanderbilt University (1994).

COMMITTEE ON WOMEN, POPULATION AND THE ENVIRONMENT. (1999). *CRACK uses unethical tactics to stop women with substance abuse problems from becoming pregnant*. Amherst, MA: Population and Development/SS, Hampshire College.

EGAN, T. (1999, September 19). A drug ran its course, then hid its users. *New York Times*, pp. A1, A46.

GOLDKAMP, J. (1993). Justice and treatment innovation: The drug court movement. Presented at the First National Drug Court Conference, Miami, Florida. http://www.ncjrs.org/txtfiles/drugctmov.txt

HALL, S., CRITCHER, C., JEFFERSON, T., CLARKE, J., & ROBERTS, J. (1978). *Police and the crisis: Mugging, the state, and law*. London: Macmillan.

HUELSMAN, J. (1998, June 16). Press releases: Gov signs "cocaine mom" bill in Waukesha. http://www.legisl.state.wi/senate/sen11/news//pr1998-4.htm

HUMPHRIES, D. (1993). Crack mothers, drug wars, and the politics of resentment. In K. D. Tunnel (Ed.), *Political crime in contemporary America: A critical approach* (pp. 39–41). New York: Garland Publishing.

HUMPHRIES, D. (1999). *Crack mothers: Pregnancy, drugs, and the media*. Columbus, OH: Ohio State University Press.

HUMPHRIES, D., DAWSON, J., CRONIN, V., WISNIEWSKI, C., & EICHFELD, J. (1991). Mothers and children, drugs and crack: Reactions to maternal drug dependency. *Women and Criminal Justice, 3*, 81–99.

JENNINGS, P. (Anchor). (1986a, July 15). Cocaine. *ABC Evening News*. Accessed through *Media services videotape, 1983–1994* (compilation tape). Nashville, TN: Vanderbilt University (1994).

JENNINGS, P. (Anchor). (1986b, September 17). Cocaine. *ABC Evening News*. Accessed through *Media services videotape, 1983–1984* (compilation tape). Nashville, TN: Vanderbilt University (1994).

JENNINGS, P. (Anchor). (1988a, July 13). Drugs/Starr death/ "crack" cocaine rush. *ABC Evening News*. Accessed through *Media services videotape, 1983–1994* (compilation tape). Nashville, TN: Vanderbilt University (1994).

JENNINGS, P. (Anchor). (1988b, October 13). Medicine: Cocaine and pregnancy/Florida "cocaine babies." *ABC Evening News*. Accessed through *Media services videotape, 1983–1994* (compilation tape). Nashville, TN: Vanderbilt University (1994).

JENNINGS, P. (Anchor). (1989, November 14). Medicine: Cocaine babies. *ABC Evening News*. Accessed through *Media services videotape, 1983–1994* (compilation tape). Nashville, TN: Vanderbilt University (1994).

JENNINGS, P. (Anchor). (1990a, January 13). Medicine: Infant mortality/Washington, D.C. *ABC Evening News*. Accessed through *Media services videotape, 1983–1994* (compilation tape). Nashville, TN: Vanderbilt University (1994).

JENNINGS, P. (Anchor). (1990b, March 7). American agenda (Drugs: Crack babies). *ABC Evening News*. Accessed through *Media services videotape, 1983–1994* (compilation tape). Nashville, TN: Vanderbilt University (1994).

JENNINGS, P. (Anchor). (1993, June 10). American agenda (Drugs: Sisters program). *ABC Evening News*. Accessed through *Media services videotape, 1983–1994* (compilation tape). Nashville, TN: Vanderbilt University (1994).

KASINSKY, R. G. (1994). Child neglect and "unfit" mothers: Child savers in the progressive era and today. *Women and Criminal Justice, 6*, 97–129.

LEVINE, H. G. (1978). The discovery of addiction: Changing conceptions of habitual drunkenness in America. *Journal of Studies on Alcohol, 39*, 143–174.

MAHER, L (1991). Punishment and welfare: Crack cocaine and the regulation of mothering. *Women and Criminal Justice, 3*, 35–70.

MAHER, L. Z., & CURTIS, R. (1992). Women on the edge of crime: Crack cocaine and the changing contexts of street-level sex work in New York City. *Crime, Law and Social Change, 18*, 221–258.

MUSTO, D. F (1987). *The American disease: Origins of narcotic control*. New York: Oxford University Press.

NATIONAL ASSOCIATION OF DRUG COURT PROFESSIONALS. (1998). *Defining drug courts: The key components*. Washington, DC: Drug Courts Program Office, Office of Justice Programs, U.S. Department of Justice.

NATIONAL INSTITUTE OF DRUG ABUSE. (1996). *National pregnancy and health survey: Drug use among women delivering live births, 1992* (NIH Publ. 96-3819). Rockville, MD: National Institute of Health, U.S. Department of Health and Human Services.

PALMER, J. (Anchor). (1985, December 1). Cocaine/crack. *NBC Evening News*. Accessed through *Media service videotape, 1983–1994* (compilation tape). Nashville, TN: Vanderbilt University (1994).

PHILLIPS, S. (Anchor). (1992a, December 29). American close-up: Crack/cocaine: Part I. *NBC Evening News*. Accessed through *Media services videotape, 1983–1994* (compilation tape). Nashville, TN: Vanderbilt University (1994).

PHILLIPS, S. (Anchor). (1992b, December 30). American close-up: Crack/cocaine: Part II. *NBC Evening News*. Accessed through *Media services videotape, 1983–1994* (compilation tape). Nashville, TN: Vanderbilt University (1994).

RATHER, D. (Anchor). (1989a, January 9). Medicine: Florida/cocaine babies. *CBS Evening News*. Accessed through *Media service videotape, 1983–1994* (compilation tape). Nashville, TN: Vanderbilt University (1994).

RATHER, D. (Anchor). (1989b, May 10). Norfolk, Virginia/child abuse case/cocaine babies. *CBS Evening News*. Accessed through *Media service videotape, 1983–1994* (compilation tape). Nashville, TN: Vanderbilt University (1994).

RATHER, D. (Anchor). (1989c, May 26). Illinois/Greene cocaine case. *CBS Evening News*. Accessed through *Media service videotape, 1983–1994* (compilation tape). Nashville, TN: Vanderbilt University (1994).

RATHER, D. (Anchor). (1989d, June 20). An American crisis: Cocaine's victims. *CBS Evening News*. Accessed through *Media service videotape, 1983–1994* (compilation tape). Nashville, TN: Vanderbilt University (1994).

RATHER, D. (Anchor). (1990a, April 5). War on drugs: Crack cocaine. *CBS Evening News*. Accessed through *Media service videotape, 1983–1994* (compilation tape). Nashville, TN: Vanderbilt University (1994).

RATHER, D. (Anchor). (1990b, June 13) Drugs/child welfare/Philadelphia, Pa. *CBS Evening News*. Accessed through *Media service videotape, 1983–1994* (compilation tape). Nashville, TN: Vanderbilt University (1994).

RATHER, D. (Anchor). (1990c, December 17). Medicine: Pregnancy and cocaine. *CBS Evening News*. Accessed through *Media service videotape, 1983–1994* (compilation tape). Nashville, TN: Vanderbilt University (1994).

RATHER, D. (Anchor). (1994, May 31). Cocaine: Part II. *CBS Evening News*. Accessed through *Media service videotape, 1983–1994* (compilation tape). Nashville, TN: Vanderbilt University (1994).

REEVES, J. L., & CAMPBELL, R. (1994), *Cracked coverage: Television news, the anti-cocaine crusade, and the Reagan legacy*. Durham, NC: Duke University Press.

REINARMAN, C., & LEVINE, H. G. (1995). The crack attack: America's latest drug scare, 1986–1993. In J. Best (Ed.), *Images and issues* (pp. 147–190). New York: Aldine.

ROBERTS, D. E. (1991). Punishing drug addicts who have babies: Women of color equality, and the right to privacy. *Harvard Law Review, 104*, 1419–1482.

ROTZOLL, B. W. (2000, April 23). Costs increase as babies mature. *Chicago-Sun Times*, p. 12.

SAWYER, D. (Anchor). (1989, July 12). American agenda (Medicine/crime: Pregnant women and drugs). *ABC Evening News*. Accessed through *Media services videotape, 1983–1994* (compilation tape). Nashville TN: Vanderbilt University (1994).

STINGL, J. (2000, May 2). Pregnant woman ordered detained. *Milwaukee Journal Sentinel*, p. 1A.

CASES

Roe v. *Wade*, 410 U.S. 113 (1973).

Whitner v. *South Carolina S.C.* LEXIS 120*2 (1996).

8

Women, AIDS, and the Criminal Justice System

Joan Luxenburg and Thomas E. Guild

Women as offenders and women as victims have played a significant role in the shaping of criminal justice policy to deter the spread of AIDS. For the woman as offender, we look at prostitutes and their association with the AIDS epidemic. For the woman as victim, we look at the offense of sexual assault and the controversy surrounding mandatory HIV testing (and disclosure).

In the misguided belief that female prostitutes transmit the virus to their male clients, several states have enacted AIDS-specific statutes that target prostitutes for HIV-antibody testing as well as for enhanced criminal penalties for HIV-positive prostitutes who know their serostatus and continue to engage in prostitution. With no scientific evidence indicating that prostitutes are a vector for transmission of the virus, they are incarcerated for periods longer than necessary.

The criminal justice system has targeted sexual assault defendants for mandatory HIV-antibody testing and disclosure to victims. With further expansion of these laws, women as the victims of rape will be granted medical information regarding their rapists. This seemingly necessary intrusion into the rights of defendants has been challenged unsuccessfully on constitutional grounds.

The epidemic of acquired immune deficiency syndrome (AIDS) has had an impact on every facet of the criminal justice system (Blumberg, 1990b). We address two legal issues surrounding AIDS that are very specific to women. One topic (prostitution) involves women as criminal offenders. The other topic (sexual assault) involves women as the victims of crime. Although men are also arrested for prostitution, the offense is clearly a female-dominated activity. In 1999, of the approximately 64,000 arrests for prostitution and commercialized vice, almost 61 percent were of females. Similarly, we recognize that males are the victims of rape. However, only an estimated 10 percent of rapes occur to

117

males (*Face-to-Face*, 1990). This percentage may be larger, since overall, three to ten rapes go unreported for every one rape that is reported (President's Commission on the Human Immunodeficiency Virus Epidemic, 1988).

Our focus on prostitution and AIDS will deal with whether prostitutes are at greater risk than other sexually active women for contracting the AIDS virus [also known as the human immunodeficiency virus (HIV)] and whether prostitutes are vectors for transmitting the virus to their customers. We examine legislation that targets prostitutes for mandatory HIV-antibody testing or that targets HIV-antibody-positive prostitutes for enhanced criminal penalties. For the issue of sexual assault, we look at the debate over requiring HIV-antibody testing of accused and/or convicted rapists and disclosure of such test results to the alleged and/or proven victims.

WOMEN AND AIDS

Women's concerns in the AIDS epidemic had gone virtually ignored until 1990. During the 1980s (the first decade of the AIDS epidemic), the public minimized the role of women and their relationship to this public health crisis. Women were merely viewed as the principal caregivers for persons living with AIDS (PLWAs), for example, as nurses in hospitals or as mothers welcoming their homosexual sons home to spend their remaining days with family. This picture changed when in 1990, AIDS was recognized as the leading cause of death among black women in New York and New Jersey, and it was predicted to become by 1991 the fifth-leading cause of death among U.S. women of childbearing age ("AIDS deaths soaring," 1990; "More women getting AIDS," 1990). During the summer of 1990, the World Health Organization (WHO) estimated that 3 million women and children would die of AIDS during the 1990s, a figure representing more than six times their numbers of AIDS deaths in the 1980s ("More women, children," 1990). The rising death rate for women with AIDS became apparent. Whereas only 18 women between the ages of 18 and 44 in the United States died of AIDS during the year 1980, for the year 1988 the number was 1430 ("AIDS deaths soaring," 1990). Prior to 1983 only 90 women 13 years and older in the United States had been diagnosed with AIDS (Miller, Turner, & Moses, 1990, pp. 50–51). However, by November 1990, the cumulative figure for all females in the United States (regardless of age) was 16,394 (Oklahoma State Department of Health, 1991).

In recognition of the increase in the number of women with HIV infection, World AIDS Day (held December 1, 1990) proclaimed its focus to be on women and AIDS. Earlier that year, the Sixth International AIDS Conference (held in San Francisco in June) became a forum for the Women's Caucus of the AIDS Coalition to Unleash Power (ACT-UP) to voice their grievances about women's issues related to HIV infection. By November 1990, the American Civil Liberties Union (ACLU) added to its staff a lawyer assigned to work exclusively with issues involving HIV infection among women and children (Herland Sisters Resources, 1990).

In the 1990s, women were among the new wave of HIV infection. By the end of the year 2000, 20 percent of PLWAs in the United States were females (Centers for Disease Control, 2001a). Of the 774,467 cumulative reported cases of AIDS in the United States (1981 to 2000), 134,411 were among women. Of the cumulative 448,060 deaths from AIDS during the same period, 66,448 were among women. Of the approximately 40,000 new HIV infections occurring in the United States annually, 30 percent are among women. Of these annual new infections for women, 75 percent were from heterosexual exposure and 25 percent were from injection drug use (Centers for Disease Control, 2001b).

PROSTITUTION AS A TRANSMISSION CATEGORY

The AIDS literature on prostitution has concentrated almost exclusively on female hetero-sexual prostitutes rather than on male (homosexual) prostitutes. Because the clientele of male prostitutes are principally males, the AIDS literature treats male prostitutes for discussion under the heading of homosexuals (Centers for Disease Control, 1987b; Turner, Miller, & Moses, 1989, p. 14). Stereotypically, prostitutes have been cast as injection drug users (IDUs) or the sexual partners of IDUs when, in fact, only a small percentage may fall into the category of IDUs. In actuality, street prostitution accounts for an estimated 20 percent of all prostitution; and an estimated 5 to 10 percent of prostitutes are addicted (Cohen, Alexander, & Wofsy, 1990, p. 92; Leigh, 1987, p.180). It is likely that those who are addicted (to injection drugs or to crack) disregard safer sex practices in order to support their habit. For HIV-infected women in general, by the end of the 1980s, 75 percent had acquired the virus through injection drug use or through sexual relations with IDUs ("AIDS deaths soaring," 1990).

Self-reported findings suggest that prostitutes may be more likely to use a condom with their customers rather than with their regular sex partners (Cohen et al., 1990; Miller et al., 1990; Rowe & Ryan, 1987, pp. 2–20). However, when Project AWARE (Association of Women's AIDS Research and Education) conducted its San Francisco General Hospital comparison of prostitutes and other sexually active women, it found a slightly lower seropositive rate for prostitutes (Leigh, 1987). The association between HIV-antibody-positive status and injection drug use (rather than with prostitution) was clearly found in the Centers for Disease Control (CDC)–coordinated seroprevalence studies of prostitutes in 10 U.S. cities, including New York, San Francisco, Jersey City, Miami, and Los Angeles (Centers for Disease Control, 1987a).

Although our discussion focuses on street prostitution, it is worthwhile to note seroprevalence findings from other types of prostitution. In a study of New York City call girls, one in a sample of 80 was HIV-antibody positive, and that person was an IDU (*Geraldo*, 1990). When Nevada conducted testing of all prostitutes employed in legal brothels, not a single case of HIV-antibody-positive results occurred in over 4500 tests of approximately 500 prostitutes (Hollabaugh, Karp, & Taylor, 1987, p. 135). Licensed houses of prostitution in Nevada (in addition to screening prospective employees for injection drug use) are required by law (since March 1986) to conduct preemployment HIV-antibody screening and monthly testing after employment; and employment is denied to HIV-antibody-positive applicants (Centers for Disease Control 1987a; "Infection not reported," 1987).

Several years into the AIDS epidemic, the CDC had not reported any documented cases of HIV transmission from a female prostitute to a male customer through sexual contact (Cohen et al., 1990). Probably the most common means of an infected prostitute transmitting the virus to another person is through sharing infected injection drug paraphernalia (AIDS and Civil Liberties Project, 1990). In the United States, female-to-male transmission of the AIDS virus through sexual contact is less efficient than is male-to-female transmission

(Eckholm, 1990a). For the period 1981 to October 1985, the CDC concluded that only one-tenth of 1 percent of all U.S. cases of AIDS were the result of female-to-male sexual transmission (Schultz, Milberg, Kristal, & Stonebruner, 1986, p. 1703). In January 1988, only six of the 11,000 cases of AIDS in New York City males traced back to female-to-male sexual contact, although it was impossible to ascertain from the published data whether prostitutes were involved (AIDS and Civil Liberties Project, 1990). Randy Shilts (1987, pp. 512–513) reported on a case of a San Francisco injection drug–using prostitute who continued working while carrying the AIDS virus for 10 or 11 years until her death in 1987, yet during that period, only two male heterosexual contact cases of AIDS had occurred in San Francisco.

In a CDC study of spouses of transfusion-acquired PLWAs, 16 percent of wives were infected, while only 5 percent of husbands were infected; and although 10 percent of those studied had more than 200 sexual contacts with an infected partner, the uninfected spouse remained seronegative (Stengel, 1987). It must be remembered that the chances of becoming infected are greater for repeated sexual contact (e.g., with a spouse), as opposed to a one-time encounter (e.g., with a street prostitute). The ACLU estimated that 200,000 female prostitutes participate in some 300 million sexual transactions per year in the United States, yet the incidence of males contracting the AIDS virus from prostitutes in the United States was virtually nil (AIDS and Civil Liberties Project, 1990, p. 102). Early reports among U.S. servicemen are probably most responsible for having implicated prostitutes in the spread of the AIDS virus (Redfield et al., 1985). Critics of these reports were quick to reply that military men would be reluctant to report injection drug use or homosexual behavior (Potterat, Phillips, & Muth, 1987).

AIDS LAW AND PROSTITUTES

The ACLU's position on coercive measures against prostitutes is that such measures are futile and serve to drive the disease farther underground (AIDS and Civil Liberties Project, 1990). History reveals that government crackdowns on prostitutes to stop the spread of other sexually transmitted diseases (STDs) have been ineffective (Brandt, 1985, 1988, p. 370). Nevertheless, prostitutes have been the target in several states for mandatory HIV-antibody testing and for enhanced criminal penalties for HIV-antibody-positive prostitutes who continue to practice their trade while knowing their seropositive status.

By 1990, approximately 22 states had criminalized the act of knowingly exposing another person to the AIDS virus ("More states," 1990). From the authors' own observations in Oklahoma, the utility of an AIDS-specific law seems questionable. The Oklahoma law (Okla. Stat. Ann. tit. 21, § 1192.1), which took effect July 1, 1988, states:

A. It shall be unlawful for any person to engage in any activity with the intent to infect or cause to be infected any other person with the human immunodeficiency virus.

B. Any person convicted of violating the provisions of this section shall be guilty of a felony, punishable by imprisonment in the custody of the Department of Corrections for not more than five (5) years.

In January 1990, the first person to be charged under this new law was a 34-year-old Tulsa prostitute, Lynnette Osborne (a.k.a. Lynette Love). Osborne had apparently been reported to police by other prostitutes who work in the same general location (Tulsa's red light district). Four undercover Tulsa police officers had interactions with Osborne, resulting in four counts of soliciting between October 1989 and January 1990. Upon Osborne's arrest (under the then-new law), a search warrant was issued allowing authorities to test her blood for the HIV antibodies (Brus, 1990; "Charge filed," 1990). Unfortunately, the Osborne case did not lend itself to us for analysis of the first trial of its kind in Oklahoma, because the defendant pled guilty in February 1990 to all four felony counts in exchange for four three-year prison terms, to run concurrently ("Prostitute goes to jail," 1990).

Several states enacted AIDS legislation that specifically targeted prostitutes. Among the earliest laws was Florida's 1986 statute, which mandated that convicted prostitutes be tested for HIV antibodies (and other STDs). In that state, engaging in prostitution after having been informed of one's seropositivity resulted in a misdemeanor, separate from the charge of prostitution [Bowleg and Bridgham, 1989; Centers for Disease Control, 1987a; Fla. Stat. Ann. 14A, § 381.609, 3(i)(1)(a) (West 1990)]. Georgia law provided that a person who was aware of his or her seropositivity and subsequently offers to engage in sexual intercourse or sodomy for money, without disclosing (prior to the offer) the presence of the HIV infection, was guilty of a felony punishable upon conviction by not more than ten years. Georgia law also permitted HIV-antibody testing by court order for anyone convicted of or pleading no contest to any HIV-transmitting crime, including prostitution (Bowleg and Bridgham, 1989). Idaho law mandated HIV-antibody testing for defendants being held in any county or city jail who are charged with certain offenses, including prostitution (Bowleg and Bridgham, 1989).

Illinois law required HIV-antibody testing for those convicted of a sex-related offense, including prostitution, solicitation, patronizing a prostitute, and operating a house of prostitution (Thomas, 1988). One may question the relevance of testing the operator of a house if he or she is not exchanging his or her own bodily fluids with the customers. Similarly, the state of Washington's law required anyone convicted of prostitution or "offenses relating to prostitution under chapter 9A.88 RCW" to submit to HIV-antibody testing. Included (in 9A.88 RCW) were the offenses of "promoting prostitution" and "permitting prostitution" [Wash. Rev. Code, § 70.24.340, 70.24.340(1)(b) (Supp. 1988)]. Under this law, even persons who engaged in no actual sexual act, but who advanced prostitution, were required to take the HIV-antibody test. (Weissman and Childers, 1988–1989).

Michigan's law provided that those convicted of crimes capable of transmitting the AIDS virus (including prostitution) would be examined for HIV antibodies upon court order unless the court determined such testing to be inappropriate (Bowleg and Bridgham, 1989). Nevada law required anyone arrested for prostitution to be tested for HIV antibodies. If the arrest resulted in a conviction, the defendant was requested to pay $100 for the cost of the testing. After receiving notification of a positive test, if the person were subsequently to be arrested and found guilty of another charge of prostitution, the new conviction would be for a felony punishable by one to 20 years in prison and/or a $10,000 fine [Nev. Rev. Stat. Ann., § 201.356, 201.358 (Michie 1987)]. Rhode Island and West Virginia each enacted laws requiring any person convicted of prostitution to be tested for HIV antibodies (Bowleg and Bridgham, 1989).

California's law required convicted prostitutes (and certain other sex offenders) to be tested for HIV antibodies. If a prostitute received positive test results and later received a subsequent conviction for prostitution, the subsequent conviction would be for a felony [Calif. Penal Code, § 647 f (West Supp. 1989)]. Despite California's law, some counties in that state opted not to conduct such testing. For instance, the Alameda County Health Department declined to test convicted prostitutes, partly because that county's budget did not permit it. Alameda County's policy came into the public limelight surrounding the highly publicized case of an Oakland prostitute, Linda Kean. Kean had posed for a picture in a *Newsweek* article in which she claimed to be an HIV-antibody-positive heroin-using prostitute who continued to service customers (Cowley, Hager, & Marshall, 1990). A zealous Oakland vice-squad sergeant, Mike Martin, read the *Newsweek* article and promptly arrested Kean for attempted murder, after he witnessed her getting into a car with a suspected customer. Robert Benjamin, Director of the Communicable Disease Division of the Alameda County Health Department, referred to Kean's arrest as "scapegoating" and a "witch hunt." According to Benjamin, it is the customer's personal responsibility to use a condom. Benjamin further pointed out that testing prostitutes for HIV antibodies would send a "false message," suggesting to the public that those prostitutes who are still on the street have a clean bill of health.

In the 1990s, state supreme courts in California and Illinois upheld the constitutionality of laws involving mandatory HIV-antibody testing of convicted prostitutes, and at least two states passed laws requiring such testing for merely accused (not yet convicted) prostitutes (Anderson, 1998). In upholding the Illinois law, the state supreme court opined that such a warrantless and suspicionless search was allowable because the intrusion on the offender's privacy was minimal and convicted offenders have a diminished expectation of privacy. Further, the government's "special need" in protecting the public health overrides the individual's interest in requiring individualized suspicion that the prostitute might be HIV positive ("AIDS testing for convicted," 1992).

Critics of AIDS-specific laws targeting prostitutes suggest that enhancing penalties for subsequent convictions of HIV-antibody-positive prostitutes is an unproductive, punitive strategy aimed at a politically powerless group who show no epidemiological evidence that they are contributing significantly to sexual transmission of the AIDS virus. The laws clearly originated from a false perception that prostitutes pose a major risk to their customers.

ALTERNATIVES TO COERCION

The government's paternalistic concern can be helpful in assisting grassroots efforts to educate disenfranchised segments of the population to reduce risk behaviors. Among IDUs, the Community Health Outreach Worker (CHOW) has been most successful in educating this population; CHOWs are usually recovering addicts indigenous to the community and ethnically matched to the population they try to reach. CHOWs provide referrals for drug treatment programs, condoms, instructions for cleaning drug paraphernalia, and so on. Several organizations, such as Cal PEP (California Prostitutes Education Project), have utilized prostitutes and ex-prostitutes in a similar manner (*Geraldo*, 1990). Funding and expansion of such programs appear to be worthy areas in which the government can invest its resources wisely. Education with dignity appears to have worked in Pumwani, a crowded slum in Kenya, where in 1990 some 400 prostitutes could be found working on any given day (Eckholm, 1990b). More than 80 percent of Pumwani prostitutes had tested positive for HIV antibodies. Knowing that HIV reinfection or other STDs could worsen their health, these woman had cooperated with health officials and began using condoms, reportedly 80 percent of the time (Eckholm, 1990b). Since African prostitutes are transmitters of the AIDS virus, thousands of new HIV infections were being avoided by these efforts. Only about 30 percent of the male truckers at a nearby weighing station (outside Nairobi) reported that they "sometimes" used the free condoms handed to them; and one in four of those drivers (who consented to testing) showed HIV antibodies (Eckholm, 1990b). Stubborn male customers are not confined to Pumwani. In the United States, there is a need to educate the clients of prostitutes as well as to monitor these men to learn the incidence and prevalence of HIV infection among them (Miller et al., 1990). Although noncoercive government intervention shows promise for persuading prostitutes to reduce high-risk behaviors, the strategy may work only because we are dealing with consensual (although commercialized) sexual relations. For nonconsensual sexual relations, coercive measures may be appropriate.

AIDS LAW AND SEXUAL ASSAULT

By the mid-1990s, at least 45 states had enacted legislation which required either accused or convicted sexual offenders to submit to HIV-antibody testing (Stine, 2000). Prior to the enactment of AIDS-specific laws to address this topic, courts found themselves inconsistently deciding whether or not to permit testing of defendants accused of sexual assaults. In 1987, a Texas Court of Appeals ruled that a district court did not have the statutory (or constitutional) power to order an HIV-antibody test for a defendant charged with aggravated sexual assault, nor did the district court have the authority to release the results to alleged victims on a "need to know basis" (*Shelvin* v. *Lykos*, 1987). Subsequent to this appellate decision, Texas passed legislation (during a second special session in 1987) granting statutory power to trial courts to order such tests and to disclose the results to alleged victims [Tex. Crim. Proc. Code Ann., Art. 21.31 (Vernon 1988); Thomas, 1988]. According to the Texas law, a person indicted for sexual assault and aggravated sexual assault could be directed by a court to be examined and/or tested for STD, AIDS, or HIV antibodies. The court could direct such examination and/or testing on its own motion or at the request of the alleged victim. The results were not to be used in any criminal proceeding regarding the alleged assault. The court was not allowed to release the results to any parties other than the accused and the alleged victim.

In New York State, before similar legislation was introduced and defeated, that state's courts appeared to favor the victim's need to know over the defendant's right to privacy. In 1988, the New York Supreme Court ruled that it was not violative of a defendant's right to privacy for the state to divulge a rape defendant's HIV-antibody test results to the victim when such testing is done during routine processing of the person into the prison population (*People of New York* v. *Toure*, 1987). Further, the court, in its *balancing test*, decided that the fears and health concerns of the victim outweighed the minimal intrusion to the defendant. Similarly, a county court decided in New York in 1988 that a defendant who had pled guilty to attempted rape could be ordered to submit to HIV-antibody testing and that the victim had a right to know the results (*People of New York* v. *Thomas*, 1988). In that case, the court concluded that the testing was not an unreasonable search and seizure under the Fourth Amendment and that the intrusion to the defendant was minimal.

Two New York City cases gained national attention in 1990 on the issue of the victim's need to know the accused sexual offender's HIV-antibody status. In one case, a 17-year-old Columbia University coed was raped at knife-point in her dormitory room by former Columbia University security guard, 28-year-old Reginald Darby (Glaberson, 1990; Salholz, Springen, DeLaPena, & Witherspoon, 1990). In this case a Manhattan assistant district attorney plea-bargained a first-degree rape case for a reduced sentence, contingent upon the defendant's submitting to an HIV-antibody test and making the results available to the district attorney's office and to "other appropriate parties." The reduced sentence was for no more than five to 15 years, rather than the maximum sentence of $8\frac{1}{3}$ to 25 years. One legal expert on women's rights criticized such agreements as creating a "windfall" for defendants and their attorneys (Glaberson, 1990). It was feared that rape defendants and their attorneys would have additional leverage for striking plea agreements and could even imply an AIDS risk where there was none. Clearly, AIDS-specific legislation was seen as preferable to this type of plea bargain. However, bills requiring HIV-antibody testing of rape defendants (and disclosure to victims) were defeated in New York's legislature in 1990 (Glaberson, 1990); and a principal opponent to the proposed laws was the Lambda Legal Defense Fund, a gay rights organization (*Face-to-Face*, 1990). Lambda's position was that no one should be "forced" to take an HIV-antibody test. However, subsequently Lambda reportedly was willing to support such testing when the rape victim is pregnant (*Face-to-Face*, 1990). The other New York City case to gain attention in 1990 involved a victim of a 1988 burglary and rape, whose assailant was apprehended at the scene by police after he fell asleep in the victim's bed. The defendant (32-year-old Barry Chapman), an IDU and career offender on parole for rape and burglary, was eventually convicted. The victim, who had witnessed a hypodermic needle fall out of Chapman's jacket when police searched it, wanted him tested. Chapman refused two requests, by the Manhattan District Attorney's office, to be tested. Even after Chapman died of AIDS in Sing Sing Prison in 1990, the victim remained unaware of the cause of death, until CBS News obtained the autopsy report and informed the victim. More than two years after her attack, the victim continued to test negative for HIV antibodies.

New York eventually enacted a testing law for those convicted of felonies involving "sexual intercourse" or "deviate sexual intercourse" if the victim requests the HIV test (Fishbein, 2000). New York's law was enacted in 1995 in response to a mandate by the federal government, contained in the 1990 Crime Control Act. The act requires that states provide mandatory HIV testing schemes for convicted sex offenders at the request of their victims (Fishbein, 2000).

In 1988, when Connecticut failed to pass a bill that would have forced rape defendants to be tested, those opposing the measure pointed out the unclear message that would result from a negative test (Hevesi, 1988). Because of the long "window period," the time between becoming infected and actually showing antibodies to the virus, a negative test does not rule out the presence of the virus in the rapist. For this reason, the victim is probably the most logical one to be tested (and retested every six months). With regard to repeated testing of the rapist, legislation can be worded to include this. For instance, Kansas law provided that if the mandated test results were negative for persons convicted of offenses capable of transmitting the AIDS virus, the court would order the person to submit to another HIV-antibody test six months after the first test (Bowleg & Bridgham, 1989). This second test may actually be of dubious usefulness to the victim, because a positive test for the offender at this juncture may be the result of sexual activity after incarceration.

By late 1990, very few states provided for HIV-antibody testing of those merely accused of sexual assault (prior to conviction). Colorado law provided that those who, after a preliminary hearing, are bound over for trial for sexual offenses (involving penetration) would be ordered by court to be tested for HIV antibodies. The court would report the test results to victims upon the victim's request. If the accused voluntarily submitted to an HIV-antibody test, such cooperation would be admissible as mitigation of sentence if the offense resulted in conviction [Colo. Rev. Stat. 8B, § 18-3-415 (1990)]. Florida law provided that any defendant in a prosecution for any type of sexual battery, where a blood sample is taken from the defendant, would have an HIV-antibody test. The results of the test could not be disclosed to anyone other than the victim and the defendant [Fla. Stat. Ann. 14A, § 381.609 3(i)(6) (West 1990); "Rape suspect," 1990]. Idaho law required the public health authorities to administer an HIV-antibody test to all persons confined in any county or city jail who were charged with "sex offenses" (Bowleg & Bridgham, 1989).

In 1993, New Jersey enacted two laws in order to comply with the mandate of the 1990 Crime Control Act. The laws authorized mandatory HIV testing for accused or convicted sex offenders. A case involving three juveniles (arrested under these statutes in 1994) reached the New Jersey State Supreme Court after the juveniles had challenged the constitutionality of the statutes. The New Jersey Supreme Court upheld the constitutionality of the statutes. In so doing, the court explained that for the accused, a "formal charge" requires the state to establish "probable cause" to believe that bodily fluids could have been transferred from the accused to the victim. Such probable cause, the court felt, would be necessary to support the state's compelling interest in such testing (Runke, 1999).

The length of time between testing the accused and/or convicted offender and notifying the victim (where allowed) is a crucial consideration. A case profiled on national TV (*Face-to-Face*, 1990) illustrated the problem of timing. The case involved a victim of a rape and attempted murder in a suburban Seattle park who was three months' pregnant at the time of the knife-point attack. The conviction took place two days before the victim gave birth to a baby girl (six months after the attack). However, it took another six months until the victim was notified of the negative test results. The victim wanted to know the defendant's HIV-antibody status prior to his conviction, to decide whether to terminate the pregnancy. However, Washington was not one of the states where an accused rapist could be required to be tested prior to conviction.

The President's Commission on the Human Immunodeficiency Virus Epidemic, in its June 1988 report, made several recommendations concerning HIV-antibody testing (and disclosure) in cases of sexual assault. Among their recommendations, the commission favored mandatory testing "at the earliest possible juncture in the criminal justice process" (Blumberg, 1990b, p. 76) and that there be disclosure to those victims (or their guardians) who wish to know.

As of the late 1990s, the CDC had no documented case of a rape victim becoming infected with the AIDS virus as a consequence of a sexual assault (Blender, 1997). According to Mark Blumberg, who has written extensively on AIDS and the criminal justice system, the risk of HIV infection to female survivors of rape is remote. Most rape victims have been subjected to vaginal, rather than anal intrusion, and (citing a 1988 *JAMA* article) Blumberg asserts that the chances are 1 in 500 for a female to contract the AIDS virus from a single male-to-female episode of vaginal intercourse (Blumberg, 1990a, p. 81). Nevertheless, rape has taken on an added threat to life in the AIDS epidemic and consequently, places its survivors in a tormented frame of mind.

SUMMARY AND CONCLUSIONS

Since no scientific evidence implicates U.S. female prostitutes significantly in transmission of the AIDS virus through sexual contact with their male customers, it may be futile, politically and legally, to use punitive legislative measures to "control" such activity. Coercive and punitive measures are unlikely to alter the behavior of women engaged in consensual sexual relations with their customers, especially where such activity constitutes their livelihood. Where they exist, it is unlikely that punitive strategies will stop the spread of the AIDS virus when such strategies target prostitutes.

Noncoercive measures such as education would contribute at least as much to public health as coercive measures against such prostitutes. Since data indicate that transmission via injection drug use is a greater risk than sexual transmission as far as female prostitutes are concerned, education in this area as well as distribution of clean needles might do more to assure public health than all the coercive and punitive measures presently on the books.

Of course, proponents of punitive legislation might point out that even if the risk of sexual transmission is small, all possible measures must be taken to check the AIDS virus. They might also argue that since many female prostitutes live a somewhat urban nomadic lifestyle, statistics and documentation on their transmission role may be extremely difficult to gather.

As far as state legislation requiring either accused or convicted sexual assault offenders to submit to HIV-antibody testing, several problems are raised. First, if we are testing accused persons on an involuntary basis, we are eviscerating the presumption of innocence for the criminally accused. To conduct such testing, the government ought to have a compelling governmental interest before infringing on a criminal defendant's fundamental constitutional right to be presumed innocent. The right of a victim to obtain such information seems to fall short of such a compelling state interest. As for defendants who are convicted of sexual assault, convicts have traditionally lost many civil libertarian protections after conviction, and it seems more within the U.S. constitutional tradition to then use coercive HIV-antibody testing. The contribution to public health and the victim's peace of mind seem to be sufficient justification for such postconviction testing and limited disclosure.

Clearly, the AIDS health crisis is a serious epidemic. Rational and effective policies should be followed with a purpose of safeguarding both individual constitutional rights and public health in the United States.

REFERENCES

AIDS AND CIVIL LIBERTIES PROJECT, AMERICAN CIVIL LIBERTIES UNION. (1990). Mandatory HIV testing of prostitutes: Policy statement of the American Civil Liberties Union. In M. Blumberg (Ed.), *AIDS: The impact on the criminal justice system* (pp.101–107). Columbus, OH: Merrill Publishing.

AIDS deaths soaring among women. (1990, July 11). *Daily Oklahoman*, p. 5.

AIDS testing for convicted prostitutes upheld. (1992, July 30). *Chicago Daily Law Bulletin*, p. 1.

ANDERSON, S. (1998). Individual privacy interests and the "special needs" analysis for involuntary drug and HIV tests. *California Law Review, 86*(1); 119–177.

BLENDER, A. N. (1997). Testing the fourth amendment for infection: Mandatory AIDS and HIV testing of criminal defendants at the request of a victim of sexual assault. *Seton Hall Legislative Journal, 21*; 467–501.

BLUMBERG, M. (1990a.). AIDS: Analyzing a new dimension in rape victimization. In M. Blumberg (Ed.), *AIDS: The impact on the criminal justice system* (pp. 78–87). Columbus, OH: Merrill Publishing.

BLUMBERG, M. (ED.). (1990b). *AIDS: The impact on the criminal justice system.* Columbus, OH: Merrill Publishing.

BOWLEG, I. A., & BRIDGHAM, B. J. (1989). *A summary of AIDS laws from the 1988 legislative sessions.* Washington, DC: George Washington University, Intergovernmental Health Policy Project, AIDS Policy Center.

BRANDT, A. M. (1985). *No magic bullet: A social history of venereal disease in the United States since 1880.* New York: Oxford University Press.

BRANDT, A. M. (1988, April). AIDS in historical perspective: Four lessons from the history of sexually transmitted diseases. *American Journal of Public Health, 78*(4), 367–371.

BRUS, B. (1990, January 22). Tulsa official hopes arrest to slow AIDS. *Daily Oklahoman*, p. 1.

CENTERS FOR DISEASE CONTROL. (1987a, March 27). Antibody to human immunodeficiency virus in female prostitutes. *Morbidity and Mortality Weekly Report, 36*(11), 159.

CENTERS FOR DISEASE CONTROL. (1987b, December 18). Human immunodeficiency virus infection in the United States: A review of current knowledge. *Morbidity and Mortality Weekly Report, 36*(5–6), 8.

CENTERS FOR DISEASE CONTROL. (2001a, June 1). HIV and AIDS, 1981–2000. *Morbidity and Mortality Weekly Report, 50*(21), 430.

CENTERS FOR DISEASE CONTROL. (2001b, April 4). 20 Years of AIDS: A glance at the HIV epidemic. Accessed June 15, 2001.

http://www.cdc.gov/nchstp/od/20years.htm

Charge filed under anti-AIDS law. (1990, January 21). *Sunday Oklahoman*, p. A18.

COHEN, J. B., ALEXANDER, P., & WOFSY, C. (1990). Prostitutes and AIDS: Public policy issues. In M. Blumberg (Ed.), *AIDS: The impact on the criminal justice system* (pp. 91–100). Columbus, OH: Merrill Publishing.

COWLEY, G., HAGER, M., & MARSHALL, R. (1990, June 25). AIDS: The next ten years. *Newsweek*, pp. 20–27.

ECKHOLM, E. (1990a, September 16). AIDS in Africa: What makes the two sexes so vulnerable to epidemic. *New York Times*, p. 11.

ECKHOLM, E. (1900b, September 18). Cooperation by prostitutes in Kenya prevents thousands of AIDS cases. *New York Times*, p. 46.

Face-to-Face. (1990, December 10). Columbia Broadcasting System.

FISHBEIN, S. B. (2000). Pre-conviction mandatory HIV testing: Rape, AIDS and the fourth amendment. *Hofstra Law Review, 28*, 835–867.

Geraldo. (1990, May 11). Have prostitutes become the new Typhoid Marys? Tribute Entertainment.

GLABERSON, W. (1990, July 9). Rape and the fear of AIDS: How one case was affected. *New York Times*, p. A13.

HERLAND SISTER RESOURCES. (1990). ACLU AIDS project to focus on women and children with AIDS. *Herland Voice, 7*(10), 4.

HEVESI, D. (1988, October 16). AIDS test for suspect splits experts. *New York Times*, p. 30.

HOLLABAUGH, A., KARP, M., & TAYLOR, K. (1987). The second epidemic. In D. Crimp (Ed.), *AIDS: Cultural analysis/cultural criticism* (pp. 127–142). Cambridge, MA: MIT Press.

Infection not reported among legal prostitutes. (1987, November 18). *AIDS Policy and Law*, pp. 2–3.

LEIGH, C. (1987). Further violations of our rights. In D. Crimp (Ed.), *AIDS: Cultural analysis/cultural criticism* (pp. 177–181). Cambridge, MA: MIT Press.

MILLER, H. G., TURNER, C. F., & MOSES, L. E. (1990). AIDS: *The second decade*. Washington, DC; National Academy Press.

More states establishing laws allowing AIDS assault cases. (1990, October 22). *Daily Oklahoman*, p. 20.

More women, children expected to die from AIDS. (1990, July 29). *Edmond Sun*, p. A9.

More women getting AIDS, study says. (1990, November 30). *Daily Oklahoman*, p. 6.

OKLAHOMA STATE DEPARTMENT OF HEALTH. (1991, January). *Oklahoma AIDS Update, 91*(1), 6.

POTTERAT, J. J., PHILLIPS, L., & MUTH, J. B. (1987, April 3). Lying to military physicians about risk factors for HIV infections [To the Editor]. *Journal of the American Medical Association, 257*(13), 1727.

PRESIDENT'S COMMISSION ON THE HUMAN IMMUNODEFICIENCY VIRUS EPIDEMIC. (1988). Sexual assault and HIV transmission: Section V of Chapter 9. Legal and ethical issues. *Report of the President's Commission on the Human Immunodeficiency Virus*. Submitted to the President of the United States, June 24, 1988. Reprinted in M. Blumberg (Ed.), *AIDS: The impact on the criminal justice system* (pp. 73–77). Columbus, OH: Merrill Publishing, 1990.

Prostitute goes to jail in AIDS case. (1990, February 14). *Daily Oklahoman*, p. 31.

Rape suspect due AIDS test. (1990, July 23). *Daily Oklahoman*, p. 7.

REDFIELD, R. R., MARKHAM, P. D., SALAHUDDIN, S. Z., WRIGHT, D. C., SARNGADHARAN, M. G., & GALLO, R. C. (1985, October 18). Heterosexually acquired HTLV-III/LAV disease (AIDS-related complex and AIDS): Epidemiologic evidence for female-to-male transmission. *Journal of the American Medical Association, 254*(15), 2094–2096.

ROWE, M., & RYAN, C. (1987). *AIDS: A public health challenge: State issues policies and programs*. Vol. I. *Assessing the problem*. Washington, DC: George Washington University, Intergovernmental Health Policy Project, AIDS Policy Center.

RUNKE, J. P. (1999). Fourth amendment balancing act: Special needs of rape victims justify court-ordered HIV testing of the accused. *Seton Hall Law Review, 29*, 1094–1121.

SALHOLZ, E., SPRINGEN, K., DELAPENA, N., & WITHERSPOON, D. (1990, July 23). A frightening aftermath: Concern about AIDS adds to the trauma of rape. *Newsweek*, p. 53.

SCHULTZ, S., MILBERG, J. A., KRISTAL, A. R., & STONEBRUNER, R. L. (1986, April 4). Female-to-male transmission of HTLV-III [To the Editor]. *Journal of the American Medical Association, 255*(13), 1703–1704.

SHILTS, R. (1987). *And the band played on: Politics, people and the AIDS epidemic*. New York: St. Martin's Press.

STENGEL, R. (1987, June 8). Testing dilemma: Washington prepares a controversial new policy to fight AIDS. *Time*, pp. 20–22.

STINE, G. J. (2000). *AIDS update 2000*. Upper Saddle River, NJ: Prentice Hall.

THOMAS, C. (1988). *A synopsis of state AIDS laws enacted during the 1983–1987 legislative sessions*. Washington, DC: George Washington University, Intergovernmental Health Policy Project, AIDS Policy Center.

TURNER, C. F., MILLER, H. G., & MOSES, L. E. (1989). *AIDS: Sexual behavior and intravenous drug use*. Washington, DC: National Academy Press.

WEISSMAN, J. L., & CHILDERS, M. (1988–1989). Constitutional questions: mandatory testing for AIDS under Washington's AIDS legislation. *Gonzaga Law Review, 24*, 433–473.

CASES

People of New York v. *Thomas*, 529 N.Y.S. 2d 439 (Co. Ct. 1988).

People of New York v. *Toure*, 523 N.Y.S. 2d 622 (Sup. 1987).

Shelvin v. *Lykos*, 741 S.W. 2d 178 (Tex. App.-Houston 1987).

9

The Legal Response to Substance Abuse during Pregnancy

Inger Sagatun-Edwards

Maternal drug use during pregnancy raises complex legal and ethical questions, pitting the rights of the pregnant woman against the rights of the fetus. Important constitutional issues are involved in this debate. In this chapter we discuss the background and history of the legal response to these issues, including (1) criminalization of maternal substance abuse, (2) juvenile court involvement for the purpose of protecting the child (or fetus), and (3) civil commitment legislation. Often, two or more of these approaches may be combined. The most relevant recent court cases and state legislation are included in the discussion. We conclude that criminal prosecution of fetal abuse does not protect the well-being of the fetus enough to violate important constitutional rights for the mother. Similarly, fetal abuse should not automatically come under mandatory child abuse reporting laws, and juvenile court intervention should be used only in the most serious cases to protect the child. A comprehensive public health approach is the best way to deal with this problem.

In this chapter we focus on substance abuse during pregnancy. Numerous public policy issues are raised by the births of infants whose exposure to drugs during pregnancy may have led to long-lasting medical and developmental impairments. Should the state intervene on behalf of the unborn child? Should the criminal justice system take action to protect the fetus and punish the mother for her conduct? Should the child welfare system take action to protect the fetus, or remove the child temporarily after birth on the assumption that drug abuse during pregnancy is an indication of an unfit parent? Or should the mother be left to the medical and public health systems without court involvement?

The concept of fetal abuse raises complex legal and ethical questions. The mother's right to privacy and her autonomy must be balanced against her child's welfare. Ironically, *Roe* v. *Wade*, which established the right to abortion, has been used to argue in favor of the fetal rights movement. In this decision, the U.S. Supreme Court held that after the first trimester of pregnancy, the interests of potential life become important, and that after viability, the state has a legitimate and important interest in the unborn. After viability, the state may protect fetal life by prohibiting all abortions that are not necessary to protect the life and health of the mother. Thus, both proponents and opponents of the criminalization of fetal abuse can draw on different parts of *Roe* v. *Wade* to support their cause. Webster (1989) subsequently rejected the rigid trimester scheme for establishing viability, thus giving ammunition to those who argue that states may constitutionally criminalize pregnant women who abuse substances known to harm fetuses (Wright, 1990).

Almost a decade ago, Paltrow (1992) argued that no criminal statute on fetal abuse could be tailored narrowly enough to protect a woman's right to privacy or her due process rights. A more recent article by the Harvard Law Review Association (1998) also concluded that in balancing the maternal privacy interests against the state's interest in protecting the life and health of the fetus, courts should only uphold narrowly drawn statutes targeted at specific, egregious conduct, and that in general, prosecutions for fetal abuse will not enhance fetal health and thus serve state interests. The article argued that the constitutional body of privacy law in general, and abortion law in particular, strongly suggests the existence of a maternal privacy interest that would be infringed by such statutes, thus requiring strict scrutiny by the courts (p. 994). Fetal abuse statutes would implicate two different aspects of the right to privacy: the right to make decisions that affect the spheres of family, marriage, and procreation, and the right to control one's own body. The *Harvard Law Review* article used the viability decision in *Roe* v. *Wade* (1973) and subsequent abortion cases to provide a framework for analyzing the conflicts between maternal privacy rights and the state interest in protecting fetuses and weighting the two to determine when the latter becomes compelling. *Roe's* holding that the state's interest in the birth of a fetus does not become compelling during the first two trimesters of pregnancy does not necessarily rule out the existence of a compelling state interest in ensuring that fetuses that will be carried to term are born unharmed. States may have a greater interest in preventing future suffering of those who will be born than in ensuring that any particular fetus will be born. Conversely, *Roe's* holding that states are allowed to protect fetuses from abortion in the third trimester does not necessarily imply that states have an equally compelling interest in protecting fetuses from all other harms during that period. Furthermore, fetuses are most vulnerable in the earliest stages of pregnancy and should require more protection then. Thus prosecutions of substance abuse by pregnant women in the third trimester after viability makes less sense than do prosecutions at an earlier stage.

De Ville and Kopelman (1999) have pointed out that even the use of terminology suggests different approaches to this issue, thus the terms *unborn child* and *expectant mother* as used in recent legislation in Wisconsin elicit different feelings and content than do the terms *fetus* and *pregnant woman*. The former terms focus on the socially assumed duties of a mother and her responsibilities during pregnancy. The choice of terms reflect an underlying ideology that may affect how a legal policy is implemented and received.

In this chapter we discuss three legal approaches to the issues related to drug use in pregnancy: (1) criminalization of mother's conduct on various legal grounds, (2) juvenile dependency court involvement for the protection of the fetus or child after birth, and (3) civil commitment of pregnant women to drug treatment facilities to protect the fetus. First, I summarize briefly the current state of knowledge about the effects of prenatal drug use on the child, and the issue of the legal status of fetal rights.

MATERNAL SUBSTANCE ABUSE DURING PREGNANCY

During the late 1980s, crack/cocaine emerged as the most frightening enemy in the War on Drugs, with a media frenzy over the alleged crack epidemic (Gomez, 1997; Humphries, 1998). Early medical studies concluded that crack/cocaine had very negative effects on the fetus (Chasnoff, Burns, Burns, & Schnoll, 1986). The wisdom that sprang up in the late 1980s and early 1990s was that crack/cocaine addiction among pregnant mothers causes serious, often irreparable medical problems in their babies and that this condition was extremely widespread and extremely costly to society. According to several studies, prenatal substance abuse could cause a wide range of serious medical complications for the infant, such as withdrawal, physical and neurological deficits, low birth weight, growth retardation, cardiovascular abnormalities, spontaneous abortion, and premature delivery, as well as long-term developmental abnormalities (Howard, Kropenske, & Tyler, 1986; Petitti & Coleman, 1990; Weston, Ivens, Zuckerman, Jones, & Lopez, 1989). Early hospital studies by the National Association on Perinatal Addiction Research and Education estimated that about 375,000 drug-exposed infants are born each year, at least one of every ten births in the United States (Chasnoff, Burns, Schnoll, & Burns, 1985; Dixon, 1989). A federal study in 1991 found that the number of young foster children who had had prenatal exposure to drugs grew from 17 percent in 1986 to 55 percent in 1991 (U.S. General Accounting Office, 1994). Most states also reported dramatic increases in the numbers of children victimized by parental drug involvement (Daro & McCurdy, 1992).

However, both early estimates of the widespread nature of maternal drug use during pregnancy and the conclusion that poor fetal outcomes are caused solely by illegal drugs later came under attack. Many of the original studies that spurred fears of a generation of "crack babies" were flawed in a number of ways. One critic points out that the early hospital estimates were based on a survey of 36 hospitals, accounting for only 5 percent of all U.S. births in 1989 (Farr, 1995). Another notes that the women surveyed had used a number of different drugs and that the incidence of fetal exposure in different hospitals varied substantially (Gustafson, 1991). The extent to which the children's medical problems are actually due to illegal drugs is also difficult to determine. Many drug users are polydrug abusers, mixing illegal drugs with legal drugs such as cigarettes and alcohol, all known contributors to poor fetal outcomes. Often, such factors are compounded by family poverty, poor nutritional status and general health, sexually transmitted diseases, and little or no prenatal care (Hurt, Brodsky, Braitman, & Giannetta,1995; Lutiger, Graham, Einarson & Koren, 1991; Mathias, 1992, Richardson & Day, 1991).

A problem with early studies on the babies of mothers who used powdered cocaine and crack was that there were no control groups. The effects of cocaine are particularly difficult to identify because of the high probability of a total lack of prenatal care (Inciardi, Lockwood, & Pottieger, 1993). Studies that have only recently become available as prenatally exposed children are followed into their preschool years show that many expectations about developmental problems have not been supported (Barth & Needell, 1996; Hawley, Halle, Drasin, & Thomas, 1995). However, other recent research has found central nervous problems with behavioral dysfunctions (Kenner & D'Apolito, 1997); and language delays (Mentis, 1998). Chasnoff et al. (1998) concluded that behavioral characteristics of 4- to 6-year-olds were directly affected by prenatal exposure, resulting in higher rates of depression and anxiety, attention problems, aggressive behavior, and impulsivity and distractibility. According to Hutchins (1997), knowledge concerning the biological effects of drug exposure on the newborn is inconclusive at present. A recent examination of existing evidence on the topic concluded that "recent studies do not support the case for devastating consequences, but rather suggest that there are subtle deficits amenable to intervention" (LaGasse, Seifer, & Lester, 1999, p. 39). The dangers of the use and abuse of alcohol which may lead to fetal alcohol syndrome (FAS) remain the best documented of those for any substance (Mattson & Riley (1998).

TRADITIONAL FETAL RIGHTS

The fetal rights movement, which seeks to define the fetus as a person, grew out of the attempt to hold women liable for prenatal conduct that may cause harm to a fetus (Beckett, 1995). Within this movement, drug babies are seen as separate entities from their mothers and in need of protection from their substance-abusing parent. However, whether a fetus has any legal rights is a controversial issue. Most current laws seek to protect children from harm after their birth, and the applicability of current child abuse and neglect laws to prenatal conduct is uncertain. In most jurisdictions, fetuses have few, if any legal rights, since as fetuses they are not considered to be children. The fetus therefore has traditionally had a very precarious legal position. A much debated issue is whether pre-natal conduct that affects the fetus should come under the same legislation intended for children after birth, or if new laws should be created that are specifically directed at the protection of the fetus.

Nonrecognition of the fetus as a legal entity is embodied in the "born alive" rule, which states that the fetus has to be born alive as a precondition to legal personhood. Underlying this rule is the assumption that the mother and fetus constitute a unit whose legal interests are coextensive (McNulty, 1987–1988). Historically, the law declined to extend any legal rights to the fetus except in narrowly defined situations and except when rights were contingent on live births (*Roe* v. *Wade*, 1973). Since the law viewed the fetus as part of the mother, it was only after birth that the child acquired any legal rights independent of those of the mother (Rickhoff & Cukjati, 1989).

To be actionable child abuse under traditional criminal law, the conduct that causes the injury or creates the dangerous situation must occur after the birth of a live child (*Reyes* v. *Superior Court*, 1977). In this case the court found that child-endangerment statutes did not apply to prenatal conduct, since this was not expressly stated in the relevant statute (*California Penal Code*, 1977).

Increasingly, however, the born alive rule in child abuse and child neglect laws has come under attack. In *Commonwealth* v. *Cass* (1984), the court held that a viable fetus was a person within the protection of the state's vehicular homicide statute. Several states, including California, Illinois, Iowa, Michigan, Missisippi, New Hampshire, Oklahoma, Utah, Washington, and Wisconsin, now have "feticide" statutes.[1] In an important case from South Carolina (Condon, McInstosh, Zelenka, Avant, & DeLoach, 1997; *Whitner* v. *South Carolina*, 1997) the state court allowed criminal prosecution for fetal abuse under the South Carolina child abuse and endangerment statute. The *Whitner* court premised its decision on the "long-standing" precedents regarding fetal rights in criminal cases. This landmark case is discussed in more detail later in the chapter.

In civil law, fetal rights have already been well established. A majority of states consider a fetus that has died in utero to be a person under wrongful death statutes, and therefore parents may sue people who harmed the fetus in utero, causing the death (McNulty, 1987–1988). Courts have also long recognized "wrongful life" actions. However, most of these cases involve harm caused by a third person, not the mother, and are therefore not directly applicable to the issue of maternal substance abuse during pregnancy. In general, parents are generally protected from civil suits for fetal harm by the doctrine of parental immunity (e.g., *Chambess* v. *Fairtrace*, 1987). Some courts have refused to recognize this immunity. In *Grodin* v. *Grodin* (1981), a child brought suit against his mother for prenatal injuries because of the mother's negligence in failing to secure prenatal care. The court held that the injured child's mother should bear the same liability as a third person for negligent conduct that interfered with the child's rights to begin life with a sound mind and body (Balisy, 1987).

THE LEGAL RESPONSE TO SUBSTANCE ABUSE DURING PREGNANCY

States have used both civil and criminal statutes to address substance abuse during pregnancy. Criminally, women have been charged under drug delivery and distribution statutes and under child endangerment statutes. Civilly, states have used neglect and abuse statutes for juvenile court after the child is born, and protective custody and civil commitment orders while the woman is still pregnant (Coffey, 1997).

Criminalization of Maternal Substance Use during Pregnancy

Proponents of criminalization argue that there are three compelling interests that justify prosecuting women for their conduct during pregnancy: (1) the state's interest in protecting the fetus's right to potential life, (2) the state's interest in protecting the newborn's right to be born healthy, and (3) the state's interest in protecting maternal health (Sagatun-Edwards, 1997). There is also a fourth compelling state interest in the criminalization of fetal injury by pregnant drug users: (4) the state's interest in protecting society from the burden of providing for injured newborns (Wright, 1990). Proponents believe that even under strict scrutiny standards the state's interests in protecting the health and the life of the unborn child take precedence over maternal privacy rights.

In a series of consecutive decisions the U.S. Supreme Court has firmly established a strict scrutiny requirement in privacy decisions affecting the spheres of family, marriage, and procreation, and the right to control one's own body (*Eisenstadt* v. *Baird*, 1972; *Griswold* v. *Connecticut*, 1965; *Roe* v. *Wade*, 1973). These and subsequent abortion decisions make clear that any decision or statute that infringes upon a constitutionally protected privacy right must undergo strict scrutiny review, and it will be upheld only if it is narrowly tailored to achieve a compelling state interest (Harvard Law Review Association, 1998).

As of 1999, approximately 200 pregnant women in 24 states had been prosecuted around the country on various theories of fetal abuse (Paltrow, 1999). These prosecutions have typically involved creative applications of existing statutes, such as (1) delivery of a controlled substance to a minor, or (2) some form of child endangerment or abuse. Most prosecutions under both types of existing law have ultimately been unsuccessful, with the notable important exception of *Whitner* v. *South Carolina* (1997). The courts have concluded that these laws were not meant to apply to the situation of drug use during pregnancy, and prior to *Whitner* all cases prosecuted successfully at the trial level had been thrown out by either the appellate or superior court of the relevant state. Many of these attempts to prosecute women criminally for illicit drug use during pregnancy foundered on the question of nonrecognition of fetal rights, as discussed above, the perception that existing laws were not intended to include fetal abuse, or that the constitutionally protected maternal rights to privacy were more important than the state's interest in protecting the unborn.

Prosecution under Controlled Substance Statutes

As stated above, many criminal prosecutions have been based on existing criminal laws, which were not designed or intended to govern prenatal conduct. These include statutes that prohibit drug use, sale, possession, or delivery of drugs to minors, which apply to all adults, males and females. *Johnson* v. *Florida* (1992) was the first case of this kind that was prosecuted successfully at the trial level using a "delivery of drugs to a minor" statute to apply to drugs being transferred through the umbilical cord at birth. The mother appealed and the appellate court affirmed her conviction. The Florida Supreme Court, however, reversed the conviction on a variety of grounds, including legislative intent. The court held that the legislature did not intend the word *deliver* to include the passage of blood through the umbilical cord. The Florida Supreme Court adopted the language of the justice who dissented in the lower appellate court decision when she wrote that "the Legislature never intended for the general drug delivery statute to authorize prosecution of those mothers who take illegal drugs close enough in time to childbirth that a doctor could testify that a tiny amount passed from mother to child in the few seconds before the umbilical cord was cut. Criminal prosecution of mothers like Johnson will undermine Florida's express policy of "keeping families intact" and could destroy the family by incarcerating the child's mother when alternate measures could protect the child and stabilize the family" (*Johnson* v. *Florida*, 1992, at 1294).

The Florida Supreme Court decision noted that drug abuse is a serious national problem and that there is a particular concern about the rising numbers of babies born with cocaine in their systems as a result of maternal substance abuse. But the court pointed out the negative aspects of prosecuting pregnant substance abusers. Women who are substance abusers may simply avoid prenatal care for fear of being detected when the newborns of these women are, as a group, the most fragile and sick and most in need of hospital neonatal care. Decisions from higher courts since the Florida Supreme Court reversal in Johnson have followed the same path: The courts have consistently refused to apply drug delivery statutes to pregnant women.

Prosecution under Child Endangerment Statutes

Until the *Whitner* case, prosecutions based on criminal child abuse statutes also had infrequent success. Courts repeatedly held that a fetus is not a child within the meaning of statutes prohibiting acts endangering the welfare of children. An example of such a decision is a case from the Supreme Court of Kentucky, *Commonwealth of Kentucky* v. *Connie Welch* (1993), where the high court reversed the trial court that had found Ms. Welch guilty of a criminal child abuse count. The court of appeals affirmed her convictions for possession of a controlled substance but vacated her conviction on the criminal abuse charge. The Kentucky Supreme Court affirmed the decision of the court of appeals by noting that

> the mother was a drug addict. But, for that matter, she could have been a pregnant alcoholic, causing fetal alcohol syndrome; or she could have been addicted to self-abuse by smoking, or by abusing prescription painkillers, or over the counter medicine; or for that matter she could have been addicted to downhill skiing or some other sport creating serious risk of prenatal injury, risk which the mother wantonly disregarded as a matter of self-indulgence. What if a pregnant woman drives over the speed-limit, or as a matter of vanity doesn't wear prescription lenses she knows she needs to see the dangers of the road? The defense asks where do we draw the line on self abuse by a pregnant woman that wantonly exposes to risk her unborn baby? . . .
>
> It is inflicting intentional or wanton injury upon the child that makes the conduct criminal under the child abuse statutes, not the criminality of the conduct per se. . . . In short, the District Attorney's interpretation of the statutes, if validated, might lead to a "slippery slope" whereby the law could be construed as covering the full range of a pregnant woman's behavior—a plainly unconstitutional result that would, among other things, render the statutes void for vagueness. (*Commonwealth of Kentucky* v. *Connie Welch*, 1993, at 282)

The Supreme Court of Kentucky concluded that their state drug delivery statutes and child endangerment statutes did not intend to punish as criminal conduct self-abuse by an expectant mother potentially injurious to the baby she carries. In a similar decision, the Supreme Court of Nevada (*Sheriff* v. *Encoe*, 1994) explicitly held that the constraints of federal due process notice requirements prohibited reinterpreting the child neglect statutes to include fetal abuse.

In a departure from the state supreme court decisions noted above, a landmark case from the Supreme Court of South Carolina, *Whitner* v. *South Carolina* (1997), upheld the prosecution of a woman who ingested crack/cocaine during the third trimester of her pregnancy under child abuse and endangerment statutes by concluding that a fetus does have legal rights of its own.

The procedural history of the case is as follows: On February 6, 1992, Cornelia Whitner, a 28-year-old African-American woman, was arrested for a violation of S.C. Code Ann. 20-7-50 for "unlawful neglect of a child." Whitner had given birth to a son on February 2, 1992. The hospital test showed the presence of cocaine in his bloodstream. The Pickens County Grand Jury indicted Whitner on April 7, 1992 for the same offense and she pled guilty to "unlawful neglect of a child" on April 20, 1992. She was then sentenced to eight years' imprisonment. No objections were made to the charge or jurisdiction of the court, and Whitner did not appeal her conviction or sentence.

On May 10, 1993, Whitner filed a state postconviction application with the South Carolina Court of Common Pleas. Another judge held a hearing on November 1, 1993, and issued an order vacating the convictions on November 22, 1993. The state appealed the judge's order. Following briefing and oral argument, the South Carolina Supreme Court reversed the granting of postconviction relief on July 15, 1996, based solely on state law issues. The court later granted Whitner's petition for a rehearing and issued an amended opinion on October 27, 1997, which addressed both state and federal claims in reversing the court of common pleas conviction. The state supreme court denied rehearing from that opinion on November 19, 1997.

In its 3 to 2 opinion, the South Carolina Supreme Court noted that South Carolina law has long recognized that viable fetuses are persons holding certain rights and privileges for purposes of homicide laws and wrongful death statutes and that it would be absurd not to recognize a viable fetus as a person for the purposes of statutes proscribing child abuse. The court argued that the consequences of abuse or neglect which take place after birth often pale in comparison to those resulting from abuse suffered by the viable fetus before birth. In reaching this conclusion, the court relied on the harms reported by early articles in the *New England Journal of Medicine* (e.g., Chasnoff et al., 1985; Volpe, 1992). The perception that the defendant endangered the "life, health and comfort of her child" through ingesting crack/cocaine led the court to upheld the prosecution under the criminal child neglect statute. In contrast, the dissent argued that a fetus is not a person and that the distinction of a "viable fetus" is absurd in that it would then be legal for a woman to ingest cocaine early in the pregnancy, when presumably the fetus is most at risk for harmful substances.

The implications of the South Carolina decision were far-reaching. First, a viable fetus (24 weeks) was now treated as a child for the purposes of the South Carolina Code (*Whitner*, 328 S.C. 1, at 22). Second, this decision could render women criminally liable for a myriad of acts that the legislature had not passed into law, such as failure to obtain prenatal care or failure to quit smoking and/or drinking. As noted in the dissenting opinion, this case also highlighted the irony of incarcerating a woman up to ten years for ingesting drugs while pregnant, yet the maximum for an illegal abortion (killing a viable fetus) is only a two-year maximum (*Whitner*, at 23).

The court's majority did acknowledge that no other state has held that prenatal drug use could give rise to criminal prosecution under state child abuse and endangerment statutes, nor under illegal drug distribution statutes. The *Whitner* court reasoned that the cases that were prosecuted under statutes forbidding delivery or distribution of a controlled substance did not apply to the present situation. They also concluded that even those cases in which the court was construing the word *child* or *person* for the purposes of a child endangerment statute were distinguishable because those states in which the cases were decided did not have the same body of case law as did South Carolina.

Whitner and a woman in a parallel case, *Crawley* v. *Evatt* (1977), subsequently appealed their cases to the U.S. Supreme Court on the grounds that they had pled guilty to a crime that does not exist in South Carolina. They argued that they had been indicted for child abuse for giving birth to a child who had cocaine in his system when the child abuse statute did not apply to a fetus.[2]

Several prominent national and state medical, health, social welfare, legal services, substance abuse treatment organizations, and social policy organizations wrote briefs to the U.S. Supreme Court in support of Whitner's and Crawley's petition for a writ of certiorari urging the Court not to let the decision in South Carolina stand.[3] They argued that if left to stand, the ruling in *Whitner* would require for the first time in the nation that physicians, health care providers, and social service workers, under threat of criminal penalties, divulge to state authorities, for possible prosecution, the identities and medical information of pregnant women who engage in conduct or activities that may adversely affect the welfare of their fetuses. They warned that the *Whitner* decision would deter pregnant women from obtaining adequate prenatal care, including substance abuse treatment, and that it would seriously compromise the doctor–patient relationship. The result would be damaged health, increased suffering, escalating health care costs, and decreased life expectancy. The

Whitner decision, they argued, also created an intolerable dilemma for physicians and health care providers: Either risk jail by upholding the confidentiality of medical care, or disclose clients' identities in compliance with state reporting requirements (Tracy, Frietsche, Abrahamson, Boyd, & Risher, 1997).

Similarly, the Center for Constitutional Rights and the American Civil Liberties Union wrote briefs in support of the petition for a writ of certiorari on more legal and constitutional grounds (Olshansky, Davis, Paltrow, & Wise, 1997). They argued that *Whitner* had created an intolerable conflict among state high courts in that previous courts (e.g., Kentucky and Nevada, as described above) have refused to include fetal abuse under existing child abuse statutes without directives from state legislatures. They argued that the *Whitner* court misconstrued the federal guarantee of due process notice in that both petitioners had been unaware that fetal abuse was included in the state statutes on child abuse and neglect. Finally, they argued that *Whitner* misconstrued the prohibition against vague criminal statutes. According to the brief from the group of medical and social welfare organization, at least two alcohol and drug treatment programs in South Carolina have experienced precipitous drops in the number of pregnant women seeking admission.[4]

In a brief opposing the petition for writ of certiorari, the Attorney General of South Carolina argued that there was no conflict among the states concerning the application of child abuse laws to viable fetuses because the cases from other jurisdictions turn upon an interpretation of legislative intent (Condon et al., 1997). Since South Carolina already had included fetal rights under civil statutes, the state argued that the legislature would also have included such rights under child abuse and neglect laws. The case concerned a question of state law rather than federal law, and the *Whitner* decision had turned on interpretations of state law rather than federal constitutional grounds. Second, the petitioners' convictions satisfied due process requirements because the previous decisions of the state supreme court gave them adequate notice that a viable fetus was protected by the unlawful neglect statute. Finally, the state's brief in opposition to the petition for certiorari argued that Crawley had failed to raise her federal constitutional claims in a timely manner and that she had therefore defaulted these issues for certiorari review.

The U.S. Supreme Court declined to grant certiorari, and the decision of the South Carolina Supreme Court therefore stands (cert. denied, 1998). The South Carolina Supreme Court took an unprecedented step by expanding their child abuse and endangerment statute to include viable fetuses who are injured as a result of prenatal substance abuse. The failure of the U.S. Supreme Court to grant certiorari in the *Whitner* case means that there is now room for a broad interpretation in defining the word *child* for the purposes of statutes proscribing child abuse (Tolliver, 2000).

It remains to be seen what the far-reaching consequences of this decision will be, but it is generally expected that other state courts may follow suit and that legislation will be enacted to specifically include fetal abuse in child abuse and child neglect statutes. Indeed, within one year of the *Whitner* decision, the prosecution in a Wisconsin case urged the court to adopt the reasoning in *Whitner* as applicable to a case in which a mother had attempted to kill her unborn child by excessive consumption of alcohol (*Wisconsin* v. *Deborah J. Z.*, 1999). This case can be distinguished from other maternal substance abuse cases in that the mother clearly stated her intention to harm her fetus. The defendant in *Deborah J. Z.* filed a motion to dismiss the attempted first-degree murder charges, but the trial court denied this motion (ibid., at 491). On appeal, however, the court rejected the reasoning of *Whitner* and held that the unborn child was not a "human being" for the purposed of the attempted first-degree intentional homicide and first-degree reckless injury statute (ibid., at 494).

Although the failure of the U.S. Supreme Court to grant certiorari in the Whitner case suggested a hard line on prosecutions of maternal substance abuse, a recent U.S. Supreme Court case affirmed that there are important legal barriers to such prosecutions (*Ferguson et al.* v. *City of Charleston et al.*, 2001).

Ferguson was one of 42 women arrested under a collaborative policy between law enforcement officials in Charleston and the Medical University of South Carolina (MUSC). All but one of the women were African-American. The policy at MUSC was for hospital staff to identify pregnant patients suspected of drug abuse. Pursuant to the policy, hospital staff members tested pregnant patients suspected of drug abuse and reported positive tests to the police. When Ferguson delivered her child at MUSC, the hospital staff tested her without her consent and found traces of cocaine in her bloodstream. She was given a choice of a two-week residential drug treatment program, or face arrest and prosecution. Unable to find child care, she was unable to enter the residential program, and she was arrested for failing to comply with the order to receive drug treatment (*Ferguson et al.* v. *City of Charleston et al.*, 2001).

In 1993, nearly two years after Ferguson's arrest, the Center for Reproductive Law and Policy in New York filed a class action suit in federal district court in South Carolina against MUSC and the city of Charleston, demanding $3 million in damages for the violation of several constitutional rights (Gagan, 2000). In particular, the petitioners alleged that the warrantless and allegedly nonconsensual drug tests were unconstitutional searchers. Both the trial court and the federal appellate courts found the searches to be reasonable as a matter of law under a "special needs" doctrine. The defendants argued successfully that the testing fell within the special needs exception to the Fourth Amendment requirements. This means that a court can excuse the warrant and probable cause requirements in situations in which the existence of special needs beyond the normal need for law enforcement make the warrant and probable cause requirements impracticable. When special needs are deemed to exist, the court conducts a reasonable analysis, balancing the government interests at stake against the person's privacy interests (Gagan, 2000). In the district court, the jury found that the plaintiffs, by signing MUSC's consent to medical treatment forms, had waived the right to privacy. In the subsequent appeal to the Fourth Circuit, the court dodged the issue of consent, holding instead that the warrantless testing of pregnant women's urine when the indicia of possible cocaine use were present constituted reasonable special needs searches and therefore did not violate the Fourth Amendment (*Ferguson* v. *City of Charleston*, 1999, at 476).

The U.S. Supreme Court granted certiorari on the special needs exception only. Specifically, Ferguson posed the question whether the special needs exception to the Fourth Amendment's requirements was properly applied to a discretionary drug testing program that targeted hospital patients and was created and implemented with police and prosecutors primarily for law enforcement purposes (Gagan, 2000).

The case was argued in October 2000, and in March 2001, the U.S. Supreme Court reversed the decision of the Fourth Circuit. The court held that the MUSC policy of conducting warrantless, nonconsensual drug tests on pregnant women, and turning over positive results to the police, violates the Fourth Amendment. The five-justice majority said that the law enforcement purposes behind the policy take it outside the scope of prior rulings in which the court has been willing to uphold searches conducted under policies with the usual Fourth Amendment requirements in order to serve special needs beyond the normal need for law enforcement. For example, the court had previously applied the special needs exception to sustain drug tests for railway employees involved in a train accident and for high school students participating in interscholastic sports ("Court decisions," 2001). Writing for the court majority, Justice Stephens stressed that the critical difference in its prior drug testing cases and *Ferguson* lies in the nature of the special need asserted for the warrantless searches. In the other cases, the special need advanced was one divorced from the state's general interest in law enforcement. In this case, however, the central and indispensable feature of the policy from its inception was the use of law enforcement to coerce patients into substance abuse treatment. Even though the ultimate purpose of the policy was beneficent, the purpose it actually served was ultimately indistinguishable from the general interest in crime control. Given the extensive involvement of law enforcement officials at every stage of the policy, the case, the court majority argued, simply did not fit within the closely guarded category of special needs. The court found that in balancing the intrusion on the person's privacy interest against the special needs that supported the program, in this case the invasion of privacy, was much more substantial than in the other cases. Justice Kennedy joined in the majority judgment, but not in the reasoning. Justice Scalia wrote the dissenting opinion (joined by Rehnquist and Thomas), arguing that the drug-testing policy was valid under the court's special needs jurisprudence, and that no search occurred when urine samples that were voluntarily given to the hospital were later turned over to the police (*Ferguson et al.* v. *City of Charleston et al.*, 2001). The majority reached their judgment on the assumption that the searches were conducted without the informed consent of the patients, and in concluding that the judgment from the appellate court should be reversed, remanded the case for a decision on the consent issue. Although encouraging for those who oppose prosecution of pregnant substance abusers, *Ferguson* was primarily a Fourth Amendment case and did not deal directly with the issue of criminalizing maternal substance abuse.

Constitutional Issues Raised by Criminalization of Drug Use During Pregnancy

Although many observers who favor prosecutions of fetal abuse applaud the *Whitner* decision, many also feel that legislation specifically aimed at maternal substance abuse during pregnancy should be enacted rather than relying on courts' interpretations of existing law. Courts can only interpret the law after the fact, and "court-written" law is inherently unstable. Many states have therefore considered such new legislation, and several states have proposed statutes designed to criminalize maternal drug use during pregnancy. However, no states have yet passed a bill that explicitly criminalizes substance abuse during pregnancy. In California, a bill to define drug use in late pregnancy as criminal child abuse failed in committee in April 1998 (Pasternak, 1998). Such failures may be because there are serious social policy concerns and constitutional difficulties with such bills and because many medical and legal scholars have strongly criticized the use of any criminal sanction to address the problem of prenatal drug use. Indeed, several important medical, legal, and civil rights groups have voiced their opposition to policies aimed at the criminalization of pregnant drug users.

Criminalization of maternal conduct during pregnancy violates a woman's rights to equal protection under the law. Because evidence of a newborn's positive toxicology screen is used only in cases against women, women would be punished because of their drug use and their ability to get pregnant. A statutory requirement that women resolve all health care decisions in favor of the fetus would hold women to a much higher standard. The Harvard Law Review Association (1998) provided an in-depth analysis of the policy considerations that legislatures and courts should take into account when deciding whether to enact criminal fetal abuse statutes or to read fetal protection into existing legislation. The long-established constitutional rights of the individual to control procreative and familial decisions should also apply to maternal decisions potentially infringed upon by fetal abuse legislation. Broad fetal abuse statutes that are patterned on child abuse statutes, those that make neglecting or abusing a crime without specifying what constitutes neglect or abuse would be unconstitutional. They would be void for vagueness, and they require an infringement on maternal rights not justified by the fetal protection they offer; thus they would not be tailored narrowly enough to suvive strict scrutiny. For example, a child abuse statute that included fetuses could be interpreted to punish the taking of drugs that are essential to the mother's health but harmful to the fetus (p. 1005). One possible avenue is to add additional penalties to conduct that is already criminal: for example, on pregnant women who take heroin. As long as the state could establish that the harm to the fetus is significant and that no lesser ban would protect fetuses adequately, such a statute would be constitutional. However, limiting the imposition of criminal liability to conduct already criminalized makes little sense as a practical matter because the deterrent effect of such an extra penalty is at best unclear and would penalize pregnancy more than any other factor (p. 1007). To pass the strict scrutiny test, the state must show that any statute prohibiting fetal abuse in fact serves that interest. Because a fetal abuse statute may provide a powerful incentive to women to stay away from doctors to avoid detection and prosecution, statutes that criminalize pregnant women's conduct actually may thwart rather than serve the state's interest in protecting the fetus (p. 1008). The authors conclude, as did the authors of the briefs supporting *Whitner* and *Crawley*, that educating women and funding prenatal care are better approaches to the problem. Unlike criminal liability, these solutions foster positive social attitudes toward the role of women and family relationships.

Fein (1996) has argued in favor of prosecution of women who harm their fetuses during gestation in order to "save the unborn child from unfit mothers" (p. 31). Robertson (1989) noted that meeting obligations to the unborn child may require limitations on the mother's conduct that would not be there if she were not pregnant.

Juvenile Court (Civil Court) Involvement

Criminal prosecution is not the only method that states have employed in an attempt to reach women who put their unborn children at risk by using drugs during pregnancy. States have also used child custody statutes which provide for the temporary or permanent removal of children who have been abused or neglected by their parents or guardians to separate mothers from their children at birth, based on substance abuse during pregnancy (Clarke, 2000). Civil child abuse and neglect proceedings deal with the child after he or she is born; thus they do not implicate the same constitutional issues of privacy, bodily integrity, and personal autonomy that are raised when mother and child are one entity (Coffey, 1997).

Although criminal prosecutions of pregnant drug users have been largely unsuccessful, thousands of women have had their children removed from their custody as a result of prenatal use of drugs (Paltrow, 1993). While the stated purpose of the criminal court is to punish the offender, the stated purpose of the juvenile court is protection of the child. Until recently, juvenile law and the jurisdiction of juvenile court did not extend to unborn children. In *In re Steven S.* (1981), the court of appeals in California overturned a juvenile court decision, finding that an unborn fetus was not a person within the meaning of the child abuse or child neglect statutes. However, in Michigan (*In re Baby X*, 1980) an appellate court reasoned that since prior treatment of one child can support neglect allegations regarding another child, prenatal treatment can be considered probative of child neglect. In *In re Troy D.* (1989), the California Supreme Court let stand an earlier appellate decision that the use of drugs during pregnancy is alone sufficient basis to trigger a child abuse report and to support juvenile court dependency jurisdiction. This decision was later negated by passage of the Perinatal Substance Abuse Act in California (1991), which does not endorse the view that prenatal substance abuse is by itself indicative of future child abuse and neglect (see the description later in the chapter). However, several other states have passed civil child abuse and child neglect statutes that declare drug and/or alcohol use during pregnancy to be predictive of child abuse (Paltrow, 1992). Issues of concern for juvenile court or family court jurisdiction are the criteria for testing, whether positive tests should be included under mandatory reporting laws for child abuse and neglect and the criteria used to remove a child from the mother.

Entry to Juvenile Court.   The first point of entry of drug-exposed infants and their families into the juvenile court system is often right after birth. Some states specifically require physicians to test and report pregnant women to child protective services for illicit substance abuse when toxicology tests on newborns are positive. Many hospitals now perform neonatal toxicology screens when maternal drug use is suspected. Typically, hospital protocols dictate that such screens are performed when the newborn shows signs of drug withdrawal, when the mother admits to drug use during pregnancy, or when the mother has had no prenatal care (Robin-Vergeer, 1990). Based on a positive toxicology test, the hospital may report the case to the child protective services, which in turn may ask the court to prevent the child's release to the parents while an investigation takes place. If further investigation reveals a risk to the child, the court may assume temporary custody of the child, and in the most serious cases, parental rights may be terminated (Sagatun-Edwards, Saylor, & Shifflett, 1995).

There are several problems with testing of mothers and children for the presence of illegal drugs. First, there is the invasion-of-privacy problem. Second, such testing is notoriously unreliable, and the results may depend on what type of drug was ingested and how soon after the ingestion the drug test was administered (Gomby & Shiono, 1991). Third, there may be both racial and social class biases in both the testing procedures and the reports of the testing (Chasnoff et al., 1990).

As of this date, no states require mandatory testing for drugs of all pregnant women. Minnesota is a state that early chose universal screening of neonates while limiting maternal testing to women with pregnancy complications that suggest drug use (Sagatun-Edwards et al., 1995). In a recent case from Michigan (*Marchwinski, Konieczny, and Westside Mothers* v. *Howard*, 2000), welfare recipients challenged the constitutionality of a new law authorizing suspicionless drug testing (ibid., at 1135). The district court judge found that the law was unconstitutional where not designed to address jeopardy to public safety. Most states condition testing on a physician's suspicion of prenatal drug use, based on obstetric complications or assessment of mother and baby. Such discretionary testing is, however, most often done in public hospitals on poor and minority mothers. If routine testing is to be done at all, it should be universal testing of all newborns, thus negating the criticism of bias against minorities and the poor. However, compelling arguments against universal screening include cost, lack of informed consent, lack of reliability, and overemphasizing illegal drugs over equally dangerous drugs, such as alcohol. Most important, the threat of screening may influence a woman's decision to seek prenatal care (Sagatun-Edwards, 1997).

Mandatory Reporting under Child Abuse and Neglect Reporting Laws

In the wake of *Whitner* and the state's Child Protection Reform of 1996, South Carolina requires mandatory reporting of cases suspected of abuse or neglect involving unborn, yet viable fetuses, defined as 24 weeks' gestation with an illegal drug in their system (Condon, 1998). The policy distinguishes between a prebirth protocol and a postbirth protocol. The prebirth protocol is (1) reporting the incident; (2) investigation by the Department of Social Services; (3) treatment/intervention/documentation; and (4) after birth, continued services are provided by the Department of Social Services, as stated in the postbirth protocol. The postbirth protocol is (1) reporting/investigation; and (2) an amnesty program, with the mother asked to seek treatment and counseling voluntarily. The protocol gives the mother a chance to sober up; failure to rehabilitate will cause a mother to be prosecuted for violation of criminal child abuse and neglect.

In Minnesota the definition of child abuse includes prenatal exposure to drugs (Minnesota Statutes Annotated, 1990a. If the results on a toxicology screen of either mother or child are positive, the physicians are required to report the results to the Department of Health, and local welfare agencies are then mandated to investigate and make any appropriate referrals (Minnesota Statutes Annotated, 1990b). Other states, including Florida, Massachusetts, Oklahoma, Utah, and Illinois, have included fetal abuse under their mandatory child abuse reporting laws. Florida amended its child abuse laws to underscore the specific risks associated with maternal drug use. Simultaneously, the Department of Health and Rehabilitative Services issued a policy requiring reports of newborn drug dependency and created a specialized unit to investigate drug-affected infants. Although these laws and policies established Florida's reputation as being tough on maternal substance abuse, in a study by Pearson and Thoennis (1996), many children's protective services workers and legal personnel characterized Florida as being a lenient climate, due to gaps in the law, treatment voids, and court backlogs. Illinois amended its child abuse reporting laws in 1989 so that any child born with any illegal drug in its system would be defined as a neglected child. This eliminated the need to prove any harmful effects of maternal cocaine use and created the legal basis for filing a neglect petition. Again, the Pearson and Thoennis study (1996) reports that these statutory changes did not revolutionize case handling in this state.[5]

In California, the Perinatal Substance Abuse Services Act of 1990 emphasizes the desirability of medical services and drug treatment, and it does *not* endorse mandatory reporting of positive toxicology screens. This law modified the existing child abuse reporting laws in California to specify that a positive toxicology screen at the time of delivery of an infant is not in and of itself a sufficient basis for reporting child abuse or neglect. Instead, any indication of maternal substance abuse shall lead to an assessment of the needs of the mother and her infant. Any indication of risk to the child as determined by the assessment is then reported to county welfare departments (Perinatal Substance Abuse Services Act of 1990, effective July 1, 1991; California Penal Code § 11165.13, 2001). Although the California approach is often characterized as a fairly measured public health oriented way to deal with this problem, Noble, Klein, Zahnd, and Holtby (2000) found in an interview study of commission members that created the law, lasting concerns about gender equity and women's rights. Gomez (1997) also used the development of the law in California to study the "tug of war" between prosecutors who advocated for the rights of the fetus/child and those who argued more forcefully for the woman's rights, ultimately ending in a compromise bill between the two sides.

The state of Washington treats perinatal substance abuse as a public health issue. The state has eschewed legislation requiring routine testing of babies, relying instead on hospitals to flag, test, and report cases to children's protective services where the risk of child abuse is high. As a result of the Omnibus Drug Act of 1989, Washington made pregnant women a priority for treatment of chemical dependency (Pearson & Thoennis, 1996). The state of Oregon treats alcohol abuse and drug dependency as an illness rather than a crime, and the Oregon legislature has rejected several bills aimed at criminalizing drug use during pregnancy (Jones, 1999). Whether the decision in *Ferguson* will have any impact on reports to the child protective services as a result of positive toxicology tests remains to be seen.

Legal Criteria for Removing a Child from the Parents

In determining what to do with a child, social services and juvenile courts in all states must now follow the directives of Public Law 105-89, the Adoption and Safe Families Act of 1997. Under this law, children's safety is now the paramount concern that must guide all child welfare services. State welfare agencies are mandated to make reasonable efforts to prevent a child's placement in foster care, and if foster care is necessary, the state must make efforts to reunite the family during specified time periods, with court hearings every six months. If such reunification is not possible, the law further requires permanency planning for the child, which may include termination of parental rights to make adoption possible (Sagatun-Edwards & Saylor, 2000b). Substance abuse during pregnancy is not addressed specifically in the act, except that it calls for expansion of child welfare demonstration projects, including projects that are designed to "identify and address parental substance abuse problems that endanger children and result in the placement of children in foster care, including placement of children in residential facilities" (§ 301 of the Adoption and Safe Children's Act of 1997). Despite the mandated reunification policy, drug-exposed cases tend to show a higher risk of removal (Leslie, 1993), court involvement (Sagatun-Edwards et al., 1995), and foster care placement (Feig, 1990). Taylor (1995) found that it was much more common for a drug-abusing parent to lose the right to visitation and custody than for nonabusing parents to do so. The assumption that drug use during pregnancy causes "imminent" danger to the fetus reinforces the perception of pregnant women's drug use as child abuse and neglect (Pollitt, 1990). According to Beckett (1995), the majority of the lower and appellate civil court rulings have supported the state's removal of infants from their mother's custody based on a positive drug toxicology.

Civil Commitment Legislation and Placing the Fetus in Protective Custody

Outside the criminal context, the state may institute civil confinement for persons who present a danger to themselves or others. This procedure, called *civil commitment*, results in confinement in a hospital or treatment facility for varying lengths of time. In recent years, some states have moved toward detaining substance-abusing women during their pregnancy to protect their fetuses from harm.

In 1998 the Wisconsin state legislature amended its child protection laws so that women who abuse alcohol or drugs during pregnancy can be confined for the duration of their pregnancies [Wis. Stat., § 48.01–.347 et seq. (1998)]. The new Wisconsin fetal protection legislation revises significantly the state's child abuse law (De Ville & Kopelman, 1999). The purpose of the Wisconsin bill is "to provide a just and humane program of services to children and unborn children and the expectant mothers of those unborn children" [Wis. Stat., § 48.01 (1998)]. The statute defines an "unborn child" as a "human being from the time of fertilization to the time of birth" and stresses that provisions of the law are intended to apply throughout an expectant mother's pregnancy (ibid., § 48.01–.02). It is in the best interest of the unborn child to order the mother who abuses drugs and/or alcohol during pregnancy to receive treatment, including inpatient treatment. This treatment may include, but is not limited to, medical, psychological, or psychiatric treatment, as well as alcohol or other drug abuse treatment or other services that the court finds necessary and appropriate [ibid., § 48.01 (1)]. The legislation also specifically frees health professionals to disclose confidential information obtained within the health care relationship. An expectant mother can be taken into custody for up to 48 hours without a hearing on the grounds that there is a substantial risk to the child.

This modification of Wisconsin's child abuse and protection laws followed a 1997 Wisconsin Supreme Court ruling which declared that the then-current child abuse laws could not be used to confine a pregnant woman who had tested positive for cocaine (*Angela M. W.* v. *Kruzicki*, 1997). In this case, the Court of Appeals of Wisconsin had first affirmed a juvenile court order placing a woman's unborn child in protective custody, but the state supreme court reversed the ruling. Soon after this decision, the Wisconsin legislature amended the statute to permit such detentions under state law. [With the exception of South Carolina, as described earlier, state courts have maintained that unmodified, existing child protection laws could not be used to take pregnant women into custody for the benefit of their fetuses (De Ville & Kopelman, 1999)]. South Dakota enacted similar legislation on July 1, 1998, which gives relatives the power to place pregnant women in custody for up to nine months [S.D. Codified Laws, (2s), 34-20A-63, (1998)]. Similar bills were introduced in Alaska, California, Delaware, Georgia, Indiana, Maryland, Masschusetts, Minnesota, Tennessee, and Virginia in 1998 ("States look to detention," 1998). Norway passed similar legislation in 1996; under that country's civil laws, pregnant women can be confined to a locked residential drug treatment facility for the duration of their pregnancy if they refuse voluntary treatment and all other attempts to treat her substance abuse have failed. Norway has taken a clear stand in favor of the fetus over the woman's rights to privacy in this conflict; the legislation is based on the notion that if a woman forgoes the right to an abortion, she has a duty to protect the fetus (Sagatun-Edwards, 1999).

De Ville and Kopelman (1999) point out that by defining a fetus from conception as a child, the Wisconsin legislature shifts the balance from a woman's privacy rights versus the fetus to balancing a woman's rights against a child's rights. The inclusion of the fetus in a child abuse model is further underscored by the provision that a guardian ad litem can be appointed to represent the fetus to serve as an advocate for the best interests of the unborn child [Wis. Stat., § 48.193, .981(3)]. They also argue that the law is flawed in that it does not guarantee the evidentiary protection that it typically required when individual rights are abrogated, in that all that is needed for a social worker to report is that she/he has "reasons to believe" or "reason to suspect" that an unborn child is at substantative risk for abuse. In most child abuse and neglect proceedings, clear and convincing evidence is needed to remove a child. But the varied effects of using drugs during pregnancy and the lack of clear knowledge about such effects makes it difficult ever to reach the standard of clear and convincing evidence for fetal injury. Thus the Wisconsin legislation and others like it put substantial burdens on a pregnant woman's freedom with very low evidentiary standards. If civil commitment is to be used, it should be based on the normal evidentiary standards used for other civil commitment, such as in mental health cases (i.e., that a woman should be singled out for treatment and confinement not because she is pregnant, but because she represents a risk of harm to herself) (De Ville & Kopelman, 1999). In *Addington* v. *Texas* (1979), the U.S. Supreme Court held that when a state deprived a person of liberty through civil commitment, the state must prove the necessity to do so by at least clear and convincing evidence. The Fourteenth Amendment provides that a state shall not deprive any person of life, liberty, or property without due process of law. Until better data become available showing a clear and convincing likelihood of substantial and avoidable harm posed by women who use drugs and alcohol when they are pregnant, civil commitment based on suspicion of harm alone violates the woman's due process rights.

SUBSTANCE ABUSE TREATMENT AND PRE- AND POSTNATAL CARE

Very few adequate drug rehabilitation services are available for pregnant substance abusers or for mothers with young children, and the ones that are available may not serve their particular needs. Opponents and proponents of criminalization and/or juvenile court involvement alike agree that the most effective solution to the problem of prenatal drug abuse is drug treatment and rehabilitation. The major problem here is that appropriate drug treatment programs are often unavailable or unaffordable, and when they are available, there are long waiting lists to get in.

Existing treatment programs often discriminate against pregnant women. In a survey of 78 drug treatment programs in New York City, Chavkin found that services were inadequate for pregnant women (Chavkin, 1991). Although this survey is now several years old and more treatment facilities have become available to pregnant women, the situation is still much the same. The financial cost involved alone is one reason that court-ordered drug rehabilitation services through the juvenile court currently may be the only way that a mother can afford to undergo drug rehabilitation programs (Larson, 1991). An intervention study that provided a voluntary coordinated treatment approach for substance-abusing mothers in juvenile dependency court found that providing enhanced services to substance abusing families had a significant positive impact. Those mothers and infants who participated in drug treatment, public health service, and parenting programs were significantly more likely to keep their children and to have positive outcomes than a control group without enhanced services (Sagatun-Edwards & Saylor, 2000b). A recent study that provided residential treatment for pregnant crack users pointed to the importance of early interventions for this population (Fiocchi & Kingree, 2001).

In contrast, criminal statutes, such as in South Carolina, which punish women if they do not seek treatment may easily backfire. Women may be afraid to consider such treatment if they know that they will be detained (Cole, 1990). Ideally, what is needed are free prenatal care and drug counseling in a nonpunitive setting, available to all, and geared to different ethnic and cultural subgroups. One of the most effective weapons against infant mortality is early, high-quality, comprehensive prenatal care.

CONCLUSIONS

A wide variety of legal responses to maternal substance abuse have been discussed, from criminal prosecution under existing drug-delivery laws and criminal child abuse and neglect statutes, to juvenile court jurisdiction and mandatory testing and reporting to child protective services, and civil commitment of pregnant women to protect the fetus. Any legal response should depend on the gains to the fetuses and children relative to the harms to maternal rights that might arise from such a policy. Although the health of a fetus is important, criminalizing fetal abuse in most cases will not serve the intended purpose. It would probably jeopardize, rather than secure, the fetal health. Women at risk would not seek medical advice for fear of being punished and of losing their children. More important, the mother's constitutional guarantees of right to liberty and privacy would be violated. The constitutionally protected rights to liberty, privacy, and equality prohibit any legal recognition of the fetus that would diminish women's decision-making autonomy on their right to bear children. Criminalization of conduct during pregnancy is simply a wrong policy; it is unconstitutional, sexist, and serves no social policy purpose.

Protection of children after birth is important. The states should have the right to interfere under juvenile court jurisdiction once family maintenance programs and other treatment forms of intervention have been explored. Infants who have severe symptoms of drug addiction and whose parents are unable to care for them should be reported to the child protective services. However, this should only be a last resort, and mothers should not be detained simply for failing treatment. Any interventions on behalf of the drug-exposed infant must be predicated on other indications of future harm, not the past prenatal use. Such indicators might include a mother's failure to care for siblings, unwillingness to participate in a drug treatment program and parenting classes, and the unavailability of a support system. The goal should always be to provide pregnant women with effective drug treatment and comprehensive pre- and postnatal care so that they may maintain custody of their own children. Intervention should be limited to protect children who are at great risk, so that loss of constitutional rights and societal costs may be prevented. Civil commitment should be used only when there is clear and convincing evidence of harm.

In general, the best policy to be followed is to treat perinatal substance abuse as a public health problem. Free and nonpunitive pre- and postnatal care should ideally be available to all. Government expansion of educational and medical services aimed at all pregnant and, especially, substance-abusing women will avoid the infringement on maternal privacy rights and in the long run prove less costly and intrusive than criminal liability and/or long-term juvenile court intervention.

NOTES

1. State codes containing feticide statutes include: Cal. Penal Code, § 187 (1986); Ill. Ann. Stat., ch. 38, § 9-1.1 (1985); Iowa Code Ann., § 707.7. (1979); Mich. Comp. Laws Ann., § 705.322 (1968); Miss. Code Ann. § 97-3-37 (1973); N.H. Rev. Stat. Ann. § 585: 13 (1974); Okla. Stat. Ann. tit. 21, § 713 (1983); Utah Code Ann., § 76-5-201 (1983); Wash. Rev. Code Ann., § 9A. 32.060 (1977); Wis. Stat. Ann., § 940.04 (1987).

2. In November 1991, another woman in South Carolina, Melissa Ann Crawley, was arrested under similar circumstances and pled guilty to the same charge. She was sentenced to five years' imprisonment and did not appeal her conviction or sentence. In September 1994, Crawley filed a state petition for writ of habeas corpus. At the conclusion of her hearing, the judge vacated her conviction and sentence. The state of South Carolina appealed the judge's order. On December 1, 1997, in an unpublished opinion, relying on the decision in *Whitner*, the state supreme court reversed the granting of state habeas relief and reinstated Crawley's conviction and sentence (*Crawley* v. *Evatt*, 1997). The state supreme court denied her petition for rehearing on January 8, 1998. Both Whitner and Crawley subsequently petitioned the U.S. Supreme Court to review the decisions of the South Carolina Supreme Court (*Whitner* v. *South Carolina*, and *Crawley* v. *Moore*, 1997) in the Supreme Court of the United States, October term, 1997.

3. Organizations supporting the petition for writ of certiorari as amici curiae in *Whitner* v. *South Carolina* were the National Association of Alcoholism and Drug Abuse Counselors, South Carolina Association of Alcoholism and Drug Abuse Counselors, American College of Obstetricians and Gynecologists, National Association of Social Workers, American Nurses Association, South Carolina Nurses Association, American Medical Women's Association, National Association for Families and Addiction Research and Education, Association for Medical Education and Research in Substance Abuse, American Academy on Physician and Patient, Society of General Internal Medicine, National Council on Alcoholism and Drug Dependency, National Center for Youth Law, Legal Services for Prisoners with Children, Coalition on Addiction, Pregnancy, and Parenting, NOW Legal Defense and Education Fund, Legal Action Center, Women's Law Project, Drug Policy Foundation, and Alliance for South Carolina's Children (Tracy et al., 1997). Organizations joining in a reply brief in support of petition for a writ of certiorari for both Whitner and Crawley were the Center for Constitutional Rights and the American Civil Liberties Union of South Carolina Foundation (Olshansky et al., 1997).

4. These organizations include the Children's Defense Fund, the American Public Health Association, the American Medical Association, the American Nurses Association, the Center for the Future of Children, the National Association on Alcoholism and Drug Abuse, the National Black Women's Health Project, and the National Association for Perinatal Addiction Research.

5. Fla. Stat. Ann., § 415.503 (Supp. 1988); Mass. Laws Ann., ch.119, § 51A (West Supp. 1988); Omnibus Crime Bill, Ch. No. 290, H.F. No. 59; Minn. statutes 1988 at 626.5561 and 5562; Okla. Stat. Ann. tit. 21, sect. 846 (A) (West Supp. 1988); Utah Code Ann., § 78-36-3.5 (1989 Cum. Supp.); Ill. H.B. 2590, P.A. 86-659, § 3 (1989).

REFERENCES

Adoption and Safe Families Act of 1997, Washington, DC: Public Law 105-89.

Adoption Assistance and Child Welfare Act of 1980, 42 U.S., § 420 et seq., as amended by the Omnibus Budget Reconciliation Act of 1987, Public Law 96-271.

BALISY, S. (1987). Maternal substance abuse: The need to provide legal protection for the fetus. *Southern California Law Review, 60*, 1209–1238.

BARTH, R., & NEEDELL, B. (1996). Outcomes for drug exposed children four years post adoption. *Children and Youth Services, 18*(1–2), 37–56.

BECKETT, K. (1995). Fetal rights and "crack moms": Pregnant women in the war on drugs. *Contemporary Drug Problems, 22*, 587–612.

California Penal Code. (1977, 2001). St. Paul, MN: West Publishing.

CHASNOFF, I., ANSON, A., HATCHER, R., STENSON, H., IAUKEA, K., & RANDOLPH, L. (1998). Prenatal exposure to cocaine and other drugs: Outcome at four to six years. *Annals of the New York Academy of Science, 846*, 666–669.

CHASNOFF, I. J., BURNS, K. A., BURNS, W. J., & SCHNOTT. S. H. (1986). Prenatal drug exposure: Effects on neonatal and infant growth and development. *Neurobehavioral Toxicology and Teratology, 8*(4), 357–362.

CHASNOFF, I., J., BURNS, W. J., SCHNOLL, S. H., & BURNS, K., A. (1985). Cocaine use in pregnancy. *New England Journal of Medicine, 393*(11), 666–669.

CHASNOFF, I. J., LANDRESS, H. J., & BARRETT, M. E. (1990). The prevalence of illicit drug or alcohol during pregnancy and discrepancies in mandatory reporting in Pinellas County, Florida. *New England Journal of Medicine, 322*(17), 1202–1206.

CHAVKIN, W. (1991). Testimony presented to House Select Committees on Children, Youth and Families, U.S. House of Representatives. Columbia University School of Public Health.

CLARKE, A. (2000). FINS, PINS, CHIPS, and CHINS: A reasoned approach to the problem of drug use during pregnancy. *Seton Hall Law Review, 29*, 634–693.

COFFEY, C. (1997). *Whitner* v. *State*: Aberrational judicial response or wave of the future for maternal substance abuse cases? *Journal of Contemporary Health, Law and Policy, 14*, 211–255.

COLE, A. M. (1990). Legal interventions during pregnancy: Court-ordered treatment and legal penalties for potentially harmful behavior by pregnant women. *Journal of the American Medical Association, 264*, 2663–2670.

CONDON, C. (1998, April). *Use of illegal drugs detected pre-birth.* State of South Carolina: Office of the Attorney General.

CONDON, C., MCINTOSH, J., ZELENKA, D., AVANT, D., & DELOACH, C. R. (1997). Brief in opposition to petition for writ of certiorari, *Whitner* v. *State of South Carolina*, and *Crawley* v. *Moore*, No. 97-1562, U.S. Supreme Court, October Term.

Court decisions, search and seizure: State hospital's nonconsensual drug tests on pregnant women ruled unconstitutional. (2001, June 16). *Criminal Law Reporter, 68*(25), 551–552.

DARO, D., & MCCURDY, K. (1992, August). *Current trends in child abuse reporting and fatalities: NCPCA's 1991 annual fifty state survey.* Chicago: National Committee for Prevention of Child Abuse.

DE VILLE, K., & KOPELMAN, L. (1999). Fetal protection in Wisconsin's revised child abuse laws. *Journal of Law, Medicine and Ethics, 27*(4), 332–349.

DIXON, S. (1989). Effects of transplantal exposure to cocaine and methamphetamine on the neonate. *Western Journal of Medicine, 150*, 436–442.

FARR, K. A. (1995). Fetal abuse and the criminalization of behavior during pregnancy. *Crime and Delinquency, 41*(2), 235–245.

FEIG, L. (1990). *Drug exposed infants and children: Service needs and policy questions*. Working paper. Office of Social Services Policy, Division of Children, Youth and Family Policy, Offfice of the Assistant Secretary for Planning and Evaluation. Washington, DC: Department of Health and Human Services.

FEIN, B. (1996, September 23). Protect the unborn from unfit mothers. *Insights on the News, 12*, 31–36.

FIOCCHI, F., & KINGREE, J. B. (2001). Treatment retention and birth outcomes of crack users enrolled in a substance abuse treatment program for pregnant women. *Journal of Substance Abuse Treatment, 20*(2), 137–147.

GAGAN, B. (2000). *Ferguson v. City of Charleston, South Carolina*: "Fetal abuse," drug testing and the Fourth Amendment. *Stanford Law Review, 53*(2), 491–514.

GOMBY, D., & SHIONO, P. (1991). Estimating the number of substance-exposed infants. *The Future of Children, 1*(1), 17–26.

GOMEZ, L. (1997). *Misconceiving mothers: Legislators, prosecutors, and the politics of prenatal drug exposure*. Philadelphia: Temple University Press.

GUSTAFSON, N. (1991). Pregnant chemically dependent women: The new criminal. *Affilia: Journal of Women and Social Work, 6*, 61–73.

Harvard Law Review Association. (1998, March). Note: Maternal rights and fetal wrongs: The case against the criminalization of "fetal abuse." *Harvard Law Review, 101*, p. 994–1015.

HAWLEY, T., HALLE, T., DRASIN, R., & THOMAS, N. (1995). Children of addicted mothers: Effects of the "crack epidemic" on the caregiving and the development of preschoolers. *American Journal of Orthopsychiatry, 65*(3), 364–379.

HOWARD, J., KROPENSKE, V., & TYLER, R. (1986). The long term effects on neurodevelopment in infants exposed prenatally to PCP. *National Institute of Drug Abuse Monograph Series, 64*, 237–251.

HUMPHRIES, D. (1998). Crack mothers at 6. *Violence Against Women, 6*(1), 45–61.

HURT, H., BRODSKY, N. L., BRAITMAN, L. E., & GIANNETTA, G. (1995, July/August). Natal status of infants of cocaine users and control subjects: A prospective comparison. *Journal of Perinatology, 15*(4), 297–305.

HUTCHINS, E. (1997). Drug use during pregnancy. *Drug Issues, 27*, 463–465.

INCIARDI, J., LOCKWOOD, D., & POTTIEGER, A. (1993). *Women and crack cocaine*. New York: Macmillan.

JONES, K. (1999). Prenatal substance abuse: Oregon's progressive approach to treatment and child protection can support children, women, and families. *Willamette Law Review, 35*, 797–823.

KENNER, C., & D'APOLITO, K. (1997). Outcomes for children exposed to drugs in utero. *Journal of Obstetric, Gynecologic, and Neonatal Nursing, 26*, 595–603.

LAGASSE, L. L., SEIFER, R., & LESTER, B. M. (1999). Interpreting research on prenatal substance exposure in the context of multiple confounding factors. *Clinics in Perinatology, 26*, 39–54.

LARSON, C. (1991). Overview of state legislative and judicial responses. *The Future of Children, 1*(1), 73–83.

LESLIE, B. (1993). *Parental crack use: Demographic, familial and child welfare perspectives : A Toronto study*. North York, Ontario, Canada: Children's Aid Society of Metropolitan Toronto.

LUTIGER, B., GRAHAM, K., EINARSON, T., & KOREN, G. (1991). The relationship between gestational cocaine use and pregnancy outcome: A meta-analysis. *Teratology, 44*, 405–414.

MATHIAS, R. (1992). Developmental effects of prenatal drug exposure may be overcome by postnatal environment. *NIDA Notes, 7*(1), 14–17.

MATTSON, S. N., & RILEY, E. P. (1998). A review of the neurobehavioral deficits in children with fetal alcohol syndrome or prenatal exposure to alcohol. *Alcoholism: Clinical and Experimental Research, 22*, 279–292.

MCNULTY, N. (1987–1988). Pregnancy police: The health policy and legal implications of punishing pregnant women for harm to their fetuses. *Review of Law and Social Change, 16*(2), 277–319.

Mentis, M. (1998). In utero cocaine exposure and language development. *Seminars in Speech and Language, 19*, 147–165.

Minnesota Statues Annotated. (1990a). Section 626.556, Subd.1 (West Supp.).

Minnesota Statues Annotated. (1990b). Section 626.6661, Subd. 1 (West Supp.).

NOBLE, A., KLEIN, D., ZAHND, E., & HOLTBY, S. (2000). Gender issues in California's perinatal substance abuse policy. *Contemporary Drug Problems, 27*(1), 77–121.

OLSHANSKY, B., DAVIS, L., PALTROW, L., & WISE, C. R. (1997). Reply brief in support of petition for a writ of certiorari, *Whitner* v. *South Carolina*, and *Crawley* v. *Moore*, No. 97-1562, U.S. Supreme Court, October Term.

PALTROW, L. (1990). When becoming pregnant is a crime. *Criminal Justice Ethics, 9*(1), 41–47.

PALTROW, L. (1992). *Criminal prosecutions of women for their behavior during pregnancy.* New York: Center for Reproductive Law and Policy.

PALTROW, L. (1993, August). Winning strategies: Defending the rights of pregnant addicts. *The Champion.*

PALTROW, L. (1999). Pregnant drug users, fetal persons, and the threat to *Roe* v. *Wade. Albany Law Review, 62*, 999–1024.

PASTERNAK, J. (1998, May 2). Wisconsin o.k.'s civil detention for fetal abuse. *Los Angeles Times*, pp. A1, A13.

PEARSON, J., & THOENNIS, N. (1996). What happens to pregnant substance abusers and their babies? *Juvenile and Family Court Journal, 1*, 15–28.

Perinatal Substance Abuse Act of 1991. (1991). Sacramento, CA: California Senate.

PETITTI, D., & COLEMAN, M. (1990). Cocaine and the risk of low birth weight. *American Journal of Public Health, 80*(1), 25–28.

POLLITT, K. (1990). Fetal rights: A new assault on feminism. *The Nation, 247*(12), 455–460.

RICHARDSON, G. & DAY, N. (1991, July/August). Maternal and neonatal effects of moderate use of cocaine during pregnancy. *Neurotoxicology and Teratology, 13*, 455–460.

RICKHOFF, T., & CUKJATI, E. (1989). Protecting the fetus from maternal drug and alcohol abuse: A proposal for Texas. *St. Mary's Law Journal, 21*(2), 259–300.

ROBERTSON, J. (1989, August). *American Bar Association Journal.* p. 38.

ROBIN-VERGEER, B. I. (1990). The problem of the drug exposed newborn: A return to principled intervention. *Stanford Law Review, 42*(3), 745–809.

SAGATUN-EDWARDS, I. (1997). Crack babies, moral panic, and the criminalization of behavior during pregnancy. In E. Jensen & J. Gerber (Eds.), *The construction and impact of the war on drugs.* Cincinatti, OH: Anderson Publishing.

SAGATUN-EDWARDS, I. (1999). *Report to the Fulbright International Committee on the legal response to maternal substance abuse in Norway.* Oslo, Norway: Fulbright Association.

SAGATUN-EDWARDS, I., & SAYLOR, C. (2000a). Drug-exposed infant cases in juvenile court: Risk factors and court outcomes. *Child Abuse and Neglect, 24*(7), 925–937.

SAGATUN-EDWARDS, I. & SAYLOR, C. (Fall, 2000b). A coordinated approach to improving outcomes for substance-abusing families in juvenile dependency court. *Juvenile and Family Court Journal*, pp. 1–15.

SAGATUN-EDWARDS, I., SAYLOR, C., & SHIFFLETT, B. (1995). Drug exposed infants in the social welfare system and the juvenile court. *Child Abuse and Neglect: The International Journal, 19*(1), 83–91.

States look to detention for pregnant drug users. (1998, May 2), *Star-Tribune* (Minneapolis), p. 15A.

TAYLOR, M. (1995). Parent's use of drugs as a factor in award of custody of children, visitation rights, or termination of parental rights. *American Law Reports, 5*, 535–668.

TOLLIVER, A. (2000, Winter). Child abuse statute expanded to protect the viable fetus: The abusive effects of South Carolina's interpretation of the word "child." *Southern Illinois Law Journal, 23*, 383–412.

TRACY, C., FRIETSCHE, S., ABRAHAMSON, D., BOYD. G., & RISHER, M. (1997). On petition for writ of certiorari, *Whitner* v. *State of South Carolina*, No. 97-1562, U.S. Supreme Court, October Term.

U.S. GENERAL ACCOUNTING OFFICE. (1994, April). *Foster care: Parental drug use has alarming impact on young children*. Washington, DC: Report to the Chairman, Subcommittee on Ways and Means, House of Representatives.

VOLPE, J. J. (1992, August). Effects of cocaine use on the fetus. *New England Journal of Medicine, 327*, 399–407.

WESTON, D. R., IVENS, B., ZUCKERMAN, B., JONES, C., & LOPEZ, R. (1989). Drug exposed babies: Research and clinical issues. *National Center for Clinical Infant Programs Bulletin, 9*(5), 7.

Wisconsin Statutes, subsections 48.01.347 et seq. 1996 Wisconsin Laws 292 (A.B. 463, enacted June 16, 1998).

WRIGHT, L. (1990). Fetus vs. mother: Criminal liability for maternal substance abuse during pregnancy. *Wayne Law Review, 36*, 1285–1317.

CASES

Addington v. *Texas*, 441 U.S. 418, 420 (1979).

Angela M. W. v *Kruzicki*, 561 N.W. 2d 729 (Wis. 1997), rev'd *Angela M. W.* v. *Kruzicki*, 541 N.W. 2d 482 (Wis. Ct. App. 1995).

Chambess v. *Fairtrace*, 158 Ill. App. 3d 325, 511 N.E. 2d 839 (1987).

Commonwealth v. *Cass*, 392 Mass. 799, 467 N.E. 2d 1324 (1984).

Commonwealth of Kentucky v. *Connie Welch*, 864 S.W. 2d 280 (1993).

Crawley v. *Evatt*, Mem. Op. No. 97-MO-117 (S.C. Dec. 1, 1997).

Eisenstadt v .*Baird*, 405 U.S. 438 (1972).

Ferguson et al. v. *City of Charleston et al.* 121 S. Ct. 1281; 149 L. Ed. 2d 205; 2001 U.S. LEXIS 2460; 69 U.S.L.W. 4184.

Ferguson v. *City of Charleston*, 186 F.3d 469 (4th Cir. 1999).

Griswold v. *Connecticut*, 381 U.S. 479 (1965).

Grodin v. *Grodin*, 102 Mich. App. 369, 301 N.W. 2d 869 (1981).

In re Baby X, 97 Mich. App. 111, 293 N.W. 2d 736 (1980).

In re Steven S., 126 CA 3r 23, 178 Cal. Rptr. 525 (1981).

In re Troy D., 215 Cal. App. 3d 889, 263 Cal. Rptr. 868 (1989).

Johnson v. *Florida*, 602 So. 2d 1288 (Fla. 1992).

Marchwinski, Konieczny, and Westside Mothers v. *Howard*, 113 F. Supp. 2d 1134 (2000).

Reyes v. *Superior Court*, 75 Cal. App. 3d 214, 141 Cal. Rptr. 912 (1977).

Roe v. *Wade*, 410 U.S. 113 (1973).

Sheriff v. *Encoe*, 110 Nev. 1317, 888 P.2d 596 (1994).

Webster v. *Reproductive Health Services*, 492 U.S. 490 (1989).

Whitner v. *State of South Carolina*, 328 S.C. 1; 492 S.E. 2d 777 (S.C. 1997); *cert. denied*, 118 S. Ct. 1857 (1998); 1998 U.S. 3564.

Wisconsin v. *Deborah J. Z.*, 596 N. W. 2d 490 (Wis. Ct. App. 1999).

10

HIV Disease and Women Offenders

Arthur J. Lurigio, James A. Swartz, and Ciuinal Jones

In this chapter the topic of human immunodeficiency virus (HIV)/acquired immunodeficiency syndrome (AIDS) and women in the criminal justice system is examined. The chapter is divided into five sections. In the first the HIV/AIDS epidemic is described, with an emphasis on the disproportionate number of women of color infected with the virus. In the second section data are presented on the incidence and prevalence of HIV/AIDS among different correctional populations (e.g., jail, prison, probation, parole), broken down by gender, age, and race. Why women in the criminal justice system are especially at risk for HIV (e.g., prostitution, IV drug use) is also explored. Basic HIV/AIDS-related issues in institutional and community corrections (e.g., testing, segregation, confidentiality, and treatment) are discussed in the third section. In the fourth section original data gathered from focus groups of incarcerated women are presented, which explore the factors that impede safer sex and drug-use practices. In the final section various strategies for preventing the transmission of HIV among women offenders are described.

This chapter is about HIV disease among women in the criminal justice system. The characteristics of women under correctional supervision and those of women with HIV and AIDS mirror each other in important ways. Both groups consist of disproportionate numbers of poor women of color. Women in both groups are also more likely to use intravenous drugs and to have sex with intravenous drug users (American Correctional Association, 1990). The overlap between these two groups has influenced the content and organization of this chapter. Hence, in several places, our discussions regarding HIV transmission and prevention transcend women offenders and pertain to all women, especially women of color, particularly African-American women, one of the fastest-growing segments of both the HIV/AIDS and the criminal justice populations in the United States (Chesney-Lind,

1995). In addition, our suggestions for HIV program implementation, although discussed in the context of a HIV program for women inmates, are also germane to HIV programs for incarcerated men.

The chapter is divided into four major sections. In the first section we describe the causes of HIV and the prevalence of HIV disease in general and among women and women of color. In the second section we examine HIV and drug use, present data on HIV and women in prison, and discuss the value of drug treatment in stemming the spread of HIV. The third section focuses on HIV education and findings from a study of an HIV education program for women probationers. In the fourth section we enumerate practical guidelines for developing and implementing HIV programming for women in jail and prison settings.

SPREAD OF HIV DISEASE

Infection with HIV, the cause of AIDS, is perhaps the most profound public health crisis that the nation and the world will ever face (Institute of Medicine, 1988). In 1996, AIDS was the eighth-leading cause of death overall in this country, the second-leading cause of death among Americans aged 25 to 44, and the leading cause of death among African-Americans between the ages of 25 and 44 (Centers for Disease Control, 1996a, 1998b). Since the first AIDS cases were reported to the Centers for Disease Control in 1981, scientists have learned a great deal about the etiology, clinical manifestations, and progression of HIV disease (Cohen, 1998).

HIV is a retrovirus that destroys the body's T-1 helper cells, which are the mainstays of the immune system. Untreated HIV disease results in significant immunosuppression that is irreversible and inexorable, rendering infected persons highly susceptible to a variety of opportunistic microbes and cancers that typically are harmless to persons with healthy immune systems (Fauci, 1988). HIV is spread through unprotected sexual contact, transfusions of infected blood or blood products, and perinatal passage from infected mother to fetus. AIDS is the late or end stage of the clinical spectrum of HIV disease, which includes asymptomatic HIV infection and acute HIV-related illnesses without life-threatening sequela. Estimates suggest that 78 to 100 percent of HIV-infected persons will progress to AIDS within 15 years following their initial exposure to the virus (Douglas & Pinsky, 1992).

As of December 1997, 641,086 AIDS cases had been reported and 390,692 persons had died from AIDS in the United States (Centers for Disease Control, 1998a). An estimated 250,000 Americans are living with AIDS and between 650,000 and 900,000 are HIV positive. Because of successful prevention efforts that target persons at higher risk for HIV infection and the introduction of efficacious combination drug therapies to slow the progression of HIV disease, the incidence of AIDS is increasing at a yearly rate of 5 percent, compared with yearly rates of 65 to 95 percent during the early years of the HIV epidemic (Centers for Disease Control, 1998a).

HIV Disease and Women

Women have accounted for an increasing number of newly reported AIDS cases in the United States (Centers for Disease Control, 1997). The spread of HIV through sexual intercourse occurs more readily from men to women than from women to men. Women's risk of infection through heterosexual contact increases when they engage in anal sex or when they have a vaginal infection at the time of vaginal intercourse. Women with HIV are more likely than uninfected women to contract more often—and more severe—cases of vaginal infections, genital ulcers, genital warts, pelvic inflammatory disease, and cervical cancer.

A number of HIV-related diseases are different in women than they are in men. Men with AIDS, for example, are eight times more likely than women with AIDS to develop Kaposi's sarcoma, one of the AIDS-defining illnesses. Women with AIDS, however, are significantly more likely than men with AIDS to develop thrush as well as genital cancers, warts, and herpes (New Mexico AIDS InfoNet Fact Sheet, 1997).

HIV can be transmitted from women to children perinatally during pregnancy, labor, or delivery or postpartum through breast feeding. Exactly when transmission occurs from mother to child is unknown (World Health Organization, 2001). Women who contract HIV have approximately a 20 to 30 percent chance of having an HIV-infected child (Arras, 1990), and perinatal transmission of HIV is higher in minority women (Selik, Castro, & Pappaioanou, 1988).

AIDS is the seventh-leading cause of death among children aged 1 to 4 in the United States. By 1995, nearly 7000 cumulative pediatric AIDS cases had been reported in the United States; 82 percent of the cases involved children of color. The overwhelming majority (90 percent) of pediatric AIDS cases were the result of maternal transmission of HIV. Among women who transmitted HIV perinatally, 60 percent had contracted HIV through injection drug use or sex with an injection drug user (Centers for Disease Control, 1995b).

Rates of HIV infection and AIDS among male and female inmates in jails and prisons are significantly higher than the rates found in the general population. The rate of confirmed AIDS cases in the U.S. population is 0.08 percent, whereas the rate among state and federal prison inmates is 0.51 percent. Jail and prison inmates with the highest rates of HIV infection were arrested for drug offenses (and hence more likely to be using drugs at the time of admission) and were more likely to report that they had used drugs in the month before their current offenses (Bureau of Justice Statistics, 1997). The rate of HIV infection is higher among women state prison inmates than it is among men state prison inmates, 4.0 percent versus 2.6 percent. Moreover, between 1991 and 1995, the number of HIV-infected female prisoners increased at a rate of 88 percent; over the same time period, the number of HIV-infected male prisoners increased 28 percent.

Incarcerated females with HIV are concentrated in five northeastern states, each with infection rates among women inmates of 10 percent or higher: New York (23 percent), Rhode Island (15 percent), Connecticut (13 percent), New Hampshire (11 percent), and Massachusetts (10 percent). New York was the only state in which the infection rate among men state prison inmates exceeded 10 percent (Bureau of Justice Statistics, 1997).

Rates of HIV infection and AIDS among arrestees also have been found to be higher than the rates in the general population. A study of 831 adult male and 162 adult female arrestees in six Illinois counties, for example, found that the HIV infection rates in the sample were higher than the general population rates from the same Illinois counties. The rates for male and female arrestees were comparable: approximately 2 percent of the urine samples collected from the men and women tested positive for HIV.

HIV Disease and Women of Color

The HIV epidemic has had a devastating impact on women of color throughout the world (Maldonado, 1997). Women from developing countries constitute more than 90 percent of the cumulative AIDS cases among women worldwide (UNAIDS, 1996). Paralleling epidemiologic trends in the developing world, women of color in the United States are disproportionately affected by HIV disease. Although women of color represent approximately one-fourth of the female population in this country, they accounted for 77 percent of the new AIDS cases and 76 percent of the cumulative AIDS cases reported among women in 1995. The most rapidly expanding transmission category among women is heterosexual contact with HIV-infected men (Conrad, 1997).

The HIV epidemic has struck particularly hard at women in the African-American community. By year end 1995, for example, African-American women constituted 12 percent of the country's female population but accounted for approximately 55 percent of both the new and the cumulative AIDS cases found among women (Centers for Disease Control, 1995b). In 1995, the case rate among African-American women was 59 per 100,000, 16 times higher than the rate for white women and more than twofold higher than the rate for Hispanic/Latino women (Centers for Disease Control, 1995b). Estimates suggest that by the year 2000, African-American women will be 20 times more likely than non-African-American women to have AIDS (Walker, 1997). Valleroy (1998) recently reported that HIV prevalence among young African-American women is seven times higher than it is among young white women and eight times higher than it is among young Hispanic women.

The higher rates of HIV infection among women of color might be attributable to several factors, including their greater risk of contact with intravenous drug users, which we discuss in the next section, their negative perceptions of condom use (e.g., belief that condoms are symbols of sexual promiscuity), and their difficulty in maintaining stable sexual partnerships because of the significant gender imbalance in the African-American community, especially in the lowest-income areas (Mays & Cochran, 1988). Kline, Kline, and Oken (1992) reported that women of color weighed their chances of contracting HIV against expectations that condom use would be physically uncomfortable for them and would reduce their sexual pleasure. Among minority women who deal every day with a host of social problems such as poverty, violence, crime, and drug use, the risk of contracting HIV can seem relatively remote or trivial (Nyamathi & Lewis, 1991). In addition, Quinn (1993) found that a high percentage of poor women lacked knowledge about HIV protective behaviors but only half indicated they were "worried about getting AIDS."

Women's use of condoms to prevent HIV is quite low in general. Osmond et al. (1993), for example, estimated that the majority of women use condoms in fewer than half of the occasions in which they have sexual intercourse. To decrease their own HIV risk through condom use, women must influence the sexual practices of men, an often serious and frustrating challenge (Cochran, 1989; Ellerbrock, Bush, Chamberland, & Oxtoby, 1991). Many men, especially men of color, are reluctant to use condoms because of stereotypic cultural notions about masculinity that militate against such use (Osmond et al., 1993; Peterson, Catania, Dolcini, & Faigeles, 1993). The lack of gender equality and socially encouraged passivity in heterosexual relationships might also preclude women from asking their male partners to use condoms (Amaro, 1995; Stein, 1990). Furthermore, women might perceive that such demands imply a lack of trust in their partners' sexual fidelity, causing conflicts in relationships that can have severe financial and emotional consequences for women (Kane, 1990; Shayne & Kaplan, 1991). And studies have shown that women's demands for condom use can result in physical and sexual assaults (O'Leary & Jemmott, 1995; Wermuth, Ham, & Robbins, 1992).

Osmond et al. (1993) reported that positive attitudes toward condom use were unrelated to reductions in women's risky sexual behaviors. Instead, the researchers found that a combination of HIV knowledge, motivation to reduce HIV risk, high self-esteem, and assertiveness in their sexual relationships influenced women's HIV-related sexual practices.

HIV AND DRUG USE

Unlike the developing world, in which three-fourths of HIV infections stem from unprotected heterosexual contact, intravenous drug use plays a central role in the spread of HIV in the United States, especially among women (Maldonado, 1997). Nearly three-fourths of new HIV infections overall are directly or indirectly attributable to illicit drug use (Kolata, 1995). Illicit drug users transmit HIV to each other through sharing HIV-contaminated needles or injection paraphernalia; through heterosexual contact with their uninfected, and often unsuspecting sexual partners; and through the exchange of sex for drugs, a behavior commonly seen among women who use crack/cocaine (McCoy, Miles, & Inciardi, 1995).

Women, Drugs, and HIV

In 1995, equal percentages of new AIDS cases among women were associated with injection drug use and heterosexual contact with an HIV-infected partner: 38 percent within each mode of transmission. More than one-fourth (27 percent) of all the women infected through heterosexual contact contracted HIV from having sex with injection drug users. Nearly half (47 percent) of the cumulative AIDS cases among women by 1995 were attributable to women's injection drug use; 78 percent of the cumulative AIDS cases stemming from injection drug use were among women of color. Throughout the past decade, AIDS incidence among African-American women infected through injection drug use increased at a rate of 10 to 20 percent each year (Centers for Disease Control, 1998c). As data strongly suggest, therefore, the epicenter of the AIDS epidemic in the United States has shifted from the gay male population to drug addicts and their sex partners.

Offenders and HIV

The prevalence of drug use among offenders is significantly higher than it is among members of the general population (Leukefeld, 1985), which places offenders at greater risk for HIV infection. According to the Drug Use Forecasting Study, which has tested arrestees for drug use in more than 20 cities, the proportions of women testing positive for drugs often has equaled or exceeded those of men even for intravenous drug use (e.g., Decker & Rosenfeld, 1992).

HIV infection has been thoroughly documented among intravenous drug users, but researchers have reported increased risks of HIV disease among nonintravenous crack users as well. Booth, Watters, and Chitwood (1993), for example, reported that women who smoked crack/cocaine had more sexual partners and were more likely to engage in prostitution to obtain money for drugs than were women who did not smoke crack. Cocaine use also has been associated with the risk of contracting other sexually transmitted diseases (Rolfs, Goldberg, & Sharrar, 1990), the presence of which increases a person's susceptibility to HIV (Centers for Disease Control, 1997). Stall (1988) reported that heavy users of alcohol and noninjection drugs placed themselves at greater risk for HIV because of the disinhibitory effects that these substances exert on sexual behaviors. Whereas drug users accurately perceive their elevated HIV risk as a result of intravenous drug use, they tend to underestimate their risk of contracting HIV from unprotected sex (Kline & Strickler, 1993).

Over approximately the same time period that addicts and their sex partners have become the primary at-risk populations for HIV disease, staggering numbers of drug-abusing and drug-dependent persons have been processed through the criminal justice system (Belenko, 1990). Partly as a result of the most recent war on drugs and widely adopted mandatory minimum sentencing practices for drug crimes, state and federal prisons in the United States now house nearly 2 million offenders. Another 4 million offenders are on probation or parole supervision (Proband, 1998).

Incarcerated women are much more likely than men to be serving time for drug offenses (Bureau of Justice Statistics, 1994), an offense category that is related to higher rates of drug use. In particular, women offenders have very high rates of cocaine abuse and dependence. According to the 1997 Arrestee Drug Abuse Monitoring Program's annual report (National Institute of Justice, 1998), which is based on urinalysis results, adult female arrestees had higher rates of cocaine use in 18 of the 21 reporting sites. They also had higher rates of heroin use compared with male arrestees in 15 of the 21 reporting sites; however, these differences between men and women were not as large as they were for cocaine use.

A 1994 study of Illinois prison inmates was conducted by Treatment Alternatives for Safe Communities (TASC), which is a community-based, not-for-profit organization serving high-risk populations (including addicted offenders), and the Survey Research Laboratory of the University of Illinois. Men and women who entered the Illinois Department of Corrections at each of the state's four reception and classifications centers were randomly selected for in-depth interviews that explored their current and past drug use and their knowledge and attitudes regarding their risk for HIV infection.

Figure 1 shows the results for inmates' lifetime drug dependence. Women had a higher rate of lifetime dependence (i.e., ever dependent on the drug) on any drug (61 percent) compared with men (55 percent). Male admissions had higher rates of dependence on alcohol and marijuana. Drug-use findings for female admissions to Illinois prisons were consistent with the national ADAM result, that is, women had a much higher rate of lifetime dependence on cocaine (45 percent) than that of with men (27 percent). Moreover, according to the number of *DSM-III R* (American Psychiatric Association, 1987) symptoms reported, women had more severe drug dependencies than men.

The pattern and magnitude of the lifetime drug dependence found in the sample of Illinois prison admissions were very similar to the patterns of drug dependence found in 1995 for male and female arrestees from six Illinois counties (Illinois Criminal Justice Information Authority, 1996). Female arrestees had higher rates of lifetime dependence when all drugs were considered and were especially likely to be dependent on

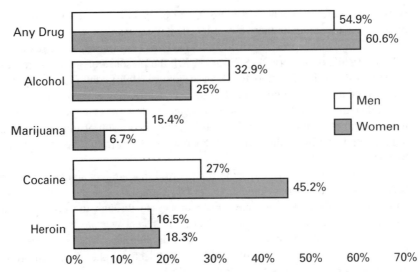

FIGURE 1   Comparison of the prevalence of lifetime drug dependence between men and women admitted to the Illinois Department of Corrections, by drug. (From Treatment Alternatives for Safe Communities, 1994.)

cocaine. And as would be expected, urinalysis results showed that women used cocaine at a much higher rate than men. In summarizing across the Illinois prisoner and arrestee studies, researchers noted that "on average, approximately two-fifths of all adult Illinois males and three-fifths of all adult Illinois females who become involved with the criminal justice system are dependent on alcohol or other drugs at or near the time of their arrests" (Illinois Criminal Justice Information Authority, 1996, p. ix).

Drug-using female offenders are different from drug-using male offenders in other respects that compound their risk for HIV infection. Data that compared Chicago men ($n = 7673$) and women ($n = 1929$) who were referred for a TASC assessment over the past two years showed that women were more likely than men to report crack cocaine (48 percent compared with 29 percent) and injection drug use (8 percent compared with 5 percent). Other studies have found that criminally involved and addicted men and women also differ on how they are initiated into drug use, the length of time between initial use and drug dependency, and the likelihood of being involved with sex partners who also use drugs (e.g., Bowis, Griffiths, Gossop, & Strang, 1996; Hser, Anglin, & McGlothlin, 1987).

Women tend to be initiated into drug use by their boyfriends or husbands, whereas men are more likely to be initiated into drug use by their friends. After drug use has been initiated, women become addicted more quickly than men and are also more likely to be involved with sex partners who use drugs. Furthermore, women who inject drugs are also more likely than their male counterparts to report that they share needles with their partners.

These results indicate that female offenders are among the groups at greatest risk for HIV primarily because of their heavy use of drugs, especially cocaine, the exchange of sex for drugs that often accompanies cocaine use (McCoy, Miles, & Inciardi, 1995), and their involvement with addicted men with whom they have sex and share injection equipment. Many women involved with addicted partners perceive themselves as being at low risk for

HIV as long as they remain monogamous with their primary sex partners. Ethnographic studies (e.g., Ramos, Shain, & Johnson, 1995), however, suggest that addicted men often deceptively live nonmonogamous lives, placing themselves and their uninformed female partners at risk for HIV infection.

Drug Treatment and HIV

As we have just discussed, elevated HIV-risk among women offenders is directly or indirectly tied to drug use. Drug treatment, therefore, is an important means for controlling the spread of HIV in this highly vulnerable population (Batki & London, 1991; Brown & Needle, 1994; Guydish, Golden, & Hembry, 1991). The criminal justice system has great potential for encouraging women offenders to enroll in drug treatment programs and to obtain HIV-related services (e.g., HIV testing and counseling), which they would be less likely to do voluntarily. Moreover, addicts are often poorly motivated for treatment, and community-based drug treatment resources typically are scarce (Brown, 1990–1991). Hence, one of the best opportunities for engaging women addicts in drug treatment occurs while they are under the control of the criminal justice system.

Drug treatment programs for addicted women offenders have, historically, been designed "by men, for men" because of the preponderance of men in the criminal justice system and in need of drug interventions. Male-oriented drug treatment programs are generally inappropriate for and ineffective with women and have been characterized as hierarchical, punitive, and psychologically destructive for addicted women, who tend to have more serious self-esteem issues than those of addicted men (e.g., Ramlow, White, Watson, & Leukefeld, 1997). Consequently, drug treatment programs that are more suitable for women offenders are less confrontational and provide more nurturing experiences for participants.

In single-parent homes, women are more likely than men to bear the primary responsibility for raising children. To participate in drug-treatment programs, many women require child-care services. Because addicted women frequently live with and are strongly influenced by their addicted partners, women's drug treatment programs also must deal with the issue of how to manage this relationship (or terminate it) so that these women can achieve lasting recovery.

Treatment programs that are more sensitive to women's needs have become more available; however, they can be expensive if they include outpatient child-care arrangements or residential services that allow children to live with their mothers during treatment. Because of this expense and because men are still the preponderant population in the criminal justice system, it appears that drug-addicted and criminally involved women, and hence women at high risk for HIV infection, remain underserved.

Attitudes toward HIV

The 1994 Illinois Department of Corrections survey findings suggest that gender-sensitive HIV programs also need to respond to women's perceptions about HIV risk. Men and women inmates were significantly different in their attitudes toward HIV risk. Women were more likely to report that they would not have sex with a *new* partner unless he wore a condom but that they would have unprotected sex with their current partners. And, in general, higher proportions of women than men indicated that they were practicing safer sex and were more concerned about infecting someone else with HIV. At the same time, the women were almost three times more likely than the men to report that no matter what they did, they were ultimately going to be infected with HIV. Thus although more of the women than men inmates reported that they practiced safer sex, the women still felt that they were at high risk for contracting HIV, and many perceived that they were powerless to prevent themselves from contracting HIV.

According to a widely used model for understanding risk behavior, individuals are less likely to change their risk behaviors if they feel that doing so will have no positive consequences (Catania, Kegeles, & Coates, 1990). Hence HIV programs for women should focus on the fatalistic sense that they have regarding HIV infection, whereas programs for men need to address their unrealistic perceptions of invulnerability to HIV.

HIV EDUCATION

In the absence of a cure for or vaccine against HIV disease, prevention is crucial in combatting the HIV epidemic (Fauci, 1988; Jemmott, Jemmott, & Fong, 1992), a goal that is best achieved through education (Fineberg, 1988). The Institute of Medicine (1988) underscored the importance of educating various target populations at high risk for HIV because of injection drug use and unprotected sex, such as criminal offenders (Lanier & McCarthy, 1989). As Hammett and Moini (1990) have noted: "Education and training programs still represent the cornerstone of efforts to prevent transmission of HIV infection in prisons and jails, as well as in the population at large. In fact, the actual and potential role of education affects decisions on virtually all of the other AIDS issues and policy options in correctional facilities."

Because of the higher HIV risk of persons who come in contact with the criminal justice system, owing mostly to injection drug use and sex work, Hammett, Hunt, Gross, Rhodes, and Moini (1991) contended that "the CJS [criminal justice system] may assemble and identify a higher concentration of persons at risk for exposure to and transmission of HIV than will any other private or public agency" (p. 106). In a similar statement, the AIDS Research Institute (1995) declared that "prisons and jails would seem to be an ideal venue for drug treatment and education. There are more injection drug users in correctional facilities in the U.S. than in drug treatment centers, hospitals, or social services" (p. 1). Nonetheless, Hammett et al. (1991) found that the majority of corrections agencies did not provide comprehensive HIV education programs for offenders. Moreover, the percentage of state and federal prisons offering HIV education declined significantly from 1990 to 1994, and a large number of the programs relied on written materials rather than live instruction, which is a more effective means of HIV prevention (Centers for Disease Control, 1996b).

Other researchers have stressed the importance of the criminal justice system in providing HIV education and referral services (e.g., Polonsky et al., 1994; Joint Subcommittee on AIDS in the Criminal Justice System, 1989; Lurigio, 1989). The relationship between high-risk behaviors and knowledge of HIV has been studied in both juvenile and adult offender populations (e.g., Morrison, Baker, & Gillmore, 1994). And HIV education programs have been implemented successfully in jail (Baxter, 1991) and in community corrections settings (Griffin, Lurigio, & Johnson, 1991).

HIV education for offenders can be quite effective. Lurigio, Petraitis, and Johnson (1992), for example, successfully educated probationers in Cook County (Chicago) about HIV. Offenders who participated in an HIV education session, compared with a control group of non-HIV-educated offenders, had more knowledge of HIV prevention and transmission and were more willing to undergo HIV testing, to use condoms, and to refrain from sharing needles. Other prevention programs aimed at increasing knowledge of HIV among offenders have had limited success, however. Among boot camp participants, for example, HIV education did not significantly affect offenders' perceived risk of HIV or attitudes toward high-risk sex activities (Burton, Marquart, Cuvelier, Alarid, & Hunter, 1993), which according to researchers, might be more difficult to change through HIV-intervention programs than are risky drug-use practices (e.g., Turner, Heather, & Moses, 1989).

HIV Education for Women Probationers

Jones and Lurigio (1996) evaluated an HIV education program for African-American women on probation. Brief education sessions, conducted as part of offenders' monthly reporting requirements, were designed to increase their knowledge about HIV and to reduce their risky behaviors. The researchers hypothesized that the participants would score significantly higher on an HIV knowledge test than a comparison group of women probationers and would retain that knowledge on follow-up assessment. Jones and Lurigio (1996) also explored why women fail to engage in risk-reduction behaviors despite their knowledge of HIV prevention strategies. To examine this question, they conducted extensive interviews with the study's participants, eliciting their attitudes toward safer sex practices and drug use and their decision-making styles in sexual relationships.

Jones and Lurigio (1996) found that the vast majority of women in the study were already knowledgeable about basic HIV facts. At pretest, more than 80 percent already knew that HIV can be transmitted by sharing needles and having unprotected sex and that it cannot be transmitted through casual contact (e.g., shaking hands). Significantly lower percentages of women at pretest gave correct responses about the chances of contracting HIV by donating blood or engaging in mutual masturbation. More important, more than two-thirds of the probationers at pretest believed than animal skin condoms were more effective than latex condoms in preventing HIV, and more than half of the women were incorrect about proper placement of a condom on a man's penis.

As predicted, the educated group's knowledge increased significantly at posttest, whereas the control group's did not. The attitudes and behaviors of the HIV-educated probationers also were more likely to change. At one-month follow-up, the educated group was more likely than the control group to report that they had bought condoms, had sex with condoms, and had asked their partners to use condoms since the education session. Moreover, the educated group was more likely to report that they were worried about contracting HIV and that they had been tested for HIV since the education session.

Interviews with women probationers identified a number of obstacles to safer sex practices. Contrary to conventional wisdom, several of the women believed that condom use would detract from *their* sexual pleasure but not necessarily from their partners' enjoyment. As found in previous research, the women stated that they were afraid to ask their partners to use condoms because of the implications and consequences of such a request. In the words of one woman, "if I ask him [boyfriend] to use a condom, you know, he will think that I don't trust him anymore. It would be insulting to him . . . we might start fighting over it." Another probationer reported that "[asking her partner] to put on a condom would piss him off. He then starts to accuse me of sleeping around and starts hittin' on me, and [might] leave me for a few days."

With regard to effective HIV education programs for women offenders, probationers made two important observations. The first was that facts about HIV risk behaviors will be largely ignored by women who are actively using or addicted to illicit drugs. The over-whelming need to use drugs precludes women from "hearing" or applying any HIV-prevention measures. The women also reported that when they were "high" and "on the streets," obtaining drugs and surviving from one day to the next were immediate concerns, whereas HIV risk seemed a distant or obscure threat.

The second was that peer educators, especially those with seropositive status, are regarded as the most credible instructors. According to probationers, the educators' back-ground and experiences are more important than the content of the sessions with regard to influencing their HIV-related behaviors. Offenders noted that messages about protection are particularly forceful when delivered by African-American women who had contracted HIV by engaging in unprotected sex or using intravenous drugs, the same behaviors that place them at risk for infection.

As Jones and Lurigio (1996) and other studies suggest, increasing HIV knowledge alone might be insufficient in decreasing women's risk of HIV contraction. Instead, inter-ventions focused on women offenders must also increase their self-efficacy in making decisions with their male partners about condom use. In addition, factors that immediate-ly affect women's well-being, such as lack of financial resources, shelter, and food, might cause them to view their risk of HIV as unimportant and far removed relative to other pressing concerns. Therefore, HIV-intervention programs in the criminal justice system must address these aspects of women's lives as well. Finally, educational efforts must focus on the power differential between men and women in sexual relationships, which has been posited as a factor in influencing women's high-risk sexual behaviors and another reason why their knowledge of HIV-prevention strategies might not affect their actual HIV-related behaviors (Stein, 1990).

HIV RISK-REDUCTION PROGRAM FOR WOMEN INMATES

TASC was awarded a three-year noncompetitive grant from the Centers for Disease Control to provide HIV education and outreach services to substance-abusing women offenders in the Cook County (Chicago) Sheriff's Female Furlough Program (SFFP). TASC's program, which is called Project Roots, was implemented in December 1997.

In partnership with the Cook County Department of Corrections, TASC serves a daily average of 70 women in Project Roots. Participants are required to report to Roots five days per week as a part of the SFFP pretrial diversion program and to remain drug-free. The program provides women from the SFFP with group HIV interventions that focus on the causes of high-risk behaviors and on participants' intimate and family relationships. The program also provides direct and referral services to participants' family members and significant others. Through a comprehensive network of community-based providers, TASC links participants to a variety of medical and habilitative services.

To assist program participants in their recovery from substance abuse, Roots holds, on site, weekly Narcotics Anonymous and Alcoholics Anonymous meetings. A stress management series also has been added to Roots. The program benefits greatly from a strong client advocacy board (peer council) and a community agency advisory committee. As Project Roots has demonstrated, HIV risk-reduction programs can be developed successfully in correctional settings by focusing on program content, staff performance, service goals, and open communication with jail administrators and personnel.

Based on our experiences in Project Roots, we discuss ways to develop and provide HIV-prevention services for female offenders and to address the challenges that such programming is likely to encounter in correctional institutions. These activities are important in the planning and implementation of a HIV risk-reduction program for women: Locate the program's funding source, select the program's target population, develop a program work plan, establish a program implementation committee, address impediments to program development and implementation, determine the role of the correctional facility in program planning and implementation, develop an educational curriculum that is age, gender, culture, and language appropriate, convene a peer council to guide and support the program, identify HIV interventions or other services that are already offered in the correctional institution, draw lessons from successful HIV programs for similar populations, and conduct evaluations of program operations and outcomes. Following these guidelines, which we describe in more detail below, can help outside agencies in planning effective HIV education and service programs for women in jails or prisons (Centers for Disease Control, 1995a).

Locate a Funding Source

Program developers must determine whether the initiative will be funded internally by the correctional institution, externally through grant funding, or by a combination of funds from both sources. If the funding source is the correctional institution, program staff can be highly confident that the institution is receptive to and supportive of the program. If an external source of funding is being sought, information about the prospective program as well as the granting agency's expectations regarding program operations, services, and matching funds should be discussed with correctional staff before any plans are made for designing or implementing the program. The most successful programs involve correctional staff from the onset in searching for funding sources and in writing grant applications.

Define the Target Population

Staff must specify the criteria that will be used to select women for the program (e.g., race, risk behaviors, sexual orientation, offense). When targeting female offenders for HIV programs, it is advantageous initially to select women who are currently participating in other self-improvement programs within the correctional institution. Long-standing drug treatment, furlough, or parenting programs afford a solid foundation on which to build an HIV program, which can benefit significantly from a strong structural base of existing programming that emphasizes participant self-control, program compliance, and skills building.

Staff should select a small group of women to pilot the HIV program. Potential participants should complete an initial HIV risk assessment to determine seroprevalance rates and participants' risks for future HIV infection. Collaboration with an institution's medical services unit will allow the program to offer confidential HIV testing with pre- and posttest counseling. HIV testing and counseling will become even more important as participants increase their knowledge of HIV and their willingness to be tested. If no HIV testing capacity exists in the institution, program administrators should contact local county or city health departments for assistance. Although correctional facilities are designed primarily for discipline and safety, AIDS advocates have always underscored the need for HIV-related health care and counseling services as well.

Determine the Role of the Correctional Facility

Most jail or prison administrators will probably choose to be highly involved in HIV program planning, implementation, and participant selection. Some administrators, however, might prefer to be minimally involved in these activities or to be consulted only on program safety or security issues. To provide good-quality HIV programming, correctional staff should strike a balance, being supportive but not overly demanding in their involvement with program planners and practitioners.

Program policies should be consistent with the larger policies of the correctional setting. The first step in ensuring compliance with facility regulations is to discuss them fully with jail or prison administrators. HIV program staff should know who to contact regarding programming issues that might affect the institution. For example, a participant of the HIV program communicates that she is HIV positive. In this case, program providers should be aware of the jail's or prison's protocol regarding HIV-positive disclosures and should use institutionally approved procedures for HIV testing and follow-up. In short, HIV program staff should be aware of all the institution's policies that affect the program directly.

Develop a Work Plan

A program work plan should be developed, providing a blueprint that identifies what will be accomplished as the program progresses. The work plan describes the roles, duties, and responsibilities of staff involved in program operations and the methods that will be employed to achieve program goals and objectives. The work plan also specifies when staff meetings occur and who should be present at those meetings, when reports and curricula should be submitted to funders, when participant recruitment should begin and end, and when and to what departments HIV referrals should be made. The work plan serves as a barometer, keeping the program staff and institutional support persons informed about program progress and needs.

Establish an Implementation Committee

An implementation committee should be formed with representatives from all areas of the jail or prison that are affected by or involved in the implementation of the HIV initiative. During the development phases of the program, representatives from all areas of the facility should be present for monthly meetings. Widespread involvement in program development fosters strong internal linkages between institutional and program staff.

The most important function of the implementation committee is to write program policies and procedures. The charge of the implementation committee is also to oversee execution of the program; however, when the program is under way successfully, the committee will probably focus its attention on larger policy issues, such as the handling of confidential HIV test results, HIV-related referrals to outside service agencies, and the housing and treatment of HIV-infected inmates.

Address Program Barriers

Barriers to HIV prevention in correctional settings are similar to those present in the community: misinformation, lack of information, and stigmatization of HIV-infected persons. To overcome these barriers, facility personnel should be educated about HIV before inmate programming begins. Furthermore, facility administrators must be cognizant of all the logistical issues surrounding program implementation in order to provide the support and assistance that is needed to make the program work effectively. A program to educate inmates about HIV risk behaviors, for example, might encounter the following questions:

- Will the length of the initial presentations to inmates interfere with any jail-related orientations?
- Can a physical space be secured that is conducive to discussing the topics of HIV and AIDS?
- Will correctional officers be present during the educational sessions?
- Are written program materials appropriate, and have they been approved by jail or prison administrators? (Prior approval might be necessary in some facilities.)
- Are latex barriers considered contraband even if they are not being distributed?

If possible, the implementation committee should address these questions during the planning phase.

Develop Curriculum and Follow-Up Activities

Specific, measurable, and attainable goals and objectives for learning should be written throughout the curriculum. The curriculum should also identify clearly the types of inmates being reached and the different modes of interventions that will be used in the program (e.g., education, case management, and medical assessment). In addition, the curriculum should include a variety of teaching methodologies that are responsive to the specific needs of particular types of learners. In correctional settings it is important to offer non-literacy based HIV education sessions for persons with reading deficiencies or learning disabilities (Kantor, 1990).

Program content should emphasize the dangers of HIV transmission posed by needle sharing and oral, anal, and vaginal sex. The curriculum should repeat basic HIV facts using consistent, simple, and easily remembered messages. Programmers should be creative in developing participant-focused and interactive curricula. For example, educators can conduct hands-on exercises in which participants practice applying a condom to a penis model, which is an effective way to demonstrate and reinforce correct condom use. Again, program staff should know in advance if this type of activity is allowed in the facility because condoms are contraband in many correctional settings.

Educators should encourage inmates to participate in group and self-exploration exercises. The program should also employ videos and lectures. Videos, however, should be used sparingly and should be no longer than 20 minutes in length. Longer films often fail to hold participants' attention and can lead to disruptive participant behaviors and lost teaching opportunities.

A follow-up program or intervention in the community must be developed to provide a continuum of care for program participants. Released inmates should be linked to supportive services in the community where they can continue to receive HIV information. Community follow-up is critical to the long-term success of any corrections-based HIV education program.

Convene a Peer Council

A peer council can facilitate greatly the success of an HIV program for incarcerated women. They can help to develop the curriculum, to encourage inmates to participate in sessions, to support HIV-infected inmates, and to identify problems or obstacles to program implementation. Peer council members should have previous experience with one or more of the following: alcohol and substance abuse; incarceration; HIV experiences on an individual, family, or community level; relationship difficulties; and decision-making skills relating to safer drug use and sex practices. Peer counselors are effective at relating directly to the participants, providing a level of support that is unmatched, even by the staff. It may be necessary initially to select women from outside the facility to join the peer council (e.g., former inmates who have made a successful adjustment in the community). After the program has been established and has worked with a group of successful inmates, the peer council can be fully constituted from within the institution.

The most important contribution that peer counselors can make is as HIV educators. Peer education has proved effective in correctional settings (e.g., Centers for Disease Control, 1996b). Peer educators can also stress to inmates the importance of HIV testing and can be instrumental in disclosing HIV-positive results to those infected. Hence the selection and training of a small group of inmates motivated to work with program staff can be a critical addition to the program. Peer educators are often the key to program success, especially if the program is lacking a racially and linguistically diverse staff that is able to relate effectively to the inmate population.

Peer groups from other jail or prison programs might be available to cover topics such as drug use or parenting problems, which are common issues among incarcerated women. Peers from other program areas must be educated fully about HIV as the necessary first step in developing a strong HIV peer council in a correctional setting. Peer council members should take their responsibilities seriously: inducting them through a special ceremony can be helpful in solidifying their commitment to the program. Peer council members also should have clearly defined job descriptions and roles.

Identify Other HIV Interventions

Many correctional settings are large, making communication difficult from one division or complex to another. The program implementation committee should determine whether similar programs are operating in the facility and should be aware of any previous barriers or obstacles that these programs faced during planning or implementation. Staff from other HIV programs can provide committee members with helpful advice and direction.

Instead of "reinventing the wheel," program developers should ascertain if other institutions have created similar HIV programs and are willing to provide technical support or consultation. Existing HIV programs can offer refreshing programmatic ideas as well as valuable community networks and resources. It might benefit program staff to join other committees or initiatives that are aimed at helping women inmates.

Evaluate the Program

An evaluation plan should be a central component of HIV programming. The plan should involve a process evaluation that studies program operations and interventions and an outcome evaluation that examines whether the program has achieved its objectives and goals. The process evaluation provides staff with useful, ongoing information for improving the content and delivery of services. The outcome evaluation provides practitioners and funders with data regarding program success, which holds the program accountable and can help to guide future programming. When coupled effectively with a process evaluation, an outcome study informs staff about the most and least effective aspects of their program and recommends strategies for better interventions.

Evaluators determine whether a program was implemented as planned and whether participants have completed the program successfully. Measures of longer-term success in changing behaviors can be particularly difficult to obtain in jails because of the highly transient nature of the population. Therefore, evaluators must formulate strategies for measuring whether women on furlough, house arrest, or released status have internalized HIV risk-reduction messages.

SUMMARY

The spread of HIV disease is a major public health problem in the United States. Women of color are one of the fastest-growing segments of the population with HIV and AIDS and also are represented disproportionately in the criminal justice system. Research demonstrates that women arrestees and inmates in jails and prisons have significantly higher rates of HIV infection compared with members of the general population mostly because of intravenous drug use and sex with intravenous drug users.

The criminal justice system can play a major role in stemming the spread of HIV among high-risk women by implementing HIV prevention and drug treatment programs. To be most effective, prevention programs must increase women's knowledge about safer sex and drug-use practices as well as change their attitudes and perceptions about condom use and their notions about personal susceptibility to HIV. Because the use of intravenous and other types of drugs contribute greatly to HIV risk, drug treatment is an essential component of HIV prevention efforts for women. HIV programming for women offenders must be gender-specific and culturally sensitive, owing to the large number of minority women under correctional control. In addition, programming should be designed to accommodate the special needs of women with self-esteem and literacy problems.

HIV programming can be implemented successfully in jails, prisons, and probation departments—settings in which high-risk women can be provided with prevention and treatment services. Programs for incarcerated women should be carefully planned and designed with the input and support of facility administrators and staff. Furthermore, HIV program staff should be aware of all facility policies and protocols that can affect program operations. HIV program curricula should contain measurable goals. Basic educational messages should be simple and factual and they should be repeated several times and in different ways. Finally, peer educators can be quite effective in educating women about HIV prevention and in communicating the results of HIV testing and therefore should be brought into HIV programming whenever possible.

REFERENCES

AIDS RESEARCH INSTITUTE. (1995). *HIV prevention needs*. San Francisco: University of California Press.

AMARO, H. (1995). Love, sex, and power: Considering women's realities in HIV prevention. *American Psychologist, 6*, 437–447.

AMERICAN CORRECTIONAL ASSOCIATION. (1990). *The female offender: What does the future hold?* Washington, DC: St. Mary's Press.

AMERICAN PSYCHIATRIC ASSOCIATION. (1987). *Diagnostic and statistical manual of mental disorders* (3rd ed. rev.). Washington, DC: APA.

ARRAS, J. (1990). AIDS and reproductive decisions: Having children in fear and trembling. *Milbank Quarterly, 68*, 353–382.

BATKI, S. L., & LONDON, J. (1991). Drug abuse treatment for HIV-infected patients. In J. L. Sorensen, L. A. Wermuth, D. R. Gibson, K. Choi, J. R. Guydish, & S. L. Batki (Eds.), *Preventing AIDS in drug users and their sexual partners* (pp. 77–98). New York: Guilford Press.

BAXTER, S. (1991). AIDS education in the jail setting. *Crime and Delinquency, 37*, 48–63.

BELENKO, S. (1990). The impact of drug offenders on the criminal justice system. In R. Weisheit (Ed.), *Drugs, crime and the criminal justice system* (pp. 27–78). Cincinnati, OH: Anderson Publishing.

BOOTH, R. E., WATTERS, J. K., & CHITWOOD, D. D. (1993). HIV risk-related sex behaviors among injection drug users, crack smokers, and injection drug users who smoke crack. *American Journal of Public Health, 83*, 1144–1148.

BOWIS, B., GRIFFITHS, P., GOSSOP, M., & STRANG, A. (1996). The differences between male and female drug users: Community samples of heroin and cocaine users compared. *Substance Use and Misuse, 31*, 529–543.

BROWN, B. S. (1990–1991). AIDS and the provision of drug user treatment. *International Journal of the Addictions, 25*, 1503–1514.

BROWN, B. S., & NEEDLE, R. H. (1994). Modifying the process of treatment to meet the threat of AIDS. *International Journal of the Addictions, 25*, 1739–1752.

BUREAU OF JUSTICE STATISTICS. (1994, March). *Women in prison* (U.S. DOJ Publ. NCJ 145321). Washington, DC: U.S. Government Printing Office.

BUREAU OF JUSTICE STATISTICS. (1997, August). *HIV in prisons and jails, 1995* (U.S. DOJ Publ. NCJ 164260). Washington, DC: U.S. Government Printing Office.

BURTON, V. S., MARQUART, J. W., CUVELIER, S. J., ALARID, L. F., & HUNTER, R. J. (1993). A study of attitudinal change among boot camp participants. *Federal Probation, 57*, 46–52.

CATANIA, J. A., KEGELES, S. M., & COATES, T. J. (1990). Towards an understanding of risk behavior: An AIDS risk reduction model (ARRM). *Health Education Quarterly, 17*, 53–72.

CENTERS FOR DISEASE CONTROL. (1995a). *Guidelines for health education and risk reduction activities*. Atlanta, GA: CDC.

CENTERS FOR DISEASE CONTROL. (1995b). *U.S. HIV and AIDS cases reported through December 1995*. Atlanta, GA: CDC.

CENTERS FOR DISEASE CONTROL. (1996a). HIV/AIDS surveillance report, February. Atlanta, GA: CDC.

CENTERS FOR DISEASE CONTROL. (1996b). HIV/AIDS education and prevention programs for adults in prisons and jails and juveniles in confinement facilities: United States, 1994. *Morbidity and Mortality Weekly Report, 45*, 27–41.

CENTERS FOR DISEASE CONTROL. (1997). *Report on the global HIV/AIDS epidemic*. Atlanta, GA: CDC.

CENTERS FOR DISEASE CONTROL. (1998a). *HIV/AIDS surveillance report: Cases reported through December 1997*. Atlanta, GA: CDC.

CENTERS FOR DISEASE CONTROL. (1998b). *CDC update: HIV/AIDS in the African American community*. Atlanta, GA: CDC.

CENTERS FOR DISEASE CONTROL. (1998c). *Geneva '98, combatting complacency: A closer look at HIV trends by gender and race*. Atlanta, GA: CDC.

CHESNEY-LIND, M. (1995). Rethinking women's imprisonment: A critical examination of trends in female incarceration. In B. R. Price & N. J. Sokoloff (Eds.), *The criminal justice system and women: Offenders, victims, and workers* (pp. 71–88). New York: McGraw-Hill.

COCHRAN, S. (1989). Women and HIV infection. In V. Mays, G. Albee, & S. Schneider (Eds.), *Primary prevention of AIDS* (pp. 27–42). Newbury Park, CA: Sage Publications.

COHEN, P. T. (1998). *Understanding HIV disease: Hallmarks, clinical spectrum, what we need to know*. Available: HIV InSite: AIDS Knowledge Base

CONRAD, R. (1997). *African Americans suffer disproportionately from AIDS*. Washington, DC: National Center for Public Policy Research.

DECKER, S., & ROSENFELD, R. (1992). Intravenous drug use and the AIDS epidemic: Findings from a 20-city sample of arrestees. *Crime and Delinquency, 38*, 492–509.

DOUGLAS, P. H., & PINSKY, L. (1992). *The essential AIDS fact book*. New York: Simon & Schuster.

ELLERBROCK, T. V., BUSH, T. J., CHAMBERLAND, M. E., & OXTOBY, M. J. (1991). Epidemiology of women with AIDS in the United States, 1981 through 1990. *Journal of the American Medical Association, 265*, 2971–2975.

FAUCI, A. (1988). The human immunodeficiency virus: Infectivity and mechanisms of pathogenesis. *Science, 239*, 617–622.

FINEBERG, H. V. (1988). Education to prevent AIDS: Prospects and obstacles. *Science, 239*, 592–596.

GRIFFIN, E., LURIGIO, A. J., & JOHNSON, B. R. (1991). HIV policy for probation officers: An implementation and evaluation program. *Crime and Delinquency, 37*, 36–47.

GUYDISH, J. R., GOLDEN, E., & HEMBRY, K. (1991). Needle sharing, needle cleaning, and risk behavior change among injection drug users. In J. L. Sorensen, L. A. Wermuth, D. R. Gibson, K. Choi, J. R. Guydish, & S. L. Batki (Eds.), *Preventing AIDS in drug users and their sexual partners* (pp. 28–42). New York: Guilford Press.

HAMMETT, T. W., & MOINI, S. (1990). *Update on AIDS on prisons and jails*. Washington, DC: National Institute of Justice.

HAMMETT, T., HUNT, D., GROSS, M., RHODES, W., & MOINI, S. (1991). Stemming the spread of HIV among IV drug users, their sexual partners, and children: Issues and opportunities for criminal justice agencies. *Crime and Delinquency, 37*, 101–124.

HSER, Y., ANGLIN, M. D., & MCGLOTHLIN, W. (1987). Sex differences in addict careers: 1. Initiation of use. *American Journal of Drug and Alcohol Abuse, 13*, 33–57.

ILLINOIS CRIMINAL JUSTICE INFORMATION AUTHORITY. (1996, July). *Results of the 1995 Illinois drug use forecasting study*. Chicago: ICJIA.

INSTITUTE OF MEDICINE. (1988). *Confronting AIDS: Update 1988*. Washington, DC: National Academy Press.

JEMMOTT, J. B., JEMMOTT, L. S., & FONG, G. T. (1992). Reductions in HIV risk-associated sexual behaviors among black male adolescents: Effects of an AIDS prevention intervention. *American Journal of Public Health, 82,* 372–377.

JOINT SUBCOMMITTEE ON AIDS IN THE CRIMINAL JUSTICE SYSTEM. (1989). *AIDS and the criminal justice system: A final report and recommendations.* New York: The committee.

JONES, M. E., & LURIGIO, A. J. (1996). *Combatting HIV in the suburbs: An intervention for African American women probationers.* Paper presented at a grantee meeting of the Cook County Department of Health, South Holland, IL.

KANE, S. (1990). AIDS, addictions and condom use: Sources of sexual risk for heterosexual women. *Journal of Sex Research, 27,* 427–444.

KANTOR, E. (1990). AIDS and HIV infection in prisoners: Epidemiology. In P. T. Cohen, M. A. Sande, & P. A. Volberding (Eds.), *The AIDS knowledge base* (pp. 86–99). San Francisco: Medical Publishing Group.

KLINE, A., KLINE, E., & OKEN, E. (1992). Minority women and sexual choice in the age of AIDS. *Social Science and Medicine, 34,* 447–456.

KLINE, A., & STRICKLER, J. (1993). Perceptions of risk for AIDS among women in drug treatment. *Health Psychology, 12,* 313–323.

KOLATA, G. (1995, February 28). New picture of who will get AIDS is crammed with addicts. *New York Times,* pp. A17–A18.

LANIER, M. M., & MCCARTHY, B. R. (1989). AIDS awareness and the impact of AIDS education in juvenile corrections. *Criminal Justice and Behavior, 16,* 395–411.

LEUKEFELD, C. G. (1985). The clinical connection: Drugs and crime. *International Journal of Addictions, 20,* 1049–1064.

LURIGIO, A. J. (1989). Practitioners' views on AIDS in probation and detention. *Federal Probation, 53,* 16–24.

LURIGIO, A. J., PETRAITIS, J. M., & JOHNSON, B. R. (1992). HIV education for probationers. *AIDS Education and Prevention, 4,* 205–218.

MALDONADO, M. (1997). Trends in HIV/AIDS among women of color. *Update special edition: Women of color and HIV/AIDS policy.* Washington, DC: National Minority AIDS Council.

MAYS, V., & COCHRAN, S. (1988). Issues in the perception of AIDS risk and risk reduction activities by black and Hispanic/Latina women. *American Psychologist, 41,* 949–957.

MCCOY, H. V., MILES, C., & INCIARDI, J. (1995). *Survival sex: Inner-city women and crack-cocaine.* New York: Roxbury Publishing.

MORRISON, D. M., BAKER, S. A., & GILLMORE, M. R. (1994). Sexual risk behavior, knowledge and condom use among adolescents in juvenile detention. *Journal of Youth and Adolescence, 23,* 271–288.

NATIONAL INSTITUTE OF JUSTICE. (1998). *ADAM 1997 annual report on adult and juvenile arrestees.* Washington, DC: NIJ.

NEW MEXICO AIDS INFONET FACT SHEET. (1997). Women and HIV. http://hivsite.UCSF.edu/medical/factsheets

NYAMATHI, A., & LEWIS, C. (1991). Coping of African American women at risk for AIDS. *Women's Health Issues, 1,* 53–62.

O'LEARY, A., & JEMMOTT, L. S. (1995). General issues in the prevention of AIDS in women. In A. O'Leary & L. S. Jemmott (Eds.), *Women at risk: Issues in the primary prevention of AIDS* (pp. 114–129). New York: Plenum Press.

OSMOND, M. W., WAMBACH, K. G., HARRISON, D. F., BYERS, J., LEVINE, P., IMERSHEIN, A., & QUADAGNO, D. M. (1993). The multiple jeopardy of race, class, and gender for AIDS risk among women. *Gender and Society, 7,* 99–120.

PETERSON, J. L., CATANIA, J. A., DOLCINI, M. M., & FAIGELES, B. (1993). Multiple sexual partners and condom use among African Americans in high-risk cities of the United States: The National AIDS Behavioral Surveys. *Family Planning Perspectives, 25,* 263–267.

POLONSKY, S., KERR, S., HARRIS, B., GAITER, J., FICHTNER, R. R., & KENNEDY, M. G. (1994). HIV prevention in prisons and jails: Obstacles and opportunities. *Public Health Reports, 109,* 615–625.

PROBAND, S. C. (1998). Corrections populations near 6 million. *Overcrowded Times, 9,* 4–5.

QUINN, S. C. (1993). AIDS and the African American woman: The triple burden of race, class, and gender. *Health Education Quarterly, 20,* 305–320.

RAMLOW, B. E., WHITE, A. L., WATSON, D. D., & LEUKEFELD, C. G. (1997). The needs of women with substance use problems: An expanded vision for treatment. *Substance Use and Misuse, 32,* 1395–1403.

RAMOS, R., SHAIN, R. N., & JOHNSON, L. (1995). "Men I mess with don't have anything to do with AIDS": Using ethno-theory to understand sexual risk perception. *Sociological Quarterly, 36,* 483–504.

ROLFS, R., GOLDBERG, M., & SHARRAR, R. (1990). Risk factors for syphilis: Cocaine use and prostitution. *American Journal of Public Health, 80,* 853–857.

SELIK, R., CASTRO, K. G., & PAPPAIOANOU, M. (1988). Racial/ethnic differences in the risk of AIDS in the United States. *American Journal of Public Health, 78,* 1539–1545.

SHAYNE, V. T., & KAPLAN, B. J. (1991). Double victims: Poor women and AIDS. *Women and Health, 17,* 21–37.

STALL, R. (1988). The prevention of HIV infection associated with drug and alcohol use during sexual activity. *Advances in Alcohol and Substance Abuse, 7,* 73–88.

STEIN, Z. (1990). HIV prevention: The need for methods women can use. *American Journal of Public Health, 80,* 460–462.

TREATMENT ALTERNATIVES FOR SAFE COMMUNITIES. (1994). *A survey of the level of need for substance abuse treatment among Illinois State Prison inmates.* Unpublished raw data.

TREATMENT ALTERNATIVES FOR SAFE COMMUNITIES. (1996). *Final results of the 1995 Illinois drug use forecasting study.* Report published by the Illinois Criminal Justice Information Authority.

TURNER, C., HEATHER, G., & MOSES, L. (1989). *AIDS: Sexual behavior and intravenous drug use.* Washington, DC: National Academy Press.

UNAIDS. (1996). *The HIV/AIDS situation in mid 1996: Global and regional highlights.* Joint United Nations Program on HIV/AIDS fact sheet. Geneva: UNAIDS.

VALLEROY, L. A. (1998). Young African American women at high risk for infection. *Journal of Acquired Immune Deficiency and Human Retrovirology, 18,* 25–48.

WALKER, J. (1997). *The AIDS crisis among African Americans.* New York: Balm in Gilead.

WERMUTH, L. A., HAM, J., & ROBBINS, R. L. (1992). Women don't wear condoms: AIDS risk among sexual partners of IV drug users. In J. Huber & B. E. Schneider (Eds.), *The social context of AIDS* (pp. 78–91). Newbury Park, CA: Sage Publications.

WORLD HEALTH ORGANIZATION. (2001). Preventing HIV transmission from mother to child: Strategic option. Geneva, Switzerland.

SECTION IV

Women in Prison

11

Women in Prison

Vengeful Equity

Barbara Bloom and Meda Chesney-Lind

The number of women in U.S. prisons has increased dramatically in recent decades, rising nearly sixfold since 1980. In addition, the increase in women's imprisonment has outstripped the male increase every year since the mid-1980s. As a result, women's share of the correctional population has also increased significantly. In the face of such increases, the authors question whether changes in the character of women's crime, measured either by arrest or commitment data, signal a change in the seriousness of women's offenses. A review of these data suggests a significant increase in the proportion of women with drug offenses serving time in state and federal prisons. Additionally, large numbers of women are imprisoned for property offenses.

A review of the conditions that women experience in prison suggests that they are experiencing the "worst of both worlds" correctionally. On the one hand, recent "parity"-based litigation has been deployed to justify treating women inmates the same as men—resulting in women on chain gangs and in boot camps. On the other hand, details of women's experience of prison underscore the persistence of gender as a theme in their situations both inside the prison and in their relationships with their families. Finally, the need to seek actively to reduce our nation's reliance on imprisonment as the primary response to women's crime is discussed.

In recent years, movie audiences have been entertained by Hollywood's newest construction of women, "the rampaging female" (Birch, 1994, p. 1). Films such as *Thelma and Louise, Fatal Attraction, Basic Instinct, Set It Off,* and *Bound,* among others, have introduced images of women—African-American and white, heterosexual and lesbian, working and middle class—seeking and apparently getting revenge, money, excitement, control, and "liberation" through criminal activity. While notions of womanhood that appear in popular culture, particularly movies, have always been problematic (Douglas, 1994; Haskell, 1973), the last two decades have seen a particular and determined focus on the lethally violent woman, who has become the "new cliché of Hollywood cinema, stabbing and shooting her way to notoriety" (Birch, 1994, p. 1; Holmlund, 1995). There is no denying the fact that women's violence fascinates the general public at the same time that it perplexes feminist scholars (White & Kowalski, 1994), but its chief attribute is its relative rarity. As an example, women killers have accounted for about 10 to 15 percent of all homicides for centuries (Holmlund, 1994, p. 131), and there is even some evidence that the number of adult women killing men actually decreased rather sharply in the last few years. One estimate of this decline is 25 percent (Holmlund, 1994, p. 131). Hollywood's female crime wave has occurred in the absence of a dramatic change in the level of women's violence or serious crime for that matter (see also Chesney-Lind, 1997). It has, however, accompanied a different change, one that may explain the need to construct women as more culpable, blameworthy, and aggressive: a dramatic increase in the number of imprisoned women.

THE NATIONAL CONTEXT: GETTING TOUGHER ON WOMEN'S CRIME

Historically, women under criminal justice supervision were correctional afterthoughts, often ignored because their numbers were extremely small in comparison to those of men under supervision (Rafter, 1990). Indeed, in the mid-1970s, only about half the states and territories had separate prisons for women, and many jurisdictions housed women inmates in male facilities or in women's facilities in other states.

This pattern shifted dramatically during the 1980s, and since then, the nation has seen the number of women in U.S. prisons increase sixfold. In 1980 there were just over 12,000 women in U.S. state and federal prisons. By 1996 there were almost 75,000 (Bureau of Justice Statistics, 1997a). Since 1985 the annual rate of growth of female prisoners averaged 11.2 percent higher than the 7.9 percent average increase in male prisoners.

Women's share of imprisonment has also increased. At the turn of the century, women were 4 percent of those imprisoned; by 1970 this had dropped to 3 percent, and women accounted for only 3.9 percent of those in prison in 1980; but by 1996, women accounted for 6.3 percent of those in prison (Bureau of Justice Statistics, 1997a, p. 6; Callahan, 1986).

California led the nation with 10,248 women in prison, followed by Texas, with 9933, New York with 3728, and Florida with 3302 incarcerated women (Bureau of Justice Statistics, 1997a, p. 6). As of October 12, 1997, the number of women incarcerated in California state prisons reached over 11,000 (California Department of Corrections, 1997).

The rate of women's imprisonment is also at an historic high, increasing from a low of 6 sentenced female inmates per 100,000 women in the United States in 1925 to 51 per 100,000 in 1996 (Bureau of Justice Statistics, 1997a, p. 5; Callahan, 1986). As we shall see, the soaring increase in the imprisonment of women is not explained by changes in the character and seriousness of women's offending. In fact, despite media images of violent women offenders, the proportion of women serving sentences in state prisons for violent offenses declined from 48.9 percent in 1979 to 32.2 percent in 1991. In states such as California, which operates the two largest women's prisons in the nation, the decline is even sharper. In 1992, only 16 percent of the women admitted to the California prison system were incarcerated for violent crimes, compared to 37.2 percent in 1982 (Bloom, Chesney-Lind, & Owen, 1994).

What does explain the increase? The War on Drugs has become a largely unannounced war on women, particularly women of color, and this has clearly contributed to the explosion in the women's prison population (Bloom et al., 1994). Over two decades ago (1979), one in ten women in U.S. prisons was serving time for drugs. Now it is one out of three (32.8 percent), and while the intent of "get tough" policies was to rid society of drug dealers and "kingpins," over a third (35.9 percent) of the women serving sentences for drug offenses in the nation's prisons are serving time solely for "possession" (Bureau of Justice Statistics, 1988, p. 3).

Under current punishment philosophies and practices, women are also increasingly subject to criminalization of noncriminal actions and behaviors. For example, large numbers of poor and homeless women are subject to criminalization as cities across the nation pass ordinances prohibiting begging and sleeping in public places. Many of these women are mothers. Additionally, pregnant drug-addicted women are increasingly being sentenced to prison. Possibly the most dramatic targets of the war on drugs are pregnant women using illegal drugs, who are characterized as "evil women" willing to endanger the health of their unborn children in pursuit of drug-induced highs.

PROFILE OF WOMEN PRISONERS

The characteristics of U.S. women prisoners reflect a population that is triply marginalized by race, class, and gender. Imprisoned women are low income, disproportionately African-American and Latina, undereducated and unskilled with sporadic employment histories. Moreover, they are mostly young, single heads of households, with at least two children (Owen & Bloom, 1995). Women prisoners have a host of medical, psychological, and financial problems and needs. Substance abuse, compounded by poverty, unemployment, physical and mental illness, physical and sexual abuse and homelessness, often propels women through the revolving door of the criminal justice system.

Table 1 describes the characteristics of state female inmates as follows: African-American women comprise 46 percent of women prisoners, white women 36.2 percent of women in prison, and Hispanic women 14.2 percent of women in prison. The median age of women in prison is approximately 31 years.

The majority of imprisoned women were unemployed prior to arrest (53.3 percent) and 22.7 percent had completed high school. The majority of incarcerated women were also unmarried (45 percent never married). More than three-fourths have children, two-thirds of whom are under age 18 (Bureau of Justice Statistics, 1994). The majority of the children of imprisoned mothers live with relatives, primarily grandparents. Approximately 10 percent of the children are in foster care, a group home or other agency. About 8 to 10 percent of women are pregnant when they are incarcerated (Bloom & Steinhart, 1993).

Women under criminal justice supervision frequently have histories of childhood or adult abuse. Forty-three percent of women inmates reported being physically or sexually abused at some time in their lives prior to incarceration. More than four in every ten women reported that they had been abused at least once before their current admission to prison (Snell & Morton, 1994, p. 5). Compared to men, imprisoned women were at least three times more likely to have been physically abused and at least six times more likely

TABLE 1   Characteristics of Female State Prison Inmates, 1991[a]

Characteristic	Percent
Race/origin	
White non-hispanic	36.2
Black non-hispanic	46.0
Hispanic	14.2
Other	3.6
Age	
17 or younger	0.1
18–24	16.3
25–34	50.4
35–44	25.5
45–54	6.1
55 and older	1.7
Median age	31.0
Marital status	
Married	17.3
Widowed	5.9
Divorced	19.1
Separated	12.5
Never married	45.1
Education	
Eighth grade or less	16.0
Some high school	45.8
High school graduate	22.7
Some college or more	15.5
Prearrest employment	
Employed	46.7
Full-time	35.7
Part-time	11.0
Unemployed	53.3

Source: Snell and Morton (1994).

[a]Number of inmates, 38,796.

to have been sexually abused since age 18. For most women under correctional supervision, their problems begin as girls; another national study of women in U.S. prisons and jails indicated that nearly half (46.7 percent) had run away as girls—and two-thirds of these women ran away more than once (American Correctional Association, 1990). Table 2 illustrates the family lives of women inmates prior to prison.

TABLE 2   Childhood Households of Female Inmates and Abuse Experienced before Prison, 1991

	Percent of Female Inmates
Grew up in a household with both parents present	58
Ever lived in a foster home or institution	17
Parents or guardians abused alcohol or drugs	34
Immediate family member ever incarcerated	47
Ever physically or sexually abused	43

Source: Snell and Morton (1994).

Incarcerated women use more drugs and use them more frequently than do men. About 54 percent of the women used drugs in the month before their current offense, compared to 50 percent of the men. Women prisoners are also more likely than their male counterparts to use drugs regularly (65 versus 62 percent), to have used drugs daily in the month preceding their offense (41 versus 36 percent), and to have been under the influence at the time of the offense (36 versus 31 percent). Nearly one in four female inmates reported committing their offense to get money to buy drugs, compared to one in six males (Bureau of Justice Statistics, 1994, p. 7).

The rate of HIV infection is higher for women prisoners than for men prisoners. At the end of 1995, 4.0 percent of female state prisoners were infected with HIV compared to 2.3 percent of male prisoners. From 1991 to 1995, the number of male state inmates infected with HIV increased 28 percent, while the number of female inmates infected with HIV increased at the much faster rate of 88 percent (Bureau of Justice Statistics, 1997b, p. 6).

MOTHERS BEHIND BARS

It is estimated that between 75 and 80 percent of women prisoners are mothers (Bloom & Steinhart, 1993) and that two-thirds of those who are mothers have at least one child under age 18 (Snell & Morton, 1994). A similar percentage of male prisoners, approximately 65 percent, are fathers (Bureau of Justice Statistics, 1994). When a father is incarcerated, responsibility for his children is typically assumed by their mother.

The problems facing incarcerated mothers and their children have been the focus of studies spanning more than three decades. The research has consistently shown that mothers who are prisoners face multiple obstacles in maintaining their relationships with their children. In addition to correctional systems, mothers in prison must also deal with child welfare agencies.

A mother's incarceration is more disruptive to children since mothers are frequently the primary caretakers of their children prior to incarceration. The majority of these mothers are single parents who had custody of their children (73 percent) prior to incarceration. Many of these women never see their children during the period that they are incarcerated.

According to a national study (see Bloom & Steinhart, 1993), over 54 percent of the children of incarcerated mothers never visited their mothers during incarceration. For mothers who were separated from their children prior to arrest, the no-visit rate was 72 percent.

Bloom and Steinhart (1993) found that 17 percent of children whose mothers were incarcerated lived with their fathers, nearly half (47 percent) lived with their grandparents, 22 percent were with relatives or friends, and about 7 percent had been placed in foster care. Incarcerated mothers whose children are in foster care must overcome numerous obstacles to maintain their parental rights (Barry, 1995). Children are often in multiple-foster-care placements and siblings are separated, making it difficult for mothers to determine the whereabouts of their children. This situation is exacerbated when the social services caseworker does not maintain timely communication with the mother. Distance from the prison, lack of transportation, and limited economic resources on the part of the caregiver can pose barriers to regular visitation by children. This, coupled with inadequate family reunification services during incarceration and inability to meet contact requirements and statutory schedules for reunification, put many incarcerated mothers at considerable risk of losing custody of their children (Gabel & Johnston, 1995).

A mother who is incarcerated may not have access to resources such as parent education, drug treatment, counseling, and vocational training to meet the other reunification requirements commonly imposed by dependency courts. Additionally, while continuing contact between mother and child may be the most significant predictor of family reunification following incarceration, as mentioned previously, mothers in prison often have little or no contact with their children while incarcerated.

Although no studies have systematically examined the extent of this issue, the Center for Children of Incarcerated Parents has found that involuntary termination of parental rights occurs disproportionately among women. About 25 percent of women offenders whose children participate in the center's therapeutic programs lost their parental rights (Johnston, 1992).

The Personal Responsibility and Work Opportunity Reconciliation Act of 1996 (PRA) is likely to cause further disruption to incarcerated women and their families. For example, PRA specifically denies federal assistance to two categories of women offenders, drug felons and probation and parole violators. First, PRA imposes a lifetime ban on receiving food stamps or assistance from the federal grant for anyone convicted of a drug felony. Pregnant women can receive benefits while pregnant but not after the child is born. PRA also prohibits benefits to persons violating the conditions of probation and parole. In 1996 there were 515,600 women on probation and 79,300 on parole (Bureau of Justice Statistics, 1997a), and many of them are at high risk of technical violations due to failure to report or drug relapse. The ban does not distinguish between minor technical violations and serious violations such as committing a new crime. These provisions pose significant consequences for women in prison and their families since women incarcerated for drug offenses are the fastest-growing population in women's prisons (Katz, 1997).

CURRENT OFFENSES

Studies have consistently shown that women generally commit fewer crimes than men and that their offenses tend to be less serious. Gilfus (1992); Bloom, Chesney-Lind, and Owen (1995); and Pollock (1994) argue that women's patterns of criminal activity differ from those of men in both the type and amount of crime committed by women. Nearly half of all women in prison are currently serving a sentence for a nonviolent offense and have been convicted in the past only of nonviolent offenses (Snell & Morton, 1994, p. 1). The offenses for which women are arrested and incarcerated are primarily property and drug offenses. When women do commit acts of violence, it is most likely against a spouse or partner and in the context of self-defense (Browne, 1987; Bureau of Justice Statistics, 1994).

As noted earlier, contrary to media-spawned images of the "new violent female criminal," the proportion of women imprisoned for violent offenses continues to decline. Meanwhile, the proportion of women in prison for drug-related offenses has increased substantially. When women do commit violent offenses, they often do so in self-defense and as a response to domestic violence. Additionally, women prisoners are far more likely to kill intimates or relatives (49 percent) than strangers (21 percent), whereas men are more likely to kill strangers (50.5 percent) than intimates or relatives (35.1 percent) (Bureau of Justice Statistics, 1994). The nature of women's violence is often intertwined with their own histories and experiences of abuse, and consequently, their acts of violence take on a different significance than men's violence (Stark & Flitcraft, 1996; Websdale & Chesney-Lind, 1997).

The war on drugs, coupled with the development of new technologies for determining drug use (e.g., urinalysis), plays another less obvious role in increasing women's imprisonment. Many women parolees are being returned to prison for technical parole violations because they fail to pass random drug tests. Of the 6000 women incarcerated in California in 1993, approximately one-third (32 percent) were imprisoned due to parole violations. In Hawaii, 55 percent of the new admissions to the Women's Community Correctional Center during a two-month period in 1991 were being returned to prison for parole violations, due largely to drug violations. Finally, in Oregon, during a one-year period (October 1992–September 1993), only 16 percent of female admissions to Oregon institutions were incarcerated for new convictions; the remainder were probation and parole violators. This pattern was not nearly so clear in male imprisonment; 48 percent of the admissions to male prisons were for new offenses (Anderson, 1994).

Nowhere has the drug war taken a larger toll than on women sentenced in federal courts. In the federal system, the passage of harsh mandatory minimums for federal crimes, coupled with new sentencing guidelines intended to "reduce race, class and other unwarranted disparities in sentencing males" (Raeder, 1993), have operated in ways that distinctly disadvantage women. They have also dramatically increased the number of women sentenced to federal institutions. In 1989, 44.5 percent of the women incarcerated in federal institutions were being held for drug offenses. Only two years later, this increased to 68 percent. Twenty years ago, nearly two-thirds of the women convicted of federal felonies were granted probation, but in 1991 only 28 percent of women were given straight probation (Raeder, 1993, p. 927). The mean time to be served by women drug offenders increased from 27 months in July 1984 to a startling 67 months in June 1990 (Raeder, 1993, p. 929). Taken together, these data explain why the number of women in federal institutions has skyrocketed since the late 1980s. In 1988, before full implementation of sentencing guidelines, women comprised 6.5 percent of those in federal institutions; by 1992 this figure had jumped to 8 percent. The number of women in federal institutions increased by 97.4 percent over a three-year period (Bureau of Justice Statistics, 1989, p. 4; 1993, p. 4).

Snell and Morton (1994) found many women are serving time in state prisons for larceny–theft. Indeed, of the women serving time for property offenses (28.7 percent of all women in prison), well over a third (36.7 percent) are serving time for larceny–theft. This compares to only 18 percent of men who are serving time for property crimes. Fraud is another significant commitment offense for women, accounting for 35 percent of women's but only 9.7 percent of men's most serious property offenses. Men serving time for property offenses are more likely to be serving time for burglary (52.4 percent).

California again gives us a closer look; over a third (34.1 percent) of women in California state prisons in 1993 were incarcerated for property offenses for which "petty theft with a prior" is the most common offense. This generally includes shoplifting and other minor theft. One women in ten in California prisons is doing time for petty theft. In total, one women in four is incarcerated in California for either drug possession or petty theft with a prior (Bloom et al., 1994, p. 3).

ARREST PATTERNS

The pattern of women's arrests provides little evidence that women's crimes are increasing in seriousness and frequency, which would, in turn, explain the dramatic increase in women's imprisonment. As an example, arrests of adult women increased by 36.5 percent between 1986 and 1995 (Federal Bureau of Investigation, 1996, p. 213). During that same period, the number of women held in state and federal prisons increased by 179 percent (Bureau of Justice Statistics, 1997a).

Most of the increase in women's arrests is accounted for by more arrests of women for nonviolent property offenses such as fraud, forgery, and theft, as well as for drug offenses. The arrest data also support the notion that the war on drugs has translated into a war on women. Between 1986 and 1995, arrests of adult women for drug abuse violations increased by 91.1 percent compared to 53.8 percent for men (Federal Bureau of Investigation, 1996, p. 213). In the last decade, arrests of women for drug offenses and other assaults have replaced fraud and disorderly conduct as the most common offenses for which women are arrested (see Table 3). Women's share of arrests for serious violent offenses went from 10.8 percent to 12.3 percent between 1983 and 1992 (Federal Bureau of Investigation, 1992).

These figures, however, should not be used to support notions of dramatic increases in women's crime. As an example, while the number of adult women arrested between 1994 and 1995 did increase, it was only by 4 percent (Federal Bureau of Investigation, 1996, p. 216). Turning specifically to trends in the arrests of women for Part One or "index" offenses (murder, rape, aggravated assault, robbery, burglary, larceny–theft, motor vehicle theft, and arson), these did increase by 16.2 percent (compared to an increase in male arrests of 4.5 percent) between 1986 and 1995 (Federal Bureau of Investigation, 1993, p. 222). While these figures may appear to be dramatic, recall that this category includes larceny–theft, which some contend often involves such minor offenses that it should not be confused with serious crime (see Steffensmeier & Allan, 1995).

Moreover, looking at these offenses differently reveals, if anything, a picture of stability rather than change over the past decade. Women's share of these arrests as a proportion of all those arrested for these offenses rose from 21.8 percent to 23.4 percent between 1986 and 1995. Women's share of arrests for serious violent offenses moved from 11 percent to 15 percent during this same period (Federal Bureau of Investigation, 1996, p. 213).

TABLE 3   U.S. Rank Order of Adult Male and Female Arrests, 1986 and 1995

Male				Female			
1986 Arrests	Percent of Total	1995 Arrests	Percent of Total	1986 Arrests	Percent of Total	1995 Arrests	Percent of Total
(1) Other offenses	24.3	(1) Other offenses	28.7	(1) Other offenses	21.0	(1) Other offenses	26.2
(2) DUI	17.1	(2) DUI	11.3	(2) Larceny–theft	18.0	(2) Larceny–theft	14.5
(3) Drunkenness	9.4	(3) Drug abuse	11.0	(3) DUI	11.3	(3) Drug abuse	9.7
(4) Drug abuse	7.9	(4) Other assaults	8.8	(4) Fraud	8.4	(4) Other assault	8.1
(5) Larceny–theft	7.4	(5) Larceny–theft	6.8	(5) Drug abuse	6.8	(5) DUI	8.0

Source: Compiled from the Federal Bureau of Investigation (1996, p. 213).

Overall, the increase in women's arrests is largely accounted for by more arrests of women for nonviolent property offenses such as shoplifting (larceny–theft), which was up 8.1 percent; check forgery (forgery or counterfeiting), which was up 41.9 percent; welfare fraud, which was up 13.5 percent; and most important, drug offenses, which were up 100.1 percent (Federal Bureau of Investigation, 1996, p. 213). Here the increases in arrests are real, since the base numbers are large, and as a result, these offenses comprise a large portion of women's official crime. Whether they are the product of actual changes in women's behavior over the last decade or changes in law enforcement practices is an important question to which we now turn.

THE NATURE AND CAUSES OF WOMEN'S CRIME

As represented in official arrest statistics, women's crime is remarkably similar to the pattern seen in girls' arrests. Essentially, adult women have been, and continue to be, arrested for minor crimes and what might be called "deportment" offenses (prostitution, disorderly conduct, and "driving under the influence"). Their younger counterparts are arrested for essentially the same crimes, as well as status offenses (running away from home, incorrigibility, truancy, and other noncriminal offenses for which only minors can be taken into custody). Like arrests of girls, arrests of adult women have shown an increase in both aggravated and other assaults. Finally, and most important, adult women's arrests for drug offenses have surged.

Where there have been increases in women's arrests for offenses that appear to be nontraditional, as in the case of assault or drug offenses, careful examination of these trends reveals the connections between these offenses and women's place.

English (1993) approached the issue of women's crime by analyzing detailed self-report surveys that she administered to a sample of 128 females and 872 male inmates in Colorado. She examined both the participation rates and crime frequency figures for a wide array of offenses. She found few differences in the participation rates of men and women, with the exception of three property crimes. Men were more likely than women to report participation in burglary, while women were more likely than men to have participated in theft and forgery. Exploring these differences further, she found that women "lack the specific knowledge needed to carry out a burglary" (English, 1993, p. 366).

Women were far more likely than men to be involved in forgery. Follow-up research on a subsample of high-crime rate female respondents revealed that many had worked in retail establishments and therefore "knew how much time they had between stealing the checks or credit cards and having them reported" (English, 1993, p. 370). The women said that they would target strip malls, where credit cards and bank checks could be stolen easily and used in nearby retail establishments. The women reported that their high-frequency theft was motivated by a "big haul," which meant a purse with several hundred dollars in it as well as cards and checks. English concludes that women's overrepresentation in low-paying, low-status jobs increases their involvement in these property crimes (English, 1993, p. 171).

English's findings with reference to two other offenses where gender differences did not appear in participation rates are worth exploring. She found no difference in the participation rates of women and men in drug sales and assault. However, when examining these frequency data, English found that women in prison reported significantly more drug sales than men reported, but this was not because they were engaged in big-time drug selling. Instead, the high number of drug sales was a product of the fact that women's drug sales were "concentrated in the small trades (i.e., transactions of less than $10)" (English, 1993, p. 372). Because they made so little money, English found that 20 percent of the active women dealers reported 20 or more drug deals per day (English, 1993, p. 372).

A reverse of the same pattern was found when she examined women's participation in assault. Here, slightly more (27.8 percent) of women than men (23.4 percent) reported an assault in the last year. However, most of these women reported only one assault during the study period (65.4 percent) compared to only about a third of the men (37.5 percent).

In sum, English found that both women's and men's crime reflected the role played by economic disadvantage in their criminal careers. Beyond this, though, gender played an important role in shaping women's and men's response to poverty. Specifically, women's criminal careers reflect "gender difference in legitimate and illegitimate opportunity structures, in personal networks, and in family obligations" (English, 1993, p. 374).

WOMEN AND THE DRUG CONNECTION

The majority of female arrests are for drug offenses and crimes committed to support a drug habit, particularly theft and prostitution. According to Drug Use Forecasting (DUF) data, more than half of women arrestees test positive for drugs. Drug-related arrests contribute to increases in the female prison population (Bureau of Justice Statistics, 1991). Federal Bureau of Investigation (FBI) data suggest that women accounted for 20 percent of the increase in drug arrests between 1980 and 1989. From 1982 to 1991, the number of women arrested for drug offenses increased by 89 percent, compared with an increase of 51 percent for men during the same period (Mauer & Huling, 1995).

Studies show that women are more likely to use drugs, use more serious drugs more frequently, and are more likely than men to be under the influence of drugs at the time of their offenses (Bureau of Justice Statistics, 1991, 1992). Although it is commonly assumed that women addicts will probably engage in prostitution to support their drug habits, their involvement in property crimes is even more common. In their sample of 197 female crack/cocaine users in Miami, Inciardi, Lockwood, and Pottieger (1993) found that in the women's last 90 days on the street, 76 percent engaged in drug-related offenses, 77 percent committed minor property crimes, and 51 percent engaged in prostitution (p. 120). The reliance on prostitution to support drug habits was also not confirmed in Anglin and Hser's sample (1987). According to the FBI, arrests for prostitution decreased between 1983 and 1992 (Federal Bureau of Investigation, 1993). Anglin and Hser (1987) found that the women in their sample supported their habits with a variety of crimes, in addition to property crimes, to raise money. Although theft is the crime of choice for women drug users, the researchers found that drug dealing was one of the criminal activities in which their respondents engaged (p. 393).

Data from state and federal court convictions also suggest that women are being arrested, convicted, and sentenced to prison for drug and property crimes but that both crime categories appear to be related to drug use. Felony conviction data for most serious offenses from state courts in 1990 illustrate that the highest percentage of women were convicted of fraud, which includes forgery and embezzlement (38 percent), followed by drug possession (17 percent) and trafficking (15 percent) (Maguire, Pastore, & Flanagan, 1993, p. 528). In terms of the numbers of offenders sentenced in the federal courts in 1992 under the U.S. Sentencing Commission Guidelines, the largest numerical category for females was drug offenses.

SENTENCE LENGTH AND TIME SERVED

Because female prisoners tend to receive shorter sentences than men overall, it has been assumed that women benefit from chivalrous treatment by sentencing judges. Recent research and available data suggest that shorter sentences for women are in fact a result in gender differences in the offenses for which women are incarcerated, criminal histories, and crime roles. On average, women incarcerated in state prisons in 1991 had fewer previous convictions than men, and their record of past convictions was less violent. Women were more likely than men to be in prison for drug and property offenses, and less likely than men to be incarcerated for violent offenses (Mauer & Huling, 1995).

The Bureau of Justice Statistics (1991, 1994) provides some information on time served and sentence length. Overall, average time served for those released in 1986 was 16 months. Violent offenders served an average of 27 months, with property offenders serving about 13 months on average and drug offenders serving around 14 months. In the 1991 sample, women received somewhat shorter maximum sentences than men, with half of the female prisoners serving a sentence of 60 months or less versus half of the men serving a sentence of 120 months or less. Twenty-four percent of the female prison population received sentences of less than 36 months. For women's drug offenses, the median sentence received was 54 months (with a mean of 79 months); property offenders received a median sentence of 44 months (with a mean of 74 months); and violent offenders received a median sentence of 180 months (mean 178 months). For all female prisoners, the median sentence received was 60 months, with a mean of 105 months (Bureau of Justice Statistics, 1994).

RACE, CLASS, AND GENDER DISPARITIES

Contemporary feminist theorists argue for the integration of race, class, and gender in any ana-lytic framework used to study the experiences of women in the criminal justice system. Without such a framework it is impossible to draw a truly accurate picture of their experiences.

Only a few research efforts, however, have focused on the combined effects of race, class, and gender disparities among women in the criminal justice system. The stark realities of race, class, and gender discrimination touch the lives of all women and appear throughout the criminal justice process. Racial bias is a factor in arrests, pretrial treatment, and differential sentencing of women offenders. Women of color are disproportionately incarcerated in the United States. African-American women are incarcerated at a rate seven times that of white women (143 versus 20 per 10,000), and women of color represent more than 60 percent of the adult women in state and federal prisons nationwide (American Correctional Association, 1990). Women of color are also disproportionately represented on the death rows of this country relative to their proportion in the general population.

Mann (1995) documents disproportionality in prison sentences by comparing arrest rates with sentencing rates of women offenders in three states, California, Florida, and New York. She found that in all three states, women of color, particularly African-Americans, were disproportionately arrested. Mann asserts that women of color face double discrimination because of their gender and race/ethnicity. When class level is included, these women often face triple jeopardy.

A recent review of the literature addressing differential sentencing of African-American women and men notes the dearth of research on the possible interactive effects of gender and ethnicity and the inconclusiveness of the available information on the influence of race and ethnicity on criminal justice dispositions (Odubekun, 1992). The few studies that do report race-specific gender differences indicate more punitive treatment of women of color.

Foley and Rasche (1979) found that African-American women received longer sentences (55.1 months) than white women (52.5 months) in their study of one Missouri institution over a 16-year period. When the same offense was committed, Foley and Rasche found differences based on race. For example, white women imprisoned for murder served one-third less time than African-American women incarcerated for the same offense.

According to Mann (1989), in 1979, 32 percent of the women arrested and sentenced to prison in California were African-American, 14.9 percent were Hispanic, 0.8 percent were Native American, and 52.4 percent were white. By 1990, felony prosecutions of women of color in California had increased to 34.4 percent for African-Americans, 19 percent for Hispanics, and 2.5 percent for other women of color; prosecutions of white female felons had decreased to 43.8 percent. California female convictions in 1990 were fairly consistent across racial and ethnic subgroups.

In a study of sentencing outcomes for 1034 female defendants processed in a northern California county between 1972 and 1976, Kruttschnitt (1980–1981, p. 256) reports that in three of the five offense categories studied, a defendant's race or income affected her sentence. "Specifically, African-American women convicted of either disturbing the peace or drug law violations are sentenced more severely than their white counterparts."

In a study of gender differences in felony court processing in California in 1988, Farnsworth and Teske (1995) found that white women defendants were more likely to have charges of assault changed to nonassault than were women of color. Also, class and race often come together, as defendants are often African-American or Latina, and poor. Similar to arrest figures, sentencing statistics may also reflect the race and gender bias that occurred in the earlier decision-making stages of the criminal justice process.

THE WAR ON DRUGS: A WAR ON WOMEN OF COLOR

The declared intention to get rid of drugs and drug-related crime has resulted in federal and state funding being allocated for more police officers on the streets, more federal law enforcement officers, and the building of more jails and prisons rather than funds for prevention, education, and treatment. Poor women of color have become the main victims of these efforts in two ways. As mothers, sisters, daughters, and partners, they are trying to hold their families and communities together while so many men of color are incarcerated, and in addition, they are increasingly imprisoned themselves.

The incarceration of women of color, especially African-Americans, is a key factor in the increase in the number of women in prison. Women serving sentences for possession and possession for sale constitute the majority of women in prison for drug offenses.

According to a recent study by the Sentencing Project, from 1989 to 1994, young African-American women experienced the greatest increase in criminal justice control of all demographic groups studied. The 78 percent increase in criminal justice control rates for black women was more than double the increase for black men and for white women, and more than nine times the increase for white men (Mauer & Huling, 1995). Nationally, between 1980 and 1992 the number of black females in state or federal prisons grew 278 percent while the number of black males grew 186 percent; overall, the inmate population increased by 168 percent (Mauer & Huling, 1995).

Mauer and Huling (1995) present compelling evidence to support their contention that much of this increase can be laid at the door of the War on Drugs, which many now assert has become a war on women, particularly women of color. Their analysis of Justice Department data shows that between 1986 and 1991, the number of black non-Hispanic women in state prisons for drug offenses nationwide increased more than eightfold, from 667 to 6193 (see Table 4). This 828 percent increase was nearly double the increase for black non-Hispanic males and more than triple the increase for white females (see Table 4).

TABLE 4   State Prisoners Incarcerated for Drug Offenses by Race or Ethnic Origin and Gender, 1986 and 1991

	1986		1991		Percent Increase	
	Male	Female	Male	Female	Male	Female
White (non-Hispanic)	12,868	969	26,452	3,300	106	241
Black (non-Hispanic)	13,974	667	73,932	6,193	429	828
Hispanic	8,484	664	35,965	2,843	324	328
Other	604	70	1,323	297	119	324
	35,930	2,370	137,672	12,633	283	433

Source: Mauer and Huling (1995).

"EQUALITY WITH A VENGEANCE":
IS EQUAL TREATMENT FAIR TREATMENT?

Pollock (1994) asks if women are receiving more equal treatment in the criminal justice system today. If equal treatment relates to equal incarceration, the answer appears to be a resounding yes. It is certainly true that many more women offenders are likely to be incarcerated than at any other time in U.S. history. The criminal justice system appears to be more willing to incarcerate women.

There is a continuing debate among feminist legal scholars about whether equality under the law is necessarily good for women. To recap this debate (see Chesney-Lind and Pollock-Byrne, 1995, for a full discussion), some feminist legal scholars argue that the only way to eliminate the discriminatory treatment and oppression that women have experienced in the past is to push for continued equalization under the law, that is, to champion equal rights amendments and to oppose any legislation that treats men and women differently. It is argued that while equal treatment may hurt women in the short run, in the long run it is the only way to guarantee that women will ever be treated as equal partners in economic and social realms. For example, MacKinnon (1987, pp. 38–39) states: "For women to affirm difference, when difference means dominance, as it does with gender, means to affirm the qualities and characteristics of powerlessness." Even those who do not view the experience of women as one of oppression conclude that women will be victimized by laws created from "concern and affection" that are designed to protect them (Kirp, Yudof, & Franks, 1986).

The opposing argument maintains that women are not the same as men and that because it is a male standard that equality is measured against, women will always lose. Therefore, the position calls for recognizing the differential or "special" needs of women. This would mean that women and men might receive differential treatment as long as it did not put women in a more negative position than the absence of such a standard.

Yet another position points out that both the equal treatment and special needs approaches accept the domination of male definitions. For example, equality is defined as rights equal to those of males, and differential needs are defined as needs different from those of males. In these cases, women are the "other" under the law; the "bottom line" is a male one (Smart, 1989). Eisenstein (1988) writes: "Difference in this instance is set up as a duality: woman is different from man and this difference is seen as a deficiency because she is not man" (p. 8).

While these scholars are identifying the limitations of an equal-treatment model in law or in research in legal practices, that model and the evidence on which it is based are the centerpiece for sentencing reforms throughout the United States. These gender-neutral sentencing reforms aim to reduce sentencing disparity by punishing like crimes in the same way. By emphasizing parity, and then utilizing a male standard, more women are losing their freedom (Daly, 1994).

PRISONS AND PARITY

Initially, the differential needs approach was the dominant correctional policy. From the outset, the correctional response to women offenders was to embrace the Victorian notion of "separate spheres" and to construct and manage women's facilities based on what were seen as immutable differences between men and women (Rafter, 1990; Singer, 1973).

Women were housed in separate facilities, and programs for women prisoners represented their perceived role in society. Thus they were taught to be good mothers and housekeepers; vocational education to prepare for employment was slighted in favor of domestic training. Women were hired to supervise female prisoners in the belief that only they could provide for the special needs of women prisoners and serve as role models to them. To some degree, this legacy still permeates women's prisons.

Sentencing practices also treated women and men differently. Women typically were much less likely to be imprisoned unless the woman offender did not fit the stereotypical female role; for example, she was a bad mother or did not have a family to care for (Chesney-Lind, 1987; Eaton, 1986).

The differential treatment of women in sentencing and prison programming was challenged by an emerging "parity" perspective during the 1970s. As a result of prisoner rights' litigation based on the parity model (see Pollock-Byrne, 1990), women offenders are being swept up in a system that seems bent on treating women "equally." This equity orientation translated into treatment of women prisoners *as if they were men*. Since this orientation did not change the role of gender in prison life or corrections, women prisoners receive the worst of both worlds.

For example, boot camps have become very popular as an alternative to prison for juvenile and adult offenders. New York operates a boot camp for women that is modeled on boot camps for men. This includes uniforms, short hair, humiliation for disrespect of staff, and other militaristic approaches.

Chain gangs for women have also become fashionable. In Alabama, male chain gangs were reinstated and corrections officials in that state were threatened with a lawsuit brought by male prisoners suggesting that the practice of excluding women from chain gangs was unconstitutional. The response from the Alabama Corrections Commissioner was to include women in chain gangs (Franklin, 1996). The corrections commissioner was ultimately forced to resign, but the debate about the value of male chain gangs continues in the state.

A serious and persistent allegation that has been associated with women's imprisonment is sexual abuse of women inmates at the hands of male correctional officers. The sexual victimization of women in U.S. prisons is the subject of increasing news coverage and, more recently, international scrutiny. Scandals have erupted in Georgia, Hawaii, California, Ohio, Louisiana, Michigan, Tennessee, New York and New Mexico (Craig, 1996; Curriden, 1993; Lopez, 1993; Meyer, 1992; Sewenely, 1993; Stein, 1996; Watson, 1992). This issue is of such concern that it has attracted the attention of organizations such as Human Rights Watch (1993).

Institutional subcultures in women's prisons, which encourage correctional officers to "cover" for each other, coupled with inadequate protection accorded women who file complaints, make it unlikely that many women prisoners will formally complain about abuse. Additionally, the public stereotype of women in prison as "bad girls" also makes it difficult for a woman inmate to support her case against a correctional officer in court. Finally, what little progress has been made is now threatened by recent legislation that has curtailed the ability of prisoners and advocates to sue about prison conditions (Stein, 1996, p. 24; see also Human Rights Watch, 1996).

Reviewing the situation of women incarcerated in five states (California, Georgia, Michigan, Illinois, and New York) and the District of Columbia, Human Rights Watch (1996) concluded:

Our findings indicate that being a woman prisoner in U.S. state prisons can be a terrifying experience. If you are sexually abused, you cannot escape from your abuser. Grievance or investigatory procedures, where they exist, are often ineffectual, and correctional employees continue to engage in abuse because they believe that they will rarely be held accountable, administratively or criminally. Few people outside the prison walls know what is going on or care if they do know. Fewer still do anything to address the problem. (p. 1)

Human Rights Watch (1996) also noted that investigators were "concerned that states' adherence to U.S. anti-discrimination laws, in the absence of strong safeguards against custodial sexual misconduct, has often come at the fundamental rights of prisoners" (p. 2).

Ironically, despite the superficial emphasis on equity in contemporary corrections, it appears that women today are also recipients of some of the worst of old separate spheres abuses, particularly in the area of social control. As an example, McClellan (1994) examined disciplinary practices at prisons housing Texas male and female inmates. McClellan constructed two samples of inmates (271 males and 245 females) from Texas Department of Corrections records and followed them for a one-year period. She found gender-related differences in treatment between the sexes. For example, she documented that while most men in her sample (63.5 percent) had no citations or only one citation for a rule violation, only 17.1 percent of the women in her sample had such records. McClellan (1994) noted that women prisoners were more likely to receive numerous citations and for different sorts of infractions than men. Most frequently, women were cited for "violating posted rules," while males were cited most often for "refusing to work" (p. 77). Women were more likely than men to receive the most severe sanctions.

McClellan (1994) notes that the wardens of the women's prisons in her study state quite frankly that they demand total compliance with every rule on the books and punish violations through official mechanisms. She concluded that there exist "two distinct institutional forms of surveillance and control operating at the male and female facilities" (p. 87).

DOING TIME: ADAPTATION AND COPING IN CONTEMPORARY WOMEN'S PRISONS

Very little research has been conducted on women prisoner subcultures in over two decades since the classic research of Ward and Kassebaum (1965), Giallombardo (1966), and Heffernan (1972). Owen (1998) describes the world of women's prisons today. As Owen explains, the day-to-day world of female prisons now requires a new description and analysis. She attempts to answer several critical questions: How do women in prison do time? How has prison culture for women changed from the findings of earlier research? How have the contemporary problems of overcrowding, the war on drugs, gangs, and racial division among prisoners affected the way women do time? Owen observed that women prisoners organize their time and create a social world that is quite different from contemporary men's prisons. She suggests that imprisonment and its subsequent response are gendered.

As cited in Owen (1998), the early work of Ward and Kassebaum (1965) and Giallombardo (1966) focused on a social structure based on the family, traditional gender roles, and same-gender relationships. Later studies (Larsen & Nelson, 1984; Leger, 1987; Propper, 1982) described the female prisoner culture in terms of pseudofamily structure and homosexual relations, following themes developed by Ward and Kassebaum and

Giallombardo. These studies suggest that women create lives in prison that reflect elements of traditional family roles and the street life. This social structure revolves around their sexual identify and attendant social roles, mirroring their relations with males on the outside.

Owen explains that Heffernan (1972) found that the existing descriptive and theoretical models of prison culture were based on a male version of the prison and therefore were inadequate for describing life in a women's prison. Employing Syke's (1958) hypotheses, Heffernan looked for key roles and norms that enable the prisoner social system to act cohesively and to reject those who don't adopt the roles and norms. Although she found no support for Syke's role adaptations among the women prisoners in her study, Heffernan described adaptation to the inmate world in terms of three orientations: "the square," a woman who was tied to conventional norms and values; "the cool," a person doing time in a way that involved control and manipulation; and "the life," someone who embraced a more deviant criminal identity based on the culture of the streets.

Similar to Irwin (1970), Heffernan argues that a woman's initial orientation to prison was often based on preprison identities. She found that women who created a family life in prison were most apt to adapt to prison life and that the family was a critical element to the social order of the prison.

The imprisonment of women is tied directly to their status under patriarchy (Kurshan, 1992). Kurshan states that while prisons are used as social control for both men and women, the imprisonment of women "as well as all other aspects of our lives, takes place against a backdrop of patriarchal relationships" (p. 230). Following this theme, Owen (1998) suggests that "the study of women in prison must be viewed through the lens of patriarchy and its implications for the everyday lives of women."

According to Owen (1998), little has changed in women's prison culture. Personal relationships with other prisoners, both emotionally and physically, connections to family and loved ones, and commitments to preprison identities continue to shape the core of prison culture among women. "The world of the women's prison is shaped by pre-prison experiences, the role of women in contemporary society, and the ways women rely on personalized relationships to survive their prison terms" (p. 7). Economic marginalization, histories of abuse, and self-destructive behavior form the pathway to women's imprisonment. The degree to which these behaviors continue to shape their lives, in turn, is dependent on the nature of one's experience in the prison and attachment to competing systems and identities (p. 8).

Contemporary women's prisons also differ from men's prisons in terms of gang activity. Owen (1998) found a lack of organized gangs at her study site, the Central California Women's Facility. She attributed this to the prison family structure and the activities surrounding this structure, which may meet the survival needs of women prisoners that are often met by street gangs.

CONCLUSIONS: PROGRAM AND POLICY IMPLICATIONS

The expansion of the women's prison population has been fueled primarily by increased rates of incarceration for drug law violations and other less serious offenses. The majority of imprisoned women in the United States are sentenced for nonviolent crimes, which often reflect their marginalized status. Women prisoners share many of the problems of their male counterparts, but they also endure unique issues as a result of their race, class, and gender. This threefold jeopardy is manifested in several ways: (1) women offenders are more likely to be victims of physical, sexual, and emotional abuse; (2) they are at greater risk of incarceration due to substance abusing behavior; and (3) they are most likely to be the sole caretakers of dependent children and they are economically marginalized.

Women prisoners have a host of medical, psychological, and financial problems and needs. Substance abuse, compounded by poverty, unemployment, physical and mental illness, physical and sexual abuse, and homelessness often propels women through the revolving door of the criminal justice system. Rather than affording an ameliorative approach to these complex issues, the law enforcement response often exacerbates these problems, causing further psychological and social stress.

Changes in criminal justice policies and practices over the last decade have clearly contributed to dramatic growth in the female prison population. Mandatory prison terms and sentencing guidelines are gender-blind, and in their crusade to get tough on crime, policymakers have gotten tough on women, drawing them into jails and prisons in unprecedented numbers.

The data summarized in this chapter, as well as other research, suggest that women may be better served in the community due to the decreased seriousness of their crimes and their amenability to treatment. By focusing on strategies that directly address the problems of women in conflict with the law, the overuse and overcrowding of women's prisons can be avoided.

Women prisoners have experienced a history of neglect in the development and implementation of correctional programming targeted to their situations. Historically, programs for women offenders were based on male program models without consideration as to their appropriateness for women. Thus we have very little empirical evidence indicating what works for female offenders.

Research supported by the National Institute of Corrections by Austin, Bloom and Donahue (1992) identified a series of effective strategies for working with women offenders in community settings. This study reviewed limited program evaluation data and found that "promising approaches" are multidimensional and deal with the gender-specific needs of women. Austin et al. found that promising community programs combined supervision and services to address the specialized needs of female offenders in safe, structured environments. These programs and strategies use an "empowerment" model of skill building to develop competencies to enable women to achieve independence.

A recent study (Koons, Burrow, Morash, & Bynum, 1997) provides characteristics of promising programs serving women offenders. "A sizable number of promising models approached the treatment of women offenders using a comprehensive and holistic strategy for meeting their needs" (p. 521). Program components included elements such as the use of continuum of care, individualized and structured programming, and an emphasis on skill building.

A review of the backgrounds of women in prison suggests more effective ways to address their problems and needs. Whether it be more funding for drug treatment programs, more shelters for the victims of domestic violence, more family-focused interventions, or more job training programs, the solutions are available. However, changes in public policy are needed so that the response to women's offending is one that emphasizes human needs rather than focusing solely on punitive sanctions. The tax dollars saved by reducing women's imprisonment could be reinvested in programs designed to meet their needs, which would enrich not only their lives but the lives of their children and future generations.

REFERENCES

AMERICAN CORRECTIONAL ASSOCIATION. (1990). *The female offender: What does the future hold?* Washington, DC: St. Mary's Press.

ANDERSON, S. (1994). *Comparison of male and female admissions one year prior to the implementation of structured sanctions.* Salem, OR: Oregon State Department of Corrections.

ANGLIN, M., & HSER, Y. (1987). Addicted women and crime. *Criminology, 25,* 359–394.

AUSTIN, J., BLOOM, B., & DONAHUE, T. (1992). *Female offenders in the community: An analysis of innovative strategies and programs.* Washington, DC: National Institute of Corrections.

BARRY, E. (1995). Legal issues for prisoners with children. In K. Gabel & D. Johnston (Eds.), *Children of incarcerated parents* (pp. 147–156). New York: Lexington Books.

BIRCH, H. (ED.). (1994). *Moving targets: Women, murder and representation.* Berkeley, CA. University of California Press.

BLOOM, B., CHESNEY-LIND, M., & OWEN, B. (1994). *Women in California prisons: Hidden victims of the War on Drugs.* San Francisco: Center on Juvenile and Criminal Justice.

BLOOM, B., & STEINHART, D. (1993). *Why punish the children? A reappraisal of the children of incarcerated mothers in America.* San Francisco: National Council on Crime and Delinquency.

BROWNE, A. (1987). *When battered women kill.* New York: Free Press.

BUREAU OF JUSTICE STATISTICS. (1988). *Profile of state prison inmates, 1986.* Washington, DC: U.S. Department of Justice.

BUREAU OF JUSTICE STATISTICS. (1989). *Prisoners in 1988.* Washington, DC: U.S. Department of Justice.

BUREAU OF JUSTICE STATISTICS. (1991). *Women in prison in 1986.* Washington, DC: U.S. Department of Justice.

BUREAU OF JUSTICE STATISTICS. (1992). *Women in jail in 1989.* Washington, DC: U.S. Department of Justice.

BUREAU OF JUSTICE STATISTICS. (1993). *Prisoners in 1992.* Washington, DC: U.S. Department of Justice.

BUREAU OF JUSTICE STATISTICS. (1994). *Women in prison.* Washington, DC: U.S. Department of Justice.

BUREAU OF JUSTICE STATISTICS. (1997a). *Prisoners in 1996.* Washington, DC: U.S. Department of Justice.

BUREAU OF JUSTICE STATISTICS. (1997b). *HIV in prisons and jails, 1995.* Washington, DC: U.S. Department of Justice.

CALIFORNIA DEPARTMENT OF CORRECTIONS. (1997, October 15). *Weekly report of population.* Data Analysis Unit, Offender Information Services Branch. Sacramento, CA: CDC.

CALLAHAN, M. (1986). *Historical corrections statistics in the United States, 1850–1984.* Washington, DC: Bureau of Justice Statistics.

CHESNEY-LIND, M. (1987). Female offenders: Paternalism reexamined. In L. Crites & W. Hepperele (Eds.), *Women, the courts and equality* (pp. 114–140). Newbury Park, CA: Sage Publications.

CHESNEY-LIND, M. (1997). *The female offender: Girls, women and crime.* Thousand Oaks, CA: Sage Publications.

CHESNEY-LIND, M., & POLLOCK-BYRNE, J. (1995). Women's prisons: Equality with a vengeance. In J. Pollock-Byrne & A. Merlo (Eds.), *Women, law and social control* (pp. 155–175). Boston: Allyn & Bacon.

CRAIG, G. (1996, March 23). Advocates say nude filming shows need for new laws. *Rochester Democrat and Chronicle,* pp. A1, A6.

CURRIDEN, M. (1993, September 20). Prison scandal in Georgia: Guards traded favors for sex. *National Law Journal,* p. 8.

DALY, K. (1994). *Gender, crime and punishment.* New Haven, CT: Yale University Press.

DOUGLAS, S. (1994). *Where the girls are: Growing up female with the mass media.* New York: Random House.

EATON, M. (1986). *Justice for women?* Milton Keynes, England: Open University Press.

EISENSTEIN, Z. (1988). *The female body and the law.* Berkeley, CA: University of California Press.

ENGLISH, K. (1993). Self-reported crime rates on women prisoners. *Journal of Quantitative Criminology, 9*, 357–382.

FARNSWORTH, M., & TESKE, R. (1995). Gender differences in felony court processing: Three hypotheses of disparity. *Women and Criminal Justice, 6*(2), 23–44.

FEDERAL BUREAU OF INVESTIGATION. (1992). *Crime in the United States, 1991*. Washington, DC: U.S. Department of Justice.

FEDERAL BUREAU OF INVESTIGATION. (1993). *Crime in the United States, 1992*. Washington, DC: U.S. Department of Justice.

FEDERAL BUREAU OF INVESTIGATION. (1996). *Crime in the United States, 1995*. Washington, DC: U.S. Department of Justice.

FOLEY, L., & RASCHE, C. (1979). The effect of race on sentence, actual time served and final disposition on female offenders. In J. Conley (Ed.), *Theory and research in criminal justice*. Cincinnati, OH: Anderson Publishing.

FRANKLIN, R. (1996, April 26). Alabama to expand chain gangs—adding women. *USA Today*, p. 3A.

GABEL, K., & JOHNSTON, D. (EDS.). (1995). *Children of incarcerated parents*. New York: Lexington Books.

GIALLOMBARDO, R. (1966). *Society of women: A study of a women's prison*. New York: Wiley.

GILFUS, M. (1992). From victims to survivors: Women's routes of entry and immersion into street crime. *Women and Criminal Justice, 4*(1), 62–89.

HASKELL, M. (1973). *From reverence to rape: The treatment of women in the movies*. New York: Holt, Rinehart and Winston.

HEFFERNAN, E. (1972). *Making it in prison: The square, the cool, and the life*. New York: Wiley.

HOLMLUND, C. (1995). A decade of deadly dolls: Hollywood and the woman killer. In H. Birch (Ed.), *Moving targets: Women, murder and representation*. Berkeley, CA: University of California Press.

HUMAN RIGHTS WATCH. (1996). *All too familiar: Sexual abuse of women in U.S. state prisons*. New York: Holt, Reinhart & Winston.

INCIARDI, J., LOCKWOOD, D., & POTTIEGER, A. (1993). *Women and crack cocaine*. New York: Macmillan.

IRWIN, J. (1970). *The felon*. Englewood Cliffs, NJ: Prentice Hall.

JOHNSTON, D. (1992). *The children of offenders study*. Pasadena, CA: Pacific Oaks Center for Children of Incarcerated Parents.

KATZ, P. (1997). The effect of welfare reform on incarcerated mothers and their families. *Family and Corrections Network Report, 14*, 3, 6.

KIRP, D., YUDOF, M. & FRANKS, M. (1986). *Gender justice*. Chicago: University of Chicago Press.

KOONS, B., BURROWS, J., MORASH, M., & BYNUM, T. (1997). Expert and offender perceptions of program elements linked to successful outcomes for incarcerated women. *Crime and Delinquency 43*(4), 512–532.

KRUTTSCHNITT, C. (1980–1981). Social status and sentences of female offenders. *Law and Society Review, 15*(2), 247–265.

KURSHAN, N. (1992). Women and imprisonment in the U.S. In W. Churchill & J. VanDer Wall (Eds.), *Cages of steel* (pp. 331–358). Washington, DC: Maisonneuve Press.

LARSEN, J. & NELSON, J. (1984). Women, friendship, and adaptation to prison. *Journal of Criminal Justice, 12*(5), 601–615.

LEGER, R. (1987). Lesbianism among women prisoners: Participants and nonparticipants. *Criminal Justice and Behavior, 14*, 463–479.

LOPEZ, S. (1993, July 8). Fifth guard arrested on sex charge. *Albuquerque Journal*, pp. A1, A2.

MACKINNON, C. (1987). *Feminism unmodified: Discourse on life and law*. London: Harvard University Press.

MAGUIRE, K., PASTORE, A., & FLANAGAN, T. (1993). *Sourcebook of criminal justice statistics, 1992*. U.S. Department of Justice, Bureau of Justice Statistics. Washington, DC: U.S. Government Printing Office.

MANN, C. (1989). Minority and female: A criminal justice double bind. *Social Justice, 16*(3), 95–114.

MANN, C. (1995). Women of color and the criminal justice system. In B. Price & N. Sokoloff (Eds.), *The criminal justice system and women* (pp. 118–135). New York: McGraw-Hill.

MAUER, M., & HULING, T. (1995). *Young black Americans and the criminal justice system: Five years later.* Washington, DC: The Sentencing Project.

MCCLELLAN, D. (1994). Disparity in the discipline of male and female inmates in Texas prisons. *Women and Criminal Justice, 5*(2), 71–97.

MEYER, M. (1992, November 9). Coercing sex behind bars: Hawaii's prison scandal. *Newsweek*, pp. 23–25.

ODUBEKUN, L. (1992). A structural approach to differential gender sentencing. *Criminal Justice Abstracts, 24*(2), 343–360.

OWEN, B. (1998). *In the mix: Struggle and survival in a women's prison.* Albany, NY: State University of New York Press.

OWEN, B., & BLOOM, B. (1995). Profiling women prisoners: Findings from national surveys and a California sample. *Prison Journal, 75*(2), 165–185.

POLLOCK, J. (1994, April). *The increasing incarceration rate of women offenders: Equality or justice?* Paper presented at Prisons 2000 conference, Leicester, England.

POLLOCK-BYRNE, J. (1990). *Women, prison, and crime.* Pacific Grove, CA: Brooks/Cole.

PROPPER, A. (1982). Make-believe families and homosexuality among imprisoned girls. *Criminology, 20*(1), 127–139.

RAEDER, M. (1993). Gender and sentencing: Single moms, battered women and other sex-based anomalies in the gender-free world of federal sentencing guidelines. *Pepperdine Law Review, 20*(3), 905–990.

RAFTER, N. (1990). *Partial justice: Women, prisons, and social control.* New Brunswick, NJ: Transaction Books.

SEWENELY, A. (1993, January 6). Sex abuse charges rock women's prison. *Detroit News*, pp. B1, B7.

SINGER, L. (1973). Women and the correctional process. *American Criminal Law Review, 11*, 295–308.

SMART, C. (1989). *Feminism and the power of law.* London: Routledge & Kegan Paul.

SNELL, T., & MORTON, D. (1994). *Women in prison.* Special report. Washington, DC: Bureau of Justice Statistics.

STARK, E., & FLITCRAFT, A. (1996). *Women at risk: Domestic violence and women's health.* London: Sage Publications.

STEFFENSMEIER, D., & ALLAN, E. (1995). Gender, age and crime. In J. Sheley (Ed.), Handbook of contemporary criminology (pp. 88–116). New York: Wadsworth Publishing.

STEIN, B. (1996, July). Life in prison: Sexual abuse. *The Progressive*, pp. 23–24.

SYKES, G. (1958). *Society of captives.* Princeton, NJ: Princeton University Press.

WARD, D., & KASSEBAUM, G. (1965). *Women's prison: Sex and social structure.* Chicago: Aldine-Atherton.

WATSON, T. (1992, November 16). Georgia indictments charge abuse of female inmates. *USA Today*, p. A3.

WEBSDALE, N., & CHESNEY-LIND, M. (1997). Doing violence to women: Research synthesis on the victimization of women. In L. Bowker (Ed.), *Masculinities and violence.* Thousand Oaks, CA: Sage Publications.

WHITE, J., & KOWALSKI, R. (1994). Deconstructing the myth of the nonaggressive woman: A feminist analysis. *Psychology of Women Quarterly, 18*, 487–508.

12

Crime Control Policy and Inequality among Female Offenders

Racial Disparities in Treatment among Women on Probation[1]

Zina T. McGee and Spencer R. Baker

In this chapter we discuss racial differences in risk factors and behavioral conditions among 1547 women placed on probation between 1986 and 1989. In seeking to account for variations in behavioral conditions imposed on female probationers by the court, attention is given to the factors that place women at a greater risk of increased incarceration, including drug abuse history, employment status, and number of prior felony convictions. Disparities in treatment measures such as community placement, alcohol treatment, drug treatment, drug testing, mental health counseling, house arrest, day program, and community service are also discussed, and special attention is paid to crime control policies that serve as the bases for disparate treatment among women on probation, particularly women of color.

LITERATURE REVIEW

In the United States, rates of female arrests and subsequent incarceration are increasing (Gowdy et al., 1998; Greenfeld & Snell, 1999; Snell, 1994). Figures released by the Bureau of Justice Statistics indicate that the female prison population has grown more than 11 percent annually since 1985, resulting from changes in arrest policies and crime patterns (Richie, 2000). In 1995, more women were arrested, convicted, and sent to prison than ever before, primarily for violating laws that prohibit the sale and possession of specific drugs (Gowdy et al., 1998). Despite the increase in female offenders, little attention has been paid to the need for specialized programs such as medical care, counseling, drug treatment, and parenting skills training, and even less is known about disparities in the availability of treatment and rehabilitation programs.

Despite the increase in research devoted to violence against women, many studies have not effectively addressed women's involvement in illegal activity, particularly as the nature and composition of female offenders have changed. Further, very few studies have explored the intersection between victimization and offending as it occurs among women, many of whom remain neglected when discussions of the criminal and juvenile justice systems arise. While self-report data on male and female offending reveal similar patterns regarding drug- and property-related offenses, studies have also shown that abused and neglected adolescent females are at a greater risk of becoming violent as they reach adulthood (Belknap, Holsinger, & Dunn, 1997; Federle and Chesney-Lind, 1992). In a study of male and female prisoners, McClellan and Farabee (1997) found that female inmates were more likely than males to report childhood maltreatment and exhibited higher levels of depression and substance abuse during adulthood. Additionally, female abuse victims were more likely to engage in criminality and often responded to their victimization status with self-blame (McClellan & Farabee, 1997).

Researchers have suggested that studies of female criminality tend to address background characteristics such as age, marital status, education, and employment while neglecting the psychosocial and mental health needs of women in the criminal justice system (MacKenzie & Browning, 1999). Further, little emphasis is placed on the conditions of women in prison, many of whom suffer from a loss of self-esteem and are at a greater risk for depression, self-harm, and suicide. This is particularly problematic since many incarcerated women have a history of social, educational, and health problems in addition to being victims of battering and sexual assault prior to arrest (McClellan & Farabee, 1997; Richie, 2000). Women of color from low-income communities, especially, continue to bear the burden of punitive philosophies within the criminal and juvenile justice systems and have experienced the greatest increase in criminal justice control of all demographic groups (Campbell, 2000; Henriques & Jones-Brown, 1998; Mann, 1995; Richie, 1996, 2000).

Studies have suggested that compared to white women in prisons and jails, black women face greater problems since they are more likely to be single, living on welfare, and responsible for young children (Mann, 1995; McGee, 2000; Pollock, 1999; Van Wormer & Bartollas, 2000). The loss of custody and contact with children poses an even greater problem in that one-half of all female inmates have at least one child under the age of 18 (MacKenzie & Browning, 1999). Richie (1996, 2000) argues that the intersection of gender, race, and violence creates a unique system that leaves many black women vulnerable to public and private subordination. Thus studies continue to suggest that the war on drugs has become a war on women of color since many of them are serving sentences for drug-related offenses.

Criminologists exploring the underlying causes of criminal activity among women have noted that the increase in incarcerated females is not the result of greater involvement in more serious crime. Instead, emphasis is placed on changes in sentencing laws and practices such as mandatory minimum sentencing. Consequently, current sentencing guidelines have resulted in higher rates of imprisonment for economic crimes, many of which involve a disproportionate number of women (Campbell, 2000; Pollock, 1999; Richie, 1996, 2000; Van Wormer & Bartollas, 2000). With the exception of larceny-theft, rates of arrest and detainment among females have increased faster for drug-related offenses than for any other category within the crime index, causing many researchers to examine the implications of crime control policy on women's participation in the criminal and juvenile justice systems (see, e.g., Bass &

Jackson, 1997; Cotton-Oldenburg, Jordan, Martin, & Kupper, 1999; Fagan, 1994; Lex, 1994; Logan, 1999; Marquart, Brewer, Mullings, & Crouch, 1999; McGee, 2000; Medrano, Zule, Hatch, & Desmond, 1999; Mieczkowski, 1994; and Tortu et al., 2000). Since the increase in felony drug charges among females can be viewed primarily as a response to deteriorating economic conditions, many impoverished women are forced to engage in drug crimes to survive since they are the primary caretakers of their children (Richie, 2000). Issues of treatment among women offenders in order to prevent further crimes are rarely addressed, and studies have shown that more than two-thirds of all women incarcerated are repeat offenders, while one-third return to prison within three years of their release (McQuaide & Ehrenreich, 1998). Researchers have argued that higher rates of repeat offending among women of color can be attributed to welfare reform and the reduction of legal sources for supporting poor families. Subsequently, these women are "recycled" through the criminal justice system with little chance for rehabilitation and treatment (McQuaide & Ehrenreich, 1998).

Although few studies have examined the conditions of confinement among women prisoners, even less is known about adjustment outcomes among women upon their release from prison. In 1998, an estimated 950,000 women were under the custody of correctional agencies, with probation or parole agencies supervising 85 percent of them in the community (Greenfeld & Snell, 1999). Further, women under the supervision of these agencies were mothers of an estimated 1.3 minor children (Greenfeld & Snell, 1999; Mumola, 2000). Despite the growth of institutional and aftercare programs designed to support recently released female offenders (see, e.g., Henriques & Jones-Brown, 1998), prison and jail administrators continue to highlight lack of funding and limited resources as barriers to successful outcomes for females on probation or parole. Further, discriminatory practices often prevent women of color from achieving outcomes relating to economic independence, family reunification, and reduced criminal involvement. Mann (1995), for example, argues that in the criminal justice system, parole is a privilege rather than a right. Women of color, in particular, are subjected to harsh stereotypes affecting the release decisions of many parole board members. In fact, African-American women convicted of property crimes and drug offenses appear to have less successful parole outcomes (Mann, 1995). Although past research has identified several factors associated with success on probation, studies addressing female probationers have found unstable employment, marital status, and number of past convictions to be the most significant predictors of failure on probation (Sims & Jones, 1997).

Studies have also shown that recent laws to fight drug-related crime have led to sharp increases in the rates of incarcerated women, most of whom were raising children at the time of their arrest. Since racial minorities comprise a larger proportion of the inmate population, the problem of child care becomes particularly problematic for women of color (Young & Jefferson-Smith, 2000). Young and Jefferson-Smith (2000), for example, argue that the concept of kinship care, in which grandparents or other relatives raise children, relates more to family preservation as opposed to child placement as mothers are imprisoned. Further, the cumulative effects of poverty, racism, and sexism experienced by many black mothers will ultimately become the experiences of their children, thus creating a new generation of youth at risk. Studies have shown that maternal incarceration is the strongest predictor of future criminal behavior and imprisonment among children. Issues of stigmatization and guilt also emerge, while research has indicated that many female teenagers will become pregnant as a result of the incarceration of their mothers (Young & Jefferson-Smith, 2000).

In this chapter, we focus on several factors that are of concern when studying female probationers, particularly African-American women. Issues central to the current study are the identification of risk factors for recidivism and disparities in treatment between European-American women and African-American women placed on probation. Our intent is to explore the linkage between race, risk factors and behavioral conditions imposed among a sample of female probationers over a four-year period. Special attention is paid to differences concerning race, and we hypothesize that these differences will be more salient for African-American females placed on probation compared to European-American female probationers. The study uses three primary sources of information: sentencing records, probation files, and criminal history files. We agree with Mann's (1995) contention that parole boards expect women to meet higher standards of proper conduct than are required of men, and that the release from prison differs significantly because of race and ethnicity. Thus it is expected that greater risk factors and fewer imposed behavioral conditions will be present among African-American women placed on probation. Suggestions for future research and policy implications are also discussed.

RESEARCH METHODOLOGY

Data for this study were collected from the *Recidivism of Felons on Probation, 1986–1989* [United States]. Information was collected on felony probationers in 32 jurisdictions between 1986 and 1989. The data set is composed of 12,369 unweighted cases. The 12,369 cases are representative of 81,927 probationers. The data include, but are not limited to, the following information: financial assessments imposed by the court, behavioral conditions, and caseloads of probation officers.

The study uses three primary sources of information: sentencing records, probation files, and criminal history files. Sentencing records provided a way for the sample to be drawn and also provided information on the cases selected in the sample. Probationer files provided information about the probationer's sex, marital status, educational level, reason for leaving probation, supervision level, and behavioral conditions (e.g., attending alcohol treatment, performing community service, and submitting to drug tests). Criminal history files were used to provide information about arrest activity of the probationer while under supervision. For the present study, emphasis is placed specifically on European-American and African-American female inmates ($n = 1547$). Drug abuse history, employment status, and number of prior felony convictions are among the risk factors influencing number of behavioral conditions imposed by the court, measured as community placement, alcohol treatment, drug treatment, drug testing, mental health counseling, house arrest, day program, and community service.

RESEARCH RESULTS

Table 1 presents background characteristics of the female probationers in the sample. Results show that at the time of their arrest, most women were between the ages of 30 to 39 (30.5 percent), were single (52.6 percent), had completed some high school (41.5 percent), and were employed less than 40 percent of the time (53.9 percent). With the exception of

TABLE 1   Characteristics of European-American and African-American Female
          Offenders on Probation

	Percent European-American Women (n = 877)	Percent African-American Women (n = 670)	Percent Total Sample (n = 1547)
Age			
Under 20	6.8	6.5	6.6
20–24	25.6	23.7	24.8
25–29	25.1	28.2	26.4
30–39	30.2	30.9	30.5
40–49	8.7	7.7	8.3
50 and older	3.6	3.1	3.4
Marital status[***]			
Married/widowed	34.2	17.8	27.3
Divorced/separated	23.3	15.6	20.1
Single	42.5	66.5	52.6
Education[*]			
Grade school	10.6	7.4	9.2
Some high school	38.4	45.7	41.5
High school (GED)	35.0	31.9	33.7
Some college	12.0	13.2	12.5
College degree	4.0	1.9	3.1
Prearrest employment[***]			
Employed more than 60% of the time	37.8	28.0	33.7
Employed 40 to 60% of the time	14.9	8.8	12.3
Employed less than 40% of the time	47.4	63.2	53.9

[*]$p < 0.05$, [**]$p < 0.01$, [***]$p < 0.001$.

age, African-American women had higher percentages in each category, further suggesting a pattern of cumulative disadvantage prior to arrest as discussed in the literature (Van Wormer & Bartollas, 2000; Young & Jefferson-Smith, 2000).

Table 2 presents a comparative analysis of risk factors for recidivism and the presence of behavioral conditions imposed by the court among European-American and African-American women in the sample. The findings are consistent with previous studies which suggest that many of the women processed through the criminal justice system are nonviolent, first-time offenders (Campbell, 2000; Pollock, 1999; Richie, 1996, 2000; Van Wormer &

TABLE 2 **Comparison of Risk Factors and Imposed Behavioral Conditions among African-American and European-American Probationers**

	Percent European-American Women ($n = 877$)	Percent African-American Women ($n = 670$)	Percent Total Sample ($n = 1547$)
Number of conviction charges			
One	84.1	84.2	84.2
Two	10.5	11.9	11.1
Three	3.2	1.7	2.6
More than three	1.2	2.4	2.2
Number of prior felony convictions[***]			
None	85.9	78.8	82.9
One	8.0	12.5	9.9
Two or more	6.1	8.8	7.2
Status of compliance with alcohol treatment[**]			
Satisfactory	44.8	24.3	38.7
Progress made	29.9	16.2	25.8
Unsatisfactory	25.3	59.5	35.5
Status of compliance with drug treatment[**]			
Satisfactory	41.4	20.9	34.5
Progress made	21.9	20.9	21.6
Unsatisfactory	36.7	58.1	43.9
Status of compliance with drug testing			
Satisfactory	32.1	21.7	29.2
Progress made	32.6	33.7	32.9
Unsatisfactory	35.3	44.6	37.9
Status of compliance with mental health counseling			
Satisfactory	43.7	40.9	42.9
Progress made	31.1	31.8	31.3
Unsatisfactory	25.2	27.3	25.8
Number of behavioral conditions imposed[***]			
Zero	35.4	53.3	43.0
One	33.3	30.0	31.9
Two	18.0	9.8	14.5
More than two	13.2	6.9	10.6

TABLE 2   *(continued)*

	Percent European-American Women (*n* = 877)	Percent African-American Women (*n* = 670)	Percent Total Sample (*n* = 1547)
Sentence imposed for first felony arrest[*]			
Prison	22.8	19.1	20.8
Jail	3.8	12.8	8.7
Jail and probation	27.8	12.8	19.7
Probation only	7.6	14.9	11.6
Other	1.3	2.1	1.7
Not guilty/case dropped	36.7	38.3	37.6
Conviction offense[***]			
Murder/nonnegligent Manslaughter	2.5	3.3	2.8
Rape	1.7	.9	1.4
Robbery	4.0	7.0	5.3
Aggravated assault	6.4	15.4	10.3
Burglary	6.6	4.6	5.8
Larceny/auto theft	23.4	28.7	25.7
Forgery/fraud/embezzlement	7.6	10.7	9.0
Drug trafficking	28.4	14.5	22.4
Drug possession	18.9	14.3	16.9
Weapon offense	.5	.6	.5
Drug abuse history[***]			
No	45.7	61.3	52.2
Occasional abuse	22.7	13.8	19.1
Frequent abuse	31.5	24.9	28.8

[*]$p < 0.05$, [**]$p < 0.01$, [***]$p < 0.001$.

Bartollas, 2000). Most women were convicted of only one charge (84.2 percent) and had no prior felony convictions (82.9 percent). African-American women, however, had more prior felony convictions than did European-American women. The most common conviction offenses were nonviolent activities, including larceny/auto theft (25.7 percent), drug trafficking (22.4 percent), and drug possession (16.9 percent). Regarding racial differences, African-American women were more likely to have been convicted of larceny/auto theft (28.7 percent), followed by aggravated assault (15.4 percent) and drug trafficking and drug possession (14.5 percent and 14.3 percent, respectively). A greater percentage of

European-American women were convicted of drug trafficking (28.4 percent), larceny/ auto theft (23.7 percent), and drug possession (18.9 percent), suggesting fewer convictions for violent offenses among this group than for African-American women. Although both groups had no drug abuse history (52.2 percent), African-American women were less likely to abuse drugs than were their European-American counterparts (61.3 percent and 45.7 percent, respectively).

Regarding the sentence imposed for a first felony arrest, results in Table 2 indicate that many women were either acquitted of the charge or had their case dropped (37.6 percent). Consistent with previous literature addressing the disparities in treatment and rehabilitation among black female offenders (Mann, 1995; Sims & Jones, 1997), the findings show that African-American women had fewer behavioral conditions imposed, including drug and alcohol treatment and mental health counseling, than did European-American women (53.5 percent and 35.4 percent, respectively). Among those women receiving alcohol and drug treatment after their arrest, a larger percentage of African-American women were unsuccessful with treatment compared to European-American women, indicating a greater risk of repeat offending and subsequent criminal justice processing among these women, many of whom are subjected to the harsh realities of poverty, racism, and sexism (Richie, 2000). In general, the findings point more toward the discrepancies in risk factors and treatment measures among African-American women than European-American women placed on probation.

SUMMARY AND DISCUSSION OF RESULTS

The findings of this study support the contention that African-American women have experienced the greatest increase in criminal justice control (Gowdy et al., 1998; Henriques & Jones-Brown, 1998; Mann, 1995; Richie, 2000). Significant racial differences exist with regard to the presence of risk factors and the number of behavioral conditions imposed by the court on female probationers. Since studies suggest continuously that increased rates of incarceration among African-American women are primarily the result of more aggressive criminal justice policies on drug offenses, it seems plausible that future research should address the unique problems of imprisoned women of color, including institutional and aftercare treatment upon release from prison.

Thirty years of "get tough on crime" policies that increase the likelihood and length of incarceration, such as mandatory minimum sentences and "three strikes" laws, appear to be either gender blind or beneficial to women. In fact, these reforms contain significant consequences for women. Cutting social services from which women benefit pays for a portion of the costs of prison construction and maintenance. In addition, since women are more likely to be employed in social services and men are more likely to be employed in criminal justice, the increase in the criminal justice system at the expense of the social service system places women's employment opportunities in jeopardy. Finally, the incarceration of parents leaves behind children who may be traumatized and whose emotional and economic care is left to women. Increased barriers to economic, emotional, and social well-being among those women who will ultimately be released from prison further exacerbate this situation, as many of them remain "forgotten offenders."

APPENDIX: ANALYSES USING STRUCTURAL EQUATION MODELING

Additional data analyses were conducted using structural equation modeling (SEM) procedures with the computer program Analysis of Moment Structures (AMOS) 4.01. These procedures allow several hypothesized relationships between measures and variables to be estimated simultaneously (see Arbuckle & Wothke, 1999; Boomsma, 2000; Hatcher, 1994; Kenny, 1999; Kline, 1998; MacCallum, Roznowski, & Necowitz, 1992; McDonald & Marsh, 1990; and Nichol & Pexman, 1999 for further discussion of structural equation modeling). A latent variable, the risk factor, consisted of measures of drug abuse history, employment, and the number of prior felony convictions. There were 923 cases that contained complete data for the variables included in the model, with 18 cases dropped based on multivariate normality, resulting in a sample size of 905. First, an overall model (Figure 1) was investigated to determine if the risk factor predicted the number of behavioral conditions imposed. To determine an adequate fit of the model to the data, the chi-square, the Tucker Lewis Index (TLI), the Comparative Fit Index (CFI), the root-mean-square error of approximation (RMSEA), and the standardized root-mean-square residual (SRMR) were reported. A subsequent analysis was conducted to determine if there were significant differences existing based on ethnicity, including European-American females ($n = 520$) and African-American females ($n = 338$). This comparison was conducted by holding structural parameter estimates constant across groups.

The overall model demonstrated a good fit to the data. The chi-square was non-significant [χ^2 (2, $n = 905$) = 4.671, $p = 0.097$], reflecting the good fit with both the TLI and CFI in the excellent range (Figure 2). The RMSEA with its confidence interval and the SRMR were indicative of the excellent fit. All of the parameter estimates were statistically significant. Table 3 contains the means, standard deviations, and covariance matrix. On request, the authors will provide additional support data for fit of the model to the data.

Based on the excellent results of the overall model, a group comparison was made. Using the same overall model (Figure 1), the sample was divided into two groups based on ethnicity, and multisample analyses were conducted. The overall model fit the data excellently for both European-American and African-American female samples (Figures 3 and 4, respectively). Again the chi-square was not statistically significant [χ^2 (4, $n = 858$) = 3.040, $p = 0.551$], indicative of an excellent fit. The TLI and CFI supported the excellent fit of the model. The RMSEA with its confidence interval and the SRMR added additional

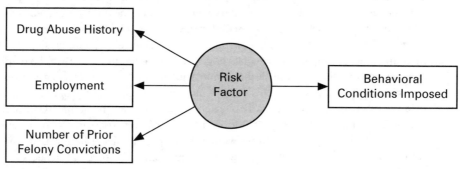

FIGURE 1   Model for analysis.

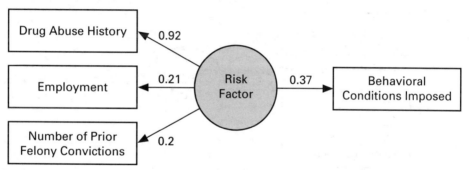

FIGURE 2   Analysis for overall sample. Chi-square (2, $n = 905$), 4.671; $p = 0.097$; Tucker Lewis Index (TLI), 0.998; Comparative Fit Index (CFI), 1.000; root-mean-square error of approximation (RMSEA), 0.038; standardized root-mean-square residual (SRMR), 0.0215.

support for the models. All parameter estimates were statistically significant. To determine if the European-American and African-American female samples differ statistically, the two models were compared by holding parameter estimates constant across analyses. This comparison was accomplished by holding the factor loadings from risk factor to the measures of drug abuse history, employment, and prior felony convictions and the factor loading from risk factor to behavioral conditions imposed invariant across samples. Using a chi-square significance test, the difference between the models is not statistically significant at the 0.05 level [χ^2 (3, $n = 858$) = 7.304, $p = 0.063$], indicating that the models are significantly different.

Table 4 provides the results of the three models. The drug abuse history reflected the greatest change between European-American and African-American females (0.79 and 0.96, respectively), but the influence of the risk factor in predicting the behavioral conditions imposed was directly reversed. For the European-American females, the risk factor had a stronger influence (0.43) on predicting behavioral conditions imposed than for African-American females (0.31), suggesting a greater likelihood of treatment measures to prevent recidivism among European-American women at risk for repeat offending than for African-American women.

TABLE 3   Means, Standard Deviations, and Covariance Matrix[a]

	Mean	s.d.	1	2	3	4
1	1.24	0.574	0.329			
2	1.75	0.866	0.089	0.749		
3	2.23	0.906	0.053	0.150	0.820	
4	1.02	1.104	0.046	0.324	0.046	1.217

[a]1, Number of prior felony convictions; 2, drug abuse history; 3, employment; 4, behavioral conditions imposed.

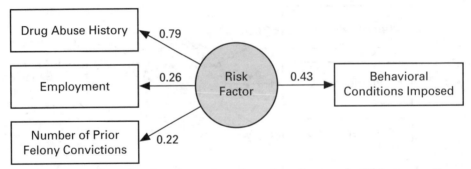

FIGURE 3   Analysis for European-American female sample. Chi-square (4, n = 858), 3.040, p = 0.551; Tucker Lewis Index (TLI), 1.001; Comparative Fit Index (CFI), 1.000; root-mean-square error of approximation (RMSEA), 0.000; standardized root-mean-square residual (SRMR), 0.0152.

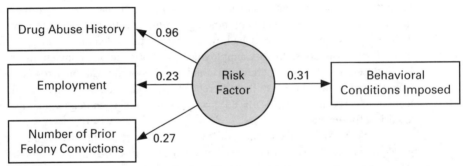

FIGURE 4   Analysis for African-American female sample. Chi-square (4, n = 858), 3.040, p = 0.551; Tucker Lewis Index (TLI), 1.001; Comparative Fit Index (CFI), 1.000; root-mean-square error of approximation (RMSEA), 0.000; standardized root-mean-square residual (SRMR), 0.0152.

TABLE 4   Comparison of Standardized Total Effects across Models[a]

	Risk Factor		
	Overall	European-American	African-American
1	0.197	0.218	0.269
2	0.923	0.787	0.962
3	0.208	0.258	0.226
4	0.367	0.429	0.309

[a]1, Numver of prior felony convictions; 2, drug abuse history; 3, employment; 4, behavioral conditions imposed

NOTE

1. Data for this project were collected from the U.S. Department of Justice, Bureau of Justice Statistics, *Recidivism of Felons on Probation, 1986–1989*. Conducted by Mark A. Cunniff and the National Association of Criminal Justice Planners, 2nd ICPSR ed. [Ann Arbor, MI: Inter-university Consortium for Political and Social Research (producer and distributor), 1994]. The original collector of the data, ICPSR, and the relevant funding agency bear no responsibility for uses of this collection or for interpretations or inferences based on such uses.

REFERENCES

ARBUCKLE, J. & WOTHKE, W. (1999). *Amos 4.0 user's guide*. Chicago: Smallwaters Corporation.

BASS, L. & JACKSON, M. (1997). A study of drug-abusing African-American pregnant women. *Journal of Drug Issues, 27*(3), 659–671.

BELKNAP, J., HOLSINGER, K., & DUNN, M. (1997). Understanding incarcerated girls: The results of a focus group study. *Prison Journal, 77*(4), 381–405.

BOLLEN, K. A. (1989). *Structural equations with latent variables* (Wiley Series in Probability and Mathematical Statistics). New York: Wiley.

BOOMSMA, A. (2000). Reporting analyses of covariance structures. *Structural Equation Modeling, 7*(3), 461–483.

CAMPBELL, N. (2000). *Using Women: gender, drug policy, and social justice*. New York: Routledge.

COTTON-OLDENBURG, N., JORDAN, B., MARTIN, S. & KUPPER, L. (1999). Women inmates' risky sex and drug behaviors: Are they related? *American Journal of Drug and Alcohol Abuse, 25*(1), 129–148.

FAGAN, J. (1994). Women and drugs revisited: Female participation in the cocaine economy. *Journal of Drug Issues, 24*(1–2), 179–211.

FEDERLE, K., & CHESNEY-LIND, M. (1992). Special issues in juvenile justice: gender, race and ethnicity. In M. Schwartz (Ed.), *Juvenile justice and public policy: toward a national agenda*. New York: Macmillan.

GOWDY, V., SUTTON, R., CAIN, T., MOSS, A., CORROTHERS, H., CAMP, A., KATSEL, T., ENGLISH, S., PARMELY, A., ZEPP, J., & SCHMIDT, A. (1998). *Women in criminal justice: A twenty year update special report*. Washington, DC: U.S. Department of Justice.

GREENFELD, L. & SNELL, T. (1999). *Women offenders*. Washington, DC: U.S. Department of Justice.

HATCHER, L. (1994). *A step-by-step approach to using the SAS system for factor analysis and structural equation modeling*. Cary, NC: SAS Institute.

HENRIQUES, Z., & JONES-BROWN, D. (1998). Self-taught empowerment and pride: A multimodal/dual empowerment approach to confronting the problems of African American female offenders. In R. Zaplin (Ed.), *Female offenders: Critical perspectives and effective interventions* (pp. 307–330). Gaithersburg, MD: Aspen Publishers.

KENNY, D. A. (1999). Causal modeling: Measures of fit. Accessed December 25, 1999. http://nw3.nai.net/~dakenny/fit.htm

KLINE, R. B. (1998). *Principles and practices of structural equation modeling*. New York: Guilford Press.

LEX, B. (1994). Alcohol and other drug abuse among women. *Alcohol Health and Research World, 18*(3), 212–222.

LOGAN, E. (1999). The wrong race, committing crime, doing drugs, and maladjusted for motherhood: The nation's fury over "crack babies." *Social Justice, 26*(1), 115–136.

MACCALLUM, R. C., ROZNOWSKI, M., & NECOWITZ, L. B. (1992). Model modifications in covariance structure analysis: The problem of capitalization on chance. *Psychological Bulletin, 111*, 490–504.

MACKENZIE, D. L. & BROWING, K. (1999). The impact of probation on the criminal activities of offenders. *Journal of Research in Crime and Delinquency, 36*(4), 423–454.

Mann, C. (1995). Women of color and the criminal justice system. In B. Price & N. Sokoloff (Eds.), *The criminal justice system and women: Offenders, victims, and workers* (2nd ed.). New York: McGraw-Hill.

MARQUART, J., BREWER, V., MULLINGS, J., & CROUCH, B. (1999). The implications of crime control policy on HIV/AIDS-related risk among women prisoners. *Crime and Delinquency, 45*(1), 82–97.

MCCLELLAN, D. S., & FARABEE, D. (1997). Early victimization, drug use, and criminality: A comparison of male and female prisoners. *Criminal Justice and Behavior, 24*(4), 455–477.

MCDONALD, R., & MARSH, H. (1990). Choosing a multivariate model: Noncentrality and goodness of fit. *Psychological Bulletin, 107*(2), 247–255.

MCGEE, Z. (2000). The pains of imprisonment: Long-term incarceration effects on women in prison. In R. Muraskin (Ed.), *It's a crime: Women and justice* (pp. 205–214). Upper Saddle River, NJ: Prentice Hall.

MCQUAIDE, S., & EHRENREICH, J. H. (1998). Women in prison: Approaches to understanding the lives of a forgotten population. *Affilia: Journal of Women and Social Work, 13*(2), 233–242.

MEDRANO, M., ZULE, W., HATCH, J., & DESMOND, D. (1999). Prevalence of childhood trauma in a community sample of substance-abusing women. *American Journal of Drug and Alcohol Abuse, 25*(3), 449–458.

MIECZKOWSKI, T. (1994). The experiences of women who sell crack: Some descriptive data from the Detroit crack ethnography project. *Journal of Drug Issues, 24*(1), 227–249.

MUMOLA, C. (2000). *Incarcerated parents and their children.* Washington, DC: U.S. Department of Justice.

NICHOL, A. A. M., & PEXMAN, P. M. (1999). *Presenting your findings: A practical guide for creating tables.* Washington DC: American Psychological Association.

POLLOCK, J. (1999). *Criminal women.* Cincinnati, OH: Anderson Publishing.

RICHIE, B. (1996). *Compelled to crime: The gender entrapment of battered black women.* New York: Routledge.

RICHIE, B. (2000). Exploring the link between violence against women and women's involvement in illegal activity. *Research on women and girls in the justice system.* Washington, DC: U.S. Department of Justice.

SIMS, B., & JONES, M. (1997). Predicting success or failure on probation: Factors associated with felony probation outcomes. *Crime and Delinquency, 43*(3), 314–327.

SNELL, T. (1994). *Women in prison.* Washington, DC: U.S. Department of Justice.

TORTU, S., BEARDSLEY, M., DEREN, S., WILLIAMS, M., MCCOY, H., GOLDSTEIN, M., STARK, M., & ESTRADA, A. (2000). HIV infection and patterns of risk among women drug injectors and crack users in low and high sero-prevalence sites. *AIDS Care, 12*(1), 65–77.

United States Department of Justice. (1995, March 31). *Recidivism of felons on probation, 1986–1989.* Bureau of Justice Statistics.

VAN WORMER, K. & BARTOLLAS, C. (2000). *Women and the criminal justice system.* Needham Heights, MA: Allyn & Bacon.

YOUNG, D., & JEFFERSON-SMITH, C. (2000). When moms are incarcerated: The needs of children, mothers and caregivers. *Families in Society: Journal of Contemporary Human Services, 81*(2), 130–146.

13

Three Strikes and It's *Women* Who Are Out

The Hidden Consequences for Women of Criminal Justice Policy Reforms[1]

Mona J. E. Danner

Thirty years of "get tough on crime" policies that increase the likelihood and length of incarceration, such as mandatory minimum sentences and three strikes laws, appear to be either gender blind or beneficial to women. In fact, these reforms contain significant consequences for women. A portion of the costs of prison construction and maintenance are paid for by cutting social services from which women benefit. In addition, since social service agencies are more likely to employ women whereas criminal justice agencies are more likely to employ men, growth of the criminal justice system at the expense of the social service system places women's employment opportunities in jeopardy. Finally, the incarceration of parents leaves behind children who may be traumatized and whose emotional and economic care is left to women.

The 1994 Federal Crime Control Act marks the twenty-sixth year of the "get tough on crime" movement initiated with the passage of the 1968 Crime Control and Safe Streets Act (Donziger, 1996, p. 14). The 1984 crime bill increased penalties for drug offenses, thereby engaging the War on Drugs and initiating the centerpiece of law-and-order legislative efforts to control crime—mandatory minimum and increased sentence lengths. "Three strikes and you're out" laws, in particular, captured the imagination of the public, the press, and politicians. State legislators in 37 jurisdictions proposed three strikes laws in 1993 and 1994, often as part of their own state crime bills. By the end of 1995, 24 state jurisdictions and the federal government had enacted these laws, and California voters had made three strikes part of their constitution (Clark, Austin, Henry 1997; Turner, Sundt, Applegate, & Cullen 1995). The new sentencing laws contained in the federal and state crime bills increased the dramatic expansion of the criminal justice system already under way, especially in corrections.

At the end of 1999, the United States recorded over 6.3 million adults in the correctional population, that is, on probation or parole, in jail or prison (U.S. Department of Justice, 2000). By midyear 2000, our nation incarcerated over 1.3 million of its citizens in federal and state prisons, more than a fourfold increase in just 20 years; another 621,000 people were in local jails. Over 163,000 of those imprisoned were women, and another 915,000 women were on probation or parole (Beck & Karberg, 2001; U.S. Department of Justice, 2000). In the 1980s, the rate of women's imprisonment increased nearly twice as much as that of men's, and 34 new women's prison units were opened (Immarigeon & Chesney-Lind 1992). African-Americans, who account for 13 percent of the population, are 45 percent of those incarcerated (Beck & Karberg 2001); 25 years ago they were 35 percent of those locked up (Maguire, Pastore, & Flanagan, 1993, p. 618). Black men and women are seven times more likely to be imprisoned than are white men and women (Beck & Karberg, 2001); the expansion of mandatory and increased sentences for drug law violations accounts for much of the increase (Mauer, 1990). The numbers of black women imprisoned for drugs has increased more than three times that of white women (Bush-Baskette, 1998). Young African-American men are particularly hard hit by the rhetoric and ensuing policies associated with the War on Drugs and three strikes laws (Tonry, 1995). Nearly all of those behind bars are poor.

The result of "lock 'em up" policies is that state and federal prisons currently operate at, respectively, up to 117 and 132 percent capacity (Beck & Karberg, 2001). Across the country, federal and state governments are engaged in an enormous and costly prison construction program. In fact, prisons represent "the only expanding public housing" in our country ("The prison boom," 1995, p. 223). One truism of prison and jail construction remains: "If you build it, they will come," so the costs associated with maintaining these facilities and incarcerating citizens, especially geriatrics as lifers age, will quickly dwarf the costs of construction.

The rationale behind the crime bills and the resulting expansion of the criminal justice system cannot be found in the crime rate. Despite political rhetoric at the national and state levels and the carnage presented daily and repeatedly in all forms of news and entertainment media, the violent crime rate remained relatively stable over the last 25 years, as measured by the National Crime Survey (Rennison, 2000).

Throughout it all, however, the consequences for women of the expansion of the criminal justice system remain largely unconsidered and invisible in public policy discussions. This chapter makes women visible in identification of the hidden costs to women of the expansion of the criminal justice system. In brief, I argue that one way or another, it is *women* who will pay the lion's share of criminal justice reform.

LOOKING FOR WOMEN

The feminist revolution in society and the academy is about making women visible, interrogating and deconstructing the manner in which women do appear, and calling for progressive action to benefit women. In criminal justice, feminist analysis has focused largely on women as offenders, victims, and workers (Price & Sokoloff, 1995), with the issues and debates centered around building theory, containing men's violence against women, and the equality/difference concern (Daly & Chesney-Lind, 1988). In this chapter, feminist perspectives in criminal justice are advanced in an analysis of the ways in which supposedly gender-blind crime control writ large affects *all* women.

Women are not readily visible in current criminal justice policy debates. The use of a baseball analogy—"three strikes and you're out"—to refer to the policy of mandatory life sentences for those persons convicted of three felonies illustrates the exclusion of women from the crime debates. Although it's called the national pastime, women don't identify with baseball much, have no significant presence in the sport, and reap few of its economic benefits (facts true of most professional sports). Yet it is in this sense that baseball represents an excellent analogy to the crime bills since women remain largely invisible from the debates surrounding criminal justice reforms. When women do appear, it is often as diversionary props which only barely suggest the realities of the lives of women and girls. Recent public debates in some states regarding increasing the availability of concealed weapons provide one illustration of this phenomenon.

During the 1995 legislative year, Virginia enacted a "right to carry" law requiring that judges grant permits for concealed weapons to nearly anyone who applies (Snider, 1995). Lobbyists for the National Rifle Association (NRA), along with sympathetic legislators, repeatedly invoked the image of the lone woman walking to her car at night who might need a gun to protect herself from the lurking stranger ready to pounce on her at any moment. This image of a woman served as a diversionary prop to obscure the protests of police and judges, who objected to the law because of safety concerns and the restriction on judicial discretion. The image also diverted attention from the vested interests of the NRA and state politicians who benefit from NRA contributions. This is simply one example of the way in which women are used in debates surrounding criminal justice policies. Women's lives and the realities of potential dangers are distorted, and in the process, women are left out of the debate and policies are enacted which will not only *not* benefit most women, but will, in fact, harm many women.

Nearly all of the political rhetoric about crime focuses on making our streets and neighborhoods safe again and protecting our homes from vicious, dangerous intruders. The focus on stranger crimes ignores the fact that it is the ones whom they know and love who represent the greatest danger to women's lives. Although women are much less likely than men to become victims of violent crimes in general, when women are assaulted, robbed, or raped, the best guess is to look to their loved ones. Of these violent crimes that women experience, the perpetrator is a husband, boyfriend, ex-husband, or ex-boyfriend 29 percent of the time; the comparable figure for men is 4 percent. Adding in other relatives increases the figure for women to 38 percent; for men, it is 7 percent. Expanding the definition to include other persons known reveals that 78 percent of the times that women are the victims of violent crimes, the assailant is known to the victim as either an acquaintance, a friend, relative, or an intimate partner; for men this figure is 51 percent. The offender is a stranger in less than one-fourth of the occasions when women are victims of violent crime by a lone offender (Bachman & Saltzman, 1995). In violent crimes occurring between spouses, lovers, ex-spouses, and ex-lovers, nearly 90 percent of the time the victim is a woman, and a woman is the victim in 70 percent of murders between intimate partners (Greenfeld et al., 1998).

Women need far less protection from strangers than from supposed protectors, especially intimate partners, relatives, and acquaintances. But the debates surrounding the crime bills and recent research demonstrate that women are also at risk from lawmakers and even some law enforcers (Kraska & Kappeler, 1995), most of whom are men, nearly all of them white, and with respect to politicians, legislators, and judges, members of the elite social classes. Lawmakers do not pay attention to the data but, like the public, fall victim to popular myths about crime, especially the myth that it is strangers who are most responsible for violent victimizations, particularly those committed against women. The result is that this myth and others like it are used to shape public debate and craft public policies that ignore women's lives and force women to bear the brunt of the financial and emotional costs for such policies.

The *New York Times* called women the "quiet winners" in the U.S. Crime Bill because of the inclusion of the Violence Against Women Act (Manegold, 1994). This portion of the national crime bill budgeted $1.6 billion for a national hot line for domestic violence victims and education programs aimed at police, prosecutors, and judges. It includes provisions that encourage mandatory arrests in domestic violence complaints, sex offender registration programs, and the release to victims of the results of rapists' HIV tests. It had also allowed women to file civil suits in cases of gender bias crimes, although this provision was overturned by the U.S. Supreme Court in *U.S. v. Morrison* (2000).

The Violence Against Women Act makes women's victimization visible and crafts public policies to assist women. The act represents an important step in public recognition of, and response to, male violence against women. But examination of the crime bills and their accompanying public debate reveals no sign of women other than as victims of domestic violence.

Feminist interrogation about how criminal justice policies affect women's lives calls us to make visible more of the ways in which the criminal justice policies affect women. Considering the unintended consequences and hidden costs of the crime bills and current public policies suggests that women are less likely to be quiet winners in criminal justice reforms as a whole than to be quiet and big-time losers.

So we return to the baseball analogy. "Three strikes and you're out" doesn't just refer to the policy of mandatory life sentences following a third felony conviction. It also refers to three ways in which women will be hurt by, and forced to pay for, criminal justice reform.

STRIKE 1: OFF THE ROLLS

The first strike against women comes in the decisions regarding which government services will be sacrificed to pay for expansion of the criminal justice system. The emphasis on budget balancing and deficit reduction at the national and state levels means that money targeted for tough-on-crime proposals comes at the expense of other government programs. RAND researchers concluded that implementation of California's three strikes law would require cuts in other government services totaling more than 40 percent over eight years, a move that would leave the state of California "spending more money keeping people in prison than putting people through college" (Greenwood et al., 1994, p. 34). The hardest-hit programs, however, are those in social services, especially those targeted to the poor, most of whom are women and children.[2]

Discussion about entitlements to the poor is to some limited extent a separate debate about the causes of poverty and the state's responsibility, or lack thereof, to help alleviate misfortune and suffering. But it is also a debate that remains close to the debates about crime and criminal justice. Like criminal offenders and prisoners, women on welfare and their families are demonized as lazy, unwilling to work for their keep, immoral, and criminal.

Both groups—composed disproportionately of poor and minority persons—are scapegoated as the source of numerous social ills while public attention draws away from inequitable economic and political conditions (Sidel, 1996). Blaming the victims of structural conditions justifies cutting welfare for the poor and funneling savings elsewhere.

Social services that benefit women are sacrificed to accommodate the expenditures associated with expansion of the criminal justice system. Chesney-Lind (1995) notes that New York continued to build beds in women's prisons at the same time that it had an insufficient number of beds for women and children in shelters. Adequate social services can reduce those life stressors associated with criminality; legal changes and battered women's shelters helped reduce the rates of women's homicide of male partners (Browne, 1990, as cited in Chesney-Lind, 1995).

The rhetoric surrounding cuts in social programs reveals class as well as race/ethnic and gender bias. The Welfare Reform Bill of 1996 imposed a limitation on the length of time that poor women may receive welfare assistance. After two years most women will be kicked off the rolls under the assumption that they will find work. Overall, few provisions are made for ensuring that either jobs or day care are available. We see social class operating here. Politicians, pundits, and religious leaders commonly argue that children should be cared for at home by the mother. Apparently, this is true, however, only for middle-class mothers and their children; poor mothers are admonished and will be legally required to leave their children so that they may return to work in order to save the tax coffers.

In 1994, at the same time that Virginia first instituted welfare reform, the state also passed its crime bill and accompanying criminal justice reforms. Plans called for the building of 27 new prisons at a cost of $1 billion over 10 years (later estimates placed these costs at $2 to 4 billion) as well as three strikes and other provisions for increasing the length of sentences for violent offenses and repeat offenses. The bill also called for the abolition of parole as of January 1, 1995, but the governor's new parole board had already, in effect, abolished parole, as it drastically reduced the number of paroles granted, at a cost of $77 million in just six months (LaFay 1994). Virginia prisons were so overcrowded that they could not accept new inmates housed in local jails awaiting transfer to the state system. This, in turn, led to such pressures in the jails that sheriffs sued the state to force it to assume its responsibility and take custody of its charges (Jackson, 1995). One way in which Virginia, like all states, deals with the problem of overcrowding is to ship inmates to other states and pay them the costs associated with incarceration (LaFay, 1995).

The expenditures associated with the expansion of the criminal justice system are being paid for in part by the savings to come from reforms that cut the social safety net of welfare. Further, an "iron triangle" of interests—politicians, job-starved communities, and businesses that build and service prisons—benefits from tough-on-crime rhetoric and policies (Thomas, 1994). Neither military, corporate, nor middle-class subsidy programs are targeted for payment in support of the prison industrial complex; rather, social service programs—with their disproportionately poor, minority, and female recipients—remain those responsible for picking up the check.

Women are the majority of direct beneficiaries of various social service programs, but we know that they steer nearly all of those benefits to their dependents, especially their children, but also the elderly and disabled adults in their lives. Simply put, women and those who depend on them will lose their economic and social safety net, in part so that politicians can appear to be tough on crime and imprison more men and women. It is poor women—who are also disproportionately minority, especially African-American women—and their families who in this way will pay a disproportionate share of the hidden costs associated with the war on crime and drugs. Strike one.

STRIKE 2: JOBS FOR WHOM?

Women are not only more likely than men to be the recipients of social services, women are also more likely to be employed in social service agencies as social workers, case workers, counselors, and support staff. The implications of this fact represent the second strike against women. Seventy-one percent of social workers are women, and women comprise an even larger portion of front-line case workers and clerical personnel (U.S. Bureau of the Census 2000, p. 416). Thus, as social services are cut back, women workers will be affected disproportionately.

Critics will respond that the expansion of the criminal justice system means increased employment opportunities for women. After all, 26 percent of law enforcement employees in the United States are women (Pastore & Maguire 2000, Table 1.56). Even greater opportunities appear to exist in corrections, where 29 percent of employees in adult corrections are women (Maguire & Pastore, 1999, p. 81). However, most women employed in law enforcement and corrections agencies work in traditional pink-collar ghettos as low-wage clerical or support staff. Practically speaking, the *only* way to advance to upper levels of administration in either policing or corrections is through line employment as a police or correctional officer. And although 71 percent of law enforcement employees are police officers, only 11 percent of police officers are women (Pastore & Maguire 2000, Table 1.56), and women make up just 19 percent of correctional guards (Maguire & Pastore, 1999, p. 81).

There remains a long-standing bias against women in policing and corrections. Even after more than 20 years of proven effectiveness as officers on the streets and in the prisons, male co-workers and supervisors persist in their bias against women. They use harassment and masculine work cultures that marginalize women to resist efforts to increase the representation of women on these forces (Martin & Jurik, 1996; Morash & Haarr, 1995).

The attacks on affirmative action in the current political climate further endanger women's employment possibilities in the criminal justice system (Martin, 1995). In addition, the definition and nature of work in criminal justice is being restructured to emphasize punitiveness and dangerousness. In Virginia, probation and parole counselors were renamed officers and may now carry weapons (§ 53.1-145 of the Code of Virginia). Virginia's Director of Corrections since 1994 insists that probation and parole clients as well as inmates be called "convicts" or "felons." These moves emphasize punishment and the untrustworthiness of offenders; they stand in sharp contrast to the need to develop positive relationships in order to encourage social adjustment. Such practices also emphasize masculinity as a requirement for the job, thereby creating a climate that further discourages women in the work.

Three strikes and no-parole policies have at least three implications for police and correctional officers. For the police, three strikes may influence people likely to be caught in the web of these laws to take more desperate measures than ever to evade arrest. For correctional guards, abolishing parole first means overcrowding in the prisons; it also means the loss of incentives and rewards for good behavior and the loss of faith in the future. In turn, these conditions produce an increase in the likelihood of prison violence and uprisings.

Thus real increases in fear and the loss of hope among offenders become coupled with politically inspired attitudes about the dangerousness of offenders and the punitive goals of the work. Combined with attacks on affirmative action, bias against women in traditionally male occupations, and the resulting stress on women employees, these factors may be surprisingly effective in bringing about actual *decreases* in women's employment in precisely those positions in policing and corrections that lead to advancement and higher pay.

The crime bills represent a government jobs program—criminal justice is, in fact, "the only growing public-sector employment" ("The prison boom," 1995, p. 223), but the new jobs created come at the cost of other public-sector jobs, such as those in social services, which are more likely to be held by women. And the new jobs created by the expansion of the criminal justice system are overwhelmingly jobs for men. Strike two.

STRIKE 3: FAMILY VALUES?

Men and women who commit crimes for which they are convicted and sentenced to prison have not lived their lives solely in criminal gangs; they do not structure their entire days around illegal activity; they are not *only* criminals. They are also sons and daughters, fathers and mothers. In short, they are responsible for caring for others who depend on them, and most of them do their best to meet these responsibilities because they do, in fact, love their families.

Sixty-five percent of women and 55 percent of men in state prisons in 1997 had children under the age of 18; most of these women (64 percent) and many men (44 percent) lived with their children before entering prison (Mumola, 2000). Imprisoned adults cannot contribute to their families' financial or psychological well-being. In a few cases children are committed to foster homes or institutions. But most of the time another family member takes over care of those children and any elderly or disabled adults left behind—and that family member is usually a woman. This fact represents the third strike against women.

Because most of those imprisoned are men, it is the women in their lives—wives, girlfriends, and mothers—who are left with the responsibility for providing for the economic and emotional needs of the children and any dependent adults, a task these women must accomplish on their own. And when women are imprisoned, it is generally their mothers who take over the care of the children.

As we imprison increasing numbers of men and women, we saddle more women with sole responsibility for care of the next generation. The problem is exacerbated when the state, due to overcrowding, moves prisoners out of its system and to other states, thereby leaving the women and children bereft of even emotional support from incarcerated parents.

Today in the United States, "there are at least 1.5 million children of prisoners and at least 3.5 million children of offenders on probation or parole" (Johnston, 1995a, p. 311). The women who care for these children, as well as the children themselves, must be recognized as paying some of the hidden costs of punitive criminal justice policies. Parental arrest and incarceration endures as a traumatic event for all involved. It can lead to inadequate child care, due to persistent and deepening poverty. In addition, children may suffer from problems with which the women who care for them must cope: developmental delay, behavioral and emotional difficulties, feelings of shame and experiences of stigmatization, distrust and hatred of police and the criminal justice system, and subsequent juvenile delinquency (Carlson & Cervera, 1992; Fishman, 1990; Johnston 1995b). In effect, children suffer from post traumatic stress disorder when their parents are imprisoned (Kampfner, 1995). Effective programs to address the needs of children of incarcerated parents and their caregivers remain few in number and endangered.

As politicians get tough on crime, it is women and children who do the time, alone. Remembering the first two strikes against women discussed earlier, it emerges as strikingly clear that women will not be able to look to the federal or state government for either public assistance or public employment. Strike three. It's *women* who are out.

FINAL THOUGHTS: AN EVERYWOMAN'S ISSUE

It remains far too easy to be lulled into complacency when it comes to women and criminal justice. After all, women represent a very small number of offenders. And despite male violence against women, most victims of crime are men. Yet the social construction of crime and criminals and the political nature of their control are neither gender blind nor gender neutral. We are finally and fully confronted by the harsh reality that criminal justice *is* about women, *all* women. Although it occasionally operates as an important resource for women, the criminal justice system most frequently represents a form of oppression in women's lives. It attacks most harshly those women with the least power to resist it. As Jean Landis and I wrote a decade ago:

> it is time to recognize that in real life . . . offenders do not exist as exclusive objects. They are connected in relationships with other people, a major portion of whom are women—mothers, wives, lovers, sisters and daughters. Any woman who fights to keep her wits, and her roof, about her as she helplessly experiences a loved one being swept away by the currents of criminal justice "knows" the true brutality of the system and the extensiveness of its destruction. If she is a racial/ethnic minority person, which she is likely to be, and/or if she is poor, which she surely is, she intuitively knows the nature of the interaction between criminal justice practices and the racist and/or classist [as well as sexist] structure of her society, as well as its impact on her life, her family, and her community. (Danner & Landis, 1990, pp. 111–112).

She also knows that precious little assistance exists for her, and those who depend on her, in the form of either welfare or employment from the larger community as represented by the state. In addition, it is every woman, no matter who she is, who will pay for the dramatic expansion of the criminal justice system. Growing the criminal justice system in an era of tax cuts and budget reductions requires shrinking other government services, such as education, health care, and roads, that benefit all members of the public. Clearly, criminal justice *is* a women's issue.

The get tough, lock 'em up, and three strikes policies will not reduce crime or women's pain associated with crime. They will only impoverish communities as they enrich politicians and those corporations associated with this new prison industrial complex. Although women have been largely left out of the debate, it is women who are the quiet losers—the big-time losers—in the crime bills. Criminal justice reforms such as these are politically motivated, unnecessary, ineffective, and far, far too costly. And finally, and most important, it is women who receive the least from the wars on crime and drugs, and it is women who bear most of their hidden burdens.

ACKNOWLEDGMENTS

The paper was originally prepared as the 1995 Women's Studies Junior Faculty Lecture, Old Dominion University; I thank Anita Clair Fellman, Director of Women's Studies, for that invitation. Thanks to Marie L. VanNostrand (formerly of the Virginia Department of Criminal Justice Services) and Lucien X. Lombardo (Old Dominion University), who were most gracious in providing me with materials. The members of Our Writing Group and COOL provided much encouragement and entertainment. An earlier version was presented at the 1995 American Society of Criminology meetings, Boston, Massachusetts.

N O T E S

1. This chapter is an updated adaptation from the author's chapter in *Crime Control and Women: Feminist Implications of Criminal Justice Policy*, edited by Susan L. Miller (Newbury Park, CA: Sage Publications, 1998).
2. Entitlements to the poor include Temporary Assistance to Needy Families (TANF), formerly known as Aid to Families with Dependent Children (AFDC); the Women, Infants and Children (WIC) nutritional program; food stamps; school breakfast and lunch programs; Medicaid; public housing and emergency grants; and social security for disabled and dependent persons, as well as other programs. Each of these programs is under attack and will almost certainly be cut back, just as has welfare.

R E F E R E N C E S

Bachman, R., & Saltzman, L. E. (1995). *Violence against women: Estimates from the redesigned survey.* Washington, DC: U.S. Department of Justice.

Beck, A. J., & Karberg, J. C. (2001). *Prison and jail inmates at midyear 2000.* Washington, DC: U.S. Department of Justice.

Browne, A. (1990, December 11). Assaults between intimate partners in the United States. Testimony before the United States Senate, Committee on the Judiciary, Washington, DC.

Bush-Baskette, S. R. (1998). The war on drugs as a war against Black women. In S. L. Miller (Ed.), *Crime control and women: Feminist implications of criminal justice policy* (pp. 113–129). Thousand Oaks, CA: Sage Publications.

Carlson, B. E., & Cervera, N. (1992). *Inmates and their wives: Incarceration and familiy life.* Westport, CT: Greenwood Press.

Chesney-Lind, M. (1995). Rethinking women's imprisonment: A critical examination of trends in female incarceration. In B. R. Price & N. J. Sokoloff (Eds.), *The criminal justice system and women: Offenders, victims, and workers* (2nd ed., pp. 105–117). New York: McGraw-Hill.

Clark, J., Austin, J., & Henry, D. A. (1997). *"Three strikes and you're out": A review of state legislation.* Washington, DC: U.S. Department of Justice.

Daly, K., & Chesney-Lind, M. (1988). Feminism and criminology. *Justice Quarterly, 5,* 497–538.

Danner, M. & Landis, J. (1990). Carpe diem (seize the day!): An opportunity for feminist connections. In B. D. MacLean & D. Milovanvovic (Eds.), *Racism, empiricism and criminal justice* (pp. 109–112). Vancouver, British Columbia, Canada: Collective Press.

Donziger, S. A. (Ed.) (1996). *The real war on crime: The report of the national criminal justice commission.* New York: HarperPerennial.

Fishman, L. T. (1990). *Women at the wall: A study of prisoners' wives doing time on the outside.* New York: State University of New York Press.

GREENFELD, L. A., RAND, M. R., CRAVEN, D., KLAUS, P. A., PERKINS, C. A., RINGEL, C., WARCHOL, G., MASTON, C., & FOX, J. A. (1998). *Violence by intimates: Analysis of data on crimes by current or former spouses, boyfriends, and girlfriends.* Washington, DC: U.S. Department of Justice.

GREENWOOD, P. W., FYDELL, C. P., ABRAHAMSE, A. F., CAULKINS, J. P., CHIESA, J., MODEL, K. E., & KLEIN, S. P. (1994). *Three strikes and you're out: Estimated benefits and costs of California's new mandatory-sentencing law.* Santa Monica, CA: RAND Corporation.

IMMARIGEON, R., & CHESNEY,-LIND, M. (1992). *Women's prisons: Overcrowded and overused.* San Francisco: National Council on Crime and Delinquency.

JACKSON, J. (1995, January 11). Sheriffs suing state to relieve overcrowding in city jails. *Virginian-Pilot*, pp. A1, A6.

JOHNSTON, D. (1995a). Conclusion. In K. Gabel & D. Johnston (Eds.), *Children of incarcerated parents* (pp. 311–314). New York: Lexington Books.

JOHNSTON, D. (1995b). Effects of parental incarceration. In K. Gabel & D. Johnston (Eds.), *Children of incarcerated parents* (pp. 59–88). New York: Lexington Books.

KAMPFNER, C. J. (1995). Post-traumatic stress reactions in children of imprisoned mothers. In K. Gabel & D. Johnston (Eds.), *Children of incarcerated parents* (pp. 89–100). New York: Lexington Books.

KRASKA, P. B., & KAPPELER, V. E. (1995). To serve and pursue: Exploring police sexual violence against women. *Justice Quarterly, 12*, 85–111.

LaFAY, L. (1994, December 9). New, low parole rate has cost Va. $77 million." *Virginian-Pilot*, pp. A1, A24.

LaFAY, L. (1995, February 17). State sends 150 inmates to Texas. *Virginian-Pilot*, pp. A1, A9.

MAGUIRE, K., & PASTORE, A. L. (EDS.). (1999). *Sourcebook of criminal justice statistics, 1998.* Washington, DC: U.S. Department of Justice.

MAGUIRE, K., PASTORE, A. L., & FLANAGAN, T. J. (EDS.). (1993). *Sourcebook of criminal justice statistics, 1992.* Washington, DC: U.S. Department of Justice.

MANEGOLD, C. S. S. (1994, August 25). Quiet winners in house fight on crime: Women. *New York Times*, p. A19.

MARTIN, S. E. (1995). The effectiveness of affirmative action: The case of women in policing. *Justice Quarterly, 8*, 489–504.

MARTIN, S. E., & JURIK, N. D. (1996). *Doing justice, doing gender: Women in law and criminal justice occupations.* Thousand Oaks, CA: Sage Publications.

Mauer, M. (1990). *Young black men and the criminal justice system: A growing national problem.* Washington, DC: The Sentencing Project.

MORASH, M., & HAARR, R. N. (1995). Gender, workplace problems, and stress in policing. *Justice Quarterly, 12*, 113–140.

MUMOLA, C. J. (2000). *Incarcerated parents and their children.* Washington, DC: U.S. Department of Justice.

PASTORE, A. L., & MAGUIRE, K. (EDS.). (2000). *Sourcebook of criminal justice statistics.* Accessed May 4, 2001.
http://www.albany.edu/sourcebook

PRICE, B. R., & SOKOLOFF, N. J. (1995). *The criminal justice system and women: Offenders, victims, and workers* (2nd ed.). New York: McGraw-Hill.

RENNISON, C. M. (2000). *Criminal victimization, 1999.* Washington, DC: U.S. Department of Justice.

SIDEL, R. (1996). *Keeping women and children last: America's war on the poor.* New York: Penguin Books.

SNIDER, J. R. (1995, December 13). Have gun, will travel. *Virginian-Pilot*.

The prison boom. (1995, February 20). *The Nation*, pp. 223–224.

THOMAS, P. (1994, May 12). Making crime pay. *Wall Street Journal*, pp. A1, A6.

TONRY, M. H. (1995). *Malign neglect: Race, crime, and punishment in America.* New York: Oxford University Press.

TURNER, M.G., SUNDT, J. L., APPLEGATE, B. K., & CULLEN, F. T. (1995). "Three strikes and you're out" legislation: A national assessment. *Federal Probation, 59*, 16–35.

U.S. BUREAU OF THE CENSUS. (2000). *Statistical abstract of the United States 2000*. Washington, DC: U.S. Government Printing Office.

U.S. DEPARTMENT OF JUSTICE. (2000, July 23). U.S. correctional population reaches 6.3 million men and women: Represents 3.1 percent of the adult U.S. population. Press release.

CASE

U.S. v. *Morrison*. 529 U.S. 598 (2000).

14

Disparate Treatment in Correctional Facilities

Looking Back

Roslyn Muraskin

As of the year 2000, there were known to be an annual average of about 2.1 million violent female offenders. Three out of four violent female offenders commit simple assault. An estimated 28 percent of violent female offenders are juveniles. An estimated 4 in 10 women who commit violent crimes are perceived as being under the influence of alcohol and/or drugs at the time the crime was committed. In 1998 alone there were an estimated 3.2 million arrests of women. And since 1990 the number of female defendants convicted of felonies in State courts has grown at more than twice the rate of increase in male defendants (U.S. Department of Justice, 2000).

The providing of services and programs is all part of good correctional practice. It ensures that those inmates returned to society can be be reintegrated into society. With the number of women incarcerated there exists the need for proper treatment within the correctional facilities. In this chapter we review the problems and cases of the past, demonstrating that services legally mandated have not been fully delivered.

CURRENT HISTORY: OVERVIEW

In the latter part of the twentieth century, an estimated 950,000 women were under the care, custody, and control of correctional agencies. This is about one woman involved with the criminal justice system for every 109 adult women within the population of the United States. In examining the racial and ethnic composition of the general population, we find that "non-Hispanic black females outnumber non-Hispanic black males by nearly 1.9 million, accounting for more than a quarter of the total difference in the number of males and females in the general population" (Bureau of Justice Statistics, 2000). The average age of females in the general population is about 2½ years higher than that of males. See Table 1 for a comparison of violent crimes committed by females and males.

TABLE 1   Comparison of Violent Crimes by Gender

Offense	Average Annual Number of Offenders Reported by Victims, 1993–1997		Women as a Percent of Violent Offenders
	Female	Male	
All	2,135,000	13,098,000	14
Sexual assault	10,000	442,000	2
Robbery	157,000	2,051,000	7
Aggravated assault	435,000	3,419,000	11
Simple assault	1,533,000	7,187,000	18

About 1 out of 7 violent offenders described by victims was a female. Women accounted for 1 in 50 offenders committing a violent sex offense, including rape and sexual assault; 1 in 14 robberies; 1 in 9 offenders committing aggravated assault; and more than 1 in 6 offenders described as having committed a simple assault. Black and white offenders accounted for nearly equal proportions of women committing robbery and aggravated assault; however, simple assault offenders were more likely to be described as white (see Table 2).

With regard to women who murder: "Since 1993 both male and female rates of committing murder have declined. Rates of committing murder in 1998 were the lowest since statistics were first collected in 1976. The estimated rate for murder offending by women in 1998 was 1.3 per 100,000, about 1 murderer for every 77,000 women. The male rate of murder offending in 1998 was 11.5 per 100,000, about 1 murderer for every 8,700 males" (Bureau of Justice Statistics, 2000, p. 10).

"In 1998 there were an estimated 3.2 million arrests of women, accounting for about a fifth of all arrests by law enforcement agencies. Women were about 17% of those arrested for Part I violent crimes (murder, rape, robbery, and aggravated assault) and 29% of those arrested for Part I property crimes (burglary, larceny, and motor-vehicle theft). Women accounted for about 16% of all felons convicted in State Courts in 1996. Women were 8% of convicted violent felons, 23% of property felons, and 17% of drug felons. Women defendants accounted for 41% of all felons convicted of forgery, fraud, and embezzlement" (Bureau of Justice Statistics, 2000, p. 11).

TABLE 2   Characteristics of Violent Female Offenders

Offense	Percent by Race of Female Offenders		
	White	Black	Other
Violent offenses	55	35	11
Robbery	43	43	14
Aggravated assault	45	46	10
Simple assault	58	31	10

According to Julie Samuels, acting director for the National Institute of Justice, there exists the common observation that the criminal behavior of women is not to be deemed an important problem. For many years it has been believed that if women were to commit any crimes, they would commit only minor crimes and therefore have always constituted a small fraction of the correctional population. But these facts have veiled a trend that has attracted everyone's attention. It is well known that although crime rates are down, there is a growing population within correctional facilities: tougher and longer sentences. For women, however, the number of female inmates is growing at a rate higher that than of men. Among academics there has been a call to redefine justice.

According to Samuels (2000), "Whether justice should promote unalloyed equality, be blind to the circumstances in which crime is committed, and consider only the gravity of offense and prior record, is still a matter of debate. In the current sentencing environment, the view of those who favor equity above all other considerations has won the day. There is another perspective, the belief that sanctions ought to be tailored to the specific characteristics and circumstances of individual offenders" (U.S. Department of Justice, p. 2).

LOOKING BACK INTO HISTORY

In the United States, no constitutional obligation exists for all persons to be treated alike. The government frequently does, in fact, treat disparate groups differently. However, this does not excuse invidious discrimination among potential recipients (Gobert & Cohen, 1981, pp. 294–295). What is required is that where unequal treatment exists, the inequalities must be rational and related to a legitimate interest of the state (Pollack & Smith, 1978, p. 206). Laws have created categories in which some people may be treated unequally. These categories have always included women incarcerated in correctional facilities. The question that still arises is "whether the inequalities by the law are justifiable—in legal terms whether the person upon whom the law's burden falls has been denied equal protection of the law" (pp. 206–207).

Since the decision in *Holt* v. *Sarver* (1970), in which the court declared an entire prison to be in violation of the Eighth Amendment and imposed detailed remedial plans, the judiciary has taken an active role in the administration of correctional facilities. Many of the landmark cases challenged the inequity of treatment between male and female prisoners.

Ostensibly, the needs of male and female prisoners would appear to be the same. They are not. Although some inmate interests are similar, others are separate and distinct. In many institutions, criteria developed for men were applied automatically to women, with no consideration given for gender differences. Research has shown that female offenders have always experienced more medical and health problems than do male inmates. Classification officials have noted that female offenders have needed help in parenting skills, child welfare, pregnancy and prenatal care, home stability, as well as an understanding of the circumstances of their crime. But typically, assignments to programs and treatment resources within correctional facilities have always been based on what is available rather than on what should be available.

A review of the literature of the cases and issues that have dealt with disparate treatment has revealed that each takes note of the fact that women historically have represented a small minority in both prisons and jails. Yet the effects of incarceration have been in many but not all respects similar for men and women. Each has suffered the trauma of being separated from family and friends. When either a man or a woman becomes imprisoned, he or she experiences a loss of identity as well as a devaluation of his or her status. Regardless of the inmate's gender, prison life has coerced conformity to an environment alien to the individual, where one's every movement is dictated each and every minute (Muraskin, 1989).

Most challenges to prison conditions have neglected the special needs of female prisoners, especially the jails, where both males and females are located together. Traditionally, correctional facilities for women have not received funding comparable to that of correctional facilities for men. Education and vocational-training programs for women have been historically and seriously underfunded. "Benign neglect [has] . . . created a situation of unequal treatment in many states" (Hunter, 1984, p. 133). Correctional administrators have insisted that "the small number of female offenders [has] made it too expensive to fund such programs." The courts, however, have ruled "that cost is not an acceptable defense for denying equal treatment" (pp. 133–134). Historically, females have been subject to policies designed for the male offender. Just as "women have deferred to males in the economic, social, political spheres of life, [i]n the legal realm, more specifically in the imprisonment of the female, women have been forced into the status of being less than equal" (Sargent, 1984, p. 83).

REVIEW OF CASES: WOMEN AND EQUALITY/PARITY

When inmates similarly situated find themselves being treated differently, there may exist a violation of equal protection. A review of the cases discussed below demonstrates what established the discrimination against women who are incarcerated.

Constitutionally, no obligation exists for the government to provide any benefits beyond basic requirements. However, this principle should not be an excuse for invidious discrimination among potential recipients (Gobert & Cohen, 1981, pp. 294–295). Case law has held that benefits afforded some cannot be denied solely on race or gender. In any equal protection challenge, the central question that has been raised is the "degree of state interest which can justify disparate treatment among offenders" (*Reed* v. *Reed*, 1971). As established, the "classification must be reasonable, not arbitrary and must bear a fair and substantial relation to the object of the legislation or practice" (ibid.). Courts, for example, have found sex classifications to be irrational because they appear to be enacted solely for the convenience of correctional administrators (see *Craig* v. *Boren*, 1976[1]; *Weinberger* v. *Wisenfeld*,1975[2]; *Eslinger* v. *Thomas*, 1973[3]. Existing differences in conditions, rules, and treatment among inmates have proven fertile ground for equal protection challenges. Administrative convenience is not an acceptable justification for disparity of treatment (*Cooper* v. *Morin*, 1979, 1980), nor is lack of funds an acceptable justification for disparate treatment (*State ex rel Olson* v. *Maxwell*, 1977).

Legal uprisings against intolerable conditions in correctional facilities and prisoners' rights litigation were initiated by male attorneys and male prisoners. In the early stages of this litigation, female inmates did not turn to the courts, nor did officials at female institutions fear lawsuits, condemnation by the public, or inmate riots. With so few women incarcerated, there was little the women felt they could do. This situation has changed. Female prisoners sued and demanded parity with male prisoners. The Fourteenth Amendment has been the source for issues of violation of privacy, and the Eighth Amendment is used for cases involving cruel and unusual punishment.

Differential sentencing of similarly situated men and women convicted of identical offenses has been found to violate the equal protection clause. A review of cases dealing generally with sentencing in correctional institutions includes prior rulings in the case of *United States ex rel Robinson* v. *York* (1968), which held that it was a violation of the equal protection clause for women who were sentenced to indeterminate terms under a Connecticut statute to serve longer maximum sentences than those of men serving indeterminate terms for the same offenses. In *Liberti* v. *York* (1968), the U.S. Supreme Court held that the female plaintiff's indeterminate sentences of up to three years violated the equal protection clause because the maximum term for men convicted of the same crime was one year. In *Commonwealth* v. *Stauffer* (1969), a Pennsylvania court held the practice of sentencing women to state prison on charges for which men were held in county jail to be a violation of a woman's right to equal protection.

In *Williams* v. *Levi* (1976), dealing with disparate treatment in the issue of parole, male prisoners in the District of Columbia were placed under the authority of the D.C. Board of Parole, whereas women prisoners were placed under the authority of the U.S. Board of Parole's stricter parole standards of violence. In *Dawson* v. *Carberry* (1973), it was held that there must be substantial equivalence in male and female prisoners' opportunities to participate in work-furlough programs.

In *Barefield* v. *Leach* (1974), women at the Women's Division of the Penitentiary of New Mexico claimed that conditions there violated their rights to an uncensored press, to have their persons free from unreasonable searches, to be free from cruel and unusual punishment, and to be allowed due process and equal protection of the law regarding disciplinary procedures and rehabilitative opportunities, respectively. The court held that "[w]hat the equal protection clause requires in a prison setting is parity of treatment as contrasted with identity of treatment, between male and female inmates with respect to the conditions of their confinement and access to rehabilitative opportunities." *Barefield* is especially important, as it was the first case to enunciate the standard against which disparity of treatment of men and women in prison was to be measured.

Still further, in *McMurray* v. *Phelps* (1982), there was a challenge to conditions for both men and women at the Quachita County jail, where the jail ordered an end to the disparate treatment of female detainees. And in *Mary Beth G.* v. *City of Chicago* (1983), a strip-search policy under which female arrestees underwent a full strip search without reason to believe that a weapon or contraband was present was ruled to be a violation of the equal protection clauses as well as the Fourteenth Amendment.

In *Bounds* v. *Smith* (1977), the court held that access to the courts by prisoners was a fundamental constitutional right. The court noted that there existed an affirmative obligation on the part of state officials to ensure court access by providing adequate law libraries or some alternative involving a legal-assistance program. It was noted further in the court's decision that females had less access to library facilities than did male inmates. This situation was ordered remedied. In *Cody* v. *Hillard* (1986), the court held that inmates at the state women's correctional facility, which had neither a law library nor law-trained assistants, were denied their constitutional right of meaningful access to the courts.

In a case dealing with the transfer of female inmates out of state because of a lack of facilities (*State ex rel Olson* v. *Maxwell*, 1977), female inmates filed a petition for a supervisory writ challenging the North Dakota practice of routinely transferring them to other states to be incarcerated, alleging a denial of equal protection and due process. It was held that North Dakota must not imprison women prisoners outside the state unless and until a due process waiver hearing was held or waived and the state admitted that it could not provide women prisoners with facilities equal to those of male prisoners.

"From a policy perspective, discriminatory distribution of prison privileges . . . will appear counter-rehabilitative, fueling inmate administration animosity and generating inmate peer jealousies" (Gobert & Cohen, 1981, p. 295). In *Canterino* v. *Wilson* (1982, 1983), it was indicated that "restrictions imposed solely because of gender with the objective of controlling lives of women inmates in a way deemed unnecessary for male prisoners" would not be tolerated. The Court concluded that "males and females must be treated equally unless there is a substantial reason which requires a distinction be made" (1982). Case law has established that discriminatory selection for work release when based on race, religion, gender, or even mental impairment is not an acceptable practice. Any arbitrary or capricious selection for participation in work programs has been prohibited by the courts.

Due to the small numbers of women in men's correctional facilities, services and treatment programs have appeared to have been reduced. Such reduced services included medical services. Generally, there has always been a wider range of medical services provided for male inmates than female inmates. Thus in both *Todaro* v. *Ward* (1977) and *Estelle* v. *Gamble* (1976), the issues were medical. In the former case, the medical system in the Bedford Hills Correctional Facility was found to be unconstitutionally defective, while in the latter, there was found to be deliberate indifference to the medical needs of the females. This was a violation of the Eighth Amendment.

In *Bukhari* v. *Huto* (1980), it was held that no justification existed for disparate treatment based on the fact that women's prisons serviced a smaller population and the cost would be greater to provide programs equivalent to the men's institutions. Cost could not be claimed as an excuse for paucity of services.

The landmark case on women's prison issues was *Glover* v. *Johnson* (1979). This was a comprehensive case challenging a dispute system of educational, vocational, work, and minimum security programs in the Michigan prison systems based on due process and equal protection. The Court ruled that female prisoners must be provided program opportunities on a parity with male prisoners. The case resulted in an order requiring the state to provide postsecondary education, counseling, vocational programs, and a legal education program (in a companion case *Cornish* v. *Johnson* 1979) as well as other relief. "Institutional size is frankly not a justification but an excuse for the kind of treatment afforded women prisoners" (*Glover*, 1979).

In a facility in Nassau County, New York, in the case of *Thompson et al.* v. *Varelas* (1985), the plaintiffs asked for

> [d]eclaratory and injunctive relief regarding the discriminatory, oppressive, degrading and dangerous conditions of . . . their confinement within the Nassau County Correctional Center. . . . [A]lleged in their action was the existence of inadequate health care, lack of private attorney visiting facilities, inadequate and unequal access to employment, recreation and training; unequal access to library facilities and newspapers, and excessive confinement; unsanitary food preparation and service; and, inadequate and unequal access to religious services. . . .

They claimed that lack of these facilities and services violated their rights as guaranteed by the First, Fifth, Sixth, Eighth, Ninth, and Fourteenth Amendments to the Constitution of the United States, but it was not until September 1985 that a consent was entered in the *Thompson* case. *Thompson* makes a further argument for the needs of a checklist of standards against which to assess what constitutes disparate treatment in the correctional facilities.

Prior to these cases the female prisoner was the "forgotten offender." Testimony by a teacher in the Glover case indicated that whereas men were allowed to take shop courses, women were taught at a junior high level because the motto of those in charge was "keep it simple, these are only women."

Although litigation has provided the opportunity for inmates to have a role in altering their conditions of confinement, a judicial opinion does not necessarily bring about change, then or now. Viewed from a nonlegal perspective, litigation is simply a catalyst for change rather than an automatic mechanism for ending wrongs found. All the cases held that invidious discrimination cannot exist.

REVIEW OF THE LITERATURE

The first penal institution for women opened in Indiana in 1873. By the beginning of the twentieth century, women's correctional facilities had opened in Framingham, Massachusetts, in Bedford Hills, New York, and in Clinton, New Jersey. The Federal Institution for Women in Alderson, West Virginia, opened in 1927, and the House of Detention for Women (the first separate jail for women) opened in New York City in 1931. These institutions all shared one thing in common, "traditional values, theories and practices concerning a woman's role and place in society. . . . The staffs, architectural design and programs reflected the culturally valued norms for women's behavior" (Feinman, 1986, p. 38).

Historically, disparate treatment of male and female inmates started when state penitentiaries first opened. "Female prisoners . . . were confined together in a single attic room above the institution's kitchen. [They] were supervised by the head of the kitchen below. Food was sent up to them once a day, and once a day the slop was removed. No provision was made for privacy or exercise and although the women were assigned some sewing work, for the most part they were left to their own devices in the 'tainted and sickly atmosphere'" (Rafter, 1983, p. 135). Female convicts were morally degraded to a greater extent than male convicts. The reformatories built for female prisoners "established and legitimated a tradition of deliberately providing for female prisoners treatment very different from that of males" (p. 148).

"From Lombroso to the present, criminological thought has been wrought with the sexism inherent in assuming that there exist only two distinct classes of women—those on pedestals and those in the gutter" (Lown & Snow, 1980, p. 195). "The differential law enforcement handling seems to be built into our basic attitudes toward woman. The operation of such attention can be called euphemistically the chivalry factor" (Reckless, 1967).

The chivalry factor meant that women should be treated more leniently than men. The nature of treatment and programs for female inmates appears to indicate the assumption of such a theory. Theories have always abounded concerning the causes of criminality by female offenders. The chivalry factor, once accepted, does not appear to be held in favor today. Once a woman enters the correctional facility, she has not necessarily benefited from the benevolence of the criminal justice system. Theories of female crime have always emphasized the natural differences between men and women but have failed to explain why women commit the crimes they do. It is clear that female prisoners have historically been treated differently and sometimes worse than male prisoners. Often, as an alternative to differential treatment, the model followed has been that of the male prisons, which has frequently ignored the obvious physical differences of female inmates. An almost total lack of enforcement of standards exist for the confinement of women.

In addition to the historically poor quality and minimal services that have been made available to female inmates, they have continued to suffer the same miserable conditions of incarceration as those of male inmates. Women have suffered even more in the jails, because of the failure to classify them according to the seriousness of their crime. Women have always lived in crowded facilities, often finding themselves under squalid conditions, lacking privacy, faced with insensitive visiting rules, callous treatment, and the threat of, or actual, sexual abuse. Stress on the female inmate also continues to stem from being separated from her family and children.

Much of the neglect in assessing disparate treatment has been attributed by writers believing that the experiences in prison for both men and women are the same and are not areas calling for special investigation. As Rafter indicated in 1983, it was not until the 1970s that literature dealing with women's prisons began to taken notice of their specialized problems (p. 130). Feinman (1982) indicated that for the most part, programs in correctional facilities for women continued to be based on the belief that "the only acceptable role for women is that of wife/mother" (p. 12). The female offender continues to be described as being poor, African-American, Hispanic, or other; undereducated; and lacking in both skills and self-confidence. Whereas nearly two-thirds of the women under probation supervision are white, nearly two-thirds of those confined in local jails and state and federal prisons are minority: black, Hispanic, and other races. The majority of the women who are incarcerated have graduated from high school. About 7 in 10 women who are in the correctional facilities have minor children. These women are reported to have an average of 2.11 children. These estimates convert into more than 1.3 million children who are the offspring of women incarcerated. Female prisoners demonstrate more difficult economic circumstances than do their male counterparts: About 4 in 10 women in state prison reported that they were employed full time prior to being arrested, while nearly 6 in 10 males had been working full time. The up-to-date figures show that about 44 percent of women who are incarcerated had been physically or sexually assaulted. About half of the women have used alcohol or drugs at the time they were caught. "About 6 in 10 women in State prisons described themselves as using drugs in the month before the offense, 5 in 10 described themselves as a daily user of drugs, and 4 in 10 were under the influence of drugs at the time of the offense" (Bureau of Justice Statistics, 2000, p. 19). In the year 1998, the highest per capita rate of women who were confined was in Oklahoma (1222), and the lowest was in Maine and Vermont (9 in each) (p. 21). There are currently about 138,000 women confined in correctional facilities, which represents a "tripling of the number of incarcerated women between the years 1985 and 1997" (latest available figures) (p. 8).

Indications are that in the twenty-first century, more women will be involved in committing crimes than ever before. Yet when women are released back into the community, studies continue to show that men still represent a disproportionate majorty in community programs. The way that community programs continue to be structured continues to provide evidence of the lack of sensitivity and the differential treatment afforded women.

Historically, the women's correctional system was not to replicate that of the men's but rather, was to differ along a "number of key dimensions, including its historical development, administrative structures, some of its disciplinary techniques and the experience of inmates" (Rafter, 1983, p. 132). Today's women's facilities have changed little from those at the beginning of the twentieth century. Today, women's prisons appear to be smaller and fewer in number (Pollock-Byrne, 1990, p. 97). Characteristically women's prisons are located farther from friends and families; their numbers being relatively small compared to that of men prisoners; with the "relatively small number of women in prison and jail [being] used to 'justify' *low levels of specialization* in treatment and failure to segregate the more serious and mentally ill offenders from the less serious offenders" (as is done in male prisons and jails) (ibid.).

The attitude that has persisted throughout the literature over these many years illustrates that women have been regarded as moral offenders, whereas men have continued to *assert* their masculinity. "[I]nstitutional incarceration needs to become more reflective of the ongoing changing social climate" (Sargent, 1984, p. 42). Most states continue to have one (in some cases, two) facilities for women, which of necessity must be of maximum security; local jails house both men and women. Population size has become a justification for ignoring the plight of women prisoners. However, as pointed out in the decision in *Glover*, size is but "an excuse for the kind of treatment afforded women prisoners" (p. 1078). The disparate treatment of female and male prisoners "is the result of habitual and stereotypic thinking rather than the following of a different set of goals for incarceration" (Lown & Snow, 1980, p. 210).

If administrators in corrections continue to assign women's corrections low priority in budget allocation, staff development, and program development, continued conflict can be expected between the needs of the correctional facilities and such treatment afforded women in this century. It may well be that because of overcrowding in both types of facilities, men's and women's equality will become less of an issue, thereby producing equality undesirable conditions for both. Regardless, disparate treatment continues to permeate correctional institutions. Adequate care and continuity in the delivery of services to all inmates is important. Standards must be applied equally. Such standards as developed over the years are meant to serve efficiency, provide greater cost-effectiveness, and establish better planning than we have at present.

According to Richie, Tsenin, and Widom (National Institute of Justice, 2000), "there is a common perception that the criminal behavior of women and girls are not serious problems. Women are more likely to commit minor offenses and have historically constituted a very small proportion of the offender population. But these facts mask a trend that is beginning to attract attention. The dramatic rise in the number of prison and jail inmates is fairly well known; less so is that the ranks of women inmates are increasing much faster than are those of their male counterparts. The pace at which women are being convicted of serious offenses is picking up faster than the pace at which women are convicted" (p. 2). These researchers have asked for a redefining of justice. "Whether justice should promote unalloyed equity, be blind to the circumstances in which crime is committed, and consider only gravity of offense and prior record, is still a matter of debate. In the current sentencing environment, the view of those who favor equity above all other considerations has won the day. . . . [W]omen and girls who are caught up in the justice system enter it as a result of circumstances distinctly different from those of men, and so find themselves at a distinct disadvantage" (p. 3).

If the cases are the catalyst for change, change must occur. Words have little meaning if actions do not follow (Muraskin, 1989, p. 126).

NOTES

1. In *Craig* v. *Boren* (1976) it was held to "withstand [a] constitutional challenge under the equal protection clause of the Fourteenth Amendment, classification by gender must serve important governmental objectives and must be substantially related to achievement of those objectives."

2. *Weinberger* v. *Wisenfeld* (1975) was a case in which a widower was denied benefits for himself on the ground that survivors' benefits were allowable only to women under 42 USCS sec. 4029g): "a provision, heard, 'Mother's insurance benefits,' authorizing the payment of benefits based on the earnings of a deceased husband and father covered by the Social Security Act, to a widow who has a minor child in her care." The Court held that "(1) the sex-based distinction of 42 USCS sec. 402(g), resulting in the efforts of women workers required to make social security contributions producing less protection for their families than was produced by the efforts of men, violated the rights to equal protection under the due process clause of the Fifth, and (2) the distinction could not be justified on the basis of the 'non-contractual' character of social security benefits, or on the ground that the sex-based classification was one really designed to compensate women beneficiaries as a group for the economic difficulties confronting women who sought to support themselves and their families."

3. *Eslinger* v. *Thomas* (1973) was an action brought by a female law student who alleged that she was denied employment as a page because of her gender. Citing *Reed*, the Court indicated that the "Equal Protection Clause (denies) to States the power to legislate that different treatment be accorded to persons placed by a statute into different classes on the basis of criteria wholly unrelated to the objective of that statute." The Court quoted from an article by Johnson and Knapp (1971) that "on the one hand, the female is viewed as a pure delicate and vulnerable citizen who must be protected from exposure to criminal influences; and on the other, as a brazen temptress, from whose seductive blandishments the innocent must be protected. Every woman is either Eve or Little Eve—and either way she loses." The decision of the lower court was reversed, there being no "fair and substantial 'relation between the object of the resolution' which was to combat the appearance of impropriety, and the ground of difference, which was sex. . . ."

REFERENCES AND BIBLIOGRAPHY

ALLEN, H. E., & SIMONSEN, C. E. (1978). *Corrections in American: An introduction* (Criminal Justice Series). Encino, CA: Glencoe.

AMERICAN CORRECTIONAL ASSOCIATION. (1985, April). *Standards for adult local detention facilities* (2nd ed.). In cooperation with the Commission on Accreditation for Corrections.

ARDITI, R.R., GOLDBERG, F., JR., PETERS, J., & PHELPS, W. R. (1973). The sexual segregation of American prisons. *Yale Law Journal, 6*(82), pp. 1229–1273.

ARON, N. (1981). Legal issues pertaining to female offenders. In N. Aron (Ed.), *Representing prisoners.* New York: Practicing Law Institute.

BELKNAP, J. (1996). *The invisible woman.* Belmont, CA: Wadsworth Publishing.

BUREAU OF JUSTICE STATISTICS. (2000, October 3). Lawrence A. Greenfeld & Tracy L. Snell. http://www.ojp.usdoj.gov/bjs/pub/ascii/wo.text

FABIAN, S. L. (1980). Women prisoners' challenge of the future. In N. Aron (Ed.), *Legal rights of prisoners.* Beverly Hills, CA: Sage Publications.

FEINMAN, C. (1982). Sex role stereotypes and justice for women. In B. R. Price & N. J. Sokoloff (Eds.), *The criminal justice system and women* (pp. 131–139). New York: Clark Boardman.

FEINMAN, C. (1986). *Women in the criminal justice system*. New York: Praeger.

GIBSON, H. (1973). Women's prisons: Laboratories for penal reform. *Wisconsin Law Review*.

GOBERT J. J. & COHEN, N. P. (1981). *Rights of prisoners*. New York: McGraw-Hill.

HUNTER, S. (1984, Spring–Summer). Issues and challenges facing women's prisons in the 1980's. *Prison Journal, 64*(1).

INCIARDI, J. A. (1984). *Criminal justice*. Orlando, FL: Academic Press.

LEWIS, D. K. (1982), Female ex-offenders and community programs. *Crime and Delinquency: Rights of Prisoners, 28*.

LOWN, R. D., & SNOW, C. (1980). Women, the forgotten prisoners: *Glover* v. *Johnson*. In S. L. Fabian (Ed.), *Legal Rights of Prisoners*. Beverly Hills, CA: Sage Publications.

MURASKIN, R. (1989) *Disparity of correctional treatment: Development of a measurement instrument*. Doctoral dissertation, City University of New York. Doctoral Dissertation Abstracts International.

MURASKIN, R. (2000). *It's a crime: Women and justice*. Upper Saddle River, NJ: Prentice Hall.

NATIONAL INSTITUTE OF JUSTICE. (2000, September). Beth E. Richie, Kay Tsenin & Cathy Spatz Widom, *Research on Women and Girls in the Justice System*.

POLLACK, H., & SMITH, A. B. (1978). *Civil liberties and civil rights in the United States*. St. Paul, MN: West Publishing.

POLLACK-BYRNE, J. (1990). *Women, prison and crime*. Belmont, CA: Brooks/Cole.

RAFTER, N. (1983). Prisons for women, 1790–1980. In M. Tonry & N. Morries (Eds.), *Crime and justice: An annual review of research*, Vol. 5. Chicago: University of Chicago Press.

RECKLESS, W. (1967). *The crime problem*. New York: Appleton-Century-Crofts.

SARGENT, J. P. (1984, Spring–Summer). The evolution of a stereotype: Paternalism and the female inmate. *Prison Journal, 1*.

SARRI, R. (1979). Crime and the female offender. In E. S. Gomberg & V. Frank (Eds.), *Gender and disordered behavior: Sex differences in psychopathology*. New York: Brunner/Mazel.

SINGER, L. (1979). Women and the correctional process. In F. Adler & R. Simon (Eds.), *The criminality of deviant women*. Boston: Houghton Mifflin.

U.S. DEPARTMENT OF JUSTICE. (2000).
www.ojp.usdoj.gov/bjs.pub/ascii/wo.txt

WILLIAMS, V. L., FORMBY, W. A., & WATKINS, J. C. (1982). *Introduction to criminal justice*. Albany, NY: Delmar Publishers.

WOOD, D. (1982). *Women in jail*. Milwaukee, WI: Benedict Center for Criminals.

CASES

Barefield v. *Leach*, Civ. Action No. 10282 (1974).

Bounds v. *Smith*, 430 U.S. 817 (1977).

Bukhari v. *Huto*, 487 F. Supp. 1162 (E.D. Va. 1980).

Canterino v. *Wilson*, 546 F. Supp. 174 (W.D. Ky. 1982) and 562 F. Supp. 106 (W.D. Ky. 1983).

Cody v. *Hillard*, 799 F.2d 447 (1986).

Commonwealth v. *Stauffer*, 214 Pa. Supp. 113 (1969).

Cooper v. *Morin*, 49 N.Y. 2d 69 (1979), *cert. denied*, 446 U.S. 984 (1980).

Cornish v. *Johnson*, No. 77-72557 (E.D. Mich. 1979).

Craig v. *Boren*, 429 U.S. 190 (1976).

Dawson v. *Carberry*, No. C-71-1916 (N.D. Cal. 1973).

Eslinger v. *Thomas*, 476 F.2d (4th Cir. 1973).

Estelle v. *Gamble*, 429 U.S. 97 (1976).

Glover v. *Johnson*, 478 F. Supp. 1075, 1078 (1979).

Holt v. *Sarver*, 309 U.S. F. Supp. 362 (E.D. Ark. 1970).

Liberti v. *York*, 28 Conn. Supp. 9, 246 A.2d 106 (S. Ct. 1968).

Mary Beth G. v. *City of Chicago*, 723 F.2d 1263 (7th Cir. 1983).

McMurray v. *Phelps*, 535 F. Supp. 742 (W.D.L.A. 1982).

Molar v. *Gates*, 159 Cal. Rptr. 239 (4th Dist. 1979).

Reed v. *Reed*, 404 U.S. 71 (1971).

State ex rel Olson v. *Maxwell*, 259 N.W. 2d 621 (Sup. Ct. N.D. 1977).

Thompson et al. v. *Varelas, Sheriff, Nassau County et al.*, 81 Civ. 0184 (JM) (September 11, 1985).

Todaro v. *Ward*, 431 F. Supp. 1129 (S.D. N.Y. 1977).

United States ex rel Robinson v. *York*, 281 F. Supp. 8 (D. Conn. 1968).

Weinberger v. *Wisenfeld*, 420 U.S. 636, 43 L. Ed. 2d 514 (1975).

William v. *Levi*, Civ. Action No. Sp. 792-796 (Sup. Ct. D.C. 1976).

15

Doing Time in Alaska

Women, Culture, and Crime

Cyndi Banks

Qualitative research was conducted in a women's prison near Anchorage, Alaska with the aim of giving voice to incarcerated Alaskan Native women who are culturally distinct and have discrete social and historical experiences. A particular focus of the research was to acknowledge these differences as well as the differences between Native cultural groups and then to make explicit the women's experiences within the prison. The articulation between the lives of the women and their "criminality," the response of the justice system to the factors that contribute to this criminalization, and the ways in which the cultural specificity of the women is appreciated and negotiated within the prison are explored with the aim of engendering an awareness of the cultural dimension of women's experience of prison. In the interaction between the Alaskan Native women and other prisoners and staff, a series of inversions and oppositions are produced and the women engage in these oppositions and inversions as a way of constructing an identity and of coping with the experience of imprisonment.

CULTURAL SPECIFICITY

Alaskan Native women constitute a discrete ethnic group whose experience as "deviants" and persons imprisoned is to be viewed in the context of a collection of cultures—those of the Yupik, Athapascan, Tlinget, Aleut, and Inupiat people of Alaska. These cultures are not homogeneous, and the values, expectations, and cultural practices of these peoples contribute to the experience of living and being, for example, a Yupik or an Inupiat person, and their acts of deviance can dramatize cultural boundaries. Through their utterances and social interactions are expressed the terms in which they define their world.

This is not the place to enter into an extended discussion of social change and the Native cultures of Alaska. Notwithstanding the constant reinterpretation of Native identity as persons relate to and interact with the broader economic, political, and cultural changes occurring in North American culture, it is sufficient to be aware that Alaskan Native cultures have generally continued to define themselves by reference to their differing cultural practices and by kinship. These practices take the form of extended families, a subsistence lifestyle,[1] notably in the rural parts of the state,[2] and a network of social practices concerned with spirituality and the reinforcement of cultural identity by the assertion of norms stressing unity, equality, and cooperation.[3]

Especially for those Alaskan Natives relocating to the urban areas of the state, interacting with the dominant culture poses the challenge of harmonizing different cultures. As one graduating high school student put it: "Because of my heritage and culture, I spend a lot of time thinking about that. I try to mix both together and take the best of the two; and try to be myself too. I don't want to forget about my past culture because of who I am. But I can't go back ten thousand years ago" (Chance, 1990; p. 191). Social change has affected Native Alaskan cultures in a manner similar to that experienced by Native Americans. Among the Alaskan Native groups, alcoholism,[4] suicide,[5] violent death, and mental illness are common and are considered by many commentators to be caused by culture change (Brod, 1975; Kraus & Buffler, 1979; Travis, 1983 in Phillips & Inui, 1986, p. 124). To these issues must be added the trauma of child abuse and sexual assault (Fienup-Riordan, 1994, p. 40). American Indian women and Alaskan Native women are more likely to die from motor vehicle accidents, homicide, and alcoholism than are other women in the United States (Lujan, 1995; p. 25).

I have argued elsewhere (Banks, 2000) that the cultural context should be a fundamental component of any criminological enterprise and that cultural specificity should implicate all relevant cultural experiences. In a discussion of the value of comparative criminology, Nelkin (1994) has also observed that "there are few topics in comparative criminology on which progress can be made without the possibility of being able to interpret the significance of crime and control in relation to other social and cultural phenomena" (p. 227). In exploring the cultural context of the lived experience of incarcerated Alaskan Native women, I argue that the interaction between Native Alaskan women and other prisoners and staff produces a series of inversions and oppositions concerning the manner in which "culture" is mediated. In their constant negotiation of prison, the women engage themselves in these oppositions and inversions as a means of constructing an identity and of coping with the experience of prison.

A major inversion is that of *observation/participation*. Here the women follow their cultural learning, which requires that they watch and learn through observation things not understood (Ross, 1996) rather than following demands for "active" participation in programs. However, inactivity or nonparticipation is regarded by staff as resistance.

Silence/noise inverts the cultural learning of silence as respect, to silence as denial and resistance. This is seen in confronting techniques in treatment programs, in relations between Alaskan women and African-Americans, who play loud rap music and who are gregarious in contrast to the silence of the Arctic tundra. The Native women may engage with this inversion by committing an infraction so that they can retreat to segregation to avoid the noise and confusion of the prison. In so doing, they paradoxically place themselves in the site of punishment to find peace within the prison.

The oppositions of *cultural sensitivity/special treatment* highlight a fundamental inversion on the part of the staff. Here, being culturally sensitive is constructed as special treatment, providing staff with a rationale for denying cultural difference altogether. Recognizing difference would place extra demands for time, energy, and resources on staff that already see themselves as overburdened, especially by women prisoners, who are seen as high-maintenance inmates always asking "why."

Respect for authority/unfriendliness is an inversion by which staff read traditional practices of respect as distancing and aloofness and as reason for not establishing relationships. Staff believe that prisoners must come to them because they see it as essential that prisoners take responsibility for their deviance and recognize that they have made wrong choices which have lead to their criminality. Staff see friendliness and approaches to them as explicit statements that prisoners have reached this stage of understanding.

In terms of treatment programs, there arises the inversion of *tearing down/building up*. On the one hand, the women's culture teaches competence through modeling, building on one's attributes and listening to and observing others; on the other hand, Western counseling practices involve confronting in order to tear down defenses so that one will recognize the personality defects that have caused the criminality. It is only after the destruction of the person's criminal identity that transformation is believed possible. Other treatment processes based on culture, such as the drumming groups and talking circles, may be tolerated but are viewed with suspicion and may be categorized as allowing sexual license and encouraging contraband.

Emotional/cognitive is an inversion associated with Native failure to respond adequately to treatment programs. Natives were condemned for spending time on the affective and spiritual dimension of their culture in the form of family obligations and cultural practices. Most staff privileged a cognitive approach and did not value Native feelings of connection to culture such as the joy, sharing of feelings, and spiritual uplift engendered by the limited cultural programs.

In the opposition of *language/no language*, Native women learn the language of treatment and of the institution. They must understand the nuances of "role model" and "above reproach" if they are to succeed in ascending the levels of the institutional status system. They must learn the language of prison rules and, if they are to complete treatment programs and qualify for early release or regain custody of their children, absorb the responses of counseling programs and recognize the grammar of treatment. Staff, however, are not trained to develop any significant understanding or appreciation of the Native culture beyond those aspects that affect their daily duties, such as differing conceptions of time. The inadequate English language skills of most Natives were, for the staff, a reflection that the Natives had not taken the trouble to learn the dominant culture.

Finally, *knowing/not knowing* signifies the obligation of Native Alaskan women to become aware of a web of practices within the dominant culture shaping the process of doing time in Alaska. Not knowing "how to do it" disqualifies the women from active participation in many areas of prison life. They simply do not possess the degree of knowledge of the dominant culture that would enable them to be treated and accepted as members of it. They do not know the jokes or how to express them.

"CRIMINAL" WOMEN

There are 15 main prison facilities in the state of Alaska, one of which, Hiland Mountain Prison, is dedicated to women offenders. On January 1, 1999, there were 240 women incarcerated at Hiland Mountain, 72 of whom were Alaskan Native women, constituting 30 percent of all women inmates (Statistical Analysis Unit, 1999). Alaskan Natives, both male and female, comprise 16 percent of the Alaska population but generally make up 34 percent of the adult inmate population (Schafer, Curtis, & Atwell, 1997).

Compared to white Alaskans, Alaskan Natives are 2.2 times more likely to get arrested, 3.3 times more likely to be arrested for a violent felony (e.g., murder, rape, aggravated assault, armed robbery), 2.9 times more likely to have a psychiatric hospitalization, and 6.9 times more likely to be treated in an alcohol treatment center (Phillips & Inui, 1986).

Although there is a considerable body of research concerning women's experience of prison, including some insight into the probable causes of their incarceration (see, e.g., Gelsthorpe, 1989; Rierden, 1997; Sommers, 1995; Watterson, 1996), research directed specifically at the Native American experience of prison is scanty and there appears to be little research on imprisoned Alaskan Native women. It is in this context that I conducted research at Hiland Mountain Correctional Center near Anchorage, Alaska. The institution was opened as a woman's institution in January 1998, having previously been used solely as a sex offender program for men. This program continues and is housed in the same building as the women's institution.

In November 1997, the average daily inmate population at Hiland was 256 persons. At the time I conducted my interviews in 1999, there were 210 women imprisoned there. Alaskan Native women's offenses ranged from probation and parole violations to drug and alcohol abuse and assault and manslaughter. Some were doing time for only a few months and others for up to 45 years.

Using qualitative interview techniques, I interviewed 21 Alaskan Native women as well as eight male and female staff members at the institution and combined with my research an analysis of institutional manuals, program materials, and records concerning Alaskan Native women inmates. Each interview lasted from 1½ to 2½ hours and was conducted in a private office located in the prison library. Interview questions were open-ended and focused generally on family and cultural background, experience of the criminal justice system and of the institution, coping strategies, staff/inmate relationships, and participation in treatment programs. My primary data source is the women themselves and the staff working with them.

In a move away from the positivistic approach[6] to research, which prescribes "hygienic research" methodologies (Stanley & Wise, 1993), feminists have recognized that research is never objective or value-free (Du Bois, 1983; Mies, 1983; Roberts, 1981; Stanley & Wise, 1993). As Liz Stanley writes: "Emotional involvement, the presence of emotions, is taboo; and an ideology exists which states that it is *possible*, not just preferable, to prevent this from happening. But we say that this is mere mythology. Emotions can't be controlled by mere effort of will, nor can adherence to any set of techniques or beliefs act as an emotional prophylactic" (Stanley & Wise, 1993, p. 160). This recognition has prompted use of a wide range of methods in feminist research generally, and specifically in research on violence (Dobash & Dobash, 1992; Gelsthorpe, 1990; Gelsthorpe & Morris,

1990; Kelly, 1988, 1990), including surveys to establish the scope of the problem, quali-tative interview techniques using open-ended questions, examination of official agency records, historical analysis, participant observation, and ethnography. No one research method is preferred over another but it is considered that a variety of methods and range of approaches will help give voice to women's experience of violence (Kelly, 1988), as long as the methods are reflective[7] (Roberts, 1981) and allow women to speak for themselves (Gilligan, 1993). As part of my effort to be reflexive in my research I attempted to use, like Burbank (1994, p. 15), "the self-consciousness of others to help me discover what is less conscious, or absent, in my own thinking."

The notion of *voice* is about language and assumes "that the way people talk about their lives is of significance, that the language they use and the connections they make reveal the world that they see and in which they act" (Gilligan, 1993, p. 2). Voice, then, is not simply what people say but is also concerned with the meaning underlying the spoken word and requires a search for the implicit. Strathern (1981) has argued that when Westerners study other cultures they must question their own assumptions since they understand the world through a Western set of concepts. In this view, although it may be possible for women's voices to enter a text that is constructed from another culture, no assumption should be made about the ability to do so (Strathern, 1988). Citing the philoso-pher Winch (1958, 1964), Hammersley (1994, p. 52) argues that it is possible to understand beliefs and actions within another culture only by viewing them within the cultural context and the rules regulating those beliefs and actions.[8] He suggests that it is important to be aware constantly that our cultural assumptions may lead us in the wrong direction.

Initially, the women interviewed were reluctant to speak openly about their lives and experiences before incarceration and wanted to know the purpose of the questions and the use to which the information would be put. Their initial concerns, of course, reflect the privileged position I hold as interviewer and as a white female. I explained that my interest was to capture their experiences and their concerns as to their criminalization and of being incarcerated and that any identifying information they shared would be kept confidential. Following the first two interviews, some of the women had discussed my research among themselves and seemed reassured that I was not part of the system that had incarcerated them and that there would be no consequences for them in terms of completing their sentences. Consequently, they responded to my questions with more openness and less suspicion. Some women subsequently approached me asking to be included in my interviews[9] so that they could provide information about their experiences, and many asked for a copy of the completed written material.

THEORETICAL CONSIDERATIONS

In considering the experience of Alaskan Native women in prison, I draw on standpoint theo-ry. Jaggar defines a *standpoint* as "a position in society from which certain features of reality come into prominence and from which others are obscured" (in Nielson, 1990, p. 24). According to Nielson: "Feminist standpoints begin with but do not end with women's expe-riences, and as in the case of other standpoint epistemologies, they are more than perspectives. They involve a level of awareness and consciousness about one's social location and this loca-tion's relation to one's lived experience" (p. 24). Feminist standpoint epistemology involves the use of methodologies that emphasize the experience of women. This is premised on the assumption that women's world view or standpoint is shaped by their social and material life. Harding (1987, p. 185) explains: "The argument here is that human activity, or 'material life,' not only structures but also sets limits on human understanding: what we do shapes and constrains what we can know." It is important to recognise that women occupy a number of standpoints at one time. As Cain (1990) puts it: "[W]e are all located within a [changing] web or configuration of relationships. We all have relationships with other people and we speak each from our own unique site in a complex configuration of interrelated people. In this sense, there is as much knowledges as there are people. And it is to deal with precisely this point that the standpoint epistemologies have been developed" (p. 129).

Some feminists have acknowledged that standpoint epistemologies provide us with another partial view of the world. They do not claim that this view is the absolute truth, as a positivistic approach to research would allege (see Caulfield & Wonders, 1994, p. 219). The importance of acknowledging difference through standpointism is that we can open ourselves up to "the potential richness of women's contributions to knowing and to welcome the challenges, both intellectual and political . . . " of this diversity (Cain, 1990, p. 134).

Standpoint theory, with its emphasis on subordinate groups, is able to draw on the lives of marginalized persons "as the starting point from which to frame research questions and concepts" and to incorporate "the perspectives of those outside the cultural center" (Wood, 1992, in Orbe, 1998, p. 27). For black women, another marginalized group, Audre Lorde observes (in Collins, 1990, p. 91) that these women "become familiar with the language and manners of the oppressor, even sometimes adopting them for some illusion of protection" and, Collins adds, "while hiding a self-defined standpoint from the prying eyes of dominant groups." As emerges from the following discussion, this perspective has validity when considering the cultural standpoint of Alaskan Native women in prison.

WOMEN'S LIVES AND CULTURAL NARRATIVES

Fifteen of the women interviewed lived in rural areas of the state, and among the entire group were Yupik, Tlinget, Inupiat, Athapascan, and Aleut women. There emerged from the women's narratives a series of themes, many of which were shared by most of the women. These included: sexual abuse as a child or teenager, the frequency of deaths in the family, depression and loneliness, alcohol consumption at an early age, running away from home or from foster homes, domestic violence and physical abuse, being placed in state custody as a child, and drug and alcohol abuse at the time of arrest and jailing. Studies have shown that a high proportion of incarcerated women generally have suffered sexual and physical abuse and that their first contact with the justice system often occurred because they were running away from that abuse (Chesney-Lind & Shelden, 1998; Flowers, 1995; Widom, 1989).

Common to the various cultural groups is the extended family. Many of the women said that their grandparents had raised them, largely as a result of their parents being unable to care for them due to their abuse of alcohol. However, a by-product of this upbringing was that a number of women said they had learned aspects of their culture, and in some cases their own language, through their relationship with their grandparents. Some also faced abuse from their grandparents, who watched their grandchildren consumed by problems caused by social change, disease, and alcohol abuse.

A subsistence lifestyle in Alaska means living off the land by hunting, fishing, and trapping, and by this means producing food and income. Today, many rural Alaskan Natives continue to practice a subsistence lifestyle. A number of the women had come from this lifestyle, from a village of perhaps a few hundred Alaskan Native people, to a city of 300,000, composed chiefly of the dominant culture. The village subsistence lifestyle, with its open spaces and interdependency on communal survival was for them the antithesis of prison life, with its confinement, discipline, structure, and rules, and many of them expressed this dimension of their experience in prison. The staff, too, remarked on the hardship that these women suffered through this process of abrupt change.

Associated with the subsistence economy is native food, which for these women was not simply a particular form of nourishment that they were unable to enjoy in prison but also represented within their culture, relationships that were enhanced and sustained through processes such as communal hunting and exchange. In this sense, therefore, a significant part of the traditional way of life and the culture was lost for these women, and this resulted in feelings of depression and homesickness while in prison.

Family disruption and dislocation as a result of constant relocation of the home and in the identity of the person responsible for their upbringing is a common motif in the women's narratives. One woman, who was half Inupiat on her mother's side with an Irish father was born in Michigan and lived with her father until he died when she was 3 years old. Her mother liked to travel and had not lived with them. Following her father's death, she was brought back to Alaska as a ward of the state. She spent a couple of years living with her mother outside Anchorage and at age 6 was adopted by white parents. An Inupiat woman explained that her family had frequently moved when she was a child; "We moved from one village to another in Bristol Bay, then moved to another village because my sister died so we could look after a nephew. One time we moved because one village didn't have a store, so we moved to a village that had a store."

Alcohol abuse in the form of drinking at an early age was common to more than half of the women. In some cases the women had felt a keen sense of loss and abandonment resulting from being placed with their grandparents so as not to interfere with their parent's drinking habits and consumption. Using and abusing alcohol to overcome or numb physical and emotional pain was a common theme.

One Yupik woman was raised by her grandparents while her mother lived apart from them and visited only infrequently. Her mother had a drinking problem and was physically abusive toward her when drinking and verbally abusive when sober. The abuse caused her to become angry and to fight at school. She started drinking at age 13 and discovered that drinking numbed any feelings of pain after she fell and hit her head on a coffee table when drunk. As she put it, "I hated the taste but liked the effect of not feeling pain."

A Tlinget woman lived with her grandparents until their death when she was 12 years old and then moved in with her mother, who was employed at a cannery. She explained that her grandparents "were not affectionate people" and she began drinking beer at age 10 after the death of her grandmother. She remembered that she felt lost and lonely at the time of their death and "drank a lot to kill the pain." An Athapascan woman said she started drinking at the age of 14 years having been brought up in a household where both parents drank heavily and where domestic violence was constant. She noted that there were many deaths in her village through alcohol consumption and commented, "alcohol is killing everyone."

Physical and sexual abuse were prominent in the women's narratives. An Inupiat woman was taken into custody by the state at 9 months of age after her alcoholic mother became angry while giving her a bath, picked her up, and threw her across the room. The state placed her in the care of her sister in Anchorage, where she suffered further physical abuse. A Tlinget woman described how she often could not attend school when she was a child because of her father's beatings and that he frequently locked her in her room until the bruises on her face, ribs, and legs had healed. Another Inupiat woman described a childhood of physical abuse at the hands of her mother. She was so angry about the beatings she and her siblings had suffered that it took her 10 years after she left home to contact her mother again.

Sexual abuse, by a grandfather, father, uncle, cousin, or other relative, figured in eight of the narratives. One Tlinget woman said that she grew up with her parents and that they drank heavily. The sexual abuse started at age 8 or 9 and stopped at age 17. If she failed to respond to her father, "he would go for my sister and I wouldn't let him touch my sister." Her father often beat her when he was drunk, leaving bruises all over her body and around her neck where he tried to choke her. Her mother also participated in the beatings and when she tried to run away to her grandparents she was beaten more. The father was charged for sexual abuse of a minor when she was 17. This woman recalled that she started drinking at age 13 and, after running away from the abuse at home at the age of 17, she spent time in a state juvenile institution as a child in need of aid under the state juvenile law.

A Yupik woman recounted the sexual abuse she experienced at the hands of her uncle starting at 8 years of age and on many occasions subsequently. She tried to tell people about the abuse but no one believed her until she was taken to the village clinic, where it was discovered that she suffered from gonorrhea. The uncle was later charged and he died in jail of cancer. She was subsequently placed in the Alaska Psychiatric Institution, which she described as being more like a jail than a hospital, for depression and suicidal tendencies since she tried many times to kill herself.

Some older women's lives were significantly affected by their experience of being taken out of the village community at a young age and placed in residential schools, some because many members of their families had died from the flu epidemic. This dislocation and subsequent isolation from the family and the village community resulted in loneliness and loss of language and culture. A Yupik woman tearfully described her feelings of depression and loneliness while in boarding school. She and the other children were forbidden to speak their own language and were forced to wear dresses in winter and eat strange food. When asked about her experience of residential school an Inupiat woman cried several times while recalling that she found life at the mission school "very hard." Due to the distance between the school and her village, she saw her father only once a year when he came to the school to visit. When she was 10 years old she returned home for the holidays, but said she soon wrote and asked her teacher to take her back because she felt so disconnected from village life and her family.

Alaskan cultures, like those of American Indians, suffer very high rates of death through suicide and excessive alcohol consumption.[10] Frequent grieving is therefore a significant part of the Alaskan Native experience, and it shaped the lives of many of the women. Depression often results from the multiplicity of family loss, both in the women's early childhood and during their teens and adulthood. Their narratives show a pattern of frequent family death and resulting trauma, depression, and feelings of loss. A Yupik woman grew up with her grandfather until his death when she was 8 years old, when she moved to live with her parents. Her oldest brother drowned when he was 17 years old. She recalled her reaction: "I felt like I was on my own with no one to take care of me—everyone I loved or cared about was dying or dead—my mother was sick—a lot of people had TB (tuberculosis) and had to stay in hospital for years. I made a decision to look after myself at age 13, especially after grandfather died. I remember feeling lonely and depressed and my self-esteem was low."

In another narrative, an Inupiat village woman's father died when she was a baby and she later learned that her sister had been murdered. By the time she was 20 she lost two more brothers, one through drowning and the other through an accident. White parents adopted another Inupiat woman during her teens following the death of her grandfather and mother. As an adult, she received news that her brother had died falling through the ice, that another brother was killed in a vehicle accident, and that her sister had committed suicide. She noted several other deaths that had affected her and described how she began to drink to forget her losses.

GETTING INTO TROUBLE

Eleven of the 21 women interviewed said that they had committed offenses as teenagers, the most prevalent being consuming alcohol while a minor and shoplifting. Six women had run away or been picked up as runaways while teenagers, and some of them were taken into custody as children in need of aid (CINA), a status offense under state law.[11] Others simply ran away from home and lived on the streets of Anchorage and other places until they returned to live with one of their relatives. An Aleut woman was brought up by her sister in Anchorage and at age 13 was told to leave home when her sister discovered she was smoking marijuana, something she said she had been doing since the age of 8. She explained that while on the run, she stayed in shelters, with friends, and lived on the street, surviving through shoplifting. At the age of 15 she was placed in McLaughlin Juvenile Institution after having been taken into custody as a runaway.

A Yupik woman, who as a teenager was several times committed to the Alaska Psychiatric Institution due to depression and several suicide attempts resulting from an abusive family situation, was placed in a series of foster homes between the ages of 9 and 18 and ran away from a number of these homes. While on the street she was involved in drug and alcohol abuse and later became a crack addict.

As mentioned earlier, the offense of consuming alcohol as a minor was prevalent in the teenage years of many of the women. A Yupik woman, who was placed on probation for that offense, was subsequently placed by her grandfather in Charter North, an alcohol treatment program. After four months in the program, she remained sober for two weeks before running away from home. She was then sent to McLaughlin Institution as a child in need of aid.

During their teens nearly all the women consumed alcohol, some quite heavily and from an early age. In many cases this alcohol abuse flowed from parental alcohol abuse and the resulting family dysfunction. This teenage drinking was pursued into the adult years and many of the offenses committed as adults were alcohol related or were specifically based on alcohol abuse, such as driving under the influence of alcohol.

Drug abuse also featured in the early years of many of the younger women, who said they began smoking marijuana in their early teens, although some started when much younger. A Yupik woman abused alcohol as a teenager but stopped drinking at the age of 18. She later became a physician's assistant working for local health corporations and in 1987 was involved in a small plane crash that caused her severe back pain. She became addicted to her pain-killing medication and was involved in a common law relationship in which her partner sold heroin. She became addicted to cocaine and heroin and was diagnosed positive with the human immunodeficiency virus (HIV) in 1991. She and her partner committed crimes to support their addiction and to survive on the streets of Anchorage. Another woman took no drugs or alcohol until the age of 18 but became involved in an abusive relationship with a white man who was an alcoholic. She started drinking with him and was charged seven times with disorderly conduct in a period of six years, until she underwent a treatment program and stopped drinking for 10 years. She moved through a series of relationships and prior to her incarceration was living with another white alcoholic who abused her. She was addicted to crack/cocaine for three years and supported herself through prostitution.

Violent and abusive relationships are a common theme in the women's narratives, and some are in prison for violent offenses committed while intoxicated. A Yupik woman who started drinking at age 13 was married at 19 and then stopped drinking for four months. However, she took up drinking again, became violent when drinking, and would "steal, hide and sneak drink" and abuse her husband or anyone else present. In 1993 she drove while drunk and killed two people. An Inupiat woman, who lived in a village where there were almost no drugs or alcohol, attended the University of Alaska, Fairbanks and lost her scholarship because of bad grades. She started drinking there and tried cocaine, returned to the village and then moved to the town of Dillingham, where she lived with a boyfriend. The relationship provoked much domestic violence, leading to his receiving an eight-month sentence for assaulting her. She moved on to another boyfriend, who she slashed with a knife while drinking. She said they drank the entire time, stopping only on Sunday when the liquor store was closed.

A 60-year-old Inupiat woman is serving a 45-year sentence for first-degree murder after stabbing a female friend in the back during an argument as they were drinking and playing cards. She would not talk about the circumstances of the offense, saying that she simply could not comprehend her actions. She had been imprisoned first at the age of 21 for being an accessory to a robbery and had suffered three abusive marriages.

In terms of the women's criminality, the narratives of their teenage years illustrate that the juvenile offenses that might be said to have contributed to their criminality were minor in nature. It is apparent, however, that many began to develop a pattern of alcohol abuse that did contribute to later offenses. Also, many of the women had been in a series of relationships, whether common law or marriage, in which domestic violence was prominent and had had white partners who were often seriously abusive.

Only four women said they had no previous periods of incarceration as an adult (this could include time in the Sixth Avenue Jail for short periods), and overall, the women's previous offenses included murder (one woman), manslaughter related to driving under the influence, assault, assault with a deadly weapon, driving under the Influence, drunk and disorderly (one said that she had 26 convictions for this offense), shoplifting, forgery, probation violations, drug charges, prostitution, sexual assault, burglary, and destruction of property.

PROCESSING AND PROGRAMS

Upon entering Hiland Mountain Prison the women are given an orientation course for a minimum of 14 days, known as *phase one*. Staff told me that Alaskan Native women make up 30 to 40 percent of all new intakes. The purpose of phase one is "to orient prisoners to the rules and regulations and the available programs." According to the prison handbook, during this period the prisoners are observed and evaluated as to their behavior and attitude. This is for the purpose of determining "the prisoner's ability to maintain appropriate conduct in the general population." On completion of phase one, each prisoner is given a choice to enter either the cognitively based female offender program (FOP), the substance abuse program (RSAP)[12], or to be placed on nonproductively involved status (NPI). However, those with sentences under 60 days automatically enter NPI status. During each phase a prisoner wears a different-colored uniform (until they can afford to purchase regular clothing from the institution in phases other than NPI) and a different-colored name badge, and each phase group must eat meals apart from other phase groups.

In characterizing one choice as nonproductive while the other two choices involve programs and treatment, the prison administration signals its distaste for those in the prison who remain idle in the face of efforts to treat their deviance. The prison manual reinforces this discourse of treatment in opposition to "doing nothing" by providing that those who elect NPI status must submit a form of application and "cop-out" form to the phase one counselor and house supervisor. The Cleary settlement decision of the state superior court has determined, however, that prisoners are not required to undertake treatment programs except under court order to which they are required to consent.[13] Nevertheless, there are clear pressures by the administration to do so. Being placed on NPI status involves wearing a blue suit and being placed in the labor pool and on work crews rather than working in one of the more desirable institutional positions. Access to the commissary is limited to one day a week.

On completion of phase one prisoners pass on to *phase two* for a minimum of six months and are assigned to a room in a different wing than that occupied in phase one, based on their participation in educational, therapeutic, and work programs. Each prisoner develops a basic program schedule with the assistance of her wing counselor. This is designed to meet treatment goals, which are stated to be "developing responsibility, addressing individual needs and basic life skills."

In phase two each prisoner must satisfy 11 criteria to be eligible to move on to phase three, but failure to complete the single criterion of "court-ordered treatment and any treatment team requirements" may result in being placed on NPI status. The 11 criteria relate to attending classes and groups, including attending daily wing groups if in a program wing; maintaining a job in the institution; educational work if the prisoner has no high school diploma; an absence of management problems; an absence of disciplinary write-ups within 90 days of advancing to phase three; and progress toward treatment goals. The onus is placed on the prisoner to apply for a move to phase three, and the counselor must determine whether to support the application or whether the treatment team should make the decision.

To advance to *phase three*, the prisoner must be considered a "role model in the institution" by the treatment team. This assessment is based on participation in programs, conduct, and attitude. Phase three is less restrictive and is "designed to provide an incentive and the means to change criminal behavior patterns by the utilization of the variety of groups and/or classes available." In this phase, emphasis is placed on prisoners maintaining "consistent . . . self-control and being positive examples of behavior and attitude." By instilling and maintaining these attributes the prisoner achieves the status of "role model to other prisoners."

The minimum period in phase three is one year, and advancement from there to *honor status* is not automatic but depends on an evaluation by the treatment team based on program participation, conduct, and attitude. In honor status, the desideratum of role model is elevated to a condition of being "above reproach." This criterion is judged by the satisfactory completion of 11 tests, which include completion of treatment plan, attendance at daily wing group meetings, and "independent motivation, self-improvement, and exemplary (role model) behavior."

To enjoy honor status, a prisoner must show a minimum of 180 days without incident or rule infraction, but "inappropriate behaviors not resulting in incident report may be considered for denial of advancement." This status contains the fewest restrictions and carries extra privileges. The honor status prisoner is one who has exhibited "superior conduct, attitude and programming, with a centralized commitment to the institution and her goals." Prisoners enjoy their own rooms, hold an institutional job, will be group facilitators in counseling, and enjoy access to library classrooms and common areas until lockdown, as well as extra phone privileges.

The prison administration requires that the prisoners be counted eight times daily starting at 2:00 A.M. and finishing at 10:00 P.M. Prisoners occupy themselves with work, treatment programs, recreation, eating, and sleeping. Only visitors on the approved list may visit, but there is no limit to the number on each list, and visitors may make actual contact with prisoners. Each prisoner has a key to her room and rooms are kept locked when unoccupied.

Among the programs offered to prisoners in phase two are "36 Thinking Errors,' "19 Tactics Used by the Criminal to Avoid Change," "Criminal Personality," "Anger Management," "Goal Setting," "Expressing Feelings," "Assault Cycle," "Coping With Anger," and "Completion of an Autobiography." In phase three, prisoners may undertake modules called "Problem Solving/Conflict Resolution," "Passive Assertive and Aggressive Behaviors," "Self-Centeredness," and "Anger Management." In the substance abuse program (RSAP), which is usually court-ordered, prisoners are located separately in a special wing. The programs were said to be intensive, but staff were reluctant to provide any detailed information, as they were in the process of changing the program content.

STAFF PERCEPTIONS

Interviews with staff were shaped by issues of programming and treatment, control and discipline, and relations between staff and Alaskan Natives. Culture training did not figure largely in the staff's qualifications. A number had attended workshops of one to three days on cultural awareness, but cultural sensitivity had not been a major focus of training. Despite this, some staff clearly did recognize the need for such training. Staff identified cultural difference between Native Alaskans and others in terms of divergences in the acknowledgment of time and in the appreciation of silence. They noted that silence was often perceived by whites as passive resistance and indirect aggression. A staff person noted that Native women were written up most often for missing the count and thought that this related to their concept of time.

The staff education coordinator explained that one of her tasks was teaching cross-cultural activities with a focus on African-American culture. When asked about Alaskan Native culture, she responded that she sometimes used Native American literature and that "doing more was an issue of time and resources." She also pointed out that participation in programs did affect parole and furlough applications.

With few exceptions, staff believed that despite their cultural difference, Alaskan Natives should receive the same treatment as other groups, believing that culturally specific programs might provoke demands for special treatment by other groups. One staff member considered that liaison between Native inmates and the community about aftercare resources and options would amount to "special treatment." Two staff thought that race and ethnicity were factors affecting treatment since treatment programs were "geared to white culture." They thought that programs such as "Thinking Errors" attempted to impose white culture on Natives.

Some statements by staff indicated a lack of sensitivity toward the value placed on the extended family. For example, one response indicated that Native women were thought to spend excessive time and energy dealing with outside family issues and paid insufficient attention to the "treatment" of *their own issues*. "Women use emotions as a screen; it keeps them focused on emotion rather than on responsibility. They need to focus on the cognitive." This person did not think that Native women had a harder time than others in prison except in terms of their need for physical space. They responded with anger and depression to being "cooped up" and then with resistance by "being slower at things." "Natives act like they don't understand when they do, they act stupid when they are not, and act confused as though they don't understand. This helps get staff off their back; they can accuse you of prejudice, usually by telling someone else that they think you are and it gets back to you. It's a form of control because staff don't want to be accused."

My perception was that there was a prevailing feeling of disquiet among staff at the difference manifested by Native Alaskans in their conduct, aptly summarized by one staff person as follows: "They won't look you in the eye, don't show emotions, won't cry, some will laugh but look away. They keep to themselves. You don't even know they are there unless you go to them." As a result, another staff emphasized: "We don't have time to seek them out. If they come to us we'll talk to them; they are really hard to deal with because you don't know what's going on with them." One female staff perceived Natives as "unfriendly" because they did not come to talk to her. Yet another thought that by keeping to themselves, Alaskan Natives were perceived as a clique. It was believed that Alaskan Natives did not support the inmate code of silence but rather would come to staff about a problem immediately. This, although helpful for the Natives in their relationships with staff, did not assist them with other inmates, as they became known as snitches. A number of Alaskan Natives were classified as having mental health problems when some staff thought they were "just shy."

Staff frequently remarked that Alaskan Native women tended to be more reticent in groups in the female offender program, more comfortable sitting and letting others talk, and would participate only if they felt comfortable or were required to talk. When they "got past their resistance," they did as well as anyone else. I was told, "we're resistant to what we are not comfortable with." For Alaskan Natives, staff believed, resistance took the form of an absence of verbal and written communication, especially about feelings, but "once they allowed themselves to participate, they were often more honest than others."

As a response to lack of participation, one female staff pulled Natives aside and instructed them to participate. This was often met with the response that other people had already said what they would have said or that there was insufficient time for them to speak. She told them to repeat, if necessary, and that they would eventually learn how to participate. Differences between rural and urban Natives were observed, with the former having more difficulty opening up, but her message was the same to both groups. She did, however, take more time with the rural Natives.[14]

Staff raised the issue of communicating with Alaskan Natives, noting that for many, English was a second language or that English skills "were not honed" and this caused problems, as it was hard for the Natives to communicate their needs verbally or in writing. One effect was that Natives did not submit written complaints as often as others.

On the question of differences between male and female prisoners generally, the view was expressed that women prisoners were harder to work with because they "manipulated more than men, asked more questions, had more authority issues, and always wanted to know why." They thought men more compliant, whereas women "move into feelings" and reacted more. Women, it was suggested, regressed into teenagers in prison as though they hadn't matured, perhaps as a reaction to authority. As one staff member put it: "We make them co-dependent; they have to ask for everything."

One staff described Alaskan Native women as "quieter but angrier. They keep to themselves, don't voice their opinions, and bottle up their emotions, especially anger." Sexual abuse, alcohol and physical abuse, and domestic violence were seen as the causes of their anger. Staff tried to get them to be more assertive: to speak out and talk about the things that made them angry. All staff thought that more patience was needed with Alaskan Natives, and one suggested that this was due to "their low tolerance for anger." Some would not confront them until they had established a relationship with them. They were described as "time bombs" that had to be "handled more gently." This conclusion was based on facial expression, comments made, and their tendency to isolate themselves. Native women from the rural north were described as compliant, quiet, and introverted, as making no eye contact, and as less assertive.

It was said that Native women complained most about their roommates and were unwilling to compromise about lights being on and off, and about noise. As a consequence, staff tried to put Native women together if rooms were available because "it is always better to put the races together but not always possible." When Native women submitted complaints, they related to issues of personal space and comfort, such as discourteous treatment by roommates. Rather than write up Alaskan Natives for disciplinary infractions, some tried to deal with disciplinary matters informally.

Some staff asserted that Native women were "treated poorly" by other staff, were expected to act the same as other prisoners, and were expected to understand the structures and expectations of the institution. No allowances were made and there was no sensitivity to cultural difference. Natives were often employed in the kitchen and in other menial jobs, and very few obtained prestigious jobs within the institution.

Alaskan Native women identified a number of tensions within the institution, including frequent changes of program content; moving prisoners from room to room, resulting in the breakup of established friendships (the women said that it was particularly hard for the rural women to develop such friendships in prison); and participating in court-ordered programs involving confrontational and aggressive techniques, where there was a tendency to confront the weaker people in the groups (i.e., the Alaskan Natives). I asked staff about these tensions. According to one, whose comment was supported by some women's accounts, such tensions can have the effect that Native women will commit an infraction in order to spend time in segregation where there is peace and no pressure. This was especially true of rural Natives, whereas Natives from the city of Anchorage were more streetwise and able to deal with the noise and confusion, although they, too, sometimes made use of this strategy. In relation to being moved around, this was cited as a general problem caused by startup problems in the institution.

Staff thought that ethnic groups within the institution tended to "hang around together" and ethnicity did not become an issue unless and until it was raised to support a personality clash. Most of the Alaskan Native women identified a hierarchy of power within the institution based on ethnicity: with whites at the top, then African-Americans, Hispanics, and Natives, with Eskimos at the very bottom. A staff member denied this claim, describing it as a "typical victim stance." She did, however. agree that Natives were "pushed around" by the African-Americans. Others thought that Natives did not get along with African-Americans at all, and that this became clear when staff tried to room them together, as Natives would rather go to segregation than room with the more gregarious African-Americans.

Native coping strategies mentioned by staff included forming alliances through cultural activity such as a drumming group, which they felt helped to "ground Natives to something familiar." I was told that cultural activities for Native Alaskan women comprised an Athapascan drumming group and a talking circle. One comment made about Native sweat lodges was that they were not part of Hiland Mountain programs but that the attitude of most staff in other institutions was that "they probably do it for the sex."[15] Most thought that it was against the rules, and there was concern that contraband items might be used. One thought that the talking circle and the drumming groups provided positive role models for Native women and she had noticed that they were more peaceful for a few weeks after an event. A talking circle occurs weekly for the women and the male sex offenders together. A staff member commented that he thought the women did not participate to a great degree but did benefit from this form of counseling in addition to the cognitive programs.[16] Some thought participation in the group was merely an "excuse for developing relationships" between the men and the women.

A few staff thought the confrontational methods used in the female offender program sometimes caused more harm than good to Native women. An example was a woman who told a group she had blacked out and was unable to recall her crime. She was confronted by the other members and told she was lying. Native women were said by staff to be frightened about the FOP program and its requirement to "build relationships."

Both the women and staff are uncomfortable with the location of sex offenders adjacent to the women's institution, especially when so many of the women have been the victims of sexual abuse. The decision not to relocate the sex offenders was apparently based on administrative convenience, in that there was government and community support for the sex offenders to continue to be located at Hiland Mountain.

The segregation unit is divided into punitive and administrative segregation. The latter comprises those with health problems that might be contagious, those who might be at risk from others, those who are less mobile through pregnancy, and persons detoxing. Punitive segregation is a disciplinary sanction for acts such as contraband possession, fighting, and disruptive behavior. Recreation of one hour a day is permitted and inmates are locked down for the remainder of the day, apparently, as one staff member said, "to give them time to think and to understand what they have lost." The segregation staff told me that Natives seem to have an easier time coping with segregation because they have "a solitary lifestyle" and cope better with prison life when they are not under pressure from others.

The medical unit staff told me that depression was often a big issue for Native women, but that they generally had not sought care prior to institutionalization. However, once institutionalized, they do ask for medication. There is a psychiatric unit at Hiland, referred to as Special Needs, which generally comprises 30 to 40 percent Native Alaskans. A psychiatrist or psychologist makes assignments to the unit. Commenting on the cognitively based treatment programs, the psychiatrist noted that Natives did not do well on cognitive tests but were "above average in spatial and mechanical geometry."

INMATE PERCEPTIONS

Treatment Experiences

Most women said that they would feel more comfortable if there were native counselors on staff in the prison. At present, there are none.[17] A woman who acted as the Native spiritual adviser for the institution described the prison's treatment programs as cognitively based and contrasted this with the native cultural programming, which was "spiritually, creatively, and materially task-oriented." She noted that some women "could not get a grip on the Western approach" and that arts and crafts "brought the native women out a lot."[18] She thought that more cultural programming would overcome women's shyness and that women were too proud or too scared to ask or did not know who to ask or "how to word it." This is consistent with the remark of another woman that she was not used to being around "loud people," referring to the "noisiness" of group therapy.

The women said that staff told them that despite the Cleary agreement, furlough was unlikely unless they participated in programs. They complained of a vicious cycle that began with having to take programs, and being confronted in those programs, described by one woman as "forced treatment" that was "not useful for Natives." She said that more time to carry out tasks required by programs was needed and that education and skills to build self-esteem and to "make them feel good about who they are" were more useful than treatment. She complained that the groups were "overwhelming" for Natives; there was too much homework and they were seen as not cooperating and as failing to respond to the demands of the program. This resulted in their ending up in nonproductively involved status, where they would "vegetate" and be locked down most of the time.

The women learn the techniques of participation and the language and responses of counseling in the cognitive programs. Some thought that this had the effect of lowering self-esteem because of its focus on the negative in terms of thinking errors and mistakes making rather than building on attributes. What had been learned could be located only within the prison environment and was not capable of being transformed into practices for living outside the prison. They constructed Native women as a discrete group in need of unique programs reflective of their cultures, taking account of their conception of time as being "one season ahead" and for cultural difference in the form of the extended family rather than the individualistic therapeutic approach. Time could be differentiated inside and outside the prison, and this was expressed by one woman as the shock of seeing that a child had grown, whereas in the prison, time was perceived to be in stasis. Another felt intimidated by group work because she feared that what she said might be misunderstood or wrong in some way. Time was also a factor in information courses showing video films. Here the video presentations were described as "too fast," and some suggested that more use be made of the pause control.

In talking to me, women often used treatment and counseling expressions such as:

"I learned a lot about myself and my anger."

"I learned to trust and how to have friendships and relationships."

"The 36 thinking errors made me look at my thinking."

"I learned to trust and to let go."

"I didn't like prison at first until I went to treatment and admitted to myself my role in getting here."

"I was closed at first. I used the tactic of attack."

One woman, referring to the 36 thinking errors and 19 tactics, commented: "I didn't realize I was doing all those things before!" She had constructed prison as a teaching experience for herself but appeared to be suspicious of staff, indicating that she did not talk to them unless they asked her first and that she always respected them. There was a sense in which this woman appeared to have developed a co-dependency on the experience of counseling and treatment to such an extent that she expressed concern about needing more support of this kind before she could leave the institution and succeed in life outside. Another woman saw giving personal information through the confronting practice in counseling groups as providing information that would be used against her rather than, as in counseling practice, supplying personal information in order to confront a person's self-destructive behaviors.

Noisiness in the confronting process was seen as deleterious for Native women but was applauded within the groups by those participating and by staff as being appropriately responsive to the program. Native women, referring to the group work, often commented that they did not "know how to do it" and complained that if they never spoke, they were described as "closed" and were subject to criticism.

It appears from my interviews that many women will take the substance abuse program as a means of regaining custody of their children from the state. One urban woman's experience of the program was positive in that "we are taught a new way of thinking, shown how to dig inside ourselves and our issues stemming from childhood." Another woman's perspective was that she was "forced to take a look at myself and turn it into something positive." However, another woman considered those in the program to be "outcasts" and separated from the rest of the prison population. The reason given was that those in the program were instructed to confront and inform on those who did not conform to the program rules or behaved in a manner considered adverse to its aims. This was consistent with the general approach in the institution of "breaking the inmate code of silence."[19] One woman had learned through group counseling that she "had a choice," and had "chosen to do drugs" and "to blame everyone else for her problems." Although she had been sexually abused as a child and this had led to depression and drug use, she had been "helped through counseling" to see that her problems were a "result of her own choices" and not because of her abuse.

The women told me that there were no Native programs other than a drumming group and a recently started talking circle, and most felt, in the words of one woman: "It feels good to hear the songs, to sing, to talk about our families and traditions. We feel more connected with tradition; it brings our spirits back up." Women who attended the talking circle enjoyed the "sharing of feelings." The experience of the Native programs was described by another woman as peaceful and comfortable and "they start to sing and speak; you can feel it in their face." Speaking of her experience with the drumming group, another woman liked to dance and sing, as it made her feel good and lifted her spirits. "It's sacred for us, we say prayers for each other." She felt "safe talking in front of those in the Native program."[20] She mentioned that the prison had held a potlatch for the women and that those who attended "felt more connected and good about themselves." However, one problem with the drumming program was that it was perceived as treating all Native cultures as homogeneous, that is, as composed of the Athapascan culture alone.

Some women described the talking circle as a confidential process of sharing problems and advice. For another, the talking circle and drumming group were places where she could talk about anything she wanted "without worrying that it would be shared to counselors or others." Here she suggests that these were places where she could be a Native and communicate as such, not only in her own language but also in language divorced from the treatment discourse of the prison. Another felt intimidated in the Western-style groups and would not speak because of fear of punishment. As she put it: "I wasn't my true self. In the talking circle, I realized more about myself and I needed to change more than just drug and alcohol abuse." She thought this happened "through listening to others." She said that she felt accepted when she expressed frustration and anger in the talking circle. One woman believed that programs concerned with the experience and process of grieving were an urgent need. "We are losing people because of drugs and alcohol; we need to grieve before we can move on. Alcohol is killing everyone."

Coping Experiences

A number of women with urban backgrounds or with experience of living on the streets of Anchorage distinguished between the coping experience of rural and urban Native women. Rural women missed Native foods and visits from their families, found the expectations of group therapy difficult to meet, had problems comprehending and following institutional rules, and appreciated and responded to programs that brought Native culture to the prison. Rural women were said to be "naïve and fearful of the big city and the separation from everything they know." Some urban women were uninterested in Native culture, but others said that prison was the first place they had been introduced to their culture and found the experience positive and a move toward discovering their cultural identity.

Urban women suggested that they experienced some difficulties in relating to rural women. One woman who lived with both urban and rural women in her wing exemplified this. She explained: "The young city women didn't grow up like I did, they grew up in white society with TV and computers and they don't speak their own language." It emerged that staff relied largely on Native women inmates to instruct new Native inmates on the rules and practices of the institution and to "show them the ropes." Some women found this pedagogy "overwhelming," unused to being approached by so many women and being in such a densely populated environment. Some thought that there should be a specific orientation program for Native women.

One specific coping strategy was the formation of small familylike groups[21] of Native inmates where women were encouraged to speak their own language and support each other in dealing with problems and issues within the prison, and as one woman designated as a mother put it: "They come to me with problems if they don't get along." One effect of this support was the suspicion with which others regarded the Native women when they spoke in their own language. Other women expressed the importance of the informal family as being a group of persons "you can reach out to and you know you can trust," and an older woman said that she was addressed as "Grandma" because of her gray hair. Another woman said two younger girls addressed her as "Momma."

Rural Native women lead much less regulated lives than in the detailed prison regime and have great difficulty in adjusting to the prison restrictions and multiplicity of rules. Natives who have regular contact with visitors seem to cope better with the regime. Staff pointed out that it was difficult, if not impossible, for rural Natives to receive visits, due to the distance and cost. This, staff felt, caused rural Natives to feel overwhelmed and lost, but they suffered in silence. Some urban women were able to receive visitors but chose not to do so, because, as one woman put it: "I'd rather talk to them on the phone, I don't like them to see me here; it makes me feel bad." Some cope by isolating themselves from the inmate population and even from other Native women. They are afraid that they may be written up for some rule they do not understand.

The prison experience helped some women by giving, as one woman put it, "tools to help me stay sober." She did not want to come back, saying, "I don't like being away from my kids and family." Another coped initially with what she described as her frightening prison experience—being around street girls and hearing about street life, drugs, and the use of guns for protection—by spending the $700 she received each month from her husband on purchases for other inmates, to avoid their verbal abuse and gain their acceptance. She was introduced to crack/cocaine in prison and learned to smoke it while in the substance abuse program and in the female offender program. She did what she "had to in group." "I used to cry about my crime in group but I had no feelings about it" and "I cried and acted remorseful." It was not the treatment program that influenced her to stop using drugs but thinking about her children; "that was my turning point."

"Staying to myself and keeping busy" and "keeping a low profile" were coping strategies employed by a number of women. Keeping busy involved being active in prison by undertaking prison work and activities, and for many women, making handicrafts, but some women complained of boredom even when busy. One woman said that for her the prison experience was "long, exhausting, and boring" and another that she was "going through the days angry." Native women had one specific complaint about beadwork, a popular handicraft for Natives at the prison. They were forced to buy beads through the prison but had supplies at home that could be brought in and used. They were told that the institution's concern was contraband.

Rural and urban Native women had experienced prejudice from the white women living in their wing. One woman described how white women showed this prejudice by laughing and joking about certain Native women and "talking to us like we are dumb and stupid." She said that she experienced this attitude regularly and would bring it up in groups and with staff.

The staff and inmate relationship was a major focus for most Native women. Approaches to staff ranged from giving them respect, in which case they felt that staff reciprocated; to avoiding them altogether, as staff were perceived as having the potential to impose disciplinary write-ups, which would affect an inmate's status generally, including eligibility for furlough. Disciplinary action for offenses relating to locking oneself out of one's room, falling asleep, missing count, and not doing chores were regarded by some as of minor importance. They complained that sanctions for these offenses were imposed at will rather than being dealt with through the formal machinery of the disciplinary board and that the penalties were too harsh, for example, wearing an orange suit, writing essays, and cleaning a wing for a week, all of which were perceived as humiliations. Women who had no experience of a structured lifestyle outside prison felt that they were being unfairly penalized when they failed to comply with time restrictions such as being in their wing at a specific time to be counted. Good relations with staff could be enhanced by "laughing and joking" with them, and those inmates who possessed the skill to do this would "tease, laugh, and joke" and as a result were seen to be gaining more privileges. Only a few of the Native women possess these skills.[22]

Prison practices and rules predicated on a white cultural background caused difficulties for the Native women. One example is the use of written commissary slips to effect purchases from the prison commissary. There is no exchange of money, the actual accounting being performed at a later stage. Inmates are expected to be aware of their financial resources at all times and not to write slips when they have no funds. If they do so, they face disciplinary action. Many Native women are unused to this kind of accounting, and consequently, were written up for infractions.

Women were uncomfortable being located adjacent to sex offenders, especially since many had themselves been victimized sexually. Their discomfort also incorporated a perception that the male sex offenders had better facilities, equipment, and programs. An added complaint was being forced to share dinning facilities and also staff who had previously been employed in the sex offender program.

Referring to Native values and practices, one woman said: "Silence for natives is taught as a form of respect, but in jail silence is offensive to other races. They say we are in denial—we were taught to keep our eyes down—whites say you are in denial—this is how we show respect." The same woman thought that the greatest problem that Native women faced in coping with prison was their cultural learning. "In our culture we are taught to be humble and not to say things about our problems but just to deal with it." She gave as examples women agreeing with the staff when they rejected their requests and taking the attitude that it was no use standing up for oneself: "If the guards say no, we just agree."

DISCUSSION

In the expanding literature on women's criminality and their experience as prisoners, most discussion has ignored culture, although some attention has been given to Native Americans (see, e.g., Grobsmith, 1994; Ross, 1998). A major focus of this discussion has been the centrality of culture and the standpoint of marginalized Native cultures in the Alaskan prison setting. The cultural narratives of the Alaskan Native women, combined with staff narratives and located within the framework of the prison regime at Hiland Mountain, constitute a rich body of knowledge concerning the criminality and experience of prison for these women. I adopt the view of Chesney-Lind and Sheldon (1998) that explanations for women's criminality need to be grounded in their specific life experiences and problems, and I would add, in the case of these women, in their own cultural practices and worldview. Cultural difference matters, especially when deprived of liberty in a prison setting, participating in programs designed for the dominant culture and administered primarily by members of that culture. Whatever may be the constraints, culture does not cease to define identity as it represents "a historically transmitted pattern of meanings embodied in symbolic forms by means of which men communicate, perpetuate, and develop their knowledge about and attitudes towards life"[23] (Geertz, in Kuper, 1999, p. 98). Native Alaskan women do not lose their "webs of significance," but they find that to others their culture is perceived as a set of "attitudes" demonstrating resistance, silence, and noncooperation. Social change has brought trauma to Native Alaskans generally in the form of alcoholism, high rates of depression and suicide, family dysfunction and dislocation, and violent and abusive relationships. The women's life experiences have been shaped and affected by these traumas.

Native Alaskan women, especially those from the rural areas, suffer not only deprivation of liberty but also deprivation of their cultural identity. This occurs in their dislocation from family, friends, and community, in their loss of traditional nourishment, and through severing of the spiritual and affective processes that implicate their cultures. The prison environment at Hiland reinforces feelings of powerlessness, dislocation, oppression, and distance already part of the women's social and historical experience following colonization.

From my research emerges a series of oppositions and inversions that flow from the interaction between the Native Alaskan women and other prisoners and staff. The women engage themselves in these oppositions and inversions as a means of constructing an identity enabling them to survive the prison experience. It would seem that the aim of the prison regime is creation of an "ideal prisoner" possessing assertive qualities valued by the dominant culture but showing the necessary subserveince valued within the prison environment. The achievement of this ideal presents significant problems for non-Native prisoners who are members of the dominant culture, let alone for Native Alaskans. It is likely that Alaskan Native women at Hiland Mountain prison will never measure up to this ideal, and in this respect the prison is a microcosm of Native experience of white Alaskan society, where the traumatic experience of colonization has marginalized and criminalized so many Alaskan Native women.

ACKNOWLEDGMENTS

I would like to thank the administration and staff of Hiland Mountain prison for their cooperation and assistance for this research. My appreciation also goes to David Blurton and Gary Copus of the University of Alaska Fairbanks for their administrative assistance for this project. Most of all, I would like to thank the Alaskan Native women who participated in the project by giving their time and stories.

NOTES

1. Hensel (1996) contends that for the Yupik "subsistence is the central focus in the intellectual, material and spiritual culture of both historic and contemporary Yupik society" (p. 3) and Chance (1990) writes that for the Inupiat "subsistence hunting and fishing are still fundamental to nutrition and culture" (p. 200).

2. At the end of World War II the majority of Alaskan Native people lived in isolated communities away from urban centers (Simeone, 1995, p. 43).

3. For example, Fienup-Riordan (1994) says that food sharing and gift giving constitute the core of Yupik social life (p. 49).

4. This is not the place to discuss the causes of alcohol abuse by indigenous people generally; however, Saggers and Gray (1998, p. 88) note that this excessive alcohol consumption may be perceived to have many causes and, after assessing indigenous usage in Australia, New Zealand, and Canada, are of the view that "reasons for drinking are themselves a function of relationships between indigenous and non-indigenous societies within the broader web of political and economic relationships. That is, they are symptoms of underlying inequalities."

5. The regional suicide rate has increased from 5.5 to 55.5 per 100,000 over the last 20 years. This is five times the national rate (Lenz, in Fienup-Riordon, 1994, p. 40).

6. Positivism involves using the scientific method, which is based on the assumption that there is an "objective" truth or reality which can be measured and tested through observation of the real world (Bernard, 1988, p. 12). Positivism searches for the "one truth" that can assist researchers to identify "social laws" that can "predict and control behaviour" (Stanley & Wise, 1993, p. 117). In the social sciences this search involves using the methods and procedures of the "pure" sciences.

7. Roberts (1981, p. 16) argues that within the notion of "reflexivity" is the process within which feminists incorporate their own "experience" into their work.

8. Bierne (1983) criticizes Winch's position, which suggests that researchers must "go native" if they are to achieve this goal. Like Strathern, Bierne argues that "we can only understand the social life of other cultures through the prison of our own linguistic and conceptual apparatus" (p. 385).

9. During my second period of interviews focusing on the staff, one Alaskan Native woman inmate asked why I hadn't interviewed her since she felt she had a particular point of view which should be included in my research. I assured her that the issue had been one of time, and we arranged an interview.

10. From 1980 to 1989, Alaskan Native mortality rate was 698 per 100,000 while the Alaskan non-Native mortality rate was 341 per 100,000. Injuries or suicide caused one-third of Native deaths and alcohol was implicated 98 percent of the time. The average life expectancy for Alaskan Natives rose from 48 to 68 between 1950 and 1984 but is still significantly lower than the overall U.S. average of 75 (Middaugh, 1995, and Middaugh et al., 1991, in Nader, Dubrow, and Stamm, 1999).

11. In fiscal year 1995, 1049 CINA cases were filed in Alaska's courts, about half in Anchorage. This represents an increase over the preceding year, when 713 cases were filed. Under the CINA procedures, an adjudication takes place at which a judge decides whether the Department of Family and Youth Services has shown on the evidence that the child taken into custody is a child in need of aid. A 1996 assessment found that less than half of all CINA cases statewide reached the adjudication stage, but Bethel (a Yupik area in the southeast of the state) adjudicated 77 percent of its CINA cases, almost all of which involved Indian children, as compared with Anchorage, which adjudicated 37 percent, Fairbanks 36 percent, and Sitka 43 percent (Alaska Judicial Council, 1996).

12. Many participants enter the RSAP under court order.

13. The Cleary litigation began in 1981. A class action challenged the conditions of correctional facilities in Alaska, and in January 1983 the state superior court approved a partial settlement agreement with a separate settlement agreement being concluded in February 1983 (see *Hertz v. Cleary and Alaska Board of Parole*, 1992).

14. In "The Dangerous Individual," Foucault describes a case where an accused would not respond to questions from the presiding judge as to his motivation for a series of rapes and attempted rapes other than to admit that he committed them (Foucault, 1988). Foucault argues that much more is required of an accused "beyond admission; there must be confession, self-examination, explanation of one's self, revelation of what one is" (p. 126). According to Foucault, the criminal justice system is unable to function unless "provided with another type of discourse, the one given by the accused about himself, or the one which he makes possible for others through his confessions, memories, intimate disclosures etc." (pp.126–127).

15. Ross (1998) found in Montana that the wardens frequently perceived the interest of Native prisoners in Native religion as a "step back to savage ways."

16. It may be that in the talking circle Native traditions are now mediated through Western notions of time and self-concept and the women see the talking circle as another form of therapy.

17. Less than 8.5 percent of employees of the Alaska Department of Corrections are Alaskan Native (Riley, 2000).

18. Grobsmith (1994, Chapter 5) discusses the Native experience of substance abuse treatment in prisons in Nebraska. Referring to AA meetings, she notes that "they feel conspicuous as minority members; they dislike the Judeo-Christian orientation of AA and feel it is not relevant to their Native American practices; they are often shy and reticent about speaking up in front of others, thereby drawing attention not only to themselves but to shameful acts in which they may have engaged; and finally, they do not feel that genuine self-growth can occur in an environment where correctional officers are present. Confiding personal things about one's activities—whether past or present—is too risky in a prison setting where inmates suspect that guards will not keep their confidence . . . " (p. 116). By contrast, Ross (1998) found that in Montana, Native teachings are viewed as strengthening and healing and that many Native prisoners seek out their culture while imprisoned.

19. Owen (1998) found that compared to male prison culture, female prison culture tolerated a higher level of "telling."

20. The spiritual and affective dimensions within one American Indian culture are expressed by Twylah Hurd of the Seneca, who points out that listening was a major characteristic of Native society and that "Native spirituality is connected to the heart and Earth. Foreign spirituality is connected to the head" (Kulchyski, McCaskill, & Newhouse, 1999, p. 84). He says that "Native people function from within; that is where all their gifts are, and other cultures had to have something outside, whereas a Native person will look at the outside things as adding to whatever comfort they have" (p. 89).

21. Owen (1998) discusses the formation of families by women in prison based on her own research in the largest women's prison in California. She observed two broad categories of relationships: those of play families and homosexual relationships. She argues that the play family is an "enduring feature of women's prison culture" and that they reflect the role played by women outside the prison. Although some families play a romantic couple, characteristically an older woman will take on the role of the mother, with a younger woman taking on the role of a daughter.

22. Owen (1998) observed in her study of a California women's prison that one survival mechanism used by the women is the development of "prison smarts," where a woman learns through experience how to manage the prison community resources and staff in a way that allows her to do her own time. One key aspect of prison smarts is the ability to get things done, called "juice," and some women are able to gain a reputation for this.

23. In this instance, Geertz is using the term *men* in the generic sense.

REFERENCES

ALASKA JUDICIAL COUNCIL. (1996). *Improving the court process for Alaska's children in need of aid: Executive summary*. Anchorage, AK: AJC.

BANKS, C. (2000). *Developing cultural criminology: Theory and practice in Papua New Guinea*. Sydney, Australia: Sydney Institute of Criminology.

BEIRNE, P. (1983). Cultural relativism and comparative criminology. *Contemporary Crisis, 7*, 371–391.

BERNARD, H. R. (1988). *Research methods in cultural anthropology*. London: Sage Publications.

BROD, T. M. (1975). Alcoholism as a mental health problem of Native Americans. *Archives of general psychiatry, 32*: 1385–1391.

BURBANK, V. K. (1994). *Fighting women: Anger and aggression in aboriginal Australia*. Berkeley, CA: University of California Press.

CAIN, M. (1990). Realist philosophy and standpoint epistemologies or feminist criminology as a successor science. In L. Gelsthorpe & A. Morris (Eds.), *Feminist perspectives in criminology* (pp. 124–140). Buckingham, England: Open University Press.

CAULFIELD, S., & WONDERS, N. (1994). Gender and justice: Feminist contributions to criminology. In G. Barak (Ed.), *Varieties of criminology* (pp. 213–229). Westport, CT: Praeger.

CHANCE, N. A. (1990). *The Inupiat and arctic Alaska: An ethnography of development*. Forth Worth, TX: Holt, Rinehart & Winston.

CHESNEY-LIND, M., & SHELDEN, R. (1998). *Girls, delinquency, and juvenile justice*. Belmont, CA: West/Wadsworth.

COLLINS, P. H. (1990). *Black feminist thought: Knowledge, consciousness, and the politics of empowerment*. New York: Routledge.

DOBASH, R. E., & DOBASH, R. (1992). *Women, violence and social change*. London: Routledge.

DuBOIS, B. (1983). Passionate scholarship: Notes on values, knowing and method in feminist social science. In G. Bowles & R. D. Klein (Eds.), *Theories of women's studies* (pp. 105–116). London: Routledge & Kegan Paul.

FIENUP-RIORDAN, A. (1994). *Boundaries and passages: Rule and ritual in Yup'ik Eskimo oral tradition*. Norman, OK: University of Oklahoma Press.

FLOWERS, R. B. (1995). *Female crime, criminals and cellmates: An exploration of female criminality and delinquency*. Jefferson, NC: McFarland Publishers.

FOUCAULT, M. (1988). *The dangerous individual*. In L. D. Kritzman (Ed.), *Michel Foucault: Politics, philosophy, culture: Interviews and other writings, 1977–1984* (pp. 125–151). New York: Routledge.

Gelsthorpe, L. (1990). Feminist methodologies in criminology: A new approach or old wine in new bottles? In L. Gelsthorpe & A. Morris (Eds.), *Feminist perspectives in criminology* (pp. 89–106). Buckingham, England: Open University Press.

GELSTHORPE, L., & MORRIS, A. (EDS.). (1990). *Feminist perspectives in criminology*. Buckingham, England: Open University Press.

GILLIGAN, C. (1993). *In a different voice*. Cambridge, MA: Harvard University Press.

GROBSMITH, E. (1994). *Indians in prison: Incarcerated Native Americans in Nebraska*. Lincoln, NE: University of Nebraska Press.

HAMMERSLEY, M. (1992). *What's wrong with ethnography? Methodological exploration*. London: Routledge.

HARDING, S. (1987). Introduction: Is there a feminist method? In S. Harding (Ed.), *Feminism and methodology* (pp. 1–14). Bloomington, IN: Indiana University Press.

HENSEL, C. (1996). *Telling our selves: Ethnicity and discourse in southwestern Alaska*. New York: Oxford University Press.

KELLY, L. (1988). *Surviving sexual violence*. Cambridge: Polity Press.

KELLY, L. (1990). Journeying in reverse: Possibilities and problems in feminist research on sexual violence. In L. Gelsthorpe & A. Morris (Eds.), *Feminist perspectives in criminology* (pp. 107–114). Buckingham, England: Open University Press.

KRAUS, R., AND BUFFLER, P. (1979). Sociocultural stress and the American Native in Alaska: An analysis of changing patterns of psychiatric illness and alcohol abuse among Alaska Natives. *Culture, Medicine, and Psychiatry, 3*: 111–151.

KULCHYSKI, P., MCCASKILL, D., & NEWHOUSE, D. (EDS.). (1999). *In the words of elders: Aboriginal cultures in transition*. Toronto, Ontario, Canada: University of Toronto Press.

KUPER, A. (1999). *Culture: The anthropologist's account*. Cambridge, MA: Harvard University Press.

LUJAN, C. C. (1995). Women warriors: American Indian women, crime, and alcohol. *Women and Criminal Justice, 7*(1), 9–31.

MIES, M. (1983). Towards a methodology for feminist research. In G. Bowles & R. D. Klein (Eds.), *Theories of women's studies* (pp. 177–139). London: Routledge & Kegan Paul.

NADER, K., DUBROW, N., & STAMM, B. H. (Eds.). (1999). *Honoring differences: Cultural issues in the treatment of trauma and loss*. Philadelphia: Brunner/Mazel.

NELKEN, D. (ED.). (1994). *The futures of criminology*. London: Sage Publications.

NIELSON, J. M. (1990). Introduction. In J. M. Nielson (Ed.), *Feminist research methods: Exemplary readings in the social sciences* (pp. 1–37). Boulder, CO: Westview Press.

ORBE, M. (1998). *Constructing co-cultural theory: An explication of culture, power, and communication*. Thousand Oaks, CA: Sage Publications.

OWEN, B. (1998). "In the mix": Struggle and survival in a women's prison. Albany, NY: State University of New York Press.

PHILLIPS, M., & INUI, T. (1986). The interaction of mental illness, criminal behavior and culture: Native Alaskan mentally ill criminal offenders. *Culture, medicine and psychiatry, 10*, 123–149.

RIERDEN, A. (1997). *The farm: Life inside a women's prison*. Amherst, MA: University of Masssachusetts Press.

RILEY, J. (2000). Obstacles to minority employment in criminal justice: Recruiting Alaska Natives. *Alaska Justice Forum, 16*(4).

ROBERTS, H. (1981). Women and their doctors: Power and powerlessness in the research process. In H. Roberts (Ed.), *Doing feminist research* (pp. 7–29). London: Routledge.

ROSS, L. (1998). *Inventing the savage: The social construction of Native American criminality*. Austin, TX: University of Texas Press.

ROSS, R. (1996). Leaving our white eyes behind: The sentencing of Native accused. In M. Nielsen & R. Silverman (Eds.), *Native Americans, crime, and justice* (pp. 152–169). Boulder, CO: Westview Press.

SAGGERS, S., & GRAY, D. (1998). *Dealing with alcohol: Indigenous usage in Australia, New Zealand and Canada*. Cambridge, MA: Cambridge University Press.

SCHAFER, N. E., CURTIS, R., & ATWELL, C. (1997). *Disproportionate representation of minorities in the Alaska juvenile justice system: Phase 1 report*. Justice Center, University of Alaska–Anchorage.

SIMEONE, W. (1995). *Rifles, blankets, and beads: Identity, history, and the Northern Athapaskan potlatch*. Norman, OK: University of Oklahoma Press.

SOMMERS, E. (1995). *Voices from within: Women who have broken the law*. Toronto, Ontario, Canada: University of Toronto Press.

STANLEY, L., & WISE, S. (1993). *Breaking out again: Feminist ontology and epistemology* (2nd ed.). London: Routledge.

STATISTICAL ANALYSIS UNIT. (1999). Growth in corrections: State, national and international numbers. *Alaska Justice Forum, 15*(4), 1, 4–6.

STRATHERN, M. (1981). Culture in a netbag: The manufacture of a subdiscipline in anthropology. *Man, 16*, 665–688.

STRATHERN, M. (1988). *The gender of the gift: problems with women and problems with society in Melanesia*. Berkeley, CA: University of California Press.

WATTERSON, K. (1996). *Women in prison: Inside the concrete womb*. Boston: Northeastern University Press.

WIDOM, C. S. (1989). The cycle of violence. *Science, 244*, 160–166.

WINCH, P. (1958). *The idea of a social science and its relation to philosophy*. London: Routledge & Kegan Paul.

WINCH, P. (1964). Understanding a primitive society. *American Philosophical Quarterly, 1*, 307–324.

CASE

Hertz v. *Cleary and Alaska Board of Parole*, Supreme Court of the State of Alaska (May 29, 1992).

16

Sexual Abuse and Sexual Assault of Women in Prison

Zelma Weston Henriques and Evelyn Gilbert

By the end of 1994, 794,100 women were in prison, jail, or on probation/parole. This number represents 1 of every 130 women in the total population. In 1995 the population of women in prison was 6.3 percent of the overall prison population (Bureau of Justice Statistics, 1995). As of June 30, 1996, there were 73,607 women in federal and state prisons and 63,500 women in local jails. Further, 51 percent of the female jail population were still awaiting trial (Bureau of Justice Statistics, 1997). Flowers (1987) observed that while the crimes of women in jail are mainly misdemeanors and victimless crimes, their fate behind bars is anything but victimless and is perhaps the greatest criminal justice system paradox.

The numbers are indisputable evidence that the paternalistic gloves of the criminal justice system have been removed. The public has accepted a punitive response to women who step outside the bounds of their socially prescribed role. But are women to be subjected to all the degradations of punishment that characterize male offenders? Some believe that incarcerated women have always experienced harsher punishment than men. The suggestion is that the harsh punishment of women is evidenced by the number of penal facilities; geographic placement; lack of variety in female institutions; absence of educational, treatment, and vocational programming in women's prisons; and the virtual absence of transitional or alternative programs. On the other hand, some believe that imprisonment and its accompanying deprivations are the "just deserts" of persons who violate the criminal law. Do all deprivations equal just deserts?

Since the first system of laws was developed, punishment has been officially sanctioned as a means of regulating behavior (Allen & Simonsen, 1995, p. 69). While most people agree that those who violate societal standards must be sanctioned, few understand that the significance of punishment flows from the perspective of the one being punished. If the punishment is perceived as undeserved, unjust, or too harsh, and other inmates reinforce this belief, offenders' deviant behavior is more likely to be reinforced by punishment. It is incumbent upon the state and its representatives (i.e., correctional officers) to be irreproachable paragons of community citizenship, to champion superior values, and to foster conformist behavior (Allen & Simonsen, 1995, pp. 71, 72), even in the punishment of criminals.

A century ago, women reformers advocated the creation of separate correctional institutions for women. The reformers were repulsed by the abuse of female inmates at the hands of male guards. They abhorred the widespread practice of abuses in the male-dominated prison system. Elizabeth Fry (1790–1845), a British Quaker, is attributed with early prison reform. She felt that female custodial officers in prison would prevent sexual assault of female inmates by male guards (Freedan, 1974, p. 79). According to Pollock (1990, p. 43), sexual abuse was disturbingly common in custodial prisons run by men. Women might be fondled at intake and raped in their cells by their male keepers. On other occasions, guards would make sport of their sexual encounters with their female captives ("An illustrated history," 1871).

Separate penal facilities for women are still dominated by male custodial officers, and there is no evidence that sexual assaults have diminished with the introduction of female correctional officers. According to Flowers (1987, p. 161), sexual and physical abuse and harassment of female prisoners is "a common practice" in many small jails, especially in the South. An example is the case of Joan Little, a black female inmate in a North Carolina county jail, who killed her white jailer after he tried to sexually assault her. For this woman, the penalty under law for murder was a less severe punishment than the sexual assault at the hands of the custodial officers. Patsy Sims, an investigative journalist, found Joan Little's experience not unique among incarcerated women. In interviews of more than fifty incarcerated women, Sims (1976) heard stories of oral sex through the jail bars, trespass of male trustees into women's cells, and offers of reduced sentences in exchange for sexual favors.

It would appear that sexual assault and harassment of women by male correctional officers is not an issue in correctional management. Sims (1976) describes the system response as less than apathetic. This type of response contributes to the harshness of punishment for imprisoned women. Additionally, women in custodial regimes are " . . . probably lonelier and certainly more vulnerable to sexual exploitation, easier to ignore because so few in number, and viewed with distaste by prison officials, women in custodial units were treated as the dregs of the state prisoner population" (Rafter, 1990, p. 21). The literature on imprisoned women recognizes their exploitation and the fact that they have little or no choice but to submit to the predations of their keepers (Pollock, 1997). Women are imprisoned for punishment. Their exploitation by male custodial officers is an additional degradation of imprisonment. Lack of recourse to prevent the sexual assault makes the imprisonment severe punishment. While imprisonment may be just deserts for the crime committed, forced sexual assault is undeserved, unjust, and harsh punishment. Sexual assault of female inmates by male correctional staff is inconsistent with the goals of retribution, deterrence, incapacitation, or rehabilitation.

DEFINITION OF THE PROBLEM

Sexual assault is the gender-neutral term now used to refer to the sexual violation of both women and men. It is meant to capture the traditional legal concept of rape as well as the traditional notion of homosexual rape. Rape may be defined as the forced carnal knowledge of a woman by a man. Homosexual rape referred to male-on-male sodomy. Despite the statutory differences, by state, in the term used to refer to traditional rape, a generic definition of the offense *criminal sexual assault* is "any genital, anal, or oral penetration, by a part of the accused's body or by an object, using force or without the victim's consent" (Tuite, 1992). Sexual abuse is sometimes used interchangeably with *sexual assault*. While both refer to sexual crimes, *assault* is a specific incident and *abuse* indicates a pattern of behavior. *Sexual harassment* is a pattern of sexual abuse.

Erez and Tontodonato (1992) cite the National Advisory Council on Women's Education Programs' categorization of sexual harassment into five levels. According to this categorization, the nearly total authority used by guards in their interaction with female inmates, as documented in the recent report by Human Rights Watch, equates with the third and fourth levels of sexual harassment. Level three includes a solicitation for sex with the promise of reward. Level four introduces the notion of punishment for failure to comply with a request for sexual favors. Negative consequences ensue for noncooperation. This type of situation is generally thought of as the quintessential sexual harassment (Erez & Tontodonato, 1992, p. 233).

MAGNITUDE OF THE PROBLEM

Scholars and practitioners agree that the precise number of sexual assaults committed yearly is unknown. The medical profession recognizes sexual assault as a violent crime that claims a victim every 45 seconds in this country. Based on this crime clock, more than 700,000 women are sexually assaulted yearly, resulting in two-thirds of these victims under the age of 18 (American Academy of Pediatrics Committee on Adolescence, 1994). In stark terms, one in five women has been the victim of a sexual assault by the time she reaches her twenty-first birthday (Ester & Kuznets, 1994). A former president of the American Medical Association observed that "the crime is shrouded in silence, caused by unfair social myths and biases that incriminate victims rather than offenders."

Official estimates of sexual assault closely parallel those of the medical profession. The evidence from the National Crime Victimization Survey (Bureau of Justice Statistics, 1995) is that at least 500,000 women were victims of attempted rape or rape, and the number not reported ranges from two to six times those reported. While women are 10 times more likely than men to be sexual assault victims, the Survey recorded 49,000 men as victims.[1] All women are potential victims of sexual assault; however, sexual assault victims are characteristically young, low income, and single, separated, or divorced[2]; and African-American women are disproportionate sexual assault victims (Bureau of Justice Statistics, 1994).

Sexual assault is recognized as an increasing problem in the general population. By extension, it is reasonable to believe that the number of sexual assaults among the incarcerated is astronomical. Many women were sexually abused (rape, incest) prior to their incarceration (American Correctional Association, 1990, p. 6; Arnold, 1990; Carlen, 1983; Chesney-Lind & Rodriquez, 1983; Gilfus, 1992; Greenfeld & Minor-Harper, 1991, p. 6; Immarigeon, 1987; Sargent, Marcus-Mendoza, & Yu, 1993). Their continued abuse at the hands of their keepers is therefore an issue that warrants attention and redress. The ACA reports that the average female offender has probably been a victim of sexual abuse (36 percent) a minimum of three to eleven times or more (55 percent) between the ages of 5 and

14 (57 percent). She probably was sexually abused by a male member of the immediate family (49 percent) such as a father or stepfather (23 percent). Reporting the incident resulted in no change or made things worse (49 percent). Greenfeld and Harper-Minor reported that an estimated 22 percent of the women in prison in 1984 said that they had been sexually abused prior to the age of 18. Their study found that women serving time for a violent offense are the most likely of the prisoners to report having experienced prior physical or sexual abuse.

The exact number of male and female prisoners sexually assaulted is unknown. Surveys conservatively estimate more than 290,000 inmates are sexually assaulted behind bars each year (Donaldson, 1993). In 1995, there were 69,028 women in prison and an estimated 135,000 rapes of female inmates nationwide (Bureau of Justice Statistics, 1995). The problem is serious and chronic but has not been adequately studied. Although there are no statistics to document the magnitude of sexual abuse[3] of women in jails, there is reason to believe that the majority of assaults go unreported. Sims (1976) contends that the stories she heard from incarcerated women are substantiated by attorneys, correction officers, and law enforcement personnel. A Manhattan lawyer concedes: "Inmates are in a completely vulnerable position and are very susceptible to sexual advances by guards for a variety of reasons" (Golding, 1998). For example, between January 1990 and June 1995, 76 sexual misconduct complaints were filed by inmates at the Albion State Correctional Facility near Rochester, New York. Albion is New York State's largest prison for women, and male custodial officers outnumber female correctional officers by a 3:1 ratio. Of the 76 complaints, 56 were dropped (mainly because inmates refused to talk when questioned), but 14 cases were substantiated. As a result, six officers were transferred from Albion and one officer received counseling. Six cases remain open (Williams, 1996).

Absent empirical data, anecdotal reports of custodial sexual assault of females are rich sources of the magnitude and nature of the problem. An example from New York is worthy of note. Twenty-two-year-old inmate Felita Dobbins, serving time at Bedford Hills, accused a correction officer of sexually abusing her. To substantiate her claim, she retained the officer's semen in a perfume bottle. According to the assaulted inmate, the officer threatened to kill members of her family, including her 2-year-old daughter, if she reported the incident. Upon arrest for forcible sodomy, the officer resigned from his job. He pled guilty to the lesser charge of sexual abuse and received five years' probation. Of her experience, the inmate lamented: "In their eyes I was the criminal, so why not go with the officer?" (Williams, 1996). This is a common experience among female inmates, as the following case demonstrates. A Delaware inmate, Dorothy Carrigan, accused a prison guard of raping her. When the guard finished, he tossed the used condom on the inmate's bed and told her to flush it down the toilet. The inmate turned the used condom in to prison officials. Although the custodial officer was charged under a Delaware law that prohibits sex between prisoners and correctional workers, prison officials and prosecutors alleged that the female inmate consented to engage in sex with the officer (Holmes, 1996).

Apparently, in prison there is a fine line between consensual and nonconsensual sex. Whether or not female inmates can overcome the "willing participant" hurdle, they are still punished for making the accusation. Consider the Delaware inmate. After making the accusation of rape, Dorothy was immediately transferred from a minimum-security section of the women's prison to the maximum-security section. While in maximum-security, she was beaten and harassed by guards; as a result, she jumped from the second-floor tier of cells to the floor (Holmes, 1996). In addition to assaults, inmates are sexually abused, sometimes as a matter of policy. Although required, the strip search of newly admitted prisoners may be conducted in such a way as to dehumanize inmates. LeBlanc (1996) reports a typical search as described by an inmate:

> To be searched the inmate spreads her legs while the female officer slides a mirror on the end of a long instrument, like an oversize spatula, on the floor. The inmate squats over it and coughs. She also opens her mouth, runs her fingers along her gums and under her breasts and through her pubic hairs. She folds back her ears and wiggles her toes. Then she bends over, as if to touch her toes, and spreads her buttocks and coughs again. (p. 39)

The inmate who provided the description of the search stated that she appreciates it when the officer doesn't stare. At Albion State Facility in New York, strip searches were videotaped from January 1994 to July 1994 in response to inmate complaints of abuse. However, videotaping as a solution to the problem of sexual abuse led to additional issues related to sexual harassment. According to inmates, the tapings represented a systemwide pattern of sexual harassment of women inmates (including incidents of inmates being impregnated by guards) by correctional officers (Rutenberg & Stasi, 1995). A lawsuit filed on behalf of the inmates at Albion State Correctional facility resulted in a settlement from the state in the amount of $1000 per incident to the women involved in each of 85 documented videotaped strip searches (Rutenberg & Stasi, 1995).

Perhaps, women inmates are subjected to harsh punishment because their presence in prison proves that they are not members of the "gentler sex": that is, they have violated gender-role expectations. After all, nice girls don't exhibit behaviors and engage in those activities that cause them to be incarcerated. For Sims (1976), "much of the abuse—sexual and otherwise—is due to an attitude that women prisoners, especially black ones, are little better than animals."[4]

Female inmates who become pregnant as a result of a sexual assault in prison are encouraged to have abortions, while the officers accused of the impregnation are usually allowed to resign (Holmes, 1996; Williams, 1996). If the inmate does continue the pregnancy, she will not be allowed to keep the baby. In either scenario, the woman's right to make decisions about her body and offspring is usurped by the correctional system. Even for women in the general population, being deprived of the ability to make a decision to get pregnant and keep the baby is harsh treatment. For female inmates this amounts to severe punishment and there is no corollary for incarcerated men; it is undeserved and unjust.

Experts acknowledge that it is difficult to measure the extent of the problem but admit that even one such case is too many. Many cases go unreported "partly because of fear, partly because the jailer is considered more believable" than a woman locked up for committing a crime. Dorothy Q. Thomas, director of the Human Rights Watch Women's Rights Project, says that sexual abuse of women in prison by guards is a "hidden, largely accepted, standard operation procedure, and there are very little express administrative rules or laws to prohibit, punish and remedy it." Women who had been imprisoned in the Federal Correctional Institution in Dublin, California, sued the BOP and were awarded monetary damages for their sexual victimization. The women were serving time for nonviolent crimes (drug-related and credit card conspiracy) but were isolated in the men's solitary confinement unit as discipline for fighting. In a civil rights suit, three women alleged that prison officials (guards, lieutenants, a captain, the warden, and regional director of BOP) facilitated and encouraged a prostitution ring in which "guards took money from inmates in return for access to the women" (Opatmy, 1996). Although the regional director was transferred to Denver and the guards left the Dublin prison, available information suggests that none of those named in the suit have been criminally prosecuted or fired from the BOP.

Elaine Lord, the superintendent at New York's Bedford Hills Correctional Facility, states: "The system creates a need to get things and there are too many things to be bargained for." A recent report prepared by Human Rights Watch (1996) notes that guards use their nearly total authority to provide or deny goods and privileges to female prisoners to compel them to have sex, or in other cases, to reward them for having done so.

RESPONSE TO THE PROBLEM

Even when assaults are reported, the response is usually to give more credence to the accused than to the victim. Treating the sexual assault as though it is victim-precipitated is usually a response when a female inmate does make an allegation. However, the traditional response to charges of sexual assault brought against prison employees is to subject the female inmate to punishment (e.g., administrative, disciplinary, or protective confinement).

Since 1979, New Jersey has had a statute that criminalizes sex between inmates and prison employees. Connecticut has had such a law since 1972. Delaware also has such a law. In New York, such a law was enacted in 1996. This law classifies all sex between prison employees and inmates as rape ("Ending sexual abuse," 1996; Golding, 1997). Despite the laws, sexual assaults continue. Few male[5] prison staff who engage in sexual relations with female prisoners ever face legal action (Flowers, 1987, p. 161).

Some women inmates also use sex to demand privileges and favors from guards ("Ending sexual abuse," 1996; Sims, 1976). In her investigation, Sims found women who admitted that some of the sex is by force, while others admitted that the sex was consensual or bartered to obtain better treatment, or to get needed or wanted things such as a candy bar or a Coke. In the Beaufort county jail, there were stories regarding how a jailer named Alligood offered sandwiches or whiskey in exchange for touching a breast (Sims, 1976, p. 137).

Inmates

In confinement, women have fewer resources than are available to victims of sexual assault outside prisons or jails. The victim-response protocol is well known even though most women choose not to invoke the protocol by not reporting the assault. The medical community recommends that sexual assault victims seek help within the first seventy-two hours after an attack to facilitate treatment. Treatment is critical because the victimization causes "lasting emotional distress, self-destructive behavior, interpersonal problems and behavioral disorders" (American Medical Association, 1995).

Female inmates have taken legal action in recent years (Holmes, 1996). Prisons in California, Georgia, and the District of Columbia have reached out-of-court settlements in class-action suits brought on behalf of women alleging sexual harassment and sexual assault by guards while incarcerated. The landmark class-action suit against prison officials because prison inmates were victims of sexual assault was brought by men who had been incarcerated in a Florida prison.[6] In *LaMarca* v. *Turner* (1987), ten inmates of Glades

Correctional Institution claimed that they suffered "unconstitutional conditions of confinement" because of the "deliberate indifference" of the superintendent. The alleged sexual assault or sexual abuse cases of each of the inmates were similar; LaMarca's allegations, outlined in the court's opinion, are indicative:

> On May 14, 1982, Anthony LaMarca, then an inmate at GCI, filed a handwritten *pro se* complaint in the district court stating that he had "been countlessly approached, threatened with physical violence and assaulted by other inmates at [GCI] because [he] refused to participate in homosexual activities, or pay protection to be left alone." He alleged that "a severe lack of protection" existed at GCI and that "the institution seem[ed] unable or unwilling to handle the situation."

The court agreed that conditions of confinement precipitated and sustained violence, thus were unconstitutional:

> *First*, every plaintiff was attacked or threatened with a weapon, typically a knife. The evidence establishes the prevalence of such weapons and Turner's failure to take reasonable measures designed to control such contraband. *Second*, the long duration of several of the attacks, the places in which they occurred, and possibly the fact that they occurred in the first place, are functions of Turner's failure to take even minimal steps to ensure that GCI was adequately patrolled (Aldred raped in shower for fifteen to twenty minutes; Durrance led away at knifepoint from place between bunks which was concealed by hanging blanket; Bronson raped with baseball bat on recreation field in broad daylight; Saunders raped in bathroom for twenty-five to thirty minutes; Harper raped in top bunk; Cobb stabbed in front of canteen in fight lasting ten to twelve minutes). *Third*, Turner's failure to implement adequate reporting procedures for rapes and assaults was a legal cause of plaintiff's psychological and possibly physical damage (Aldred reported rape to several officers with no results; Aldred not given protective confinement; Durrance and Bronson did not report out of fear of consequences; Saunders raped by two inmates who previously had attacked him; Saunders reported rape and received inadequate treatment and no investigation; inmates identified as assailants by LaMarca were not confined for investigation and continued to assault him; classification officer told Johnson to take protective confinement or to get a weapon and fight back). *Fourth*, Turner's callous indifference to the obvious and rampant indicia of homosexual activity was the proximate cause of rapes, attacks, or repeated harassment (Aldred, Durrance, Bronson, Saunders, and Harper raped; Bronson forced to commit nonconsensual sexual act in movie trailer; Johnson sexually harassed and later attacked four times; constant threats and sexual solicitation caused LaMarca to escape, take protective confinement, and receive disciplinary reports; Cobb injured in fight over homosexual). *Fifth*, Turner's failure to adequately supervise correctional officers up to the lieutenant level resulted in corruption and incompetence among the officers and a lack of reasonable protection of inmates (Cobb's assailant worked as an "enforcer" with GCI staff and was protected by them; LaMarca complained to Barrett about threats and assaults and was given a knife by Barrett; Bronson afraid to report rape because he had witnessed inmates exchanging money and drugs with guards).

The court accepted inmates' evidence of sexual assault or sexual abuse and said that the superintendent was aware of the problems at the prison but did not take actions to protect inmates from violence. The court found that the inmates had been subjected to cruel and unusual punishment in violation of the Eighth Amendment protection from violence and ordered monetary awards to the inmates: "[D]ue to [their] very nature as acts of violence, the rapes that occurred are not isolated incidents of sexual conduct, but rather flow directly from the lawless prison conditions at GCI. . . . [These conditions created] the background and climate which . . . preordained homosexual rapes and other inmate assault[s]."

Finally, the court established two committees to recommend additional actions. The penological committee was required to find out if there were other rape victims in the prison and to prevent further sexual assaults. A committee composed of psychiatrists and psychologists was charged with (1) prescribing treatment for the inmates who brought suit, and (2) developing a prison strategy to provide support for rape victims.

Organizations and advocacy groups have taken up the cause of female inmates sexually assaulted. Examples include the American Civil Liberties Union's Prison Project, National Women's Law Center (both in Washington, DC), California Prison Focus (based in San Francisco), National Lawyers' Guild, and Amnesty International Americas Regional Program. The inmates at Chowchilla Valley State Prison for Women sent a grievance to the California Prison Focus detailing "sexual assault, improper touching, leering at women in showers, intimidation and constant verbal harassment" (California Prison Focus, 1998) by male corrections officers. The sexual assault or sexual abuse took place in the solitary confinement unit at the prison. After an on-site investigation of the inmates' complaints, the California Prison Focus contacted the director of the prison and (1) demanded a response to the allegations, (2) asked for the removal of male custodial officers from the solitary confinement unit, and (3) requested a meeting to discuss their preliminary findings.

The inmate alone must cope with feelings of shame, anger, and guilt for being victimized. As with women who are not incarcerated, the victim of sexual assault is viewed as culpable in letting the assault happen. Similarly, the assaulted inmate experiences isolation, fear, and helplessness as she struggles with the question "Where can I go for help and protection?" The experience is most likely to be difficult to survive since the inmate may be isolated from and shunned by other female inmates.

Correctional Officers

The prison work environment requires that the corrections officer function as a social control agent who has primary responsibilities of custody, security, and control. Correctional staff are organized along rigid paramilitary lines consisting of a chain of command of structure composed of the ranks of officer trainee, officer, sergeant, lieutenant, captain, major, deputy for custody, and the superintendent or warden. Officers are the line staff responsible for the direct supervision of inmates and daily enforcement of all policy and procedures set forth by the managerial staff (Lombardo, 1981, p. 310). Lombardo used the term *people worker* to analyze the role of the correctional officer, noting that the officer must work with inmates on a personal level in an environment of physical closeness over long periods of time (p. 311).

Many correction officers are drawn to the job to help other human beings and to engage in activities that are intrinsically worthwhile. Correctional officers hunger for opportunities to improve the quality of life in the prison community and grasp them when they can. Like most of us, they want to be people who matter.

The organizational goals of U.S. prisons directly proscribe or indirectly influence the role of the correctional officer (Hepburn & Albonetti, 1980). Historically, prisons have emphasized the custody functions of control and security (Lombardo, 1981, p. 317). In recognition of the complexity of their duties, guards are now called correctional officers, and training academies routinely provide new hires with weeks of orientation and sophisticated training covering such skill areas as the use of physical force, report writing, and sensitivity to cultural diversity. In addition, there are some correctional managers who have instituted ongoing professional training for employees and membership in organizations such as the American Society of Criminology (Pollock, 1990, p. 294).

Most correctional facilities combine the dual roles of custody and treatment. This duality creates role conflict for the correctional officer. The goal of custody demands that the principal rule of interaction between officers and inmates is to maintain maximum social distance (Lombardo, 1981, p. 318). Beginning in the 1960s, rehabilitation became an important goal of prisons. The introduction of treatment as a goal required nonpunitive control of inmates, relaxed discipline, a willingness to form affective ties, informal relationships that resulted in minimized social distance with inmates, and the exercise of discretion based on individual characteristics and situations (p. 318). The central goal of the treatment role entails flexibility, the use of discretionary justice, and the ability to secure inmate compliance through informal exchange relationships that deviate from the written rules (p. 319). Administrators formally and informally create an expectation that correctional officers should define themselves as agents of change who will use discretion as they engage in the daily process of helping the treatment staff to rehabilitate inmates while maintaining security and enforcing the roles (Cressey, 1965; Poole & Regoli, 1981; President's Commission, 1967). Correctional officers are expected to exercise professional judgment and flexibility in performing their job and are subject to disciplinary action if they themselves violate the rules or permit inmates to violate the numerous official rules and procedures of the prison (Hepburn, 1985).

Yet Poole and Regoli (1981) note that introducing such rehabilitation-related practices as due process rights in disciplinary actions, limited use of solitary confinement, and formal inmate grievance mechanisms has undermined the ability of the correctional officer to use coercive power, with a corresponding loss of officer control, and provided inmates with a countervailing power. This places the officer in the stressful position of having to serve two masters. Many officers express the opinion that administrators and treatment staff have more respect and affinity for inmates than for officers, suggesting that the social distance between correctional officers and administrators may even be greater than that between officers and inmates (Lombardo, 1981, p. 321).

The relationship between the correctional officer and inmate is one of *structured conflict* (Jacobs & Kraft, 1978). Inmates do not want to be incarcerated and naturally resent the staff assigned to control them (p. 309). The corrections officer is both a manager and a worker: a low-status worker in relationship to superior officers, but a manager of inmates. As the lowest level in the correctional hierarchy, the officer is under surveillance by corrections management and the scrutiny of inmates. Officers often experience a sense of emotional isolation. They work alone or as a part of a small team, but always with the expectation that they are capable of performing the functions of the job independently (Jacobs & Kraft, 1978, p. 311). Officers possess power in relation to inmates. In discussing the bases of control, Poole and Regoli (1981) identify and define legitimate power and coercive power. These authors note that "legitimate power is rooted in the legal authority given the officer to exercise control over inmates because of their structural relationship within the prison." The position of the officer in this relationship confers the right to have orders obeyed and authority respected. The position of the inmate in the relationship conveys the duty to obey orders.

Coercive power, on the other hand, is based on the inmate perception that officers have the ability to punish rule violators, either formally (through the use of written reports of misconduct) or informally (by beating or other forms of physical and psychological abuse). Although this power is limited by the possibility of legal or administrative action against the officer, it nevertheless serves to remind the inmate that coercion is a basis of power within the prison. This is demonstrated by cell searches, assignment to disciplinary units, random strip searches, and lethal force to accomplish compliance (Poole & Regoli, 1981, p. 314). Upon arrival at the correctional facility, inmates are informed that they are expected to follow all the rules or suffer the consequences (Poole & Regoli, 1981, p. 315).

Criminal Justice System

Many states have laws criminalizing sexual assault or sexual abuse of prisoners. The effectiveness of these laws has yet to be determined, but it is interesting to note several of the laws. When New York State introduced the legislation, The New York State Department of Correctional Services took the position that because inmates are under the control of employees twenty-four hours a day, they cannot give free consent, and without consent it is a crime ("Ending sexual abuse," 1996). Prior to the enactment of the 1996 law, the union pledged support for the bill only if it included an amendment that would safeguard against false accusations made by inmates: make false accusations a felony rather than a misdemeanor. Republican Assemblyman Michael Balboni of Nassau County, New York, has expressed skepticism about accusations by inmates, acknowledging that people in prison are not particularly believable and that by their presence in prison they have demonstrated they're not going to play by the rules (Williams, 1996). Former New York City Commissioner of Corrections, State Senator Catherine Abate, one of the sponsors of the bill, resisted the amendment, arguing that further penalties on inmates may increase their reluctance to come forward since many women already submit to sex as a "condition of confinement" ("Ending sexual abuse," 1996).

In 1997, the Federal Bureau of Prisons amended its policy statement on sexual assault "to include instances of staff-on-inmate sexual abuse/assault" (Federal Bureau of Prisons, 1997) in recognition of the vulnerability of inmates to their keepers. The policy defines two types of sexual abuse or assault: inmate-on-inmate and staff-on-inmate. The BOP considers the latter type illegal and the first type a prohibited act. Annual reporting of the number of sexual assaults is required. While reporting, treatment, and investigation and prosecution protocols are established, the policy does not include specific statements about actions to be taken when the aggressor in the sexual abuse or assault is correctional staff.

The Justice Department filed lawsuits in the federal district courts in Phoenix and Detroit alleging that Arizona and Michigan failed to protect female inmates from rape and sexual assault by prison guards and staff members in violation of the federal Civil Rights of Institutionalized Persons Act of 1980. Both lawsuits seek court orders requiring that the states protect female inmates from rapes, sexual assaults, and other improper contact by the state ("Government sues," 1997).

RECOMMENDATIONS

In addressing the sexual assault or abuse of women in prison, several issues must be considered. New York State Senator Catherine Abate noted that male officers, by virtue of their position, have a great deal of power over female prisoners. Acknowledging that many of these women have been in abusive relationships, Abate identified the need for change.

She noted a need for greater numbers of female officers so that men aren't frisking women (Rutenberg & Stasi, 1995). For example, at Central California Women's Facility, only 2 percent of the guards are women. At New York State Albion Correctional Facility, male officers outnumber female officers by a 3:1 ratio. There is also a need for greater integration of the correctional workforce.

The majority of women in prison are there for drug-related crimes (Bureau of Justice Statistics, 1997). Rather than incapacitation, isolation, and confinement, treatment programs are needed. Women are considered to be less dangerous and have historically been arrested and incarcerated for fewer and less serious offenses (Muraskin & Alleman, 1993; Pollock, 1990). It is therefore important that mandatory sentencing and other sentencing policies that have had a disproportionate impact on women, especially women of color, be examined. Alternatives to incarceration should be sought. In cases where it is necessary to imprison women, and especially in cases where women are to be searched, the policy should be to have two officers conduct the search, one of whom must be female. Although this is currently the policy in some institutions (e.g., Central California Women's Facility), this should become the policy throughout the criminal justice system. LeBlanc (1996) notes that many women in prison are accustomed to coercive relationships and that the problem worsens when they are placed in a highly sexualized, paramilitary setting in the custody of mostly men.

Ethics should be emphasized as a focus of training in the academy. All staff should be trained regarding their role in preventing rape and other forms of sexual abuse. Although the possibility exists for prostitutes and others to seduce correctional employees, these people should be guided by a standard of professionalism in their dealings with all inmates. In the same way that prostitution is the crime that might have landed women in jail, rape or other sexual violations by the correctional employee should result in the violator also being sanctioned. Sexual violations by correctional employees should therefore be viewed as criminal and punished accordingly. Services, including rape counseling, should be made available to women who are victims of sexual abuse while they are in custody and upon their release to the community.

CONCLUSIONS

According to Pollock-Byrne (1990, p. 41), there were additional reasons why Fry, along with other American reformers, supported the idea that prisons should be run by women superintendents, called warders. One reason is that women warders would set a proper moral example of true womanhood for women inmates who had fallen from grace. Another reason is that warders would provide a sympathetic ear for female inmates.

Walker (1989) acknowledges women's marginality in U.S. society and cites the vast amount of violence against women as evidence of this marginality. It therefore stands to reason that if women in general are marginalized, women in prison are marginalized to a greater degree.

How then can a woman in prison convincingly report and explain that she has been raped? Among the issues to be considered are (1) trust, (2) credibility, (3) shame, guilt, anger, and (4) isolation, fear, helplessness. Trust is the most crucial issue facing the assaulted inmate who must decide: "Is it safe to tell?" and "Who can be told?" Credibility is an issue shared by the inmate and authorities. For the inmate, the question becomes "Will I be believed?" For correctional authorities, the question is: "Why should she be believed?" The justice system is designed and operated based on a male model. Men, therefore, can easily tell their stories using the rules of the legal system (Walker, 1989, p. 257).

Battered women are failed by the court system because it is based on a male model of how to determine fact. Women often have trouble "separating discrete factual events from the general patterns of their lives" (Walker, 1989, p. 258). If, for women in general, physical and sexual abuse are events that have shaped their lives from early on, it should not be difficult to understand the power of such patterns over their lives and its influence even more so when they are in prison, stripped of their freedom, and in addition, have been sexually abused. Women in prison have a right[7] not to be victims of sexual exploitation.

N O T E S

1. Although there are no official counts of sexual assaults on homosexuals, the National Gay and Lesbian Task Force (1992) reports that lesbian and gays are more likely to be targeted for violent attacks today that they were 10 years ago.
2. Marital sexual assault is a serious aspect of family violence and appears to be more common among couples living below the poverty line, particularly when men are unemployed (Crime Victims Research and Treatment Center, 1992).
3. Lesbian relationships are excluded because they have been recognized as a distinguishing feature of the female prison subculture. Lesbian relationships are voluntary and consensual and represent attempts to create family (including marital) units. The description of prison lesbian relationships by Stephen Donaldson (1990) is notable:

    The "penitentiary turnout" is the inmate who resorts to lesbian relationships because the opposite sex is unavailable; in contrast, the "lesbian" prefers homosexual gratification even in the outside world, and this is equated with the queen in the men's prison. The lesbian is labeled as sick by some of the other inmates because the preference in a situation of choice is deemed perversion. The participant in lesbian relations who does so for lack of choice is not so stigmatized.

    The "femme" or "mommy" is the inmate who takes the female role in a lesbian relationship, a role highly prized because most of the inmates still wish to play the feminine role in a significant way in prison. . . . The complement is the "Stud broad" or "daddy" who assumes the male role, which in its turn is accorded much prestige.

    When a stud and a femme have established their union, they are said to be "making it" or to "be tight," which is to say that other inmates recognize them socially as a "married" pair. Since the prisoners attach a positive value to sincerity, the "trick"—one who is simply exploited sexually or economically—is held in low esteem by the inmate subculture. Tricks are also regarded as "suckers" and "fools" because their lovers dangle unkept promises in front of them. The "commissary hustler" is the woman who establishes more than one relationship; besides an alliance with an inmate in the same housing unit, she also maintains relations with one or more inmates in other housing units for economic advantage. The other women, labeled tricks in the prison argot, supply her with coveted material items which she shares only with the "wife" in her own unit. The femme may even encourage and guide the stud in finding and exploiting tricks. The legitimacy of the primary pseudo-marriage is not contested, though the tricks may anticipate replacing the femme when a suitable opportunity arises.

4. Mauer and Huling (1995) attribute the current increase in the number of women in the criminal justice system to the war on drugs launched by the Republican administrations of Reagan and Bush. Although the United States has historically had a disproportionate number of

African-Americans in prison (Brinkley-Jackson, Carter, & Rolison, 1993; Free, 1996; French, 1983; Mann, 1993), this disparity is exacerbated by the get-tough-on-crime policies of recent decades. The 78 percent increase in the number of African-American women under criminal justice supervision between 1989 and 1994 (Mauer, 1995) has less to do with increased criminality and more to do with the social and economic environments (poverty, limited economic opportunities, and abuse) shaping the lives of African-Americans. According to Arnold (1990, p. 139), black women are victims of gender and class oppression, as well as sexual violence at the hands of stepfathers and father substitutes. The latter victimization conditions the women to rigid, patriarchal family relationships, relations that are replicated in prison with male custodial officers. This socialization contributes to the continued vulnerability to sexual assault while in confinement of African-American women.

5. Women custodial staff also sexually assault female inmates, as the following story posted on the Stop Prison Rape Web page demonstrates:

   I hear this woman's voice everyday. She has victimized other girls here as well + no one will lift a finger to stop her. She runs this + if one displeases her, they are victimized. I believe the officials are scared of her + the obvious power she holds. Knowing her the way I do, I sincerely believe she is blackmailing someone to get away with what she has + is still doing.

   No one cares what happens to a prisoner. Everyone has the attitude that prisoners complain too much + have unreal expectations in wanting to live as a human being. That we somehow deserve all that happens to us. I know this attitude well; because I used to have this view before my incarceration.

   I have done all I can possibly do to help myself . . . + it is useless. . . . No one here is interested in your organization. The major reason for that is homosexuality is blatant + 89% of the inmate population engages in free, casual sex + damn anyone who doesn't. Inmates-to-inmates + inmates-to-officials. It's sickening.—Clara, Florida.

6. Another interesting case is that of a transsexual. See *Farmer* v. *Brennan* (1970).

7. Dane County, Wisconsin (1998), has created the "Sexual assault victim's bill of rights," which is instructive as an exemplar for the criminal justice system. The bill of rights is available on the Web at http://danenet.wicip.org/dcccrsa/bill2.html.

REFERENCES

ALLEN, H., & SIMONSEN, C. (1995). *Corrections in America* (7th ed.). Englewood Cliffs, NJ: Prentice Hall.

AMERICAN ACADEMY OF PEDIATRICS COMMITTEE ON ADOLESCENCE. (1994). Sexual assault and the adolescent. *Pediatrics*, 94, 761–765.

AMERICAN CORRECTIONAL ASSOCIATION. (1990). *The female offender: What does the future hold?* Washington, DC: St. Mary's Press.

AMERICAN MEDICAL ASSOCIATION. (1995, November 6). AMA reports "silent violent epidemic" of sexual assault throughout the U.S. Press release, Chicago.

An illustrated history and description of state prison life by one who has been there. Written by a convict in a convict's cell [Prison Life, 1865–1869]. New York: Globe.

ARNOLD, R. A. (1990). Process of victimization of black women. *Social Justice, 17*, 153–166.

BRINKLEY-JACKSON, D., CARTER, V. L., & ROLISON, G. L. (1993). African American women in prison. In B. R. Fletcher, L. D. Shaver, & D. B. Moon (Eds.), *Women prisoners: A forgotten population* (pp. 65–74). Westport, CT: Praeger.

BUREAU OF JUSTICE STATISTICS. (1994, January). *Violence against women: a national crime victimization survey report*. Washington, DC: U.S. Department of Justice.

BUREAU OF JUSTICE STATISTICS. (1995). *National crime victimization survey*. Washington, DC: U.S. Department of Justice.

BUREAU OF JUSTICE STATISTICS. (1997). *Prison and jail inmates at midyear, 1996*. Washington, DC: U.S. Department of Justice.

CALIFORNIA PRISON FOCUS. (1998, June 8). California prison focus exposes sexual abuse at Valley State Prison. Press release, San Francisco.

CARLEN, P. (1983). *Women's imprisonment: A study in social control*. London: Routledge & Kegan Paul.

CHESNEY-LIND, M., & RODRIQUEZ, N. (1983). Women under lock and key. *Prison Journal, 63*(2), 47–65.

CRIME VICTIMS RESEARCH AND TREATMENT CENTER. (1992). *The national women's study*. Charleston, SC: Medical University of South Carolina.

CRESSEY, D. R. (1965). Prison organization. In J. March (Ed.), *Handbook of organizations* (pp. 1023–1070). Chicago: Rand McNally.

DANE COUNTY, WISCONSIN. (1998). *Dane County sexual assault victim's bill of rights*. http://danenet.wicip.org/dcccrsa/bill2.html

DONALDSON, S. (1990). Prisons, jails, and reformatories. In W. Dynes (Ed.), *Encyclopedia of homosexuality*. New York: Garland Publishing.

DONALDSON, S. (1993, December 29). The rape crisis behind bars. *New York Times*. Ending sexual abuse in prison. (1996, April 27). *New York Times*, 22:1.

EREZ, E., & TONTODONATO, P. (1992). Sexual harassment in the criminal justice system. In I. Moyer (Ed.), *The changing roles of women in the criminal justice system: Offenders, victims, and professionals* (2nd ed., pp. 227–252). Prospect Heights, IL: Waveland Press.

ESTER, A., & KUZNETS, N. (1994). *AMA guidelines for adolescent preventive services [GAPS]: Recommendations and rationale*. Baltimore: Williams & Wilkins.

FEDERAL BUREAU OF PRISONS. (1997). *PS 5324.04 sexual abuse/assault prevention and intervention programs*. Washington, DC: U.S. Department of Justice.

FLOWERS, R. B. (1987). *Women and criminality*. New York: Greenwood Press.

FREE, M. D. (1996). *African Americans and the criminal justice system*. New York: Garland Publishing.

FREEDAN, E. B. (1974). Their sisters' keepers: An historical perspective on female correctional institutions in the United States, 1870–1900. *Feminist Studies, 2*, 77–95.

FRENCH, L. (1983). A profile of the incarcerated black female offenders. *Prison Journal, 63*(2), pp. 80–87.

GILFUS, M. E. (1992). From victims to survivors to offenders: Women's routes of entry and immersion into street crime. *Women and Criminal Justice, 4*, 63–90.

GOLDING, B. (1997, April 25). Correction officer is charged with misconduct. *Gannett Newspaper*, pp. 1B, 12A.

GOLDING, B. (1998, January 4). Group urges action to stop sex abuse in female prisons. *Gannett Newspaper*, pp. 1A, 14A.

Government sues two states over women's prisons. (1997, March 11). *New York Times*, p. A16(2).

GREENFELD, L., & MINOR-HARPER, S. (1991). *Women in prison*. Bureau of Justice Statistics Special Report. Washington, DC: U.S. Department of Justice.

HEPBURN, J. (1985). The exercise of power in coercive organizations: A study of prison guards. *Criminology, 23*(1), 146–164.

HEPBURN, J., & ALBONETTI, C. (1980). Role conflict in correctional institutions: An empirical examination of the treatment-custody dilemma among correctional staff. *Criminology, 17*(4), 445–459.

HOLMES, S. A. (1996, December 27). With more women in prison, sexual abuse by guards becomes greater concern. *New York Times*, p. 9.

HUMAN RIGHTS WATCH. (1996). *All too familiarly: Sex abuse of women in U.S. prisons*. New York: HRW.

IMMARIGEON, R. (1987). Women in prison. *Journal of the National Prison Project, 11*, 1–5.

JACOBS, J. B., & KRAFT, L. (1978). Integrating the keepers: A comparison of black and white prison guards in Illinois. *Social Problems, 25*, 304–318.

LEBLANC, A. N. (1996, June 2). A woman behind bars is not a dangerous man. *New York Times Magazine*, pp. 33–40.

LOMBARDO, L. (1981). *Guards imprisoned: Correctional workers at work*. New York: Elsevier.

MANN, C. (1993). *Unequal justice: A question of color*. Bloomington, IN: Indiana University Press.

MAUER, M. (1995, October 16). Disparate justice imperils a community. *Legal Times*.

MAUER, M., & HULING, T. (1995). *Young black Americans and the criminal justice system*. Washington, DC: The Sentencing Project.

MURASKIN, R., & ALLEMAN, T. (1993). *It's a crime: Women and justice*. Englewood Cliffs, NJ: Regents/Prentice Hall.

NATIONAL GAY AND LESBIAN TASK FORCE. (1992). *A study of five cities: New York, Chicago, San Francisco, Boston and Minneapolis*. NGLTF.

OPATMY, D. (1996, September 29). Three women sue, allege sex slavery in prison. *San Francisco Examiner*, p. C1.

POLLOCK, J. (1990). *Prisons: Today and tomorrow*. Gaithersburg, MD: Aspen Publishers.

POLLOCK-BYRNE, J. (1990). *Women, prison and crime*. Belmont, CA: Brooks/Cole.

POOLE, E., & REGOLI, R. (1981). Alienation in prison: An examination of the work relations of prison guards. *Criminology, 19*(2), 251–270.

PRESIDENT'S COMMISSION ON LAW ENFORCEMENT AND ADMINISTRATION OF JUSTICE. (1967). *Task force report: Corrections*. Washington, DC: U.S. Government Printing Office.

RAFTER, N. H. (1990). *Partial justice: Women, prisons, and social control* (2nd ed.). Boston: Northeastern University Press.

RUTENBERG, J., & STASI, L. (1995, September 10). Prison strip. *Daily News*, pp. 4, 5.

SARGENT, E., MARCUS-MENDOZA, S., & YU, C. (1993). Abuse and the woman prisoner. In B. Fletcher, L. Shaver, & D. Moon (Eds.), *Women prisoners: A forgotten population* (pp. 55–64). Westport, CT: Praeger.

SIMS, P. (1976). Women in southern jails. In L. Crites (Ed.), *The female offender* (pp. 137–147). Lexington, MA: D.C. Heath.

TUITE, P. (1992). *Ignorance is no excuse*. Chicago: Nelson-Hall.

WALKER, L. E. (1989). *Terrifying love: Why battered women kill and how society responds*. New York: Harper & Row.

WILLIAMS, M. (1996, April 23). Bill seeks to protect inmates from guards who seek sex. *New York Times*, pp. A1, B4.

CASES

Farmer v. *Brennan*, 114 S. Ct. (1970).

LaMarca v. *Turner*, 662 F. Supp. 647 (1987).

17

Dying to Get Out

The Execution of Females in the Post-*Furman* Era of the Death Penalty in the United States

David E. Schulberg

In this chapter we examine the subject of women and the death penalty in the modern era of American capital punishment jurisprudence. Proceeding from the unusual perspective of the death penalty itself, as opposed to the more frequently referenced experiences of women on death row, we bring a unique context to an important subject deserving of careful attention.

While providing an overview of the highlights of U.S. death penalty history, we examine briefly the constitutional underpinnings of modern capital punishment jurisprudence, including Eighth and Fourteenth Amendment–related Supreme Court decisions. Attention is given to several key Supreme Court cases that have had a startling effect on the present capital punishment scheme in the United States. Particular emphasis is given to a review of several important feminist theories purporting to explain gender-centric patterns in capital punishment jurisprudence involving women, including chivalry, evil woman, and equality theory.

We discuss several gender-based factors involved in the cases of the only women executed to date in the modern death penalty era in the United States and outline the facts surrounding the offenses that caused them each to be executed. Finally, we will draw conclusions and make recommendations concerning the present and future state of female death penalty jurisprudence in the United States.

Velma Barfield asked for Cheese Doodles, a Kit Kat bar, and a Coke (B. Bass, personal communication, April 13, 2000). Karla Fay Tucker requested a banana, a peach, and a garden salad with ranch dressing (Texas Department of Criminal Justice, 2000). Judias Buenoano wanted steamed broccoli, steamed asparagus with tomato and lemon wedges, black pepper, fresh strawberries, and hot tea (Debra Buchanan, personal communication, March 3, 2000). Betty Lou Beets (Texas Department of Criminal Justice, 2000), apparently having little appetite, made no special request whatsoever (Texas Department of Criminal Justice, 2000). Christina Riggs selected Supreme pizza, garden salad with Ranch dressing, pickled okra, strawberry shortcake, and cherry limeade (D. Taylor, personal communication, May 1, 2000). Wanda Jean Allen, also apparently lacking appetite, asked for nothing (A. Taylor, personal communication, May 31, 2001). Marilyn Kay Plantz, comparing only with Christina Riggs in the appetite department, ordered a chicken taco salad, a Mexican pizza, two encharitos, two chicken soft tacos, an order of cinnamon twists, a piece of pecan pie, and two cans of Coca-Cola (A. Taylor, personal communication, May 31, 2001).

What made each of these meals unique, even macabre, and each of the women eating them noteworthy, was not, however, what they ate. Nor, perhaps, even where they ate. What was special was what these meals themselves were. Each woman, although time separated their fate from one another, was about to be executed for murder, and these meals were their last.

Barfield, Tucker, Buenoano, Beets, Riggs, Allen, and Plantz remain the only women put to death in the United States since the Supreme Court cleared the way for executions to resume, with the 1976 decision in *Gregg* v. *Georgia* (Death Penalty Information Center, 2000).

THE DEATH PENALTY: AN OVERVIEW

As the new millennium dawns, capital punishment remains our society's ultimate ritual for reclaiming power from those who murder (Carroll, 1997). Capital punishment also remains one of society's two most hotly debated topics, comparing, in this regard, only with abortion (Maloney, 2000). When questioned concerning their opinion on capital punishment, the average person is either definitely for or against it (Smith, 1999, p. 5).

Capital punishment remains part of our national crime control policy even as we find ourselves the only Western nation still to execute our own citizens (Maloney, 2000). From a low of 42 percent in 1966 (Death Penalty Information Center, 2000a), the death penalty has steadily climbed in popularity to between 66 percent (Death Penalty Information Center, 2000d) and 77 percent (Maloney, 2000), although this approval drops to 50 percent when life without the possibility of parole is introduced as an alternative (Death Penalty Information Center, 2000d).

Historical Highlights

The number of executions conducted in American history is not known. Executions were often local affairs, and permanent records were generally not centrally kept. Despite the national shift to prisons, some states conducted official hangings at local jails well into the twentieth century (Maloney, 2000).

Official statistics on lawful executions were first collected in the United States in the 1930s (University of Alaska, 2000). Between 1930 and 1967, when an unofficial moratorium on executions was agreed to by those jurisdictions having a death penalty, a total of 3859 had taken place, of which 32 women were lawfully executed in the United States (Smith, 1999). These figures do not include extrajudicial executions—lynching—which, in the

United States between 1882 and 1951 accounted for at least 4730 additional deaths (Maloney, 2000). Such factors preclude a complete and accurate account of persons executed, officially and otherwise, much less the number of women (Schmall, 1996).

Although one report "confirmed" 18,309 executions, including those of 501 women (Schmall, 1996), another estimated 18,000 to 20,000 executions, with 400 believed to be of women (Rapaport, 1990). Victor Streib, a noted writer on women and the death penalty, estimates that fewer than 400 females were lawfully executed in the history of U.S. capital punishment (Carroll, 1997). Although the number of executions in the United States remains unclear (Carroll, 1997), the first and last executions of women in the earlier era of death penalty jurisprudence is known. In 1632, Jane Champion became the first woman executed in the new colonies (Death Penalty Information Center, 2000a), with Elizabeth Ann Duncan, in August 1962, the last (Streib, 2000).

CONSTITUTIONAL UNDERPINNINGS OF THE DEATH PENALTY

The Eighth Amendment

In *Trop* v. *Dulles*, the U.S. Supreme Court noted that the contours of what constituted cruel and unusual punishment were not clearly defined but could not be limited to harms the framers had experienced (*Trop* v. *Dulles*, 1958). Although *Trop* was not a capital case (Reggio, 2000), opponents of the death penalty applied the court's logic to their cause, arguing that capital punishment should no longer be allowed (Death Penalty Information Center, 2000b). Following closely on *Trop*, the Supreme Court entered a watershed period in the history of capital punishment jurisprudence, beginning in 1962 when the Court held that the Eighth Amendment was "incorporated" and applied to the states. This case, *Robinson* v. *California* (1962), profoundly affected capital jurisprudence, leading to increased federal appeals, and a noticeable decline in executions (Smith, 1999). This culminated in the previously mentioned unofficial moratorium on executions, which lasted from 1967 (Death Penalty Information Center, 2000) until 1977 (Streib, 2000a), while the federal courts decided the constitutionality of existing death penalty statutes (Smith, 1999).

Fine Tuning the Death Penalty

In 1968 the U.S. Supreme Court began to "fine tune" the way in which capital punishment was administered (Death Penalty Information Center, 2000c). The Court held that a law mandating death, upon jury recommendation, was unconstitutional in that it encouraged waiving a jury trial (*U.S.* v. *Jackson*, 1968) and also held that a juror could be disqualified only where the person's attitude toward capital sentencing would prevent even an impartial decision (*Witherspoon* v. *Illinois*, 1968).

In 1970, again addressing jurors and juror discretion in capital cases (Death Penalty Information Center, 2000), the Court considered two cases consolidated under *McGautha* v. *California* (under *Crampton* v. *Ohio* and *McGautha* v. *California*, 1971). Both cases were premised on Fourteenth Amendment claims of violation of due process (Death Penalty Information Center, 2000). Rendering their decision, the Court approved of unfettered jury discretion and nonbifurcated trials (*McGautha*, 1971).

Although the Court has been active over the past 20 years defining the relationship of the Eighth and Fourteenth Amendments to capital punishment (Smith, 1999), it seems clear that the present Court remains strongly supportive of capital punishment and will remain so for at least the foreseeable future (Maloney, 2000). But this was not always so.

SUPREME COURT GUIDANCE

Furman v. *Georgia*

In 1972 the Supreme Court heard three cases that rocked the underpinnings of the U.S. criminal justice system (Smith, 1999). Consolidated under *Furman* v. *Georgia* (1972), these cases considered the Eighth Amendment–based argument that unfettered jury discretion resulted in arbitrary and capricious sentencing (Death Penalty Information Center, 2000b). All nine justices tried to define the contours of "cruel and unusual" punishment, each filing separate opinions and thus leaving no clear standard with which states could harmonize their death penalty laws (Smith, 1999). Justice White, concurring in *Furman*, neatly summed up the capital punishment situation, noting that "there was no meaningful basis for distinguishing the few cases in which it was imposed from the many cases in which it was not" (Maloney, 2000, p. 14).

Furman held punishment to be cruel and unusual if the sanction was too severe, applied arbitrarily, offended the sense of justice, or was no more effective than a less severe penalty (Reggio, 2000). Although over 600 death sentences were commuted as a direct result, the number of persons sentenced to death built again, as states revised their laws to conform to *Furman* (University of Alaska, 2000). A new and invigorated death penalty era was taking shape (Streib, 1990).

Gregg v. *Georgia*

In 1976, the Supreme Court consolidated the cases (University of Alaska, 2000) of *Gregg* v. *Georgia*, *Jurek* v. *Texas*, and *Proffitt* v. *Florida*, reinstating the death penalty under the model of guided discretion. The Court ruled that the death penalty did not violate the Eighth Amendment (Death Penalty Information Center, 2000d) if it was administered so as to protect against arbitrariness and discrimination (Maloney, 2000). *Gregg* confirmed the constitutionality of new capital punishment statutes in Florida, Georgia, and Texas (Death Penalty Information Center, 2000).

On January 17, 1977, Gary Gilmore became the first person to be executed (Death Penalty Information Center, 2000) in the modern death penalty era (Streib, 1990). Although capital punishment was again an American legal reality, several key Supreme Court decisions modifying its application were to follow (Smith, 1999).

Additional Key Decisions

In the related 1976 cases of *Woodson* v. *North Carolina* (1978) and *Roberts* v. *Louisiana* (1976), the Court declared that statutes mandating the death penalty for certain offenses were unconstitutional. These two decisions invalidated mandatory capital punishment statutes in 21 states and reduced the capital sentences of hundreds of inmates to life imprisonment (University of Alaska, 2000).

In *Coker* v. *Georgia* (1977), the Court held that the death penalty for rape of an adult female was disproportionate to the offense and therefore unconstitutional. The decision lead to the reduction of 20 rape-based death sentences across the United States. The 1978 Supreme Court decision in *Lockett* v. *Ohio* (1978) required sentencing authorities to consider broadly every possible mitigating factor relating to the offense before them rather than being limited to those on a specified list. *Lockett* resulted in the release of 99 condemned inmates from Ohio's death row (University of Alaska, 2000).

In unrelated challenges between 1986 and 1989 (University of Alaska, 2000), the Supreme Court held it unconstitutional to execute the mentally insane (*Ford* v. *Wainwright*, 1986) as well as those under 16 at the time they killed (*Thompson* v. *Oklahoma*, 1988). The Court also held it not categorically unconstitutional to put to death the mentally retarded (*Penry* v. *Lynaugh*, 1989), although it has recently agreed to revisit this issue later this year (Death Penalty Information Center, 2001a).

THE DEATH PENALTY AND GENDER

Feminist Theories and Capital Punishment

Although scholarly writing sometimes concerns itself with women on death row, little has been written about females and the death penalty (Carroll, 1997). This may have to do with the few women sentenced to death, or the cultural anomaly of actually executing them (Rapaport, 1990). As deftly indicated by Carroll (1997, p. 1413): "Why focus on capital punishment when death row is roughly as open to women as is the United States Senate?"

Although the number of women contemporarily sentenced to die, or actually executed, is perhaps too low to be of much statistical interest (Carroll, 1997), the disparity between the risk of male and female execution might support the belief that there is "a chivalrous disinclination to sentence women to die" (Rapaport, 1990, p. 504). If true, however, this disinclination dissipates rapidly and in proportion to the type and degree of violent conduct exhibited by these females.

Concentrating on prosecutorial discretion and juror disposition to sentence women to death, gender-based theories account for much discussion as to why some women are executed and others not. No gender-based theory, however, can boast the long and detailed support that race- or class-based theories enjoy (Carroll, 1997), although theories based on race or class may not consider gender-centric causative factors unique to female criminality.

The Chivalry Theory

The chivalry theory argues that women are safeguarded by traditional and protective notions of femininity, which preclude jurors from seeing women as "death eligible" despite the vicious nature of the act with which they are charged. Gender assumptions that stereotype women as being weak, passive, submissive, and dependent on men are viewed as creating a protective shield that makes females less attractive to imprison and less eligible to execution (Carroll, 1997).

As Victor Streib notes: "It's like a girl playing on the football team. Knocking her on her butt doesn't give you the same thrill as it would if it was a big guy. The death penalty is partly man against man" (Phillips, 2000), a notion echoed by Leigh Beinen, a Northwest

University law professor who studies death–penalty related gender bias (Rueter, 1996). Beinen believes that few women face execution because of the symbolism central to capital punishment, saying: "Capital punishment is about portraying people as devils, but women are usually seen as less threatening."

The Evil Woman Theory

The basis of the evil woman theory is that a female who acts particularly violently, or in gender-defying or forbidden ways, is denied the protections of gender afforded others of her gender, making her more eligible for death sentencing if she commits a capital crime. To fit this model, a woman must violate the important social values of humanity with her criminal act, and the strictures of femininity with her "unladylike" conduct. Such behavior allows judges and juries to put aside notions of these defendants as the "gentler sex" and to see them as dangerous monsters (Carroll, 1997).

Chivalry versus Evil Woman: A Commonality

According to Carroll (1997), supporters of the chivalry and evil woman theories agree that the death penalty really acts to enforce the outer bounds of acceptable feminine behavior by marking gender-acceptable boundaries. The penalty of death and the act of execution are viewed by these proponents as proof that the law enforces social conformity. To be executed, murderers must represent the power of evil. Because women rarely descend to such levels, and because of the ritualistic, reclaiming aspects associated with execution, women are rarely put to death. It is the rare woman, and the rare act of evil by women, that is sufficiently powerful to make executing her reassure us about our own personal safety. To reach this level, these theorists agree, a woman must frighten, behaving completely in opposition to the female norm expectations of others. Death eligibility for women implies not only the cessation of womanly conduct, but also the taking on of typically male violence (Carroll, 1997).

The Equality Theory

Women tend to commit different kinds of crime and have less extensive criminal records than men, which might account for fewer women being sentenced to death and ultimately executed. These factors suggest that forces other than gender may influence which women are subject to capital sanction, and that a theory of equality may be more representative than either the chivalry or evil woman theories as a reason why women receive the death penalty (Carroll, 1997).

The equality theory proposes that females are sentenced to death only when their offenses are particularly egregious and uses their scarcity on death row to suggest that few women commit the type of offense that warrants capital punishment for either gender. Noted gender researcher Elizabeth Rapaport suggests that equality theory may be the most accurate explanation concerning women on death row, given the limited information available, because it most neatly reflects the stories of men on death row, suggesting an overall equality in sentencing (Carroll, 1997).

Putting Theory to the Test

Five of the women executed in the present death penalty era clearly fit the mold agreed upon by experts as providing "a better chance of being sentenced to death" (Streib, 2000a), having committed "Bonnie and Clyde types of things" (Streib, 2000, p. 3), "coldblooded [*sic*], very atrocious type of crime" (Phillips, 2000, p.3). Juries and judges who might otherwise have found mitigation related to gender (Rueter, 1996) were unable or unwilling to in their cases. The cases of Velma Barfield, Christina Riggs, and Wanda Jean Allen, however, are arguably different in these respects.

Evidence that gender-neutral factors may account for the same results as those more gender-centric exists (Rueter, 1996), although the continuing sociolegal migration toward actual gender equality may eventually make all gender-based factors concerning women and capital punishment moot (Streib, 1990). As for Karla Fay Tucker, Judias Buenoano, Betty Lou Beets, and Marilyn Kay Plantz, the sheer brutality of their crimes appears to have done that for them.

Velma Barfield's execution, on the other hand, may have resulted as much from incredibly poor timing as any other factor, including the nature of her crime. Support for the death penalty was high in North Carolina and the governor was running for a hotly contested senatorial seat, the election for which was just four days after the scheduled execution date (Rapaport, 1990). Barfield may have been as much a victim of politics as of her own bad acts.

As for Christina Riggs, her execution remains a bizarre anomaly of the U.S. justice system. Initially, Riggs requested the trial jury to sentence her to death (Death Penalty Information Center, 2000), later mounted a very limited appeal of her murder conviction, but not her sentence (*Riggs* v. *Arkansas*, 1999), and finally chose to actively decline all further appeals of both her conviction and sentence (Death Penalty Information Center, 2000).

Although it fits the rubric of the evil woman theory, Wanda Jean Allen's case arguably does so more due to her own nature than that of the murder for which she was put to death. Unlike Tucker, Buenoano, Beets, and Plantz, Allen's violation of the strictures of femininity hurt her at least as much, and probably more, than any perceived violation of the objective rules of humanity. Joanne Bell, executive director of the Oklahoma chapter of the American Civil Liberties Union, pointed out that had Allen been part of a straight couple, she probably would have been tried for manslaughter, not murder, and therefore not faced the death penalty (Simo, 2001). Allen was a lesbian convicted of killing her live-in lesbian lover. This was a fact exploited by the prosecution during her trial (Kirby, 2001) and used by the gay and lesbian media to point out perceived homophobic attitudes, but rarely mentioned outside that forum (Simo, 2001). As Tonya McClary, program director for the National Coalition to Abolish the Death Penalty said, "Oklahoma is in the Bible Belt; it's very homophobic" (Kirby, 2001). None of this, however, minimizes the cold-blooded nature of the murder for which Allen was put to death.

SEVEN WOMEN

Velma Barfield

Velma Barfield, executed in North Carolina on November 2, 1984 (Death Penalty Information Center, 2001c), was the first woman to die in the United States in the modern era of the death penalty and the first woman to be executed in 22 years. Put to death for killing her boyfriend with arsenic, Barfield admitted to poisoning three other persons, including her mother, and was suspected in the poisoning death of her husband (Death Penalty Information Center, 2000a).

Barfield poisoned her boyfriend to prevent his filing forgery charges related to checks for prescription drugs to which she had long been addicted. This followed a pattern evidenced in several of her previous murders. Her jury found aggravating circumstances in that the murder was based on pecuniary gain as well as the desire to avoid criminal liability (Death Penalty Information Center, 2000a).

Barfield's sentence was not only carried out—unique enough, regardless of gender, when so many death sentences are commuted for a variety of reasons—but also went forth despite what was characterized as her "miraculous" transformation while in prison (Carroll, 1997). This "born-again christian [*sic*] grandmother, now drug free, well adjusted and extraordinarily well liked, even loved, at Women's Prison," perhaps should have been granted clemency, and indeed might have been were it not, many believe, for the proximity of the election (Rapaport, 1990).

Karla Fay Tucker

Karla Fay Tucker became the second woman put to death in the modern death penalty era and the first executed in Texas since the Civil War (CNN Interactive, 1998). Although there is no doubt of her readily admitted guilt (Gwynne, 1998), it remains unclear whether the enormous coverage surrounding her case was due more to her gender or profound conversion to Christianity (Agitator, 1998b), or to the fact that she was "an attractive young woman" (Maloney, 2000, p. 8). Tucker may not have been "the same person who had coldly participated in two murders 15 years earlier" (Maloney, 2000, p. 9), but the facts surrounding her case epitomize her as perhaps the very essence of the "evil woman" (Carroll, 1997, p. 1421). Her crimes have been characterized as "particularly brutal" (Horn, 1998).

Tucker and her boyfriend, after consuming "an astonishing quantity of heroin, Valium, speed, percodan, mandrax, marijuana, dilaudid, methadone, tequila and rum" (Gwynne, 1998), broke into an occupied apartment, where Tucker's boyfriend struck the male victim with a hammer (*Tucker* v. *Texas*, 1988). As the victim begged for his life, Tucker struck him repeatedly with a pickax until he was dead, the pair later repeating the process on a female found hiding under a blanket in the apartment (Rapaport, 1990). Afterward, Tucker told her sister that "she got a thrill while 'picking' Dean," and that "every time she 'picked' Jerry, she looked up and she grinned and she got a nut and hit him again." Both bodies suffered over 20 wounds (CNN, Interactive, 1998), and the female victim still had the pickax embedded in her when later discovered (Rapaport, 1990).

Were the details of the two murders not enough to seal Tucker's fate, her own penalty phase testimony most certainly was. Tucker's admission of a personal history of vicious fights, planned robbery-murders, and two planned witness killings clearly showed that she represented a continuing danger to society (Rapaport, 1990). Despite the perhaps meritorious argument that she found religion and changed remarkably since her conviction (Maloney, 2000), Karla Fay Tucker was executed on February 3, 1998 (CNN, Interactive,1998). The following month, Judias Buenoano became the third woman executed in the modern death penalty era.

Judias Buenoano

Judias Buenoano might never have been suspected of murder were it not for her 1983 attempt to kill her fiancé by a car bomb (Agitator, 1998a). He survived, had some pills she had previously given him analyzed, and discovered that they contained deadly poison (*Buenoano v. Florida*, 1988). When police investigated the bombing they realized that "Buenoano" was Spanish for "Goodyear," learned of her previous marriage under that name, and discovered that her former husband's body contained lethal amounts of arsenic (Agitator, 1998a).

Testimony at Buenoano's murder trial revealed that she had told two friends how to kill with poison, admitting to them that this was how she murdered Goodyear. One of these women also testified that Buenoano told her that she should heavily insure her husband and then poison him, to escape her poor marriage (*Buenoano v. Florida*, 1988).

Although convicted only of murdering Goodyear, there was evidence that Buenoano had poisoned a previous boyfriend, as well as her own son (Agitator, 1998a). Buenoano had her mortgage paid, and additionally collected $118,000 in insurance and other compensation from money gained from the three murders. Had she succeeded in killing her fiancé, Buenoano would have received over $510,000 in life insurance, plus 60 percent of his estate (*Buenoano v. Florida*, 1988).

Executed by Florida on March 30, 1998 (Death Penalty Information Center, 2001c), Buenoano holds the dubious distinction of being the first woman to die in that state's electric chair (Florida Department of Corrections, 2000). Arguably, she could also be the poster-child for the evil woman theory. Her conviction resulted in virtually no publicity (Maloney, 2000). The same was not true, however, for Betty Lou Beets. Beets was a great-grandmother, and virtually none of the rather extensive international coverage of her execution let the world forget it.

Betty Lou Beets

When executed by Texas [British Broadcasting Corporation (BBC), 2000] on February 24, 2000 (Death Penalty Information Center, 2000d), Betty Lou Beets was a 62-year-old great-grandmother, a fact that the world media mentioned prominently in almost every report concerning her (Time.com, 2000). Also mentioned, although less prominently, were unsubstantiated allegations by Beets that she had been a battered wife (BBC, 2000).

Mentioned as an afterthought in many articles, however, was that Beets had been convicted of murdering her fifth husband (Yahoo!News, 2000) for his insurance and pension (BBC, 2000), shooting her second husband and charged but not tried for the murder of her fourth husband. Dubbed the "Black Widow" (APBNews, 2000) due to her fatal propensity toward eliminating her mates, Beets's two dead husbands were found buried around her home, both encased in sleeping bags and both shot in the backs of their heads (BBC, 2000). Beets was the second woman executed in Texas since statehood and the fourth in the modern death penalty era (Yahoo!News, 2000).

Christina Riggs

Christina Riggs's execution came about so suddenly that virtually no news coverage or protests resulted from it. Foregoing additional appeals that may have preserved her life indefinitely, and refusing to ask the governor for clemency (Death Penalty Information

Center, 2000b), Riggs became the first woman ever executed by the state of Arkansas and the fifth woman in the United States to be executed since *Furman* (Death Penalty Information Center, 2001c), succumbing to lethal injection on May 2, 2000 (D. Tyler, personal communication, May 1, 2000).

Convicted of the premeditated murders of her 5-year-old son and 2-year-old daughter in November 1997, Riggs readily admitted to suffocating each child when drugs she had administered failed to kill them. Admittedly despondent due to personal problems over which she planned to kill herself, Riggs admitted to killing her children to prevent them from thinking she did not love them and to prevent a custody battle that might have separated the children due to their differing fathers (*Riggs* v. *Arkansas*, 1999).

Wanda Jean Allen

When executed by the state of Oklahoma on January 11, 2001, Wanda Jean Allen became the sixth woman put to death since U.S. executions resumed in 1977 (Death Penalty Information Center, 2001c). She also became a woman of many dubious firsts. The first lesbian executed in the United States in the twenty-first century (Simo, 2001), Allen was also the first woman executed by Oklahoma since statehood (Death Penalty Institute of Oklahoma, 2001) and the first black woman put to death in the United States since Betty Jean Butler was executed in Ohio in 1954 (Fight the Death Penalty, 2001).

Ending their relationship after a domestic dispute, Gloria Leathers left the house that she and Allen shared and rode with her mother to the police station to file a report arising from the breakup. Allen followed, and after trying unsuccessfully to reconcile (Pro Death Penalty, 2001), shot Leathers once in the abdomen with a handgun she held concealed under her sweatshirt. Allen fled but was arrested four days later, the same day that Leathers succumbed to her wound (Pro Death Penalty, 2001).

Approaching the execution, much of the world's media (Simo, 2001) focused on the defense contentions that Allen had an IQ of 69, which placed her within the range of mental retardation (Kirby, 2001). Ignored was that a psychologist placed her IQ at 80 in the mid-1990s (Fight the Death Penalty, 2001). Also ignored was Allen's mother's testimony that Allen had done well in school (Rueter, 1996).

Virtually ignored was the manslaughter conviction (Carroll, 1997) that Allen was on probation for when she killed Leathers (Fight the Death Penalty, 2001), her written threat to kill Leathers were she to end their relationship, and her having told Leathers's son, on the day of the shooting, that she would not rest until Leathers was dead (Carroll, 1997).

Marilyn Kay Plantz

Marilyn Kay Plantz, the seventh woman executed since Furman ushered in the present U.S. death penalty era (Death Penalty Information Center, 2001c), and the second female put to death by Oklahoma in less than four months (Yahoo!News, 2001), remains as of this writing, the last woman executed in the United States (Death Penalty Information Center, 2001c).

Executed May 1, 2001, for the murder of her husband, Jim Plantz, a death planned to look like an accident (Doucette, 2001a), in order to cash in on approximately $219,000 in life insurance (*Plantz* v. *Oklahoma*, 1994), Marilyn Kay Plantz epitomizes all that the evil woman theory implies. After several failed attempts to have her husband killed (*Plantz* v. *Oklahoma*, 1994), Marilyn Plantz arranged for her lover (Doucette, 2001a) and another man (*Plantz* v. *Oklahoma*, 1994) to ambush Mr. Plantz as he entered the house that he and Marilyn shared. Both men beat Mr. Plantz repeatedly with baseball bats that she provided (*Plantz* v. *Oklahoma*, 1994). Although the victim cried out for her as he was being struck, his cry went ignored. Marilyn Plantz was waiting in her bedroom for the attackers to finish (Doucette, 2001b).

After severely beating Mr. Plantz, the assailants carried their now-moaning victim outside, where Marilyn commented that her husband's "head was busted open" and that his injuries did not appear accidental. Marilyn then ordered the men "to burn him" (*Plantz* v. *Oklahoma*, 1994) and returned to the house to clean up the blood (Doucette, 2001a).

With one assailant driving Jim Plantz's pickup, and the other following in Marilyn's car, the killers drove to a rural area (Doucette, 2001a), placed the victim behind the truck's steering wheel, doused him and the cab with gasoline, and set him on fire. Both men admitted seeing the victim rise up as they drove away, and evidence indicated that Mr. Plantz had tried to escape from the burning truck before being felled by smoke and flames (*Plantz* v. *Oklahoma*, 1994).

The killers returned to find Marilyn still cleaning up blood, and at her direction, exchanged their bloody clothing for that of their victim. The killers left the Plantz home, disposed of the bloody clothing, which had been put into a sack by Mrs. Plantz, and then bought sandwiches and drinks with money from Jim Plantz's trouser pockets (*Plantz* v. *Oklahoma*, 1994).

The Plantz's then 9-year-old daughter and 5-year-old son, asleep in the next room throughout the attack, reacted to their mother's death sentence quite differently. Whereas her daughter reconciled with her and appealed for mercy on her behalf, Plantz's son visited her but without reconciliation. In fact, her son wrote the following to the Oklahoma Pardon and Parole Board: "Can you even try to imagine in your worst nightmares, having your father killed in the very next room with the T-ball bat he taught you to hit with the day before?" (Doucette, 2001a).

One of the killers that Marilyn Plantz hired testified for the prosecution in exchange for his life (Peebles, 2001). Her former lover (Doucette, 2001a), later executed for his part in the murder (Mullen, 2001), testified that while he had no particular reason to kill Jim Plantz, he thought of the abuse Marilyn told him she suffered at the hands of her husband, including blackened eyes which he himself had seen (Peebles, 2001). Although Marilyn Plantz told the police that she and her husband had enjoyed a perfect marriage, and during her trial steadfastly denied any role in the murder of her husband (Peebles, 2001), she eventually confessed to her part in the killing (Yahoo!News, 2001).

Although mounting questions continue to develop concerning the forensic work and related testimony of Oklahoma City police chemist Joyce Gilchrist (Yahoo!News, 2001), neither Gilchrist nor her work were seen as a deciding factor in Plantz's conviction (ChannelOklahoma, 2001b) or execution (Yahoo!News, 2001). Any controversy which might have been raised in the Plantz case became, as noted by Oklahoma Governor Frank Keating, outweighed by the damning testimony of one of her co-conspirators, additional and unchallenged evidence of her guilt, and her own confession (Yahoo!News, 2001).

CONCLUSIONS

One recent death penalty–related study showed that not only was there no evidence of any deterrent effect following Oklahoma's reinstitution of the death penalty after a 25-year moratorium, but killings between strangers actually increased significantly after that state again began executions. Strikingly similar results were shown in a California study, following the first execution in that state in 25 years, although the increased murder rate was more modest than in Oklahoma and was studied for only eight months following the particular executions. Research in Texas found that the infliction of capital punishment had no effect on the number of murders in that state despite the fact that Texas had been conducting executions at a relatively steady rate for many years (*Riggs* v. *Arkansas*, 1999).

As for gender, the issue becomes even murkier. The United States holds the dubious distinction of housing more women condemned to death than any other country in the world, although this population remains virtually invisible unless a woman is scheduled for imminent execution. This comparatively small population, coupled with its invisibility (Thompson, 1997), are two major reasons why gender is not studied more, and this lack of study is why gender-centric reasons for women committing capital crimes, and being put to death for these crimes, are still, to this day, greatly unknown. If these reasons are to become known, research must be undertaken to pinpoint the reasons why women commit capital offenses, especially in light of the few gender-centric theories that purport to account for what is a varied and growing death row population in the United States.

What has been a much hidden and ignored problem must not be permitted to remain so (Thompson, 1997), at least if we, as a society, are not to have this population continue to grow until, by sheer numbers, it forces us to conduct such important research. By then, of course, any steps taken will have been too little and too late for the even larger number of women who find themselves on this country's death rows, as well as their victims.

Although the population of women on death rows in the United States is infinitesimal compared with similarly situated males (Thompson, 1997), it remains inconceivable, especially in this so-called modern age, that such a unique and identifiable population can simply be ignored. Their identifiability, if not also their low numbers, make them an almost ideal class for particularly accurate and effective research and for results implementation.

The worst crime may not be the comparatively few murders committed by these women, although each in itself is tragic, as much as the almost larger evil represented by our ignorance of why they were committed. This is especially true in considering a population as generally nonthreatening, well adjusted to incarceration, and unbelievably amenable to rehabilitation, as are the vast majority of females sentenced to death row.

Perhaps their very amenability, adjustment, and nonthreatening status is their worst enemy, robbing these women of the possibility of advanced treatment modalities that could better support their approach to normalized, if not also productive lives while remaining imprisoned. This would almost assuredly be the result if this population were larger, or their behavior more noticed.

As for the women executed since the reinstitution of the death penalty, excluding Velma Barfield, Christina Riggs, and possibly Wanda Jean Allen, for the reasons stated earlier, each stands apart as a stark exception that reinforces the probability of the points noted above. Tucker, Buenoano, Beets, and Plantz each killed while not needing to kill. They killed out of evil intent and design, not from necessity; and in each of the cases described, these women did so particularly coldbloodedly. These four women stand as stark exceptions to every stricture that would have allowed them to remain indistinguishable within the limited "crowd" that are women sentenced to die in the United States. They set themselves apart from the group by their overt viciousness, and they paid for this ferocity with their lives.

POSTSCRIPT

As of this writing, there are no female executions scheduled imminently anywhere in the United States (Death Penalty Information Center home page, 2001). This could change at any time, depending on the progress of individual cases.[1] There remains no general moratorium on public execution, including the execution of women, and no such moratorium, formal or informal, is projected. Retired Supreme Court Justice Harry Blackmun, commenting on the effectiveness of capital punishment, said he felt "morally and intellectually obligated to concede that the death penalty experiment has failed" (Maloney, 2000). Although this may or may not be true intellectually, realistically such concerns are made virtually mute by the polemic that the death penalty inspires.

Immediately after the execution of Barbara Graham and two accomplices following an infamous 1950s murder, reporter Al Martinez told the arresting detective outside the execution area that their deaths will make little overall difference. "Others will go on killing," Martinez said. The detective looked at Martinez for some time before he replied: "But *they* won't" (Martinez, 2000).

Although neither side involved in the death penalty debate may ever prove that theirs is the right argument, or perhaps even the better argument, one fact seems undeniable. As long as states continue to spend more money on prisons than on education, there will remain a need to argue the effectiveness of capital punishment, with or without regard to the issue of gender.

NOTES

1. Since this paper went to print, the state of Oklahoma had, in fact, executed Lois Nadeau Smith for the murder of her son's former girlfriend.

REFERENCES

AGITATOR (1998a). Case of Judias V. Buenoano, execution of Judias V. Buenoano. Accessed February 2000.
  http://www.agitator.com/dp/98/judibuen.html
AGITATOR (1998b). Case of Karla Faye Tucker, execution of Karla Faye Tucker. Accessed February 2000.
  http://www.agitator.com/dp/98/karlatuck.html
APB NEWS. (2000, February 24). Texas executes "Black Widow." Accessed February 24, 2000.
  http://www.apbnews.com/cjsystem/justicenews/2000/02/24BEETS0224_01.html

BRITISH BROADCASTING CORPORATION. (2000, February 25). U.S. grandmother executed for murder. Accessed February 25, 2000.
http://news.bbc.co.uk/hi/english/world/Americas/newsid_655000/655686.stm

CARROLL, J. E. (1997). Images of women and capital sentencing among female offenders: Exploring the outer limits of the Eighth Amendment and articulated theories of justice. *Texas Law Review, 75,* 1413.

CHANNELOKLAHOMA. (2001a, January 12). State executes Wanda Jean Allen. Accessed April 30, 2001.
http://www.channeloklahoma.com/okl/news/stories/news-20010111-165311.html

CHANNELOKLAHOMA. (2001b, May 1). Gilchrist problems won't stop Plantz execution. Accessed June 18, 2001.
http://www.channeloklahoma.com/okl/news/stories/news-74885020010501-110518.html

CNN INTERACTIVE. (1998). Profile: Facing death with memories of murder. Accessed March 3, 2000.
http://www.cnn.com/SPECIALS/1998/tucker.execution/profile

DEATH PENALTY INFORMATION CENTER. (2000a). Arkansas executes despondent woman.
http://www.deathpenaltyinfo.org/index.html

DEATH PENALTY INFORMATION CENTER. (2000b). Facts about deterrence and the death penalty. Accessed April, 2000.
http://www.deathpenaltyinfo.org/index.html

DEATH PENALTY INFORMATION CENTER. (2000c). History of the death penalty. Accessed February 2000.
http://www.deathpenaltyinfo.org/index.html

DEATH PENALTY INFORMATION CENTER. (2000d). What's new (last updated February 25, 2000). Accessed February 25, 2000.
http://www.deathpenaltyinfo.org/index.html

DEATH PENALTY INFORMATION CENTER. (2001a). Upcoming executions. Accessed May 26, 2001.
http://www.deathpenaltyinfo.org/index.html

DEATH PENALTY INFORMATION CENTER. (2001b). What's new (last updated June 15, 2001). Accessed June 18, 2001.
http://www.deathpenaltyinfo.org/index.html

DEATH PENALTY INFORMATION CENTER. (2001c). Women and the death penalty. Accessed May 26, 2001.
http://www.deathpenaltyinfo.org/index.html

DEATH PENALTY INSTITUTE OF OKLAHOMA. (2001, February 27). Wanda Allen executed January 11, 2001. Accessed April 30, 2001.
http://www.dpio.org/inmates/Allen_Wanda.html

DOUCETTE, B. (2001a, May 1). Woman awaits her execution. Oklahoma Online. Accessed May 1, 2001.
http://www.oklahoman.com/cgi-bin/show_article?ID=677729&pic=none&TP=getarticle

DOUCETTE, B. (2001b, May 2). Woman dies for husband's 1988 slaying. In the news: Corrections news from around the world. Accessed May 26, 2001.
http://www.doc.state.ok.us/DOCS/News/010502itn.htm

Fight the Death Penalty in USA. (2001). Executions, 1996–2000. Accessed June 18, 2001.
http://fdp.dk/uk/exec/exe-0101.htm

FLORIDA DEPARTMENT OF CORRECTIONS. (2000). Death row fact sheet: Facts and fallacies. Accessed February 2000.
http://www.dc.state.fl.us/oth/deathrow

GWYNNE, S. C. (1998, January 19). Why so many want to save her. Time.Com. Accessed March 3, 2000.
http://www.time.com/time/magazine/1998/dom/900119/crime.a_time_investigati7.html

HORN, R. (1998, January 20). Outspoken jurist says death penalty needs to be consistent.
http://www.reporternews.com/local/poe0120.html

KIRBY, D. (2001). Was justice served? *Advocate.* Accessed April 30, 2001.
http://www.advocate.com/html/stories/832/832_wandajean.asp

MALONEY, J. J. (2000). The death penalty. *Crime magazine: An encyclopedia of crime.* Accessed March 3, 2000.
http://www.crimemagazine.com/cp101.htm

MARTINEZ, A. (2000, March 12). The long, cold mile. *Los Angeles Times,* p. B1.

MULLEN, T. (2001, April 18). *Daily Oklahoman.* Board rejects woman's bid for clemency. Accessed June 18, 2001.
http://www.ocadp.org/plantz.html

PEEBLES, R. (2001). Clemency denied on April 17. Death Penalty Institute of Oklahoma. Accessed June 20, 2001.
www.dpio.org/inmates/Plantz_Marilyn.html

PHILLIPS, R. A. (2000, February 25). No gender equality on death row. APBNews. Accessed February 25, 2000.
http://www.apbnews.com/cjsystem/findingju_/women0226_01.html?s=syn.yahoofc_women022, 1, 2

PRO DEATH PENALTY. (2001). January 2001 executions. Accessed June 1, 2001.
http://prodeathpenalty.com/Pending/01/jan01.htm

RAPAPORT, E. (1990) Some questions about gender and the death penalty. *Golden Gate University Law Review, 20,* 501–538.

REGGIO, M. H. (2000). History of the death penalty. Frontline: The execution. Accessed March 2000.
http://www.pbs.org/wgbh/pages/frontline/shows/execution/readings/history.html

RUETER, T. (1996). Why women aren't executed: gender bias and the death penalty.
www.abanet.org/irr/hr/genderbias.html

SCHMALL, L. (1996). Forgiving Guin Garcia: Women, the death penalty and commutation. *Wisconsin Women's Law Journal, 11,* 283–315.

SIMO, A. (2001). Oklahoma kills black lesbian. The Gully. Accessed April 30, 2001.
http://www.thegully.com/essays/gaymundo/010115allen.html

SMITH, S. C. (1999, December 2). Capital punishment in the United States. Close Up Foundation: Capital Punishment in the United States.
www.closeup.org/punish/org

STREIB, V. (1990). Death penalty for female offenders. *University of Cincinnati Law Review, 58,* 845–867.

STREIB, V. (2000a). Death penalty for female offenders: January 1973 to June 1999.
http://www.law.onu.edu/faculty/streib/femdeath.htm

STREIB, V. (2000b, February 26) No gender equality on death row. APBNews. Accessed March 2000.
http://www.apbnews.com/cjsystem/findingjustice/2000/02/26/women0226_02.html

TEXAS DEPARTMENT OF CRIMINAL JUSTICE. (2000). Final meal requests. Accessed March, 2000.
http://TDCJ.ST.TX.US/stat/finalmeals.htm

THOMPSON, C. (1997). The invisibility of women on death row: A personal view. Lifelines Ireland Newsletter. Accessed April, 2000.
http://www.sun.soci.niv.edu/~critcrim/dp/dp-wom1

Time.com. (2000, February 24). Improbably, Betty Lou Beets' death is news. Accessed February 24, 2000.
http://www.time.com/time/daily/0,2960,39849-101000224,00.html

UNIVERSITY OF ALASKA–ANCHORAGE. (2000). Focus on the death penalty. Justice Center Web site. Accessed March 2000.
http://www.uaa.alaska.edu/just/death/history.html

YAHOO!NEWS. (2000, February 25). Texas executes grandmother.
sg.dailynews.yahoo.com/headlines/world/afp/article.H..../Texas_executes_evidence.htm

YAHOO!NEWS. (2001, May 1). Oklahoma executes woman despite evidence dispute. Accessed May 28, 2001.
http://dailynews.yahoo.com/h/nm/20010501/ts/usa_execution_oklahoma_dc_1.html

CASES

Allen v. *Oklahoma*, No. 99-6033 (1999) WL 49284 (10th Cir., July 13, 1999). Unpublished opinion.

Buenoano v. *Florida*, 527 So. 2d 194 (Fla. Sup. Ct., 1988).

Coker v. *Georgia*, 433 U.S. 584 (1977).

Crampton v. *Ohio & McGautha* v. *California* (consolidated under) 402 U.S. 183 (1971).

Ford v. *Wainwright*, 477 U.S. 399 (1986).

Furman v. *Georgia*, 408 U.S. 238 (1972).

Gregg v. *Georgia*, 428 U.S. 153 (1976).

Jurek v. *Texas*, 428 U.S. 262, (1976)

Lockett v. *Ohio*, 438 U.S. 586 (1978).

Penry v. *Lynaugh*, 492 U.S. 302 (1989).

Plantz v. *Oklahoma*, 876 P.2d 268 (1994).

Proffitt v. *Florida*, 428 U.S. 242 (1976).

Riggs v. *Arkansas*, 3 S.W. 3d 305 (1999).

Roberts v. *Louisiana*, 428 U.S. 325 (1976).

Robinson v. *California*, 370 U.S. 660 (1962).

Thompson v. *Oklahoma*, 487 U.S. 815 (1988).

Trop v. *Dulles*, 356 U.S. 86 (1958).

Tucker v. *Texas*, 771 S.W. 523 (1988).

U.S. v. *Jackson*, 390 U.S. 570 (1968).

Witherspoon v. *Illinois*, 391 U.S. 510 (1968).

Woodson v. *North Carolina*, 428 U.S. 280 (1976).

18

Women on Death Row

Etta F. Morgan

❖

Capital punishment is a controversial issue in society, yet it is the most severe punishment that our courts and administer. The purposes of this chapter are to (1) provide an historical overview of capital punishment; (2) explain capital punishment using Girard's theory of culture; (3) examine the influence of the U.S. Supreme Court regarding capital punishment; (4) discuss the importance of gender in the criminal justice process; and (5) review the literature on executed females as well as share some of the experiences and problems of female death row inmates.

Ironically, every aspect of our society is influenced by the social and cultural perspectives that dominate our being. These influences are also prevalent in the administration of our prisons. Women, as second-class citizens in society, carry this status into the penal system, which openly ignores their needs in more ways than one. One prime example would be that most states have only one prison for women, and some have none. Female criminality and experiences have often been described based on men's experiences. Previous research (Erez, 1989; Kruttschnitt, 1982; Mann, 1984; Pollock-Byrne, 1991; Visher, 1983; Zingraff & Thompson, 1984) suggests that as a group, women have been treated more leniently than men in the criminal justice system. If this is true, it may explain the disproportionate number of women sentenced to death in relation to the number of men sentenced to death. Female offenders have often been a forgotten population in research as well as in reality.

Limited research has focused on women sentenced to death. Streib publishes a quarterly report, which details demographics about the offender, a brief statement about the offense, and the current status of the inmates (i.e., reversals, commutations, etc.). O'Shea (1999) has provided an expanded view of women on death row by examining the penal codes of the states in which they were sentenced and by sharing stories of women under the sentence of death, those on death row, and women who have been executed. Other authors (Fletcher, Dixon, Shaver, & Moon, 1993; Lezin, 1999; Mann, 1984) tend to devote only a few pages in textbooks to a discussion of women on death row. Gillespie and Lopez (1986a,b) were instrumental in providing insight into the executions of women, and Baker (1999) and Rapaport (2000) have renewed the research on the execution of women since it is apparent that women will once again be executed in the United States. Perhaps this limited body of literature is due to the fact that women do not commit violent crime at the same rate as men, and therefore we have tended not to focus our research efforts on women and violent crimes.

There appears to be an increase in female crime based on the current *Uniform Crime Reports* (UCR), but it is unclear whether this increase is due to actual offenses or changes in reporting practices by law enforcement agencies. Cautiously interpreting the UCR data, there seems to be an increase in violent crimes by females, but basically, female crime is still concentrated in the area of property crimes. Upon closer examination of violent crimes, it is found that women homicide offenders tend to kill persons of the same race, usually an intimate male associate. As a group, women murderers are not as common as their male counterparts, which could possibly influence the treatment they receive in the criminal justice system. In examining the imposition of death sentences in this country, it is obvious that women are not sentenced to death or executed at the same rate as men.

The death penalty has and continues to be a controversial issue in the United States. It is the ultimate sentence that can be imposed for a criminal offense. Proponents of the death penalty suggest that it is needed in order to deter would-be criminals, while opponents believe that it is an inhumane act on the part of society in administering justice. In the past, the death penalty was withdrawn because some states were unfairly targeting specific populations of offenders. Although it was reinstated by the Supreme Court in 1976, the controversy has not been settled as to whether or not the death penalty should be used as a form of punishment.

HISTORICAL OVERVIEW

Capital punishment is a controversial issue nationally as well as internationally. It is believed to have been in existence before societies became organized. After the organization of society, legal codes were established in an attempt to provide rules and regulations for social control. Capital punishment has been included in legal codes since the period of the Old Testament continuing on to the Code of Hammurabi, Assyrian laws, Athenian Codes, European laws, and the code established in the American colonies (Koosed, 1996).

Capital punishment in the United States has been greatly influenced by English traditions and research has shown it to be an Anglo-American custom (Paternoster, 1991). The practice of capital punishment in the colonies reflected the ideology of the American people in regard to the types of crime that were considered capital offenses. Because there was no uniform criminal code throughout the colonies, each state had different capital statutes (Kronenwetter, 1993; Paternoster, 1991). In some instances, states declared fewer offenses (five to eight) capital offenses if committed by whites while identifying 70 offenses as capital offenses if committed by blacks. After the American Revolution, states begin to restrict the number of offenses that could be classified as capital offenses. States also narrowed the application of capital punishment by establishing degrees of murder and giving juries more discretion in sentencing, thereby permitting the jury to sentence people to death in only the most serious murders (Paternoster, 1991).

Along with the passage of discretionary statutes for capital crimes, this period of American capital punishment has two distinct characteristics. First, executions were public events and second, local authorities were responsible for performing all executions. Executions were performed as public events until the end of the nineteenth century, although some public executions were performed as late as 1936 and 1937. At the turn of the century we find a shift from public executions controlled by local authorities to executions controlled and conducted by the state (Paternoster, 1991).

Capital punishment's historical significance is not only related to punishment but also to social control. Capital punishment was often administered upon those identified as members of problem populations. It was believed that these populations did not respect established authority. In many instances, these populations were viewed as threatening or dangerous to established authority. Capital punishment also had an extralegal form, that was lynching. According to Paternoster (1991), "[l]ynching, primarily by vigilante groups, was frequently used by majority groups to keep minorities oppressed" (p. 8). The use of this extralegal form of capital punishment claimed more lives than legal executions. Although we experienced a decline in lynchings with the centralization of the death penalty, there were more executions between 1930 and 1940 than were noted for the following 20 years. During the 1960s and 1970s, there was a decline in executions followed by a moratorium on capital punishment (Paternoster, 1991).

Over time, there have been regional differences in the imposition of the death penalty. Historically, the South has performed more executions than any other region. In examining capital offenses and capital statutes during the pre-modern era, Paternoster (1991) states: [O]ne interesting feature about the imposition of capital punishment for different offenses is that the region of the country and the race of the offender has been, at least in the past, an important correlate" (p. 15). Statistics (Flanagan & Maguire, 1989) suggest that race may have been an overriding factor in the imposition of the death penalty for particular offenses in the South, resulting in racially biased applications of the death sentence. It has also been suggested, as in previous years, that capital punishment continued to be used as a form of social control for specific groups.

Capital punishment, as the ultimate sentence, has also created problems for juries. Specifically, juries were at odds with the harshness of the laws and as a result found themselves mitigating that fact instead of the case. In later years, juries were given discretionary powers with the understanding that they were to consider any and all factors related to the case that could support a death sentence as well as factors supportive of a noncapital sentence (Paternoster, 1991). This unbridled reign led to irrational and discriminatory practices in the imposition of death sentences. The uncontrolled sentencing freedom enjoyed by juries and the misapplication of death sentences "led to the temporary suspension of the death penalty in the United States" (p. 17).

The modern era of capital punishment represents a return to the imposition of death sentences. During the moratorium on capital punishment, the U.S. Supreme Court ruled that the discretionary powers given to juries were unconstitutional along with the procedures used for the imposition of death sentences. A thorough examination of the Supreme Court's position as it relates to capital punishment will be examined in more detail later using Girard's theory of culture.

THEORETICAL ANALYSIS

The debate over capital punishment remains unresolved in American society. Some believe that capital punishment deters would-be criminals, while others contend that persons should be punished based on the doctrine of retribution. Another possible explanation for the existence of capital punishment in our society may be the need for ritualized violence as a method of social control. Although controversial, René Girard's theory of culture (1977) based on religious thought, anthropology, psychology, literary criticism, and other social sciences appears to explain the importance of the death penalty in our society. According to Girard (1987):

> In the science of man and culture today there is a unilateral swerve away from anything that could be called mimicry, imitation, or mimesis. And yet, there is nothing, or next to nothing, in human behavior that is not learned, and all learning is based on imitation. If human beings suddenly ceased imitating, all forms of culture would vanish. . . . The belief is that insisting on the role of imitation would unduly emphasize the gregarious aspects of humanity, all that transforms us into herds. There is a fear of minimizing the importance of everything that tends toward division, alienation, and conflict. If we give a leading role to imitation, perhaps we will make ourselves accomplices of the force of subjugation and uniformity. (p. 7)

The theory that human behavior is to some extent learned behavior resulting from imitating the behavior of others has also been advanced by theorists, such as Aristotle, Plato, Tarde, and Sutherland. Although Plato's description of imitation, as well as his followers, failed to identify specific behaviors involved in appropriation, Girard (1987) states that "if imitation does indeed play the fundamental role for man, as everything seems to indicate, there must certainly exist an acquisitive imitation, or, if one prefers, a possessive mimesis whose effects and consequences should be carefully studied and considered" (p. 9), not overlooked. It is indisputable that imitation brings about conflict, but in many instances, persons have learned to control and dispense imitated behavior in acceptable ways.

Society determines which behaviors are authorized, thereby identifying behaviors that may or may not be imitated. In other words, there are restricted imitations. These prohibitions exist because some behaviors are just plain absurd or they threaten the safety of society (Girard, 1987). It has been suggested that primitive societies understood that unlike modern society, there was a relationship between mimesis and violence (Girard, 1987). The theory of culture advanced by Girard claims that "there is a connection between conflict and acquisitive mimesis. Modern society tends to view competition and conflict differently from primitive society mainly because we tend to see difference emerge from the outcome of a conflict [and] we tend to focus on the individual act" (pp. 11–12).

By focusing on the individual act, instead of the act and its context, we (modern society) are able to view violence as an isolated crime. In doing so, we fail to truly understand the context in which the act was committed and its relationship to the violence experienced. Instead, we depend on the power of our judicial institutions to mandate adherence to the rules of social order, which does little, if anything, to increase our understanding of imitative violence or the importance of external factors to violent behavior(s). The purpose of these judicial institutions seems to imply that all persons in a society will abide by the laws that have been established and agreed upon by the members of society, but this is not true, especially since laws tend to represent the wishes of those persons who have power and wealth in society (the elite) in an attempt to control the masses.

It has been suggested that without these institutions, "the imitative and repetitious character of violence becomes manifest once more; the imitative character of violence is in fact most manifest in explicit violence, where it acquires a formal perfection it had not previously possessed" (Girard, 1987, p. 12). For example, in previous societies, a murder expanded substantially in the form of blood feuds. Violent acts, such as the blood feuds and other rivalries, had to be curtailed to reunite the community, and the solution had to be dramatic and violent. Basically, the idea was and remains: Violence begets violence.

In *McGautha* v. *California* (1971), a violent solution was also suggested by one justice as the only means by which violence could be ended even though it was noted that violence is self-propagating. Fortunately or unfortunately, our society has established a judicial institution in the form of the death penalty as a means to end violence (sanctioned self-propagating violence). Society has proscribed the method, time, and deliverer of the punishment for the sanctioned ritualized killing of another person (Girard, 1987). As such, the death penalty is a dramatic and violent solution used to reunite the community, but fails unless the targeted community is the victim's family, not society as a whole. Beschle (1997) states: "[M]odern legal systems seek to break the cycle of imitative violence by directing the punitive urge of all members of society toward a common enemy" (p. 521). The common enemy becomes the "new victim" in the community-sanctioned ritualized violence.

To proceed through the various phases of the ritualized killing, there must first be some type of relationship established between the "new victim" and the community. As part of the ritualized killing, it is important that the person to be executed (the new victim) be viewed as the cause of the community's discord and that his or her death will somehow restore peace in the community. Girard (1987) also suggests that "at the moment when violence ceases and peace has been established, the community has the whole of its attention fixed on the victim it has just killed" (p. 81), which leads one to surmise that in some instances, there is a fascination with some executed persons, such as Gary Gilmore and Ted Bundy.

In addition to the symbol of intense interest in the executed victim, there are many symbols associated with the death process. For example, the tradition of the *last meal* is viewed as a special privilege or a ritualized privilege granted by the community to one who for a brief period is perceived as special and worthy of this treatment. Additionally, the person who has received the death sentence most often is a typical member of the community but is also significantly different because of his or her criminal act. This being the case, most members of the community lack compassion for and do not identify themselves with the offender. Having used Girard's theory of culture to explain the symbolism in the death process, we now use his theory to examine the shift in the rulings of the U.S. Supreme Court.

Girard's (1987) theory can be used as a plausible explanation for the shift in the courts from being concerned with guilt to focusing more on expediting executions. As justices are replaced on the Court, we find that the new member is expected to bring to the Court a particular view that is shared by the controlling political party. The justice, then, merely advances the opinions shared by those who are not in office who share the same beliefs. In many instances, justices have been accused of relying on personal feelings or previous policy decisions, which purportedly expressed the public's desires, in order to write opinions for various cases. This being the case, it is safe to assume that some of the opinions rendered by the Court have not only been influenced by public opinion, but also mirror public opinion, thereby extending the theory of imitation to the Court. For this reason, we are able to link Girard's theory of culture to the shift in Supreme Court decisions based on the makeup of the Court and the political climate under which it has operated. Girard (1987) noted that society does not desire to be perceived as in a state of constant revenge, but is more interested in providing an effective judicial system, which allows permissible social constraints. The apparent shift in the Supreme Court suggest that some, if not all, of the justices believe that there must be little or no interference from the Supreme Court in lower-court decisions. This "hands-off" approach has evolved over time as the Supreme Court has decided various cases. In the following sections we discuss briefly this evolutionary process of the Supreme Court.

INFLUENCE OF THE SUPREME COURT

One phase that the Supreme Court entered into can be identified as the period of constitutionality. By this we mean that the Court was concerned with the issue of whether or not the death penalty itself was against the Constitution of the United States. *Powell* v. *Alabama* (1932) (the right to appointed counsel in capital cases) is said to represent the beginning of the Court's reform efforts concerning the death penalty. It is during this period that the Court used broad interpretations of the Fourteenth Amendment to bring about changes in criminal justice systems throughout the states in relation to capital cases. However, the main issue of whether or not the death penalty was in violation of the Constitution was often *not discussed*. It was not until Justice Goldberg's dissenting opinion in *Rudolph* v. *Alabama* (1963) that there was even any hint of a constitutional issue.

The Court continued to avoid the issue of constitutionality until there was an active campaign against the death penalty initiated by the National Association for the Advancement of Colored People (NAACP) Legal Defense Fund, which resulted in a moratorium against executions. During this period, the Court, in *Witherspoon* v. *Illinois* (1968), ruled that juror exclusion could not be based solely on a person's own objections to the death penalty. It is also in *Witherspoon* that we find the first written opinion (by Justice Stewart) in a case decision that questions the propriety of the death penalty. Without ruling specifically on whether or not the death penalty was against the Constitution of the United States, the Court suggested that morally sound jurors would not impose the death penalty upon another human being, and therefore a decision concerning the matter was not warranted by the Court (Burt, 1987). The Court presumed that American society was harmonious and stable and would work in such a manner as to maintain social order (Burt, 1987). The implication was that the maintenance of social order would deter and/or reduce crime and there would be no need to administer the death penalty. Therefore, the Court would not have to address the constitutional issue concerning the death penalty.

However, four years later, in *Furman* v. *Georgia* (1972), the majority of the justices declared that the death penalty as administered was in violation of Eighth Amendment protection against cruel and unusual punishment. The rationale for this conclusion varied among the justices, but the main concern was application of the death penalty under the existing standards at that time. The Court failed, however, to declare the death penalty unconstitutional based on a different set of standards. By 1976, the Court in *Gregg, Proffitt*, and *Jurek* ruled that the sentence of death was not an unconstitutional punishment and for a brief period began scrutinizing imposed death sentences upon appellate review. According to Burt (1987), "this kind of closely detailed, sustained observation by the Supreme Court was itself 'aberrational'" (p. 1780).

Beginning in 1983, the Court turned resolutely away from this pursuit, instead appearing intent on affirming capital punishment in order to suppress 'the seeds of anarchy-of self help, vigilante justice, and lynch law'" (Burt, 1987, p. 1780). The Court not only seemed to support capital punishment but also began closing avenues previously open to inmates seeking federal constitutional relief. State appellate courts were encouraged to (1) spend less time reviewing cases, (2) overlook admitted errors in death penalty proceedings, and (3) disregard the proportionality review process (Burt, 1987). Then, in 1985, the Court made another shift in the capital punishment debate.

In *Wainwright* v. *Witt* (1985) the Court dismantled the opinion it rendered in *Witherspoon* concerning death-qualified jurors and instead, concluded that there was a presumption of correctness on the part of state judges in excluding jurors. This action by the Court blocked federal constitutional review unless the defense attorney could show that the trial judge had erred. Given the resources available to defense attorneys in capital cases, the likelihood of a challenge to the presumption of correctness lies moot. The Court continued to tear down the tenets of the *Witherspoon* decision in its ruling in *Lockhart* v. *McCree* (1986). It ruled that even if a death-qualified jury is more conviction-prone than other juries, that fact alone *does not* raise a constitutional issue for review by the Court. According to Burt (1987), the Court's ruling in *Lockhart* reveals that "the Court is now content on suppressing rather than exploring doubts about capital punishment" (pp. 1788–1789).

It is not surprising that the controversy surrounding capital punishment continues when the justices of the Supreme Court cannot deal effectively with the issue. If there are constitutional safeguards to ensure that inmates are afforded those rights, why should judges be instructed to overlook such safeguards? Does this mean that the justices of the Supreme Court view persons convicted and sentenced to death as less than human and therefore that such persons should not be afforded the rights guaranteed by the Constitution? It seems fair to say that the chaos that has plagued the Court concerning capital punishment is representative of the confusion and inconsistencies that prevail in society about capital punishment. Perhaps the chaos that plagues us (society) could be diffused by simply treating those persons sentenced to death as human beings until death, if an execution is forthcoming. After all, what does society have to lose if death is what one seeks? Does acknowledging that these people are human stir up emotions that one tries hard to suppress? Is that why we prefer not to read or hear about the conditions of incarceration? Facing the reality that death row inmates are humans just like any of us makes it hard to accept the inadequacies of prison life.

THE ADMINISTRATION OF LAW

Laws in any society define behaviors deemed unacceptable based on the morals and values of the community at large. They also determine who will be punished (Price & Sokoloff, 1995). In societies that are not very complex, informal rather than formal methods are used as means of social control. Both society and individuals are presumably protected by the laws. These laws may prescribe punishments, direct or restrain certain actions, and access financial penalties (Reid, 1995). Price and Sokoloff (1995) state "the law protects what those in power value most" (p. 14). Laws are created and passed by legislative bodies composed mainly of rich white men and persons who share their interests (Price & Sokoloff, 1995). Laws are the mechanism by which the dominant class ensures that its interests will be protected (Quinney, 1975). However, challenges to specific laws are not uncommon (Price & Sokoloff, 1995).

Historically, women have been considered the property of their fathers or husbands without full acknowledgment of them as individuals with rights granted by the Constitution (Price & Sokoloff, 1995). Several cases have come before the Supreme Court concerning the rights of women. In the landmark case of *Reed* v. *Reed* (1971), the Supreme Court ruled that women were indeed persons and should be treated as such under the U.S. Constitution. The Court stated that the Fourteenth Amendment clause "does not deny to States the power to treat different classes of persons in different ways. . . . [it] does, however, deny to States power to legislate that different treatment be accorded to persons placed by a statute into different classes on the basis of criteria wholly unrelated to the objective of that statute. A classification must be reasonable, not arbitrary, and must rest upon grounds of difference having a fair and substantial relation to the object of the legislation . . ." (*Reed* v. *Reed*, 1971).

According to the justices, preference based on gender which is used merely to reduce the number of court hearings that could arise because two or more persons are equally entitled is directly in violation of the Fourteenth Amendment clause forbidding arbitrariness, nor can gender be used as a preventive measure against intrafamily controversies (*Reed* v. *Reed*, 1971). Based on this ruling, the Court recognized women as individuals with the right to individualized treatment, but it did not identify gender in relation to the suspect-classification argument under the Fourteenth Amendment.

It was not until *Frontiero* v. *Richardson* (1973) that the Court ruled by a 4–4 plurality vote—gender was not to be a suspect classification (at 677). This case involved differential treatment of men and women in the military with regard to their respective spouses being classified as dependents. The ruling by the Court also stated that the current statute was in violation of the due process clause of the Fifth Amendment. Justice Powell suggested that the Court should not rule on gender as a suspect classification because the Equal Rights Amendment (ERA) had been approved by Congress and it would eliminate the need for such a classification (*Frontiero* v. *Richardson*, 1973). Unfortunately, the states did not ratify the ERA.

Women were still seeking equal rights during the Ford and Carter administrations. Although the Court ruled in *Craig* that "classification by gender must serve important governmental objectives and must be substantially related to achievement of those objectives" (*Craig* v. *Boren*, 1976). Yet this case did not a have true impact on constitutional law; instead, it most notably suggested that there were changes in alliances among the justices. These cases represent only small legal gains by women.

According to Hoff (1991): "[S]ome of the most disturbing gender-biased decisions the Supreme Court has reached in the last seventeen years have involved pregnancy cases. . . . other recent decisions are either discouraging or disquieting for the cause of complete female equality, especially where redistributive economic issues are at stake" (p. 251).

Knowing that many households are now headed by women has not moved Congress or the Supreme Court to address the comparable worth issue properly. Instead, they avoid the comparable worth issue as though it were a plague. Women must decide "whether they prefer equal treatment as unequal individuals (when judged by male standards) or special treatment as a protected (and thus implicitly) inferior group" (Hoff, 1991, p. 274). The legal system has not always treated women and girls fairly, and this could be due in part to the perceptions that men (who are the majority in the legal system) have of females (Price & Sokoloff, 1995). Roberts (1994) states: "[T]he criminal law most directly mandates socially acceptable behavior. Criminal law also helps to shape the way that we perceive women's proper role" (p. 1). Women who do not adhere to prescribed gender roles and commit criminal offenses are viewed differently by our criminal justice system. This issue is discussed more fully in the following section.

FEMALE CRIMINALITY

Female crime is not as prevalent as that of males and previously had not been considered a social problem (Belknap, 2001). Women are also more likely to commit fewer and less serious violent crimes than are males (Belknap, 2001; Mann, 1984; Pollock-Byrne, 1991; Simon & Landis, 1991). Yet we have been led to believe that female crime has reached outlandish proportions and far exceeds male crime. The basis for this information has been the *Uniform Crime Reports* (UCRs) complied by the FBI from data supplied by law enforcement agencies.

According to Steffensmeier (1995), these data (the UCRs) are problematic in assessing female crime patterns. Steffensmeier suggests the following: (1) the changes in arrest rates may be related more to "public attitudes and police practices . . . than to actual behaviors," (2) because of the broadness of categories they include "dissimilar events and . . . a range of seriousness," and (3) the definition of serious crime as used by the UCRs tends to lead one to believe that serious female crime has risen dramatically, when, in fact, women have been arrested more for the crime of larceny, "especially for shoplifting" (p. 92) than for any other type I offense. Previous research (Mann, 1984; Naffine, 1987; Simon & Landis, 1991; Steffensmeier, 1980) has revealed that overall, female crime rates have remained fairly stable in most areas. The notable changes are in the areas of "less serious property offenses and possibly drugs" (Belknap, 2001, p. 58).

To better assess the rate of female crime, Steffensmeier (1995) completed a 30-year study of arrest statistics. Although the study examined trends in individual offenses, of particular importance here are the trends by type of crime based on male/female arrests. The type of crimes chosen to develop trends for male/female arrests were "violent, masculine, Index ('serious'), and minor property" (Steffensmeier, 1995, p. 94). He found that female participation in masculine crimes increased slightly, which led to more arrests, but this was not the case for violent crimes. Steffensmeier again attributes the increase in arrests for index crimes to an increase in the number of women committing larcenies. Women have also had an increase in arrest rates for minor property crimes (Belknap, 2001; Steffensmeier, 1995). Simpson (1991) suggests that violent behavior varies among females and it is difficult to separate the individual influences of race, class, and gender because they are so intermingled. For the purposes of this chapter, we examine only the influence of gender in the administration of law.

Having examined briefly female criminality, we now turn our attention to the processing of female criminal cases by the criminal justice system. It has been suggested (Chesney-Lind, 1982; Farnworth & Teske, 1995; Frazier, Bock, & Henretta, 1983; Harvey, Burnham, Kendall, & Pease, 1992; Spohn & Spears, 1997; Steffensmeier, 1980) that women receive differential treatment during the processing of criminal cases. The differential treatment may be negative or positive. For example, Steffensmeier (1980) suggested that the likelihood of future offending and the perceived danger to the community influenced the preferential treatment of women in the criminal justice process and as a result increased their chances of receiving probation instead of prison. Yet Chesney-Lind (1982) discovered that female juveniles have always received negative differential treatment . She noted that the females were processed into the juvenile justice system as a result of status offenses and received institutionalization more often than did male juveniles.

Frazier, Bock, and Henretta (1983) examined the effect of probation officers in determining gender differences in sentencing severity. In their study, they collected data from presentence investigation reports with various information concerning the offender, as well as recommendations from the probation officers regarding sentences. According to Frazier et al., "there is a strong relationship between gender of offender and final criminal court disposition. . . . [P]robation officers' recommendations have major effects and . . . being female greatly increases the likelihood of receiving a nonincarceration sentence recommendation " (pp. 315–316). In an international comparison of gender differences in criminal justice, Harvey, Burnham, Kendall, and Pease (1992) found that women were processed out of the criminal justice system more often than men. Their study also revealed that men who were processed through the criminal justice system were convicted and imprisoned at a higher rate than were women worldwide. Harvey et al. note "that criminal justice worldwide operates differentially by gender (but not necessarily in a discriminatory way)" (p. 217).

In another study, Farnworth and Teske (1995) found some evidence of gender disparity in relation to charge reductions if there was no prior criminal history. The absence of prior offending was noted to increase the possibility of probation for females. Based on the selective chivalry thesis, Farnworth and Teske discovered "that white females were twice as likely as minority females to have assault charges changed to nonassault at sentencing" (p. 40). There was also supportive evidence which suggested that the use of discretionary powers influenced informal rather than formal decisions.

More recently, Spohn and Spears's (1997) study of the dispositions of violent felonies for both men and women revealed that more men (71.4 percent) than women (65.0 percent) were prosecuted but that their conviction rates were very similar and major differences appeared in sentencing. For example, males were incarcerated 77.4 percent of the time versus 48.2 percent for females. Overall, females normally served "428 fewer days in prison" (p. 42) than did males. This study also found that charge reduction or total dismissal of charges was more likely for females than for males. Spohn and Spears state: "Females were more likely than males to have injured their victims. . . Female defendants were much less likely than male defendants to have a prior felony conviction. Females were charged with and convicted of less serious crimes and were less likely . . . to be charged with or convicted of more than one offense . . . less likely than males to have used a gun to commit the crime or to have victimized a stranger. . . . [F]emales were more likely to have private attorneys and to be released prior to trial" (p. 42). Based on their findings, Spohn and Spears suggest that violent female offenders are looked upon differently by judges for various reasons, such as: (1) females may be perceived as less dangerous to the community; (2) females may have acted as an accomplice instead of being the primary perpetrator; (3) the risk of recidivism is less for females; and (4) there is a better chance of rehabilitating female offenders.

WOMEN AND CAPITAL PUNISHMENT

Imposition of the death penalty is not just racially biased but is also gender biased. Streib (1990) states that gender bias is associated with two main sources: "(1) the express provisions of the law and (2) the implicit attitudes, either conscious or subconscious, of key actors involved in the criminal justice process" (p. 874). Although gender is not mentioned specifically in state statutes, there are certain considerations that may be applied differently based on gender (Streib, 1990). For example, most male criminals have prior criminal histories that include violent acts whereas women do not have significant prior criminal histories and tend to be less violent than their male counterparts. When women are arrested for murder, it is usually their first offense. Because there tends to be an absence of criminal behavior on the part of women, Mann (1984) and Steffensmeier (1980) suggest that women are not viewed as a threat to society. Another factor considered in capital cases is the defendant's mental state. Allen (1987) suggests that a commonly held belief is that female murderers are emotionally unbalanced at the time of the crime. Additionally, women are usually not the primary perpetrator, therefore, they are able to request consideration for this mitigating factor. According to Streib (1990), "even when all of the specific aggravating and mitigating factors are the same for male and female defendants, females still tend to receive significantly lighter sentences in criminal cases generally" (p. 879).

In examining the treatment of female defendants in the criminal justice system, Gillespie and Lopez (1986b) found that "in one area, however, women have constantly been treated with unquestionable deference because of their sex—that of the death penalty. Women have been traditionally been considered a separate class, deserving of a brand of "justice" all their own. Rather than execute them, they have been lectured, even released to the supervision of their husbands, and often never brought to trial" (p. 2).

It has been suggested that this deference is related directly to the paternalistic attitudes of male power brokers in the criminal justice system. However, this idea only explains why some women receive preferential treatment. It is not useful in explaining the absence of the same treatment toward other women. It is this difference which makes these other female defendants susceptible to harsh treatment in the criminal justice system. Research (Mann, 1984; Streib, 1990) has shown that women who are uneducated, poor, members of a racial minority group, and of a lower socioeconomic group tend not to receive preferential treatment in the criminal justice system. It is women who have any or all of the aforementioned factors that are more likely to be condemned to death and in some instances, executed in our society.

Historically, we find that there is and has been in this country an acceptance of executing female offenders. Although executions of female defendants are rare, there have been 561 confirmed executions of women since 1632. This represents 2.8 percent of all executions in the country. Yet when we examine executions of females from other centuries, we find that fewer executions take place today than in the past. For example, women comprised only 0.7 percent of the executions during the modern era (Streib, 2001). In the following section, we discuss briefly the characteristics of women executed.

PROFILE OF WOMEN EXECUTED

We find that 68 percent of women who have been executed in the United States were white and 32 percent were black. Although some defendants were over 50, the average age was 38.7 years old. In terms of previous criminal history, only one had a prior homicide conviction; the others had only minor criminal histories. The motivation for the crimes was profit and emotion, but they were not always domestic situations (Gillespie & Lopez, 1986a). Several patterns emerged related to executed women and the crimes. First, there was usually nothing unique or particularly heinous about the crime. Second, collecting insurance was the primary motive for the murder in many cases, and in most instances there was a male accomplice. Next, there seemed to be no established relationship between the victim and the defendant. Finally, the South has executed more women than any other region, while New York leads the states in the execution of women (Gillespie & Lopez, 1986a).

In examining death sentences imposed from January 1, 1973 through December 31, 2000, we find that women received only 137 death sentences compared to over 7031 death sentences for men (Death Penalty Information Center, 2001a; Streib, 2001). During the 1970s women received only 22 death sentences, but there was a dramatic increase (51) in the number of death sentences imposed on women in the 1980s. During 1989, there were 11 death sentences given to women, representing the single highest total of death sentences given women in any one year from 1973 through 2000. In the 1990s we find a total of 57 death sentences imposed (Streib, 2001). It is interesting to note that 72 of the death sentences imposed from 1973 through 1997 were either commuted to life imprisonment or reversed; three of the death sentences were actually fulfilled (Death Penalty Information Center, 1998; Streib, 1998).

As of January 1, 2001 there were 3669 males and 57 females on death row (Death Penalty Information Center, 2001a; Streib, 2001). Of the 57 females currently on death row, five have had their sentences overturned. Women constitute 1.53 percent of the total death row population (NAACP Legal Defense and Educational Fund, 2001). Since capital punishment was reinstated in 1976, there have been 683 executions. Of these executions, only seven women (Velma Barfield, 1984; Karla Faye Tucker and Judy Buenoano, 1998; Betty Beets and Christina Riggs, 2000; and Wanda Jean Allen and Marilyn Plantz) have been executed, representing .074 percent of the total number of executions (Death Penalty Information Center, 2001a).

Upon closer examination, we find that the women on death row range in age from 23 through 71. The time spent on death row spans a period of a few weeks to almost 19 years. Thirty-five percent of the women on death row were between the ages of 20 and 29 at the time of the criminal act; 28 percent were between 30 and 39 years old. The racial breakdown of defendants reveals that 60 percent of the inmates are white and 33 percent are black. Latinas represent only 7 percent of the female death row population (Death Penalty Information Center, 1998, 2001a).

Briefly, we should note that the victims were nearly 82 percent white, 12 percent black, 3 percent Latino/a, and 2 percent Asian. More often, the victim was male (53 percent), with females representing 47 percent of the victims. Interestingly, Native American defendants only killed white victims and Asian defendants killed only Asian (four) and white (one) victims, while white, black, and Hispanic defendants killed victims of all four racial groups (white, black, Hispanic, and Asian) (Death Penalty Information Center, 2001b).

The women who are currently serving a death sentence are subjected to the same inadequate environmental conditions as other women in prison: poor medical care, inhumane treatment, and isolation from family. In many instances, people who are in correctional facilities become socialized to believe that they are (1) not human, (2) worthless, and (3) cannot be rehabilitated. In other words, they will always be criminals. Some critics also suggest that we should not permit persons on death row access to rehabilitative programs because they are serving a death sentence. We disagree, especially since the reversal rate on appeals for women is 97 percent (Streib, 1998).

Although the reversal rate for women is high, until their sentences are reversed, these women must survive within the confines of the institution. A major concern for death row inmates is medical care. First, a death row inmate has to wait until an officer makes a security check in order to secure a form requesting a doctor's visit. Then a nurse decides whether or not the request will be granted. In many instances, this decision is based solely on the nurse's opinion, not on a preliminary evaluation of the inmate's medical condition. Inmates state that they often do not seek medical assistance because the officers accuse them of trying to get attention. One inmate was so worried that the officers were going to accuse her of trying to get attention that she did not seek medical assistance at the onset of a heart attack. Her cellmate finally called an officer, against the sick woman's wishes, to take her to the infirmary. Unfortunately, the nurse in the infirmary said that there was nothing wrong with her and had the inmate returned to her cell. The inmate died later that night of a massive heart attack. This is only one story of the lack of concern shown by some people who are employed to provide medical care to inmates. Yet the media suggests that inmates have the best medical care available.

Like other inmates, death row inmates are seldom treated as persons by correctional officers and staff. Instead, they are made to feel like a burden that everyone wishes would go away. Because death row is isolated from the general population, the correctional officers are the only people these inmates interact with during the day. If an inmate is housed in the same cell unit as another death row inmate, they may visit and talk to each other. Some correctional officers speak to inmates in a manner that creates problems. By this we mean that inmates expect to be treated as human beings, not as animals or objects. Although their daily activities are programmed by the institution, some correctional officers add to the humiliation of the inmates by their conduct and handling of inmates. It is at times like these that inmates need to be able to turn to family to cope with the dehumanization characteristic of prison life.

In some instances, families cannot withstand the pressures associated with having a family member incarcerated. In far too many cases, family relationships are strained because there is little to no contact with the incarcerated person. Research (Mann, 1984; Pollock-Byrne, 1991) shows that women tend to lose contact with their families more often than men because states normally have only one women's prison and it is located in a remote, rural area of the state. As a result, visitation is more difficult and more restricted for death row inmates. Women also experience a severe emotional separation from family and friends due to their socialization process. Family support adds to an inmate's sense of humanity. Without this support, inmates do not have a buffer from the institutional process of dehumanization.

CONCLUSIONS

The reversal rate on appeal for women sentenced to death is approximately 97 percent (Streib, 1998). Because of the high reversal rate associated with female offenders, we have been lulled into believing that women will not be executed. Given the current attitude toward executing women, we can expect an increase in the number of women executed. We believe that this increase is inevitable because of the ever-lingering "get tough on crime" mentality presently dominant in our society along with recent legislation in Congress limiting appeals for defendants. Perhaps instead of a get-tough reactive crime policy, we should have a get tough proactive crime policy and there would be no need for death rows in this country.

REFERENCES

ALLEN, P. (1987). Rendering them harmless: The professional portrayal of women. In P. Carlen & A. Worrell (Eds.), *Gender, crime and justice*. Philadelphia: Milton-Keynes.

BAKER, D. (1999). A descriptive profile and socio-historical analysis of female executions in the United States: 1632–1997. *Women and Criminal Justice, 10*(3), 57.

BELKNAP, J. (2001). *The invisible woman: Gender, crime and justice* (2nd ed.). Belmont, CA: Wadsworth Publishing.

BESCHLE, D. (1997). What's guilt (or deterrence) got to do with it? The death penalty, ritual, and mimetic violence. *William and Mary Law Review, 38*(2), 487–538.

BURT, R. (1987). Disorder in the court: The death penalty and the Constitution. *Michigan Law Review, 85*, 1741–1819.

CHESNEY-LIND, M. (1982). Guilty by reason of sex: Young women and the juvenile justice system. In B. Price & N. Sokoloff (Eds.), *The criminal justice system and women* (pp. 77–105). New York: Clark Boardman.

DEATH PENALTY INFORMATION CENTER. (1998). *Facts about the death penalty*. Washington, DC: DPIC.

DEATH PENALTY INFORMATION CENTER. (2001a). *Women and the death penalty*. Washington, DC: DPIC.

DEATH PENALTY INFORMATION CENTER. (2001b). *Death row U.S.A.: Execution update*. Washington, DC: DPIC.

EREZ, E. (1989). Gender, rehabilitation, and probation decisions. *Criminology, 27*(2), 307–327.

FARNSWORTH, M., & TESKE, R., JR. (1995). Gender differences in felony court processing: Three hypotheses of disparity. *Women and Criminal Justice, 6*(2), 23–44.

FLANAGAN, T., & MAGUIRE, K. (1989). *Sourcebook of criminal justice statistics*. Washington, DC: U.S. Department of Justice, Bureau of Justice Statistics.

FLETCHER, B., DIXON-SHAVER, D., & MOON, D. (1993). *Women prisoners: A forgotten population*. Westport, CT: Praeger.

FRAZIER, C., BOCK, E., & HENRETTA, J. (1983). The role of probation officers in determining gender differences in sentencing severity. *Sociological Quarterly, 24*, 305–318.

GILLESPIE, L., & LOPEZ, B. (1986a). Differential death: Executed women. Paper presented at the annual meeting of the Western Society of Criminology, Newport, CA.

GILLESPIE, L., & LOPEZ, B. (1986b). What must a woman do to be executed: A comparison of executed and non-executed women. Paper presented at the annual meeting of the American Society of Criminology, Atlanta, GA.

GIRARD, R. (1977). *Violence and the sacred* (Patrick Gregory, Trans.). Baltimore: Johns Hopkins University Press.

GIRARD, R. (1987). *Things hidden since the foundation of the world*. London: Athlone Press.

HARVEY, L., BURNHAM, R., KENDALL, K., & PEASE, K. (1992). Gender differences in criminal justice: An international comparison. *British Journal of Criminology, 32*(2), 208–217.

HOFF, J. (1991). *Law, gender and injustice: A legal history of U.S. women.* New York: New York University Press.

KOOSED, M. (1996). *Capital punishment: The philosophical, moral, and penological debate over capital punishment.* New York: Garland Publishing.

KRONENWETTER, M. (1993). *Capital punishment: A reference handbook.* Santa Barbara, CA: ABC-CLIO.

KRUTTSCHNITT, C. (1982). Respectable women and the law. *Sociological Quarterly, 23*(2), 221–234.

LEZIN, K. (1999). *Finding life on death row: Profiles of six inmates.* Boston: Northeastern University Press.

MANN, C. (1984). *Female crime and delinquency.* Tuscaloosa, AL: University of Alabama Press.

NAACP LEGAL AND EDUCATION FUND. (1998). *Death row, U.S.A.* New York: NAACP.

NAFFINE, N. (1987). *Female crime: The construction of women in criminology.* Sydney, Australia: Allen & Unwin.

O'SHEA, K. (1999). *Women and the death penalty in the United States, 1900–1998.* Westport, CT: Praeger.

PATERNOSTER, R. (1991). *Capital punishment in America.* New York: Lexington Books.

POLLOCK-BYRNE, J. (1991). *Women, prison, and crime.* Pacific Grove, CA: Brooks/Cole.

PRICE, B., & SOKOLOFF, N. (1995). The criminal law and women. In B. Price & N. Sokoloff (Eds.), *The criminal justice system and women: Offenders, victims, and workers* (pp. 11–29). New York: McGraw-Hill.

QUINNEY, R. (1975). *Class, state and crime: On the theory and practice of criminal justice.* New York: Longman.

RAPAPORT, E. (2000). Equality of the damned: The execution of women on the cusp of the 21st century. *Ohio Northern University Law Review, 26,* 581.

REID, S. (1995). *Crime and criminology* (7th ed.). Madison, WI: Brown & Benchmark.

ROBERTS, D. (1994). The meaning of gender equality in criminal law. *Journal of Criminal Law and Criminology, 85*(1), 1–14.

SIMON, R., & LANDIS, J. (1991). *The crimes women commit, and the punishments they receive.* Lexington, MA: Lexington Books.

SIMPSON, S. (1991). Caste, class, and violent crime: Exploring differences in female offending. *Criminology, 29*(1), 115–135.

Spohn, C., & Spears, J. (1997). Gender and case processing decisions: A comparison of case outcomes for male and female defendants charged with violent felonies. *Women and Criminal Justice, 8*(3), 29–59.

STEFFENSMEIER, D. (1980). Assessing the impact of the women's movement on sex-based differences in the handling of adult criminal defendants. *Crime and Delinquency, 26,* 344–357.

STEFFENSMEIER, D. (1995). Trends in female crime: It's still a man's world. In B. Price & N. Sokoloff (Eds.), *The criminal justice system and women: Offenders, victims, and workers* (pp. 89–104). New York: McGraw-Hill.

STREIB, V. (1990). *American executions of female offenders: A preliminary inventory of names, dates, and other information* (3rd ed.). Cleveland, OH: Author.

STREIB, V. (1990). Death penalty for female offenders. *University of Cincinnati Law Review, 58*(3), 845–880.

STREIB, V. (1998). *Capital punishment for female offenders: Names, dates, and other information* (3rd ed.). Cleveland, OH: Author.

STREIB, V. (2001) *Death penalty for female offenders: January 1, 1973 to December 31, 2001.* Cleveland, OH: Author.

VISHER, C. (1983). Chivalry in arrest decisions. *Criminology, 21*(1), 5–28.

ZINGRAFF, M., & THOMPSON, R. (1984). Differential sentencing of men and women in the U.S.A. *International Journal of the Sociology of Law, 12,* 401–413.

CASES

Craig v. *Boren*, 429 U.S. 190, 197 (1976).

Frontiero v. *Richardson*, 411 U.S. 677 (1973).

Furman v. *Georgia*, 408 U.S. 238 (1972).

Gregg v. *Georgia*, 428 U.S. 153 (1976).

Jurek v. *Texas*, 428 U.S. 262 (1976).

Lockhart v. *McCree*, 106 S. Ct. 1758 (1986).

McGautha v. *California*, 402 U.S. 183 (1971).

Powell v. *Alabama*, 287 U.S. 45 (1932).

Proffitt v. *Florida*, 428 U.S. 242 (1976).

Reed v. *Reed*, 404 U.S. 71, 92 S. Ct. 251, 30 L. Ed. 2d 255 (1971).

Rudolph v. *Alabama*, 375 U.S. 889 (1963).

Wainwright v. *Witt*, 469 U.S. 412 (1985).

Witherspoon v. *Illinois*, 391 U.S. 510 (1968).

SECTION V

Women: Victims of Violence

19

Arrest Policies for Domestic Violence

Their Implications for Battered Women

Susan L. Miller

❖

Historically, the criminal justice system has failed to respond adequately to woman battering. In response to criticisms, the system has moved toward emphasizing pro-arrest policies. Much of this redirection resulted from an outcry from feminist groups and the findings from the Minneapolis Domestic Violence Experiment, which indicated that arrest deters offenders at higher rates than separation does or mediation. Consequently, in the ensuing years, many police departments have restructured their policies and procedures. Replication efforts have tested the deterrence hypothesis using different samples and geographic sites. Several particular concerns have been raised as a result of these shifts in policy. First, the replication studies have failed to demonstrate convincingly that arrest of batterers deters repeat offenses from occurring in sites other than Minneapolis; arrest may, in fact, make the situation worse. Second, under mandatory arrest statutes, often both the victim and offender are arrested despite preemptive aggression from the offender. Finally, pro-arrest policies may introduce disproportionately negative ramifications for women of lower socioeconomic classes and minority women.

In this chapter, the changes in how the criminal justice system responds to woman batterers, beginning with a review of the policy changes since the 1980s, are explored. Next, the research conducted to evaluate pro-arrest policies is addressed. The implications for victims are assessed in terms of these studies and the differential impact that these policies may have for lower-class and minority women. Finally, a brief review of alternatives and supplements to arrest is conducted, such as coordinated community and criminal justice system response efforts.

Historically, the crime of intimate violence has been shrouded in secrecy, viewed as a private matter and not as a social problem. Both legal and social institutions have reinforced the "hands-off approach" that has characterized responses to woman battering. However,

307

since the 1970s, efforts initiated by the battered women's movement have propelled the issue of intimate violence into the national spotlight (see Dobash & Dobash, 1977; Schechter, 1982).[1] Much of the research and political activism has focused on identifying the correlates of abuse, providing services for victims, creating or strengthening domestic violence legislation, and improving the criminal justice system's responses to woman battering. One of the most compelling criticisms concerning the handling of woman battering has been leveled against police officers' failure to arrest woman batterers and protect victims adequately. Consequently, in the 1980s, innovative laws were introduced and policy efforts were designed to improve the criminal justice system's treatment of domestic disputes. Included was the move toward pro-arrest policies. In this chapter we focus on the problems that facilitated these policy innovations, the pro-arrest strategies themselves, and review the current status of pro-arrest strategies. Special attention is paid to the different impacts that these policies may have for lower-class and minority battered women. We conclude with a brief review of alternative dispositions (other than arrest) and their value to battered women.[2]

CRIMINAL JUSTICE SYSTEM'S RESPONSES TO WOMAN BATTERING

The handling of domestic disputes evokes deep feelings of frustration both from police officers responding to these calls and from battered women responding to police officers' inaction.[3] Since mediation or separation were the common modes of police response, batterers were not punished for their actions and victims of their violence were not adequately protected (Stanko, 1985). These official responses were justified by cultural norms and gender-role expectations, despite the accumulated evidence showing that unchecked intimate violence escalates in frequency and intensity, with some episodes resulting in the death of the victim (Walker, Thyfault, & Browne, 1982).[4]

For years, battered women faced police officers who routinely supported the offender's position, challenged the credibility of the victim—often blaming her for her own victimization—and trivialized her fears (Gil, 1986; Karmen, 1982). Police officer training manuals reinforced officer behavior, stressing the use of family crisis intervention or separation tactics (International Association of Chiefs of Police 1967; Parnas, 1967). This policy emphasis sanctioned the discretion of police officers; it thus also sanctioned their reluctance to initiate criminal justice proceedings when officers thought that a reconciliation might occur and make arrest actions futile (Field & Field, 1973; Lerman, 1986). Not only did the police fail to respond formally to battering by invoking arrest, but other components in the system responded similarly (e.g., prosecutors and judges).[5] Taken together, the failure of the system to respond appropriately to woman battering perpetuated the silence surrounding intimate violence.

Statistics indicate that when police *do* retain the discretion to arrest in domestic-assault incidents, officers largely do *not* arrest.[6] For example, three different studies indicate that for domestic-violence incidents, police arrest rates were 10, 7, and 3 percent (see Buel, 1988). In Milwaukee, although 82 percent of battered women desired arrest of their abusers, police arrested only 14 percent of these offenders (Bowker, 1982). Similarly, in Ohio, police arrested only 14 percent of the cases, even though in 38 percent of these incidents, victims were either injured or killed (Bell, 1984). Overall, police in jurisdictions with pro-arrest policies still fail to arrest batterers (Balos & Trotzky, 1988; Ferraro, 1995; Lawrenz, Lembo, & Schade, 1988).

As a result of police departments' inadequate responses to treat battering as a serious offense, class-action suits were introduced against police departments by victims (Martin, 1978, Paterson, 1979). In fact, battered women who felt unprotected by police have received some satisfaction from this kind of court action, arguing successfully that the equal protection clause of the Fourteenth Amendment is violated when police treat women who are assaulted by an intimate partner differently from people assaulted by strangers.[7] Class-action suits, political activism by feminists, and victims' advocacy groups proved instrumental in challenging the efficacy and unresponsiveness of police departments (Schechter, 1982). The stage was set for researchers to explore new and different responses by police to battering, including advocating for pro-arrest or mandatory arrest policies.

MANDATORY ARREST POLICIES

Movement away from discretionary arrest policies and toward mandatory or pro-arrest policies is attractive for a variety of reasons. First, the psychological benefit to battered women cannot be overstated: Arrest demonstrates a willingness to assert officially that battering will not be tolerated. Second, some police officers believe that mandatory-arrest laws assist in clarifying police roles by providing more guidance and training (Loving, 1980). Third, evaluations of jurisdictions that enact mandatory-arrest laws indicate that rather than making police officers more vulnerable, police injuries decrease (National Criminal Justice Association, 1985); this decrease may be due to the advance notice or warning about the consequences of abusive behavior once mandatory arrest policies are in effect. Fourth, the onus of responsibility is transferred to police and does not remain solely on the battered woman's shoulders. Thus, many believe that officer-initiated arrest empowers the victim (Buel, 1988): "Arrest can kindle the battered woman's perception that society values her and penalizes violence against her. This perception counteracts her experience of abuse. . . . When a battered woman calls the police and they arrest the man who beats her, her actions, along with the officer's actions, do something to stop her beating. . . . Now her actions empower. The woman may begin to believe in herself enough to endeavor to protect herself" (Pastoor, 1984).[8]

A fifth advantage of mandatory arrest policies is the feeling that more equitable law enforcement will result than with a discretionary-based arrest system. Buel (1988, p. 224) argues that mandatory arrest that is conducted whenever specific, objective conditions are met will "ensure that race and class distinctions are not the basis for determining how police intervene in family violence situations."[9] Sixth, strong police action can contribute to purposeful follow-through by the other components of the criminal justice system.

Finally, some early research findings indicate that recidivism of batterers decreases dramatically after instituting mandatory arrest policies. For instance, homicides decreased from 12 or 13 annually to 1 in the first six months of 1986 in Newport News, Virginia (Lang, 1986); in Hartford County, Connecticut, the number of calls for police service for domestic violence incidents decreased by 28 percent (Olivero, 1987). Perhaps the most conclusive research finding has been attributed to the Minneapolis Domestic Violence Experiment, conducted by Sherman and Berk (1984).

The Minneapolis experiment manipulated types of police response to misdemeanant domestic assault.[10] The research findings revealed that arrest is twice as effective a deterrent for batterers than the more traditional police strategies of separation or mediation (Sherman

& Berk, 1984).[11] A subsequent national survey of police departments indicates that jurisdictions supporting arrest for minor domestic assault are increasing in numbers (from 10
percent in 1984 to 31 percent in 1986); eleven states attribute these policy changes to the
publicized results of the Minneapolis experiment's success (Cohn & Sherman, 1986).[12]

NEW CONCERNS ABOUT MANDATORY ARREST POLICIES

Ostensibly, mandatory arrest policies appear to solve many of the dilemmas faced by
battered women. In fact, it is difficult not to embrace wholeheartedly such a transformation
of police procedure in dealing with women battering. However, there are at least three
considerations that limit unconditional acceptance of the interpretation that arrest deters
battering or that mandatory arrest eliminates disparity in arrest practices. First, there are
methodological problems associated with the original (first-wave) research, the
Minneapolis Domestic Violence Experiment (MDVE) (Binder & Meeker, 1996; Sherman
& Berk, 1984), which was instrumental in generating additional evaluations of mandatory-
arrest policies. Second, there are problems identified with the NIJ-funded replication studies
and contrary results reported from other (second-wave) studies (Dutton, Hart, Kennedy, &
Williams, 1996). Third, there may be unintended negative consequences of mandatory
arrest for battered women themselves, particularly for women of color or women from lower
socioeconomic groups (Miller, 1989; Rasche, 1995). These concerns raise hesitations
about fully accepting the conclusion that arrest of woman batterers deters subsequent acts
of intimate violence.

METHODOLOGICAL PROBLEMS

Since the Minneapolis Domestic Violence Experiment remains the seminal study to inform
public policy on police response to domestic violence, it is important to review the experiment
and its findings. Methodological problems associated with the MDVE are now legion
(see, e.g., Binder & Meeker, 1988; Fagan, 1989; Lempert, 1984). The most salient problem
concerns the sample. The deterrent effect attributed to mandatory arrest was based on a
small number of follow-up interviews completed by the battered women: Sherman and
Berk (1984, p. 265) report a 62 percent completion rate for the initial face-to-face interviews
and a 49 percent completion rate for the biweekly follow-ups for six subsequent months
(161 respondents from a sample of 330 victims). Sherman and Berk (1984) contend that the
experimental design of the research had no effect on the victim's participation decisions
during the follow-up phase. It may be likely that further violence occurred but is undisclosed
in follow-up interviews, or is simply lost due to case attrition. If these problems escape
detection, a research artifact may be created during the follow-up stage or, the observed
deterrent effect may be only temporary, contingent on pending charges (Jaffe, Wolfe,
Telford, & Austin, 1986).

Victims may display reluctance in requesting police service after experiencing the
consequences of official intervention once a mandatory-arrest policy becomes effective
(Sherman & Berk, 1984, p. 269). This dynamic would mask continued violence in follow-up
interviews and in official records, demonstrating a deterrent effect in reporting practices
but not actual battering incidences (Berk & Newton, 1985). In fact, Buzawa (1982) contends

that once a woman loses control over the outcome of a domestic dispute, she may be deterred from calling the police.[13] Battered women who call the police for help may only desire cessation of the immediate abuse; in these cases, arrest may be acknowledged by the woman as a possible alternative but one that is not desirable. An unintended consequence may be that battering *escalates* as a result of an arrest, with increased intimidation, threats, or retaliation from the abuser, causing the victim to be silent (Goolkasian, 1986, p. 35).[14]

Findings of a deterrent effect may really be a result of displacement in which the original violent relationship has terminated but the batterer simply moves into a violent relationship with a new partner (Fagan, 1989; Reiss, 1985). This displacement effect is related to selective attrition problems identified by Elliott (1989, p. 453). These may occur if arrest affects the termination of the relationship, thereby limiting the deterrent interpretation of lower recidivism rates after a pro-arrest policy goes into effect. Ford (1984) offers support for this hypothesis with evidence that arrest may be correlated with breaking up, which is one successful way of stopping further violence. A displacement effect could also exist under the guise of a deterrent effect if the violence shifts its focus to other family members. If a relationship remains intact but the couple moves away from the area, their absence in official records may be misleading if it is interpreted as a deterrent effect (Lempert, 1984).

Given the plausibility of alternative explanations, some researchers have suggested caution in adopting such dramatic policy shifts based on the "success" of the Minneapolis experiment, fearing that the changes are not well thought out, not well grounded in empirical support, and are generated from research that is methodologically problematic (Binder & Meeker 1988; Elliott, 1989; Gelles & Mederer, 1985; Lempert, 1984; Zorza, 1994; Zorza & Woods, 1994).[15]

FAILURES AND PROBLEMS WITH REPLICATION STUDIES AND OTHER PRO-ARREST EVALUATIONS

In this section we explore the policy impacts of mandatory or presumptive arrest in a number of jurisdictions.[16] Researchers examining the impact of a pro-arrest policy change in London, Ontario found that the numbers of cases in which the police initiated criminal charges of woman abuse increased dramatically (2.7 percent in 1979 to 67.3 percent in 1983), the numbers of cases dismissed or withdrawn decreased substantially, and victim self-reports revealed a decrease in subsequent violence for the year following the policy change and police intervention (Jaffe et al., 1986). However, results from a police officer survey indicated that only 21 percent of the police surveyed believed that the new policy was effective in stopping intimate violence, and 32 percent thought women stopped calling the police after the policy was enacted (Jaffe et al., 1986). Elliott (1989) addresses this contradiction, maintaining that the study is plagued by serious methodological problems that question the success of the new arrest policy, such as the absence of control groups to use for comparisons and the unrepresentativeness of the sample of victims used. In light of these problems, it is difficult to conclude with any confidence that pro-arrest policies in Ontario facilitated victim reporting or that the deterrent effects indicated were really *true* ones.

Buzawa and Buzawa (1990) contend that police officers are generally distrustful of police-policy directives designed by outside political leaders or nonpolice personnel. This distrust is manifested in officer circumvention of laws or policies, which "extends to ignoring or subverting recognized rules of criminal procedure or explicit organizational goals and directives" (p. 100). Research that evaluates the impact of a presumptive arrest policy adopted by the Phoenix, Arizona police supports the idea that police circumvent policy (Ferraro, 1989b); despite the change in law and department policies, arrests were made in only 18 percent of the domestic assault cases. Ferraro (1989b) suggests that most noncompliance by the police was related to legal, ideological, and political considerations, which led them to ignore the policy change. In this analysis, Ferraro was able to gather detailed qualitative data through interviews with victims. These provided explanations as to why some battered women, particularly those from lower-class positions, would be less inclined to call the police if it meant their partners would be arrested, creating financial hardship for the family, including possible job loss.

In 1987, the District of Columbia's police department enacted new legislation that directed officers to arrest batterers. However, an evaluation conducted two years after its imposition found that police had failed to enforce the guideline, continuing to resort to mediating domestic disputes and keeping arrests at a minimum (Baker, Cahn, & Sands, 1989). These findings are based on interviews with almost 300 victims who sought protection at either the Superior Court or the Citizens Complaint Center. Similar to other pro-arrest policy implementation evaluations, police circumvented the policy. In the DC study, only 5 percent of the cases resulted in arrest; this rate remained low even when the complainant was seriously injured (requiring medical treatment) or had been threatened with knives, guns, or other weapons.[17] The most commonly cited reasons offered by police to explain their failure to arrest were that they believed nothing could be done (23.7 percent), the police thought the case was "domestic" or the couple lived together (22.6 percent) (and thus the police did not want to get involved), or the victim was instructed to go to the Citizens Complaint Center (20.1 percent) to explore civil remedies.

Based on the questions and concerns generated by Sherman and Berk's Minneapolis experiment, the National Institute of Justice[18] funded six different replication studies to explore the deterrent effects of police response to battering (U.S. Department of Justice, 1985). It was hoped that these new studies would address and correct some of the important issues and problems raised by the Minneapolis experiment.[19] The replication studies have achieved equivocal results and in fact suggest that arrest may have no effect or even might escalate violence (see Berk, Campbell, Klap, & Western, 1992a,b; Dunford, 1990; Dunford, Huizinga, & Elliott, 1990; Garner, Fagan, & Maxwell, 1995; Hirschel, Hutchinson, & Dean, 1992a,b; Pate & Hamilton, 1992; Sherman, Smith, Schmidt, & Rogan, 1992; Sherman et al., 1991).[20]

The NIJ-funded replication studies evaluated various interventions; the results demonstrated different outcomes. For instance, the Milwaukee project used three treatment responses: arrest with a mean jail detention of 11.1 hours, arrest that resulted in an average release time of 2.8 hours, and no arrest (only issued a warning). An analysis of 1200 cases revealed no significant differences in arrest effects after a six-month follow-up period (Hirschel et al., 1992a), although there was a slight deterrent effect after 30 days. The researchers concluded that arrest affects people differently, with persons who have a greater stake in conformity because of their employment being more deterred by arrest than unemployed persons with little stake in conformity (Sherman, 1992).

In its replication, the Omaha Police Experiment followed the design of the MDVE by randomly assigning cases to one of three police interventions: separation, mediation, or arrest. They developed two types of outcome measures: official recidivism (measured by new arrests or complaints noted in police records) and victim reports of repeat acts of violence (fear of injury, pushing-hitting, and physical injury) (Dunford et al., 1990, p. 188). Victims were interviewed twice over a six-month period, with the overall completion rate being 73 percent ($n = 242$).[21]

Several comparisons between the two experiments concerning the victim interview data are important to highlight. The proportion of initial interviews completed in Minneapolis was 62 percent, and in Omaha, the proportion was 80 percent; the proportion completing the six-month follow-up interview for Minneapolis was 49 percent, whereas in Omaha, the proportion was 73 percent. Additionally, only the Omaha experiment used face-to-face interviews. The researchers concluded that there are virtually no differences in the prevalence and frequency of repeat offending regardless of the police intervention assigned to the case (Dunford et al., 1990). Thus the Omaha experiment was unable to replicate the Minneapolis findings. Omaha researchers also sought to determine if one of the interventions (separation, mediation, or arrest) could delay a repeat of violence for a longer period of time than the other interventions. After conducting time-to-failure analyses, Dunford and others (1990, p. 202) present that "[a]fter six months at risk, no one treatment group could be described as requiring more time to fail than any other treatment group." The conclusion reached in the Omaha Police Experiment provides ample caution for mandatory or presumptory arrest policies to be adopted in other jurisdictions: "[A]rrest in Omaha, by itself, did not appear to deter subsequent domestic conflict any more than did separating or mediating those in conflict. Arrest, and the immediate period of custody associated with arrest, was not the deterrent to continued domestic conflict that was expected. If the Omaha findings should be replicated in the other five sites conducting experiments on this issue, policy based on the presumptory arrest recommendation coming out of the Minneapolis experiment may have to be reconsidered" (p. 204).[22] The last line in their article offers an admonition to both researchers and practitioners interested in the reduction of woman battering to begin considering new or additional strategies to cope with this problem.

Similar to findings reported in Milwaukee and Omaha, the Charlotte study found that arrest increased domestic violence recidivism rather than deterring it. The Charlotte replication retested three treatments: immediate arrest, issuing a citation for court at a later date, and no formal action (separate and advise). An analysis of 650 cases revealed an increase in the proportion of repeat arrests across each group. Hirschel et al. (1992a) offered five reasons why the Omaha, Milwaukee, and Charlotte experiments failed to find evidence supporting arrest as an effective deterrent. First, a majority of offenders in these studies had previous criminal records, so arrest failed to deter because it was not a new experience. Second, many of the offenders studies were chronic abusers or had criminal histories, so arrest was unlikely to have any impact. Third, arrest may not be associated with a change in behavior, especially when the time served is relatively short and offenders have been arrested before. Fourth, the data revealed that few offenders were found guilty and sentenced to jail. Finally, these studies focused on whether arrest was an effective deterrent for all offenders and ignored the possibility that arrest may be effective for only certain types of abusers.

Researchers in Colorado Springs and Metro-Dade found limited support for the MDVE findings, but only with victim interview data (Schmidt & Sherman, 1996), and the response rate was low. Sherman (1992) suggests that if the response rate in Colorado experiment was higher among the more stable, employed group of criminals (30 percent of offenders were known to be employed), the difference could be due to the kinds of people tapped by victim interviews versus official records. Conversely, Hirschel et al. (1992b) argue that extensive comparisons conducted on interviewed versus noninterviewed cases showed the two groups to be similar. Confounding the interpretation of results in the Colorado experiment was the fact that the majority of crimes in the sample (58 percent) were based on the offender's nonviolent, harassing, or menacing behavior toward the victim (Sherman, 1992). These measures may be different from the physical attack required to arrest for battery in other replication studies.

Overall, these studies reviewed indicate that for a variety of reasons, mandatory (or presumptive) arrest policies do not provide the anticipated panacea to the woman-battering problem. Additionally, Buzawa and Buzawa (1990, pp. 102–105) cite several reasons for not supporting mandatory arrest policies: first, they argue that the benefits do not outweigh the costs because convictions will not increase dramatically. A victim may refuse to comply with prosecutorial efforts voluntarily; or if forced to testify, her recall ability may be deliberately vague or too incomplete to warrant further prosecution efforts (Ferraro, 1989b). Second, police may engage in arrest-avoidance techniques that would limit assistance to victims: "The net result may therefore be to shift help from some victims who receive no police assistance to another group who obtain the degree and type of help that a paternalistic system believes is appropriate, whether desired or not" (Buzawa & Buzawa, 1990, p. 103). Third, in cases in which a victim is not desirous of an arrest, mandatory policies perpetuate the belief that police disregard victims' preferences.[23] Buzawa and Buzawa suggest that victim preferences must be elicited out of earshot from the offender and that police should be trained in other victim-sensitive skills. Fourth, these policies entrust too much power to police departments; *dual arrests* (of both the victim and offender) or threats of such an outcome might result.[24] For example, both Connecticut and Rhode Island experienced a significant increase in dual arrests for the first several years following the change to mandatory arrests. Some jurisdictions, such as Washington, DC, include specific language in their statutes, such as *primary aggressor*, in order to reduce the likelihood of a dual arrest; Massachusetts requires written justification for the arrest of both the offender and the victim. Qualitative interviews with police administrators from 24 police departments across Massachusetts revealed that dual arrests were more likely to occur when it was difficult for the officers to assign blame or the officer was assaulted by the victim (Mignon & Holmes, 1995). These last two reservations involve the potential for police to misuse their arrest powers; critics point out that police may make more trivial arrests of victims if they are called repeatedly to the same house. Policies may as well encourage judges not to treat the cases seriously. To support this last claim, the researchers refer to Ferraro's (1989a) finding that policies "created great uncertainty both for the judiciary and the department and tended to trivialize cases clearly warranting arrest" (Buzawa & Buzawa, 1990, p. 105).

Statutes that guide police to distinguish between the primary physical aggressor and the party who used violence in self-defense may be a fruitful avenue to pursue. However, these changes may not be enough to solve the problem of dual arrests. Hooper (1996) explains that the self-defense and primary aggression paradigms were developed to accommodate male (to male) violence and may not be the most helpful for women's violence, which is essentially different from men's violence. Women's violent acts are often not immediately precipitated by the violent acts of their partners (Hooper, 1996).

Rather, domestically violent women can be viewed as caught up in a pattern of violence that they did not initiate and do not control (Hamberger & Potente, 1994). Better training and education of police officers in both the dynamics of domestic violence and in communication with victims may help with the dual arrest problem (Saunders, 1995).

RACE AND CLASS IMPLICATIONS

Another potential problem with mandatory arrest policies is that they may produce unanticipated and negative consequences for some women. Due to limited opportunities, resources, and alternatives, men who abuse women from minority or low socioeconomic groups may be disproportionately arrested in jurisdictions favoring pro-arrest policies, creating added problems for battered women.[25] However, a discussion acknowledging the differential concerns of battered women from minority and low-income groups is largely absent from the domestic violence literature.[26] The responses of women from different racial, ethnic, class, and religious groups may indicate that policies designed to assist them may prove to be inadequate or inappropriate based on their cultural or community needs. Lockhart (1985) contends that any mainstream research on battering suffers from major shortcomings in design: "[R]acial comparisons made by these researchers were based on an implicit assumption that all groups in this country are homogeneous, regardless of their political, socio-historical, and economic experiences. *Researchers who ignore the fundamentally different realities of racial groups commit serious methodological and theoretical errors*" (p. 40, emphasis added).

Hagan and Albonetti (1982) report that blacks and lower-socioeconomic-status persons are more likely than whites and higher-socioeconomic-status persons to perceive injustice operating against them by police, juries, and court personnel. Minority groups indeed have a long history of uneasy relations with police (see Overby, 1971; Rossi, Berk, & Edison, 1974). If a legacy of distrust exists between the minority community and law enforcement agents, minority women may not embrace the new arrest polices. Some minority-group women may object "to mandatory arrest laws because they are viewed as providing police with yet another means of harassing minority group men rather than as protection for battered women" (Goolkasian, 1986, p. 37).

Many black women themselves may be ambivalent about seeking relief from the criminal justice system: "The effects of racism and sexism seem too great to tackle in the face of having been victimized by a loved one. The woman often times feels powerless to change her situation, tending to feel she is being forced to tolerate the situation longer because the very system which has historically served to subjugate and oppress her is the only system which can save her from the immediate abusive system" (Hearing on Violence Prevention Act, 1978, p. 521).[27] This testimony echoes informal conclusions regarding black women's reluctance to involve police in their personal lives: "All [abusive] men, regardless of race, should be dealt with, but black men are going to be dealt with more severely. Naturally, this troubles [black] victims. Black women know they don't want him (the abuser) in jail—all they want is for the abuse to stop. . . . There's a lot of guilt involved when you're talking about reporting a man. There's a fear that it's not supporting black and other minority men and that they shouldn't be punished" (Williams, 1981, p. 22).

McLeod (1984) discusses two competing hypotheses concerning disproportionate representation of minority citizens and calls to the police. First is the differential participation hypothesis, which states that statistics accurately reflect that minorities are more involved in domestic violence incidents; second is the differential notification hypothesis, which suggests that these statistics are misleading in that they only reflect *reporting* rates, not participation rates.

Research conducted by Block (1974) found that black victims have higher reporting rates than whites with assault-and-battery incidents and so are overrepresented in official police statistics. Similarly, Hindelang (1976) claims that the statistics are misleading: They reflect assaults known to police only. National Crime Survey (NCS) data also seem to support the differential notification hypothesis: The data show overrepresentation of minorities in abuse victimizations (11.3 percent of population are black; 17 percent of male victims are black) (McLeod, 1984).

With any assessment of pro-arrest policies, it is necessary to discern whether or not there are class differences in victims' reporting of intimate violence to the police. Schwartz (1988) tackles the issue of differential representation of minority and lower-class citizens reflected in victimization surveys. Essentially, he argues that there is evidence suggesting that the NCS is more likely to be biased in favor of showing more middle- and upper-class women's victimizations rather than overrepresenting lower classes, citing Sparks' (1981) research: "[He] argues that black and lower-class persons systematically underreport assaults in NCS interviews, and that any findings which show a greater incidence of victimization of lower-class persons are in fact stronger than would be indicated by these data" (Schwartz, 1988, p. 378).

Additionally, Schwartz challenges the pervasive argument that there are *not* class differences in intimate violence vulnerability. He argues that this issue is largely ignored by feminists conducting research on battered women because they do not want to advance the myth that battered women are located primarily in the lower end of the economic spectrum. Schwartz contends that since feminist ideology embraces framing the issue within a context which insists that all women are equally oppressed and vulnerable to victimization in a patriarchal society, they refuse to investigate class distinctions. Feminists (and other researchers) are able to criticize effectively the methodology of studies that do find greater incidence rates among lower-class women. Schwartz contends that this is very easy to do (e.g., reporting artifacts–data sources–oversample poorer persons, who are more likely to use services such as the police, courts, shelters, or other social service agencies; see Okum, 1986, p. 48).[28]

Conspicuously absent in the District of Columbia's mandatory arrest policy evaluation is any mention of the racial breakdowns of victims and offenders.[29] However, the study does offer some relevant economic information: 55.5 percent of the battering victims earned $15,000 or less; 79 percent earned less than $20,000. The authors assert that "[c]ontributions from other household members do not significantly increase these victims' financial security: Even with other family member's income, 63 percent of the victims lived in households whose income was $20,000 or less per year" (Baker et al., 1989, pp. 29–30). Even more important is the finding that the victim whose abusers were arrested was even poorer. "These results reflect the fact that victims who have lower incomes do not have resources, other than the police and the Citizens Complaint Center, to escape domestic violence. They do not have lawyers to commence legal action, they do not have the option of moving their families to separate homes; they do not have the income to enter family counseling designed to stem the violence. The police response to their plight is possibly their only protection" (p. 30).

Both minority and lower-class women have traditionally placed greater reliance on police intervention to resolve conflicts within their intimate relationships. Social class may be inextricably linked to race in the study of intimate violence; this is because nonwhites are overrepresented in the lower socioeconomic groups, and socioeconomic status affects options (Lockhart, 1985, 1987). Women with more income have greater access to resources to assist them in keeping their abuse private; they have the ability to afford private physicians and safe shelters, which results in their being able to escape detection from law enforcement, hospital emergency rooms, or social service agencies (Asbury, 1987; Prescott & Letko 1977; Stark, Flitcraft, & Frazier, 1979; Washburn & Frieze, 1981).

Findings from the National Commission on the Causes and Prevention of Violence suggest that "lower-class people are denied privacy for their quarrels: neighborhood bars, sidewalks, and crowded, thin-walled apartments afford little isolation" (Eisenberg & Micklow, 1977, p. 142). Therefore, it is entirely plausible that mandatory and pro-arrest policies may affect disproportionately minority women and women from lower socioeconomic statuses, who may have fewer opportunities and alternatives available for settling disputes privately (Stanko, 1985). The economic consequences of arrest may be more devastating for lower socioeconomic households. If the batterer is jailed, income may be lost, thus increasing the probability that a woman may not call the police if arrest would be imminent. Thus it seems clear that limited alternatives exist for economically disadvantaged battered women, especially women from minority groups, who are faced with the dilemma of being dependent on the police for assistance whenever their partners engage in violence against them.

BRIEF REVIEW OF ALTERNATIVES AND SUPPLEMENTS TO ARREST

Early efforts of the battered women's movement were designed to assist the victims of domestic violence by establishing shelters and crisis lines. Not all of these programs received unanimous support; shelters have been viewed (mostly by pro-family groups) as instrumental to the destruction of the family. Empirical assessments refute these contentions (Stone, 1984).[30] By the early 1980s, domestic violence legislation was enacted in most states (Morash, 1986). Included were a variety of programs or remedies: civil protection orders were established to provide effective procedures to ensure victim safety;[31] legal advocacy and job-training programs designed to empower women became readily accessible in shelters. However, not all of these options have been successful. Grau, Fagan, and Wexler (1984) report that restraining orders designed to provide civil court alternatives to formal sanctions are largely ineffective. Based on 270 victim interviews in four states, they argue that civil protection orders do little to prevent or reduce future violence, and the potential helpfulness of these orders is limited by implementation problems (e.g., long waiting periods and little or no protection offered to cohabitators or unmarried individuals), circumvention by police officers who fail to enforce the orders, and an overall lack of coordination and integration of civil and criminal remedies (Grau et al., 1984). Harrell and Smith (1996), Klein (1996), and others have reported that although civil restraining orders were ineffective in protecting victims from future violence, they served an important symbolic feature. These conclusions are particularly important given Harlem and Smith's (1996) finding that the majority of women who seek restraining orders were victims or more seriously abused by their partners. In addition, researchers found that the potential helpfulness of these orders was hampered by the cumbersome process of obtaining a permanent restraining order, low arrest rates, and the lack of vigorous prosecution and significant sanctioning of offenders (Klein, 1996).

More recently, attention has shifted toward exploring the relationship dynamics of battering, concentrating on providing treatment for offenders.[32] Many of these intervention or treatment efforts apply a feminist, antisexist, psychotherapeutic approach that challenges male batterers to examine traditional gender-role socialization, responses, and practices (see, e.g., Adams, 1989). Evaluations of counseling programs indicate much variability in recidivism rates, often as low as 2 percent in programs in which batterers were eager to participate (Dutton, 1987) to as high as 39 percent (Gondolf, 1984). Some of this variability is attributed to small sample sizes and different measures of recidivism. Deterrence may be most effective when both social and legal penalties are utilized (Fagan, 1989). For instance, one study that followed batterers who were arrested and participated in court-mandated counseling demonstrated low recidivism rates (as measured by wives' reports) after 30 months (Dutton, 1986b). Gondolf (1998) examined batterer treatment programs of varying interventions and lengths and concluded that shorter programs may be just as effective as longer, more intensive programs. His research used a 15-month follow-up period, and he argues for the use of much longer follow-ups to determine the impact of programs.

Police policy changes cannot exist in a vacuum. Arrest is only the initial step in the criminal justice system continuum and can easily be circumvented by unresponsiveness from other key players in the system (Dutton et al., 1996; Elliott, 1989). There has been some demonstrated success in reducing battering through innovative programming that provides a combination of services, including policies that involve the prosecutor taking responsibility for initiating prosecution, not the victim [see Lerman (1981, 1982, 1986) for a comprehensive review of these types of programs]. Fostering links between the criminal justice system and social service agencies might be helpful, especially for women with limited opportunities to explore other alternatives (see Hirschel et al., 1992a,b). Mandated counseling programs may provide this link; they would add another official component, besides the arrest itself, to the increasing societal and institutional recognition that woman battering is an act of criminal proportions. It has been suggested that a collaboration of legal sanctions and social services, such as court-mandated counseling, generally tend to complement each other and correct power imbalances between victims and offenders, rather than being coercive (Dutton, 1986a; Miller & Wellford, 1997).[33] Third-party mediation programs are also being used as a method to mediate interpersonal disputes formally with the assistance of a trained mediator who strives to develop a way to solve disputes nonviolently.[34] Prosecutors' offices have introduced pretrial mediation programs as an alternative to formal criminal processing. The idea behind mediation is to educate both the victim and the offender informally as to more effective methods for resolving conflict and to inform both parties about their legal rights. Some preliminary evaluations of mediation programs indicate they offer reductions in recidivism similar to those of more formal case processing (Bethel & Singer, 1981–1982). However, mediation programs have been criticized for their failure to assign blame and for allowing violence to be seen as part of a dysfunctional family rather than as violence directed against women (Lerman, 1984).

Many prosecutors' offices have adopted a "pro-prosecution" policy to augment pro-arrest, which entails aggressive prosecution of domestic violence cases even without victim cooperation and the enhanced use of civil protection orders. However, prosecutors feel that protection orders are not very effective and that violators receive minimal punishment. Prosecutor's offices are very supportive of domestic violence diversion programs, offender counseling programs, and victim advocacy programs (Rebovich, 1996). Research in Indianapolis, however, found that court-mandated counseling as a condition of either probation or diversion was no more effective in reducing recidivism than was prosecution with conviction using presumptive sentencing (Ford & Regoli, 1992).

Despite training, it is still very rare for police to refer battered women to outside agencies (Donlon, Hendricks, & Meagher, 1986; Loving, 1980). Consistent police training for handling domestic violence cases, proper control over training course content, and funding support for this training are virtually nonexistent (Buzawa & Buzawa, 1990). Other research indicates that policy changes exert little influence over officer beliefs and practices: Ferraro (1989a) found that most male officers disliked the presumptive arrest policy enacted in Phoenix, Arizona, with most female officers feeling similarly. For women who perceive the consequences of arrest to represent a greater hardship than the actual physical battering itself, some intermediate interventions will be necessary. Otherwise, the possibility exists of women being left without effective remedies after the failure of official ones. Cromack (1996) asserts that interagency cooperation is necessary to deal effectively with domestic violence; for instance, some police trainings use role-playing exercises while civilian volunteers act as peer advocates (Defina & Wetherbee, 1997). Interagency effectiveness rests on the police officers' commitment to arrest batterers. For instance, recent research indicated that in Florida, under a pro-arrest policy, offenders' presence at the scene increased the likelihood of arrest (44 percent when offender was present; 8 percent when offender was absent) (Feder, 1996).

Another fruitful avenue to explore involves the procedure of arrest itself. Paternoster, Brame, Bachman, and Sherman (1997) found that when police acted fairly, the rate of rearrest for domestic violence was significantly lower regardless of the outcome. McCord (1992) calls for examining the sequentialization of domestic violence when an offender leaves a current violent situation and begins with a new target. She also believes that researchers have overlooked important victim characteristics, such as education, occupation, family, or emotional resources, that may affect relationship durability following interventions or arrests (p. 233). It seems clear that to devise ways to deter domestic violence, policies, experiments, and ideas need to include studies that encompass victim characteristics, displacement concerns, interagency and coordinated community responses, treatment programs, and issues of procedural justice.

CONCLUSIONS

Mandatory arrest policies or laws may exacerbate an already difficult problem, despite good intentions or conventional wisdom. Given the inconsistent research findings and the negligible deterrence effects found in policy evaluation research, it appears that many battered women may not benefit from mandatory-arrest policies, and that these policies might be particularly detrimental for battered women of color and/or women from lower socioeconomic groups. Given these findings, expansion of state authority to intrude into peoples' lives may be unwarranted in the area of domestic violence unless a victim specifically requests such action. Efforts to improve police responses must be embedded within the context of emerging knowledge of the range of intimate violence remedies and the entire criminal justice system. Otherwise, operational changes that dictate police response to battering incidents will remain largely fractured, rhetorical, and ineffective.

ACKNOWLEDGMENT

Special thanks to Michelle L. Meloy for her helpful comments regarding an earlier draft of this chapter.

NOTES

1. Although methodologies vary, incidence rates of woman battering range from 16 percent using nationally representative household surveys (Straus, Gelles, & Steinmetz, 1980) to 50 percent based on victimization surveys and interviews (Freize, Knoble, Washburn, & Zomnir, 1980; Russell, 1982; Walker, 1979). According to national household survey data, these percentages suggest that 1.5 million women are battered each year (Straus et al. 1980; Straus & Gelles, 1986), while victimization data from the National Crime Survey provides estimates that 2.1 million women are battered annually, with violence recurring in 32 percent of the cases within six months of reporting (Langan & Innes, 1986).

2. Although this chapter's emphasis is explicitly focused on heterosexual violence perpetrated by men against women, there are other studies that explore similar issues for different samples [see Lobel (1986) and Renzetti (1987) for research on battered lesbians. See McLeod (1984) and Island and Letellier (1991) for discussions about battered heterosexual men and battered gay men, respectively.] Samples of battered lesbians or battered men, although different, share some commonalties, such as reasons that would inhibit victims' disclosure of violence.

3. Both battered men and battered lesbians may fear social stigmatization; this fear compounds disclosure issues and isolation. For battered lesbians and gay men, reporting may be particularly risky, especially if their relationships are not socially desirable or institutionally sanctioned. Additionally, traditional sources of help that are available for victims, such as shelters and laws, have been designed primarily to benefit women engaged in heterosexual relationships.

4. More thorough reviews of police responses to women battering are available elsewhere (see Buzawa & Buzawa, 1992, 1996; Elliott, 1989; Hirschel, Hutchinson, & Dean, 1992a,b).

5. For instance, a study in Kansas City (Missouri) revealed that in 85 percent of domestic assault or homicide incidents, police were called in at least once before, and police had been called in at least *five* times before in 50 percent of these cases (Police Foundation, 1977).

6. For instance, see Bowler, 1983; Ellis, 1984; Field & Field, 1973; Klein, 1981; Kuhl & Saltzman, 1985; Laszlo & McKean, 1978; Lerman, 1981; Lerman & Livingston, 1983; Parnas, 1970; Paterson, 1979; Stanko, 1982; Truninger, 1971; Vera Institute of Justice, 1977.

7. However, see Smith's (1987) analysis of interpersonal violence, which found that particular extralegal factors, such as race, gender, victim's preference, economic status of neighborhood, and demeanor of combatants toward officer, influenced police arrest decisions.

8. For more details on litigation by battered women, see Eppler (1986) and Moore (1985).

9. However, an alternative interpretation challenging Pastoor's empowerment hypothesis has been raised by MacKinnon (1983). Essentially, she argues that police intervention increases dependency on the state by battered women. Additionally, MacKinnon argues that manipulating

police responses fails to "address . . . the conditions that produce men who systematically express themselves violently toward women, women whose resistance is disabled, and the role of the state in this dynamic (p.643). See also Rifkin (1980) for a discussion of the limitations as to what the law can accomplish since it remains embedded in patriarchal foundations which do not challenge sexual stratification in society.

10. Buel (1988, p. 224) contends that officers disproportionately arrest batterers who are men of color and/or from the lower socioeconomic classes; mandatory arrest would restructure this traditional police response.

11. The Minneapolis Domestic Violence Experiment randomly assigned police officers to deliver one of three possible responses to misdemeanant domestic assaults: mediation, separation, or arrest. Using a six-month follow-up period, both victim reports and police reports indicate that arrest deterred offenders significantly more than the alternative interventions (Sherman & Berk, 1984).

12. At least one effort to replicate this finding in a nonexperimental setting has been successful (see Berk & Newton, 1985).

13. However, a reexamination of the mandatory arrest policy enacted in Minneapolis revealed that despite the policy, out of 24,948 domestic assault calls in 1986, fewer than 3635 resulted in arrest; instead of arrest, officers used mediation techniques to dispense with cases (Balos & Trotzky, 1988; see also Buzawa & Buzawa, 1996; Sherman, 1993).

14. Buzawa's (1982) position stems from an examination of aggregate domestic-assault arrest data from Detroit after an aggressive arrest policy went into effect. Considerably *fewer* calls for police assistance were made by victims *after* the policy was in place. This effect of victim deterrence may be more magnified in jurisdictions that have mandatory-arrest policies because victims would have even less power to state their preference (Buzawa, 1982).

15. One way of assessing this hypothesis is to keep track of calls to domestic violence hot lines or shelters to see if these more informal responses increase after mandatory-arrest policies go into effect. This would seem to indicate that battered women still desire help, but not in terms of official intervention. This issue might be even more complicated for some battered women (e.g., women of color or women from lower socioeconomic groups).

16. However, it is not always feasible to stall policy decisions while awaiting for results of replication studies, in light of public sentiment and political pressures (see Sherman & Cohn, 1989).

17. As of 1990, thirteen states had enacted mandatory arrest policies for domestic violence offenders (the application of arrest varies, depending on whether the offense is a felony or a misdemeanor, whether or not the crime is a first offense, for violation of a restraining order, if the victim is in danger, and for primary aggressor only) (Buzawa & Buzawa, 1982).

18. In fact, the police filed a report in only 16.4 percent of the incidents; arrests were made if the victim had broken bones or was taken to the hospital for her injuries; and only 27.2 percent of the abusers were arrested when they had threatened or attacked their partner with weapons (e.g., knives or guns), even if the weapon was visible to the police. "When the incident included an attack on a child, arrests were made only 11 percent of the time. However, when the incident included damage to the victim's car, the police made arrests in 25 percent of the cases. . . . The single factor most highly correlated with whether an arrest is made is *whether the abuser insulted the police officer*. The arrest rate for such incidents was 32 percent" (Baker et al., 1989, pp. 2–3; emphasis is original).

19. The National Institute of Justice was the original funding source for the Minneapolis Domestic Violence Experiment (Sherman & Berk, 1984).

20. The replication sites were Dade County, Florida; Atlanta, Georgia; Charlotte, North Carolina; Milwaukee, Wisconsin; and Colorado Springs, Colorado.

21. Mandatory arrests limit police officer discretion while dictating arrest action; presumptive arrest is designed to strongly guide police officer discretion in the direction of arrest.

22. Follow-up interviews were also conducted after 12 months, but these findings are not reported in their 1990 article.

23. Dunford and others (1990, p. 204) also report that victim-based measures of repeat violence indicated that victims who called the police were not placed in greater danger of being recipient of subsequent violence: "what the police did in Omaha after responding to cases of misdemeanor domestic assault (arrest, separate, mediate) neither helped nor hurt victims in terms of subsequent conflict."

24. On this point, Buzawa and Buzawa (1990, p. 103) suggest that "a mandatory-arrest policy merely appears to make victims and assailants pawns to larger policy goals formulated by administrative and well-meaning 'victim advocates,' whose goals may not be shared. Despite her emotional involvement and trauma, the victim is usually in a better position than patrol officers to determine the likely impact of an offender's arrest." It is likely that this consideration is magnified for certain groups of battered women.

25. Buzawa and Buzawa (1990) acknowledge that adding "primary aggressor" clarifications to the statutes may eliminate this problem, but in doing so, police discretion would increase.

26. There are some exceptions in the research on battered women where differences in culture and their relationship to battering have been addressed; see Ashbury (1987), Coley and Beckett (1988), and Lockhart (1985, 1987) for research concerning black women; Scarf (1983) on battered Jewish women; and Carroll (1980) for a comparison of battered Mexican-American and Jewish families; Lobel (1986) and Renzetti (1987) on battered lesbians; Feinman (1987) on battered Latino women; and "Response to wife abuse" (1985) on battered women in New Zealand.

27. In the same vein, Tong (1984) contends that black women, especially, may question arrest policies with regard to the treatment of black men, based on other experiences with the law; for example, black rapists historically have received harsher treatment than white rapists (Davis, 1981; Wolfgang & Riedel, 1975).

28. There exists even more of a split in the discourse between feminist analysis and more mainstream analysis regarding the issue of class differences in intimate-violence victimizations. Several researchers refuse to even raise the issue, positing that the question is inherently sexist and a form of victim blaming because of its assumption that victimization can be avoided if only one changed the victim's personal characteristics (see Davis, 1987; Dobash & Dobash, 1979; Klein, 1982; Stark et al., 1979; and Wardell, Gillespie, & Leffler, 1983). However, see Breines and Gordon (1983) for an opposing—and more courageous—position.

29. According to 1990 Census population counts for the District of Columbia, the racial distribution is 26.6 percent white, 65.8 percent black, and 4.6 percent other (American Indian, Eskimo or Aleut, Asian or Pacific Islander, and combined other races) (U.S. Department of Commerce, Bureau of the Census, 1991).

30. Stone (1984) conducted interviews of shelter residents to determine if shelters can be blamed for dissolving marriages. This research is important, given the recent pro-family criticisms that shelters persuade battered women to leave their spouse and family. Stone (1984) found that women who had made the decision to file for a divorce had decided *prior* to going to the shelter. Overwhelmingly, the battered women interviewed indicated that the shelter provided an opportunity to feel safe and protected while recovering from physical and emotional trauma, and a place where they could think and make rational decisions about their futures.

31. Since 1976, thirty-one states have enacted some form of civil protection order for battered women (Grau, 1982).

32. See Saunders and Azar (1989) for a review of treatment programs for family violence in general.

33. Similar to the research concerns raised by pro-arrest policies, research would need to be conducted with mandated counseling programs to discern any inherent class or race biases (see, generally, Marsella & Pedersen, 1981). Self-help style books that employ a multicultural perspective and are written by women from similar backgrounds which are designed to assist minority battered women may also benefit practitioners and policymakers who may

not understand the role that racism and racist stereotypes may play, or the value of support systems within different cultural communities [for good examples of this, see White (1985) and Zambrano (1985)].

34. See Ray (1982) for a thorough review of such mediation programs.

REFERENCES

ADAMS, D. (1989). Stages of anti-sexist awareness and change for men who batter. In L. J. Dickstein & C. C. Nadelson (Eds.), *Family violence: Emerging issues of a national crisis* (pp. 63–97). Washington, DC: American Psychiatric Press.

ASBURY, J. (1987). African-American women in violent relationships: An exploration of cultural difference. In R. L. Hampton (Ed.), *Violence in the black family*. Lexington, MA: Lexington Books.

BAKER, K., CAHN, N., & SANDS, S. J. (1989). *Report on District of Columbia police response to domestic violence*. Washington, DC: D.C. coalition against domestic violence and the women's law and public policy, Georgetown University Law Center.

BALOS, B., & TROTZKY, I. (1988). Enforcement of the domestic abuse act in Minnesota: A preliminary study, *Law and Inequality, 6*, 83–125.

BELL, D. J. (1984). The police response to domestic violence: An exploratory study, *Police Studies*, 23–30.

BERK, R. A., CAMPBELL, A., KLAP, R., & WESTERN, B. (1992a). Bayesian analysis of the Colorado Springs spouse abuse experiment. *Journal of Criminal Law and Criminology, 83*, 170–200.

BERK, R. A., CAMPBELL, A., KLAP, R., & WESTERN, B. (1992b). The deterrent effect of arrest in incidents of domestic violence: A Bayesian analysis of four field experiments. *American Sociological Review, 57*, 698–708.

BERK, R. A., & NEWTON, P. J. (1985). Does arrest really deter wife battery? An effort to replicate the findings of the Minneapolis spouse abuse experiment. *American Sociological Review, 50*, 253–262.

BETHEL, C. A., & SINGER, L. R. (1981–1982). Mediation: A new remedy for causes of domestic violence. *Vermont Law Review, 6*(2) and *7*(1), 1981–1982.

BINDER, A., & MEEKER, J. W. (1988). Experiments as reforms. *Journal of Criminal Justice, 16*, 347–358.

BINDER, A., & MEEKER, J. W. (1996). Arrest as a method to control spouse abuse. In E. S. Buzawa and C. G. Buzawa (Eds.), *Domestic violence: The criminal justice response*, pp. 129–140. Thousand Oaks, CA: Sage Publications.

BLOCK, R. (1974). Why notify the police? The victim's decision to notify the police of an assault. *Criminology, 11*, 555–569.

BOWKER, L. H. (1982). Police service to battered women: Bad or not so bad? *Criminal Justice and Behavior, 9*, 476–486.

BREINES, W., & GORDON, L. (1983). The new scholarship on family violence. *Signs: Journal of Women in Culture and Society, 8*(3), 490–531.

BUEL, S. M. (1988). Recent developments: Mandatory arrest for domestic violence. *Harvard Women's Law Journal, 11* (1988), 213-226.

BUZAWA, E. S. (1982). Police officer response to domestic violence legislation in Michigan. *Journal of Police Science and Administration, 10*(4) 415–424.

BUZAWA, E. S., & BUZAWA, C. G. (1990). *Domestic violence: The criminal justice response*. Newbury Park, CA: Sage Publications.

BUZAWA, E.S., & BUZAWA, C. G. (Eds.). (1996). *Domestic violence: The criminal justice response* (2nd ed.). Thousand Oaks, CA: Sage Publications.

CARROLL, J. C. (1980). A cultural-consistency theory of family violence in Mexican American and Jewish-ethnic groups. In M. A. Straus & G. T. Hotaling (Eds.), *The social causes of husband-wife violence* (pp. 68–81). Minneapolis, MN: University of Minnesota Press.

COHN, E. G., & SHERMAN, L. W. (1986). Police policy on domestic violence, 1986: A national survey. *Crime Control Reports, No. 5*. Washington, DC: Crime Control Institute.

COLEY, S. M., & BECKETT, J. O. (1988). Black battered women: A review of empirical literature. *Journal of Counseling and Development, 66*, 266–270.

CROMACK, B. (1996). The policing of domestic violence: An empirical study. *Policy and Society, 5*, 185–199.

DAVIS, A. Y. (1981). *Women, race and class*. New York: Random House.

DAVIS, N. J., HATCH, A. J., GRIFFIN, C., & THOMPSON, K. (1987). Violence against women in the home: A continued mandate of control. *Violence, Aggression and Terrorism, 1*(3), 241–276.

DEFINA, M. P., & WETHERBEE, L. (1997, October). Advocacy and law enforcement: Partners against domestic violence. *FBI Law Enforcement Bulletin, 66*(10), 22–24.

DOBASH, R. E., & DOBASH, R. P. (1977). Love, honor and obey: Institutional ideologies and the struggle for battered women. *Contemporary Crises, 1*, 403–415.

DOBASH, R. E., & DOBASH, R. P. (1979). *Violence against wives: A case against the patriarchy*. New York: Free Press.

DONLON, R., HENDRICKS, J., & MEAGHER, M. S. (1986). Police practices and attitudes toward domestic violence. *Journal of Police Science and Administration, 14*, 187–192.

DUNFORD, F. W. (1990). System-initiated warrants for suspects of misdemeanor domestic assault: A pilot study. *Justice Quarterly, 7*, 631–653.

DUNFORD, F. W., HUIZINGA, D., & ELLIOTT, D. S. (1990). The role of arrest in domestic assault: The Omaha police experiment. *Criminology, 28*(2), 183–206.

DUTTON, D. (1986a). The outcome of court-mandated treatment for wife assault: A quasi-experimental evaluation. *Violence and Victims, 1*, 163–176.

DUTTON, D. (1986b). Wife assaulters' explanations for assault: The neutralization of self-punishment. *Canadian Journal of Behavioral Science, 8*(4), 381–390.

DUTTON, D. (1987). The prediction of recidivism in a population of wife assaulters. Paper presented at the 3rd International Family Violence Conference, Durham, NH.

DUTTON, D., HART, S. D., KENNEDY, L. W., & WILLIAMS, K. R. (1996). Arrest and the reduction of repeat wife assault. In E. S. Buzawa & C.G. Buzawa (Eds.), *Domestic violence: The criminal justice response* (2nd ed., pp. 111–127). Thousand Oaks, CA: Sage Publications.

EISENBERG, S. E., & MICKLOW, P. L. (1977). The assaulted wife: "Catch 22" revisited. *Women's Rights Law Reporter, 3*, 142.

ELLIOTT, D. S. (1989). Criminal justice procedures in family violence crimes. In L. Ohlin & M. Tonry (Eds.), *Family violence* (pp. 427–480). Chicago: University of Chicago Press.

ELLIS, J. W. (1984). Prosecutorial discretion to charge in cases of spousal assault: A dialogue. *Journal of Criminal Law and Criminology, 75*(1), 56–102.

EPPLER, A. (1986). Battered women and the equal protection clause: Will the constitution help them when the police won't? *Yale Law Journal, 8*, 788–809.

FAGAN, J. (1989). Cessation of family violence: Deterrence and dissuasion. In L. Ohlin & M. Tonry (Eds.), *Family violence* (pp. 377–425). Chicago: University of Chicago Press.

FEDER, L. (1996). Police handling of domestic calls: The impact of offender's presence in the arrest decision. *Journal of Criminal Justice, 24*(6), 481–490.

FEINMAN, C. (1987). Domestic violence in Australia. Paper presented at the annual meeting of the American Society of Criminology, Montreal, Quebec, Canada.

FERRARO, K. (1989a). The legal response to women battering in the United States. In J. Hamner, J. Radford, & E. Stanko (Eds.), *Women, policing, and male violence* (pp. 155–184). London: Routledge & Kegan Paul.

FERRARO, K. (1989b). Policing women battering, *Social Problems, 36*(I), 61–74.

FERRARO, K. (1995). Cops, courts and woman battering. In B. R. Price & N. J. Sokoloff (Eds.), *The criminal justice system and women: Offenders, victims, and workers* (pp. 262–271). New York: McGraw-Hill.

FIELD, M. H., & FIELD, H. F. (1973). Marital violence and the criminal process: Neither justice nor peace. *Social Service Review, 47*, 221–240.

FORD, D. A. (1984, August). Prosecution as a victim power resource for managing conjugal violence. Paper presented at the annual meeting of the Society for the Study of Social Problems, San Antonio, TX.

FORD, D. A., & REGOLI, M.J. (1992). The preventive impacts of policies for prosecuting wife batterers. In E. S. Buzawa & C. G. Buzawa (Eds.), *Domestic violence: The changing criminal justice response* (pp. 180–207). Westport, CT: Greenwood Press.

FRIEZE, I. H., KNOBLE, J., WASHBURN, C., & ZOMNIR, G. (1980). Types of battered women. Paper presented at the annual research conference of the Association for Women in Psychology, Santa Monica, CA.

GARNER, J., FAGAN, J., & MAXWELL, C. (1995). Published findings from the spousal assault replication program. *Journal of Quantitative Criminology, 11*, 3–28.

GELLES, R., & MEDERER, H. (1985). Comparison or control: Intervention in the cases of wife abuse. Paper presented at the annual meeting of the National Council on Family Relations, Dallas, TX.

GIL, D. G. (1986). Sociocultural aspects of domestic violence. In M. Lystad (Ed.), *Violence in the home: Interdisciplinary perspectives* (pp. 124–149). New York: Brunner/Mazel.

GONDOLF. E. W. (1984). *Men who batter: An integrated approach stopping wife abuse*. Holmes Beach, FL: Learning Publications.

GONDOLF, E. W. (1998). Do batterer programs work? A 15 month follow-up of multi-site evaluations. *Domestic Violence Reporter, 3*(5), 65–80.

GOOLKASIAN, G. A. (1986). *Confronting domestic violence: A guide for criminal justice agencies*. Washington, DC: U.S. Government Printing Office.

GRAU, J. L. (1982). Restraining order legislation for battered women: A reassessment. *University of San Francisco Law Review, 16*, 703–741.

GRAU, J., FAGAN, J., & WEXLER, S. (1984). Restraining orders for battered women: Issues of access and efficacy. *Women and Politics, 4*(3), 13–28.

HAGAN, J., & ALBONETTI, C. (1982). Race, class, and the perception of criminal injustice in America. *American Journal of Sociology, 88*(2), 329–355.

HAMBERGER, L.K., & POTENTE, T. (1994). Counseling heterosexual women arrested for domestic violence: Implications for theory and practice. *Violence and Victims, 9*(2), 125–137.

HARRELL, A., & SMITH, B. E. (1996). Effects of restraining orders on domestic violence victims. In E. S. Buzawa & C. G.Buzawa (Eds.), *Do arrests and restraining orders work?* (pp. 214–242). Thousand Oaks, CA: Sage Publications..

Hearing on Violence Prevention Act, Formal Testimony, Harriet Tubman Woman's Shelter presented by Kenyari Bellfield in U.S. Congress, House Subcommittee on Select Education of the Committee on Education and Labor, Domestic Violence: Hearing on H.R. 7297 and H.R. 8498, 95th Congress, 2nd session, March 17, 1978; 1985.

HINDELANG, M. J. (1976). *Criminal victimization in eight American cities: A descriptive analysis of common theft and assault*. Cambridge, MA: Ballinger.

HIRSCHEL, J. D., HUTCHINSON, I. W., III, & DEAN, C. W. (1992a). The failure of arrest to deter spouse abuse. *Journal of Research in Crime and Delinquency 29*, 7–33.

HIRSCHEL, J. D., HUTCHINSON, I. W., III, & DEAN, C. W. (1992b). Female spouse abuse and the police response: The Charlotte, North Carolina experiment. *Journal of Criminal Law and Criminology, 83*, 73–119.

HOOPER, M. (1996, February). When domestic violence diversion is no longer an option: What to do with the female offender. *Berkeley Women's Law Journa*l, pp. 168-181.

INTERNATIONAL ASSOCIATION OF CHIEFS OF POLICE (1967). *Training key 16: Handing disturbance calls*. Gaithersburg, MD: IACP.

ISLAND, D., & LETELLIER, P. (1991). *Men who beat the men who love them: Battered gay men and domestic violence*. New York: Harrington Park Press.

JAFFE, P., WOLFE, D. A., TELFORD, A., & AUSTIN, G. (1986). The impact of police charges in incidents of wife abuse. *Journal of Family Violence, 1*, 37–49.

KARMEN, A. (1982). Women as crime victims: Problems and solutions. In B. R. Price & N. J. Sokoloff (Eds.), *The criminal justice system and women* (pp. 185–201). New York: Clark Boardman.

KLEIN, A. (1996). Re-abuse in a population of court-restrained male batterers: Why restraining orders don't work. In E. S. Buzawa & C. G. Buzawa (Eds.), *Do arrests and restraining orders work?* (pp. 192–213). Thousand Oaks, CA: Sage Publications.

KLEIN, D. (1981). Violence against women: Some considerations regarding its causes and its elimination. *Crime and Delinquency, 27*(1), 64–80.

KUHL, A., & SALTZMAN, L. E. (1985). Battered women in the criminal justice system. In I. L. Moyer (Ed.), *The changing role of women in the criminal justice system* (pp. 180–196). Prospect Heights, IL: Waveland Press.

LANG, P. (1986, July 21). How to stop crime the brainy way. *U.S. News and World Report*, pp. 55–56.

LANGAN, P.A., & INNES, C. A. (1986). *Preventing domestic violence against women*. Special report. Washington, DC: U.S. Department of Justice, Bureau of Justice Statistics.

LASZLO, A. T., & MCKEAN, T. (1978). Court decision: An alternative for spousal abuse cases. In *Battered women: Issues of public policy* (pp. 327–356). Washington, DC: U.S. Commission for Civil Rights.

LAWRENZ, F., LEMBO, J. F., & SCHADE, T. (1988). Time series analysis of the effect of a domestic violence directive on the numbers of arrests per day. *Journal of Criminal Justice, 16*, 493–498.

LEMPERT, R. (1984). From the editor. *Law and Society Review, 18*(4), 505–513.

LERMAN, L. (1981). Criminal prosecution of wife beaters. *Response, 4*(3), 1–19.

LERMAN, L. (1982, May/June). Court decisions on wife abuse laws: Recent developments. *Response*. (May/June 1982). Washington, DC: Center for Women's Policy Studies.

LERMAN, L. (1984). Mediation of wife abuse cases: The adverse impact of informal dispute resolution of women. *Harvard Women's Law Journal, 7*, 65–67.

LERMAN, L. (1986). Prosecution of wife beaters: Institutional obstacles and innovations. In M. Lystad (Ed.), *Violence in the home: Interdisciplinary perspectives* (pp. 250–295). New York: Brunner/Mazel.

LERMAN, L., & LIVINGSTON, F. (1983). State legislation on domestic violence. *Response, 6*, 1–28.

LOBEL, K. (1986). *Naming the violence: Speaking out against lesbian battering*. Seattle, WA: Seal Press.

LOCKHART, L. L. (1985). Methodological issues in comparative racial analyses: The case of wife abuse. *Social Work and Abstracts, 21*, 35–41.

LOCKHART, L. L. (1987). A reexamination of the effects of race and social class on the incidence of marital violence: A search for reliable differences. *Journal of Marriage and the Family, 49*(3), 603–610.

LOVING, N. (1980). *Responding to spouse abuse and wife beating: A guide for police*. Washington, DC: Police Executive Research Forum.

MACKINNON, C. (1983). Feminism, Marxism, method, and the state: Toward a feminist jurisprudence. *Signs, 8*, 635.

MARSELLA, A., PEDERSEN, P. (1981). *Cross cultural counseling and psychotherapy: Foundations, evolutions, and cultural considerations*. Elmsford, NY: Pergamon Press.

MARTIN, D. (1978). Overview: Scope of the problem. In *Battered women: Issues of public policy*. Washington, DC: U.S. Commission for Civil Rights.

MCCORD, J. (1992). Deterrence of domestic violence: A critical review of research. *Journal of Research in Crime and Delinquency, 29*(2), 229–239.

MCLEOD, M. (1984). Women against men: An examination of domestic violence based on an analysis of official data and national victimization data. *Justice Quarterly, 2*, pp. 171–193.

MIGNON, S. I., & HOLMES, W. M. (1995). Police response to mandatory arrest laws. *Crime and Delinquency, 41*(4), 430–442.

MILLER, S. L. (1989). Unintended side effects of pro-arrest policies and their race and class implications for battered women: A cautionary note. *Criminal Justice Policy Review, 3*(3), 299–316.

MILLER, S. L., & WELLFORD. C. F. (1997). Patterns and correlates of interpersonal violence. In A. P. Cardarelli (Ed.), *Violence between intimates: Patterns, causes, and effects* (pp. 16–28). Boston: Allyn & Bacon.

MOORE, T. (1985). Landmark court decisions for battered women. *Response, 8*(5).

MORASH, M. (1986, June). Wife battering. *Criminal Justice Abstracts,* pp. 252–271.

NATIONAL CRIMINAL JUSTICE ASSOCIATION. (1985). Domestic violence arrests deter batterers. Police Agencies Report. *Justice Bulletin, 5*(3).

OKUM, L. (1986). *Women abuse: Facts replace myths.* Albany, NY: State University of New York Press.

OLIVERO, A. (1987, November 16). Connecticut's new family violence may be one of the toughest— But is it tough enough? *Hartford Advocate,* p.6.

OVERBY, A. (1971). Discrimination against minority groups. In L. Radzinowicz & M. E. Wolfgang (Eds.), *The criminal in the arms of the law* (pp. 569–581). New York: Basic Books.

PARNAS, R. E. (1967). The police response to the domestic disturbance. *Wisconsin Law Review, 31,* 914–960.

PARNAS, R. E. (1970). The judicial response to intra-family violence. *Minnesota Law Review, 54,* 585–645.

PASTOOR, M. K. (1984). Police training and the effectiveness of Minnesota "domestic abuse" laws. *Law and Inequality, 2,* 557–607.

PATE, A., & HAMILTON, E. E. (1992). Formal and informal deterrents to domestic violence: The Dade County spouse assault experiment. *American Sociological Review, 57,* 691–697.

PATE, A., HAMILTON, E. E., & ANNAN, S. (1991). *Metro-Dade spousal abuse replication project draft final report.* Washington, DC: Police Foundation.

PATERNOSTER, R., BRAME, R., BACHMAN, R., & SHERMAN, L. W. (1997). Do fair procedures matter? The effect of procedural justice on spouse assault. *Law & Society Review, 31*(1), 163–204.

PATERSON, E. J. (1979). How the legal system responds to battered women. In D. M. Moore (Ed.), *Battered women* (pp.79–100). Beverly Hills, CA: Sage Publications.

POLICE FOUNDATION. (1977). *Domestic violence and the police: Studies in Detroit and Kansas City.* Washington, DC: PF, p. 9.

PRESCOTT, S., & LETKO, C. (1977). Battered: A social psychological perspective. In M. M. Roy (Ed.), *Battered women: A psychosociological study of domestic violence* (pp. 72–96). New York: Van Nostrand Reinhold.

RASCHE, C. E. (1995). Minority women and domestic violence: The unique dilemmas of battered women of color. In B. R. Price & N. J. Sokoloff (Eds.), *The criminal justice system and women* (pp. 246–261). New York: McGraw-Hill.

RAY, L. (1982). *Alternative means of family dispute resolution.* Washington, DC: Author.

REBOVICH, D. J. (1996). Prosecutorial responses to domestic violence: Results of a survey of large jurisdictions. In E. S. Buzawa & C. G. Buzawa (Eds.), *Do arrests and restraining orders work?* (pp. 176–191). Thousand Oaks, CA: Sage Publications.

REISS, A. J., JR. (1985). Some failures in designing data collection that distort results. In L. Burstein, H. E. Freeman, & P. H. Rossi (Eds.), *Collecting evaluation data: Problems and solutions.* Beverly Hills, CA: Sage Publications.

RENZETTI, C. (1987). Building a second closet: Official responses to victims of lesbian battering. Paper presented at the annual meetings of the Academy of Criminal Justice Sciences, San Francisco.

Response to wife abuse in four western countries. (1985). *Response to violence on the family and sexual assault, 8*(2), 15–18.

RIFKIN, J. (1980). Toward a theory of law and patriarchy. *Harvard Women's Law Journal, 3,* 83.

ROSSI, P., BERK, R. A., & EDISON, B. (1974). *The roots of urban discontent.* New York: Wiley.

RUSSELL, D. E. H. (1982). *Rape in marriage.* New York: MacMillian.

SAUNDERS, D. G. (1995). The tendency to arrest victims of domestic violence: A preliminary analysis of officer characteristics. *Journal of Interpersonal Violence, 19*(2), 147–158.

SAUNDERS, D. G., & AZAR, S. T. (1989). Treatment programs for family violence. In L. Ohlin & M. Tonry (Eds.), *Family violence* (pp. 481–546). Chicago: University of Chicago Press.

SCARF, M. (1983). Marriages made in heaven? Battered Jewish wives. In S. Heschel (Ed.), *On being a Jewish feminist.* New York: Schocken Books.

SCHECHTER, S. (1982). *Women and male violence: the visions and struggles of the battered women's movement.* Boston: South End Press.

SCHWARTZ, M. D. (1988). Ain't got no class: Universal risk theories of battering. *Contemporary Crisis, 12,* 373–392.

SHERMAN, L. W. (1993). *Policing domestic violence: Experiments and dilemmas.* New York, NY: Free Press.

SHERMAN, L., & BERK, R. (1984). The specific effects of arrest for domestic assault. *American Sociological Review, 49,* 261–272.

SHERMAN, L., & COHN, E. G. (1989). The impact of research on legal policy: The Minneapolis domestic violence experiment. *Law and Society Review, 23*(1), 117–144.

SHERMAN, L. W., SCHMIDT, J. D., ROGAN, D. P., GARTIN, P. R., COHN, E. G., COLLINS, D., & BACICH, A. R. (1991). From initial deterrence to long term escalation: Short custody arrest for poverty ghetto domestic violence. *Criminology, 29,* 821–850.

SHERMAN, L. W., SCHMIDT, J. D., ROGAN, D. P., SMITH, D. A., GARTIN, P. R., COHN, E. G., COLLINS, D. J., & BACICH, A. R. (1992). The variable effects of arrest on criminal careers: The Milwaukee domestic violence experiment. *Journal of Criminal Law and Criminology, 83.*

SHERMAN, L. W., SMITH, D. A., SCHMIDT, J. D., & ROGAN, D. P. (1991). *Ghetto poverty, crime and punishment: Legal and informal control of domestic violence.* Washington, DC: Crime Control Institute.

SMITH, D. A. (1987). Police responses to interpersonal violence: Defining the parameters of legal control. *Social Forces, 65*(3), 767–782.

SPARKS, R. (1981). Surveys of victimization: An optimistic assessment. In M. Tonry & N. Morris (Eds.), *Crime and justice: An annual review of research, 3* (pp. 1–60). Chicago: University of Chicago Press.

STANKO, E. A. (1982). Would you believe this woman? Prosecutorial screening for "credible" witnesses and a problem of justice. In N. H. Rafter & E. A. Stanko (Eds.), *Judge, lawyer, victim, thief: Women, gender roles and criminal justice* (pp. 63–82). Boston: Northeastern University Press.

STANKO, E. A. (1985). *Intimate intrusions: Women's experience of male violence.* London: Routledge & Kegan Paul.

STARK, E., FLITCRAFT, A., & FRAZIER, W. (1979). Medicine and patriarchal violence: The social construction of a "private" event. *International Journal of Health Services, 9,* 461–493.

STONE, L. H. (1984). Shelters for battered women: A temporary escape from danger or the first step toward divorce? *Victimology, 9*(2), 284–289.

STRAUS, M.A., & GELLES, R. (1986). Societal change and change in family violence from 1975 to 1985 as revealed by two national surveys. *Journal of Marriage and the Family, 48,* 465–479.

STRAUS, M. A., GELLES, R., & STEINMETZ, S. K. (1980). *Behind closed doors: Violence in the American family.* New York: Anchor Press.

TONG, R. (1984). *Women, sex, and the law.* Totowa, NJ: Rowman and Allanheld.

TRUNINGER, E. (1971). Marital violence: The legal solution. *Hastings Law Journal, 23,* 259–173.

U.S. DEPARTMENT OF COMMERCE. (1991). Bureau of the Census. Washington, DC: Government Printing Office.

U.S. DEPARTMENT OF JUSTICE. (1985). *Replicating an experiment in specific deterrence: Alternative police responses to spouse assault: A research solicitation.* Washington, DC: U.S. Department of Justice, National Institute of Justice.

VERA INSTITUTE OF JUSTICE. (1977). *Felony arrests: Their prosecution and disposition in New York City's court.* New York: Vera Institute of Justice.

WALKER, L. (1979). *The battered woman.* New York: Harper & Row.

WALKER, L., THYFAULT, G., & BROWNE, A. (1982). Beyond the juror's ken: Battered women. *Vermont Law Review, 7.*

WARDELL, L., GILLESPIE, D., & LEFFLER, A. (1983). Science and violence against wives. In D. Finkelhor, R. Gelles, G. Hotaling, & M. Straus (Eds.), *The dark side of families: Current family violence research* (pp. 69–84). Beverly Hills, CA: Sage Publications.

WASHBURN, C., & FRIEZE, I. H. (1981, July). *Methodological issues in studying battered women.* Paper presented at the First National Conference for Family Violence Researchers, University of New Hampshire, Durham, NH.

WHITE, E. C. (1985). *Chain change: For black women dealing with physical and emotional abuse.* Seattle, WA: Seal Press.

WILLIAMS, L. (1981, January–February). Violence against women. *Black Scholar,* pp. 18–24.

WOLFGANG, M. E., & RIEDEL, M. (1975). Rape, race and the death penalty in Georgia. *American Journal of Orthopsychiatry, 45,* 658–668.

ZAMBRANO, M. M. (1985). *Mejor sola que mal acompanada: For the Latino in an abusive relationship.* Seattle, WA: Seal Press.

ZORZA, J. (1994). *Must we stop arresting batterers? Analysis and implications of new police domestic violence studies.* New York: National Center on Women and Family Law.

ZORZA, J., & WOODS, L. (1995). *Mandatory arrest: Problems and possibilities.* New York: National Center on Women and Family Law.

20

Likelihood of an Arrest Decision for Domestic and Nondomestic Assault Calls[1]

Do Police Underenforce the Law When Responding to Domestic Violence?

Lynette Feder

Domestic violence has historically been selectively ignored by both those within as well as outside the criminal justice system. Prior to the 1980s, research contrasted these incidents to comparable nondomestic assaults and found that police typically treated domestic violence cases more leniently. More recent research, however, has focused on the police's likelihood to arrest in jurisdictions that specify mandatory or presumption in favor of arrest statutes. These studies consistently find a low rate of arrest, which, in turn, leads many to conclude that police are continuing to practice a subtle and insidious policy of nonenforcement when responding to domestic violence offenders. But an actual and current comparison of police response to domestic and nondomestic assault calls is lacking. Without a basis for comparison, one cannot assume that police are selectively underenforcing domestic violent laws.

LITERATURE REVIEW

Historical analysis indicates that wife assault has a long and honored tradition in Western civilization (Davidson, 1977; Hilberman, 1980). Under English common law, the doctrine of coverture stated that when a man and woman married, they became a single entity. Accordingly, that entity was the husband's, as the wife thereafter lost all legal standing (Dobash & Dobash; 1978; Eisenberg & Micklow, 1977). This led, quite logically, to the view that the husband had a right to control his wife. As Blackstone noted: "For, as he is to answer for her misbehaviors, the law thought it reasonable to entrust him with the power of restraining her by chastisement" (Davidson, 1977).

The husband's right to beat his wife had a more circuitous legal history in the United States. Probably because the colonists were originally dependent on women to help sustain the family, combined with the fact that they were not well versed in the ways of the English common law, Puritans deviated from this tradition (Taub, 1983). However, by the nineteenth century, Blackstone's *Commentaries of the Laws of England* gained wider influence in the United States (Davidson, 1977; Taub, 1983). The result was that some state courts explicitly recognized a husband's right to chastise his wife, while others prohibited it (Eisenberg & Micklow, 1977; Fields, 1977–1978; Stedman, 1917). Gradually, though, a judicial shift took place and by the late nineteenth century most states disallowed wife beating (Davidson, 1977; Taub, 1983). Still, even as courts rejected this right, they held that "if no permanent injury has been inflicted, nor malice, cruelty or dangerous violence shown by the husband, it is better to draw the curtain, shut out the public gaze, and leave the parties to forget and forgive" (*State* v. *Oliver*, 1873). Thus, although wifebeating was illegal in most states by the late nineteenth century, few incidents resulted in arrest or prosecution of the offender.

Given this contradictory legal history in the United States, it can hardly be surprising that law enforcement's response showed similar ambivalence in treating cases of wife abuse seriously. Furthermore, those outside the criminal justice system showed equal disinterest on the subject of domestic violence. Yet the magnitude of the problem has long suggested that this was a subject warranting serious attention.

Government figures based on domestic violent incidents reported to the police indicate that among all female victims of murders, more than one-fourth are believed to have been slain by their husbands or boyfriends (Harlow, 1991). Furthermore, approximately 2.1 million women are beaten each year (Friedman & Shulman, 1990). However, we know that these numbers greatly undercount the true amount of spousal violence, since they rely only on incidents that come to the police's attention. One well-regarded study indicated that victim interview surveys provided higher numbers of domestic violence incidents than those reported by the police (Hirschel, Hutchinson, & Dean, 1992). But victim interviews have also been shown to undercount the true incidence of violence committed at the hands of intimates (San Jose Methods Test, 1972).

Although the numbers indicated a large problem, research was surfacing which demonstrated that police were not responding as seriously to domestic assault cases as to comparable nondomestic assault calls. Black's critical study observed police–citizen encounters in three cities in 1966 and found that the victim–offender relationship was more important than the severity of the crime in accounting for variation in police likelihood to arrest (Black, 1978). He concluded that "[w]hen an offender victimizes a social intimate the police are most apt to let the event remain a private matter . . . " (p. 54).

Data from another large police observational study conducted in several cities in 1977 concluded that although police were as likely to arrest domestic as nondomestic offenders, legal variables (such as severity of offense and victim's cooperation) would argue for a higher rate of arrest in domestic assault cases. Therefore, the police were practicing a policy of underenforcement when responding to these calls (Oppenlander, 1982). Another researcher analyzed this same data set and found that a variety of extralegal factors entered into the police's decision to arrest, including the gender of the victim. Specifically, where the victim was female, police were less likely to invoke the law (Smith, 1987).

In summary, most of these earlier studies observed police handling of calls and found that police were less likely to arrest in cases of domestic versus nondomestic calls, even after legal variables had been taken into account. Probably these studies provided fuel for women's groups and other concerned citizens to lobby for changes in the laws. Simultaneously, a plethora of other factors were coalescing around this issue. For instance, results from an important study, the Minneapolis experiment, indicated that arrest led to lower rates of recidivism among domestic violent offenders (Sherman & Berk, 1984).

At the same time, litigation was also leading police to respond more proactively when dealing with domestic violence. Specifically, several important lawsuits were brought against large police departments alleging denial of equal protection under the law when the police failed to respond vigorously to assaults perpetrated upon women by their husbands and boyfriends (*Bruno* v. *Codd*, 1976). Although police responded to these lawsuits by agreeing to treat domestic assault as a crime in the future, many observers still did not see any significant changes in police's handling of these cases. A few years later, though, the courts went even further. In *Thurman* v. *City of Torrington* (1984), the police were held liable (for the sum of $2.3 million) for the injuries that a battered wife sustained when the police failed to respond vigorously to her requests for help.

Previously, statutes had largely neglected the problem of spousal abuse. But in response to these and many other factors, beginning in the 1980s, state legislatures began to directly address the problem of domestic violence (Lerman, Livingston, & Jackson, 1983). These new statutes varied greatly, although most dealt with ways in which the government could respond to the problem more effectively. As legislators wrote laws that mandated or presumed arrest when responding to domestic assault calls, researchers followed up with investigations on the impact of these laws on police behavior. Implicitly, there was an assumption that these agencies were not treating domestic violence cases as seriously as they were comparable nondomestic assault cases. Perhaps this implicit assumption explains why these newer studies did not explicitly compare police reactions to domestic versus nondomestic assault calls.

A variety of research approaches were used to assess police response to domestic violence in these jurisdictions. Researchers directly observed the police's handling of domestic calls (Ferraro, 1989; Smith, 1987; Worden & Pollitz, 1984), surveyed police on their self-reported likelihood to arrest (Breci & Simons, 1987; Dolon, Hendricks, & Meagher, 1986; Homant & Kennedy, 1985; Saunders & Size, 1986; Waaland & Keeley, 1985; Walter, 1981), analyzed police records (Bell, 1987; Berk & Loseke, 1980-1981; Erez, 1986; Lawrenz, Lembo, & Schade, 1988), or interviewed victims of domestic violence (Balos & Trotzky, 1988; Berk, Fenstermaker, & Newton, 1988; Bowker, 1984; Brown, 1984; Gondolf & McFerron, 1989; Kennedy & Homant, 1983) to determine the law's success in getting police to respond legally to domestic assault calls.

The results from these studies consistently indicated a low rate of arrest, typically between 11 and 15 percent (Bell, 1985; Blount, Yegidis, & Maheux, 1992; Buzawa, 1982; Erez, 1986). This led those working in the field to conclude that the police were engaged, either implicitly or explicity, in a process of selective nonenforcement when responding to domestic assault calls (Davis, 1983; Ferraro, 1989; Oppenlander, 1982). For instance, Lerman (1982) noted that "[t]hough written law gives the appearance that protection is available through the criminal justice system [for battered wives], many court and law enforcement officials whose duty it is to enforce the laws still believe that domestic violence is a private matter—that most abuse is too trivial to warrant intervention" (p. 3). And Taub (1983) stated: "As the preceding overview indicates, domestic violence has not merely been ignored by the legal system. Rather, it has been the subject of sex-based exemptions from laws of general applicability" (p. 165).

As already noted, these studies failed to make comparisons to police's likelihood to arrest when confronting similar nondomestic assault calls. However, it is widely known in criminological circles that arrest is a highly uncommon response in most police–citizen encounters (Sherman, 1992). Evidence of illegal behavior does not result automatically and inevitably in an arrest for a wide range of offenses (Black, 1978). As Sherman et al. (1992) aptly note: "The problem with the use of these facts as evidence of discrimination against women victims of domestic violence is that they are silent about disparity. One must look at whether there is a difference of probability of arrest for domestic violence and other offenses" (p. 141).

This study seeks to address this serious omission in the research literature.[2] Police handling of domestic assault calls will be compared to nondomestic calls with controls introduced for legal and extralegal variables. The study seeks to determine (1) the likelihood of an arrest response for domestic and nondomestic assault calls in one police jurisdiction, and (2) whether different factors account for an arrest response when police deal with these two types of calls.

RESEARCH METHODOLOGY

As if to combat police's resistance to arrest when responding to domestic assault calls in Florida, a new law was implemented as of January 1, 1992. Florida State Statute 741.29 mandated several changes, including requiring a report to be made in all cases involving domestic violence calls, whether or not an arrest was effected. Additionally, the new law directed the officer to document and justify why an arrest was not made in cases where probable cause existed. Therefore, while Florida continues to have a nonmandatory arrest policy, it is clear that the intent of the statute is to combat the resistance that laws on police handling of domestic violence were meeting in various jurisdictions within the state.

The jurisdiction out of which the study was based represents one of the largest police agencies in South Florida. The department has achieved recognition for its professionalism and has gone on record, from the very top of the hierarchy, in support of a pro-arrest law enforcement stand in the handling of domestic assault. In fact, this agency had a written pro-arrest departmental policy long before the new legislation was implemented.

This research is part of a larger study whereby police in this jurisdiction were surveyed after implementation of the new law about their likelihood to arrest when responding to domestic violence calls (Feder, 1997). Later, in an attempt to compare different research approaches used to assess police response to domestic violence, the researcher returned to this jurisdiction and requested police records for the same 17-day time period (Feder, 1998a,b). The data from this survey come exclusively from the police records.

Research indicates that domestic calls may be handled differently from the time the call is received by the police (Oppenlander, 1982). Additionally, it is possible that police records may be little more than after-the-fact reconstructions justifying previous police responses

(Dutton, 1988). This speaks to the problem of research relying exclusively on written police records. To circumvent this potential danger, the starting point for the sampling procedure was all calls for service received by this police department.

Whenever a citizen calls for help in this jurisdiction, the call is taken through their computer-assisted dispatch system (CADS). Regardless of whether or not an officer is dispatched to the site or makes a subsequent written police report, the CADS unit makes a written record of the call, which includes cursory information about the incident. Therefore, all calls for service coming into the department, and the records some of them generated subsequently, were collected. In this way, a comparison can be made between those calls where an officer was dispatched and a written police record made, and all other calls. This then allows for the possibility that domestic calls may be subtly winnowed out at an early point in the process, which would then go unrecognized if the research began at a later point in the system.

In ongoing conversations with the dispatchers it became clear that domestic assaults might originally be classified under many different headings. Therefore, it was decided to include all incoming calls for service labeled as *disturbance, domestic, fight,* or *assault.* For purposes of this research, *domestic* is defined according to Florida law. As such, it includes incidents where the victim and offender are or have been married, cohabiting, or romantically involved. Therefore, cases involving parent–child or sibling relationships would not be included under this operationalization.

Several comparisons were conducted using this research methodology. First, a comparison was made between those calls for service that received the police's attention, along with a subsequent police record (referred to as the CADS and police records group), and those calls that did not receive further investigation (referred to as CADS with no police records group). Once again, this was necessary to ensure that domestic assault calls were not being devalued by the police at an early point in the process. We hypothesize that there are no significant differences in these two groups in terms of the type of call, their priority ratings, the victim–offender relationship, estimated level of violence, and similar factors.

Next we look at the profile of domestic assault calls and compare it to nondomestic assault calls (this includes all calls for service labeled *disturbance, fight,* and *assault*). We do this when the call is first received and the only available information comes from the CADS. This process is then repeated for information that becomes available through the police's follow-up visit and subsequent report. Once again, our null hypothesis is that there are no significant differences between the two groups in terms of legal and extralegal variables as reported in the CADS or police reports.

Finally, we conduct a logistic regression equation to assess those variables that are significant in accounting for variation in police's likelihood to arrest. Since the dependent variable is dichotomous (police's decision to arrest versus not arrest), logistic regression analysis was thought to be more suitable than multiple regression (Alba, 1987; Aldrich & Nelson, 1984; Knoke & Burke, 1980). This procedure is similar to multiple regression in that it allows an examination of the individual effects of several, simultaneously considered, independent variables on the dependent variable—the probability of being arrested. Conceptually, logit analysis fits a logistic function to the data in which the dependent variable is the natural logarithm of the odds of being arrested versus all other outcomes (e.g., mediated, separated, referred, etc.). We hypothesize that the victim–offender relationship will not be significant in accounting for variation in the police's decision to arrest.

RESEARCH RESULTS

During that 17-day period, the police received 627 calls for service that were classified as *disturbance, assault, fight,* or *domestic assault.* Of these calls, 57 percent ($n = 356$) involved incidents where the police were dispatched and wrote subsequent reports. The information that comes from CADS is cursory and sometimes proves to be incorrect once the police arrived. Still, that was the information that the CADS unit was working with when they made their decisions to dispatch officers. Therefore, that is the information that we follow in determining whether calls that received a police visit were different from those where no officer was dispatched.

Comparison of Calls Receiving and Not Receiving Police Dispatch

As can be seen from Table 1, significant differences maintained between those calls for service that received police dispatch ($n = 356$) and those where police did not attend to the call ($n = 271$). Those that received a police visit were more likely to be calls for service that CADS had classified as an assault or domestic assault [χ^2 (3, $n = 627$) = 89.12, $p < 0.001$]. Additionally, those where police were dispatched were more likely to be in progress when the call came into the station [χ^2 (1, $n = 627$) = 3.91, $p < 0.05$]. Although those with higher-priority ratings were more likely to incur a police visit, calls with the lowest-priority ratings also received this follow-up response [χ^2 (3, $n = 627$) = 46.32, $p < 0.001$]. However, contrary to previous research findings (Berk & Loseke, 1980–1981; Berk et al., 1988), this jurisdiction is more likely to dispatch police when the victim placed the call for service versus when anyone other than the victim called (63 versus 54 percent, respectively) [χ^2 (3, $n = 464$) = 26.62, $p < 0.001$]. Additionally, those calls where police are dispatched are more likely to involve female victims [χ^3 (3, $n = 627$) = 21.71, $p < 0.001$]. According to these data, police are also more likely to be sent to an incident where the victim–offender relationship has been classified by the dispatcher as a domestic assault [χ^2 (1, $n = 340$) = 6.05, $p < 0.05$]. But the data also indicate that legal variables are significant in accounting for the variation in police treatment. Specifically, dispatchers are more likely to send police to calls that are determined to be more violent [χ^2 (8, $n = 539$) = 65.23, $p < 0.001$].

Comparison of Domestic and Nondomestic Assault Calls on CADS Variables

Next we turn our attention to whether significant differences appear in the CADS variables between those determined by the dispatchers to be domestic related and those classified as other than domestic. The dispatchers classified fully 57 percent ($n = 195$) of the incoming calls for service as domestic related. And once again, there were significant differences between these two groups.

As can be seen from a cursory review of Table 2, calls classified as domestic assaults were significantly more likely to be in progress when called in [χ^2 (1, $n = 340$) = 4.76, $p < 0.05$] and were given a higher priority rating than nondomestic assault calls [χ^2 (3, $n = 340$) = 24.85, $p < 0.001$]. Additionally, there was a tendency for the victim to have placed the call for service in a domestic assault. In terms of victim and offender characteristics,

TABLE 1   Comparison of Calls for Service with and without Police Reports[a]

	CADS with No Report ($n = 271$) [% (no. cases)]		CADS and Police Report ($n = 356$) [% (no. cases)]	
Type of call*				
Disturbance	74	(98)	26	(35)
Assault	21	(25)	79	(96)
Fight	67	(24)	33	(12)
Domestic assault	37	(124)	63	(213)
Call in progress*				
Not in progress	46	(215)	55	(258)
In progress	36	(56)	64	(98)
Priority rating*				
Highest priority	42	(79)	58	(109)
Second highest	33	(8)	67	(16)
Second lowest	72	(76)	28	(29)
Lowest priority	35	(108)	65	(202)
Who called*				
Victim	37	(109)	63	(188)
Family/friend	22	(13)	78	(47)
Neighbor	68	(38)	33	(19)
Other	52	(26)	48	(24)
Victim gender*				
Male	43	(62)	57	(83)
Female	34	(88)	66	(173)
Unknown	55	(121)	45	(100)
Offender gender*				
Male	37	(114)	63	(195)
Female	31	(22)	69	(50)
Unknown	55	(135)	45	(111)
Victim–offender relationship*				
Not domestic	42	(61)	58	(84)
Domestic	29	(57)	71	(138)
Highest level of violence*				
None	65	(58)	35	(31)
Shouting	59	(66)	41	(46)
Threatened, no weapon	48	(13)	52	(14)
Property damage	37	(7)	63	(12)
Minor/moderate physical	30	(61)	71	(146)
Threatened, with weapon	13	(2)	87	(13)
Used weapon	29	(2)	71	(5)
Severe physical harm	0	(0)	100	(18)
Weapon present				
No weapon present	40	(29)	60	(44)
Weapon present	16	(5)	84	(26)

[a]No correction factors were employed in the statistical tests where the numbers in the cell sizes were small.

*Significance at the 0.05 probability level.

TABLE 2   Comparison of Domestic and Nondomestic Assault Calls on CADS Variables (n = 340)[a]

	Domestic Assault Calls (n = 195) [% (no. cases)]		Nondomestic Assault Calls (n = 145) [% (no. cases)]	
Call in progress*				
Not in progress	69	(134)	79	(115)
In progress	31	(61)	21	(30)
Priority rating*				
Highest	33	(64)	23	(33)
Second highest	7	(13)	4	(6)
Second lowest	6	(12)	24	(35)
Lowest	54	(106)	49	(71)
Who called*				
Victim	79	(149)	69	(87)
Family/friend	13	(24)	18	(23)
Neighbor	5	(9)	5	(6)
Other	3	(6)	9	(11)
Victim gender*				
Male	20	(38)	37	(54)
Female	73	(143)	39	(56)
Unknown	7	(14)	24	(35)
Offender gender*				
Male	73	(143)	59	(86)
Female	19	(37)	16	(23)
Unknown	8	(15)	25	(36)
Highest violence level*				
No violence	14	(17)	24	(38)
Shouting	28	(34)	15	(24)
Threatened, no weapon	8	(10)	6	(9)
Property damage	8	(9)	4	(6)
Minor/moderate physical harm	34	(41)	44	(71)
Threatened, with weapon	3	(3)	6	(9)
Used weapon	3	(3)	1	(1)
Severe physical harm	3	(3)	1	(2)
Weapon present				
No weapon present	73	(35)	68	(21)
Weapon present	27	(13)	32	(10)

[a]In the remaining cases, missing data precluded their use in subsequent analyses.

*Significance at the 0.05 probability level.

domestic assaults were more likely to involve female victims [χ^2 (3, n = 340) = 63.47, p < 0.001] and male offenders [χ^2 (3, n = 340) = 4.12, p < 0.001]. Once again, there is a significant difference in terms of violence level: In all but a few cases, domestic assaults are classified as being less violent than nondomestic assaults [χ^2 (7, n = 280) = 17.27, p < 0.05].

Comparison of Domestic and Nondomestic Assault Calls on Police Report Variables

Victim Characteristics.   Of the 356 calls for service where an officer was dispatched and a report was made, fully 94 percent ($n = 334$) provided information in the police's report on the victim–offender relationship. Table 3 provides an overview of those classified as domestic and those recorded as nondomestic in terms of victim characteristics. Domestic assault calls are significantly more likely than nondomestic calls to involve female victims [χ^2 (1, $n = 228$) $= 43.32$, $p < 0.001$]. No other significant differences emerge in terms of victim's age, race, belligerence to police, or use of drugs or alcohol for domestic and nondomestic calls.

Offender Characteristics.   Table 4 indicates that there are few significant differences in terms of offender characteristics for domestic and nondomestic calls. The only differences that achieve significance is that offenders in the nondomestic groups are more likely to become physical in front of the police (although the numbers involved are very small) [χ^2 (1, $n = 226$) $= 4.01$, $p < 0.05$], while those in the domestic group are more likely to be known to their victims [χ^2 (1, $n = 226$) $= 19.43$, $p < 0.001$]. However, there are no meaningful differences between the two groups in terms of the offender's gender, age, race, presence at the scene when police arrive, noted use of drugs or alcohol, or belligerence to the police.

Incident Characteristics.   A comparison of domestic and nondomestic calls was also investigated in terms of characteristics related to the incident. As Table 5 indicates, there are very few variables that significantly differentiate between these two groups on

TABLE 3   Comparison of Domestic and Nondomestic Assault Calls on Police Report Variables: Victim Characteristics

	Domestic Assault Calls ($n = 189$) [% (no. cases)]		Nondomestic Assault Calls ($n = 145$) [% (no. cases)]	
Victim gender*				
Male	17	(21)	58	(59)
Female	84	(106)	42	(42)
Victim age	31.4 years		31.9 years	
Victim race				
White	83	(99)	81	(69)
Black	17	(20)	19	(16)
Victim belligerent	2	(2)	0	(0)
Victim use of drugs/alcohol	3	(4)	5	(5)

*Significance at the 0.05 probability level.

TABLE 4   **Comparison of Domestic and Nondomestic Assault Calls on Police Report Variables: Offender Characteristics**

	Domestic Assault Calls ($n = 189$) [% (no. cases)]		Nondomestic Assault Calls ($n = 145$) [% (no. cases)]	
Offender gender				
Male	84	(107)	81	(75)
Female	16	(21)	19	(18)
Offender age	32.8 years		31.3 years	
Offender race				
White	85	(98)	78	(55)
Black	15	(17)	23	(16)
Offender present				
Offender present	52	(66)	47	(46)
Offender not present	48	(62)	53	(52)
Offender use of drugs/alcohol	9	(12)	9	(9)
Offender belligerent	6	(8)	8	(8)
Offender physical in front of police*	1	(1)	5	(5)
Offender known*				
Offender known	98	(126)	82	(80)
Offender not known	2	(2)	18	(18)

*Significance at the 0.05 probability level.

incident-related variables. Specifically, domestic assaults are less likely to involve a physical fight [χ^2 (1, $n = 314$) = 5.26, $p < 0.05$], and therefore not surprisingly, amount to less severe injury[2] to the victim [χ^2 (2, $n = 228$) = 8.93, $p < 0.05$]. However, the analysis did not find differences in the level of violence involved or in the time required for police arrival between the two types of incidents. Additionally, no differences appeared in terms of victim preference for arrest, police effort to contact the offender, whether the offender was contacted, and the time police required to complete the call.

Police Handling of Domestic and Nondomestic Assault Calls

Looking at the call's outcome indicates that domestic and nondomestic calls could not be differentiated in terms of the police disposition (e.g., did nothing, separate or mediate, refer, or arrest). However, Table 6 does show an interesting twist. Where police outcome is dichotomized into those resulting in an arrest and those with all other possible outcomes (e.g., did nothing, separate or mediate, or refer), a significant difference is seen [χ^2 (1, $n =$

TABLE 5   Comparison of Domestic and Nondomestic Assault Calls on Police
Report Variables: Incident Characteristics

	Domestic Assault Calls ($n = 189$) [% (no. cases)]		Nondomestic Assault Calls ($n = 145$) [% (no. cases)]	
Arrival time	10.58 minutes		11.04 minutes	
Highest level of violence				
No violence	14	(25)	8	(11)
Harassing	5	(9)	7	(9)
Shouting	22	(39)	17	(23)
Threatened, no weapon	5	(9)	5	(7)
Property damage	6	(10)	4	(5)
Physical fighting	36	(63)	42	(59)
Threatened, with weapon	6	(10)	7	(9)
Used weapon	2	(4)	2	(3)
Severe physical harm	3	(6)	9	(13)
Involves physical fight*				
No physical fight	53	(92)	40	(55)
Physical fight	47	(83)	60	(84)
Victim injuries*				
No injuries	50	(63)	46	(46)
Some injuries	47	(60)	41	(41)
Severe injuries	3	(4)	14	(14)
Victim preference				
Does not want arrest	49	(53)	41	(40)
Prefers arrest	51	(55)	59	(57)
Police effort to contact offender				
No effort	55	(39)	61	(37)
Some effort	9	(6)	13	(8)
Great effort	37	(26)	26	(16)
Offender contacted				
Not contacted	41	(53)	47	(46)
Contacted by phone	1	(1)	2	(2)
Contacted in person	58	(74)	51	(49)
Completion time	44.07 minutes		44.5 minutes	

*Significance at the 0.05 probability level.

TABLE 6   **Comparison of Domestic and Nondomestic Assault Calls on Police Disposition**

	Domestic Assault Calls ($n = 189$) [% (no. cases)]		Nondomestic Assault Calls ($n = 145$) [% (no. cases)]	
Police disposition				
Did nothing	61	(102)	64	(72)
Separate or mediate	11	(18)	15	(17)
Refer to another agency	5	(9)	7	(8)
Arrest	23	(38)	13	(15)
Arrest outcome*				
Did not arrest	77	(151)	86	(130)
Offender arrested	23	(38)	13	(15)

*Significance at the 0.05 probability level.

334) = 5.86, $p < 0.05$). Specifically, domestic calls are almost twice as likely to result in an arrest of the offender than are nondomestic calls, although the rates of arrest are still fairly low (23 versus 13 percent, respectively).

Table 7 lists the independent legal and extralegal variables used in this logistic regression analysis. Examining the main effects of the independent variables reveals that offenders who were present when the police arrived at the scene, offenders whose victims preferred an arrest response from the police, offenders who had physically injured their victims, and those who were belligerent to police were significantly more likely to face an arrest response. Odds ratios are provided to simplify interpreting the logit coefficients in this analysis. The odds ratio is the ratio of the probability that offenders with one characteristic will be arrested to the probability that others without this characteristic will be arrested, while controlling for all other factors.

As Table 7 indicates, offender's presence at the scene when police arrive had the largest impact on police response. Persons who were present were more than nineteen times more likely to be arrested than those who were not present when police arrived at the scene, even once all other variables in the equation were controlled. Continuing to review Table 7 indicates that where the victim preferred the police to arrest, the offender was more than twelve times more likely to be arrested. In a similar fashion, those offenders who injured their victims, and those who were belligerent to the police, were each six times more likely to face an arrest.

Surprisingly, the analysis also indicates that although not significant, where the victim–offender relationship can be characterized as "domestic" (e.g., current or past marital or romantic relationship), there is a tendency for police to be more likely to arrest the offender. Specifically, offenders in domestic assaults are almost three times more likely to face an arrest response than those in equivalent nondomestic assaults.

TABLE 7   Logit Model Statistics Describing Main Effects of Independent Variables on Decision to Arrest

	Logit Coefficient	S.E.	Odds Ratio
Individual variables			
Offender belligerent*	1.829	0.943	6.23
Offender use drugs/alcohol	0.099	0.873	1.10
Offender known to victim	5.990	21.507	399.42
Victim gender	0.533	0.717	1.70
Incident-related variables			
Offender present when police arrive*	2.961	0.642	19.31
Level of violence	0.146	0.930	1.16
Victim injured*	1.853	0.815	6.38
Domestic versus nondomestic[a]	1.066	0.641	2.90
Victim preference for arrest*	2.523	0.635	12.46
	$n = 155$		
	chi squared $= 76.691$		

*Significance at the 0.05 probability level.

[a]A tendency, although not significant.

Just as important in this analysis is what failed to achieve significance in explaining an arrest decision by the police. The logistic regression indicates that offender's use of drugs or abuse of alcohol, offender being known to the victim, and victim's gender did not significantly affect the police's decision to arrest. Finally, the level of violence did not significantly distinguish between those cases where the police responded with an arrest and those where they disposed of the case using other than an arrest response. Although this seems surprising at first, it must be remembered that the extent of victim injuries significantly distinguished an arrest from a nonarrest response. Therefore, police seem to be gauging the outcome of the violence rather than the level of the violence displayed.

Overall, this model correctly predicts 87 percent of the arrest decision. In fact, of the inmates who were not arrested, 94 percent were predicted correctly (of those arrested, 65 percent were predicted correctly) by this model. The formula

$$R^2 = \frac{\chi^2}{n + \chi^2}$$

provides an R^2 statistic for logistic regression which is analogous to the familiar R^2 statistic of OLS regression analysis. Although extreme caution should be exercised in using this statistic (Aldrich & Nelson, 1984), calculations indicate that entering these variables simultaneously into this model accounts for fully 33 percent of the variance in the police's decision to arrest when responding to these calls.

As a check of the logistical regression, a multiple regression analysis was conducted using police response (arrest versus nonarrest) as the dependent variable and entering all the other legal and extralegal independent variables into the equation. This procedure yields a less conservative estimate than the logit model and is being used only for comparative purposes. The results indicate that the equation explains 38 percent of the variation in the police's decision to arrest. Additionally, the offender's presence when the police arrive, victim preference for a police arrest, extent of victim injuries, and the offender's demeanor to the police were all associated significantly and positively with an arrest decision.

SUMMARY AND DISCUSSION OF RESULTS

We originally hypothesized that there would be no significant differences between calls where police are dispatched and those where a police officer is not sent for follow-up investigation. The results of the analysis squarely indicate that there are significant differences leading to the conclusion that these are two very different types of incidents. Specifically, calls in which police are dispatched are more likely to be determined by CADS to be domestic related, they are more likely to be in progress at the time of the call, with a higher-priority rating and with the victim having placed the call for service. There are additional factors distinguishing the two types of calls. Those that receive police follow-up are more likely to involve female victims and to be judged by the dispatchers to involve a higher level of violence.

We also found that contrary to the null hypothesis, domestic and nondomestic calls could be differentiated significantly in terms of the CADS variables. Specifically, domestic assault calls were more likely to be in progress. Perhaps this is why they received a higher-priority rating from the dispatchers despite the fact that nondomestic calls involved a higher level of violence. Finally, victims were more likely to place the call to the police in domestic calls than in nondomestic calls.

Contrary to previous research indicating that dispatchers underreport the severity of domestic assaults (Oppenlander, 1982), this study finds no proof of this occurrence. Although a skeptic could point to the fact that the rating for the level of violence was significantly lower for domestics and argue that it was due to underreporting by the dispatchers, there seems to be no substance to such a charge in light of the fact that police were dispatched to 71 percent ($n = 138$) of the domestic calls and to only 58 percent ($n = 84$) of the nondomestic calls.

Finally, we hypothesized that there would not be significant differences in terms of victim, offender, or incident characteristics between domestic and nondomestic calls that police responded to upon assignment by the dispatchers. The null hypothesis stands in terms of victim and offender characteristics, with minor exceptions. Specifically, victims of domestic assaults are more likely to be female. This finding is consistent with previous research indicating that women are much more likely to be the victims of domestic violence than are men (Dutton, 1988; Gelles, 1979; Kurz, 1991).

There was little which significantly differentiated between the two offender groups. They showed no differences in terms of the gender, age, race, drug or alcohol use, belligerence to the officer, or their presence at the scene when police arrived. However, and not surprisingly, domestic offenders were more likely to be known by their victims than were nondomestic offenders.

Additionally, many incident-related variables also failed to achieve significance. Contrary to previous research findings (Oppenlander, 1982), police demonstrated similar arrival and completion times in handling domestic and nondomestic calls. There were no significant differences in terms of the highest level of violence, as indicated on the police report or in the victim's preference for an arrest. The fact that no significant differences were shown between domestic and nondomestic assault calls in terms of victim preference for arrest is noteworthy. It is commonly held that police failure to arrest domestic violent offenders reflects, to some extent, this particular victim's ambivalence (Dutton & Levens, 1977; Sherman, 1988). However, this study indicates that victims of domestic assault were not significantly less likely to desire an arrest outcome than were nondomestic assault victims.

Police also demonstrated about the same amount of effort, and met with similar amounts of success, in contacting domestic and nondomestic assault offenders. This finding does raise a question, however. Since the offender in a domestic call was known by his victim, we might expect significantly more effort and greater success on the police's part to contact a known rather than an unknown offender. Additionally, since fear of retaliation would seem to be more of an issue for victims of domestic assault, one would hope that the police would make an even greater effort to find the offender who has fled the scene. However, although we cannot know what this finding truly means, it is possible that it represents a shortage of personnel on the police's part (and therefore an inability to follow up) rather than a policy of treating domestic offenders leniently. Obviously, further research is necessary. Finally, only two variables significantly distinguished domestic from nondomestic calls: (1) nondomestic calls were more likely to involve a physical fight, and (2) therefore more likely to involve severe injuries to the victim.

The data indicate that police are almost twice as likely to arrest when responding to a domestic call than to a nondomestic call (23 versus 13 percent, respectively). Two things must be noted about this rate of arrest. First, the arrest rate for domestic assault calls in this study (23 percent) is significantly higher than found in previous studies (usually between 11 and 15 percent). What this increase represents cannot be ascertained by these data. Second, even though higher than indicated in past research, the rates of arrest remain relatively low. However, whereas previous research indicated that an arrest outcome was atypical when police responded to domestic assault calls, this research finds that police only infrequently utilize an arrest in all cases of assault, both domestic and nondomestic.

The logistic regression indicates that four variables, all incident related, were significant in accounting for this variation in police's likelihood to arrest: offender's presence at the scene when police arrive, victim's preference for an arrest outcome, extent of victim injuries, and offender's demeanor toward police. These findings are fairly consistent with previous findings. For instance, victim's preference for an arrest outcome has been found to be a leading correlate in the police's decision to arrest (Berk & Loseke, 1980–1981; Black, 1978; Smith & Visher, 1981). Additionally, the findings that extent of victim's injuries (Gondolf & McFerron, 1989; Waaland & Keeley, 1985) and offender's demeanor toward police (Smith, 1987; Smith & Klein, 1984; Worden & Pollitz, 1984) affect an arrest likelihood had been demonstrated in other research studies.

Less usual is the impact of the variable offender's presence at the scene on the police's decision to arrest. Although this variable made an arrest 19 times more likely even once all other variables had been controlled, with few exceptions (see, e.g., Feder, 1996;

Ferraro & Pope, 1993) it has received very little attention in recent years. This contrasts with earlier studies of this variable's impact on arrest outcome (Berk & Loseke, 1980–1981; Worden & Pollitz, 1984). Although the importance of studying offender's presence in the arrest decision may at first seem self-evident, its impact is critical to bear in mind. It must be remembered that in domestic cases the offenders were always known by their victims and therefore to police. Yet this study indicates that an offender could easily escape the consequences of his illegal behavior merely by ensuring that he was not there when police arrived.

Finally, although not significant, there was a tendency for the victim–offender relationship to affect the likelihood of an arrest response. Specifically, those victim–offender relationships that involved past or current marital or romantic relationships (i.e., domestics) were associated with a higher likelihood of arrest than were nondomestic calls, even after all other variables were controlled.

Perhaps these results should not come as such a big surprise. Despite claims that the family is treated as a sacred entity (Lerman, 1981), and assertions that police and prosecutors do not want to get involved in domestic cases (Buzawa, 1982; Buzawa & Buzawa, 1985; Davis, 1983), previous research comparing police response to domestic and nondomestic calls found no statistically significant differences in the police's likelihood to arrest (Smith & Klein, 1984). Dutton, after conducting an extensive review of the research literature, concluded "that the winnowing effect of the criminal justice system for wife assault cases does not appear to be appreciably different than for other crimes" (Dutton, 1988, p. 199). Finally, a comparison of domestic and nondomestic cases and prosecutorial likelihood to prefer charges also failed to show significant differences in the handling of these cases (Schmidt & Hochstedler-Steury, 1987).

None of this is meant to argue that the police's rate of arrest when responding to domestic violence is sufficient. Instead, this research merely indicates that it is comparable to, and even a bit higher than, the rate for nondomestic calls. This finding probably should not come as a surprise. The legislation enacted made a nonarrest response difficult when responding to domestic rather than nondomestic calls, and this police department had gone on record in support of this legislative mandate. Therefore, perhaps we should not be surprised to find a higher rate of arrest when police responded to domestic violence calls in this particular department.

Two important points must be noted about this study and its results. First, the research methodology limits the generalizability of the study's findings. Specifically, we deal here with data from one specific police agency in South Florida—a state without a presumptive arrest statute—during a 17-day period. The department represents a highly professional law enforcement agency that had gone on record before the legislation was passed in support of an arrest policy when responding to domestic assault calls. There is no reason to believe that this particular jurisdiction is representative of police agencies nationwide. Instead, the study is intended to be exploratory, with the hope of encouraging additional research in other jurisdictions.

Furthermore, although this research indicates that police are more likely to arrest in domestic assault cases in comparison to nondomestic assault calls, all other things being equal, it still cannot answer whether police are arresting domestic violent offenders in sufficient numbers relative to the new legislation's intent. Only the public, through their legislators, can make that decision.

NOTES

1. A shortened version was presented in an earlier article published in *Crime and Delinquency* (1998), "Police handling of domestic and non-domestic calls: Is there a case for discrimination?"
2. Severe injury was operationalized in this study as an injury requiring hospitalization for any length of time.

REFERENCES

ALBA, R. (1987). Interpreting the parameters of log-linear models. *Sociological Methods and Research, 16*, 45–77.

ALDRICH, J., & NELSON, F. (1984). *Linear probability, logit, and probit models.* Beverly Hills, CA: Sage Publications.

BALOS, B., & TROTZKY, K. (1988). Enforcement of the domestic abuse act in Minnesota: A preliminary study. *Law and Inequality, 6*, 83–125.

Bell, D. (1985). Domestic violence: Victimization, police intervention, and disposition. *Journal of Criminal Justice, 13*, 525–534.

BELL, D. (1987). The victim–offender relationship: A determinant factor in police domestic dispute dispositions. *Marriage and Family Review, 12*(1), 87–102.

BERK, R., FENSTERMAKER, S., & NEWTON, P. (1988). An empirical analysis of police responses to incidents of wife battering. In G. Hotaling, D. Finkelhor, J. Kirkpatrick, & M. Straus (Eds.), *Coping with family violence: Research and policy perspectives* (pp. 158–168). Newbury Park, CA: Sage Publications.

BERK, S. F., & LOSEKE, D. (1980–1981). "Handling" family violence: Situational determinants of police arrest in domestic disturbances. *Law and Society Review, 15*(2), 317–346.

BLACK, D. (1978). Production of crime rates. In L. Savitz & N. Johnston (Eds.), *Crime in society* (pp. 45–60). New York: Wiley.

BLOUNT, W., YEGIDIS, B., & MAHEUX, R. (1992). Police attitudes toward preferred arrest: Influences of rank and productivity. *American Journal of Police, 9*(3), 35–52.

BOWKER, L. (1984). Battered wives and the police: A national study of usage and effectiveness. *Police Studies, 7*, 84–93.

BRECI, M., & SIMONS, R. (1987). An examination of organizational and individual factors that influence police response to domestic disturbances. *Journal of Police Science and Administration, 15*(2), 93–104.

BROWN, S. (1984). Police responses to wife beating: Neglect of a crime of violence. *Journal of Criminal Justice, 12*(3), 277–288.

BUZAWA, E. (1982). Police officer response to domestic violence legislation in Michigan. *Journal of Police Science and Administration, 10*(4), 415–424.

BUZAWA, E., & BUZAWA, C. (1985). Legislative trends in the criminal justice response to domestic violence. In A. Lincoln & M. Straus (Eds.), *Crime in the family* (pp. 134–147). Springfield, IL: Charles C Thomas.

DAVIDSON, T. (1977). Wifebeating: A recurring phenomenon throughout history. In M. Roy (Ed.), *Battered women: A psychosociological study of domestic violence* (pp. 2–23). New York: Van Nostrand Reinhold.

DAVIS, P. (1983). Restoring the semblance of order: Police strategies in the domestic disturbance. *Symbolic Interaction, 6*(2), 261–278.

DOBASH, R. E., & DOBASH, R. (1978). Wives: The "appropriate" victims of marital violence. *Victimology: An International Journal, 2*(3–4), 426–442.

DOLON, R., HENDRICKS, J., & MEAGHER, S. (1986). Police practices and attitudes toward domestic violence. *Journal of Police Science and Administration, 14*(3), 187–192.

DUTTON, D. (1988). Research advances in the study of wife assault: Etiology and prevention. *Law and Mental Health, 4*, 161–220.

DUTTON, D., & LEVENS, B. (1977). Domestic crisis intervention attitude survey of trained and untrained police officers. *Canadian Police College Journal, 1*(2), 75–92.

EISENBERG, S. & MICKLOW, P. (1977). The assaulted wife: "Catch 22" revisited. *Women's Rights Law Reporter, 3*, 138–164.

EREZ, E. (1986). Intimacy, violence, and the police. *Human Relations, 39*(3), 265–281.

FEDER, L. (1996). The importance of offender's presence in the arrest decision when police respond to domestic violence calls. *Journal of Criminal Justice, 24*(6), 1–10.

FEDER, L. (1997). Domestic violence and police response in a pro-arrest jurisdiction. *Women and Criminal Justice, 8*(4), 79–98.

FEDER, L. (1998a). Police handling of domestic and non-domestic violence calls: Is there a case for discrimination? *Crime and Delinquency, 44*(2), 139–153.

FEDER, L. (1998b). Police handling of domestic violence calls: An overview and further investigation. *Women and Criminal Justice, 10*(2).

FERRARO, K. (1989). Policing woman battering. *Social Problems, 36*(1), 61–74.

FERRARO, K., & POPE, L. (1993). Irreconcilable differences: Battered women, police and the law. In N. Z. Hilton (Ed.), *Legal responses to wife assault: Current trends and evaluation* (pp. 96–123). Newbury Park, CA: Sage Publications.

FIELDS, M. (1977–1978). Wife beating: Facts and figures. *Victimology, 2*(3–4), 643–647.

FRIEDMAN, L., & SCHULMAN, M. (1990). Domestic violence: The criminal justice response. In A. Lurigio, W. Skogan, & R. Davis (Eds.), *Victims of crime: Problems, policies, and programs* (pp. 87–103). Newbury Park, CA: Sage Publications.

GELLES, R. (1979, October). The myth of battered husbands and new facts about family violence. *Ms., 66*, 71–75.

GONDOLF, E., & McFERRON, J. R. (1988). Handling battering men: Police action in wife abuse cases. *Criminal Justice and Behavior, 16*(4), 429–439.

HARLOW, C. W. (1991). *Female victims of violent crime*. Washington, DC: U.S. Department of Justice, Bureau of Justice Statistics.

HILBERMAN, E. (1980). Overview: The "wife-beater's wife" reconsidered. *American Journal of Psychiatry, 137*(11), 1336–1347.

HIRSCHEL, J. D., HUTCHINSON, I., & DEAN, C. (1992). The failure of arrest to deter spouse abuse. *Journal of Research in Crime and Delinquency, 29*(1), 7–33.

HOMANT, R., & KENNEDY, D. (1985). Police perceptions of spouse abuse: A comparison of male and female officers. *Journal of Criminal Justice, 13*, 29–47.

KENNEDY, D., & HOMANT, R. (1983). Attitudes of abused women toward male and female police officers. *Criminal Justice and Behavior, 10*(4), 391–405.

KNOKE, D., & BURKE, P. (1980). *Log linear models*. Beverly Hills, CA: Sage Publications.

KURZ, D. (1991). Corporal punishment and adult use of violence: A critique of "Discipline and Deviance." *Social Problems, 38*(2), 155–161.

LAWRENZ, F., LEMBO, J., & SCHADE, T. (1988). Time series analysis of the effect of a domestic violence directive on the number of arrests per day. *Journal of Criminal Justice, 16*, 493–498.

LERMAN, L. (1981). Criminal prosecution of wife beaters. *Response to Violence in the Family and Sexual Assault, 4*(3), 1–19.

LERMAN, L. (1982). Court decisions on wife abuse laws: Recent developments. *Response to Family Violence and Sexual Assault, 5* (3–4), 21–22.

LERMAN, L., LIVINGSTON, F., & JACKSON, V. (1983). State legislation on domestic violence. *Response to Violence in the Family and Sexual Assault, 6*(5), 1–27.

OPPENLANDER, N. (1982). Coping or copping out. *Criminology, 20*(3–4), 449–465.

SAN JOSE METHODS TEST OF KNOWN CRIME VICTIMS. (1972). *Statistics Technical Report 1.* Washington, D.C.: National Institute of Law Enforcement and Criminal Justice Statistics Division, Law Enforcement Assistance Administration.

SAUNDERS, D., & SIZE, P. (1986). Attitudes about woman abuse among police officers, victims and victim advocates. *Journal of Interpersonal Violence, 1*(1), 25–42.

SCHMIDT, J., & HOCHSTEDLER-STEURY, E. (1987). Prosecutorial discretion in filing charges in domestic violence cases. *Criminology, 25*(1), 487–510.

SHERMAN, L. (1988). *Domestic violence.* Washington, DC: U.S. Department of Justice, National Institute of Justice.

SHERMAN, L. (1992). The influence of criminology on criminal law: Evaluating arrests for misdemeanor domestic violence. *Journal of Criminal Law and Criminology, 83*(1), 1–45.

SHERMAN, L., & BERK, R. (1984). The specific deterrent effects of arrest for domestic assault. *American Sociological Review, 49*, 261–272.

SHERMAN, L., SCHMIDT, J., ROGAN, D., SMITH, D., GARTIN, P., COHN, E., COLLINS, D., & BACICH, A. (1992). The variable effects of arrest on criminal on criminal careers: The Milwaukee domestic violence experiment. *Journal of Criminal Law and Criminology, 83*(1), 137–169.

SMITH, D. (1987). Police response to interpersonal violence: Defining the parameters of legal control. *Social Forces, 65*(3), 767–782.

SMITH, D., & KLEIN, J. (1984). Police control of interpersonal disputes. *Social Problems, 31*(4), 468–481.

SMITH, D., & VISHER, C. (1981). Street-level justice: Situational determinants of police arrest decisions. *Social Problems, 29*(2), 167–177.

STEDMAN, B. (1917). Right of husband to chastise wife. *Virginia Law Reporter, 3*(4), 241–248.

TAUB, N. (1983). Adult domestic violence: The law's response. *Victimology: An International Journal, 8*(1–2), 152–171.

WAALAND, P., & KEELEY, S. (1985). Police decision making in wife abuse: The impact of legal and extralegal factors. *Law and Human Behavior, 9*(4), 355–366.

WALTER, J. (1981). Police in the middle: A study of small city police intervention in domestic disputes. *Journal of Police Science and Administration, 9*, 243–260.

WORDEN, R., & POLLITZ, A. (1984). Police arrests in domestic disturbances: A further look. *Law and Society Review, 18*(1), 105–119.

CASES

Bruno v. *Codd*, 90 Misc.2d 1047, 396 N.Y.S.2d (Sup Ct 1997).

State v. *Oliver*, 70 N.C. 60 (N.C. 1874).

Thurman v. *City of Torrington*, 595 F. Supp. 1521 (D. Conn. 1984).

21

Victims of Domestic Stalking

A Comparison of Black and White Females

Janice Joseph

S talking has gained recognition and credibility as a serious crime in the United States. Victims of stalking include those currently at risk of physical and/or emotional harm, and those in constantly pending danger but not immediately at risk. Women are the victims of stalking in disproportionate numbers (Puente, 1992).

The actions of stalkers can be extremely threatening and dangerous to their victims. Stalking can escalate to violence, so stalking victims frequently live in fear and terror. Often, they are forced to alter their lives significantly in attempts to find safety and freedom from the harassing behavior of former spouses, ex-partners or strangers (National Institute of Justice, 1996). In this chapter we focus on the extent and nature of domestic stalking among black and white victims, critically examine New Jersey's stalking legislation, and make some recommendations.

DEFINITIONS OF STALKING

Legal definitions vary from state to state, but most states define stalking as willful, malicious, threatening, and repeated conduct for the purpose of causing fear in the victim. The types of acts that states identify as stalking behaviors include the following: terrorism, surveillance, harassment, nonconsensual communication, trespass, and threats. It can also include written and verbal communication, unsolicited and unrecognized claims of romantic involvement, loitering, following, or appearing within the sight of another, contacting the victim by telephone; sending mail or electronic mail; and appearing at the workplace or residence of the victim.

EXTENT OF STALKING

Unlike most violent crimes, the Federal Bureau of Investigation and many state law enforcement officials do not categorize the incident of stalking as a separate offense. Consequently, no one knows just how common stalking is in the United States. With the passage of the 1994 Crime Bill by the U.S. Congress, which mandated the tracking and compilation of stalking crime statistics, experts will be able to determine the prevalence of this crime in the future.

It is estimated that 200,000 people in the United States stalk someone each year, and this figure is rising (Guy, 1993). Five percent of women in the general population will be a victim of stalking at some time in their lives, 51 percent of stalking victims are ordinary citizens, and 75 to 80 percent of stalking is domestic-related. Ninety percent of the stalkers suffer from some kind of mental disorder, 9.5 percent suffer from erotomania, and 43 percent have love obsession with their victims (U.S. Congress Senate Committee on the Judiciary, 1992).

The first national survey on stalking was recently conducted by the U.S. Justice Department. The study was conducted on 8000 women and 8000 men regarding their experiences with stalking. The study found that stalking was more prevalent than previously thought; 8 percent of women and 2 percent of the men have been stalked at some time in their lives. Eighty percent of the stalking victims were women and most were between 18 and 29 years old. About 87 percent of the stalkers were men. The study estimated that about 1 million women and 400,000 men are stalked every year and that women were more likely to be stalked by their male intimate partners, while men were more likely to be stalked by a stranger or an acquaintance. In most cases, the episodes lasted a year or less. Less than half of the victims were directly threatened, although the victim experienced a high level of fear. The results also indicated that there was a strong relationship between stalking and other forms of violence in intimate relationships (Tjaden & Thoennes, 1998).

DOMESTIC STALKING

Most victims of stalking are victimized by acquaintances. This represents 70 to 80 percent of all stalking cases and is distinguished by the fact that some previous personal or romantic relationship existed between the stalker and the victim before the stalking behavior began. The victims may be ex-spouses, ex-lovers, relatives, or co-workers. Perpetrators are often out for revenge and will stop at nothing to get it (Zona, Sharma, & Lane, 1993). The majority of stalking victims are victims of domestic stalking.

Domestic stalking cases that arise from domestic violence situations constitute the most common type of stalking and usually culminate in violent attacks against the victims. Victims of domestic stalking at one time shared a personal relationship with the perpetrators as an intimate or member of the same household. This includes common-law relatives as well as long-term acquaintances. The domestic stalker is often motivated by a desire to continue or reestablish a relationship after it had ended, or is out for revenge. In addition, there is usually a history of prior abuse or conflict between the victim and the stalker. The stalker intends to hurt the victim physically, and the confrontation between the two often results in tragic consequences. Domestic stalkers are most dangerous when they are first deprived of their source of power and self-esteem (Holmes, 1994); in other words, the time when their victims determine to remove themselves physically from the offender's presence on a permanent basis by leaving the relationship is very critical for victims.

The Cycle of Domestic Stalking

Schaum and Parrish (1995) identified a cycle of domestic stalking which is similar to the cycle of domestic violence. The first phase, the tension-building phase, may move from relatively innocuous invasions to more dangerous efforts to control the victim. In this phase, the victim is harassed, threatened, and terrorized by behaviors such as annoying phone calls, unsolicited letters, odd gifts, actual threats, surveillance of the victim, following the victim, and acts of vandalism.

In the second phase, the explosive or acutely violent phase, the stalker uses violence against the victim, including physical assault, kidnapping, rape, violence against family members and friends, and the perpetrator's final act of control: murder, suicide, or both.

The third phase is the hearts and flowers phase, in which the stalker either changes his techniques and asks for forgiveness or may leave the victim alone for a period of time, making the victim feeling temporarily safe. The victim may even take this to mean that the stalking is over. However, this phase is often only a new tactic in the cycle of stalking, and the stalking starts all over again.

This cycle of domestic stalking may continue for years. In some cases, the stalker may murder the victim in an attempt to have control over her. Some stalkers, however, abandon their current victim and redirect their fixation to more challenging and vulnerable females (Schaum & Parrish, 1995). Although this progression of the stalking cycle is common, no stalker is completely predictable. Some stalkers may never escalate past the first stage. Others move from the first stage to the last stage with little warning. Still others regress to previous stages before advancing to the next. Some stalkers may engage in episodes of threats and violence with alternating flowers and love letters. A few stalkers will progress to later stages in only a few weeks or even days. In other cases, some stalkers who have engaged in the most serious stalking behaviors may go months or even years without attempting a subsequent contact (National Victim Center, 1995). It is this unpredictability that makes stalkers very dangerous to their victims.

VICTIMS OF DOMESTIC STALKING: THE STUDY

In this section we present information from a sample of 86 female stalking victims. Some victims were interviewed at a courthouse. Others were referred to the researchers by other victims and were interviewed at their homes or a place that was convenient for them.

Measuring Instrument

The items on the interview schedule were developed from research of the literature on stalking. The interview schedule was divided into three parts: part I focused on the nature and extent of the stalking experienced by the victims; part II included items on the response of the victims to the stalking; and part III examined the effects of the stalking on the victims.

Description of Sample

More of the victims (41 percent) were between 25 and 29 years old than other ages. Sixty-eight percent were Catholics, 26 percent Protestant, and 6 percent of other religions. The average annual income was between $20,000 and $29,999. Fifty-three percent were African-Americans and 47 percent were white. None of the victims were living with the stalker, but 48 percent were ex-wives, 22 percent of them were still legally married to the stalker, 17 percent were former girlfriends, and 13 percent were strangers.

Nature of Stalking

The nature and extent of the stalking are shown in Table 1, which indicates that the most common activities of the stalker were following the victim (78 percent), intruding on the victim (73 percent), sending unwanted gifts to the victim (72 percent), stalking the victim's children (65 percent), and verbally threatening the victim (64 percent). Most stalkings lasted over seven months (68 percent). Table 1 also indicates that significantly more white victims than black victims were harassed on the telephone and followed. On the other hand, significantly more blacks than whites were threatened verbally and had their children stalked.

Responses to Stalking

Victims of stalking responded in several ways to their stalking, including preventive measures against the stalking. In responding to the stalking, many of the victims used preventive measures. Table 1 indicates that many of the victims bought a security system (61 percent), changed their address (60 percent), changed their behavior (54 percent), alerted the neighbors (52 percent), and documented the stalker's behavior (50 percent). The data indicate that more whites than blacks alerted their neighbors or bought a security system. On the other hand, more blacks than whites purchased caller identification for their telephones.

The majority of the victims (94 percent) said that they believed that they were stalked because the stalker wanted to control them or instill fear in them. In addition, 21 percent of the victims believed that their stalker was psychotic or delusional. Many of the victims clearly stated that the stalker knew what he was doing. Fifty-four percent of the victims also experienced domestic violence when they were intimately involved with the stalker.

Effects of Stalking

The experience of being stalked over a period of time can be described as psychological terrorism. Victims live in constant fear and are often forced to alter their lifestyle (change their address, move, and give up social activities). The results of the survey indicated that the stalking had a negative impact on many of the victims, as shown in Table 2. The majority of victims experienced sleeplessness (81 percent), anger (82 percent), fear (73 percent), self-blame (70 percent), anxiety (62 percent), and depression (62 percent). Sixty percent were forced to changed their address, and 54 percent had to change their behaviors, such as walking out late at night or going certain places alone. Table 2 also shows that whites were significantly more likely than blacks to change their address, be fearful, and experience sleeplessness, nightmares, and anxiety.

TABLE 1   Characteristics of the Stalking by Race (percent)

	Total (n = 87)	White (n = 40)	Black (n = 47)	χ^2 (df = 1)
Nature of the stalking				
Invade privacy	39	28	49	3.12
Intrude	73	75	68	0.49
Threaten verbally	64	50	80	8.85**
Harass on the telephone	48	66	25	13.70***
Threaten physically	29	3	40	21.13***
Show up unexpectedly	60	53	66	1.47
Perform surveillance	49	53	46	0.29
Hurt victim physically	52	50	53	0.08
Send unwanted gifts	72	100	51	24.37***
Follow victim	78	75	81	0.73
Stalk children	65	53	75	4.14*
Duration of the stalking				
Less than 1 month	8	11	4	
1–6 months	25	17	30	
7–12 months	35	46	28	
1–4 years	32	26	38	5.53
Responses to the stalking				
Documented stalker's behavior	50	54	50	0.15
Alerted neighbors	52	75	36	12.34***
Used caller ID	41	25	53	6.70**
Bought security system	61	98	34	37.90***
Got bodyguard	10	15	3	3.44
Bought dog	51	49	52	0.75
Bought a gun	25	30	21	0.93

*Significance at 0.05.

**Significance at 0.01.

***Significance at 0.001.

Use of Social Services

The majority of the victims utilized social service agencies to deal with the stalking. Sixty percent of the respondents reported the stalking to the police; 74 percent obtained a restraining order, 69 percent took the stalker to court, 61 percent went to a battered women shelter, 41 percent were counseled, and 31 percent went to a psychiatrist (Table 3). Many

TABLE 2   Social and Psychological Effects of Stalking by Race (percent)

	Total (n = 87)	White (n = 40)	Black (n = 47)	χ^2 (df = 1)
Changed address	60	77	50	6.20**
Changed behavior	54	64	47	2.40
Self-blame	70	51	85	11.28***
Anger	82	77	84	0.77
Fear	73	100	51	24.93***
Nighmare	41	57	28	6.88**
Sleeplessness	81	95	65	15.17***
Anxiety	62	74	50	4.91*
Depression	62	51	70	2.77
Posttraumatic syndrome	41	49	34	1.83

*Significance at 0.05.

**Significance at 0.01.

***Significance at 0.001.

of the victims who reported the perpetrator to police indicated that arrest by the police (94 percent) did not deter the stalker. Similarly, the majority of those who took out a restraining order against the stalker (91 percent) said that the stalker continued his stalking.

The data indicate that whites were more likely than blacks to call the police, go to a shelter, or visit a counselor or psychiatrist. The reason for this disparity could be that blacks are distrustful of the social system, including the police, and so are reluctant to seek help from these agencies.

TABLE 3   Use of Social Services (percent)

Agency	Total (n = 87)	White (n = 40)	Black (n = 47)	χ^2 (df = 1)
Police	60	78	27	14.06***
Restraining order	74	74	74	1.00
Court	69	77	58	3.16
Shelter	61	70	50	4.04*
Counselor	41	52	26	5.76**
Psychiatrist	31	51	15	12.87***

*Significance at 0.05.

**Significance at 0.01.

***Significance at 0.001.

Perceptions of the Stalking Legislation

The victims were asked to assess the effectiveness of the state of New Jersey's stalking legislation, which was enacted in 1993. In 8 percent of cases, the legislation was not enacted during the stalking incidents. In 13 percent of the cases, the legislation did not exist at the onset of the stalking. Over three-fourths (83 percent) of the victims claimed that they did not believe that the legislation was effective in protecting them. Of those who took the perpetrator to court (69 percent), 41 percent claimed that the charges were downgraded to a lesser offense, such as harassment, 23 percent reported that the perpetrator spent only a few weeks in jail, 28 percent that the charges were dropped because of insufficient evidence, and only 8 percent felt that the perpetrator was justly punished.

CRITICAL ANALYSIS OF NEW JERSEY STALKING LEGISLATION

Since the passage of that first antistalking law in 1990 in California, all 50 states have enacted stalking statutes. These new laws were intended to give law enforcement agencies more powerful tools to arrest and prosecute stalkers and to offer victims of stalking much greater protection than was previously available for them (National Institute of Justice, 1993).

The New Jersey antistalking law went into effect on January 5, 1993. It is intended to protect victims who are repeatedly followed and threatened and is modeled after the 1990 California statute. The bill states that a person is guilty of stalking if he or she purposely and repeatedly follows or harasses another person and makes a credible threat with the intent to place that person in reasonable fear of death or serious bodily injury (New Jersey Statute Annotated, 1997). There are, however, some problems with the law.

Legal Elements of State Antistalking Legislation

There are certain legal elements in New Jersey's state antistalking legislation, including a course of conduct requirement, a purposeful or intentional behavior requirement, a threatening behavior requirement, a fear of physical harm requirement, and a reasonable person requirement.

Course of Conduct.   New Jersey's antistalking law requires that the alleged perpetrator engage in a "course of conduct involving repeatedly maintaining a visual or physical proximity to a person or repeatedly conveying verbal or written threats or threats implied by conduct or a combination thereof directed at or toward a person" (New Jersey Statute Annotated, 1997, p. A1). New Jersey does not clearly identify the behaviors that constitute a course of conduct, although the law was intended to prosecute persons who follow or harass others. The definition of course of conduct should have been much more precise and broader. Many states specify the prohibited behaviors and include surveillance, following, "lying in wait," harassing, approaching, pursuing, and intimidating of a victim, trespassing, showing a weapon, vandalizing, disregarding warning by a victim, and confining or restraining another person (U.S. Department of Justice, 1998). Statutes that narrowly define the course of conduct and the circumstances that constitute stalking may provide only limited protection for female victims. The New Jersey legislation defines "repeatedly" as two or more occasions. What this seems to imply is that one act of stalking, no matter how serious it may be, does not constitute stalking.

Purposeful or Intentional Behavior Requirement.   According to New Jersey, stalking is "purposeful," "reckless," and "negligent." What this law requires is criminal, that is, the perpetrator is aware of what he or she is doing and has a conscious desire or objective to engage in the conduct or engages in the behavior irresponsibly. This requirement of criminal intent creates a loophole for the mentally disturbed offender. A stalker with erotomania, psychosis, or an antisocial personality disorder (all suffering, therefore, from mental disturbances) may well believe that he is merely showing the victim how much he loves her, despite the fact that his intentions may be creating fear in the victim. A prosecutor may have difficulty establishing such a stalker's guilt through criminal intent (Schaum & Parrish, 1995).

Threatening Behavior Requirement.   Like most states, New Jersey requires that the stalker pose a threat or act in a way that causes a person to be fearful. These threats could be verbal or written. This is an important element because nonverbal acts can be as threatening as written threats. The context in which certain gestures are made can make them suggestive and frightening. For example, a stalker can convey a threat by forming his hand into the form of a gun and pointing it a woman, or delivering a dead animal on a victim's doorstep. These cues are subtle but powerful enough to cause fear, especially in domestic stalking cases (National Institute of Justice, 1996).

Fear of Physical Harm Requirement.   The New Jersey statute stipulates that the stalker's acts must cause the victim to be fearful of bodily harm or death to "himself" or a member of "his" immediate family. This requirement means that the victim has to believe that the stalker will injury, disfigure, or even kill him/her or his/her immediate family before the behavior can be considered stalking. Such a restrictive requirement ignores behaviors that may not be perceived as causing such extreme violence but, nevertheless, are frightening. Why should a threat of such extreme violence be required before a victim can be protected? What is also interesting about this legislation is that it uses the terms *himself* and *his* when the majority of the victims of stalking are women (New Jersey Statute Annotated, 1997).

Reasonable Person Requirement.   In New Jersey the victims of stalking have to meet the reasonable fear or reasonable person's standard of fearfulness for their perpetrator to be charged with stalking. The statute states that the behavior should cause a "reasonable person" to fear bodily injury (New Jersey Statute Annotated, 1997, p. B1). The reasonable standard requirement is based on what a reasonable person would feel rather than on the victim's personal feelings and experiences. This is a critical element for many victims, especially victims of domestic stalking. An ex-wife, for example, who has had a prior violent relationship with the perpetrator may react fearfully to minor harassing incidents, whereas others might ignore similar incidents. Does this mean that the ex-wife's fear is unreasonable? Not necessarily, but she could be viewed as overly sensitive, and thus a judge could consider her fear unreasonable. A stalker may whisper to his former wife: "Remember the gift I gave you last year for your birthday?" To a casual listener this may seem nonthreatening, but only the victim would be able to understand the real meaning of this statement, which could be: "Remember the beating that I gave you on that day." The determination as to who is a reasonable person or what is reasonable fear is left to the discretion of the judge. However, the victim's perception of reasonable fear should be taken into consideration rather than how a reasonable person would respond to threats of a stalker. Lawmakers are now beginning to realize that the victim's perception of possible violence is the most accurate indicator of whether such violence will occur and are amending their laws (Schaum & Parrish, 1995). In addition to the criticism noted above, the term *reasonable* is not defined in New Jersey's legislation.

Persons Covered by the Antistalking Legislation.   New Jersey extends its antistalking legislation to the victim's immediate family members. The statute defines immediate family as spouse, child, sibling, or any person who regularly resides in the household or who within the preceding six months resided regularly in the household (New Jersey Statute Annotated, 1997). This restrictive definition therefore does not apply to anyone who has not resided in the household for over six months. Ten states mention stalking or harassing of a minor in their antistalking statutes, and nine of them provide for enhanced penalties against persons who stalk or harass minors. In five of these states, minors under the age of 16 are covered by the law; in three other states, coverage is extended to minors under the age of 18; and in the ninth state, only minors under the age of 12 are covered (U.S. Department of Justice, 1998). New Jersey does not cover minors in its legislation. Sometimes victims of stalking seek the assistance of close friends and co-workers who themselves may become victims of the stalker as well. However, none of the states' antistalking legislation covers close friends and co-workers of the victims.

Criminal and Civil Remedies

In New Jersey, stalking is a crime of the fourth degree, which is punishable by a term of imprisonment of up to 18 months, a fine of up to $7500, or both. A second or subsequent offense of stalking which involves an act of violence or a credible threat of violence against the same victim would be punishable as a crime of the third degree. If the defendant commits the crime of stalking in violation of an existing court order prohibiting the behavior, the offense would be classified as a crime of the third degree, which is punishable by a term of imprisonment of three to five years, a fine of up to $7500, or both (New Jersey Statute Annotated, 1997). New Jersey has both misdemeanor and felony classifications of stalking, but felony penalties for stalking are restricted to stalking where there is bodily harm, the presence of a weapon, or where the stalking constituted a violation of a protective order. It does appear, then, that the state takes the crime of stalking seriously only when the stalker threatens the victim violently.

In 1996, the New Jersey Stalking Law was amended to allow "victims" to obtain permanent restraining orders against stalkers. The permanent order can (1) restrain the defendant from entering the residence, property, school, or place of employment of the victim and require the defendant to stay away from any specified place that is named in the order and is frequented regularly by the victim, and (2) restrain the defendant from making contact with the victim, including an order forbidding the defendant from personally or through an agent initiating any communication likely to cause annoyance or alarm, including, but not limited to, personal, written, or telephone contact with the victim, the victim's employers, employees, or fellow workers, or others with whom communication would be likely to cause annoyance or alarm to the victim (New Jersey Statute Annotated, 1997). This amendment is an improvement over the original legislation passed in 1993, but restraining orders are very limited. Protective orders allow the women partial protection in that they can go to court to get the orders before anything violent actually happens as long as there is a sufficient likelihood that it will happen. These orders can serve as the first formal means of intervention in a stalking situation, but protective orders have several inherent limitations, especially if they are not enforced.

Challenges to New Jersey's Legislation

Like most stalking legislation, New Jersey's statute is open to constitutional challenges that can make it difficult to prosecute successfully perpetrators of stalking and to protect victims. The legislation can be challenged on the grounds of vagueness and overbreadth.

Vagueness and Overbreadth.   The vagueness doctrine under the due process clauses for the Fifth and Fourteenth Amendments of the U.S. Constitution requires that all persons be given fair notice of what conduct is against the law and may subject them to criminal liability. This doctrine provides that a statute is void if the conduct forbidden by it is so poorly defined that persons of common intelligence must guess at its meaning and differ as to its application. Further, courts condemn vague statutes because they may result in arbitrary enforcement of the statutes.

A similar, yet distinct ground for voiding statutes as unconstitutional is the concept of overbreadth. The doctrine of overbreadth states that the government may not pursue satisfaction of a proper governmental purpose by means that sweep unnecessarily broadly and thereby invade protected freedoms. The danger of overly broad statutes is twofold: that they may deter citizens from engaging in constitutionally privileged activities and that they give law enforcement officials the power to select certain citizens and punish them. The test for determining overbreadth is whether the statute substantially restricts constitutionally protected conduct.

Many of the elements in the state's stalking legislation can be viewed as being too vague. For example, such words as *followed, threatened, knowingly, recklessly*, and *negligently* are not clearly defined in New Jersey's law. Similarly, such phrases as *explicit or credible threat, visual or physical proximity*, or *threats implied by conduct* have been used without sufficient definition or clarity. The statute also prohibits behaviors that can be considered protected constitutionally.

In 1999, Anthony Cardell, who was convicted of stalking, appealed his conviction on the grounds that the 1996 amended New Jersey's stalking law was too broad and too vague. He argued also that the present New Jersey's stalking law limited his First Amendment rights to freedom of speech, association, and assembly, specifically in its definition of course of conduct, which makes reference to "maintaining a visual or physical proximity to a person" and to "conveying verbal threats." His arguments were that these conditions duly restrict his ability to go where he wishes and to say what he wants to say.

The defendant also argued that the antistalking statute was unconstitutionally vague in general and as applied to his conduct in this case. His argument again focused on the phrase "repeatedly maintaining a visual or physical proximity" to the victim. In essence, he complained that the phrase fails to inform how close one must get to be in violation of the law. The court ruled against both his arguments on the vagueness and overbreadth of the statute, thereby upholding the law as constitutional (*State* v. *Cardell*, 1999). In *State* v. *Saunders* (1997), the court also upheld the stalking legislation on the grounds that it was not vague or or too broad.

Despite the fact that challenges to New Jersey's stalking legislation have failed, if challenges continue, it may one day be struck down as being unconstitutional. It appears that in responding to the concerns of stalking victims, New Jersey, like so many other states, has had to walk a narrow line. On the one hand, it has to protect individuals' rights and freedoms of expression and travel and movement, and on the other hand, it cannot permit one person to place another person or his or her family in fear of physical or emotional harm. In trying to reconcile these two issues, New Jersey may have failed to balance these competing interests properly by drafting legislation that may have legal and constitutional problems. More constitutional challenges to this law are to be expected. Unless New Jersey amends its stalking law, it will be subjected to constitutional scrutiny. A challenge to this law, if successful, would result in further victimization of stalking victims.

RECOMMENDATIONS

Based on the problems in New Jersey's stalking statute, New Jersey should enact stalking legislation that:

- Is comprehensive, enforceable, and not open to constitutional scrutiny. To accomplish this, New Jersey needs to revise the present antistalking law, removing all legal loopholes.
- Protects a broad category of persons, including extended family members, minors, acquaintances, co-workers, friends, or anyone who is likely to assist the victim.
- Reforms the procedures that impede victims from taking legal actions against perpetrators of stalking, especially in the case of protection orders. States should provide easy access to long-term protection orders that prohibit the perpetrator from stalking the victim.
- Establishes severe penalties, both criminal and civil, for the crime of stalking, but at the same time avoids the possibility of any constitutional challenges under the Eighth Amendment.

One of the major difficulties with the prosecution of stalkers appears to be the lack of clear procedures, training, and the seriousness given to the crime by criminal justice professionals. Therefore, New Jersey should:

- Develop clear and comprehensive procedures for the filing, investigation, and prosecution of complaints involving the crime of stalking.
- Provide law enforcement officers, attorneys, judges, and other professionals, such as physicians and social workers, with proper training on the crime of stalking. With comprehensive training, criminal justice professionals and other professionals can become important sources of assistance for stalking victims.

- Penalize officials who do not follow the proper procedures and protocols for the enforcement of antistalking legislation.
- Utilize a collaborative approach to stalking by developing a multidisciplinary team of professionals from the criminal justice system, social services, mental health system, victim advocates, legal services, and other agencies. Multidisciplinary teams are more effective in preventing crimes and protecting victims.

The foregoing recommendations are not a panacea for preventing the crime of stalking or for protecting stalking victims but if implemented, can be useful and helpful to victims of stalking. Stalking is a serious crime and should be treated as such if states want to deal with it effectively and protect victims from stalkers.

SUMMARY

In the past several decades, the crime of stalking has gained attention due primarily to the victimization of some well-known celebrities. It is a crime of terrorism and obsession. The most common victims of stalking have had an intimate relationship with the perpetrator—they are victims of domestic stalking. The results of this small sample of stalking victims clearly indicated that stalking involves a variety of behaviors, which can range from mild to serious. The study also indicated that stalking had a physical and psychological impact on the victims. In comparing the white victims with the black victims, the study indicated that the nature of the stalking differed among the two groups and that the two groups responded differently to the stalking. One of the interesting findings is that significantly more white victims than black victims used social services. It would appear that the black victims were distrustful of social services.

In an attempt to deal with stalking, states like New Jersey have enacted antistalking legislation designed to provide protection for victims of stalking. However, there is some question as to whether these laws can be effective in protecting victims. New Jersey's stalking legislation is open to constitutional challenges and could some day be found unconstitutional. New Jersey's stalking law needs to be amended so that stalkers can be prosecuted and convicted successfully and their victims protected effectively.

REFERENCES AND BIBLIOGRAPHY

ASSOCIATED PRESS. (1999, May 17). Supreme Court to decide validity of law that keeps driver's data private.

California Penal Code, § 646.9 (1993).

DIETZ, P. E., MATHEWS, D. B., VAN DUYNE, C., MARTELL, D. A., PERRY, C. D. H., STEWART, T., WARREN, J., & CROWDER, J. D. (1991). Threatening and otherwise inappropriate letters to Hollywood celebrities. *Journal of Forensic Sciences, 36,* 185–209.

FIRST AMENDMENT NEWS PRESS. (1997, November). Federal judge reopens motor-vehicle records. http://www.fac.org/fanews/fan9710/press.htm

GEBERTH, V. (1992). Stalkers. *Law and Order, 40*(10), 138–143.

GUY, R. A. (1993). Nature and constitutionality of stalking laws. *Vanderbilt Law School, 46,* 991–1029.

HOLMES, R. M. (1994, May). Stalking in America. *Law and Order, 12,* 89–92.

JORDAN. T. (1995). The efficacy of the California stalking law: Surveying its evolution, extracting insights from domestic violence cases. *Hasting Women's Law Journal 6*(2), 363–383.

LINGG, R. A. (1993). Stopping stalkers: A critical examination of antistalking legislation. *Saint John's Law Review, 67*(2), 347–381.

Michigan Compiled Laws Annotated, § 650. 411 h(d) (1993).

MILLER, N. (1998). *State by state analysis*. Alexandria, VA: Institute of Law and Justice.

Mississippi Code Annotated, § 97-3-107 (1997).

MORIN, K. S. (1993). The phenomenon of stalking: Do existing state statutes provide adequate protection? *San Diego Justice Journal, 1*, 123.

MUSTAINE, E. E. (1999). A routine theory explanation of women's stalking victimization. *Violence Against Women, 5*(1), 43–62.

NATIONAL INSTITUTE OF JUSTICE. (1993). *Project to develop a model of antistalking code for states. Final summary report*. Washington, DC: U.S. Department of Justice.

NATIONAL INSTITUTE OF JUSTICE. (1996). *Domestic violence, stalking, and antistalking legislation*. Washington, DC: U.S. Department of Justice.

NATIONAL VICTIM CENTER. (1995). *Stalking: Questions and answers*. Arlington, VA: INFOLINK.

NATIONAL VICTIM CENTER. (1997). *Stalking and the law*. Arlington, VA: INFOLINK.

New Jersey State Annotated, 2C:12-10, § B (1) (1995).

New Mexico Statute Annotated, § 30-3A-3, 3-1 (1993).

New York Penal Law, 120:14(3) (1993).

Public Law 103-322, Title IV, Subtitle B, Chapter 110A , 2261-2266 (1994a).

Public Law 103-322, Title 18 U.S.C. 108 Stat. 2102 (1994b).

Public Law 104-201, 1069, Title 18 U.S.C. 2261, 2261A, and 2262 (1996).

PUENTE, M. (1992, July 21). Legislators tackling the terror of stalking. *USA Today*, p. 9.

SCHAUM, M. & PARRISH, K. (1995). *Stalked: Breaking the silence on the crime of stalking in America*. New York: Simon & Schuster.

SOHN, E. (1994). Antistalking statutes: Do they actually protect victims? *Criminal Justice Bulletin, 30*(3), 203–241.

Texas Penal Code Annotated, § 42-072 (1997).

THOMAS, K. R. (1993). How to stop the stalker: State antistalking laws. *Criminal Law Bulletin, 21*, 124–136.

TJADEN, P., & THOENNES, N. (1998). *Stalking in America: Findings from the national violence against women survey*. Washington, DC: U.S. Government Printing Office.

TOPLIFFE, E. (1992). Why civil protection orders are effective remedies for domestic violence but mutual protective orders are not. *Indiana Law Journal, 67*, 1039–1047.

U.S. CONGRESS SENATE COMMITTEE ON THE JUDICIARY. (1992). *Antistalking legislation hearing before the Senate Judiciary Committee*. Washington, DC: U. S. Government Printing Office.

U.S. DEPARTMENT OF JUSTICE. (1997). *Domestic violence and stalking: The second annual report to Congress under the Violence Against Women Act*. Washington, DC: U.S. Government Printing Office.

U.S. DEPARTMENT OF JUSTICE. (1998). *Stalking and domestic violence: Third annual report to Congress under the Violence Against Women Act*. Washington, DC: U.S. Government Printing Office.

WALLACE, H. (1995). Stalkers, the Constitution, and victims' remedies. *Criminal Justice, 10*, 16.

West Virginia Code, § 61-2-9a (1995).

WRIGHT, J. A., & BURGESS, A. G. (1996). A typology of interpersonal stalking. *Journal of Interpersonal Violence, 11*(4), 487–502.

Wyoming Statutes Annotated, § 6-2-605 (1993).

ZONA, M. A., SHARMA, K. K., & LANE, J. (1993). A comparative study of erotomanic and obsessional subjects in a forensic sample. *Journal of Forensic Sciences, 38*, 894–903.

CASES

State v. *Cardell*, 318 N.J. Super. Ct. App. Div., 175 (1999).
State v. *Saunders*, 302 N.J. Super. Ct. App. Div., 509 (1997).

22

Forced Sexual Intercourse

Contemporary Views

Robert T. Sigler, Ida M. Johnson, and Etta F. Morgan

In this chapter we aim to introduce with some degree of clarity an area noted for its lack of clarity. Forced sexual intercourse is generally treated as a single phenomenon. We suggest that this term is used to label four types of behavior that are substantially different. *Stranger rape* occurs when someone who is not known or who is casually known to the victim uses force to gain sexual access. *Courtship* or *date rape* occurs when someone who is developing a legitimate relationship with a victim uses force to gain sexual access. *Predatory rape* occurs when someone uses force to gain sexual access while pretending to engage in a legitimate courtship or dating activity (the pretense is used to maneuver the victim into a vulnerable position). *Spousal rape* occurs when someone uses force to gain sexual access with a spouse or with someone with whom he has a relatively permanent relationship. We argue that these are different sets of phenomena, which require different explanatory models and interventions. Each type is defined with reference to the relevant literature when appropriate. Recommendations are made for research foci for each type. A previously published model that addresses forced sexual intercourse in courtship and dating is presented.

Forced sexual intercourse has been growing steadily in importance as an area of concern for scholars. The definition of women's roles and the social values that define the relationships between men and women have been changing. Social service and criminal justice agencies have responded to these changes by moving to adopt policies and practices that are more sympathetic to female victims of domestic violence, courtship violence, and forced sexual intercourse. In the process, rape, the intentional or planned use of physical force to obtain sexual access against the wishes of a woman who was not intimately involved with her assailant, has been redefined to the extent that rape is no longer an accurate characterization of the behaviors that can be addressed by the justice system on the complaint of a victim.

Although the focus of this chapter is on the definition of types of forced sexual intercourse, it should be noted that the definition of rape that was common in the first half of this century has slowly evolved to include types of forced sexual intercourse which in the past were held to be of no interest to the justice system and to include offensive sexual behaviors that were less than intercourse. *Sexual assault*, the emerging concept, is broad, has been widely accepted, and specifies degrees of offensiveness. There is some recognition that offensive sexual behavior and forced sexual intercourse can be placed on a continuum based on degree of unacceptability of the behavior. Although this evolution may have positive effects on the ability of the justice system to protect women from male offenders, it increases the confusion in definition which has characterized forced sexual intercourse by including a wide range of behaviors under one label. At the same time, the perspective that will be presented here suggests that the continuum of those behaviors identified as forced sexual intercourse is broader than generally accepted and may include offensive sexual behaviors that are tolerated by some of the victims. Specifically, some offensive sexual behavior occurs in the context of courtship and dating and is accepted, to some degree, by some of the victims.

Historically, theories that sought to explain rape focused on those cases in which a stranger sexually assaulted a relatively unknown victim. Sexual assaults were explained in terms of mental illness and generally asserted that rape was more a matter of serious mental defect or a matter of dominance and control of women than a matter of gaining sexual access.

Three major works, published in the 1980s, sought to explain the broader range of behaviors that had become defined as behaviors that were sufficiently unacceptable that they should be subjected to the control of the justice system. Sunday and Tobach (1985) addressed the sociobiological approach to violence against women, including rape. Ellis (1989) shifted the emphasis from predatory stranger rape to acquaintance rape and recognized the influence of the feminist perspective as originally advanced by Brownmiller (1975). He grouped explanations for forced sexual intercourse into three general theoretical perspectives: feminist theory, learning theory, and evolutionary theory. Baron and Straus (1989) also sought to present theories that reflected the broader definition of rape that had emerged by the 1980s. They grouped explanations for sexual assault into four general theoretical perspectives: gender inequality, pornography, social disorganization, and legitimate violence. Readers who seek more comprehensive coverage of these perspectives should review these three earlier works as well as Brownmiller's 1975 book, *Against Our Will: Men, Women, and Rape.*

THEORETICAL PERSPECTIVES

The Feminist Perspective

The feminist movement produced, or at least influenced, much of the reform in the manner in which society relates to women. Feminists argue that sexual assault is defined as a legitimate or normal product of male-dominated societies. From this perspective offensive behaviors that control women are defined as acceptable to the males who control the society. Feminist theorists argue that patriarchal societies define men as dominant over women.

Women are assigned inferior social status, with relatively little power, while men are socially superior and dominate and control women (Dobash, 1979; Friedan, 1963). Men's power over women historically was defined as not subject to control by society in even the most severe of instances, thus came to be perceived as a right or, at least, as a privilege exercised by men. In this context, forced sexual intercourse becomes more a matter of dominance and control than a matter of sex (Brownmiller, 1975; Goth, 1979; Holdstrom & Burgess, 1980; Riger & Gordon, 1981; Scarpitti & Scarpitti, 1977). Men (male-dominated society) use the fear of rape to allow men to assert their dominance over women and rape to control nonconforming women as a means of maintaining the patriarchal system of male dominance (Adamec & Adamec, 1981; Barry, 1979; Brownmiller, 1975; Goth, 1979; Persell, 1984; Riger & Gordon, 1981; Russell, 1975; Thompson & Buttell, 1984; Weis & Borges, 1977).

Studies supporting the feminist perspective have tended to measure the incidence of rape in relation to incidents of violence in general (Baron & Straus, 1984; Benderly, 1982; Cauffman, Feldman, Jensen, & Arnett, 2000; Kutchinski, 1988; Sanday, 1981; Schwendinger & Schwendinger, 1985; Sigelman, Berry, & Wiles, 1984). Self-report studies that ask rapists to report their motivation tend to contradict the feminist model. They find that rapists report motivation by desire for excitement, risk taking, and sex (Scully & Marolla, 1984) and report high levels of deviant sexual fantasies (Walker & Meyer, 1981) with high levels of sexual arousal reported by date rapists (Yegidis, 1986). More recent research finds that sexually aroused males are more likely to report that they would be more likely to behave in a sexually forceful manner on a date (Cowling, 1998)

In the feminist model, behaviors such as forced sexual intercourse are defined as acceptable or justified. It is possible, however, to argue within the feminist perspective that the behaviors themselves are not defined as acceptable, but rather, they are defined as personal or private and not of interest to those outside the family. That is, men who force their wives or female friends to engage in sex are not defined as good or tolerated for the purposes of controlling women, but the offensive behavior which they exhibit is defined as private and personal and not suitable for control by society.

The feminist perspective can be seen as an application of social learning theory. Some authors suggest that traditional gender roles and expectations that define forced sexual intercourse as a normal aspect of male–female interaction thus encourage rape (Burt, 1980; Check & Malamuth, 1983a; Cherry, 1983; Curtis, 1975; Ewoldt, Monson, Langhinrichsen-Rohling, & Binderup, 2000; Russell, 1975; Vogel, 2000; Weis & Borges, 1977). Norms that define masculinity in terms of dominance and control and femininity in terms of passivity and submission define the use of force by men to control women as gender–role expectations that support or encourage forced sexual intercourse (Gagnon & Simon, 1973).

Social Learning Theory

From a learning theory perspective, forced sexual intercourse and the attitudes that support it are learned in the same ways that other behaviors are learned. Men who force women to have sex do so because they (and in some perspectives their victims) have learned that this is appropriate behavior. For the feminists, this learning is related to or associated with the set of values that supports the socioeconomic and political exploitation of women by men; nonfeminist social learning theorists see forced sexual intercourse as related to or associated with cultural traditions linked with interpersonal aggression, masculine roles, and sexuality.

Learning theory is a general term encompassing theories developed in a number of traditions, including symbolic interaction and cognitive attitude theory; however, much of the work that addresses rape is derived from Bandura's (1973) drive-based, psychoanalytic modeling theory, which addresses aggression. Ellis (1989, pp. 12–13) states that social learning theories of rape which assert that rape is a form of aggression state that these behaviors are learned in four ways: by imitating or modeling aggressive sexual behaviors which the learner has observed in real life or in media presentations (Huesman & Malamuth, 1986; Nelson, 1982); by observing sex and violence in the same context or presentation (Check & Malamuth, 1983b; Malamuth 1981, 1984, 1986, 1988; Malamuth, Briere, & Check, 1986); by repeating or portraying rape myths that make rape acceptable (Burt, 1980); and by the desensitization of the learner to the victim's perspective through repetition of exposure to incidents of sex and violence or of violent sex (Donnerstein, Linz, & Penrod, 1987).

The Sociobiological Perspective

The sociobiological perspective asserts that humanity is a product of evolution in which both physical and social traits conducive to survival are selected and survive through a process of natural selection. Propagation is key to survival of a trait, as a genetic predisposition can be passed on only through offspring. The linkage of sexual selection and rape with trait survival was first made by Deutsch (1944). Social traits that have been selected include female emphasis on child care and male emphasis on mating with as many partners as possible (Bateman, 1948; Chamove, Harlow, & Mitchell, 1967; Daly & Wilson, 1978; Hagen, 1979; Leshner, 1978; Smith, 1978; Symons, 1979; Trivers, 1972; Williams, 1975; Wilson, 1975). From a sociobiological perspective, men have a lower commitment to gestation than women (Quinsey, 1984) but have a disadvantage in that they cannot definitely identify their children (Daly & Wilson, 1978; Dawkins, 1976; Durden-Smith & deSimone, 1983); thus an inclination to impregnate as many females as possible has gene survival value. In this model, forced sexual intercourse increases the survival of a male's genes, thus selecting a tendency to rape (Gibson, Linden, & Johnson, 1980; Hagen, 1979; Quinsey, 1984; Symons, 1979). On the other hand, females who resist males who impregnate them and move on to other females are more likely to pass on their genes. The use of force to gain sexual access reduces the ability of a female to choose a mate who will stay with her after insemination. The absence of a male partner decreases the likelihood of survival of her children (Mellen, 1981; Richard & Schulman, 1982; Symons, 1979; Thornhill, 1980; Wilder, 1982). From this, rape would be a particularly effective strategy in modern times for men who have limited resources with which to attract a mate (Shields & Shields, 1983; Thornhill & Thornhill, 1983).

Social Disorganization and Legitimate Violence

Baron and Straus (1989) advance two additional theoretical perspectives for explaining rape: social disorganization and legitimate violence. Social disorganization occurs when social institutions and norms that regulate social conduct become ineffective (Blumer, 1937; Martindale, 1957; Mower, 1941; Thomas & Zaniecki, 1927; Wirth, 1940). When society's social control is weakened, deviant behavior and crime, including rape, are more likely to occur. Baron and Straus (1989) constructed a social disorganization index and discovered that when their measure of social disorganization is high, rates of rape are high.

Legitimate violence begins with the recognition that some theoretical perspectives define rape as normatively permitted rather than as beyond the control of society. Baron and Straus (1989) note that the feminists argue the presence of such norms (Brownmiller, 1975; Scully & Marolla, 1985).

Baron and Straus (1989) also note that a number of perspectives suggest that the legitimacy of rape might be supported indirectly. They cite violent subculture theories (Gastil, 1971; Hackney, 1969; Messner,1983; Wolfgang & Ferracuti, 1967) and cross-cultural theories that demonstrate a link between types of violence (Lambert, Triandis, & Wolf, 1959; Archer & Gartner, 1984; Huggins & Straus, 1980) and between violence and sexual violence (Sanday, 1981) as well as between violence and sexual violence in the United States (Amir, 1971). These findings are taken by Baron and Straus to support a cultural spillover theory of criminal violence. As the extent to which society approves the legitimate use of violence in some areas increases, the use of violence in rape and in collateral areas, such as personal assault, increases.

STATE OF THE ART

The theories that have been developed to explain forced sexual intercourse tend to treat forced sexual intercourse as a single type of behavior. Because forced sexual intercourse is seen as a single phenomenon, scholars have sought to develop a single theory. The theories that have been developed tend to be most effective in explaining incidents of forced sexual intercourse in which a man intends to force a women to have sex when she does not want to have sex, when physical force or the threat of physical force is used, and when the woman defines her victimization as rape. If the nature of the interaction between the victim and offender is such that forced sexual intercourse produces different sets of phenomena, a single model theory will not be sufficient to describe accurately the phenomena under study.

The criminal status of forced sexual intercourse in marriage is still evolving. Historically, forced sexual intercourse in marriage was specifically excluded in definitions of rape to the extent that the "marital exemption" was an accepted legal principle (LaFave & Scott, 1972; Palmer, 1997; Yllo, 1998).

The rationales for the adoption of the marital rape exemption include the following:

1. The marriage contract, which some people would argue dissolves the woman's rights and enhances the rights of the husband as the head of the house. A woman's consent to marriage has been extended to imply consent to submit to the wishes of the husband and can only be revoked by divorce.

2. The legal definition of rape. Historically, rape has been defined as a property crime and women were considered the property of their husbands or fathers. In *People* v. *Liberta* (1984), the court stated: "[T]he purpose behind the proscriptions [against rape] was to protect the chastity of women and thus their property value to their husbands and fathers" (at 567).

3. Marital unity (the belief that husbands and wives become one after marriage). If this is true, a man cannot rape himself (Brown, 1995; Sitton, 1993).

These rationales are no longer applicable to married women because the roles of women in society have changed dramatically.

Contemporary proponents of marital rape suggest that marital rape is not as serious as other types of rape (Sitton, 1993). It is argued that the closer the relationship between the victim and the perpetrator, the more a victim feels violated both physically and mentally. In fact, the victim may be more traumatized because of the relationship. Additionally, some proponents fear that having a marital rape classification would cause false rape claims to be made by angry wives who seek to damage or destroy their husband's reputation. Another issue raised in opposition to the inclusion of a marital rape classification was the possible impact on marital stability (Sitton, 1993). It is hard to imagine a marriage that is stable if the husband is raping his wife.

Regardless of which argument one examines concerning marital rape, the result is the same: Women are not equal beings in our society. According to Sitton (1993), "throughout our legal and cultural tradition, the woman is either a virgin or a whore, alternatively someone to be placed on a pedestal or in the bedroom" (p. 268). Again, previous views and role expectations associated with women are no longer applicable. Fortunately, in *Trammell* v. *United States* (1980), the Court ruled that women are not chattel and are no less than other human beings. Other reform measures toward gender equality have assisted in solidifying the legal status of women. Challenges to the marital rape exemption have been based on the constitutional right to privacy, a broad and private-sphere interpretation of the Thirteenth Amendment, and the Fourteenth Amendment. For a more thorough examination of the arguments regarding marital rape based on the Constitution and its amendments, see Dailey (1986), *Merton* v. *State* (1986), McConnell (1992), *People* v. *Liberta* (1984), *Reed* v. *Reed* (1971), and West (1990).

The lines are clearly drawn from a social activist perspective: Forced sexual intercourse in marriage is either rape or a husband's privilege, depending on the perspective of the speaker. It is more likely that this is an issue of public versus private interest rather than a matter of male rights. That is, few will actually believe that men who force their wives to engage in sex are behaving in a legally acceptable manner. The behavior is perceived as wrong but not a matter that should be resolved by the police and the criminal courts. Confusion is added by the prospect that there is an expectation of sexual access in marriage and a corresponding obligation of the wife to submit to her husband that is endorsed by both many men and many women (endorsement of "traditional values") (Bullough, 1974; Williams, 1979). Setting the legal arguments aside, the question of behavioral similarity remains. Is forced sexual intercourse in marriage the same or more similar to the behavior exhibited when a stranger forces an unwilling victim, or the same as or more similar to forced sexual intercourse in a courtship setting? It is possible that forced sexual intercourse in marriage is not a matter of sexual access but a matter of power and domination. It is also possible that there are two types of forced sexual intercourse in marriage: the first reflecting power and dominance, the second reflecting forcing sexual access from an unwilling spouse.

TYPES OF FORCED SEXUAL INTERCOURSE

Some scholars have focused on the development of theoretical models that address forced sexual intercourse in dating or courtship settings. Most studies with a theoretical base attempt to identify factors that make types of assault more or less likely to occur. One effort (Shotland, 1992) develops a basic typology of date rape. Five different types of date rape are characterized, based on time, courtship violence, and degree of development of a relationship. Felson (1992) has developed a model that seeks to explain sexual assaults in terms of motives and goals. He identifies five paths, using factors such as social identity, bodily pleasure, personal justice, domination, sexual relations, and harm to target.

The present theories that focus on rape are not effective in describing all of the events that presently are included under the terms *date rape, acquaintance rape*, and *marital rape*. In some incidents that are identified as date rape, a man intentionally forces a woman to have sex when she doesn't want to, using substantial force, and the woman defines her victimization as rape. In other instances that are identified as date rape, the man may not intend to force the woman to have sex, the degree of force may be less substantial, and the woman may not define her victimization as rape. In the first instance, a rape has occurred that can be explained with one or more of the existing models; the incident just happened to occur in a dating context. In the second instance, the behavior is offensive and unacceptable by standards that are emerging today, but the behavior cannot be explained accurately with existing theories. The inability to describe the nature of the phenomenon reduces the ability to address effectively what is clearly a contemporary social problem.

The data available from studies of forced sexual intercourse consistently have identified sets of incidents in which the forced sexual intercourse reported by victims is not identified as rape, beginning with Russell's (1984) early study. About one-half of the women who indicated that they had experienced incidents that met the legal definition of rape in use at that time did not respond affirmatively when asked if they had been raped. Similar results were reported by a leading study in the area of date rape. Koss, Dinero, Seibel, and Cox (1988) reported 23.1 percent of the women victimized by men they knew labeled their victimization as rape, and 62 percent of these victims indicated that they did not view their victimization as any type of crime. Similar results have been reported by Johnson, Palileo, and Gray (1992), Doyle and Burfeind (1994), Johnson and Sigler (1997), and other studies that report findings for women's characterizations of their victimization.

A BEGINNING MODEL

We argue that all instances of forced sexual intercourse are not the same—that there are substantial differences among various sets of sexually offensive behaviors. Although existing theories provide an effective basis for dealing with those cases in which a man intends to rape a woman who realizes that she is being raped, they are less effective in explaining many of the victimizations which are presently included under the labels of date or acquaintance rape.

At this point we suggest that alternative models should be developed to explain different types of forced sexual intercourse. Based on the knowledge available today, four types of forced sexual intercourse can be identified that are substantially different from each other. These models are biased in that they assume that the victim is always a woman and the offender is always a man. Although the same models might apply to homosexual relationships or to cases in which a woman victimizes a man, the limited information available in these areas makes it difficult to attempt model development. We identify four types of forced sexual intercourse: rape, spousal rape, forced sexual intercourse in a dating or courtship context, and predatory rape.

Rape occurs when a man who is unknown or known casually to the victim uses physical force or threat of physical force to secure sexual access against the wishes of the victim. Both the offender and the victim tend to identify the behavior as rape. This form of forced sexual intercourse has been studied more extensively than other forms of forced sexual intercourse, and several models are available to explain the behavior, many of which suggest that the behavior is not sexual in nature.

Spousal rape occurs when a man uses physical force or the threat of physical force against a woman to secure sexual access against her will from a partner with whom he has established a relatively permanent relationship. Definition of the behavior as rape will vary from offender to offender and from victim to victim. A relatively permanent relationship is defined as a relationship that includes sexual intimacy as a part of the relationship and is not limited to couples who share the same living area (cohabitation). Very little information is available about this form of behavior. Most of the literature that addresses this issue focuses on the legal and ethical dimensions of the issue rather than on understanding the nature of the interaction between the actors. Placing this behavior in the context of marital disputes and spouse abuse may be more effective than addressing the issue in the context of forced sexual intercourse as a sexual act, even when sexual access is the primary goal of the offender.

Forced sexual intercourse in a dating or courtship context occurs when a man uses physical force to secure sexual access without her consent from a woman with whom he is developing a relationship while the couple is engaged in a consensual intimate social context. Definition of the behavior as rape will vary from offender to offender and from victim to victim. This type of forced sexual intercourse applies only to events that occur as the relationship is developing. It is probable that sexual access is the primary motivator in these types of exchanges. In most cases, the man does not enter the exchange with the intent of using force. These events tend to be characterized as involving loss of control and may be better understood in the context of courtship than as independent acts of sexual assault.

Predatory rape occurs when a man pretends to engage in legitimate dating or courtship behavior with the intent of using force to gain sexual access against the will of the woman if he cannot gain consent. The offender will tend to identify his behavior as rape, but the victim may or may not define the behavior as rape. In these cases the offender is not seeking a personal or intimate relationship; rather, he is seeking sexual relief and has no concern for the feelings, rights, or needs of his victim. He intends to maneuver the victim into a comprising position so that she will not protest after the act has been completed, and he will use almost any means necessary to achieve his goal. Very little is known about this behavior; thus the development of an accurate model is difficult. These men are identifiable in data that have been collected by the authors (Johnson & Sigler, 1997).

FORCED SEXUAL INTERCOURSE IN A COURTSHIP OR DATING CONTEXT

Sufficient data are now available to permit the development and testing of a model designed to explain the nature of forced sexual intercourse in a dating context. Although all factors that might operate in instances of forced sexual intercourse in these situations have not been clearly identified by contemporary efforts to examine forced sexual intercourse, sufficient information has been gleaned to permit the development of a tentative model that can be used to guide further research. The model only addresses behavior that has generally been characterized as date or acquaintance rape and does not address stranger rape, spousal rape, or predatory rape.

The model advanced here suggests that some forms of forced sexual intercourse should be examined in the context of courtship or dating. Courtship is defined as a set of activities that are undertaken with the intent of establishing a fairly permanent relationship. Although some undetermined portion of dating is primarily temporary and recreational in nature, much of dating has a courtship function. Participants in recreational dating are, in many instances, evaluating their partners in terms of potential suitability as long-term partners. Dating is an activity that leads to courtship when a potential partner is identified. Although this shift in emphasis is usually not noted formally, most of those who actively date are aware of the potential in their activity.

A couple progresses from casual dating to a committed, long-term, relatively permanent relationship in a process that can be characterized by degrees of increasing intimacy. Both partners tend to assume that at some point, sexual intimacy will become a part of the relationship as the relationship matures. For most couples, this assumption is not overtly recognized, the stages through which a relationship moves to maturity are not specified, and the circumstances under which sexual intimacy will occur are not addressed overtly. The process, in terms of increasing commitment, is one of advancing and retreating as the relationship moves toward the development of a relatively permanent relationship. Forced sexual intercourse can occur when the process of relationship formation gets out of control.

In Western society, women are expected to control the degree of sexual intimacy at each stage in the development of the relationship. Men are expected to seek increasing degrees of sexual intimacy as a relationship develops and women are expected to resist male pressure until the relationship matures to the point at which the women feels comfortable committing to sexual intimacy. Women have personal standards that must be met before they are willing to engage in increased sexual intimacy, particularly sexual intercourse. Couples generally do not discuss the conditions that must be met before complete sexual intimacy becomes a part of the relationship. Although these standards are individual, they can include such things as a determination with a high degree of certainty by the woman that this man is the person with whom she wishes to establish a permanent relationship; he will not abuse her at a later date, he is as committed to her as she is to him, and he (as well as her friends, his friends, and other significant others) will not label her negatively if she agrees to complete sexual intimacy. Men who are aware that such standards exist usually are not aware of the standards held by the person with whom they are seeking to establish a relatively permanent relationship.

"Real" men are expected to be aggressive. Men who express an unwillingness to be physically aggressive are generally labeled negatively. Aggression by men in the courtship process produces a situation in which men attempt assertively to move the courtship process to increasing levels of sexual intimacy, while women resist these efforts in favor of a more deliberate and cautious development of the relationship. Men place pressure on women to move forward with commitment to the relationship while women want to move forward but not as fast as the men are requesting. Moving toward sexual intimacy is an interactive process frequently involving a trial-and-error process or advancing and retreating from complete sexual intimacy as the couple works to develop a long-term, stable, relatively permanent relationship. An out-of-control situation can develop that can produce forced sexual intercourse when unclear expectations produce unacceptable behavior, biological arousal reduces rational behavior for one or for both parties, or the level of male aggression is greater than the woman anticipated.

Some women consent to sexual intimacy when they do not really want to be intimate. There are a number of circumstances under which unwilling consent is given. This behavior may be more common in established sexually intimate relationships. Once a relationship has moved to a level including sexual intimacy, the man may desire sexual intimacy at times when the woman does not or more frequently than the woman prefers. Women sometimes will agree to sexual intimacy when they would rather not, in order to meet the man's needs. In cases in which a relationship is developing, at times a woman may hesitate to commit to complete sexual intimacy although she has decided that she will become sexually intimate at some point in the relationship with the man she is dating. As the relationship develops, she may respond to the man's pressure to agree to sexual intimacy before she is certain that she is ready for the relationship to move to that particular level of intimacy. Men generally believe that if they are persistent, some women will consent when they are not certain about their decision. Some men are not sufficiently sensitive to realize that they are forcing the women with whom they have a relationship to be sexually intimate.

The factors that have been advanced as important to a model which seeks to explain incidents of nonpredatory forced sexual intercourse include (1) the relationship formation process in which couples become increasingly intimate, (2) role expectations for aggressive behavior in courtship (more rapid development of the relationship), (3) role expectations for women to resist male aggression in courtship (less rapid development of the relationship), (4) women control (decide) when the relationship will move to more intense levels of sexual intimacy, (5) women have standards (conditions) that must be satisfied before they agree to sexual intimacy, (6) some women will consent to sexual intimacy when they don't really want to be sexually intimate, and (7) men are aware that women will consent at times when they don't want to be sexually intimate, but men are usually not aware of or sensitive to the existence of or nature of the standards or conditions that women hold for their own commitment to sexual intimacy. When these factors are applied to instances of forced sexual intercourse in courtship and dating, a number of patterns emerge (Johnson & Sigler, 1997).

In some situations, both the man and the woman anticipate and are moving toward eventual intense sexual intimacy. They engage in preliminary sexually intimate behavior, and at a point in the relationship, the situation gets out of control. The man forces the woman to have sex while they are engaging in consensual sexual activity. In these cases, it is probable that neither the man nor the woman will label the behavior as rape, psychological damage will be minimal, and both the man and the woman may choose to continue to develop a long-term relationship and have positive images of each other (Johnson & Sigler, 1997).

In some instances, the woman considers intense sexual intimacy a possibility at some point, but she has not yet committed to the development of a permanent relationship. She engages in some exploratory sexual activity even though she may not anticipate a permanent relationship. During a period of intimacy, the man forces the woman to have intercourse. In these cases, both the woman and the man might or might not define the incident as rape. If the woman defines the incident as rape, she will terminate the relationship and have mixed or negative opinions of the man. Psychological damage will be moderate to high. If the woman does not define the incident as rape, she may continue the relationship and have mixed opinions of the man. Psychological damage will be low to moderate (Johnson & Sigler, 1997).

In some situations, the woman will hold a value that prohibits sexual intercourse before a firm permanent relationship is established, but she engages in some intimate sexual behavior in the process of seeking a relationship. During a period of consensual sexual activity the man forces the woman to have sexual intercourse. In these cases the woman will define the incident as rape and the man may or may not define the incident as rape. The woman will terminate the relationship and have mixed but predominately negative opinions of the man in that there are characteristics that she found attractive that were not related to his sexual aggression. She will not continue the relationship, and in most cases psychological damage will be high (Johnson & Sigler, 1997).

This model suggests that the development of an agreement to engage in consensual sexual intercourse in a dating or courtship setting is a negotiated process in which the woman grants sexual access to the man when specific personal conditions (personal standards) are met. It is acceptable for men to actively pursue sexual intercourse, and this pursuit is not channeled by the woman's conditions for agreeing to sexual intimacy, because these conditions (woman's expectations) frequently are not clear.

The development of a relatively stable intimate relationship involves exploratory sexual behavior in which the couple approaches but does not necessarily engage in sexual intercourse. If this process gets out of control, forced sexual intercourse might occur because the man is larger and stronger and/or because the woman cannot manage to withdraw without permanently damaging a relationship she may want to preserve. When forced sexual intercourse occurs in this context, the woman may accept responsibility for the outcome, and the man might see this as an acceptable/anticipated outcome.

This model only addresses forced sexual intercourse that occurs during a legitimate pursuit of a relatively long-term relationship and does not address forced sexual intercourse labeled as predatory, blitz, or confidence rape. In the latter, a male predator engages in dating or courtship behavior to gain a position from which he can relatively safely force a woman to submit to sexual intercourse. He does not intend to develop a long-term relationship but pretends to pursue a relationship in order to gain sexual access by trick or fraud. If his efforts to gain consensual sexual access are not successful, he might use whatever degree of force is necessary to gain sexual access. The characterization of this behavior as courtship behavior provides some protection from sanctioning for the offender. It should be noted that research to date has not indicated that women are able to distinguish between the predatory rapist and the legitimate suitor until after she has been victimized successfully, and it is possible that she may not be certain after her victimization. This behavior can be explained more successfully by traditional theories of rape than by a courtship model of forced sexual intercourse.

The model will not effectively address marital rape or rape that occurs in relatively stable relationships in which sexual intercourse has been accepted as a normal part of the relationship. Although sufficient empirical attention has not been devoted to an examination of these phenomena to permit preliminary model development, it is probable that models that stress dominance and control rather than sexual access are more appropriate than other models. Power and dominance or sexual needs may drive the offender, but the behavior occurs in the context of a relatively permanent relationship and may be better understood in the context of the dynamics of the relationship, particularly the dynamics of conflict resolution, than in the context of rape or the context of courtship and dating.

The courtship model advanced here will not effectively address situations in which sexual intercourse is a potential form of recreation rather than an activity that occurs in a relatively permanent relationship. In situations in which both the man and the woman define sexual intercourse as a recreational option in casual dating, the behavioral patterns might be similar but accelerated with different interpretations of expectations and processes held by the actors. If a man forces a woman to have sex in this setting, new models might need to be developed or traditional theories of rape may be more effective in understanding and investigating the behavior. Little empirical attention has been directed toward these phenomena, so any assessment is pure speculation at this point.

The model advanced here is a simplification of a very complex system of interactions that comprise dating and courtship. There is a need for extensive further research directed toward increasing our understanding of all forms of forced sexual intercourse. An effort must be made to determine if different types of phenomena are addressed under the labels of date rape and under the more general category of rape. If there are differences, are they such that if they were fully understood, effective strategies to protect women could be developed? The questions that must be addressed are extensive. What are the factors in the individual settings that are more likely to precipitate the use of physical force? What are the interactional characteristics of these situations? What are the factors that cause some people to be more likely than others to use physical force in intimate situations? When the relevant variables are identified, patterns can be defined and resources can be allocated effectively and efficiently. The model presented here can provide a focus for this research once it is articulated and tested more fully.

SUMMARY

Forced sexual intercourse has been perceived as a single phenomenon throughout history. There has been a great deal of evolution in the reaction of the justice system with many acts of forced sexual intercourse that were considered private matters becoming criminalized. All forms of forced sexual intercourse have been defined as parts of a social problem that has emerged because changing social values regarding the roles of women and men in society and in intimate relationships have created a change in the degree of public interest in women's victimization.

Before effective responses to all forms of forced sexual intercourse can be developed, these phenomena must be understood. A first step in increasing understanding of the phenomena is to recognize that the same behaviors may be different phenomena in different social contexts. Some forms of forced sexual intercourse occur between relatively intimate partners, and one form of forced sexual intercourse might be substantially different from other forms of forced sexual intercourse. That is, types of forced sexual intercourse must be examined in the social context in which they occur.

Rape has consistently been evaluated in terms of aggression, dominance, control, and violence rather than in terms of sexual access. Historically, rape has been a crime that has been condemned, if not effectively prosecuted. Reforms in the past decade have introduced changes in the law that create different levels of sexual assault and that make cases of sexual assault easier to prosecute successfully. Social concern that accompanied reform efforts on intimate violence as well as on forced sexual intercourse has focused attention on the prevalence and nature of forced sexual intercourse.

Most theories that attempt to explain rape treat rape as a single phenomenon. All forms of forced sexual intercourse are seen as the same thing. The feminist perspective argues that rape is a characteristic of male-dominated patriarchal societies. Threat of rape functions to control and dominate women, forcing them into passive submissive roles.

Learning theories, from a number of perspectives, specify that the use of force in sexual encounters is learned in the same way that other behaviors and values are learned. The most prominent of these are drive-based psychoanalytic theories that are related to the work of Bandura (1973). Most other learning theorists, sociologists, and criminologists have not applied their perspectives directly to the explanation of forced sexual intercourse.

Sociobiologists argue that males who use force in sexual intercourse will be more likely to pass their genes on to future generations, in that access to the greatest number of partners maximizes gene survival. Women, on the other hand, maximize the transmission of their genes to future generations by attracting males who will remain with them after insemination to care for the children. Baron and Straus (1989) added models based on social disorganization and on legitimate use of violence to other existing traditional models to advance an integrated model to explain rape. Although their model effectively combines the elements of many of the traditional theories, it still treats rape as a single phenomenon in which a male intends to use force to obtain sex from an unwilling resisting female who sees herself as being raped.

The argument advanced in this chapter is that there are types or sets of related forms of forced sexual intercourse that are sufficiently different as to require separate explanatory models if the phenomena are to be understood and examined effectively. In rape, a man forces a women whom he does not know or whom he does not know very well to have sex with him. In spousal rape, a man who is in a fairly long-term sexual relationship with a woman forces her to have sex. In predatory rape, a man pretends to engage in a legitimate dating relationship with a woman in order to manipulate her into a position in which he can force her to have sex with him. In forced sexual intercourse during courtship and dating, a man and a woman are developing a long-term relationship. In the process, one or both of the actors loses control and the man forces the woman to have sex.

An expanded model for forced sexual intercourse in dating or courtship has been developed that can be used to frame future research in this area. This model assumes that the process of establishing a relatively permanent or long-term relationship involves progressively more intimate interaction as the relationship matures, with sexual inter-course anticipated at some point in the relationship. The point at which sexual intercourse becomes a part of the relationship and the conditions that must be met before this level of commitment to the relationship is accepted is determined by the woman. As the rela-tionship moves to increasingly intimate contact, the potential for loss of control and the use of force increases. In these cases, neither the man nor the woman is likely to define the behavior as rape.

This model will be refined and assessed through empirical examination. As the model develops, a more thorough and accurate understanding of the use of force in intimate relationships will emerge. As conceptualization of the phenomenon becomes more thorough and accurate, more effective responses will be developed for the justice system, and more effective educational materials can be developed to reduce the victimization of women at the hands of those with whom they seek to develop long-term, relatively permanent relationships.

REFERENCES

ADAMEC, C. S., & ADAMEC, R. E. (1981). Aggression by men against women: Adaptation or aberration? *International Journal of Women's Studies, 1*, 1–21.

AMIR, M. (1971). *Patterns in forcible rape*. Chicago: University of Chicago Press.

ARCHER, D., & GARTNER, R. (1984). *Violence and crime in cross-national perspective*. New Haven, CT: Yale University Press.

BANDURA, A. (1973). *Aggression: A social learning analysis*. Englewood Cliffs, NJ: Prentice Hall.

BARON, L., & STRAUS, M. A. (1984). Sexual stratification, pornography, and rape in the United States. In M. N. Malamuth & E. Donnerstein (Eds.), *Pornography and sexual aggression* (pp. 185–209). Orlando, FL: Academic Press.

BARON, L., & STRAUS, M. A. (1989). *Four theories of rape in American society: A state level analysis*. New Haven, CT: Yale University Press.

BARRY, K. (1979). *Female sexual slavery*. Englewood Cliffs, NJ: Prentice Hall.

BATEMAN, A. J. (1948). Introsexual selection in *Drosophila. Heredity, 2*, 349–68.

BENDERLY, B. L. (1982). Rape free or rape prone? *Science, 82*(3), 40–3.

BLUMER, H. (1937). Social organization and individual disorganization. *American Journal of Sociology, 42*, 871–877.

BROWN, E. (1995). Changing the marital rape exception: I am chattel; hear me roar. *American Journal of Trial Advocacy, 18*(3), 657–671.

BROWNMILLER, S. (1975). *Against our will: Men, women, and rape*. New York: Simon & Schuster.

BULLOUGH, V. L. (1974). *The subordinate sex: A history of attitudes toward women*. Baltimore: Penguin.

BURT, M. R. (1980). Cultural myths and supports for rape, *Journal of Personality and Social Psychology, 38*, 217–234.

CAUFFMAN, E., FELDMAN, S., JENSEN, L., & ARNETT, D. (2000). The (un)acceptability of violence against peers and dates. *Journal of Adolescent Research, 15*(6), 652–673.

CHAMOVE, A., HARLOW, H. F., & MITCHELL, G. D. (1967). Sex differences in the infant-directed behavior of preadolescent *Rhesus* monkeys. *Child Development, 38*, 329–355.

CHECK, J. V. P., & MALAMUTH, N. M. (1983a). Sex-role stereotyping and reactions to stranger vs. acquaintance rape. *Journal of Personality and Social Psychology, 45*, 344–356.

CHECK, J. V. P., & MALAMUTH, N. M. (1983b). Can participation in pornography experiments have positive effects? *Journal of Sex Research, 20*, 14–31.

CHERRY, F. (1983). Gender roles and sexual violence. In E. R. Allgeier & N. B. McCormick (Eds.), *Changing boundaries: Gender roles and sexual behavior* (pp. 245–260). Palo Alto, CA: Mayfield Publishing.

COWLING, M. (1998). *Date rape and consent*. Brookfield, VT: Ashgate Publishing.

CURTIS, L. A. (1975). *Violence, race, and culture*. Lexington, MA: Lexington Press.

DAILEY, A. (1986). To have and to hold: The marital rape exemption and the Fourteenth Amendment. *Harvard Law Review, 99*, 1255.

DALY, M., & WILSON, M. (1978). *Sex, evolution, and behavior*. North Scituate, MA: Duxbury Press.

DAWKINS, R. (1976). *The selfish gene*. New York: Oxford University Press.

DEUTSCH, H. (1944). *The psychology of women*, Vol. 1, *Girlhood*. New York: Bantam Books.

DOBASH, R. E. (1979). *Violence against wives: A case against the patriarchy*. New York: Free Press.

DONNERSTEIN, E., LINZ, D., & PENROD, S. (1987). *The question of pornography*. New York: Free Press.

DOYLE, D. P., & BURFEIND, J. W. (1994). *The University of Montana sexual victimization survey executive summary*. Missoula, MT: Author.

DURDEN-SMITH, J., & DESIMONE, D. (1983). *Sex and the brain*. New York: Warner Publishing.

ELLIS, L. (1989). *Theories of rape: Inquiries into the causes of sexual aggression*. New York: Hemisphere Publishing.

EWOLDT, C. A., MONSON, C. M., LANGHINRICHSEN-ROHLING, J., & BINDERUP, T. (2000). Youth dating violence. *Adolescence, 35*, 455–465.

FELSON, R. B. (1992). *Motives for sexual coercion.* Paper presented at the annual meeting of the American Society of Criminology, Tucson, AZ.

FRIEDAN, B. (1963). *The feminine mystique.* New York: W.W. Norton.

GAGNON, J. H., & SIMON, W. (1973). *Sexual conduct: The sources of sexuality.* Chicago: Aldine.

GASTIL, R. D. (1971). Homicide and a regional culture of violence. *American Sociological Review, 36,* 412–427.

GIBSON, L., LINDEN, R., & JOHNSON, S. (1980). A situational theory of rape. *Canadian Journal of Criminology, 22,* 51–63.

GOTH, A. N. (1979). *Men who rape: The psychology of the offender.* New York: Plenum Press.

HACKNEY, S. (1969). Southern violence. *American Historical Review, 74,* 906–925.

HAGEN, R. (1979). *The bio-social factor.* Garden City, NJ: Doubleday.

HOLDSTROM, L. L., & BURGESS, A. W. (1980). Sexual behavior of assailants during reported rapes. *Archives of Sexual Behavior, 9,* 427–439.

HUESMAN, L. R., & MALAMUTH, N. M. (1986). Media violence and antisocial behavior: An overview. *Journal of Social Issues, 42,* 1–6.

HUGGINS, M. D., & STRAUS, M. A. (1980). Violence and the social structure as reflected in children's books from 1850 to 1970. In M. A. Strauss & G. T. Hotaling (Eds.), *The social causes of husband–wife violence* (pp. 51–67). Minneapolis, MN: University of Minnesota Press.

JOHNSON, D. G., PALILEO, G. J., & GRAY, N. B. (1992). Date rape on a southern campus: Reports from 1991. *Sociology and Social Research, 76*(2), 37–41.

JOHNSON, I. M., & SIGLER, R. T. (1997). *Forced sexual intercourse in intimate relationships.* Brookfield, VT: Ashgate Publishing.

KOSS, M. P., DINERO, T. E., SEIBEL, C. A., & COX, S. (1988). Stranger and acquaintance rape: Are there differences in the victim's experience? *Psychology of Women Quarterly, 12,* 1–24.

KUTCHINSKI, B. (1988). Towards an exploration of the decrease in registered sex crimes in Copenhagen. *Technical report of the Commission on Obscenity and Pornography,* Vol. 7. Washington, DC: U.S. Government Printing Office.

LAFAVE, W. R., & SCOTT, A. W. (1972). *Handbook on criminal law.* St. Paul, MN: West Publishing.

LAMBERT, W. W., TRIANDIS, L. M., & WOLF, M. (1959). Some correlates of beliefs in the malevolence and benevolence of supernatural beings: A cross cultural study. *Journal of Abnormal and Social Psychology, 58,* 162–169.

LESHNER, A. L. (1978). *An introduction to behavioral endocrinology.* New York: Oxford University Press.

MALAMUTH, N. M. (1981). Rape proclivity among males, *Journal of Social Issues, 37*(4), 138–157.

MALAMUTH, N. M. (1984). Aggression against women. In N. A. Malamuth & E. Donnerstein (Eds.), *Pornography and sexual aggression.* Orlando, FL: Academic Press.

MALAMUTH, N. M. (1986). Predictors of naturalistic sexual aggression. *Journal of Personality and Social Psychology, 50,* 953–962.

MALAMUTH, N. M. (1988). Predicting laboratory aggression against female and male targets: Implications for sexual. *Journal of Personality and Social Psychology, 50,* 330–340.

MALAMUTH, N., BRIERE, J., & CHECK, J. V. P. (1986). Sexual arousal in response to aggression: Ideology, aggressive, and sexual correlates. *Journal of Personality and Social Psychology, 50,* 330–340.

MARTINDALE, D. (1957). Social disorganization: The conflict of normative and empirical approaches. In H. Becker & A. Boskoff (Eds.), *Modern sociological theory in continuity and change* (pp. 340–367). New York: Rinehart & Winston.

MCCONNELL, J. (1992). Beyond metaphor: Battered women, involuntary servitude and the thirteenth amendment. *Yale Law Review, 4,* pp. 207–249.

MELLEN, S. L. (1981). *The evolution of love.* San Francisco: Freeman Press.

MESSNER, S. F. (1983). Regional and racial effects on the urban homicide rate: The subculture of violence revisited. *American Journal of Sociology, 88,* 997–1007.

MOWER, E. R. (1941). Methodological problems in social disorganization. *American Sociological Review, 6,* 639–649.

NELSON, E. (1982). Pornography and sexual aggression. In M. Yaffee & E. Nelson (Eds.), *The influence of pornography on behavior*. London: Academic Press.

PALMER, S. (1997). Rape in marriage and the European Convention on Human Rights. *Feminist Legal Studies, 5*, 91–97.

PERSELL, C. H. (1984). *Understanding society*. New York: Harper & Row.

QUINSEY, V. L. (1984). Sexual aggression: Studies of offenders against women. In D. Weisstub (Ed.), *Law and mental health: International perspectives*, Vol. 1. New York: Pergamon Press.

RICHARD, A. F., & SCHULMAN, S. R. (1982). Sociobiology: Primate field studies. *Annual Review in Anthropology, 11*, 231–255.

RIGER, S., & GORDON, M. T. (1981). The fear of rape: A study in social control. *Journal of Social Issues, 37*(4), 71–92.

RUSSELL, D. E. (1975). *The politics of rape: The victim's perspective*. New York: Stein and Day.

RUSSELL, D. E. H. (1984). *Sexual exploitation: Rape, child sexual abuse, and workplace harassment*. Beverly Hills, CA: Sage Publications.

SANDAY, P. R. (1981). The socio-cultural context of rape: A cross-cultural study. *Journal of Social Issues, 37*, 5–27.

SCARPITTI, F., & SCARPITTI, E. (1977). Victims of rape. *Transaction, 14*, 29–32.

SCHWENDINGER, J., & SCHWENDINGER, H. (1985). Homo economics as the rapist in sociobiology. In S. R. Sanday & E. Toch (Eds.), *Violence against women* (pp. 85–114). New York: Gordian Press.

SCULLY, D., & MAROLLA, J. (1984). Convicted rapists' vocabulary of motives: Excuses and justifications. *Social Problems, 32*, 530–544.

SCULLY, D., & MAROLLA, J. (1985). Riding the bull at Gilly's: Convicted rapists describe the rewards of rape. *Social Problems, 32*, 251–262.

SHIELDS, W. M., & SHIELDS, L. M. (1983). Forcible rape: An evolutionary perspective. *Ethnology and Sociobiology, 4*, 115–136.

SHOTLAND, R. L. (1992). A theory of the causes of courtship rape. *Journal of Social Issues, 48*, 127–144.

SIGELMAN, C. K., BERRY, C. J., & WILES, K. A. (1984). Violence in college students' dating relationships. *Journal of Applied Social Psychology, 14*, 530–548.

SITTON, J. (1993). Old wine in new bottles: The "marital" rape allowance. *North Carolina Law Review, 72*(1), 261–289.

SMITH, J. M. (1978). *The evolution of sex*. New York: Cambridge University Press.

SUNDAY, S. R., & TOBACH, E. (1985). *Violence against women: A critique of the sociobiology of rape*. New York: Gordian Press.

SYMONS, D. (1979). *The evolution of human sexuality*. New York: Oxford University Press.

THOMAS, W. I., & ZANIECKI, F. (1927). *The Polish peasant in Europe and America*. New York: Knopf & Company.

THOMPSON, W. W. E., & BUTTELL, A. J. (1984). Sexual deviance in America. *Emporia State Research Studies, 33*, 6–47.

THORNHILL, R. (1980). Rape in *Panorpa* scorpionflies and a general rape hypothesis. *Animal Behavior, 28*, 55–59.

THORNHILL, R., & THORNHILL, N. W. (1983). Human rape: An evolutionary analysis. *Ethnology and Sociobiology, 4*, 137–173.

TRIVERS, R. (1972). Parental investment and sexual selection. In B. Campbell (Ed.), *Sexual selection and the descent of man* (pp. 136–179), Chicago: Aldine Publishing.

VOGEL, B. L. (2000). Correlates of pre-college males' sexual aggressions. *Women and Justice, 11*(3), 25–47.

WALKER, P. A., & MEYER, W. J. (1981). Medroxyprogesterone acetate treatment for paraphiliac sex offenders. In J. R. Hays (Ed.), *Violence and the violent individual*. New York: Spectrum.

WEIS, K., & BORGES, S. S. (1977). Victimology and rape: The case of the legitimate victim. In D. R. Nass (Ed.), *The rape victim* (pp. 35–75). Dubuque, IA: Kendall/Hunt.

WEST, R. (1990). Equality theory, marital rape and the promise of the Fourteenth Amendment. *Florida Law Review, 42,* 45.

WILDER, R. (1982, July). Are sexual standards inherited? *Science Digest,* p. 69.

WILLIAMS, G. C. (1975). *Sex and evolution.* Princeton, NJ: Princeton University Press.

WILLIAMS, J. E. (1979). Sex role stereotypes, women's liberation, and rape: A cross-cultural analysis of attitudes. *Sociological Symposium, 5*(1), 61–97.

WILSON, E. O. (1975). *Sociobiology: The new synthesis.* Cambridge, MA: Belknap Press of Harvard University.

WIRTH, L. (1940). Ideological aspects of social disorganization. *American Sociological Review, 5,* 472–482.

WOLFGANG, M., & FERRACUTI, F. (1967). *The subculture of violence.* London: Tavistock.

YEGIDIS, B. L. (1986). Date rape and forced sexual encounters among college students. *Journal of Sex Education and Therapy, 12,* 51–54.

YLLO, K. (1998). Wife rape: A social problem for the 21st century. *Violence Against Women, 5*(9), 989–1085.

CASES

Merton v. *State,* 500 So. 2d 1301-05 (Ala. Crim. App. 1986).

People v. *Liberta,* 474 N.E. 2d 567, 576 (1984).

Reed v. *Reed,* 404 U.S. 71, 92 S. Ct. 251, 30 L. Ed. 2d 255 (1971).

Trammell v. *United States,* 445 U.S. 40, 52 (1980).

23

Battered Women
on Mandatory Arrest Laws

A Comparison across Three States

Alisa Smith

In the 1960s and early 1970s, the needs of domestic violence victims were not being met by the criminal justice system. Arrests and prosecutions for domestic violence were not being conducted because the police and prosecutors viewed domestic violence as a "family problem" and inappropriate for criminal justice intervention. In response, feminists and victim advocates challenged these views and championed reform to strengthen the criminal justice response (Fagan, 1996). Several large civil case verdicts against police departments for their lack of response to domestic violence [e.g., *Thurman* v. *City of Torrington* (1984), and Sherman and Berk's (1984) report that arrest reduced the rate of recidivism compared to other responses to domestic violence] were also catalysts for change.

Victim advocates used the Sherman and Berk (1984) arrest findings to support legislative and policy changes. The Attorney General's Task Force on Family Violence endorsed the study's findings and recommended that state and local agencies adopt a pro-arrest policy toward domestic violence (Fagan, 1996; U.S. Attorney General, 1984). Mandatory and pro-arrest polices were adopted nearly nationwide. It was *assumed* that mandatory and pro-arrest laws would protect women from violence by increasing law enforcement involvement in the crime of domestic violence.

Evaluation research was conducted on the effectiveness of mandatory and pro-arrest laws after the nationwide implementation (Berk, Campbell, Klap, & Western, 1992; Dunford, Huizinga, & Elliott, 1990; Hirschel & Hutchinson 1992; Pate & Hamilton, 1992; Sherman et al., 1992; Steinman, 1988, 1990). The research findings were mixed. The replication studies failed to confirm the deterrence findings. Other research, however, found a reduction in recidivism rates (Steinman, 1991) and an increase in the number of arrests after the implementation of mandatory arrest laws (Jones & Belknap, 1999; Zorza & Woods, 1994). Little research, however, has explored the perceptions of battered women on mandatory arrest and its impact on *women's* actions. Few studies explore the potential and unintended consequences of mandatory arrest laws to deter battered women from contacting law enforcement (Buzawa, Hotaling, & Klein, 1998; Melton, 1999), and the findings that do exist have been contradictory (Martin, 1997; Smith, 2001).

In this chapter we explore battered women's perceptions on mandatory arrest laws in three states with different arrest policies. It also assesses the presumption that mandatory or pro-arrest policies increase criminal justice involvement in domestic violence cases. This research fills a gap in prior research by focusing on the views of battered women on mandatory arrest laws and by examining whether mandatory and pro-arrest laws increase the likelihood that battered women will report cases to the police, the likelihood of an arrest, and the number of cases pending prosecution. In essence, this study examines whether there is an increase in the criminal justice response to domestic violence in states with mandatory arrest laws (Utah, Missouri) as compared to a state without such a law (Hawaii).

MANDATORY ARREST LAWS AND BATTERED WOMEN

Most research has focused on the impact of mandatory arrest on the batterer (Berk, Campbell, Klap, & Western, 1992a; Chalk & King, 1998; Dunford et al., 1990; Hirschel & Hutchinson, 1992; Pate & Hamilton, 1992; Sherman & Berk, 1984; Sherman et al., 1992a). Little research has explored the impact of this law on battered women. Some research has found that arrests have increased in states with mandatory arrest policies (Jones & Belknap, 1999; Zorza & Woods, 1994), whereas others have found no such increase (Ferraro, 1989; Holmes, 1993; Martin, 1997). In either case, underreporting of domestic violence remains a problem (Coulter, Kuehnle, Byers, & Alfonso, 1999; Ferraro, 1989; Fluery, Sullivan, Bybee, & Davidson, 1998). Bennett, Goodman, and Dutton (1999), Coulter et al. (1999), Fleury et al. (1998), and Robinson and Chandek (2000) have found that battered women, even in mandatory arrest states, are reluctant to call the police for assistance. If battered women are not calling the police, the recidivistic effect of mandatory arrest laws is less significant. The primary reason given by battered women to explain "why they just don't call the cops" include their prior negative experience with the police and the extent of violence (Fleury et al., 1998). Others report fear of their abusers and a belief that the criminal justice system simply cannot stop the violence (Belknap, Fluery, Melton, Sullivan, & Leisenring, 2001; Bennett et al., 1999; Erez & Belknap, 1998; Hoyle & Sanders, 2000).

Another reason, overlooked by prior research, that women may not contact the police in mandatory arrest states is that this law strips battered women of the power to make decisions about police involvement and arrest. The disempowerment of battered women may undermine the goals of mandatory arrest to increase criminal justice involvement, deter violence, and protect victims (Goolkasian 1986; Sherman & Berk, 1984; Stanko, 1992). On the contrary, these laws may generate an antagonism between victims and the criminal justice system. Battered women who may not want their abuser arrested (for a variety of reasons) may become antagonistic toward a criminal justice system that ignores this desire (Cannavale & Falcon, 1976). When this is the case, battered women may actually be deterred from calling the police or requesting an arrest when their preference will be ignored by law enforcement. Some research lends support to this notion by demonstrating that victims may be more satisfied and safer when police and prosecutors take their preferences into consideration (Buzawa, Austin, Bannon, & Jackson, 1992; Ford & Regoli, 1993).

VICTIMS' OPINIONS AND SATISFACTION
WITH THE CRIMINAL JUSTICE RESPONSE

There has been a great deal of research that explores public opinion and preferences concerning the seriousness of wife abuse (Sigler, 1989), the appropriateness of arrest in domestic violence cases (Hilton, 1993; Robinson, 1999), and public preferences for the judicial handling of batterers (Sigler, 1989; Stalans & Lurigio, 1995). Some of the research on preferences and satisfaction has shown that victims of intimate violence hold different views from victims of stranger violence (Brandl & Horvath, 1991; Byrne, Kilpatrick, Howley, & Beatty, 1999; Hagan, 1983; Robinson, 1999; Stalans & Lurigio, 1995). Despite these differences, little research has been conducted which focuses on the opinions and preferences of domestic violence victims on mandatory arrest laws or their satisfaction with this criminal justice response.

Two studies examined domestic violence victims' views concerning satisfaction with the police response (Buzawa et al., 1992; Radford, 1987) and another study examined battered women's perceptions about the assistance of police, prosecutors, and judges in punishing abusers (Erez & Belknap, 1998). Buzawa et al. (1992) found that police action consistent with domestic violence victim preference related significantly to victim satisfaction. It was not an arrest *per se* that satisfied victims, only an arrest when this was the victim's preference. This finding suggests the importance of victims' views. Erez and Belknap (1998) found that victims perceived the criminal justice system as limited in its ability to provide help or relief from their abusers. Battered women's fear of their batterers was found to be a significant barrier to cooperation with criminal justice agents, and this fear perpetuated the belief that the system could not protect against violence (Bennett et al., 1999; Erez & Belknap, 1998).

Victim's perceptions of and satisfaction with the police, prosecution, and criminal justice system has been found to be essential to the system's ability to control crime (Brandl & Horvath, 1991). Since the participation and cooperation of victims is necessary to process crime and cases efficiently and effectively, domestic violence victims' perceptions and support for public policies, including mandatory arrest, is essential to an assessment of their effectiveness in protecting victims and increasing law enforcement involvement (Davis, Henlen, & Smith, 1990; Hagan, 1983; Macleod, Prescott, & Corson, 1996 McLaughlin, 1984; Smith, 1983; Wilson, 1993).

Only three studies have examined the opinions of domestic violence victims about mandatory arrest laws (Martin, 1997; Smith, 2000; forthcoming). Battered women in all three studies reported general support for mandatory arrest laws, but contrary to expectation, they did not believe that these laws would benefit them or increase their chance of reporting future domestic violence (Martin, 1997; Smith, 2000, forthcoming). Also, Smith (forthcoming) found differences in support for mandatory arrest laws based on race, marital status, and injury. Black, married, separated, and uninjured women were less supportive of mandatory arrest laws than were white, divorced, single, and injured women (Smith, forthcoming). These findings suggest that universalistic policies may not be appropriate to address domestic violence (Buzawa et al., 1992; Melton, 1999; Smith, forthcoming). One standard response that treats all battered women the same may not universally result in greater protection.

None of the prior research studies examine the opinions of women across states with different arrest policies. Similar to analyses on data disaggregated by race, marital status, and other situational circumstances, it is important to examine whether the opinions of women who live in states with different laws vary in their support and outcomes (arrest rates, requests for arrest, desires for arrest, restraining order, and prosecution). Based on prior research and using the data collected by Smith (2000) in this chapter we explore and compare differences among battered women in Hawaii, Missouri, and Utah on their support for mandatory arrest laws, outcomes, and preferences on their last incident of violence.

METHODS

The research presented is part of a larger study of battered women's perceptions of domestic violence policy. The findings here are the result of a survey ($n = 187$) given to women staying in battered women shelters and residents of three states—Hawaii ($n = 40$), Missouri ($n = 89$), and Utah ($n = 58$)—during the summer of 1998. The surveys were distributed by the State Coalition Against Domestic Violence in each state. The victim advocates in each shelter distributed the surveys to the shelter residents and returned the completed surveys to the coalition. The coalition returned the surveys to the author. Participation in the survey was nonrandom, voluntary, and confidential.

Surveying women located in battered women's shelters was intentional. The shelter provided a safe environment for the women, and it allowed for time to pass since the last victimization and survey participation. Both reduced the likelihood of "other" factors influencing the women's responses (e.g., fear of retaliation, "heat of passion" responses, and abuser threats). Tables 1 and 2 show the demographic characteristics and the situational circumstances of the sample by state, respectively.

ARREST POLICIES IN HAWAII, MISSOURI AND UTAH

Hawaii does not have a mandatory arrest law for domestic violence (Miller, 1998). In Hawaii, "any police officer, with or without a warrant, may arrest a person if the officer has reasonable grounds to believe that the person is physically abusing, or has physically abused, a family or household member and that the person arrested is guilty thereof. [Haw. Stat., § 709.906(2), (2000)]. There are several actions that a police officer may take when there exist reasonable grounds to believe that domestic violence has occurred [§ 709.906(4)]. Among the actions, police officers may order an abuser to leave the premises for 24 hours (and longer on weekends) and prohibit any direct or indirect (e.g., telephone) contact with the victim [§ 709.906(4)(b)]. If there is a violation of this order or the person refuses to comply, "the person shall be placed under arrest" [§ 709.906(4)(e)].

Missouri has a pro-arrest policy in place for a first domestic violence call, but mandates an arrest for a second domestic violence incident within 24 hours (Miller, 1998).

> When a law enforcement officer has probable cause to believe a party has committed a violation of law amounting to abuse or assault . . . against a family or household member, the officer may arrest the offending party whether or not the violation occurred in the presence of the arresting officer. . . . Any law enforcement officer subsequently called to the same address within a twelve-hour period, who shall find probable cause to believe the same offender has again committed a violation as stated in this subsection against the same or any other family or household member, shall arrest the offending party for this subsequent offense. . . . [Mo. Stat., § 455.085(1) (2000)]

TABLE 1   Demographic Characteristics [percent (number)]

	Hawaii	Missouri	Utah
Race			
African-American	2.9 (1)	16.9 (15)	3.6 (2)
Caucasian	34.3 (12)	76.4 (68)	67.4 (37)
Hispanic	2.9 (1)	2.2 (2)	10.9 (6)
Oriental	11.4 (4)	1.1 (1)	0
Other	48.6 (17)	3.4 (3)	18.2 (10)
Number of children			
0	23.7 (9)	29.7 (27)	27.5 (14)
1	18.4 (7)	23.1 (21)	19.6 (10)
2	36.8 (14)	28.6 (26)	27.5 (14)
3 or more	21 (8)	18.7 (17)	25.5 (13)
Relationship to abuser			
Spouse	35.3 (12)	35.3 (30)	37 (20)
Ex-spouse	20.6 (7)	11.8 (10)	16.7 (9)
Boy/girlfriend	14.7 (5)	17.6 (15)	13 (7)
Ex-boy/girlfriend	17.6 (6)	12.9 (11)	16.7 (9)
Other[a]	11.7 (4)	22.3 (19)	16.7 (9)
Age of respondent			
17–25 years	15 (6)	14.3 (14)	15.6 (10)
26–34 years	37.5 (15)	27.6 (27)	31.3 (20)
35–43 years	17.5 (7)	27.6 (27)	20.3 (13)
More than 44 years[b]	15 (6)	8.2 (8)	14.1 (9)
Education			
High school graduate or more education	97.3	78.9	83.3
Not a high school graduate	2.7	21.1	16.7
Respondent income			
Less than $10,000	67.3 (23)	54.5 (48)	64.7 (33)
$10,000 to $20,000	17.6 (6)	28.4 (25)	23.5 (12)
More than $20,001[c]	14.7 (5)	17 (15)	11.7 (6)

[a]Includes cohabitants, partners, friends, and other family members.

[b]The oldest person in the sample was 75 years of age.

[c]Only one person reported earning between $40,001 and $50,000; the remaining earned between $20,001 and $40,000.

TABLE 2   Situational Circumstances [percent (number)]

	Hawaii	Missouri	Utah
Prior history of abuse (yes)[*]	56.8 (21)	77.5 (69)	63.8 (37)
Abuse by more than one partner (yes)	36.8 (14)	53.3 (49)	40 (22)
Injury in last incident of violence (yes)	57.9 (22)	71.4 (65)	58.9 (33)
Time in relationship (months)			
0 to 12	7.5 (3)	17.2 (15)	16.4 (9)
13 to 24	2.5 (1)	11.5 (10)	7.3 (4)
25 to 48	17.5 (7)	19.5 (17)	21.8 (12)
49 to 60	7.5 (3)	13.8 (12)	7.3 (4)
61+	65 (26)	37.9 (33)	46.7 (26)
Number of times abused in relationship			
0 to 3	52.5 (21)	34.7 (34)	45.5 (30)
4 to 8	12.5 (5)	19.4 (19)	13.6 (9)
9 to 29	12.5 (5)	16.3 (16)	10.6 (7)
30+	7.5 (3)	16.3 (16)	6.1 (4)

[*]Differences significant across states at the 0.05 level.

Utah has a mandatory arrest law (Miller, 1998). The law states that "when a peace officer responds to a domestic violence call and has probable cause to believe that an act of domestic violence has been committed, the peace officer shall arrest without a warrant or issue a citation to any person that he has probable cause to believe has committed an act of domestic violence" [Utah Stat., § 77-36-2.2(2)(a), (2000)].

THIS STUDY

For purposes of this study, mandatory arrest was defined for respondents as follows: "Some communities have 'mandatory arrest' policies. This means that in the situation where an individual threatens to hit or actually hits a family member (e.g., a wife or husband), the officers must arrest. This is the case even though the 'victim' may not want this person arrested." In response to this definition, the battered women were asked four questions about mandatory arrest laws:

1. Do you think mandatory arrest policies should be adopted?
2. Do you think this policy would help you?

3. Do you think this policy would help others in your situation?
4. Do you think you would be more or less likely to report future domestic violence incidents in a community that has a mandatory arrest policy?

In response to the first three questions, the potential responses were: yes, no, no opinion, and not sure. In response to the fourth question, the potential responses were: more likely, less likely, no difference, and not sure.

The battered women were also asked a series of questions about the last incident of violence (prior to shelter admission). They were asked whether the police were called, whether an arrest was made, whether an arrest was requested, whether they desired an arrest, whether there was a temporary restraining order against the abuser, and whether the woman had a case pending in court against her abuser. These questions were intended to determine the amount and type of criminal justice response to domestic violence.

RESULTS

Perceptions on Mandatory Arrest Laws

The findings on the women's opinions are shown in Figure 1. Similar to prior research, battered women's support for the implementation of mandatory arrest laws is mixed. Whereas 75 percent of women in Missouri and Utah and 63 percent of women in Hawaii reported support for mandatory arrest laws, fewer believed the laws would actually help them (Hawaii 57.5 percent, Missouri 63.3 percent, and Utah 57.1 percent). Interestingly, the respondents from the state (Hawaii) without a mandatory arrest law also demonstrated the least support for its adoption and opinions on its effective benefit. Far fewer Utah respondents, although supportive of the law's adoption, reported that a mandatory arrest law would increase reporting future violence. Fewer Missouri respondents also believed the law would increase reporting future domestic violence to the police. Similar to the

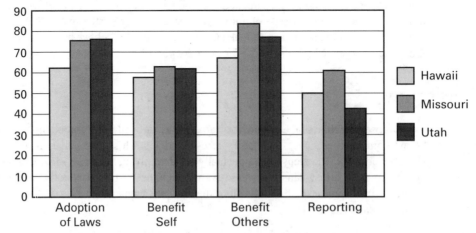

FIGURE 1   Perceptions about mandatory arrest laws.

findings of Smith (2001), battered women in these three states believed that a mandatory arrest law would be more beneficial to others (Hawaii 67.5 percent, Missouri 83.5 percent, and Utah 76.7 percent) than to themselves.

To examine whether the differences in support for mandatory laws vary depending on a battered woman's response to her violence (i.e., requesting or desiring an arrest) and the outcome of the last incident of violence (abuser arrest), comparisons (not disaggregated by state) were conducted. As expected, battered women who requested an arrest, desired an arrest, and had her abuser arrested during their last incident of violence were much more supportive of mandatory arrest policies than were women who did not request an arrest, desire an arrest, or have her abuser arrested. These findings are shown in Figure 2. More than three-fourths of battered women who requested, desired, or had her abuser arrested supported the adoption of mandatory arrest laws. Between 72 and 78 percent of these battered women believed that the law would benefit themselves, and more than 80 percent perceived that the laws would be a benefit to others. However, and in contradiction to these findings, these same women did not believe as strongly that these laws would increase the likelihood that they would report future violence to the police. Only 63 percent of women who requested an arrest, 64 percent of those who desired an arrest, and 56 percent of those whose abusers were arrested thought that the law would increase future reporting.

Impact of Mandatory Arrest Laws on the Criminal Justice Response

To assess the presumption that mandatory arrest laws increase criminal justice involvement, the percent of battered women reporting a police response, an abuser arrest, a temporary restraining order, and a case pending against her abuser for the last incident of violence were

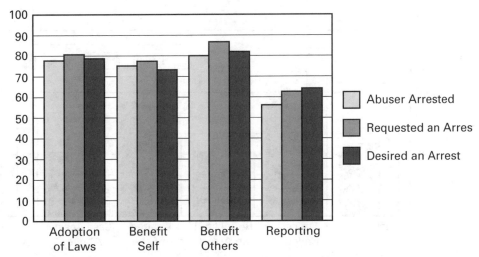

FIGURE 2   Perception on mandatory arrest laws and request for arrest, desire for arrest, and abuser arrest.

compared across the three states: Hawaii, Missouri, and Utah. In addition, the battered woman's request for an arrest and her desire for an arrest were also compared to examine whether mandatory arrest laws were consistent with the battered woman's preferences. The findings are shown in Figure 3. Contrary to expectation, Hawaii had the highest rate of temporary restraining orders (43.6 percent), police officer responses (81.6 percent), and abuser arrests (47.4 percent). Missouri and Utah had very similar rates of temporary restraining orders issued (Missouri 36 percent, Utah 31.5 percent), police response (Missouri 62 percent, Utah 64.3 percent), and abuser arrests (Missouri 29.3 percent, Utah 35.2 percent). The only response consistent with expectation concerned the percent of battered women with cases against their abusers. Hawaii had by far the fewest (12.5 percent); Missouri had 35.4 percent and Utah had 31.1 percent.

Interestingly, fewer Hawaiian women reported a request for an arrest (31.6 percent) than women from Missouri (38.9 percent) and Utah (32.1 percent), but had the highest rate of arrest (47.4 percent). Another disparity emerged when examining the percent of battered women who desired an arrest. Many more women wanted their abusers arrested (Hawaii 40.5 percent, Missouri 53.7 percent, Utah 54.9 percent) than requested an arrest. The greatest differences are in Missouri and Utah. Since the latter two are states with mandatory arrest laws and battered women need not ask for an arrest, at first blush this seems consistent with expectations. However, the fewest number of arrests also were effected in Missouri and Utah.

DISCUSSION AND CONCLUSIONS

Although these findings are not generalizable to all battered women, they shed some light on battered women's views on mandatory arrest laws. The results begin to explore differences in the views of battered women based on the status of mandatory arrest laws in three states.

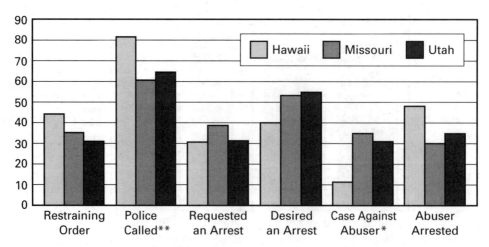

* Differences significant at the 0.5 level   ** Differences significant at the .10 level

FIGURE 3   Criminal justice response.

This research also demonstrates the importance of battered women's preferences on their support for mandatory arrest policies and the likelihood that they will initiate a criminal justice response.

In addition to generalizability, there are several additional weaknesses to this research. First, the battered women were not asked whether they were aware of the mandatory arrest laws in their state. This would have been important to fully understand women's perceptions and support for these laws. Second, the surveys were distributed to women in battered women shelters. These women have, at least while in the shelter, made the decision to separate from their abusers. This may substantially influence their opinions regarding arrest.

Perceptions

Similar to prior research, there seems to be a gap between women's general support for a mandatory arrest law, their beliefs about the helpfulness of the law, and the likelihood the law would increase future reporting of violence. Explanations for these mixed results may be found in two divergent theories concerning domestic violence: learned helplessness and survivor theories.

Walker's (2000) theory of *learned helplessness* suggests that battered women, over time, begin to believe that nothing can help them in their situation. Batterers take on an omnipotent role in the lives of battered women. Consistent with this explanation, in other studies battered women have reported that arrest would not help or protect them (Erez & Belknap, 1998; Hoyle & Sanders, 2000; Martin, 1997) and others feared that an arrest would simply anger abusers further and place them at greater risk (Coulter & Chez, 1997). Thus battered women may support mandatory arrest laws in theory and may believe that the laws could help other women, but do not believe that the laws will lead to change in their lives.

An alternative and opposing theory that may explain these mixed responses to arrest policies proposes that battered women are not helpless but that they are *survivors* (Gondolf & Fisher, 1988; Hoff, 1990). The latter theory has not been as well received by researchers, policymakers, and victim advocates as Walker's theory of learned helplessness. The survivor research identifies the numerous times that battered women attempt to leave their abusers, survive abuse successfully, and engage in a significant amount of help seeking (Gondolf & Fisher, 1988; Hutchinson & Hirschel, 1998). According to Gondolf and Fisher (1988) and Hoff (1990), it is not the battered women that fail in their attempts, but the help seekers, including the criminal justice agents, that fail battered women. Some of the findings of this research lend support to this view. For instance, there is a disparity between the percent of women contacting the police, as well as requesting and desiring an arrest, and the actual percent of abusers arrested and prosecuted. This gap demonstrates that battered women make an effort to stop the violence by relying on criminal justice agents, but the follow-through by law enforcement is lacking. Based on these differences, many of the battered women may support the adoption of mandatory arrest laws, but not see the point since officers are not making arrests when called or when requested to do so. The battered women's perceptions may be a reflection of their losing faith in the criminal justice system (Fleury et al., 1998; Ford, 1983).

Consistent with that observation, women who desired an arrest, requested an arrest, and had their abusers arrested were more supportive of mandatory arrest policies than were women who did not (Figure 2). These are probably not helpless women. More likely, they are women who are actively using law enforcement to stop their abusers. Women who, however, did not desire, request, or have their abuser arrested were less supportive of mandatory arrest policies. These women were not necessarily helpless, but clearly support for mandatory arrest varied according to their views. Battered women are not all the same. They vary in race, age, marital status, situation, and so on. One would expect that no single theory or policy would explain or assist all battered women. The findings here are consistent with other research that questions the wisdom and effectiveness of a "one size fits all" approach to battered women (Buzawa et al., 1998; Melton, 1999). Policy should be reexamined and reconsidered in light of these findings and a more individualistic approach to battering developed.

Impact

Contrary to the expected goals of mandatory arrest laws, the criminal justice response, with the exception of prosecutions, was not greater or more involved in the states with some type of mandatory arrest laws (Missouri and Utah). In particular, the highest rate of contacting the police was in Hawaii (almost 82 percent), and this difference was significant at the 0.10 level. This finding lends some support to the assertion that mandatory arrest laws may have the unintended effect of deterring battered women from calling the police in response to domestic violence. Far fewer women in mandatory arrest states (about a 20 percent differential) reported their last incident of abuse to the police. Arrest policies can only deter (assuming they do) if the police are contacted. Perhaps policies that provide more alternatives to police and battered women—other than arrest—may encourage women to contact the police or utilize other empowering options.

According to the survivor theory, battered women engage in a great deal of help seeking. This sample may be a reflection of battered women who make efforts to survive abuse and separate from their abusers. These women were located in battered women shelters and report a very high rate of contacting the police. To a much lesser extent and with a great deal of variability across use, battered women reported holding a restraining order and having a case pending against their abusers. This variability in help seeking again raises questions about the efficacy of a "one size fits all" policy approach, particularly when the exclusive response to battering is "arrest."

Also important is the difference in abuser arrests across the three states. Despite a mandatory arrest law in Utah and a pro-arrest, mandatory arrest (after the second incident in a 12-hour period) law in Missouri, the highest rate of arrest was in Hawaii. In Hawaii, there is a list of actions that may be taken by the police in response to domestic violence. It may be that these actions and follow-up with victims increases the likelihood of an abuser arrest. Prior research has suggested that low arrest rates in domestic violence cases may be explained by the absence of the abuser at the scene when the police arrive (Robinson & Chandek, 2000). Failing to arrest assailants simply because they are absent is not consistent with the objective goals of mandatory arrest policies. Further, across all states, the rate of prosecutions was woefully low. This was especially true in Hawaii. Arrest without prosecution may not effect a reduction in domestic violence and may leave battered women feeling vulnerable (Bennett et al., 1999; Davis, Smith, & Nickles, 1998; Ford, 1983; Thistlewaite, Wooldredge, & Gibbs, 1998).

In terms of a survivor explanation, battered women may see the lack of effort on the part of police to make an arrest, particularly when one is requested by battered women, as another failure of the criminal justice system. The same holds true for the failure of the system to follow up with a prosecution. In fact, failures of the criminal justice system and a lack of response by criminal justice agents may actually empower the batterer (Ptacek, 1999). A batterer may perceive a failure to pursue sanctions as a "wink and a nod" approval of the batterer's behavior. This same message conveyed to battered women reinforces a belief that the criminal justice system cannot change their situation, disempowers victims, and decreases the likelihood that domestic violence will be reported to law enforcement in the future (Ford, 1983, 1991). Although this research did not explore the differences in police response in terms of follow-through, the findings here suggest that policy that focuses on following up on an arrest may achieve greater results. Mandatory arrest policies will not achieve deterrence or empower women unless the abuser is actually arrested and prosecuted, and battered women are provided more extensive alternatives and options to deal with battering.

REFERENCES

BELKNAP, J., FLEURY, R. E., MELTON, H. C., SULLIVAN, C., & LEISENRING, A. (2001). To go or not to go? Preliminary findings on battered women's decisions regarding court cases. In H. M. Eigenberg (Ed.), *Woman battering in the United States: Till death do us part* (pp. 319–326). Prospect Heights, IL: Waveland Press.

BENNETT, L., GOODMAN, L., & DUTTON, M. (1999). Systemic obstacles to the criminal justice prosecution of a battering partner: A victim perspective. *Journal of Interpersonal Violence, 14*, 761–772.

BERK, R. A., CAMPBELL, A., KLAP, R., & WESTERN, B. (1992). A Bayesian analysis of the Colorado Springs spouse abuse experiment. *Journal of Criminal Law and Criminology, 83*, 170–200.

BRANDL, S. G., & HORVATH, F. (1991). Crime-victim evaluation of police investigative performance. *Journal of Criminal Justice, 19*, 293–305.

BUZAWA, E. S., AUSTIN, T. L., BANNON, J., & JACKSON, J. (1992). Role of victim preference in determining police response to victims of domestic violence. In E. Buzawa C. & Buzawa (Eds.), *Domestic violence: The changing criminal justice response* (pp. 255–270). Westport, CT: Auburn House.

BUZAWA, E. S., HOTALING, G., & KLEIN, A. (1998). The response to domestic violence in a model court: Some initial findings and implications. *Behavioral Sciences and the Law, 16*, 185–206.

BYRNE, C. A., KILPATRICK, D. G., HOWLEY, S. S., & BEATTY, D. (1999). Female victims of partner versus nonpartner violence: Experiences with the criminal justice system. *Criminal Justice and Behavior, 26*, 275–292.

CANNAVALE, F. J., & FALCONE, W. D. (1976). *Witness cooperation.* Lexington, MA: Lexington Books.

CHALK, R., & KING, P. A. (1998). *Violence in families. Assessing prevention and treatment programs.* Washington, DC: National Academy Press.

COULTER, M., & CHEZ, R. A. (1997). Domestic violence victims support mandatory reporting: For others. *Journal of Family Violence, 12*, 349–356.

COULTER, M., KUEHNLE, K., BYERS, R., & ALFONSO, M. (1999). Police reporting behavior and victim– police interactions as described by women in a domestic violence shelter. *Journal of Interpersonal Violence, 14*, 1290–1298.

DAVIS, R. C., HENLEN, M., & SMITH B. (1990). *Victim impact statements. Their effects on court outcomes and victim satisfaction.* New York: NYC Victim Service Agency.

DAVIS, R. C., SMITH, B. E., & NICKLES, L. B. (1998). The deterrent effect of prosecuting domestic violence misdemeanors. *Crime and delinquency, 44*(3), 434–442.

DUNFORD, F. W., HUIZINGA, D., & ELLIOTT, D. S. (1990). The role of arrest in domestic assault: The Omaha experiment. *Criminology, 28*, 183–206.

EREZ, E., & BELKNAP, J. (1998). In their own words: Battered women's assessment of the criminal processing system's responses. *Violence and Victims, 13*, 251–268.

FAGAN, J. (1996). *The criminalization of domestic violence: Promises and limits.* Washington, DC: U.S. Department of Justice, National Institute of Justice.

FERRARO, K. J. (1989). Policing woman battering. *Social Problems, 36*, 61–74.

FLEURY, R., SULLIVAN, C. M., BYBEE, D., & DAVIDSON, W. S. (1998). "Why don't they just call the cops?": Reasons for differential contact among women with abusive partners. *Violence and Victims, 13*, 333–346.

FORD, D. A. (1983). Wife battery and criminal justice: A study of victim decision-making. *Family Relations, 32*(4), 463–475.

FORD, D. A. (1991). Prosecution as a victim power resource: A note on empowering women in violent conjugal relationships. *Law and Society, 25*(2), 313–334.

FORD, D. A., & REGOLI, M. J. (1992). The prevention impacts of policies for prosecuting wife batterers. In E. Buzawa & C. Buzawa (Eds.), *Domestic violence: The changing criminal justice response* (pp. 161–180). Westport, CT: Auburn House.

GONDOLF, E. W., & FISHER, E. R. (1988). *Battered women as survivors: An alternative to treating learning helplessness.* New York: Lexington Books.

GOOLKASIAN, G. A. (1986). *Confronting domestic violence: A guide for criminal justice agencies.* Cambridge, MA: Abt Associates.

HAGAN, J. (1983). *Victims before the law.* Toronto: Butterworths.

HILTON, N. Z. (1993). Police intervention and public opinion. In N. Z. Hilton (Ed.), *Legal responses to wife assault* (pp. 37–61). Newbury Park, CA: Sage Publications.

HIRSCHEL, J. D., & HUTCHINSON, I. W. (1992). Female spouse abuse and the police response: The Charlotte, N.C. experiment. *Journal of Criminal Law and Criminology, 83*, 73–119.

HOFF, L. A. (1990). *Battered women as survivors.* New York: Routledge.

HOLMES, W. M. (1993). Police arrests for domestic violence. *American Journal of Police, 12*, 101–125.

HOYLE, C., & SANDERS, A. (2000). Police response to domestic violence: From victim choice to victim empowerment? *British Journal of Criminology, 40*, 14–36.

HUTCHINSON, I. W., & HIRSCHEL, D. J. (1998). Abused women: Help-seeking strategies and police utilization. *Violence Against Women, 4*, 436–456.

JONES, D. A., & BELKNAP, J. (1999). Police response to battering in a progressive pro-arrest jurisdiction. *Justice Quarterly, 16*, 249–273.

MACLEOD, M. D., PRESCOTT, R. G. W., & CORSON, L. (1996). *Listening to victims of crime.* Scotland: Scottish Office of Central Research Unit, Secretary of State.

MARTIN, M. E. (1997). Policy promise: Community policing and domestic violence victim satisfaction. *Policing, 20*, 513–531.

MCLAUGHLIN, A. (1984). *An analysis of victims/victim witness needs of Yukon.* Yukon, CA: Yukon Department of Justice.

MELTON, H. C. (1999). Police response to domestic violence. *Journal of Offender Rehabilitation, 29*, 1–21.

MILLER, N. (1998). Domestic violence: Review of state legislation defining police and prosecution duties and powers. Alexandria, VA: Institute for Law and Justice.

PATE, A., & HAMILTON, E. E. (1992). Formal and informal deterrents to domestic assault: The Dade County experiment. *American Sociological Review, 57*, 691–697.

PTACEK, J. (1999). Battered women in the courtroom: The power of judicial responses. Boston: Northeastern University Press.

RADFORD, J. (1987). Policing male violence—policing women. In J. Hanmer & M. Maynard, (Eds.), *Women, violence and social control* (pp. 30–45). London: Macmillan.

ROBINSON, A. (1999). Conflicting consensus: Public reaction to a domestic violence pro-arrest policy. *Women and Criminal Justice, 10*, 95–120.

ROBINSON, A., & CHANDEK, M. (2000). The domestic violence arrest decision: Examining demographic, attitudinal and situational variables. *Crime and Delinquency, 46*, 18–37.

SHERMAN, L. (1992). The influence of criminology on criminal law: Evaluating arrests for misdemeanor domestic violence. *Journal of Criminal Law and Criminology, 83*, 1–34.

SHERMAN, L., & BERK, R. A. (1984). The specific deterrent effects of arrest for domestic assault. *American Sociological Review, 49*, 261–272.

SIGLER, R. (1989). *Domestic violence in context: An assessment of community attitudes.* Lexington, MA: Lexington Books.

SMITH, A. (2000). It's my decision, isn't it? A research note on battered women's perceptions of mandatory intervention laws. *Violence Against Women, 16*(12). 1384–1402.

SMITH, A. (2001). Domestic violence laws: The voices of battered women. *Violence and Victims, 16*(2), pp. 91–111. New York: Springer.

SMITH, B. (1983). *Non-stranger violence: The criminal court response.* Washington, DC: U.S. Department of Justice, National Institute of Justice.

STALANS, L. J., & LURIGIO, A. J. (1995). Public preferences for the court's handling of domestic violence situations. *Crime and Delinquency, 41*, 399–413.

STANKO, E. A. (1992). Domestic violence. In G. W. Cordner & D. C. Hale (Eds.), *What works in policing: Operations and administration examined* (pp. 49–61). Cincinnati, OH: Anderson Publishing.

STEINMAN, M. (1988). Evaluating a system-wide response to domestic violence: Some initial findings. *Journal of Contemporary Criminal Justice, 4.* 172–186.

STEINMAN, M. (1990). Lowering recidivism among men who batter women. *Journal of Police and Administration, 17*, 124–132.

STEINMAN, M. (1991). Arrest and recidivism among women batterers. *Criminal Justice Review, 16*, 183–197.

THISTLEWAITE, A., WOOLDREDGE, J., & GIBBS, D. (1998). Severity of dispositions and domestic violence recidivism. *Crime and Delinquency, 44*(3), 388–398.

U.S. ATTORNEY GENERAL. (1984). *Final report.* Task Force on Family Violence. Washington, DC: U.S. Government Printing Office.

WALKER, L. (2000). *The battered woman syndrome* (2nd ed.). New York: Springer.

WILSON, R. I. (1993). *Supporting victims in the criminal justice system: A study of a Scottish sheriff court.* Edinburgh, Scotland: Scottish Office, Home and Health Department.

ZORZA, J., & WOODS, L. (1994). *Mandatory arrest: Problems and possibilities.* New York: National Battered Women's Law Project.

CASE

Thurman v. *City of Torrington*, 595 F. Supp. 1521 (1984).

24

Immigration Context of Wife Abuse

A Case of Vietnamese Immigrants in the United States

Hoan N. Bui

In this chapter we examine the immigration context of wife abuse among Vietnamese in the United States. Data drawn from 22 in-depth interviews with Vietnamese women victims, social workers and community members suggest that the interaction between economic opportunities for men and women, social policies, American culture, and Vietnamese culture creates changes in family dynamics among Vietnamese immigrants and affects women's experiences of abuse. Feelings of powerlessness, depression, resentment, and jealousy among men who experience downward mobility, changes in gender practices, and role reversal, as well as the inconsistency between men's and women's gender-role expectations, can cause family conflicts and men's use of force against their wives. On the other hand, economic hardship, language barriers, cultural isolation, ethnic relations, immigrant status, and immigration policies can put constraints on women's responses to abuse.

Feminist scholarship in the United States has addressed the issue of wife abuse and intimate-partner violence, but it has largely neglected the experiences of women from diverse ethnic backgrounds. A lack of research on domestic violence in ethnic minority groups, especially recent immigrant groups, has created a gap in understanding the effects of structural and cultural factors upon women's experiences of battering. The proposition that gender-based oppression is the primary cause of the social problem of battering served a purpose for the early battered women's movement, but it has also limited the consideration of race/ethnicity and other factors as significant in understanding the phenomenon of domestic violence (Kanuha, 1996; Lee & Au, 1998). Recent scholarship on domestic violence has warned against a single vision of women's experiences and argued for a contextual analysis of battered women's experiences that includes women's unique individual and social contexts (Dutton, 1996; Lee & Au, 1998).

The impact of immigration and cultural transition on family dynamics has been seen as central to the assessment of domestic violence in immigrant families (Almeika & Dolan-Delvecchio, 1999). Because domestic violence is rooted in an unequal power relationship between men and women (Bograd, 1988; Dobash & Dobash, 1979; Kurz, 1993), changes in gender relations following migration can have a major impact on the likelihood of violence at home. Immigrant families, however, respond differently to the process of adaptation, due to factors specific to their histories, including their preimmigrant and current immigrant statuses (Almeika & Dolan-Delvecchio, 1999). Immigrants also possess different types of human capital and resources, as well as cultural legacy, and face different socioeconomic situations during the process of resettlement and adaptation. Thus research on discrete experiences of particular groups will help produce additional explanations of domestic violence that capture diverse experiences of women and men.

In this chapter we examine the immigration context of wife abuse among Vietnamese immigrants in the United States.[1] Immigrants perceive, interpret, and respond to violence within the contexts of their systems of values and their experiences with the labor market, the criminal justice system, and social services; their experiences are often different from those of mainstream Americans (Gondolf, 1997). Domestic violence advocates have emphasized the need to understand cultural attitudes toward gender and stressed the importance of addressing special needs of domestic violence victims (Chalk & King, 1998). Therefore, research regarding factors that affect the likelihood of wife abuse in immigrant families and victims' responses not only contributes to the understanding of women's diverse experiences but also helps develop theory to guide interventions.

THEORETICAL ORIENTATION

Violence against women has been viewed as rooted in the patriarchal structure (Bograd, 1988; Dobash & Dobash, 1979; Kurz, 1993; Schechter, 1982; Yllo, 1993). However, a single concept of patriarchy, which assumes a universal, trans-historical, and trans-cultural phenomenon, cannot deal with different forms of gender inequality at different places and times, nor with the diversity of women's experiences (Acker, 1989; Walby, 1989). For immigrants, structural and cultural changes can affect power dynamics in the family (Gold, 1992; Hondagneu-Sotelo, 1994; Kibria, 1993; Rumbaut, 1989). Because gender relations are shaped by culture as well as men's and women's access and control of economic, political, and social resources, central to understanding the process of changes in family dynamics among immigrants are socioeconomic and cultural backgrounds as well as socioeconomic and cultural contexts of immigration resettlement (Almeika & Dolan-Delvecchio, 1999; Kibria, 1993; Mehrotra, 1999). Because of racism and classism, the interrelation between class and race/ethnicity also has important implications for power dynamics in immigrant families

The core dynamics of spouse abuse are male dominance and the quest for control and power in intimate relationships. However, the ways in which those power dynamics are constructed and manifested are influenced by structural and cultural factors. Different forms of masculinity and femininity are constructed in different economic and historical settings and are culturally honored and glorified to create a structure of gender relations (Connell, 1987; Lee & Au, 1998). While the socioeconomic context of immigration resettlement can affect men's power, cultural beliefs and practices that immigrants transported from their countries of origin can influence the manifestation of masculinity and forms of abuse. Immigration-related stress may have a negative impact on a couple's relationship and trigger or exacerbate violence in intimate relationships (Lee & Au, 1998). Changes in power dynamics as a result of adaptation to a new environment may also affect the likelihood of domestic violence. Research showed that some immigrant men reasserted their loss of power in new settings by denigrating women or abusing their wives as a way to vent their frustration (Espiritu, 1997). Recent scholarship has emphasized the need to focus on both the construction and manifestation of masculinity to understand different pathways of abuse (Abraham, 1999).

Migration itself creates situations that affect women's responses to violence and their experiences of abuse. Women who have left behind in their countries of origin the social networks of the extended family and who lack the familiarity with the new environment often feel isolated and have a need to be attached to family relationships through their husbands (Dasgupta & Warrier, 1996; Huisman, 1996; Perilla, 1999; Rimonte, 1989). Language barriers and a lack of occupational skills can cause women to depend on their husbands/partners (Chin, 1994; Perilla, 1999). Language barriers also make women misinformed or unaware of the availability of supportive services that may help them (Mehrotra, 1999; Rimonte, 1989).

In summary, because of men's and women's different locations in the hierarchies of class, race, and gender, women's experiences of male dominance, including battering, are not uniform. An understanding of immigration contexts in which violence occurs will contribute to the development of theories that can explain multiple pathways of abuse, as well as pathways to avoid abuse, and provide inputs for the design of social policies to address specific needs of immigrant victims of domestic violence.

VIETNAMESE IN THE UNITED STATES

The Vietnamese population in the United States has increased substantially during the last two decades and become a major segment of America's immigrant population (Nguyen & Haines, 1996). Following the end of the Vietnam War and the collapse of South Vietnam, more than 120,000 Vietnamese were resettled in the United States in 1975 (Do, 1999). By 1997, the foreign-born Vietnamese population in the United States had reached nearly 800,000 (U.S. Bureau of the Census, 1997). Although most Vietnamese immigrants entered the United States after the collapse of South Vietnam in 1975, they came in three different periods, each of which had its own unique features. The first wave of Vietnamese immigrants who left Vietnam shortly after the collapse of South Vietnam consisted mostly of high-ranking officers in the South Vietnamese military and government and their families. Members of this group tended to be urban and professional in background, well educated, and fluent in English (Nguyen & Haines, 1996). The second flow of Vietnamese immigrants included "boat people," who escaped Vietnam following the outbreak of the Vietnam–China conflict of 1978 and were likely to have rural backgrounds (Gold, 1992). The final exodus from Vietnam involved Vietnamese Amerasians, people coming under the family reunification program, and former political detainees and their families. The second- and third-wave immigrants tended to have low levels of education and English proficiency and few occupational skills that could be useful in the U.S. labor market (Gold, 1992; Nguyen & Haines, 1996).

The traditional Vietnamese culture, family, and gender relations were modeled on Confucian teachings that stressed the subordination of women to men. The rule of Three Obediences dictated that women obey their fathers, husbands, and oldest sons (Nguyen, 1987). Women's lives were oriented toward the family, and motherhood was the height of women's ambitions. A typical woman was expected to be married, bring to the world as many children as possible, and devote her life to serving her husband and children (Tran, 1959). On the other hand, men were prepared to work outside the home, serve the community, and become the heads of their families. For men, social positions were extremely important because "a man only exists for the community. Outside the community he has *no raison d'être*" (p. 45).

The majority of Vietnamese in the United States are first-generation immigrants and are likely to be influenced by Vietnamese cultural values and practices. However, Vietnamese culture has undergone tremendous changes in the last century. Urbanization and contacts with Western culture during French colonization and the Vietnam War have undermined some old manners and customs in the traditional Vietnamese family. Resettlement in the United States has created additional changes in family life as men and women adapt to the new environment and culture. Thus it is important to recognize the process of continuity as well as the process of change within the social context of immigration to learn how both can affect family dynamics and women's experiences of abuse.

METHOD

Data for the study were drawn from interviews with Vietnamese immigrants in two large Vietnamese communities in northern and southern California in 1998 and 2000 (see Tables 1 to 4). Because wife abuse is traditionally viewed as a private matter, most Vietnamese women are reluctant to reveal their experiences of abuse to people outside their families (Bui & Morash, 1999). Therefore, to select a sample for the study, I used the snowball technique and referrals from Vietnamese social workers and community leaders with whom I had personal relationships. Feminist scholars have emphasized the reliance on women subjects' experiences to understand social phenomena (Gorelick, 1991; Harding, 1991; Smith, 1990). However, the views of those who are knowledgeable of community life and who have contacts with victims and batterers can provide additional understanding

TABLE 1   Interview Sample: Age

Years of age	Women	Men	Total
20–30	3	—	3
31–40	3	—	3
41–50	4	3	7
51–60	3	1	4
Over 60	1	—	1
Total	14	4	18

TABLE 2   Interview Sample: Educational Attainment

Educational Attainment	Women	Men	Total
Fewer than 12 grades	3	—	3
High school	6	2	8
College	5	2	7
Total	14	4	18

of the social setting and the cultural context of battering experienced by a hard-to-reach victim population. Writing about rape, Campbell (1996, p. 39) reasons that people who advocate for rape victims can provide unique information because they stand with "one foot in the world of the . . . victims and one foot in the world of community help systems, and carry the responsibility of mutual translation." Therefore, I conducted interviews with women victims as well as social workers and community members who were knowledgeable of the domestic violence issue through their jobs and their community activities.

A total of 22 in-depth interviews were conducted with 16 women victims of wife abuse, three social workers, and three community members; all study participants were first-generation immigrants. The ages of the women victims ranged from 26 to 50 years; their time in the United States ranged from 2 to 25 years. Of 16 women, seven had been married in Vietnam before migration; the rest began their married lives in the United States. At the time of the interview, 11 women were legally married; one was in a common-law husband/wife relationship, two were separated, and two were divorced. With regard to education and occupation, one had a college degree and worked as a professional, two had some college education and worked in business (salesperson) and in the Vietnamese media (reporter), two were housewives, and 11 worked in manual jobs. Their legal status varied: Five were American citizens; seven were permanent U.S. residents, and four were legal aliens.

All three community members and one social worker were men; two other social workers were women. Among the social workers and community members, four had a college degree earned in Vietnam, and one had a college degree earned in the United States. One social worker had direct contacts with Vietnamese batterers through a batterers' counseling program; two social workers had contacts with Vietnamese women victims

TABLE 3   Interview Sample: Occupation

Occupation	Number of Persons
Housewife	2
Manual job	8
White-collar job	4
Business	1
Professional	3
Total	18

TABLE 4   Interview Sample: Years of U.S. Residence

Years of U.S. Residence	Number of Persons
1–10	13
11–15	1
16–20	1
Over 20	3
Total	18

through their jobs as a translator in a hospital and a caseworker in a welfare office. Two community members were active members of local ethnic associations (associations of former military officers); the other worked in the Vietnamese media.

The interviews, guided by a semistructured questionnaire with open-ended questions, were conducted in the Vietnamese language via telephone or face to face.[2] The women victims were asked to describe the context of their immigrant lives, changes in family dynamics during their resettlement in the United States, and their experiences of and responses to abuse. Respondents who were social workers and community members were asked about their perceptions and their knowledge of domestic violence in their communities. Most interviews with the women victims lasted at least two hours; three woman victims participated in two interview sessions. Interviews with the social workers and community members were shorter, taking slightly more than an hour. There were also several short follow-up interviews with two social workers.

All interviews were recorded in writing in Vietnamese, and the Vietnamese interview transcripts were translated into English for data processing. Because there were Vietnamese terms and idioms that could not be translated into English without losing some original meanings, both the Vietnamese and English versions of interview transcript were used for analysis. All names used in this report are pseudonyms to protect the anonymity of respondents; all quotes are translations from the Vietnamese version of the transcript.

IMMIGRATION CONTEXT OF WIFE ABUSE

Resettlement in the United States has brought about changes in the family lives of many immigrants. Leaving the familiar country of origin to venture into a new culture involves drastic changes and disruption in one's life (Lee & Au, 1998). The values and expectations that immigrants have brought with them and the discrepancy between their expectations and the actual quality of life in the United States influence how well they adjust to the life and culture of the new country (Drachman, 1992; Haines, 1996). Domestic violence is rooted in male dominance and the quest for power and control, but the contexts in which men use violence against women vary, depending on differences in economic settings, cultures, and politics that affect gender dynamics (Connell, 1987). Data drawn from interviews with the study participants showed that wife abuse among Vietnamese immigrants occurred in the contexts of changes in social and economic statuses of Vietnamese immigrant men and women, the inconsistency between men's and women's gender role expectations, cultural isolation, and immigration policies.

Men's Downward Mobility and Role Reversal

The move to the United States has created a profound loss of social and economic status among Vietnamese immigrants. Because of limited language and occupational skills, discriminatory requirements of experience and certifications in the United States, and ethnic minority status, many Vietnamese immigrant men cannot obtain employment that is commensurable with their education and training in Vietnam. Therefore, many experience a loss of status in the dominant society (Gold, 1992; Kibria, 1993). This is particularly true for a large number of former military officers who have skills that are not marketable in the United States (Gold & Kibria, 1993). A general pattern of employment among Vietnamese immigrants is that in sharp contrast to their position in middle-class occupations in pre-1975 South Vietnam, the majority of them start with menial jobs, working in the lower tiers of the occupational structure in the United States (Nguyen, 1987).

Besides a lack of language and occupational skills, Vietnamese immigrant men who felt betrayed by the United States when South Vietnam was lost to the communists also experience a "Vietnam syndrome" similar to the one experienced by American veterans of the Vietnam War (Nguyen & Haines, 1996). The syndrome that was felt most acutely by those who had been heavily involved in the Vietnam War, such as former military officers and soldiers in the South Vietnamese government, causes withdrawal, a pessimistic outlook, and a negative attitude toward social participation. As a result, many members of this group have lost motivation to improve their own adjustment to U.S. society (Nguyen & Haines, 1996).

My interviews with the women victims showed a pattern of downward mobility and blocked opportunities experienced by most of their husbands. Among husbands of 16 women, only two had a college education and worked as professionals. Six other husbands who had been professionals or military commanding officers in Vietnam and four husbands who came to the United States as teenagers or in their early 20s, but received little or no formal education and vocational training in the United States, worked in manual, temporary, and low-status jobs, such as courtesy clerk, factory assembler, auto mechanic, and school tutor. Two husbands held only part-time jobs, and two were unemployed.

Men's downward mobility was accompanied by a role reversal and a shift of power in the family. In most cases, because the husbands' salaries alone were not sufficient to meet the high cost of living, the wives had to work to supplement their family incomes, and many women earned more than their husbands. This might be because the structure of the labor market made unskilled, female-oriented jobs, such as house cleaning, hotel services, and food services, more available than male-oriented jobs (Gold, 1992). In addition, although many women were willing to learn vocational and language skills, their husbands, especially those who experienced the Vietnam syndrome, felt disinterested in learning skills to improve their earning ability and occupational status. As a result, many women could make more money and could have a higher occupational status than their husbands. For example, a 48-year-old woman (Xuan) worked in two jobs as a hotel chambermaid and earned three times as much as her husband, who held only a part-time job in a garment factory; a 49-year-old woman (Hue) was a professional with a college degree, but her husband was an auto mechanic; a 38-year-old woman (Ly) was a salesperson who could make $50,000 a year while her husband worked as a courtesy clerk and could make only around $10,000 a year. In many cases, women's ability to earn money and provide for the family shifted the roles between husband and wife, with the wives taking on the role of the primary wage earner.

The erosion of men's status, the inversion of elements of the traditional gender order in families, as well as the humiliating conditions of working in menial jobs and status inconsistency often caused distress and provoked hostility and resentment among men. According to a social worker (Hanh), many men escaped economic and family distress through alcoholism and gambling, which often triggered family conflicts, and many men used force against their wives/partners who complained about their gambling and alcohol problems or who refused to give them money they needed to gamble and drink.

Violence also occurred within the context of unfulfilled expectations. Many women continued to value men's meeting obligations despite the decline in men's actual ability to perform the task of the family provider. Some women felt disappointed, and even frustrated because they perceived that their husbands had changed and failed to fulfill the norms of masculine behavior. As one woman (Xuan) put it:

> He [Xuan's husband, who had been a captain in the South Vietnamese military] didn't want to learn English or a vocation to find a better job and make more money to support the family. While other people worked two or three jobs to make ends meet, he worked less than one job. Instead, he spent most of his time to meet with his former military fellows and discuss politics. I wish his politics could bring home some money to buy food for our children. I don't know what made them [her husband and his friends] change so much; they don't act like [good] men and husbands any more.

Hoang, a member of an association of former Vietnamese military officers, reported that many of his friends used force against their wives who complained about their lack of responsibility as family providers.

Changing Culture and Gender Norms

Across all ages, immigrants experience more or less cultural shock (Nguyen, 1987). It is quite apparent that the traditional role of the Vietnamese woman and her relationship to her husband according to the Confucian norms is likely to clash with the reality of the American environment. Adapting to new economic conditions of immigration resettlement in which the earnings of many Vietnamese men are not enough to support the family, Vietnamese women have quickly moved into the workforce and earned money. Although in Vietnam women often worked to supplement family incomes during wartime when their husbands served in the battlefields, women's position in the family and society was still subordinate to men's under the traditional gender norms shaped by Confucian teachings. In the United States, however, Confucianism has to compete with the ideology of gender equality. Vietnamese immigrant women, especially young women, are less enthusiastic about traditional gender roles, but many Vietnamese immigrant men do not change their view of feminine behavior and still expect women to perform the traditional role of homemaker (Gold, 1992, Nguyen, 1987).

Data from the study showed that the conflict between men's conservative expectations and the role of women in American society often precipitated marital problems. Many Vietnamese-American women changed their attitudes toward gender equality as a result of being exposed to American culture that supports gender equality. For instance, most women felt that household decisions should be made jointly and that housework should be shared fairly between husband and wife, because wives also worked and contributed income to the family. However, many women reported that their husbands did not change their view toward gender roles. A woman's request for a fair share of family decision making could be seen by her husband as arrogant and disrespectful behavior, and force could be used to reinstate the husband's status and restore his shattered power. One woman (Hue) explained her situation as follows:

> My husband lived here but his mind was back in Vietnam. He often talked about his "golden years" back there and complained about Vietnamese women in the United States having too much freedom and becoming disrespectful to their husbands. He usually tried to control family money and often spent large amounts of money without my consent. I felt very angry about his spending. . . . One time, I discovered that he had secretly sent a large amount of money to his friends in Vietnam. When I asked why he hadn't talked with me about this spending, we got into a verbal fight. At one point my husband tried to end the argument by taking out a gun and telling me that if I continued to talk against his friends and his use of money, he would kill me and my [3-year-old] daughter."

Women's complaints about husbands' failure to do housework also caused family conflicts and violence. As one woman (Cuc) put it:

> I also worked like him [Cuc's husband]. . . . I even worked overtime, but I had to do all house-work and take care of two children. I did not have time to watch TV or read newspapers, but he never thought about my hard work [or] gave me a hand, so I could have some time to rest. . . . He came home from work and watched TV until dinner was served. He often ignored the division of household chores we had agreed upon. When I complained, he became angry and said that I wanted to be the boss. . . . We often had arguments in situations like this. In one incident, he said that because I wanted to be the boss, he would let me know who was the boss in the house. He then hit me to make me shut up.

Literature has indicated that men's jealousy and subsequent violence is viewed as an expression of men's sexual possessiveness and control of women's sexuality and body (Campbell, 1992; Dobash & Dobash, 1979). Because men's ability to control women's sexuality is a major feature of masculinity (Messerschmidt, 1993), feelings of sexual jealousy may be stronger among Vietnamese immigrant men who feel threatened by the stereotype [in American society] that Asian men are weak and nonmasculine, and Asian women are feminine and adorable (Lin, Tazuma, & Masuda, 1979).

Data from my study indicated that that women's changing status and behavior as a result of adapting to the new life caused men's jealousy that could lead to family conflict and violence. Men's fear of losing their wives or partners was based on their perception that women in the United States, including Vietnamese women, had more freedom to engage in intimate relationships, contrary to the Vietnamese norm of feminine behavior. According to a social worker (Trinh), after settlement in the United States, Vietnamese immigrant men and women have been in inverse situations with regard to sexual jealousy. As Trinh explained:

> In Vietnam, married women were often worried about their husbands' disloyalty because most married men had either girlfriends, mistresses, or concubines at some point in their marriages. In the United States, [Vietnamese] men become very jealous and are usually worried about their wives or partners leaving them to go with American men. Their concerns are unfounded because there is a very small number of [Vietnamese] women who are married to "American" men. However, [Vietnamese] men have become paranoid because they probably think that they are less attractive than their American counterparts and that [Vietnamese] women have more freedom to engage in intimate relationships in the United States than they did in Vietnam.[3]

When men lost social and family status, they often had a fear of losing their wives or partners to other, more successful men. Violence occurred when men tried to control the behavior of their wives, who actually disregard this controlling effort. Adapting to the new norm of gender equality in the United States, many Vietnamese-American women came to doubt their husbands' right to dominate them. A financially successful woman (Ly) was beaten by her husband because she disregarded and sometimes opposed her husband's jealousy and criticism of her mode of dressing and gesture. Her husband, who was a courtesy clerk, thought that she was arrogant and disrespectful and that she provoked him to have a reason for divorce. Another woman (Oanh) was physically attacked by her husband because she protested to him when he tried to prevent her from pursuing a career goal. As Oanh recounted, "He [Oanh's former husband] just wanted me to stay home, take care of children and do housework. But I wanted to be a lawyer and decided to go to college. When he learned that I had been accepted to a law school, he felt angry. . . . We argued for several days. When he finally told me, 'No more school. Period' I felt furious and I told him, 'You cannot prohibit me from pursuing my career. If you want to stop me from studying, you have to step over my dead body.'"

Some kinds of job that required women to work at night and some working environments also aroused the suspicions of their husbands. Many factory and restaurant jobs required night-shift work, and hotel services, such as cleaning and chambermaid, were among the few jobs available for immigrant women who did not have vocational and English skills. However, under Vietnamese gender norms, women should not to go out alone at night, and hotels were not a good place for women because of prostitution activities. A misperception about some jobs in the United States often made men suspect their wives' disloyalty and beat them out of jealousy. One woman [Xuan] explained her experience of violence as follows:

> We got married in Vietnam, but I have never seen him become so jealous; only after we came to the United States . . . I was almost 50 years old, but he usually thought that I acted like a 20-year-old, trying to "get" other men. I was working at two hotels in downtown, but he did not like it. He told me to change jobs many times because under his view only prostitutes worked in hotels. . . . He got mad when I brought home good money from tips. Then, he started scrutinizing the way I dressed; he even prohibited me from wearing makeup and certain kinds of clothing. When I disregarded his unreasonable demands, he beat me and even threatened to kill me.

According to two social workers (Trinh and Hanh), many men did not want their wives to work night shifts. Due to the demand of the family economy, especially when men did not have jobs or did not earn enough to support the family, many women still worked on night shifts. However, women's work schedules often caused family conflicts that could lead to men's use of violence against them.

Economic Constraint, Isolation and Immigration Policy

Women's experiences of family violence are strongly affected by how they respond to it. Having a divorce to leave a violent husband can be one way to avoid abuse. Relying on the protection from the criminal justice system may stop violence and prevent future attacks, because arrests and prosecutions can deter some violent men (Dutton, Hart, Kennedy, & Williams, 1992).

Data from the present study indicated that police intervention into family violence could be a new resource that Vietnamese-American women could use to protect themselves from physical attacks by their husbands/partners. According to a community member

(Hoang), who was an active member of an association of Vietnamese former military officers, many Vietnamese immigrant men were aware of the prohibition of wife beating in the United States, and some tried to avoid using physical force against their wives/partners because "those who beat their wives in the United States will have a good chance to go to jail." However, economic constraint, isolation, and immigration policy could also have negative impacts on women's use of new resources to respond to abuse.

Limited language and occupation skills could affect Vietnamese-American women's help-seeking behavior in many ways. Due to a traditional view of women's primary role as homemaker, many women did not have the opportunity to learn the language or a vocation. A substantial majority of women in the present study considered their English proficiency as weak. Some of these women did not call the police when violence occurred because they could not communicate with the police. Some other women did not understand the law and were worried about what would happened if the police came. Particularly, a majority of women did not know whether there were services for abused women in their local areas. Some women were aware of these services but could not communicate with service agents who did not speak Vietnamese.

In addition, a lack of ability to live independently also affected women's help-seeking behavior. Women who depended on their husbands financially were reluctant to seek help from the police because they were afraid that their husbands would be arrested and would not be able to provide support for their families. Women who relied on public assistance were also reluctant to report abuse to the authorities. According to a social worker (Hanh), a number of women lived with their common-law husbands but claimed their single status to qualify for public assistance. When beaten by their husbands, they did not report the abuse for fear that police interventions could disclose the de facto marital relationships with their abusers and could make them unqualified for welfare benefits.

Isolation and a desire for intimate companionship also affected Vietnamese-American women's response to violence. A number of women in the present study who had no relatives in the United States openly expressed their concern that their husbands would leave home and abandon them. One woman (Ly) had obtained a personal protective order to "teach him a lesson" but finally terminated the order voluntarily and asked her husband to come back home after she learned that he had begun a relationship with another woman. As Ly explained "After he was released from jail, he came to stay with his sister because of the PPO [personal protective order]. . . . Several months later, I learned that he had moved in with another woman who was his co-worker. I felt hurt and sad. My children urge me to remove the order, and I did what they wanted, hoping our family life would resume normally. . . ."

Fear of discrimination and a sense of ethnic solidarity emerging from feelings of alienation and isolation could make many Vietnamese-American women feel reluctant to use the criminal justice system to deal with abuse. Many women did not want their co-ethnic husbands/partners to be arrested and involved in the criminal justice system that they perceived as oppressive and racially discriminatory. According to a social worker (Trinh) and a community member (Cong), Vietnamese women, their children, or their neighbors did call the police in a number of cases. Most Vietnamese women, however, only wanted the police to stop the violence but did not want the police to press charges against their husbands/partners. Trinh reported that in one local area, domestic calls by Vietnamese immigrants reduced substantially for a period of time following the news that a violent Vietnamese husband was shot to death by police officers who responded to his wife's call.

Immigration laws and policies also affected immigrant women's responses to abuse. The Immigration Marriage Fraud Amendments, which were enacted in 1986 to prevent marriage fraud, inadvertently have become a power tool for abusive spouses to use against their alien partners and children (Chin, 1994). The law requires that aliens married to U.S. citizens receive conditional residency for two years and must file another petition *with* their U.S. citizen partners at the end of the two-year period to gain lawful permanent resident status. Although the law has changed to provide relief for battered spouses by creating a special waiver for battered immigrants and allowing them to finish the process for gaining status without the help of their abusers, many women are still intimidated by their abusers' threat due to their lack of understanding of the law.

Two women in the present study had come to the United States under the sponsorship of their husbands, who were American citizens. One woman (Oanh) reported that her abusive husband had refused to do the paperwork as required by the law and often threatened to report her to the Immigration and Naturalization Service every time they had conflicts, so that she could be sent back to Canada, which was her first place of migration resettlement. Another woman (Lien) kept staying with her abuser for several years with a hope that he would help her obtain permanent U.S. residency. As she said, "I was afraid that he would retaliate [if I called the police], and no one could help me obtain a green card."

In addition, when American citizenship has become a condition for public assistance and other social benefits, and when domestic offense has been a ground for deportation of aliens, police intervention may lead to the deportation of abusive spouses.[4] For most Vietnamese immigrants, especially for those who had spent time in communist reeducation camps, resettlement in the United States was the only chance in their lifetimes to escape the communist regime. Therefore, many women may not want to call the police to report domestic abuse and take a risk of having their husbands deported because of committing a domestic offense. According to a social worker (Hanh), Vietnamese immigrants in her community were aware of a case in which a man was denied U.S. citizenship while being on probation for a domestic offense. Consequently, battered women whose husbands did not have U.S. citizenship were unlikely to call the police for fear that a conviction for a domestic violence offense would cause their husbands to be denied U.S. citizenship for a period of time, or worse, deported to their home country.

CULTURAL SETTING OF THE IMMIGRANT COMMUNITY

Immigrants frequently bring to a new country cultural beliefs and practices from their country of origin. Because cultural values influence a person's problem perception, perceived problem solutions, and help-seeking behaviors, the influence of traditional culture on immigrant life has important implications for immigrant women's experiences of abuse (Abraham, 1999; Lee & Au, 1998). Immigrants also adapt to the culture of the receiving society, and the influence of each culture varies depending on the context of resettlement. A large, concentrated immigrant community often offers an opportunity to reassert certain family practices deemed traditional in a new setting (Sanchez, 1999). In addition, a desire to maintain traditional values is also reinforced by some immigrants' efforts to recreate an authentic community and an ethnic identity in the United States in order to resist assimilation (Abraham, 1999).

Two large Vietnamese communities in northern and southern California have provided a context for the reinforcement of Vietnamese traditional culture and gender practices. According to two social workers (Hanh and Trinh) and one community member (Cong), those who worked in the Vietnamese media in both communities continued to promote Vietnamese traditional family values, women's exemplary conduct (women's Four Virtues), and the Three Obediences in books, newspapers, magazines, radio, and TV programs.[5]

According to one social worker (Chung), in a community where women were expected to be subordinate to men, calling the police to have one's husband arrested would be "unthinkable" for many Vietnamese-Americans. Most women victims in the present study did not call the police when violence occurred, although they had positive attitudes toward domestic violence laws in the United States and favored government intervention (e.g., most women agreed with the statement "Domestic violence should not be seen as a private matter, and the government should intervene to protect women"). As one abused woman (Oanh) explained: "I didn't call [the police] because I was afraid of reaction from friends and families on both sides. . . . Under our [Vietnamese] family traditions, husband and wife should protect each other, and family matters should be solved by family members, not outsiders. . . Also, because of the Three Obediences and Four Virtues traditions, I was afraid that other people would criticize me for stepping out of the norms of women's appropriate behavior."

Another social worker (Trinh) reported that most people in the community saw police intervention as necessary to prevent death or severe injuries in domestic violence incidents, but they also perceived that police intervention would widen the rift between husband and wife and lead to family breakup. Women who used the criminal justice system to deal with domestic abuse sometimes had to pay a price. A woman (Hue) bitterly reported that her call to the police for help when her husband threatened to shoot her and her daughter with a gun led to her isolation from friends and relatives, who criticized her for being "too Americanized." As Hue explained: "After I called the police, my family life became more strained. . . . His family took sides with him, and they didn't welcome me to family gatherings. Some of his friends also criticized me, and they didn't want their wives to socialize with me."

Leaving an abusive relationship was also difficult for many Vietnamese immigrant women. Although most women victims did not have a negative attitude toward divorce, many did not leave their abusive husbands because they feared that a divorce would bring shame to their own families (their parents and siblings). According to these women, some parents did feel sympathetic toward daughters who experienced family problems, but they did not want to intervene because they perceived that married women should belong to their husbands. In addition, some women felt that they had to stay in an abusive relationship because the welfare of their children depended on the presence of the father in the family, as indicated by a Vietnamese proverb: "A child without a father is like a house without roof."

CONCLUSIONS

Data obtained from 22 in-depth interviews with Vietnamese immigrants, including women victims of wife abuse, social workers, and community members, suggest that women's experiences of family violence cannot be fully understood outside their own contexts. Although men from many cultural groups construct masculinity to include the domination of women, the manifestations of men's power and control and women's responses are culturally specific and shaped by the groups' experience (Morash, Bui, & Santiago, 2000). Findings from this study also suggest that a multifactor framework that takes into account the effects of social structure, culture, and men's and women's different locations in the hierarchy of class, race/ethnicity, and gender is required to understand women's various experiences.

Immigration has created changes in gender dynamics among Vietnamese immigrants that in turn have a major impact on the likelihood of domestic violence and on women's responses to abuse. New social and economic conditions as well as American ideological belief in gender equality are new resources for Vietnamese immigrant women to change family dynamics. Whereas women have more economic opportunities in the United States than in Vietnam, many men lose economic power and social status, as well as cultural resources to support male dominance. Men's downward mobility and failure to adjust economically and culturally to the new society often clash with women's new economic roles and elevated status. Feelings of powerlessness, depression, resentment, and jealousy among men resulting from economic and cultural stress as well as the inconsistency in gender-role expectations between men and women often create family conflicts leading to men's use of force against their wives to vent frustration or to reaffirm male authority.

The interaction between economic opportunities, social policies, U.S. culture, and Vietnamese culture creates a complex structure of gender relations that provides resources for women's protection but also puts constraints on women's choice of approaches to avoid violence. Laws that prohibit violence against women, economic opportunities, and the availability of divorce without stigma are new resources that Vietnamese immigrant women can use to deal with violence. At the same time, specific conditions of immigration resettlement, including economic constraints resulting from language barriers, cultural isolation, immigration policies, immigrant status, and ethnic relations, are impediments to women's use of new resources to escape violence.

Understanding specific contexts of male abuse and women's responses to it has implications for intervention strategies. Increasing men's and women's economic opportunities, eliminating language barriers and cultural isolation, and improving ethnic relations are ways to reduce economic and cultural stress among men and to empower women to deal with abuse. However, because domestic violence is rooted in gender inequality and male dominance, interventions into domestic violence also need to focus on changing the construction of gender ideology based on the reality of migrant life, new socioeconomic conditions, and positive attitudes toward gender equality to eliminate a belief in male supremacy and the quest for power and control among men.

NOTES

1. In this chapter the term *immigrants* is used to indicate both immigrants and refugees. Although the U.S. government and immigration policies often regard refugees and immigrants as fundamentally different social groups, the literature shows that differences between the two groups are a continuum (Gold, 1992). For Vietnamese-Americans, the difference in immigration status (immigrants or refugees) is based largely on the means they used to get out of their home country (escape or official departure), but there are many similarities between Vietnamese immigrants and refugees with regard to their experiences of political oppression in Vietnam and resettlement and adaptation in the United States.

2. Ten interviews were conducted via telephone partly because of geographical distance and partly because of the preference of women victims who wanted to talk by phone so that they could discuss sensitive issues freely without facing the interviewer.

3. The term *American* was used broadly by Vietnamese immigrants to indicate non-Asian Americans.

4. The Illegal Immigration Reforms and Responsibility Act of 1996 provides that domestic violence can be a ground for deportation of aliens, and legal aliens do not qualify for most welfare benefits, except for refugees who could receive public assistance no more than five years.

5. The Four Virtues of women are derived from Confucian teachings and include good working habits, agreeable appearance, polite speech, and exemplary conduct (Nguyen, 1987).

REFERENCES

ABRAHAM, M. (1999). Sexual abuse in South Asian immigrant marriages. *Violence Against Women, 5*, 591–618.

ACKER, J. (1989). The problem with patriarchy. *Sociology, 23*, 235–240.

ALMEIKA, R. & DOLAN-DELVECCHIO, K. (1999). Addressing culture in batterers' intervention: The Asian Indian community as an illustrative example. *Violence Against Women, 5*, 654–683.

BOGRAD, M. 1988. Feminist perspectives on wife abuse. In K. Yllo & M. Bograd (Eds.), *Feminist perspectives on wife abuse* (pp. 11–27). Newbury Park, CA: Sage Publications.

BUI, H., & MORASH, M. (1999). Domestic violence in the Vietnamese immigrant community: An exploratory study. *Violence Against Women, 5*, 769–795.

BUZAWA, E. S., & BUZAWA, G. S. (1990). *Domestic violence: The criminal justice response*. Newbury, CA: Sage Publications.

CAMPBELL, J. (1992). Wife-battering: Cultural context versus Western social sciences. In D. A. Counts, J. K. Brown, & J. C. Campbell (Eds.), *Sanctions and sanctuary: Cultural perspectives on the beating of wives* (pp. 229–249). Boulder, CO: Westview Press.

CAMPBELL, R. (1996). The community response to rape: An ecological concept of victims' experiences. Unpublished dissertation. Michigan State University.

CHALK, R. & KING, P. (1998). *Violence in families: Assessing prevention and treatment programs*. Washington, DC: National Academy of Press.

CHIN, K. (1994). Out-of-town brides: International marriage and wife abuse among Chinese immigrants. *Journal of Comparative Family Studies, 25*, 53–69.

CONNELL, R. W. (1987). *Gender and power: Society, the person and sexual politics*. Stanford, CA: Stanford University Press.

DASGUPTA, S. & WARRIER, S. (1996). In the footsteps of "Arundhati": Asian Indian women's experience of domestic violence in the United States. *Violence Against Women, 2*, 238–259.

DO, H. (1999). *The Vietnamese Americans*. Westport, CT: Greenwood Press.

DOBASH, R. E., & DOBASH, R. P. (1979). *Violence against wives: A case against the patriarchy*. New York: Free Press.

DRACHMAN, D. (1992). A stage-of-migration framework for service to immigrant populations. *Social Work, 37*, 68–72.

DUTTON, M. (1996). Battered women's strategic response to violence: The role of context. In J. Edleson & Z. Eisikovits (Eds.), *Future interventions with battered women and their families* (pp. 105–124). Thousand Oaks, CA: Sage Publications.

DUTTON, D., HART, S., KENNEDY, L., & WILLIAMS, K. (1992). Arrest and the reduction of repeat wife assault. In E. S. Buzawa & C. G. Buzawa (Eds.), *Domestic violence: The changing criminal justice response* (pp. 111–127). Westport, CT: Auburn House.

ESPIRITU, Y. L. (1997). *Asian American women and men: Labor, laws, and love*. Thousand Oaks, CA: Sage Publications.

GOLD, S. (1992). *Refugee communities.* Newbury Park, CA: Sage Publications.

GOLD, S., & KIBRIA, N. (1993). Vietnamese refugees and blocked mobility. *Asian and Pacific Migration Journal, 2,* 27–56.

GONDOLF, E. (1997). Batterer programs: What we know and need to know. *Journal of Interpersonal Violence, 12,* 83–98.

GORELICK, S. (1991). Contradictions of feminist methodology. *Gender and Society, 5,* 459–477.

HAINES, D. (1996). Patterns of refugee resettlement and adaptation. In D. Haines (Ed.), *Refugees in America in the 1990s* (pp. 28–59). Westport, CT: Greenwood Press.

HARDING, S. (1991). *Whose science? Whose knowledge? Thinking from women's lives.* Ithaca, NY: Cornell University Press.

HONDAGNEU-SOTELO, P. (1994). *Gendered transitions: Mexican experiences of immigration.* Berkeley, CA: University of California Press.

HUISMAN, K. (1996). Wife beating in Asian American communities: Identifying the service needs of an overlooked segment of the U.S. population. *Violence Against Women, 2,* 260–283.

KANUHA, V. (1996). Domestic violence, racism, and the battered women movement in the US. In J. Edleson & Z. Esikovits (Eds.), *Future interventions with battered women and their families* (pp. 34–50). Thousand Oaks, CA: Sage Publishing.

KIBRIA, N. (1993). *Family tightrope: The changing lives of Vietnamese Americans.* Princeton, NJ: Princeton University Press.

KURZ, D. 1993. Physical assaults by husbands: A major social problem. In R. Gelles and D. R. Loseke (Eds.), *Current controversies on family violence* (pp. 88–103). Newbury Park, CA: Sage Publications.

LEE, M., & AU, P. (1998). Chinese battered women in North America: Their experiences and treatment. In A. Roberts (Ed.), *Battered women and their families: Intervention and treatment programs.* New York: Springer.

LIN, K., TAZUMA, L., & MASUDA, M. (1979). Adaptation problems of Vietnamese refugees. *Archives of General Psychiatry, 36,* 955–961.

MEHROTRA, M. (1999). The social construction of wife abuse: Experiences of Asian Indian women in the United States. *Violence Against Women, 5,* 619–640.

Messerschmidt, J. (1993). *Masculinities and crime.* Boston: Rowman & Littlefield.

MORASH, M., BUI, H., & SANTIAGO, A. (2000). Cultural-specific gender ideology and wife abuse in Mexican-descent families. *International Review of Victimology, 7* (special issue), 67–91.

NGUYEN, L. (1987). Cross cultural adjustment of Vietnamese in the United States. In L. B. Triàng (Ed.), *Borrowings and adaptations in Vietnamese culture* (pp. 1–21). Manoa, Hawaii: University of Hawaii at Manoa.

NGUYEN, H., & HAINES, D. (1996). Vietnamese. In D. Haines (Ed.), *Refugees in America in the 1990s* (pp. 305–327). Westport, CT: Greenwood Press.

PERILLA, J. (1999). Domestic violence as a human right issue: The case of immigrant Latinos. *Hispanic Journal of Behavior Sciences, 21,* 107–133.

RIMONTE, N. (1989). Domestic violence among Pacific Asians. In Asian Women United of California (Ed.), *Making waves: An anthology of writings by and about Asian American women* (pp. 327–337). Boston: Beacon Press.

RUMBAUT, R. G. (1989). Portraits, patterns, and predictors of the refugee adaptation process: Results and reflections from the IHARP Panel Study. In D. Haines (Ed.), *Refugees as immigrants: Cambodians, Laotians, and Vietnamese in America* (pp. 144–175). Totowa, NJ: Rowman & Littlefield.

SANCHEZ, G. (1999). Excerpts from Becoming Mexican American: Ethnicity, culture, and identity in Chicano Los Angeles, 1900–1945. In S. Coontz (Ed.), *American families: A multicultural reader* (pp. 128–152). New York: Routledge.

SCHECHTER, S. (1982). *Women and male violence: The visions and struggles of the battered women's movement.* London: Pluto Press.

SMITH, D. (1990). Women's experience as radical critique of sociology. In D. Smith (Ed.), *The conceptual practices of power* (pp. 11–28). Boston: Northwestern University Press.

TRAN, T. (1959). *Vietnam*. New York: Frederick A. Praeger.

U.S. BUREAU OF THE CENSUS. (1997). Annual demographic survey (March CPS supplement). http://www.bls.gov/cps/pub/1997/for_born.htm

WALBY, S. (1989). Theorizing patriarchy. *Sociology, 23,*213–234.

YLLO, K. (1993). Through a feminist lens: Gender, power, and violence. In R. Gelles & D. Loseke (Eds.), *Current controversies on family violence* (pp. 47–62). Newbury Park, CA: Sage Publications.

SECTION VI

Women in Criminal Justice Professions

25

Women on the Bench: Mavericks, Peacemakers, or Something Else?

Research Questions, Issues, and Suggestions

Susan L. Miller and Michelle L. Meloy

Judicial sentencing is the outcome of a cumulative process reflecting many earlier decisions and stages. One question raised by researchers is whether or not male and female judges bring different perspectives and methods of case resolution to the bench. Most of the research conducted on sentencing outcomes thus far has been quantitative, and as such, may mask subtle distinctions between how male and female judges operate. What may be needed in studying gender and judicial decision making, then, is a *deeper*, qualitative examination of the social context of the judiciary through an exploration of individual attitudes of female judges and their role orientations, as well as of the organizational/social factors that affect them. There are two related parts to this chapter: First, we examine what we know about women judges in general according to studies conducted by state and federal gender task forces and related literature; and second, we explore what "woman judge" means and what this experience implies as described by a sample of women judges.

Despite the unprecedented numbers of women judges at the local, state, and federal level today, including two U.S. Supreme Court Justices, women on the bench remain a token percentage of the judiciary. Currently, 23 percent of state appellate court justices are women (Flango, 1998) and less than 15 percent of federal judgeships are held by women[1] (Merlo & Pollock, 1995). For most elective state judiciary positions, women had to wait until after passage of the Nineteenth Amendment to be eligible (Cook, 1978; Feinman, 1986). The first attorney-trained woman in the United States was elected to a state trial court (Ohio) in 1920, and the first woman was appointed to the federal bench in 1934. Even after that, the numbers remained small and it was not until 1979 that all states had at least one attorney-trained woman on their courts (Berkson, 1981–1982). For the state in which our sample of female judges was selected, the number of female attorney-judges increased from eight in 1980 to 20 in 1990.

The chapter begins with an overview of the state and federal gender task force findings and an examination of factors and circumstances that have shaped many of the contemporary beliefs, behaviors, and working environments of women judges. In particular, we explore the ramifications of a male-dominated justice profession for women who join, the dynamics of personal and professional conflicts, and gender-related issues in judicial decision making. Within this broader framework, we also specifically examine women's own words about their judicial experiences and actions.

GENDER TASK FORCES

Fighting the war against gender bias is nothing new for women, and the battles won have afforded them the right to vote, to enter traditionally male-dominated occupations, and lifted legal prohibitions against sex-based discrimination. Although progress has been made on many fronts, the courts and the legal profession remain one of the most impervious bastions of patriarchy and bias. If women do not yet enjoy fair and equitable treatment under the law and in the justice system, their struggles and triumphs remain "bittersweet and incomplete" (Kearney & Sellers, 1996, p. 586).

Beginning in 1983, under the urging of the National Organization for Women's Judicial Educational Program, publication of the first gender task force (New Jersey Task Force on Women and the Courts) was released. To date, more than 40 states and nine of the 13 federal circuits have established task forces to study the degree to which gender bias exists within the court system and to propose ways of eliminating it. The primary questions the task forces sought to answer include: Is justice gender blind? Is equal treatment extended to all players? Does the context in which women fight against injustices ironically engage in its own discriminatory practices?

Generally, the task force findings can be categorized into two groups. The first dealt with gender bias as a constant factor in the daily operations of the courtroom and in the judicial decision-making process. In other words, the gender task forces of the state and federal judiciary closely examined how the perceptions *of* and *about* women (i.e., as jurors, witnesses, attorneys, judges, plaintiffs, defendants, etc.) affect not only women's experience in the courtroom but potentially the legal outcome as well. The second category looked at how gender bias affected the occupational positions available to women within the legal profession and court administration. Stated differently, the gender task forces investigated the extent to which professions within judicial circles remained segregated by gender (Kearney & Sellers, 1997).

Time and again, the reports cited the "pervasiveness" of gender bias in the judiciary specifically, in regard to issues of domestic violence, divorce economics, child custody, courtroom dynamics (Riger, Foster-Fishman, Nelson-Kuna, & Curran, 1995), sexual harassment and discrimination, occupational and pay range segregation, haphazard commitment to affirmative action principles, and employee benefit packages that are insensitive to the needs of women (Kearney & Sellers, 1997, p. 8). Therefore, rather than being a repository of justice and fairness, the courts, at times, engage in their own form of discrimination (Resnik, 1996).

Traditionally, the courts have viewed women in stereotypical fashion. For instance, according to the task force findings, many courts continue to believe that women are partially, if not primarily, responsible for their own domestic violence and sexual harassment victimization and also prejudge the type of juror or witness a woman will be based solely on her gender. Additionally, women's performance as mothers and wives are critiqued by the courts according to conventional expectations. These images of women remain apparent today, in that the "sex of females somehow defines their role and nature" (Kearney & Sellers, 1996, p. 9).

Gender stereotypes may help explain the courtroom insensitivity male professionals exhibit toward female professionals. The task force reports revealed a consistent pattern: women employed by the court, including those sitting on the bench, stated that men addressed them by terms of endearment (i.e., honey, sweetheart, dear), and subjected women to jokes, at their own expense, emphasizing gender and sexuality (Rosenberg, Pearlstadt, & Phillips, 1993). Female lawyers and judges were often referred to by their first name, whereas men of equal or lower stature were called "your honor" or "counselor" (Kearney & Sellers, 1997, p. 10). Therefore, women are seen as women, first and foremost, regardless of their formal or actual powers. "That women judges and lawyers who possess the privilege of formal authority can still be subjected to minor and major harassment bears testament to the pervasive modes by which [male] domination continues" (Resnik, 1996, p. 972).

Gender bias and sexism in the courts are enduring despite the fact that women enter law school at nearly the same rate as those of their male counterparts, come from similar backgrounds, attend the same law programs, and perform equally well in their academic endeavors. However, the similarities between female and male lawyers end after graduation. Female lawyers are overrepresented in lower prestige ranks (government, legal aid, and public defender work), and males are overrepresented in the higher-prestige positions (large law firms and the judiciary) (Coontz, 1995). The higher echelons of the court remain dominated by white men (Resnik, 1996). Unfortunately, this trend does not appear to be dissipating, and law, as an occupation, remains highly stratified by gender. For instance, one study found that as more women enter the profession, the career gap between women and men deepened (Tienda, Smith, & Ortiz, 1987).

This career gap is true not only for attorneys but also for other female court employees. Court personnel systems are plagued by rampant gender bias, with some states (Rhode Island, Connecticut, Utah, Colorado, and Massachusetts) reporting upward of 95 percent of female court personnel sharing in the lowest seven pay grades and none in the top seven. Men dominate key administrative positions throughout the court system, whereas the low-paying "clerical ghetto" is reserved, almost exclusively, for women (Kearney & Sellers, 1996).

The task force reports have made a significant impact on the administration of justice at the state and federal level and offer many recommendations to eliminate gender bias in the courts. Several states have published follow-up reports that track the court's progress in implementing change.[2] Some examples of these judicial revisions are: education and training highlighting gender bias, new sexual harassment policies, revamped personnel procedures designed to include family-sensitive measures for court employees and witnesses, increased emphasis on affirmative action procedures to encourage the recruitment of minorities and women, and the elimination of gender bias terminology in legal statutes and court documents. Some jurisdictions have also initiated "court watching programs" to serve as overseers of gender bias in courtrooms (Kearney & Sellers, 1996). However, perhaps the single greatest achievement of the task force movement has been its ability to make women's voices heard and to illustrate that women suffer from gender bias in courts and the legal system differently than men (Resnik, 1996). We turn now to an overview of the organizational and professional barriers that women face when entering the legal and judicial professions.

Breaking into All-Male Domains: Women's Entrance into the Criminal Justice Profession

The far-reaching influence of "separate spheres" mentality [which divided the world into the public sphere of economic and intellectual pursuits for men, and the private sphere of (supposedly) tranquil domesticity for women] confined women—both perceptually and structurally—to differential utilization in the labor market (Flynn, 1982). Rigid gender-role expectations, socialization practices, and institutionalized exclusionary practices operate to perpetuate the dearth of job opportunities for women in the criminal justice and legal fields, with the notable exception of supportive roles such as staff positions. These practices were eventually challenged by women who sought entrance into policing, corrections, and the courts in the 1970s (see Belknap, 1991; Martin, 1980; Price & Sokoloff, 1995; Zimmer, 1986).

Even when successful, as in the past 20 years, women often have found that once inside, their roles and advancement opportunities are severely curtailed because of stereotypes, differently applied performance and evaluation standards, and lack of access to the "old boys network" (see Epstein, 1995; Schafran, 1987). "Although these problems are not peculiar to criminal justice, they are keenly felt among women in this area, perhaps because crime and crime control are so closely associated with traditionally 'masculine' values" (Flynn, 1982, p. 344). Masculine traits, such as power, force, authority, and aggressiveness, are seen as belonging only to men and as the central qualifications for professions such as police officers, lawyers, judges, and correctional officers, and therefore used to justify maintaining them as male-only domains: "The link between masculinity and criminal justice is so tightly bound that we may say it is true not merely that only men can be crime fighters, but even that to be a crime fighter means to be a man" (Wilson, 1982, p. 361). Some scholars suggest, however, that the *most* resistance to admitting women to positions of traditional male power has been by the courts due to the law degree requirement (Baunach & Rafter, 1982). Mandating additional educational credentials— when structural access to law schools have not been equal for men and women until recently—exacerbates an already lopsided gatekeeping process. Nowhere is women's underrepresentation more glaring than in the courts (Githens, 1995).

Access to the "Old Boys Network" and Gatekeeping of Political Power

There is an inclination on the part of male gatekeepers to maintain judicial selection criteria that favor men. For instance, the American Bar Association embraces career paths that are typically male dominated. Older, wealthy, corporate attorneys are awarded high judicial selection ratings at the expense of women who are less likely to share similar background characteristics, career patterns, and political activism (Beiner, 1999; Githens, 1995). "No doubt the key to judicial selection lies in the political system. Since federal and state bar associations exert substantial influence over judicial appointments, it is significant that women are largely excluded from the boards of governors of bar associations and from executive positions within these organizations. Rather, political party leaders who slate judicial candidates tend to follow value systems that invariably favor the selection of male candidates" (Flynn, 1982, p. 319).

Criminal justice agencies generally are regarded as "bastions of classical male chauvinism which operate in a variety of unspoken ways to effectively exclude women" (Lamber & Streibe, 1974; see also Martin & Jurik, 1996). One way that antiwomen attitudes emerge is through the operating stereotypical assumption that the "male" characteristics of brute force, physical prowess, and toughness are the desirable characteristics of the job. These stereotypical characteristics are emphasized in the courts as well: Women are viewed as not being tough, analytical, or unemotional enough to function successfully as attorneys, or make the hard decisions that judges face (Merlo & Pollock, 1995).

Another way that such attitudes emerge is through development of the "all-male clubhouse," where "[i]n such work environments, participants often value the exclusivity of totally male companionship as a desirable goal in itself" (Wilson, 1982, p. 366). The process is informal, with old boys networks established through which favors are exchanged, barriers to inclusion are constructed, and bonding among the dominant male players is facilitated (Farr, 1988). Socializing and other informal interactions with colleagues contribute to a more satisfying working environment. Women are typically more isolated than men in the criminal justice profession, given the scarcity of female colleagues. This isolation is exacerbated for women occupying high positions in their professions, such as judgeships (Merlo & Pollock, 1995). Apart from the job morale/satisfaction issue, informal exchanges with colleagues also offer opportunities to learn important job-related information. Women become disadvantaged if they are excluded from these: "[I]f you don't sit down and talk with your colleagues, you miss an awful lot of information: What's going on? What bills are pending in the legislature? Who's going to be the next director or something or other? If you just go about your business, you'll be the only one who doesn't know that something critical is about to happen and you'll look foolish because you ask stupid questions. It's a big dilemma" (Baunach & Rafter, 1982, pp. 351–352).

Unfortunately, despite growth in the numbers of women entering criminal justice professions today, in the decade and a half since these early studies were conducted, not much has changed in the restructuring of gendered patterns in male-dominated organizations (Belknap, 1996; Martin and Jurik, 1996; Messerschmidt, 1993; Moyer, 1992).

LISTENING TO THE WORDS OF FEMALE JUDGES

In this section we explore the perceptions and experiences of a small sample of female judges. A total of 20 active female judges were identified in 1990 using state bar association information on all attorney-judgeships in any capacity (civil, criminal, administrative, appellate, etc.) in the state under investigation.[3]

These 20 female judges represent 8.4 percent of the available attorney-judgeships in the state. Although all 20 judges were invited to participate by responding to a written survey and to in-depth interviews, only five judges comprised the final sample.[4] The sample of judges who participated include an illustrious group: an appellate court judge, two district court judges, and two circuit court judges, some of whom hold high-ranking positions in the state bar association. We explored judges' demographic characteristics, educational experiences, aspects of their private lives, political and legal philosophies, and other attitudes concerning the intersection of their personal and professional lives.

The judges are all white, range in age from 41 to 68, represent various religious orientations, are either currently married or were married, and have children. In addition, the judges come from families steeped in the legal professions, which may play a role in facilitating the women's interest in law. This type of familial influence may be typical of the women who headed for higher education before the great changes of the 1970s.

Parents, teachers, and Eleanor Roosevelt were most often cited as people who served as role models for the participants as they were growing up. However, when asked specifically about who the role models were who encouraged and supported their decision to enter law school, those most often mentioned were *male* family members, *male* bosses, and *male* lawyers and judges. Despite current statistics indicating that 40 to 50 percent of all students enrolled in law schools are women, the judges in this sample remember the numbers of women in their graduating law school class (between the years of 1951 and 1975) never exceeding more than 10 percent. Survey responses indicate that none of these judges encountered a female law professor or advisor. Male classmates and male professors gave no support or only moderate support. For instance, one respondent was asked while in law school why she was taking up a chair that "rightly" belonged to a male.

All of the judges self-identified as feminists, Democrats, and liberal in philosophy. The political or social causes in which they indicated the most interest include women's rights, domestic violence, gender bias in the courts, women in the law, and financial problems experienced by economically dependent spouses. We focus on three areas revealed as significant to the judges: first, we examine the women's entrance process into the judiciary. Next, we explore the intricacies involved in balancing public and private lives and the isolating effects of the bench. Finally, we examine the judges' own perceptions of how being female might affect judicial decision making as well as their opinion on criminal justice/legal issues.

Impressions of the Gatekeeping Process

The judges were asked if they faced any gender-related difficulties in becoming a judge (including earlier phases of their legal careers) and whether or not their access to the bench was limited in any way.[5] All judges indicated that they faced discrimination; actions addressing these instances of discrimination, however, were rarely taken because of the possibility of jeopardizing one's future. Several were also unwilling to risk financial security by challenging such discrimination. One judge said she took no action "although I could have. I knew it would ruin my reputation if I did." Another judge said: "Depending on the circumstances, I would ignore it or respond with humor or challenge the treatment." Still another judge said that her strategy was to find a different job. These discriminatory experiences are confirmed by the findings of the state committee formed to study gender bias in the courts. Specifically, the committee found that 13 percent of the male attorneys, 20 percent of the female attorneys, 15 percent of the male judges, and 69 percent of the female judges responded that they were aware of gender bias in the selection process.[6]

In contrast to the obstacles identified that curtailed or discouraged women from pursuing the bench, judges were also asked to identify the specific factors that *helped* them to become judges and what kinds of support or reactions they received from their male colleagues:

First, a plan. The plan was to cultivate the Judicial Nominating Committee, place myself in a position of prominence, in continuing legal education and in Bar Association and cultivate the person best known to have the Governor's ear. (Judge A)

Motherhood! Of course, being a Master because it was a courtroom situation; also, being the first woman Bar president, having worked around the judges for years, political activities, affiliations with individuals and groups. (Judge E)

I always knew that they did not want the women getting, you know, these positions. But, they were always very cordial. . . . I find that the younger lawyers (when I say younger I mean in their 40s and younger) don't have, I don't think, the hang-ups as much. You know, they went through law school together, accept women, and are just used to women being in everything they do and it's just a very normal thing. But, [the older men] are falling back and re-grouping. In other words, the women have a very tough time. . . . Every time a woman tried to get on the Circuit Court, they kind of close forces and really resist because you're getting to the top of the pinnacle, see, and they're very afraid that they're going to lose their strong-hold. Gender bias is still there. We're breaking down the barriers, you know, it takes time. I see these young women coming on, 35, 38 years old, you know, it's going to be a different world for them as they go through, I think. (Judge C)

These statements demonstrate that the women are "savvy" to the political networking process even if their access to this network is more restricted than members of the male political in-group. Overall, three of the judges believed that their gender played a role to get them on the bench because "those in power" finally agreed to consider women and began to search deliberately for qualified female candidates. In fact, the state committee explicitly recognized the harm created when the number of female appointments were limited: It "reinforces the discriminatory environment women face" (based on the state's Special Joint Committee, 1989), and this recognition may have stimulated judicial nominations of female candidates.[7]

Reconciliation of Personal and Public Lives and the Isolating Effects of the Bench

The judges discussed at length the difficulties in juggling and combining career and family roles. Without prompting, the judges indicated that motherhood was one of the best preparatory jobs they could have experienced before becoming a judge. The judges repeatedly stressed that "motherhood" prepared them best for the bench, for it taught them "to be patient, to listen, to be firm, and to be fair." One judge said:

I think that being a mother has got to be a good background for being a judge. You do a lot of decision-making when you're raising a family—all the time. I raised a family from a desk. Also, at the dinner table, when you're trying to find out something, you learn never to act surprised. You learn skills that are very, very useful on the bench. (Judge C)

Similarly, being a "working mother" helped the following judge to appreciate the dilemmas that many women face when balancing family and professional responsibilities.

Child care problems. I am certainly very sympathetic to child care problems. And I've had women write to me thanking me for understanding that they have to go, for example, at 5:00 pm. because they have to have their kids picked up by 5:30 pm. and they've gone in front of other judges who don't understand. And I understand that, and I would never make a lawyer who couldn't stay for those reasons really stay. I'm almost shocked, this is almost the 21st century, I mean, we've got to get in line here. Not everybody can afford care in the house and they don't choose that method and kids need to be dealt with and it's a societal issue. So, in that respect, I certainly think my gender and experience as a working mother have played a big role. . . . I've had people thank me profusely and I think other magistrates they wouldn't even ask, but they somehow know they can ask me. (Judge C)

The judges were also queried about whether they found their positions socially isolating as well as the reaction they received from strangers upon discovering their occupation. The judges responded as follows:

The black robe is isolating. . . . Reactions I received from others? Surprise. You go into a group with a man and someone will say you know Judge _____. They will invariably look at the man and shake his hand. (Judge A)

I feel less isolated because there is fairly good representation of women and blacks. But I do feel isolated from my former lawyer friends and bar associate friends. People are standoffish and reserved about what they say in my presence. . . . Some men are disrespectful or don't show deference. They are usually litigants. Some lawyers make inappropriate jokes to ingratiate themselves. (Judge B)

Isolated? Yes. Appearance of impropriety rules mandate isolation; only lawyers you *know* have no chance of appearing before you can you see socially on a court day (e.g., lunch!). Reaction from others? Surprise, dismay, respect. . . . What I enjoy least about being a judge is the isolation from other lawyers; isolation from my friends, particularly lawyers. (Judge D)

This isolation may be related to *both* professional position and gender. Increased professional envy of female judges by their male colleagues may also be a factor related to women's isolation.

Gender-Related Attitudes and Justice-Based Philosophies

The judges were asked to discuss a variety of topics related to gender, such as: Does being a woman play a role in decision making? Do women judges impose harsher sentences to overcompensate for any stereotype that women are more lenient? The judges explicitly acknowledged that being a woman did play a positive role in how they responded to some cases. The judges generally felt that *they* behaved more patiently, more humanely, and possessed the ability to admit when *they* don't always have all the answers. These traits were not perceived as weaknesses, however, but as positive skills and strengths that women judges bring to the bench to complement their legal knowledge and professional experiences.

We're all a product of who we are, and I think there's a difference somehow in the way we do our jobs as judges. I'm not unhappy, as being perceived to be reasonable, I think it's what I really am. I am quite willing to admit when I don't know the answer. I don't feel hung up on not being able to admit that. I don't feel I have to pretend that I know everything. (Judge C)

I think any woman has an empathy for a woman that comes before her who has been beaten. I think that we can relate to what this woman is going through; how embarrassed she is to stand up in front of the world and talk about being beaten by her husband. . . . I feel like my gender helps me a lot in criminal cases; you have these young people who come before you, you know, first time offenders, I look at them, I see my children, or their friends. I'm sure men have their skills and I think women look at things—we make just as good decisions, but, many times we're not as objective as the men because we have that emotional quotient that comes in there just naturally. It gives us a different view. You know, I think we all come up with the same decision at the end, but we come to it from a different way. (Judge E)

I do sometimes have a reflection . . . that I am being tough because I don't want to be perceived as being soft and I try to examine whether that is what I am doing and I usually decide that it is not. I enumerate the reasons for my sentence. I write down what the sentence is and the basis. But I'm just giving myself a margin of error and I'm suggesting that I don't think we know ourselves absolutely and that there is a possibility that sometimes that concern about how others perceive us is more weighty than I think it is. But I believe and I hope that generally my sentences are fair and are based on objective reasons and not on any fear that I have on how people will perceive me. (Judge B)

During the in-depth interviews, judges responded to a variety of questions pertaining directly to issues of law that affect women. Time after time, the judges responded that although gender should *not* play a role, nonetheless, it might. They expressed that women judges may be able to empathize more, particularly with female victims. Actions by male judges, on the other hand, particularly the ones who continue to operate within a historical and stereotypical context of victim blaming when facing violent crimes committed by men against women, might reflect their own (male) assumptions and experiences in a culture that often trivializes women's experiences and victimizations. For instance, the women were asked if they believed that it makes a difference for male judges or female judges to preside over rape cases.

I don't know. I would hope not. I would hope that any judge would be able to look at the evidence fairly and impartially and direct the jury in the same way. It's not as much of an issue if you realize that 99 percent of the time rape cases are going to be tried by a jury. And, a jury is made up, generally, of both men and women and we assume that all members of that jury will decide the case fairly and impartially according to the evidence presented. If we can assume that in laypeople, why should we not assume that of judges who are not only trained in the law, but through their experience as judges, expected to behave in a fair and impartial manner? (Judge D)

Whether it does or not, I don't know. I suppose that the reality is I suppose on some level, it's probably even on a subconscious level more frightening for a female because you can imagine it happening to yourself. (Judge C)

Yes I do. Now there again, there are of course I think our new breed of males may be a little different, but so many men I've heard them say "oh, she asked for it," or "what's the big deal" and things like that. I don't know that the men have caught on yet that rape is such a violent act, it's not really a sexy act; It's an act of violence against the woman. . . . I can only tell you of how I can translate these into domestic violence cases that we hear all the time and some of my own colleagues, some of the comments they make, make me realize how insensitive they are. You know, I've even heard them say [she pretends to sound like a man while saying this], "well, you know, women like to be roughed up," and "you don't understand—a lot of women *like* that." Until they get away from that attitude, until they realize, then, we have a problem. (Judge E)

Domestic violence had been earlier identified as an area in which all of the judges expressed strong interests. The judges focused on the enforcement aspect, reflecting the trend to arrest batterers rather than relying on alternatives to law enforcement, such as separation, and mediation. The female judges' responses sharply contradicted empirical research that has shown in the past that the male judiciary has not treated domestic violence cases with any more seriousness than other players in the criminal justice system (i.e., police and prosecutors) (cf. Dobash & Dobash, 1992 Price & Sokoloff, 1995).

> Well, it depends on the circumstances. I think that the arrest option must be available to the victim. In other words, we have fought for many years now to finally get a law on the books that requires an officer to make the arrest and that permits such cases to be brought into criminal court in a manner that's workable and effective. That's not to say that there aren't other alternatives, or that other alternatives aren't appropriate in many cases. But sometimes, nothing short of arrest is going to work. And I think that that has to absolutely be available. (Judge A)

> If someone has committed an act of domestic violence or if the victim has legitimate reasons of being in imminent danger or fear of imminent danger, then absolutely—we can't find out later that we should have had a warrant. . . . If I have a domestic violence case on my docket and I put someone on probation and an order as a condition he has to move or stay away from the victim, not threaten, intimidate, harass or annoy.

> If I get a call, I don't take a chance. We've learned, I think, we have to make sure. I think, too, too many times these cases are not taken seriously, and people are really injured. (Judge E)

> I have for years felt that it was important that victims of those kinds of crime be treated like victims of other crimes. I don't think just because it's between people who know one another that the option shouldn't be available. . . . But I think that the option of an arrest and a trial and conviction is one that ought to be accessible to victims of domestic violence. And it ought to be used. (Judge B)

Overall, our interview data reveal a marked difference in judges' philosophies about gender-crime issues that may be atypical of traditional male judicial attitudes (for in-depth discussions of feminist jurisprudence related to gender differences in philosophical orientations, see Fineman and Thomadsen, 1991; Frug, 1992; and Hoff, 1991). For years, advocates of women's rights, lawyers, and others have opposed and challenged the manner in which the criminal justice and legal systems treat female victims of violent crimes committed by male offenders. The extant literature demonstrates that the enforcers (police), interpreters (lawyers and judges), and punishers (corrections) are primarily male and have been socialized and trained to believe assumptions and expectations about appropriate gender roles in society (Price & Sokoloff, 1995; Stanko, 1985). The judges in this sample seem to recognize the results of this institutionalized and systemic sexism: victim blaming and differential treatment of women. Part of this heightened understanding is shaped by their own experiences.

In summary, the judges' responses indicate the salience of the role that gender plays not only in the dynamics of specific crimes but also in the responses to these crimes by members of our social and legal institutions (Allen & Wall, 1993; "Different voices," 1990; Merlo & Pollock, 1995). These beliefs are consistent with findings revealed in research on state supreme court justices which suggested that female judges tend to have a "pro-woman" stance on a large range of issues that directly affect women and often vote against the male majority on matters related to sex discrimination, sexual conduct and abuse, medical malpractice, and property settlements (Allen & Wall, 1987, 1993). The data in this series of research indicated that female judges held steadfast to their beliefs when it came to expanding women's rights, even in the face of opposition from the majority of the court (Allen & Wall, 1993). Future research could explore whether or not judges respond to consciousness raising about general social problems identified by society at large, or whether judges highlight specific issues because of their personal backgrounds, experience, and world views (cf. Tobias, 1990, 1991).

DISCUSSION AND CONCLUSIONS

In this chapter we explore women judges in light of the gender task force findings as well as offered insight into the way that women judges view themselves within social and judicial contexts. For the component relating to women judges, the depth and richness of the interview data, despite its small sample size, provides more detailed information than that typically collected by close-ended survey instruments. The judges describe *their* own experiences and perceptions, which serves as a starting point in refining questions that should also be asked of male judges in future comparative studies, as well as providing a complementary data set to quantitative research exploring sentencing decisions and gender.[8]

Most prior research that has identified gender-related differences among judges has focused exclusively on the types of sentences they impose. This kind of research hides the importance of background factors and experiences that shape one's world views and also ignores differences in the social construction of gender roles and expectations in our society. Gender alone may not exert significant influences on sentencing decisions per se, but the different experiences and philosophies that men and women have create a contextualized construct that may exert distinctions in judicial decision making (Davis 1992–1993; Rush, 1993; Sherry, 1986; West, 1991). The differences that men and women may bring to the bench typically remain unacknowledged because they contradict the model of the "impartial" arbiter. The information gleaned from the judges' voices here lend support to hopes that women's "emphasis on connection and contextuality might similarly transform law" (Sherry, 1986, p. 165), as well as to hopes of interrupting gender bias operating against women in the courts.

The judicial gender task forces succeeded in prioritizing the issue of gender bias at the state and federal levels. The reports and follow-up studies generated by this movement emphasize women's experiences in the court system and legal profession and portray how these experiences differ by gender. Collectively, the task force findings have demanded that the "halls of justice" take judicial notice of the problems created by gender discrimination within its courtrooms, administrative organizations, and legal profession as well as validating the perceptions of women (Resnik, 1996, p. 963).

For the women judges interviewed here, several important findings emerge. First, the voices of the women judges indicate that although they experience multiple obligations, they have succeeded in reconciling these diverse role-strain pressures. The judges have reconceptualized the "traditional" caretaking role of motherhood to be one that offers excellent preparation for the bench. This interpretation differs greatly from "male" attributes of detachment and autonomy because it explicitly recognizes the benefits of familial and intimate experiences (Anleu, 1995).[9] This kind of characterization permits women judges to use their conventional sexual roles to claim legitimacy in their nontraditional career choice.

The women assert that they have been successful at negotiating and balancing their personal and professional obligations. In fact, by imbuing women's traditional female roles with honor, and insisting that these attributes are the reason for their greater clarity of judicial vision, the women judges present themselves as innovative mavericks who are more sensitive to situations of personal, familial, and/or economic injustice.

A second important finding that emerged concerns the judges' explicit perceptions about how they believe that being a woman contributes to their decision making. Although the judges are quick to emphasize that their decisions are fair, equal, strict, and just, they recognize that being female may bring a uniquely feminine understanding to the situation. The judges interviewed in this study stressed that they believe that both male and female judges ultimately reach the same legal conclusion but that they follow different paths to get there—paths that are indeed related to gender.[10] The judges describe their judicial style as patient, empathic, reasonable, with a willingness and openness to hear all sides, and they recognize that these characteristics may be misperceived or misunderstood by others as indicating that they are lenient or coddle criminals (i.e., are "soft" on crime). The judges, however, insisted that this was not the case. Their rulings were simply shaped by different understandings of the situations and were *enhanced* by these understandings, not harmed or weakened. It is likely that defendants and victims felt that they were treated with more respect because of the judges' demeanor and style, regardless of case outcome. In fact, other research suggests that offenders treated with more respect perceive greater levels of procedural justice and satisfaction (Paternoster, Brame, Bachman, & Sherman, 1997). Nowhere are these unique understandings more apparent then when we examine the judges' opinions concerning women's rights. Their willingness to resist assimilation pressures to adopt male professional norms when confronting women's issues is noteworthy. Unlike the younger "careerist" women lawyers studied by Rosenberg, Perlstadt, and Phillips (1990), who rejected feminist objectives and labels and viewed gender as "inconsequential to their careers," the women judges in this study self-labeled as feminists and endorsed the centrality of gender and its role in shaping legal discourse and judicial action.[11]

Similar to the task force findings, the judges in our sample believed that the sexist comments and actions they experienced did contribute to an inhospitable working environment throughout their legal and judicial careers. They also described feeling isolated and alienated from males in the field as well as from other lawyers and judges. These working conditions may reflect the consequences of being treated as tokens due to their scarcity in numbers and heightened visibility, so that their "non-achievement characteristics . . . eclipse performance" (MacCorquodale & Jensen, 1993, p. 583). As such, these findings echo those of Rosenberg, et al. (1993) in their research on sexist work experiences of women lawyers: Gender disparagement and sexual harassment are manifestations of "gendered systems that maintain and reinforce inequalities between men and women on the job" (p. 415).

By bringing their personal and professional experiences into the courtroom, the women revealed that they were able to dispense justice with a gentleness as well as a firmness that belied their own imaginings and expectations of a more humane courtroom setting. In fact, these views are consistent with findings reported in other studies which demonstrate that women judges opt for more participatory management styles, in contrast to men's preference for more hierarchical courtroom styles, and that women judges are more likely to acknowledge others' emotions and fears than are male judges (Judicature, 1990). Although quantitative studies may demonstrate that female judges' sentencing outcomes could be comparable or dissimilar to male judges' outcomes, the gendered paths that these follow—paths that are strikingly apparent in qualitative research, yet masked in statistical analyses—are distinctly different. Furthermore, an analysis of the task force findings provides insight into the "gendered machinery" of the court system and complements the interviews of the female judges. Hearing the voices of women and the nature of their thinking and experiences offers a much richer context in which to explore the judicial process.

NOTES

1. According to the National Center for State Courts, there are no current hard data on the percentage of female judges at the state trial level (personal communication, 2001). Furthermore, the 1995 data cited here on the percentage of women justices serving at the federal level represent the most accurate information available. However, since these statistics are not updated annually and because many federal judgeships are vacant due to judges retiring or leaving office for other reasons (Beiner, 1999), it is difficult to ascertain precisely the current demographics of the federal judiciary.

2. Colorado, Connecticut, Florida, Kentucky, Maryland, Massachusetts, New York, Minnesota, Vermont, and the state of Washington have all published procedural guidelines on how to address various types of gender bias. Additionally, judicial education programs, designed to eliminate gender bias and sexual harassment in the courts, have been enacted in at least 26 different states.

3. The state of this study will not be identified, to ensure confidentiality of the judges.

4. The other judges declined to participate because they were either too busy or because they were too concerned about confidentiality. Being approached to reveal examples of gender bias may have been perceived as threatening to their professional positions.

5. In the state of this study, the judicial selection process follows two steps: first, a nominating committee screens candidates and develops a list that is sent to the governor for each judicial vacancy. The nominating committees are comprised of attorney and lay members. Next, the governor makes appointments from these lists within a year of the occurrence of the vacancy.

6. Whereas the females indicated that the nominating committee discriminates against women in terms of initial selection and criteria, the males contended that women have been given preferential treatment in the appointment process. The data reflect, however, that despite sufficient numbers of eligible women lawyers who are of an appropriate age for appointment, women are consistently overlooked at judicial appointment time.

7. According to the state committee, many lawyers and judges believed that a quota system applied to women judges in that "once 'enough' women have been appointed, no more need apply" (Special Joint Committee, 1989). The women believed that higher standards (especially with respect to professional experience) applied to women, and inappropriate questions concerning family responsibilities, financial need, and spouse's occupations were asked of female candidates but not of male candidates, and these criteria disadvantaged women. Male attorneys, however, believed that women were selected over males who were far better qualified, and women were favored "out of a misplaced sense of imbalance on the bench" (Special Joint Committee, 1989). The committee found no substantiation for these claims, and in fact, discovered that the opposite was true. (Due to honoring the request of the judges for confidentiality, the state special joint committee is not identified or listed in the references.)

8. Obviously, our research does not attempt to *compare* women's experiences and perceptions with those of their male counterparts on the bench, although this avenue may be a potentially fruitful inquiry to pursue in future studies.

9. Feminist scholars no doubt recognize that just as essentialist positions about women are problematic, there are also potential problems when introducing essentialist characteristics of men.

10. This is a puzzling contradiction: At the same time that the women judges admit that they may have greater insight and empathy related to women's legal issues, they maintain that these strengths do *not* influence their final outcomes.

11. It may also be the case that as women attain higher-status positions, such as judgeships, they feel "safe" in being more outspoken compared to aspiring "careerist" lawyers.

REFERENCES AND BIBLIOGRAPHY

ALLEN, D., & WALL, D. (1987). The behavior of women state supreme court justices: Are they tokens or outsiders? *Justice System Journal. 12*(1), 232–244.

ALLEN, D., & WALL, D. (1993). Role orientations and women state supreme justices. *Judicature, 77*, 156–161.

ANLEU, S.L.R. (1995). Women in law: Theory, research, and practice. In B. R. Price & N. J. Sokoloff (Eds.), *The criminal justice system and women offenders, victims, and workers.* New York: McGraw-Hill.

BAUNACH, P. J., & RAFTER, N. H. (1982). Sex-role operations: Strategies for women working in the criminal justice system. In N. H. Rafter & E. A. Stanko (Eds.), *Judge, lawyer, victim, thief.* Boston: Northeastern University Press.

BEINER, T. (1999). What will diversity on the bench mean for justice? *Michigan Journal of Gender and Law, 6*(113), 1–36.

BELKNAP, J. (1996). The invisible woman: Gender, crime and justice. Cincinatti, OH: Wadsworth.

BELKNAP, J. (1991). Women in conflict: An analysis of women correctional officers. *Women and Criminal Justice, 2*, 89–115.

Cook, B. B. (1978). Women judges: The end of tokenism. In W. Hepperle & L. Crites (Eds.), *Women in the courts.* Williamsburg, VA: National Center for State Courts.

COONTZ, P. (1995). Gender bias in the legal profession: Women "see" it, men don't. *Women and Politics, 15*(2), 1–22.

DAVIS, S. (1992–1993). Do women judges speak "in a difference voice"?—Carol Gilligan, feminist legal theory, and the Ninth Circuit. *Wisconsin Women's Law Journal, 7–8*, 143–173.

DAVIS, S., HAIRE, S. & SONGER, D. R. (1993). Voting behavior and gender on the U.S. courts of appeals. *Judicature, 77*(3), 129–133.

DOBASH, R. E., & DOBASH, R. P. 1992. *Women, violence and social change.* New York: Routledge.

EPSTEIN, C. F. (1981). *Women in law.* New York: Basic Books.

EPSTEIN, C. F. (1983). The role strain of balancing political and professional responsibilities with family and personal responsibilities. In W. Hepperle & L. Crites (Eds.), *Women in the courts.* Williamsburg, VA: National Center for State Courts.

EPSTEIN, C. F. (1988). *Deceptive distinctions: Sex, gender, and the social order.* New Haven, CT: Yale University Press.

EPSTEIN, C. F. (1990). Faulty framework: Consequences of the difference model for women in the law. *New York Law School Law Review, 35*, 309–336.

EPSTEIN, C. F., SAUTE, R., OGLENSKY, B., & GEVER, M. (1995). Glass ceilings and open doors: Women's advancement in the legal profession. *Fordham Law Review, 64*(2), 291–449.

FARR, K. A. (1988). Dominance bonding through the good old boys sociability groups. *Sex Roles, 18*, 259–277.

FEINMAN, C. (1986). *Women in the criminal justice system* (2nd ed.). New York: Praeger.

Final Report of the Special Committee on Gender to the D.C. Circuit Task Force on Gender, Race and Ethnic Bias. (1996). *Georgetown Law Review, 84*(5), 1657.

FINEMAN, M. A., & THOMADSEN, N. S. (1991). *At the boundaries of law: Feminism and legal theory.* New York: Routledge.

FLANGO, C. (1998). *Appellate court procedures.* Williamsburg, VA: National Center for State Courts.

FLYNN, E. E. (1982). Women as criminal justice professionals: A challenge to tradition. In N. H. Rafter & E. A. Stanko (Eds.), *Judge, lawyer, victim, thief.* Boston: Northeastern University Press.

FRUG, M. J. (1992). *Postmodern legal feminism.* New York: Routledge.

GILLIGAN, C. (1982). *In a different voice.* Cambridge, MA: Harvard University Press.

GITHENS, M. (1995). Getting appointed to the state court: The gender dimension. *Women and Politics, 15*(4), 1–24.

HOFF, J. (1991). *Law, gender, and injustice.* New York: New York University Press.

Different voices, different choices? The impact of more women lawyers and judges on the judicial system. (1990). *Judicature, 74*(3), 138–146.

KEARNEY, R., & SELLERS, H. (1996). Sex on the docket: Reports of state task forces on gender bias. *Public Administration Review, 56*(6), 587–593.

KEARNEY, R., & SELLERS, H. (1997). Gender bias in court personnel administration. *Judicature, 81*(1), 8–14.

LAMBER, J. S. & STREIBE, V. L. (1974). Women executives, managers, and professionals in the Indiana criminal justice system. *Indiana Law Review, 8,* 353.

MACCORQUODALE, P., & JENSEN., G. (1993). Women in the law: Partners or tokens? *Gender & Society, 7,* 582–593.

MACKINNON, C. (1982). Towards a feminist jurisprudence. *Stanford Law Review, 34,* 703–737.

MARTIN, E. (1990). Men and women on the bench: Vive la difference? *Judicature, 73*(4), 204–208.

MARTIN, S. E. (1980). *Breaking and entering: Policewomen on patrol.* Berkeley, CA: University of California Press.

MARTIN, S. E., & JURIK, N. C. (1996). *Doing justice, doing gender: Women in law and criminal justice occupations.* Thousand Oaks, CA: Sage Publications.

MCCORMICK, P., JOB, T., & BROCKMAN, J. (1993). Do women judges make a difference? An analysis by appeal court data. *Canadian Journal of Law and Society, 8*(1), 135–148.

MENKEL-MEADOW, C. (1985). Portia in different voice. *Berkeley Women's Law Journal, 1,* 39.

MERLO, A. V., & POLLOCK, J. M. (1995). *Women, law, and social control.* Boston: Allyn & Bacon.

MESSERSCHMIDT, J. W. (1993). *Masculinities and crime: Critique and reconceptualization of theory.* Lanham, MD: Rowman & Littlefield.

MOYER, I. L. (1992). *The changing roles of women in the criminal justice system.* Prospect Heights, IL: Waveland Press.

MURRAY, F. K. (1990). Women and the law: Have we really come a long way? *Judge's Journal,* 19–23.

PATERNOSTER, R., BRAME, R., BACHMAN, R., & SHERMAN, L. (1997). Do fair procedures matter? The effect of procedural justice on spouse assault. *Law and Society Review, 31*(1). 163–204.

PRICE, B. R., & SOKOLOFF, N. J. (1995). *The criminal justice system and women: Women offenders, victims, and workers.* New York: McGraw-Hill.

RESNIK, J. (1996). Asking about gender in courts. *Signs: Journal of Women in Culture and Society, 21*(4), 952–990.

RIGER, S., FOSTER-FISHMAN, P., NELSON-KUNA, J., & CURRAN, B. (1995). Gender bias in courtroom dynamics. *Law and Human Behavior, 19*(5), 465–480.

ROSENBERG, J., PERLSTADT, H., & PHILLIPS, W. R. F. (1990). Politics, feminism and women's professional orientations: A case study of women lawyers. *Women and Politics, 10,* 19–48.

ROSENBERG, J., PERLSTADT, H., & PHILLIPS, W. R. F. (1993). Now that we are here: Discrimination, disparagement, and harassment at work and the experience of women lawyers. *Gender and Society, 7,* 415–433.

RUSH, S. E. (1993). Feminist judging: An introductory essay. *California Review of Legal and Women's Studies, 609,* 627–632.

SCHAFRAN, L. H. (1987). Practicing law in a sexist society. In L. L. Crites & W. L. Hepperle (Eds.), *Women, the courts, and equality*, Newbury Park, CA: Sage Publications.

SHERRY, S. (1986). The gender of judges. *Law and Inequality, 4,* 159.

STANKO, E. A. (1985). *Intimate intrusions: Women's experience of male violence.* London: Routledge & Kegan Paul.

The Effects of Gender in the Federal Courts: The Final Report of the Ninth Circuit Gender Bias Task Force. (1994). *Southern California Law Review, 8,* 745.

TIEDNA, M., SMITH, S., & ORTIZ, V. (1987). Industrial restructuring, gender segregation, and sex differences in earning. *American Sociological Review, 52,* 195–210.

TOBIAS, C. (1990). The gender gap on the federal bench. *Hofstra Law Review, 19*(1), 171–184.

TOBIAS, C. (1991). More women named federal judges. *Florida Law Review, 43,* 477–486.

WEST, R. L. (1991). The difference in women's hedonic lives: A phenomenological critique of feminist legal theory. In M. A. Fineman & N. S. Thomadsen (Eds.), *At the boundaries of law: Feminism and legal theory.* New York: Routledge.

WEST, C., & ZIMMERMAN, D. H. (1987). Doing gender. *Gender and Society, 1,* 125–151.

WIKLER, N. J. (1987). Educating judges about gender bias in the courts. In L. L. Crites & W. L. Hepperle (Eds.), *Women, the courts, and equality.* Newbury Park, CA: Sage Publications.

WIKLER, N. J., & SCHAFRAN, L. H. (1991). Learning from the New Jersey Supreme Court task force on women in the courts: Evaluation, recommendations and implications for other states. *Women's Rights Law Reporter, 12,* 313–385.

WILSON, N. K. (1982). Women in the criminal justice professions: An analysis of status conflict. In N. H. Rafter & E. A. Stanko (Eds.), *Judge, lawyer, victim, thief.* Boston: Northeastern University Press.

ZIMMER, L. E. (1986). *Women guarding men.* Chicago: University of Chicago Press.

26

Women in the Legal Profession

Does Bias Still Exist?

Jody Clay-Warner

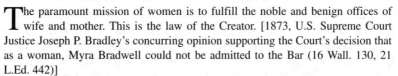

The paramount mission of women is to fulfill the noble and benign offices of wife and mother. This is the law of the Creator. [1873, U.S. Supreme Court Justice Joseph P. Bradley's concurring opinion supporting the Court's decision that as a woman, Myra Bradwell could not be admitted to the Bar (16 Wall. 130, 21 L.Ed. 442)]

Despite Supreme Court rulings and great opposition from some male attorneys, women have made significant gains in the legal profession in the United States. These gains have not been attained easily, however. Women's early attempts to enter the profession were met with resistance, and once they were admitted to practice, women experienced discrimination in hiring, salary, and promotion. Even after gains in the 1970s, women continued to face barriers to both entry and advancement. The 1980s and 1990s saw both the growth of the profession and the growth of task forces designed to study and address women's disadvantaged position. Today, women are vocal and visible members of the legal profession and, by some estimates, will soon comprise the majority of law school students (Glater, 2001). As a result, scholars have begun to examine the "feminization" of the profession and what effect this large influx of women will have on the practice of law itself (Chiu & Leicht, 1999; Menkel-Meadow, 1988). Research reveals, however, that women continue to be both accepted into the profession and excluded from it. To understand this phenomenon, I examine the history of women's entry into the profession as well as current studies of gender discrimination.

THE EARLY YEARS

Women's Entry into the Profession

Despite the resistance of the legal profession to recognize women officially as attorneys, a number of women did practice as lawyers before the American Bar Association admitted its first female members in 1918 (Feinman, 1986). Margaret Brent is known as the first woman to serve as an attorney in America (Feinman, 1986; Morello, 1986). Brent, generally recognized as an attorney by the Maryland judiciary although not officially admitted to practice, served as an attorney in colonial Maryland as early as 1648. Her most famous assignment was the administrator of the estate of Leonard Calvert, Governor of Maryland. Brent's role in Maryland's power structure was so firmly entrenched that the colonists generally referred to her as "Gentleman Margaret Brent" (Morello, 1986, p. 3). Ironically, Brent ultimately left Maryland because the legislature refused to grant her the right to vote. Morello (1986) and Bernat (1992) state that little is known about other women who may have participated in the legal system during colonial times, although there is evidence that several women represented themselves in court.

It was not until 1869, when Arabella Mansfield was admitted to the Iowa State bar, that a woman was officially recognized as an attorney in the United States. Mansfield's admission to practice, however, did not have immediate consequences for women in other states. Three years after Mansfield was licensed to practice law, the U.S. Supreme Court upheld a ruling by the Illinois State Supreme Court denying Myra Bradwell admission to the state bar after she had passed the state bar exam successfully.[1] The Illinois Supreme Court initially argued that Bradwell could not practice as an attorney, since under common law a married woman has no legal rights apart from her husband and thus could not enter into third-party contracts, as is required for attorneys (Feinman, 1986). Bradwell appealed the case, but the Supreme Court held that the states possessed the authority to determine professional qualifications and thus it was legal for the state of Illinois to bar women from serving as attorneys. *Bradwell* v. *Illinois* forced women to fight for their right to serve as attorneys on a state-by-state basis. Women were not permitted to practice in federal courts until 1879 (Morello, 1986).

Gender and Law School Admission

Around the time of the *Bradwell* decision, a few law schools also began to admit women. In 1868, Phoebe W. Couzins and Lemma Barkaloo became the first women in the United States to enter law school when they matriculated at Washington University Law School in St. Louis (Feinman, 1986; Morello, 1986). Ada Kepley enrolled in the University of Chicago Law School the next year and in 1870 became the first woman graduate of a U.S. law school. Slowly, schools around the country began to admit women, and in 1915, two institutions in Boston, Cambridge Law School and the Portia School of Law, became the first law schools designed specifically for women (Epstein, 1993).

Eastern and Ivy League schools, however, were reticent to admit women. In 1885, Alice Rufie Jordan entered Yale University Law School under a technicality—the catalog did not explicitly state that women were not allowed to enter. Once Yale's administrators recognized their mistake, they quickly amended the catalog to exclude women. They did, however, allow Jordan to graduate, but it was not until 1919 that the faculty voted to consider women applicants. Other elite law schools slowly began to admit women. Almost ten years after Yale, Columbia Law School admitted its first female student. Harvard finally admitted women in 1950, and Notre Dame enrolled women in 1969. In 1972, Washington and Lee became the last major law school in the country to open its doors to women (Slotnick, 1984).

Once women gained admission to law schools, informal quotas existed that limited women's enrollment. Admissions officers, however, denied that quotas existed and insisted that women simply were uninterested in the practice of law. This argument became more difficult to support when the *Harvard Law Record* published a report in 1965 that showed that while the number of women admitted to law school was held constant, the number of applications from women had been increasing steadily (Epstein, 1993). Epstein notes that in her 1972 survey she found that women comprised a constant proportion of students in major law schools over a 20-year period, despite an increasing number of applications.

As there were very few women in any law school class, female law students were acutely aware of their status as women. It is not surprising that many of these women experienced isolation. Women who attended law school in the first half of the twentieth century tell of being alternately ignored and castigated. Male students would frequently stamp their feet when female students responded in class to make it difficult for the professor to hear the women (Morello, 1986). Ida Klaus, who entered Columbia Law School in 1928, tells of classes in which the professor refused to call on her, despite her raising her hand repeatedly. A classmate, Helen Robinson, noted that male students refused to sit next to her in class (Morello, 1986).

As Harrington (1993) states, this inhospitable atmosphere existed at the highest levels and continued through the 1950s. She tells of attending the annual dinner that the Harvard Law School dean held to "welcome" incoming women students in 1957. At this dinner the dean told the women that they should not be there and that since women would certainly practice fewer years than men that female students were wasting the valuable resources of Harvard Law School. In interviews with Cynthia Fuchs Epstein (1993), many Harvard Law School alumnae recounted stories of in-class discrimination throughout the 1960s. A 1965 graduate stated that at the end of the term a professor announced that he believed that he had called on all class members. This woman then raised her hand and told the professor that he had not called on her or any other woman in the class. Another woman told Epstein that professors rarely called on women and seemed to fear "provoking overt (i.e., feminine) emotional collapse" (p. 66).

One of the most egregious examples of bias occurred routinely during predetermined days at a number of law schools. These days, termed Ladies Days, were popularized at Harvard University, although several other schools also held them. These days were announced in advance, and students understood that on these days the professor would call only on women. Some professors insisted that the women sit in front of the class or all congregate on the first row. On these days, the cases being discussed were often of a sexual nature or emphasized the role of women as property in English common law (Epstein, 1993; Harrington, 1993). Harvard Professor W. Barton Leach was particularly well known for his Ladies Day. On Ladies Day, Leach would tell a joke related to the case under discussion in which the punch line was "underwear." His goal appeared to be to mock the women students. Leach finally ended Ladies Day in 1968 after a group of women students "dressed in black, all wore glasses and [carrying] black briefcases" stood up during the punch line "opened [their] briefcases, and threw fancy lingerie at the 'boys,'" greatly embarrassing Leach (Epstein, 1993, p. 67, quoting from the Harvard Alumnae Directory).

Women in Legal Practice

Women graduates also faced a hiring process fraught with gender bias. Typical of other female graduates of elite law schools, Sandra Day O'Connor, who graduated third in her class at Stanford Law School in 1953, was offered only one job, as a legal secretary (Epstein, 1993).[2] Epstein notes that minority women and poor women faced even more serious barriers. She cites one Italian-American woman who was told by a Wall Street firm that they would not hire her because she was Italian, Catholic, and a "girl." This discrimination did not end with the advent of the feminist movement. It was common in the 1960s and 1970s for law firm recruiters to tell female graduates of elite schools that they didn't hire women or ask them when they planned on having children (Sassower, 1971). Morello (1986) reports that many law firms would refuse to interview women applicants and began perfunctory interviews only when placement offices insisted that they do so after a barrage of complaints from female law students.

Once women began work as attorneys, they continued to face discrimination. When women were hired, they were often hired in low-paying positions in low-prestige specialties (Epstein, 1993; Harrington, 1993). Women in private firms could expect to be paid less upon initial appointment and for the salary disparity to grow (Feinman, 1986). As White found in his 1967 study (cited in Feinman, 1986) of 2600 law school graduates (all respondents had graduated in the same year), women on average earned $1500 less than men in their first year and earned more than $8000 less than men after ten years. White found no objective reason, such as number of hours worked, experience, or prestige of law school, to account for these differences.

Women in the Judiciary

Women have also lagged behind in appointments to judgeships. Morello (1986) states that Esther McQuigg Morris became the country's first female judge when she was named justice of the peace in Wyoming in 1870. Unfortunately, Morris was one of only a handful of women to serve as a judge before the 1970s. By 1930 only 12 states had any female judges; by 1950 the number had risen to only 29 (Feinman, 1986). It was not until 1979, when Diana Barz was named a district court judge in Montana, that every state in the union had at least one sitting female state judge (Berkson, 1982).

The situation on the federal bench was even more distressing. Before the Carter administration (1976–1980), very few women served as federal judges. Slotnick (1984) notes that "more women (and non-whites) were appointed to the federal courts by Jimmy Carter. . . . than had been seated on the bench in the nation's entire history" (p. 521). Carter ultimately placed 40 women on the federal bench, which was 20 percent of all his judicial appointments. Although these gains were significant, they fell short of women's goals. By the time that Ronald Reagan appointed Sandra Day O'Connor as the first female U.S. Supreme Court justice, only 5.4 percent of all federal judges were female (Morello, 1986).

These facts are reflected in Slotnick's (1984) view that O'Connor's landmark appointment was a "pyrrhic victory," in that the vast majority of Reagan's other less-publicized appointments were all drawn from the traditional pool of conservative white males.

Despite women's underrepresentation on the bench and the barriers that women continued to face in law school and as practicing attorneys, by the end of the 1970s women had made surprising gains in the legal profession. Many of these gains were attributable to changes within the legal profession that increased opportunities for women and minorities. The demand for lawyers had increased greatly, owing largely to social movements initiated in the 1960s (Abel, 1986) and to the growth in the economy and increasing government regulations (Epstein, 1993). From 1970 to 1980, the number of women lawyers increased by 300 percent (Curran, 1986), and in 1980 women composed 50 percent of the law students at some schools (Epstein, 1993). Although women were still concentrated in government positions and in smaller firms (Epstein, 1993), by 1984 women composed one-fourth to one-third of associates in blue-chip firms (Sylvester, quoted in Morello, 1986). As a result of these gains, by the mid-1980s some claimed that there was no longer any discrimination against women in the legal profession (see Morello, 1986). Significantly, some powerful gatekeepers hold this view. Rhode (1997) tells of a conversation with a dean of an elite law school who stated that although racial bias remained a problem in the legal profession, the "woman problem" had been solved (p. 141) (see also Morello, 1986).

WOMEN'S RECENT EXPERIENCES AS LEGAL PROFESSIONALS

Women's recent experiences in the legal profession, however, suggest that although advances have been made, gender equality has not been reached. There is considerable evidence that women's position in the legal profession continues to be different from that of men. Research finds that a gender gap in salary remains, that women face barriers to promotion that men do not, and that subtle forms of discrimination impede women's advancement in the profession.

Salary Discrimination

A number of studies found that through the 1970s women lawyers earned significantly less than did their male counterparts (Adam & Baer, 1984; Glancy, 1970; White, 1967). Many expected, however, that with women entering the profession in such great numbers, disparity would soon end. Hagan's study (1990) analyzing data from over 1000 lawyers in Toronto in 1985 challenged this assumption. Hagan found that male lawyers, on average, earned approximately $40,000 a year more than women. After controlling for a variety of human capital variables, he found that almost 30 percent of the gender gap in earnings was due to discrimination. Hagan also found that as men moved into more prestigious specializations, their salary increased measurably. These increases did not occur for women. Similarly, women's salary did not increase as much as men's with increasing years of experience. He estimated that men earned about $4400 more with each additional year of experience, while women earned only $3000.

A number of studies conducted in the United States confirm Hagan's findings. The Indiana State Bar Association's Commission on Women in the Profession (Gellis, 1991) found that "even controlling for variables such as experience and type of organization, women earn significantly less than men" (p. 947). Not surprisingly, far fewer women in the Indiana survey indicated that they were very satisfied with their financial compensation than did men. The New Hampshire Bar Association's study, conducted in the mid-1980s, also found that after controlling for experience and work setting, a significant gender gap in salary remained [Report of the Task Force on Women in the Bar (New Hampshire), 1988]. The study conducted by the Florida Gender Bias Commission in 1986 also found that female assistant public defenders and assistant state attorneys earned less than their male colleagues (Florida Supreme Court Gender Bias Study Commission, 1990). These differences are particularly disturbing, as it is often thought that there is less salary discrimination in government agencies than in private firms. [For a contrasting view, see Lentz and Laband (1995).]

Even the most recent studies find a significant gender gap in earnings. Huang (1997) surveyed law school graduates in 1992. He found that women earned approximately the same as men upon graduation, but that a wage gap soon emerged and that the gap grew over time. He reports that men receive significantly greater compensation than do women for attending a prestigious law school and receive a much less severe penalty for time taken out of the labor force. Interestingly, marriage is also correlated with increased earnings for men but is associated with decreased earnings for women. Huang also found that part of the wage gap is due to occupational segregation, in which women are more likely to work in lower-paid specialties such as public interest and family law. Huang concludes that although the wage gap is smaller among more recent graduates, suggesting that the wage gap is narrowing over time, women continue to face lower returns on their human capital investments than do their male colleagues. Chiu and Leicht (1999) also find that although the wage gap between male and female lawyers has narrowed, a gap still exists. They found that this gap is most pronounced at upper income levels, prompting them to proclaim that a "glass ceiling" exists that limits women's earnings in the upper echelon of the profession.

Barriers to Partnership and Promotion

Not only does a gendered wage gap continue to exist, but there also appears to be a "partnership" gap. According to Abramson and Franklin (1986), only 23 percent of women graduates of Harvard Law School in 1974 had made partner by 1985, whereas 51 percent of their male classmates had done so. Well into the 1980s, many firms still had no women partners. In 1997 only 14 percent of law firm partners nationwide were female (National Association for Law Placement, 1998).

The difficulties that women have faced in partnership decisions are illustrated by Elizabeth Anderson Hishon's attempts to be made partner at King & Spalding, a prestigious Atlanta firm which in 1984 had yet to have a female partner. Hishon had received mixed evaluations during her seven years as an associate and had brought in a number of new clients but was passed over for partner. Among the reasons her colleagues gave for failing to give Hishon a partnership was that she was too abrasive and difficult to get along with. After being denied a partnership, she filed a complaint with the Equal Employment Opportunity Commission and sued King & Spalding. The lower court concluded that partnership decisions were private relationships that must be entered into under mutual agreement and, as a result, did not fall under the purview of the Civil Rights Act. In the majority opinion, Judge Newell Edenfield compared partnerships to marriages and stated that "to coerce a mismatched or unwanted partnership too closely resembles a statute for the enforcement of shotgun weddings" (Morello, 1986; p. 216). Hishon appealed the case, however, and in 1984 it reached the U.S. Supreme Court. The Court unanimously reversed the lower court's decision and ruled that partnership decisions were covered under the 1964 Civil Rights Act, giving Hishon permission to take legal action against the law firm (Morello, 1986). Hishon finally settled out of court with King & Spalding. This landmark decision put law firms on alert that they must practice gender fairness in both hiring and promotion decisions.

Despite the impact of the Hishon case, research continues to find that not only are women making partner at lower rates than men, but that women are judged by different standards than those used for men when partnership decisions are being made. Kay and Hagan (1998) found in their survey of Canadian attorneys in law firm practice that 46 percent of the men who had begun their careers on a partnership track had made partner, whereas only 25 percent of the women had done so. Human capital variables did not explain the different partnership rates between men and women, leading Kay and Hagan to conclude that "women associates are required to embody standards that are an exaggerated form of the partnership ideal, and these standards are imposed uniquely on women" (p. 741). In a longitudinal study of attorneys from 1990 through 1996, Kay and Hagan (1999) confirm that women must be exceptional in order to be made partner, as men received a greater return on their billable hours, rainmaking, and service to clients than did women when going up for partner.

In a report on women's position in the profession, Epstein, Saute, Oglensky, and Gever (1995) suggest a number of reasons why women continue to face barriers to promotion. In their interviews with associates, partners, and alumni of eight New York law firms, they found that negative stereotypes about women continue to plague female attorneys, making it difficult for them to advance. In particular, they note the general expectation that women will be less productive and committed to their work once they become mothers, no such assumption exists for men who become fathers. It is not the families themselves that impede women's advancement, however. Instead, Epstein et al. argue that it is the lack of support that women receive in attempting to balance work and careers, as well as the self-fulfilling prophesy created by the expectation that women cannot combine career and motherhood successfully.

Epstein et al. (1995) also found that lack of mentoring is a problem for women. Firms continue to be dominated by males who prefer to mentor other males, leaving female associates without advocates and advisors. They find that women who have strong relationships with senior mentors have a significant advantage over women who lack such resources.

Many women, of course, leave a firm before a partnership decision is made, as they perceive the barriers to be too great to overcome (Epstein et al., 1995). Others recognize the difficulties they would face in a private firm and choose to pursue other employment options. These women are not willing to make the sacrifices necessary to reach the superstar status often necessary for a women to be made partner and, as a result, either retreat into government work or into the less stressful world of in-house counsel (see Hull & Nelson, 2000). These sectors are generally considered to be less prestigious than are private firms and salary levels are certainly lower. As Hull and Nelson (1990) find, the segregation of women into such lower-paying areas of practice is only partly a result of personal preference. They suggest that constraints that law firms place on employees that disproportionately affect women are also responsible for the exodus of women from private firms. As a result, women and men continue to follow different careers paths, such that women are concentrated in less prestigious fields, thus perpetuating gender inequality.

Lawyers also receive prestige in the field through election or appointment to the bench. Women have made strides in the judiciary in the past decade, although the number of women judges still does not reflect the proportion of women in the legal profession. According to Martin and Jurik (1996; citing the ABA Commission), by the early 1990s women composed 10 percent of state court judges, 14 percent of federal circuit court judges, and 13 percent of district court judges. As Martin and Jurik (1996) point out, women continue to face barriers to judicial appointments. Echoing Kanter (1977) and Epstein (1981), Martin and Jurik suggest that male gatekeepers continue to exclude women, because they prefer to work with persons who are similar to themselves. Women are also less likely to achieve the credentials that are the unwritten qualifications for becoming a judge, such as graduation from an elite school, federal clerkship, and partnership in a prestigious law firm (Martin & Jurik, 1996).

Sexual Harassment and Gender Bias

There is little doubt that women once faced serious barriers in the legal profession. As the studies above indicate, women continue to face discrimination in hiring, promotion, and salary, although the discrimination does appear to be on the decline. Now that women have gained some degree of influence within the legal profession, legal scholars have also turned their attention to sexual harassment as well as to the more subtle forms of bias that many female attorneys may experience. A number of these scholars and legal professionals have examined whether or not male and female attorneys/judges are treated differently on an interactional level. This research explores the level of respect accorded male and female legal professions. Kuhn (1987, 1990) argues that young professional women are particularly likely to report "nonstatistical" discrimination. By this, Kuhn is referring to an inhospitable workplace in which women are accorded less respect than men. These more subtle forms of gender bias have become a focus of social science research and state and federal task forces. In most cases, the research has focused on perceptions of bias and has relied on a survey approach. These surveys consistently find that women and men hold very different perceptions about the extent of harassment and bias that exists.

In the early 1980s a number of female legal professionals, social scientists, and legal scholars began to call for studies of bias in the legal system. In 1980, the NOW Legal Defense Fund, in conjunction with the National Association of Women Judges, established the National Judicial Education Program (NJEP) to Promote Equality for Women and Men in the Courts (Schafran, 1985). The NJEP appointed sociologist Norma Wikler its first director. One of Wikler's first acts as director was to ask the judiciary to take a close look at sexism in both the legal system and the legal profession. Wikler's call was answered by a flurry of activity at the state level, as bar associations began conducting studies of gender bias in state and local courts.

The first study was conducted by the New Jersey Supreme Court Task Force on Women in the Courts (1984). In the New Jersey survey, 50 percent of female attorneys reported that they had often or sometimes experienced unfair treatment by state court judges (Eich, 1986). Forty-nine percent of the male attorneys and 78 percent of female attorneys also stated that they had observed incidents in which male attorneys treated female counsel unfairly as a result of gender (Loftus, 1984). Some of the most common behavior reported included referring to female attorneys as "little lady," "dear," or by their first names. Women also reported frequent remarks about their physical appearance, which they felt detracted from their professional role. An alarming 86 percent of women and 68 percent of men reported hearing male counsel making sexist jokes or hostile remarks about women. Although some men did report observing these behaviors, overall far fewer men reported these behaviors than did women. This fact is clearly in evidence by the 77 percent of male attorneys who reported that they had never seen a judge treat a woman in a disadvantaged manner; only 33 percent of female attorneys agreed (Loftus, 1984).

The New Jersey report served as a wake-up call to many other state bar associations and court systems, which then began their own studies of gender bias. Since that time, over 30 state courts and bar associations have completed gender bias studies ("Update: Gender bias in the courts," 1991). In 1993 the Ninth Circuit published a report of its gender bias study (Ninth Circuit Gender Bias Task Force). In 1994 the Judicial Conference in the United States encouraged all federal circuits to conduct such a study (Resnik, 1996). Four years later, a special issue of the *University of Richmond Law Review* was devoted to the study of gender bias in the federal courts, presenting a report from each federal circuit. The findings of these studies have been surprisingly consistent. As Gellis (1991) notes, task forces from states as different as California, New Hampshire, and Indiana all report that female attorneys detect a significant amount of bias in their professional lives. Male attorneys are much less likely to report that women are treated unfairly (see also Czapansky, 1990).

In their review of these reports, Hemmens, Strom, and Schlegel (1998) state that female attorneys report demeaning treatment, being subjected to sexist jokes and remarks, and frequent questions about their status as attorneys. One attorney from Minnesota noted that when she appears in court with a senior partner, other attorneys and judges often assume that she is his daughter. Males rarely report such experiences. Female attorneys are also subject to comments about their appearance, as well as criticism if they appear overly aggressive.

Similar bias affects female judges. As Hemmens et al. (1998) note, the task force reports find that female judges report being treated with less respect than their male colleagues and are frequently addressed by their first names or by "Mrs." when male judges are appropriately addressed as "Your Honor." Apparently, the status accorded to judges is not enough to counterbalance the bias associated with being female. As Resnik states with respect to the task force findings, "the intersection of woman and judge turns out to equal woman a good deal of the time, and she is other" (p. 972).

The findings of the task force reports are echoed in a number of independent studies of gender bias in the legal system. MacCorquodale and Jensen (1993) also found significant differences between men's and women's perceptions of the prevalence of bias in their survey of 48 male and 64 female attorneys in Arizona. They reported that female lawyers were more likely than males to report hearing sexist jokes from both judges and attorneys, as well as to perceive that judges use inappropriate forms of address to female counsel. MacCorquodale and Jensen concluded that female attorneys were subject to these behaviors as a result of their status as "tokens" within the male-dominated legal system.

Similarly, Lentz and Laband (1995; see also Laband & Lentz, 1993) found that male and female attorneys held different perceptions about the frequency of sexual harassment. Women believed that female attorneys experienced unwanted sexual remarks and jokes significantly more often than did male attorneys. Women were also more likely to report sexual gestures, unwanted touching, and other forms of sexual harassment than were their male colleagues.

Of course, one criticism of these studies and the task force reports is that some women are hypersensitive to gender bias and thus, since they expect that it exists, they perceive that it does. In answer to this criticism, Rosenberg, Perlstadt, and Phillips (1993) examined the way in which women attorneys' professional role orientation affected their perceptions of gender bias. They divided women into two categories based on their answers to an attitude survey. *Feminists* were women who supported feminist objectives, who believed that women must unite to upset the balance of power within the legal system, and who feel that the "feminist perspective is fundamental to their professional identity" (p. 420). By contrast, *careerists* did not identify themselves as feminists, believed that their skills and hard work would be rewarded, and felt that it was not necessary to make women's position in the legal profession a political issue.

In general, both groups of women believed that they were treated fairly. A number of women, however, reported being "verbally disparaged." This includes inappropriate address and many of the other behaviors addressed by the state and federal task forces. Two-thirds of the women reported being called "honey" or "dear," and 32 percent reported being addressed by their first name. Rosenberg et al. found that careerists were more likely to perceive these behaviors than were the feminists, regardless of their work setting (e.g., private firm, government, etc.). Thus the careerists, who generally do not want to believe that gender bias exists, reported greater amounts of gender bias than did the feminists, many of whom expect to find gender bias. Rosenberg et al. suggest that men may be more likely to engage in sexist behaviors when they are around women who they believe will not retaliate. They conclude that "reports of sexism at work are not subjective accounts that have been filtered through an ideological lens" (p. 431).

CONCLUSION

Historically, women have faced discrimination in the legal profession. Women's entry into the profession was blocked either formally or informally by courts and law schools until only the last few decades. Women also have faced discrimination in hiring and in promotion, and evidence indicates that salary discrepancies still exist. Most recently, studies find that female attorneys and judges are frequently treated in a disrespectful manner by some colleagues. Nonetheless, women have made impressive advances, owing largely to the tremendous expansion of the legal profession in the last two decades. Currently, 30 percent of attorneys practicing in the United States are female (Bureau of Labor Statistics, 2001), and more women than men now enter law school (Glater, 2001). However, the Bureau of Labor Statistics (2000) predicts that growth within the profession will slow at least through 2008 and suggests that competition for jobs will increase substantially. We must keep a watchful eye on the profession to ensure that women's gains are not lost due to changes in the labor market. We must also continue to work for the elimination of gender discrimination at every level of the profession to ensure that men and women have equal opportunities for success.

Thus, challenges remain for women entering the legal profession in the twenty-first century. The *Judges' Journal* recently asked the Honorable Margaret H. Marshall, Chief Justice of the Supreme Judicial Court of the Commonwealth of Massachusetts, whether or not gender bias still exists in the legal system. Judge Marshall replied that women lawyers today "will face far fewer obstacles than the women pioneers who came before them; but they will receive far fewer breaks than my generation. They are coming into their own; but they will be on their own" ("Gender bias in the legal system," 2000, p. 8).

NOTES

1. Bradwell was recommended for the bar after passing an oral exam in front of a judge and a practicing attorney. This type of examination was customary at the time.
2. Morello (1986) quotes Lawrence Bodine (1983), who stated that O'Connor's only job offer was as a stenographer.

REFERENCES

ABEL, R. L. (1986). The transformation of the legal profession. *Law and Society Review, 20*, 7–17.

ABRAMSON, J., & FRANKLIN, B. (1986). *Where they are now? The story of the women of Harvard Law*. New York: Doubleday.

ADAM, B., & BAER, D. (1984). The social mobility of women and men in the Ontario legal profession. *Canadian Review of Sociology and Anthropology, 21*, 22–46.

BERKSON, L. (1982). Women on the bench: A brief history. *Judicature, 68*, 286–293.

BERNAT, F. P. (1992). Women in the legal profession. In I. L. Moyer (Ed.), *The changing roles of women in the criminal justice system* (2nd ed.), pp. 307–321. Prospect Heights, IL: Waveland Press.

BODINE, L. (1983, October). Sandra Day O'Connor. *American Bar Association Journal*, p. 1384.

BUREAU OF LABOR STATISTICS. (2000). *Occupational outlook handbook, 2000–01* (Bulletin 2520).

BUREAU OF LABOR STATISTICS. (2001). *Employment and earnings*, vol. 48, no. 1.

CHIU, C., & LEICHT, K. T. (1999). When does feminization increase equality? The case of lawyers. *Law and Society Review, 33*, 557–583.

CURRAN, B. (1986). American lawyers in the 1980's: A profession in transition. *Law and Society Review, 20*, 19–52.

CZAPANSKY, K. (1990, Summer). Gender bias in the courts: Social change strategies. *Georgetown Journal of Legal Ethics, 4*, 1–22.

EICH, W. (1986, April/May). Gender bias in the courtroom: Some participants are more equal than others. *Judicature, 69*, 339–598.

EPSTEIN, C. F. (1993). *Women in law* (2nd ed.). New York: Basic Books.

EPSTEIN, C. F., SAUTE, R., OGLENSKY, B., & GEVER, M. (1995). Glass ceilings and open doors: Women's advancement in the legal profession. *Fordham Law Review, 64*, 291–449.

EPSTEIN, C. F. (1981). *Women in law*. New York: Basic Books.

FEINMAN, C. (1986). *Women in the criminal justice system* (2nd ed.). New York: Praeger.

FLORIDA SUPREME COURT GENDER BIAS STUDY COMMISSION. (1990). Report. *Florida Law Review, 42*, 803–981.

GELLIS, A. J. (1991). Great expectations: Women in the legal profession, a commentary on state studies. *Indiana Law Journal, 66*, 941–976.

Gender bias in the legal system: Does it still exist? (2000, Spring). *Judges' Journal*, pp. 6–8.

GLANCY, D. (1970). Women in law: The dependable ones. *Harvard Law School Bulletin, 21*(5), 23–33.

GLATER, J. D. (2001, March 26). Women are close to being majority of law students. *New York Times*.

HAGAN, J. (1990). The gender stratification of income inequality among lawyers. *Social Forces, 63*, 835–855.

HARRINGTON, M. (1993). *Women lawyers: Rewriting the rules*. New York: Plume.

HEMMENS, C., STROM, K., & SCHLEGEL, E. (1998). Gender bias in the courts: A review of the literature. *Sociological Imagination, 35,* 22–42.

HUANG, W. R. (1997). Gender differences in the earnings of lawyers. *Columbia Journal of Law and Social Problems, 30,* 267–311.

HULL, K. E., & NELSON, R. L. (2000). Assimilation, choice, or constraint? Testing theories of gender differences in the careers of lawyers. *Social Forces, 79,* 229–264.

KANTER, R. M. (1977). *Men and women of the corporation.* New York: Basic Books.

KAY, F. M., & HAGAN, J. (1998). Raising the bar: The gender stratification of law firm capital. *American Sociological Review, 63,* 728–743.

KAY, F. M., & HAGAN, J. (1999). Cultivating clients in the competition for partnerships: gender and the organizational restructuring of law firms in the 1990s. *Law and Society Review, 33,* 517–555.

KUHN, P. (1987). Sex discrimination in labor markets: The role of statistical evidence. *American Economic Review, 77,* 567–592.

KUHN, P. (1990). Sex discrimination in labor markets: The role of statistical evidence—Reply. *American Economic Review, 80,* 290–297.

LABAND, D. N., & LENTZ, B. (1993). Is there sex discrimination in the legal profession? *Journal of Human Resources, 28,* 230–258.

LENTZ, B. L., & LABAND, D. N. (1995). *Sex discrimination in the legal profession.* Westport, CT: Quorum Books.

LOFTUS, M. (1984). The first year report of the New Jersey Supreme Court Task Force on Women in the Courts, June 1984. *Womens' Rights Law Reporter, 9,* 129.

MACCORQUODALE, P., & JENSEN, G. (1993). Women in the law: Partners or tokens? *Gender and Society, 7,* 582–593.

MARTIN, S. E., & JURIK, N. C. (1996). *Doing justice, doing gender.* New York: Sage Publications.

MENKEL-MEADOW, C. (1988). The feminization of the legal profession: The comparative sociology of women lawyers. In R. Abel & P. Lewis (Eds.), *Lawyers in society* (Vol. 3, pp. 196–255). Berkeley, CA: University of California Press.

MORELLO, K. B. (1986). *The invisible bar: The woman lawyer in America, 1638 to the present.* New York: Random House.

NATIONAL ASSOCIATION FOR LAW PLACEMENT. (1998, February). Press release. Washington, DC: National Association for Law Placement.

NEW JERSEY SUPREME COURT TASK FORCE ON WOMEN IN THE COURTS. (1984). Final report.

NINTH CIRCUIT GENDER BIAS TASK FORCE. (1993, July). The effects of gender in the federal courts.

Report of the Task Force on Women in the Bar. (1988, Summer). *New Hampshire Bar Journal, 29,* 4.

RESNICK, J. (1996). Asking about gender in the courts. *Signs, 21,* 952–990.

RHODE, D. L. (1997). *Speaking of sex: The denial of gender inequality.* Cambridge, MA: Harvard University Press.

ROSENBERG, J, PERLSTADT, H., & PHILLIPS, W. R. F. (1993). Now that we are here: discrimination, disparagement, and harassment at work and the experience of women lawyers. *Gender and Society, 7,* 415–433.

SASSOWER, D. L. (1971, April). Women in the law: The second hundred years. *American Bar Association Journal, 57,* 332.

SCHAFRAN, L. H. (1985). Educating the judiciary about gender bias: The National Judicial Education Program to promote equality for women and men in the courts and the New Jersey Supreme Court Task Force on women in the courts. *Women's Rights Law Reporter, 9,* 109–124.

SLOTNICK, E. E. (1984). Gender, affirmative action and recruitment to the federal bench. *Golden Gate University Law Review, 14,* 519–571.

Update: Gender bias in the courts. (1991, July). *Trial,* 112–118.

WHITE, J. (1967). Women in law. *Michigan Law Review, 65,* 1051–1118.

27

Early Policing in the United States

"Help Wanted—Women Need Not Apply!"

Martin L. O'Connor

In the early nineteenth century the United States was a collection of agriculturally based communities. Although these communities employed sheriffs, constables, and a night watch (Bartollas & Hahn, 1999, p. 7), there were no police departments per se. Nevertheless, these communities were strongly influenced by English traditions and practices. Therefore, in 1829, when the English Parliament created the London Metropolitan Police Department and organized a paid police force, the United States took notice. The need and desire for a paid police force in U.S. communities became apparent. In 1833, the city of Philadelphia created its first police department, and in 1844 the New York State Legislature authorized municipalities to create police forces. Soon police departments were created throughout New York (Bartollas & Hahn, 1999). Similar police departments were created in Baltimore, Boston, Cincinnati, Newark, and New Orleans (Richardson, 1974). The personnel policies of the newly created police departments mirrored the discrimination in U.S. society. Simply stated, all police departments were composed exclusively of white males (Bouza, 1992). During the nineteenth and most of the twentieth centuries, the recruitment efforts of American police agencies with respect to women could be summarized as: "Help wanted—women need not apply!"

WOMEN BEGIN TO KNOCK AT THE POLICE DOOR

In the mid-nineteenth century the prison system in the United States was staffed almost exclusively by males. Their male guards sexually exploited a number of female inmates and the attendant publicity created efforts for change. Under pressure from the American Female Moral Reform Society to reform the system, in 1845 the city of New York hired six female matrons for its jails (Schultz, 1995). Later, the same effort to place female matrons in police stationhouses to assist in processing female arrestees was opposed by the Men's Prison Association (Berg & Budnick, 1986). Although women were not welcome in the male club of policing, the growing need for women to assist police agencies with some of the problems of delinquent children and prostitutes led to the police appointment of a woman "safety worker" in Portland, Oregon in 1905. Safety worker Lola Baldwin, although not classified as a police officer, was the first documented appointment of a woman with some police power (Bartollas & Hahn, 1999). In 1910, Alice Stebbins Wells, a social worker, was appointed by the Los Angeles Police Department as a detective to work with women and children. Soon thereafter, police departments throughout the country began employing police-women in support positions to assist in police work associated with women and children. These women were welcomed into police departments in their support roles (Hale, 1992). In 1922, there were 500 policewomen in the United States, and by 1960 their number had grown to 5617 (Schultz, 1995). Although women began to see a crack in the police personnel door, the resistance of the male police culture to an expanded role for women in policing was strong and well organized (Martin, 1994). Most of the 17,000 U.S. police agencies did not employ women. Sixty years after the appointment of Alice Stebbins Wells as the first police woman, the role of women in policing was still confined to support functions or work with juveniles and women. Furthermore, women employed in these positions were frequently required to have greater education than male police officers, and women were not permitted to compete with male officers for promotions (Milton, 1972). Some major U.S. police departments did not employ female officers in any capacity until 1966.[1]

During the 1960s a great wave of social change took place in the United States. The civil rights movement, the antiwar movement, the due process revolution, and the feminist movement were seriously questioning the nation's values. The patriarchal order that dominated society for thousands of years was under sustained attack.

> The resistance toward women in policing must be ultimately viewed in terms of the patriarchal society. . . . Western society, as well as most other cultures, has been based on social, philosophical, and political systems in which men by force, direct pressure, or through tradition, ritual, custom, language, etiquette, education, and law determine what part women shall or shall not play. . . . In policing, women had the "audacity" to desire entrance to an all male occupation, one that male officers perceived to demand the traditionally masculine attributes of dominance, aggressiveness, superiority and power. . . . " (Bartollas & Hahn, 1999, p. 286)

In the United States, women were kept in check by social norms, and legislatures created statutes embodying social values that restricted various opportunities for women. These statutes were generally approved by the courts (*Minor* v. *Happersett*: women do not have the right to vote in federal elections; *Hoyt* v. *Florida*: women can be exempted from jury service and do not have to fulfill the duties of citizenship; *Bradwell* v. *Illinois*: qualified women can be excluded from certain occupations, such as lawyer, simply because of their gender; *Goesaert* v. *Cleary*: access of women to certain occupations can be limited; *Radice* v. *New York*: women can be prohibited from working nights; *U.S.* v. *St. Clair*: women can be exempted from the responsibilities of military service). In the 1960s and 1970s a feminist wave began sweeping the United States. The feminist movement gained the attention of the U.S. Supreme Court when it ruled for the first time that sex-based classifications were "subject to scrutiny under the equal protection clause" (*Reed* v. *Reed*, 1971). In addition, the feminist movement was given powerful impetus by Betty Friedan, who touched a nerve by what she called "The Problem That Has No Name." In essence, she described the role of American women and their dissatisfaction with a nation that limited their roles in society. She raised the question: "Is this all?" (Friedan, 1963). The same question "Is this all?" could be applied to the second-class role of women in policing where they were principally confined to clerical positions and working with children. The issue was: Are woman going to be able to compete in a police career on an equal footing with their male counterparts? The resounding answer from the police organizational culture in the United States was clear, direct, and powerful. No! In the late 1960s, police officers in the New York City Police Department were asked what they thought about women becoming patrol officers. Some of their responses included the following: "Ptl. Paul DiStephano said, 'The idea of a woman driving a radio car is enough to make you want to quit the job. . . . ' Ptl. James Miller said, 'It's a bad arrangement. A woman just isn't built to handle situations that confront policemen. They're not physically equipped to do a job that sometimes demands muscle. . . . ' Ptl. George Hall said, 'A woman's place is definitely not in a radio car—it's in an office. I'll even go a little further than that—a woman belongs at home, taking care of the kids. . . . '" (Fyfe, Greene, Walsh, Wilson, & McLaren, 1997). The attitude voiced by these officers in the 1960s fairly reflects the overwhelming sentiment of the U.S. police culture of its day. Women were simply not wanted as full partners in the policing enterprise.

LEGAL FORCES BEGIN TO OPEN POLICE DOORS TO WOMEN

In 1964, Congress passed the most historic and sweeping civil rights legislation ever enacted, 42 U.S.C., § 2000. Title VII of this legislation dealt with discrimination in employment on the basis of race, color, religion, national origin, and sex. It is of interest to note that the legislation was designed primarily to address racial discrimination and the word *sex* was added to the bill at the last minute on the floor of the House of Representatives by opponents of the measure in an attempt to prevent its passage (Freeman, 1991, p. 163). Notwithstanding enormous opposition in Congress, the Civil Rights Bill became law in July 1965. The legislation did not affect discrimination against women in most police departments immediately because the act exempted municipal governments from its coverage. However, the act was a very important legal force with respect to discrimination in U.S. society. Women began to believe that it might be possible for the barriers to equal employment in policing to be removed. In 1968, two women in Indianapolis became the first in the nation to be appointed to regular patrol duties in a marked police car (Lord, 1995). Very few municipalities followed the Indianapolis lead. In fact, in some states legal statutes still prohibited women from becoming patrol officers.[2] Therefore, even if an enlightened police official in these states wanted to appoint a female to patrol duties, state statutes and civil service requirements prevented such action. Finally, in 1972, Title VII was amended to apply to state and municipal governments, thereby providing protection against discrimination in employment for women seeking entry to police departments. However, the legal battle was not yet over. Women soon found that there were additional barriers preventing them from assuming the role of police officer. These hurdles were the numerous police height, weight, and physical fitness standards that were in effect in police departments across the nation. It was not uncommon for these standards to require that applicants be 5 feet 7 inches to 5 feet 10 inches in height. In addition, it was not uncommon to require applicants to pass an obstacle course requirement, a standing broad jump, pull-ups, a sit-up while holding a weight on one's shoulders, and one-handed dumbbell presses (Fyfe et al., 1997). These standards excluded most women from entering the police profession. The relevancy of these standards was highly questionable and almost all of these standards were eliminated as a result of the U.S. Supreme Court decision in *Griggs* v. *Duke Power Company* (1971). In *Griggs*, the Court unanimously approved the disparate impact method of analyzing discrimination claims. Therefore, a policy or practice may be discriminatory if it has a disproportionate effect upon a particular group and is not job related or justified by business necessity. Hence, height, weight, and physical fitness standards that were facially neutral in their treatment of different groups but, in fact, fell more harshly on women violated Title VII because these standards could not meet the test of *Griggs*. Since *Griggs*, law enforcement agencies have repeatedly tried to justify some measure of height, weight, and physical fitness requirements but have been unable to do so (see also *Dothard* v. *Rawlinson*, 1977).[3]

THE POLICE DOOR IS LEGALLY OPEN TO WOMEN

After state laws banning women from policing were overturned by the mandates of Title VII and height, weight, and physical fitness standards were removed because they could not meet the test of *Griggs*, women began entering the police profession in increasing numbers. Some women entered some police departments and did not encounter great difficulties.[4] Nevertheless, many women encountered enormous resistance from the police organizational culture. Women experienced this resistance very early in their police careers and frequently upon their entry to police academies. In some police academies the physical fitness routine that was geared to male officers was used to demonstrate that females lack the physical strength to be police officers. The lack of upper body strength prevented many female recruits from doing as well as their male counterparts on some physical fitness regimes. In addition, some police academy trainers reluctantly agree to provide remedial firearms training to female recruits because of a female's unfamiliarity with weapons and a lack of hand strength. It has been said that inequality in police training may also be fostered by "an emphasis on meeting physical fitness standards that do not have to be maintained beyond the academy . . . [thus magnifying] the importance of physical differences. [In addition], informal coddling of women by some physical education instructors who are protective or unable to deal with some women's manipulative efforts also negatively affects all women. . . . It also undermines the confidence of male officers in women officers in general, and divides the women. . . . "

Occasionally, police academy instructors have stood in front of police academy classes and stated, "I don't care what they say, women don't belong on the job."[5] In police academy role-play exercises, female recruits who did not act in an aggressive manner like their male counterparts were considered to have "no command presence." Civility by female recruits was viewed as a sign of weakness. In some police academies it was required that recruits get into a boxing ring with boxing gloves and actually fight a male officer. One training officer in a major police agency suggested that this was necessary to see if a female officer "could take a punch."[6] Some women claimed that they were boxed right out of the police academy (*Newsday*, December 1986).

When female officers graduated from police academies and assumed their role as patrol officers, it was not uncommon for male officers to continue their hostility. Male officers viewed patrol work as "men's work" (Balkin, 1988; Milton, 1974). The hostility toward women on patrol has been based primarily on stereotypes regarding the ability of women to do what is considered a man's job (Bell, 1982). A number of studies were conducted in several cities throughout the United States to determine whether women can perform patrol work as effectively as men. The results of these studies demonstrated overwhelmingly that women are capable of successful performance as patrol officers (Bartell & Associates, 1978; Bartlett & Rosenblum, 1977; Bloch & Anderson, 1974; Sherman, 1975). The problem with these studies is the question that is raised: Can women perform patrol work as successfully as men? This question presupposes that there is a male way of policing. There is not. Although some males may be more aggressive than some females, both males and females bring their own individuality to the problems of policing. Some males are not suited for police work and some females are not suited for police work. Individual knowledge, skills, and abilities are the most important determinants of whether a person can be an effective patrol officer, not gender.

WOMEN IN POLICING: THE TWENTY-FIRST CENTURY

In 2001 the Bureau of Labor Statistics indicated that women account for almost 47 percent of the workforce in the United States. Approximately 30 percent of the legal profession is now comprised of women. Yet in policing, women hold approximately 14 percent of our nation's law enforcement positions, 8.8 percent of supervisory positions and just 7.4 percent of the top command positions (International Association of Chiefs of Police [IACP], 1998). Policing continues to be an overwhelmingly masculine enterprise. Some argue that the gains for women in policing have been very slow and that women will not reach a gender balance in policing for another seventy years ("Equality denied," Martin, 1990, p. 3). There are those who believe that widespread bias in police hiring, selection practices, and recruitment policies keep women out of law enforcement. The National Center for Women & Policing argue that entry exams with an overemphasis on upper body strength still wash out many qualified women and that women are discouraged from entering policing because of the aggressive authoritarian outdated paramilitary model of law enforcement. In addition, it is suggested that once on the job, women face discrimination, harassment, intimidation, and are maliciously thwarted as they attempt move up in rank. There is no question that the military model of policing is still widespread in the United States. Furthermore, some large police agencies employ the psychoauthoritarian stress-training model of recruit training that is closely associated with the training in some military boot camps. This "in-your-face" training model frequently involves screaming, extraordinary profanity, and demeaning actions by police trainers toward police recruits and it turns off a certain number of males and females who may be interested in police careers. This psychoauthoritarian training model has been criticized by some of the most prominent members of the police community.[7] Hopefully, during the twenty-first century, police administrators will finally realize that this Neanderthal model of police training keeps talented men and women from the police profession, is incompatible with the concept of community policing, and is detrimental to effective policing in a free society. There is an urgent need for improved police training, with a focus on human communication to develop officers who are capable of helping citizens identify and solve problems in their communities (Birzer & Tannehill, 2001). Hopefully, in the near future, job-related police training programs will be instituted so that more women will be encouraged to bring their exceptional skills to our nation's policing problems.

Recently, the International Association of Chiefs of Police (IACP) established an Ad Hoc Committee on Women in Policing to examine the role of women in policing. The committee, utilizing the resources of the Gallup Organization, conducted a survey of some of its 14,000 members. The survey confirmed critical information regarding the status of women in policing. While recognizing that the number of women in policing is growing, it also revealed:

- There are few women in policing compared to their male counterparts.
- Women still face bias from male officers.
- Many police departments lack strategies for recruiting women.
- Women officers may face gender discrimination and a "glass ceiling" that inhibits promotion.
- Sexual harassment still occurs in many police departments.
- Although the need is great, there are very few mentoring programs for women officers.

Early in the twentieth century, the IACP supported women only in support roles in policing, not in patrol functions. Therefore, it is an extraordinary change for this major international police organization to now state that "it is essential to strengthen the position of women in policing—their professional development, their progress to positions of leadership, and their contribution to the public service and safety. . . . " (IACP, 1998).

Some of the specific recommendations of the IACP study are as follows:

1. Police agencies should be educated regarding the value of gender diversity in policing.
2. Police agencies should advertise and recruit qualified women.
3. Police agencies should train members regarding gender discrimination and sexual harassment and adopt a zero-tolerance approach to discrimination and sexual harassment.
4. Police agencies should establish policies to improve the role of women in policing.
5. Police agencies should mentor female officers and strengthen their potential for longevity.
6. Police agencies should improve promotional strategies for women and move women into police leadership positions.

The IACP has concluded that while a number of agencies have welcomed women officers, "many simply have not . . . [and] women have often had to bring litigation against departments to overcome resistance . . . " (IACP, 1998). The IACP survey disclosed that 17 percent of the agencies surveyed had no female officers and 55 percent of the agencies surveyed had between one and four female officers. Ninety-one percent of the police departments surveyed had no female officers in policymaking positions. In addition, 28 percent of the departments surveyed express concern that "women lack sufficient physical strength, capacity for confrontation, size, strength and force . . . " (p. 13). This finding is troubling in light of the overwhelming evidence that policing is more cerebral than physical and it suggests that the myth that one must be big, strong, and physical to be a police officer still has support in the police organizational culture.[8] Perhaps that is why women continue to be disproportionately assigned to support positions rather than patrol (Martin, 1990).

Another factor may be paternalism, which involves male officers protecting or excusing women from undesirable tasks. This practice of assigning women to nonline functions suggests that women can't be "real cops," and it stigmatizes female officers in general and creates resentment among male officers (Padavic & Reskin, 1990).

It has taken almost 150 years for women to represent 14 percent of our nation's police forces. The police road they have traveled in the latter half of the twentieth century has been difficult for many. Nevertheless, despite the pessimistic views of some regarding the future of women in policing, there is much to be optimistic about in the twenty-first century. A number of legal and cultural barriers to women in policing have been jettisoned. Women are showing increasing interest in police careers. Research regarding the role of women in policing is very positive. Research has demonstrated that women rely on a policing style that uses less physical force, and women excel at defusing and deescalating potentially violent confrontations with citizens and are less likely to become involved in problems of excessive force. In addition, female officers often possess better communication skills than their male counterparts and are better able to facilitate the cooperation and trust required to implement community policing (Lonsway, 2000). Furthermore, in the later half of the twentieth century, for the first time women became chiefs of police in several major police departments, including Houston, Atlanta, and Portland. At least one study found that female police executives were more flexible, emotionally independent, self-assertive, self-confident, and creative than their male counterparts (Price, 1974). A number of studies demonstrate that female officers utilize a less authoritarian style of policing and rely less on physical force (Worden, 1995). The cult of machismo in policing is changing, albeit at a glacial pace. Unlike their predecessors, it is now not uncommon for male officers to recognize reluctantly that women make "good cops." Major police departments and police organizations have expressed the desire to recruit, employ, and promote more women in policing.[9] The U.S. Supreme Court has established guidelines regarding sexual harassment that significantly increase the chance of employer liability if employers do not rid their workplace of sexual harassment (*Burlington Industries* v. *Ellerth*, 1998; *Faragher* v. *City of Boca Raton*, 1998). The Court has said that even a sitting president of the United States is not immune from charges of sexual harassment (*Clinton* v. *Jones*, 1997). Almost all police departments have established sexual harassment policies (IACP, 1998). In some areas of the country, the wages, fringe benefits, and working conditions have improved significantly, thereby making policing a very attractive profession for both men and women. With these changes, it is almost certain that during the twenty-first century the number of women in policing will grow exponentially. The increased representation of women is almost certain to transform the authoritarian military climate of police agencies and hopefully make American policing kinder, gentler, and more sensitive to individual rights and the envy of the world.

NOTES

1. The Nassau County Police Department in New York is the seventh largest police department in the United States, with a force of more than 3000 sworn officers. This department did not hire women in any supporting role until the mid-1960s.

2. See New York Civil Service Law, § 58, which specifically provided that only a "male" could become a patrol officer in New York. The male restriction was not removed by the New York State legislature until 1972, when Title VII of the Civil Rights Act of 1964 was amended so that it applied to state and municipal governments.

3. The Civil Rights Act of 1991 further strengthened Title VII after the decision of the U.S. Supreme Court in *Wards Cove Packing Co.* v. *Antonio* (1989).

4. The author has interviewed several female officers in different police departments who believe that they were treated quite fairly. However, some women in the same police academy class have had very different experiences and perceptions regarding their acceptance by the male police culture.

5. The author was involved as a police administrator in two major police agencies in the United States. During a career of more than 30 years there were several occasions in which statements like this were reported to have occurred during formal training sessions. In some cases, police instructors readily admitted making the statements. In addition, anecdotal information of similar statements being made in other police academies across the country was not uncommon.

6. By parity of reasoning, one police observer suggested (tongue in cheek) that trainers should shoot police recruits to see if they can take a shot.

7. Herman Goldstein, former chief of police Joseph McNamara, and the late Daniel P. Guido, the former commissioner of police of the Nassau County New York Police Department, and the Suffolk County New York Police, the Westchester County New York Police Department, the Yonkers New York Police Department, and the Stamford Connecticut Police Department. Numerous other police officials have also condemned this extreme paramilitary model of police training.

8. Physical strength has not been shown to predict general police effectiveness (Sherman, 1973), or the ability to handle dangerous situations successfully (Bell, 1982).

9. Police departments in Albuquerque and Tucson have dramatically increased their female recruits (Polisar & Milgram, 1998) and 25 percent of the Madison, Wisconsin Police Department now is composed of female officers. In addition, the International Association of Chiefs of Police is making a major effort to encourage its members to recruit, employ, and promote women in policing.

REFERENCES

BALKIN, J. (1988). Why policemen don't like policewomen. *Journal of Police Science and Administration, 16*(1): 29–38.

BARTELL & ASSOCIATES. (1978). *The study of police women competency in the performance of sector police work in the city of Philadelphia.* Bartell.

BARTLETT, H. W., & ROSENBLUM, A. (1977). *Policewomen effectiveness in Denver.* Denver, CO: Civil Service Commission.

BARTOLLAS, C., & HAHN, L. D. (1999). *Policing in America.* Needham Heights, MA: Allyn & Bacon.

BELL, D. J. (1982). Policewomen: Myths and reality. *Journal of Police Science and Administration, 16*(1), 29–38.

BERG, B. L. & BUDNICK, K. J. (1986). Defeminization of women in law enforcement: A new twist in the traditional police personality. *Journal of Police Science and Administration*, p. 314.

BIRZER, M. L, & TANNEHILL, R. (2001, June). A more effective training approach for contemporary policing. *Police Quarterly, 4*(2), 233–252.

BLOCH, P. B., & ANDERSON, D. (1974). *Policewomen on patrol: Final report.* Washington, DC: Urban Institute, pp. 1–67.

BOUZA, A. V. (1992). *The police mystique: An insider's look at cops, crime and the criminal justice system.* New York: Plenum Press.

FREEMAN, J. (1991). How "sex" got into Title VII: Persistent opportunism as a maker of public policy. *J.L. & Equality, 9*, 163.

FRIEDAN, B. (1963). *The feminine mystique.* New York: W.W. Norton.

FYFE, J. J., GREENE, J. R., WALSH, W. F., WILSON, O. W., & McLAREN, R. C. (1997). *Police administration* (5th ed.). New York: McGraw-Hill. Quoting *Spring 3000*, the magazine of the New York City Police Department, December 1969, p. 48.

HALE, D. C. (1992). Women in policing. In G. W. Cordner & D. C. Hale (Eds.), *What works in policing? Operations and administration examined*. Cincinnati, OH: Anderson Publishing and the Academy of Criminal Justice Sciences.

INTERNATIONAL ASSOCIATION OF CHIEFS OF POLICE. (1998). *The future of women in policing: Mandates for action*.

LONSWAY, K. A. (2000, Summer). *Hiring and retaining more women: The advantages to law enforcement agencies*. Washington, DC: National Center for Women and Policing.

LORD, L. K. (1995). Policewomen. In *The Encyclopedia of Police Science* (2nd ed.). New York: William Bailey.

MARTIN, S. E. (1990). *On the move: The status of women in policing*. Washington, DC: Police Foundation.

MARTIN, S. E. (1994, August). Outsider within the station house: The impact of race and gender on black women police. *Social Problems, 41*.

MILTON, C. (1972). *Women in police*. Washington, DC: Police Foundation.

MILTON, C. (1974). *Women in policing: A manual*. Washington, DC: Police Foundation.

PADAVIC, I., & RESKIN, B. (1990). Men's behavior and women's interest in blue-collar jobs. *Social Problems, 37*, 613–628.

POLISAR, J., & MILGRAM, D. (1998, October). Recruiting, integrating and retaining women police officers: Strategies that work. *Police Chief*.

PRICE, B. R. (1974). *A study of leadership strength of female police executives: Police perspectives, problems, prospects*. New York: Praeger, pp. 96–107.

RICHARDSON, J. F. (1974). *Urban police in the United States*. Port Washington, NY: Kennikat Publishing.

SCHULTZ, D. M. (1995). *From social worker to crime fighter: Women in United States municipal policing*. Westport, CT: Praeger.

SHERMAN, L. J. (1975). An evaluation of policewomen on patrol in a suburban police department. *Journal of Police Science and Administration, 3*(4), 434–438.

WORDEN, R. E. (1995). The causes of police brutality: Theory and evidence on police use of force. In *And justice for all: Understanding and controlling police abuse of force*. Washington, DC: Police Executive Research Forum.

CASES

Bradwell v. *Illinois*, 88 U.S. 130 (1873).

Burlington Industries v. *Ellerth*, 524 U.S. 742 (1998).

Clinton v. *Jones*, 520 U.S. 681 (1997).

Dothard v. *Rawlinson*, 433 U.S. 321 (1977).

Faragher v. *City of Boca Raton*, 524 U.S. 775 (1998).

Goesaert v. *Cleary*, 335 U.S. 464 (1948).

Griggs v. *Duke Power Co.*, 401 U.S. 424 (1971).

Hoyt v. *Florida*, 368 U.S. 57 (1961).

Minor v. *Happersett*, 88 U.S. 162 (1875).

Radice v. *New York*, 264 U.S. 292 (1924).

Reed v. *Reed*, 404 U.S. 71 (1971).

U.S. v. *St. Clair*, 291 F. Supp. 122 (1968).

Wards Cove Packing Co. v. Antonio, 490 U.S. 642 (1989).

28

The Dislike of Female Offenders among Correctional Officers

The Need for Specialized Training

Christine E. Rasche

> Work with *women* offenders? Oh, they are the worst! I hate to admit it, but I would rather have a caseload of male rapists than a caseload of WOMEN petty offenders! (female community corrections officer)

There is a widespread phenomenon in corrections that has not been well researched scientifically. Anecdotally, this phenomenon shows up in conversations with correctional line staff, both those who work in prisons and those who work in community corrections. Although correctional leaders seem mostly to regard it as a curiosity with little real relevance to correctional practice, this phenomenon does have an impact on correctional officers and administrators alike. More important, it also has a direct impact on inmates at prison facilities for women. This phenomenon is the pervasive tendency among correctional workers to dislike working with female offenders or to avoid working at women's prisons, and to view such duty as undesirable.

This dislike of female offenders appears to be very widespread in corrections and is well known by almost all those who work in the field. As Pollack (1984) has noted, "There is informal agreement among correctional personnel that female offenders are somehow 'harder to work with' than male offenders" (p. 84). One has only to ask correctional officers whether they prefer working with male or female offenders. Spontaneously, most correctional officers (both male and female) tend to state a clear preference for working with male offenders.

Logically, this preference might seem somewhat counterintuitive. After all, male inmates are much more likely than female inmates to be housed in very large facilities where supervision is somewhat more difficult, and male inmates are also more likely to physically attack and injure correctional staff. A layperson might well expect that correctional staff would prefer to work in smaller facilities with inmates who are unlikely to harm them physically. However, all the available evidence suggests that the opposite is true.

The layperson might also expect that a preference for working with male inmates would be widespread only among male correctional officers, given the macho-oriented nature of our culture in general and criminal justice professions in particular. A layperson might easily assume that at least female correctional officers would prefer working with female inmates, either for ideological reasons or because of a desire for less physically risky work. Again, however, this does not seem to be true. With a few notable exceptions discussed below, most female correctional officers also seem to express a clear preference for working with male rather than female inmates. For purposes of this discussion, this widespread phenomenon is called the *male inmate preference*.

As far as can be determined, the male inmate preference is found among both male and female correctional officers, among both high- and low-ranking officers, among officers working at both male and female inmate facilities, and among officers in all regions of the country. It appears among both those correctional personnel working in prisons and those in community corrections. When this preference is expressed, it usually seems to be articulated immediately, seeming to require little or no thought on the part of respondents. Indeed, a question about their working preferences usually elicits from correctional staffers a prompt, strong, even passionate response, such as the quotation that opened this chapter. Laughter and boisterous exclamations about their working experiences often result, along with unsolicited explanations for their preferences in the form of horror stories.

In fact, often the only correctional staff who do not seem to express the male inmate preference, at least in my experience, are long-time female staff members working at female-only correctional facilities. Such staff are often women who began their careers before institutional staffs were gender-integrated, and many have spent their entire careers working at institutions for female offenders. In general, their preference for working with female inmates seems to arise from long and successful experience in working with female offenders. However, some also express a strong ideological commitment to working with women offenders. This ideological commitment among the older, long-time female staffers is sometimes feminist in nature, but it can also be religious. It should be noted that some younger correctional female staff members at female facilities (as well as a few male staffers) also express such an ideological commitment to working with female offenders. But outside of these comparatively few ideologically committed or long-time women's prison staff members, my experience is that most other correctional personnel clearly express the male inmate preference, even though they will often simultaneously agree that male inmates are more likely to represent a hazard to their own personal safety.

The fact that the male inmate preference has not been well researched scientifically does not mean that it represents a new phenomenon. Observations about the comparatively greater difficulty of working with female inmates appear in literature dating back at least to the mid-nineteenth century. For example, Pollack (1986) cites one prison matron's description of female inmates in the 1860s: "It is a harder task to manage female prisoners than male. . . . They are more impulsive, more individual, more unreasonable and excitable than men; will not act in concert, and cannot be disciplined in masses. Each wants personal and peculiar treatment, so that the duties fall much more heavily on the matrons than on the warders; matrons having thus to deal with units, not aggregates, and having to adapt themselves to each individual case, instead of simply obeying certain fixed laws and making others obey them, as in the prison for males" (Pollack, 1986, citing a prison matron in *Female Life in Prison*, 1862).

Somewhat more recently, Charles Turnbo, who served as the warden of the female prison at Pleasanton, California from the late 1970s to the early 1980s, recalled that when he was made the warden in 1978 he "received as many condolences as congratulations." He was also subjected to hearing the war stories of other colleagues who had pulled duty in women's facilities, since "many wardens want nothing to do with an all-female prison population" (Turnbo, 1993, p. 13). By way of explanation, Turnbo quoted Heffernan in observing that "Women are seen as a persistent and continuing problem in corrections for two reasons: one, their small numbers, and two, their perceived nature" (Heffernan, 1978, cited in Turnbo, 1993, p. 13).

By far the most exhaustive scientific research on this phenomenon has been done by Pollack (1984, 1986). Her research on correctional officers' attitudes revealed that what I call the male inmate preference is a real component of what she calls the prevailing modern "CO culture." Two-thirds (68 percent) of her sample of 45 experienced correctional officers who had worked in both male and female facilities stated preferences for working with male inmates, and two-thirds (67 percent) also agreed that female inmates were harder to supervise. Interestingly, female correctional officers generally expressed a stronger preference for working with male inmates than did male correctional officers (female 72 percent, male 66 percent) and were more likely than their male colleagues to agree that women inmates were more difficult to manage (female 83 percent, male 55 percent) (Pollack, 1986).

However, male and female correctional officers may not always have the same reasons for holding the same preference. As shown on Table 1, Pollack (1986) found that the reasons given by male officers for a male inmate preference included perceived difficulties in supervising the opposite sex and fear of being framed for rape. Male officers also perceived the need to modify their normal behavior when working with women inmates (e.g., curbing their speech, being careful about the use of force). By contrast, the reasons given by female

---

TABLE 1   Reasons Given by Correctional Officers for the Male Inmate Preference

Reasons given by male officers for preferring to work with male inmates included:

1. Difficulties in supervising the opposite sex and fear of being framed for rape.
2. The need to modify their behavior toward women inmates (e.g., curb their speech, be careful about the use of force).

Reasons given by female officers for preferring to work with male inmates included:

1. Male inmates were seen as more likely to treat women officers with respect.
2. Male inmates were seen as appreciating them as women, which made the job more enjoyable.

Reasons given by both male and female officers for the male inmate preference included:

1. Women inmates are more demanding.
2. Women inmates complain more.
3. Women inmates are more likely to refuse orders.

Source: Pollack (1986).

officers for a male inmate preference included perceptions that male inmates were more likely to treat women officers with respect and that male inmates seemed to appreciate them as women, which made the job more enjoyable. In short, male correctional officers were likely to perceive more potential penalties for working with female inmates, while female correctional officers saw more rewards in working with male inmates. Interestingly, however, reasons given by both male and female officers for disdaining work with female inmates included perceptions that women inmates are more demanding and tended to complain more than male inmates, and that women inmates are more likely to refuse orders.

Pollack (1986) also found that there were a few correctional officers in her sample who preferred to work with women inmates, even though they agreed that women inmates were more difficult to supervise. These officers indicated that they enjoyed the challenge of trying to deal with the demands and problems of female inmates. These atypical correctional officers also stated that they enjoyed the "variety, unpredictability, and constant turmoil that was likely to be present in settings for women" (p. 99). Normally, qualities such as "constant turmoil" are not listed as desirable job attributes!

As part of her research, Pollack (1984, 1986) explored correctional officers' views of male and female inmates by giving officers lists of adjectives which they apply to different types of inmates. As Table 2 shows, Pollack found that some adjectives were applied frequently to both male and female inmates. Thus, both male and female prisoners were seen as being defensive, distrustful, and manipulative (1986). However, female inmates specifically were characterized as emotional, temperamental, moody, manipulative, quarrelsome, demanding, changeable, complaining, argumentative, excitable, immature, and noisy. By comparison, choosing from this same list of adjectives, male inmates were characterized by correctional officers as active, defensive, boastful, aggressive, and manipulative. Pollack noted that "only three adjectives for males were agreed upon by more than 60 percent of the officers, whereas 60 percent or more officers agreed on twelve adjectives for females" (1986, 34–35). This greater consensus among the correctional officers about which adjective labels to apply to female inmates "raises the possibility that officers possess a stereotype of females. It is not unusual to obtain a high rate of agreement among those who possess a common stereotype of a group; likewise, one is less likely to get consensus on a description of any group for which a stereotype is not operating, since people interact and perceive each other differently" (p. 35).

Ultimately, Pollack found three themes emerging from the adjective descriptions of female inmates selected by correctional officers. As shown on Table 3, the first theme was *defiance*, which involved selecting descriptions of women inmates as being likely to oppose the officers in various ways. This included descriptions of women inmates as being argumentative, less likely to follow rules, demanding, and harder to handle. In the closed world of the prison, defiant inmates are uniformly disliked by correctional officers, whose jobs often hinge on the degree to which they are able to manage inmates smoothly.

The second theme Pollack (1986) found emerging from the adjectives that correctional officers chose to describe female offenders was *open display of emotion*. This involved characterizations of women inmates as expressing more feeling, being louder and noisier, having a greater tendency to cry, erupting in spur-of-the-moment outbreaks, fighting spontaneously and easily, and losing their tempers easily. Clearly, such boisterous displays are viewed by correctional officers as management problems, particularly when the emotional outburst of one inmate can result in emotional displays among others.

TABLE 2   Adjectives Used by Correctional Officers to Describe Female and Male Inmates

---

Some adjectives were applied frequently to both male and female inmates:

   Defensive (54.5%)

   Distrustful (50%)

   Manipulative (65%)

But female inmates also were characterized as:

   Emotional (83%)

   Tempermental (76%)

   Moody (74%)

   Manipulative (71%)

   Quarrelsome (64%)

   Demanding (69%)

   Changeable (67%)

   Complaining (81%)

   Argumentative (69%)

   Excitable (64%)

   Immature (62%)

   Noisy (64%)

By comparison, male inmates were characterized as:

   Active (64%)

   Defensive (60%)

   Boastful (57%)

   Aggressive (55%)

   Manipulative (60%)

Source: Pollack (1986).

The third theme characterizing female offenders in the eyes of correctional officers, according to Pollack (1986), was that female inmates were seen as *gratification seeking*. This described women inmates as needing and wanting both material and personal commodities such as attention, friendship, or sympathy more than males, and wanting things immediately with little or no patience or willingness to wait. Such impatient and demanding inmates are, once again, viewed by correctional officers as management problems who tend to create a major fuss over minor problems and who therefore make supervision more difficult. Overall, Pollack (1986) found that there was strong agreement among her respondents that men and women inmates required different styles of supervision (91 percent) and that there could be situations where they as correctional officers needed to respond to men and women in different fashions (73 percent).

Interestingly, when asked to account for why these perceived differences between male and female inmates exist, Pollack (1984, 1986) found that correctional officers referred to general "sex differences (whether biological or socialization) rather than institutional

---

TABLE 3   Themes in the Description of Female Inmates by Correctional Officers

---

1. *Defiance:* descriptions of the women as opposing the officers, which included women inmates described as being argumentative, less likely to follow rules, demanding, harder to handle, questioning rules, more troublesome, more complaining, confronting verbally, more critical, less respectful, and harder to reason with.

2. *Open display of emotion:* descriptions of women inmates as expressing more feelings, being louder/noisier, screaming/hollering more, having a greater tendency to cry, having spur-of-the-moment outbreaks, fighting spontaneously and easily, being ready to explode, being crybabies, being explosive, losing their tempers easily.

3. *Gratification seeking:* described women as needing and wanting more from their environment, needing/wanting both material and personal commodities such as attention, friendship, or sympathy, wanting things with little or no patience, emotionally demanding, less independent, more childish, having critical demands, and having a greater need for friends.

Source: Pollack (1986).

factors" (1986, p. 116). In other words, women inmates and women in general were seen as being similar. "The inmates' behavior, in other words, is taken for granted, and the officers see themselves as doing their best within the confines of that assumption. Attempts to change behavior by changing procedures, policies, or other situational components are unlikely to be viewed as effective since it is assumed that the behavior is not situationally induced. We could, therefore, expect the officers to view inmate-generated problems with exasperated resignation, which indeed, appears to be their attitude" (Pollack, 1986, p. 116). In short, correctional officers did not think there was anything they could do about the greater difficulty posed by female inmates because it was a product of nature. Women inmates were just being women.

Pollack's (1984, 1986) reports on correctional officer's different attitudes toward male and female inmates are by far the most scientific analysis of a sentiment which both experienced correctional workers and outside observers readily assert runs throughout the field. This tendency to view female inmates as more difficult to manage leads to the perpetuation of what I have called the male inmate preference.

PERCEPTIONS VERSUS REAL DIFFERENCES

The question that follows is whether there are real differences between male and female inmates in terms of supervision and management requirements, or whether correctional officers are merely articulating unfounded prejudices and stereotypes. As it turns out, there is considerable literature on the differences between men and women in captivity. There are at least three dimensions of this difference.

The first dimension of difference between male and female inmates is their *demographic profiles*. The demographic characteristics of women who are in prison are different in some important ways from those of males who are in prison. First, while African-Americans are clearly overrepresented in U.S. prisons in general, there is some evidence that there may be a larger percentage of African-Americans among women in prison than among men (Binkley-Jackson, Carter, & Robinson, 1993: Goetting & Howsen, 1983; Rafter, 1985; Sarri, 1987). Overall, women inmates have tended to be slightly older than male inmates as a group. Women inmates have also tended to be slightly better educated than their male counterparts, although this is not saying much, since both male and female inmates tend to be less academically skilled when tested than their respective completed years of formal education would suggest. Women inmates are highly likely to have minor children in the home prior to imprisonment and were usually the primary caregivers for their dependent children, which is much less true of male inmates with dependent children (Koban, 1983). Compared to male inmates, female inmates have tended to be imprisoned more often for economic and drug-related crimes than for assaultive crimes. Women inmates are less likely to have been legitimately employed than their male counterparts, despite the fact that they were often the sole support for their minor children.

In recent years, women prisoners also have been shown to have a higher likelihood of drug addiction/abuse than males, especially addiction to heroin, cocaine, and other intravenous drugs. In the light of this, it is perhaps not so surprising to find out that new women prisoners have had higher levels of human immunodeficiency virus (HIV) infection than those of new male prisoners. Also in recent years, women prisoners have been found to have had very high levels of sexual and/or physical abuse as either children or adults, or both; usually these are much higher levels than even the high levels reported for males (American Correctional Association, 1990; Arnold, 1990; Carlen, 1983; Chesney-Lind & Rodriguez, 1983; Fletcher. Shaver, & Moon, 1993; Gilfus, 1992; Immarigeon 1987a,b; Sargent, Marcus-Mendoza, & Yu, 1993).

A second dimension of difference between male and female inmates is that they have quite dissimilar *needs during incarceration*. Some differences between the sexes are obvious and expected. For example, women have needs for gynecologically related goods and services, such as menstrual supplies, annual gynecological checkups, prenatal care for those who are pregnant, and postnatal care and counseling for those who give birth in prison. Only recently have prison systems begun to acknowledge that pre- and postnatal care and counseling need to be both of the normal variety, which might be given to any woman before and after giving birth, and somewhat specialized care, given to women with greater needs. Such specialized care is needed partly because of the large proportion of prison pregnancies which are "high risk" in nature. That is, women who are pregnant in prison are more likely than those in the general population to have been in ill health previously, to have received little prior prenatal care, and to suffer from a variety of chronic conditions that increase risk during pregnancy or afterward (Resnick & Shaw, 1980; Ross & Fabiano, 1986). However, specialized care is also required because following a prison birth there is (in all but a few women's prisons) an inevitable "loss" of the newborn, who will immediately be taken away from the mother and placed outside the prison with foster caregivers. Although the child lives, its physical loss immediately following birth may be experienced as almost "deathlike" by the imprisoned mother. Special health care, both physical and mental, is required under such considerations. Male inmates, obviously, do not require such services.

Also among the obvious and expected differences between the sexes in needs during incarceration are that women inmates need different sorts of routine health and beauty aids, and different types of clothing. Women prisoners also express a much higher need for privacy than do male inmates. Furthermore, women generally need a different kind of diet, with fewer calories and carbohydrates overall and more of certain vitamins and minerals than men require.

Less obviously, it is only recently that we have begun to realize that women inmates need specialized counseling for sexual and/or physical abuse which most received as children and/or adults. Indeed, women are more likely than men to be in prison precisely for killing an adult abuser, particularly a spouse, lover, or other family member. They are also somewhat more likely to be imprisoned for having killed their own children; many women who kill their own children explain their actions as a form of "mercy" killing in the face of what they saw as intolerably brutal conditions. Also, because they were often the primary caregivers to their minor children prior to their imprisonment, women inmates seem to need more help than do male inmates in dealing with the separation from their children, which many view as the harshest single aspect of being imprisoned. There is now considerable evidence that for all these reasons women inmates need more counseling and psychiatric services overall than do male inmates.

In part because of all these unique stressors, women inmates seem to need different kinds of supervision techniques from correctional officers. Because so many women inmates have an abusive history, correctional staff may unwittingly trigger "flashbacks" of painful past abuses if they utilize the common in-your-face approach favored for handling male inmates. Male correctional staff may be more likely to run into this problem, since women inmates are likely to have been abused primarily by the males in their lives, but it should be noted that even female staff can employ supervisory tactics which backfire when used with female offenders. In discussing these first two dimensions of difference between male and female inmates, *demographic profile differences* and *different needs during incarceration*, it is noteworthy that we have *not* made any references to the third dimension, *differences in personality*. This is important because we have already seen that there are big differences in the ways staff perceive the personalities and behaviors of incarcerated men and women in general. As it turns out, there is evidence to suggest that some of these perceived differences are real. For example, some researchers (Joesting, Jones & Joesting, 1975; McKerracher, Street & Segal, 1966) have found that women prisoners are more likely than male prisoners to engage in what is usually called "acting out" behaviors (e.g., extremely emotional outbursts). A higher level of emotionality is, indeed, a consistent theme among writers describing women prisoners, including higher levels of emotional attachment between female inmates than is usually found between male inmates (Giallombardo, 1966; Lekkerkerker, 1931; Ward & Kassebaum, 1965). This higher level of emotionality is perceived by correctional officers as problematic because "emotions displayed by the inmates may translate into hostility toward the officer . . . " (Pollack, 1984).

It seems clear that there are many real differences between male and female offenders in prison that could translate into differences in required management and supervisory approaches. If we add the third dimension, *differences in personality*, it would seem that not only must the overall management of an institution be revised in certain significant ways to accommodate female offenders, but the day-to-day business of direct inmate supervision might need to be altered significantly for things to go as smoothly as possible.

SHOULD INMATE DIFFERENCES LEAD TO SPECIALIZED STAFF TRAINING?

In year 2000 there were at least 85 state prisons in the United States that housed only female offenders, plus at least another 48 state prisons housing both male and female inmates (American Correctional Association, 2001). Four additional female-only prisons were run by the Federal Bureau of Prisons, which also operated 12 co-correctional penal institutions (*Sourcebook of Criminal Justice Statistics Online*, 2001). In short, at least 145 major penal institutions in the United States housed female inmate populations, either alone or in conjunction with male inmate populations. Most of these facilities housed hundreds of inmates each, although in 2000 the numbers ranged from as few as two female inmates in Nome, Alaska to as many as 3605 in Chowchilla, California. In addition, there were also scores of state and federal prerelease centers, work release centers, halfway houses, medical facilities, forestry camps, detention centers, and other facilities housing one or more female prisoners (American Correctional Association, 2001).

Of course, men still vastly outnumber women behind bars in the United States (by about 20 to 1). But the number of women incarcerated by the states and the federal government has increased at a much faster rate than did the number of men during the 1980s and 1990s, resulting in most states now having record-high numbers of women prisoners. Prior to 1980, most states had only one separate women's prison facility, and some states did not even have that, continuing instead to house women in small separate units within larger men's prisons, in coeducational facilities, or even sending them to women's prisons in adjoining states. Due to the huge population growth of prisoners in the 1980s, however, some states had opened multiple women's institutions by the 1990s. Indeed, by 2000 at least 17 states had two or more separate women's prisons, and six states had four or more separate female-only institutions (American Correctional Association, 2000). Most states added to their correctional workforce exponentially in the 1980s and 1990s in the effort to keep pace with burgeoning prison populations, and thousands of correctional staff are now employed by these women's institutions and coeducational facilities. Add to this the correctional officers in the thousands of jails around the nation that house one or more women detainees, and the numbers of correctional officers affected by the management differences required for female versus male inmates is enormous.

Furthermore, the inmate population boom of the 1980s led to some remarkable and dramatic facilities changes. Within the span of just a few years, facilities in some states changed from housing male inmates only to housing co-correctional inmate populations, to then housing only females as inmate populations grew or shifted. This meant that correctional officers who were experienced in working with male inmates have sometimes found themselves suddenly supervising female offenders with little or no advanced preparation.

Given all the differences between male and female inmates noted above, we might expect that correctional systems would be concerned about providing specialized preparation to those correctional staff members assigned to work with female offenders. However, there seems to be little evidence of specialized training for correctional staff assigned to female facilities. The American Correctional Association recognized this in the mid-1980s when it noted that the "requirements and opportunities for staff development often overlook the needs of administration and staff for professional, on-going training in managing the female offender" (American Correctional Association, 1986, p. 29.). Modern researchers on women in prison, similarly, have also noted the lack of specialized training for staff in women's prisons: "Typically, state correctional systems have moved from an approach that isolates and differentiates the women's institution to an approach that alleges that all inmates and all prisons are the same in terms of rule, supplies, assignments and other factors. This latter approach is no more helpful than the benign neglect that previously characterized the central office's attention to facilities for women; women's prisons obviously have unique needs, different from men's institutions" (Pollack-Byrne, 1990, p. 115).

Of course, the counterargument to the claim that specialized training is needed for staff working in women's prisons is that regular correctional training is sufficient. That is, if the routine training given to new correctional officers includes training for the different supervisory requirements of female versus male inmates, no specialized training would be needed for those assigned to women's institutions.

THE CONTENT OF ROUTINE CORRECTIONAL TRAINING

The idea of requiring any training at all for correctional officers to prepare them for their duties is not a very old one. The first correctional training school was begun in New York in 1930 by the Federal Bureau of Prisons (Schade, 1986). Both prior to and after that, the states apparently hired correctional officers directly into their jobs, with little or no formal training of any kind except that received on the job. Official reviewers and reform-minded critics of corrections often complained about the quality of the correctional staff, but they usually recommended remedies in the form of taking more care about *who* was hired—rather than expressing concern about what preparation was given to that person *after* hiring.

For example, shortly after the Civil War, prison reformers Wines and Dwight (1867) set forth guidelines for the hiring of prison officers, in which they asserted that:

> Prison officers should be men of strict and uniform sobriety. . . . They should be men of mild temper, quiet manners, and pure conversation. . . . They should be men of decision and energy. . . . They should be men of humane and benevolent feelings. . . . They should be men having a sincere interest in those placed under their care. . . . They should be men of high moral principle, and distinguished by habits of industry, order and cleanliness. . . . They should be men possessing a knowledge of human nature in its various aspects and relations . . . They should be men of sterling and incorruptible honesty. . . . They should be men of experience. . . . They must be men of a just and steadfast purpose, free from prejudice and partiality. . . . They should be men of untiring vigilance. . . . They should have a liking for the occupation in which they are employed. . . . Finally, prison officers should be men duly impressed with religious principles; men who fear God, and are in the habit, as the expression of that reverence, of attending the services of some religious body. (pp. 120–122)

It is only after this long recitation about what kind of men corrections should seek to hire that Wines and Dwight provide a brief paragraph on *female* officers, about whom they recommend: "The qualifications of female officers are, in many respects, the same as those of males. It is especially important, however, that female officers should be distinguished for modesty of demeanor, and the exercise of domestic virtues, and that they should possess that intimate knowledge of household employment, which will enable them to teach the ignorant and neglected female prisoners how to economize her means, so as to guard her from the temptations caused by waste and extravagance" (pp. 123–124).

These are certainly descriptions of outstanding prospective employees. Such exemplary persons, both then and now, might possibly be attracted to high-paying high-prestige jobs. But what was the likelihood that corrections was able to attract large numbers of such inherently good and skilled workers in the nineteenth century—or could even do so now? Modern writers Hawkins and Alpert (1989) have provided a much more brutally frank description of a modern correctional officer's job:

> A candid job description for a correctional officer position would read something like this: Excellent employment opportunity for men and women who are willing to work eight-hour shifts at varying times (early morning, afternoon, and late nights) on a rotating basis. Applicants must enforce numerous rules with few guidelines. They must be willing to risk physical harm, psychological harassment, and endure the threat of inmate law suits, which could involve civil liability. They must be willing to spend eight hours each day among people who do not like them. They will not be allowed to fraternize with these people, but are expected to control as well as help them. Applicants must accept that they have little or no input into the rules they will be asked to enforce, not will they be privy to the policy rationale for these rules. They should realize that management will probably not listen to their complaints. Work superiors, located in a military chain of command, are likely to have a great deal of time invested in organizational rules and therefore will resist employee innovations. The person at the top of the chain of command is likely to be a political appointment, but applicants are not allowed to engage in political activity. Promotion is infrequent and opportunities for advancement in the organization are very limited. All applicants are considered untrustworthy: frequent questioning and searches of private possessions are designed to reduce corruption. Applicants must give up some civil rights for employment to continue. Women and minority groups are encouraged to apply, but will be discriminated against once on the job (pp. 338–339).

This job description of a correctional officer is exaggerated, of course, but there is some evidence that persons who seek correctional employment are entering into an employment area that does not have much inherent attractiveness. For example, Smith (1974) found that the social position of the correctional officer had very little prestige compared with other occupations or careers (cited in Farmer, 1977, p. 239). This low prestige may not be so much a reflection of the low pay and minimal qualifications which corrections work has traditionally involved as it is a reflection of the object of that work: prison inmates. Jacobs and Retsky (1975) observed that the job of prison guard is not entirely unlike that of other guard jobs, except that "bank guards and Secret Service agents derive some measure of esteem from the objects they guard, while 'close contacts with convicted felons seems morally profaning for the (prison) guard'" (Jacobs & Retsky, 1975, p. 10, as cited in Farmer, 1977, p. 238).

There is ample evidence that the commitment to the job at the lower levels of correctional work is not generally very great and that the field suffers from relatively high turnover rates. This may be because of the lower prestige of the field and its less desirable working conditions. But it also may be because there is some evidence that a significant proportion of persons who enter correctional work do so out of economic necessity (Shannon, 1987); in other words, most people do not enter correctional work out of a zeal to work with prisoners. Interestingly, the degree to which economic necessity plays a role in correctional recruitment may vary somewhat by gender. In at least one study, a much larger proportion of women indicated that they had sought correctional employment because they were interested in human service work (female 55 percent, male 14 percent) whereas males more frequently indicated that they took the job because there was not alternative work available to them (male 14 percent, female 3 percent) (Jurik & Halemba, 1984). Overall, however, it may be concluded that the dedication of correctional officers to their work varies greatly and that there is little internal incentive to seek more difficult or challenging posts, such as assignment to women's prisons.

As of the spring of 1993, preservice correctional training in the United States varied from a minimum of two weeks (in Louisiana, North Dakota, and Wyoming) to a maximum of 16 weeks (only in Michigan), with the average being about five and a half weeks (for 48 states plus the Federal Bureau of Prisons) (Maquire & Pastore, 1994, pp. 101–107). What is the content of that training? Wicks (1980) has noted that the emphasis in recent decades has been on standardizing correctional training in the United States, so that there can be some assurance that all correctional officers have received basic training in certain skills and knowledge areas which are consistent with state policies and procedures. Shaver (1993) observed that training in Oklahoma, for example, consisted of four weeks of intensive, centralized group training of new recruits, followed by another three to five days of in-house training and orientation once new correctional officers arrived at their actual work site. However, "Very little of this training is directly related to their new positions. Rather, the training focuses on the policies, rules, regulations and values of the correctional agency" (p. 122).

There is no reason to assume that Oklahoma is a training aberration in this regard. Shannon (1987) found that only 85 percent of his Ohio correctional officer respondents reported that they had received 40 hours of training prior to starting their position, although the American Correctional Association (ACA) has stipulated that 40 hours of preservice training is the *minimum*. Only 60 percent of Shannon's respondents indicated that they had received 120 hours of training during their first year on the job as required by the ACA. Even fewer (42 percent) indicated that they had received the required 40 hours of in-service training per year since starting their jobs.

When asked about the content of the training they had been given, Shannon's respondents indicated that the training they most frequently received had to do with firearms training, housing and body searches, contraband hunting, report writing, rules and regulations of the institution, self-defense training, key and tool control, riot control tactics, and CPR certification (Table 4). In general, Shannon (1987) notes that: "The officer's formal training consists primarily of instruction in the skills and mechanics of security procedures and the handling of inmates to maintain order and prevent trouble. The real learning (training) occurs on the job under inmate testing and manipulation attempts" (p. 173).

Of course, it is after formal preservice training that the new correctional officer learns about and enters into the officer subculture, which may well train the recruit somewhat differently than did the academy. For example, while the academy trains rookies in approved ways to handle inmates, the officer subculture "encourages officers to use intimidating behavior to establish authority over inmates" (Shannon, 1987, p. 173). It also provides working definitions of kinds of inmates the new correctional officer can expect to confront, and anecdotal evidence of what techniques work best with different kinds of inmates.

In short, while most academy training focuses on mechanical skills and operational procedures, the real "wisdom" about inmate handling comes from on-the-job inculcation into an officer subculture which may emphasize stereotypes and extreme examples. It is perhaps not at all surprising that such training leaves most correctional officers ill prepared to deal with the unique needs and demands of working with female offenders in custody.

TABLE 4   Specific Training Reportedly Received by Correctional Officers[a]

Subject	Percent
Firearms training	97
Housing and body searches	93
Contraband hunting	92
Training in report writing	88
Rules and regulations of the institution	85
Self-defense training	84
Key and tool control	78
Riot control tactics	67
Valid CPR certification	66
Legal authority training	64
Suicidal inmate recognition	62
Emergency prevention training	61
Techniques for protecting prison property	59
Inmate's rights training	57
Valid first-aid certification	56
How to behave if taken hostage	56
Radio communications	54
Identifying mental illness	52

[a]All other specific training was completed by less than half of respondents.

Source: Shannon (1987, p. 174).

THE NEED FOR SPECIALIZED TRAINING FOR STAFF WORKING WITH FEMALE OFFENDERS

So far we have seen that there is a variety of circumstances which combine to produce the widespread presence of the male inmate preference among correctional officers: the perceptions of and stereotypes about female inmates which are conveyed in the correctional officer subculture; the very real supervisory differences posed by the needs of female inmates compared to their male counterparts; and the limited and largely operations-oriented training given to officer recruits. All these conspire to virtually ensure that most correctional officers are somewhat biased against, and certainly unskilled in dealing with, female offenders in custody.

Little wonder, then, that so many correctional officers report unsatisfactory experiences in working with female offenders or, in the absence of any actual experience in female prisons, much anticipatory prejudice against such assignments. Little wonder, additionally, that women inmates continue to be viewed as more difficult to manage, since little (if any) routine training is aimed at helping correctional officers understand their female inmate charges or what supervisory techniques might be more effective with this population. And finally, little wonder that charges of sexual harassment and inappropriate behavior from correctional officers toward inmates has emerged in the 1990s as one of the more problematic features of managing female institutions. Many state correctional systems have found themselves facing such charges—either in the media or in the courtroom—from individual inmates, interest groups representing inmates, or the federal government.

Suffice it to say that confronting the problem of male inmate preference and all that it means should become a high priority for all correctional systems housing female offenders. The costs of defending the system against lawsuits and media reports are high. But there is little evidence that absent media attacks or lawsuits, most correctional systems are taking preventive measures by providing appropriate specialized training to their correctional staff members in women's institutions. Although the costs of such specialized training would be comparatively modest, it appears that most correctional leaders still regard the male inmate preference as an anecdotal curiosity with little effect on daily operations. Since their systems are always populated predominantly by male inmates, the fact that correctional officers overwhelmingly prefer duty with male inmates does not seem to be a problem. Those comparatively few correctional officers assigned to women's institutions, and their discontent with such duty, seems like a small problem in an ocean of correctional difficulties facing the modern correctional administrator.

The result, however, is that those correctional staff members who are assigned to women's prisons continue to work with inmates about whom they hold highly negative perceptions and for whose management they have never been properly trained. If nothing else, it is these correctional officers and the female inmates they supervise who are the losers.

REFERENCES

AMERICAN CORRECTIONAL ASSOCIATION. (1986). *Public policy for corrections: A handbook for decision makers.* Laurel, MD: ACA.

AMERICAN CORRECTIONAL ASSOCIATION. (1990). *The female offender: What does the future hold?* Arlington, VA: Kirby Lithographic Company.

AMERICAN CORRECTIONAL ASSOCIATION. (2001). *2001 directory of juvenile and adult correctional departments, institutions, agencies, and probation and paroling authorities.* Laurel, MD: ACA.

ARNOLD, R. (1990). Processes of victimization and criminalization of black women. *Social Justice, 17,* 153–166.

BINKLEY-JACKSON, D., CARTER, V. L., & ROLISON, G. L. (1993). African-American women in prison. In B. R. Fletcher et al. (Eds.), *Women prisoners: A forgotten population* (pp. 65–74). Westport, CT: Praeger.

CARLEN, P. (1983). *Women's imprisonment: A study in social control.* London: Routledge & Kegan Paul.

CHESNEY-LIND, M., & RODRIGUEZ, N. (1983). Women under lock and key. *Prison Journal, 63,* 47–65.

FARMER, R. E. (1977). Cynicism: A factor in corrections work. *Journal of Criminal Justice, 5,* 237–246.

FLETCHER, B. R., SHAVER, L. D., & MOON, D. G. (1983). *Women prisoners: A forgotten population.* Westport, CT: Praeger.

GIALLOMBARDO, R. (1966). *Society of women: A study of a women's prison.* New York: Wiley.

GILFUS, M. E. (1992). From victims to survivors to offenders: Women's routes of entry and immersion into street crime. *Women and Criminal Justice, 4,* 63–90.

GOETTING, A., & HOWSEN, R. M. (1983). Women in prison: A profile. *Prison Journal, 63,* 27–46.

HAWKINS, R., & ALPERT, G. P. (1989). *American prison systems: Punishment and justice.* Englewood Cliffs, NJ: Prentice Hall.

HEFFERNAN, E. (1978). Female corrections: History and analysis. Paper presented at the Confinement of Female Offenders Conference, Lexington, Kentucky. Cited in Turnbo (1993).

IMMARIGEON, R. (1987a). Women in prison. *Journal of the National Prison Project, 11*, 1–5.

IMMARIGEON, R. (1987b). Few diversion programs are offered female offenders. *Journal of the National Prison Project, 12*, 9–11.

JACOBS, J., & RETSKY, H. (1975). Prison guard. *Urban Life, 4*, 5–29.

JOESTING, J, JONES, N., & JOESTING, R. (1975). Male and female prison inmates' differences on MMPI scales and revised beta I.Q. *Psychological Reports, 37*, 471–474.

JURIK, N., & HALEMBA, G. J. (1984, Autumn). Gender, working conditions and job satisfaction of women in non-traditional occupations: Female correctional officers in men's prisons. *Sociological Quarterly, 25*, 55–56.

KOBAN, L. (1983). Parent in prison: A comparative analysis of the effects of incarceration on the families of men and women. *Research in Law, Deviance and Social Control, 5*, 171–183.

LEKKERKERKER, E. (1931). *Reformatories for women in the United States*. Groningen, The Hague, The Netherlands: J.B. Wolters.

MAQUIRE, K., & PASTORE, A. L. (EDS.). (1994). *Sourcebook of criminal justice statistics, 1993*. Washington, DC: U.S. Department of Justice, Bureau of Justice Statistics.

MAQUIRE, K., & PASTORE, A. L. (EDS.). (1997). *Sourcebook of criminal justice statistics, 1996*. Washington, DC: U.S. Department of Justice, Bureau of Justice Statistics.

MCKERRACHER, D. W., STREET, D. R. K., & SEGAL, L. S. (1966). A comparison of the behavior problems presented by male and female subnormal offenders. *British Journal of Psychiatry, 112*, 891–899.

POLLACK, J. M. (1984). Women will be women: Correctional officers' perceptions of the emotionality of women inmates. *Prison Journal, 64*, 84–91.

POLLACK, J. M. (1986). *Sex and supervision: Guarding male and female inmates*. New York: Greenwood Press.

POLLACK-BYRNE, J. M. (1990). *Women, prison and crime*. Pacific Grove, CA: Brooks/Cole.

PRISON MATRON. (1862). *Female life in prison*. New York: Hurst & Blackett. Cited in Pollack (1986).

RAFTER, N. H. (1985). *Partial justice: Women in state prisons, 1800–1935*. Boston: Northeastern University Press.

RESNICK, J., & SHAW, N. (1980). Prisoners of their sex: Health problems of incarcerated women. In I. P. Robbins (Ed.), *Prisoners' rights sourcebook*. New York: Clark Boardman.

ROSS, R. R., & FABIANO, E. A. (1986). *Female offenders: Correctional afterthoughts*. Jefferson, NC: McFarland.

SARGENT, E., MARCUS-MENDOZA, S., & YU, C. H. (1993). Abuse and the woman prisoner. In B. R. Fletcher et al. (Eds.), *Women prisoners: A forgotten population* (pp. 55–64). Westport. CT: Praeger.

SARRI, R. (1987). Unequal protection under the law: Women and the criminal justice system. In J. Figueira-McDonough and R. Sarri (Eds.), *The trapped woman: Catch-22 in deviance and control* (pp. 55–64). Newbury Park, CA: Sage.

SCHADE, T. (1986). Prison officer training in the United States: The legacy of Jesse O. Stutsman. *Federal Probation, 50*(4), 40–46.

SHANNON, M. J. (1987, April). Officer training: Is enough being done? *Corrections Today, 49*, 172–175.

SHAVER, L. D. (1993). The relationship between language culture and recidivism among women offenders. In B. R. Fletcher, L. D. Shaver, & D. G. Moon, (Eds.), *Women prisoners: A forgotten population*. Westport, CT: Praeger.

SMITH, W. (1974). Some selective factors in the retention of prison guards. Unpublished masters thesis written in 1963 and reported in E. Johnson, *Crime, corrections and society*. Homewood, IL: Dorsey Press. Cited in Farmer (1977).

Sourcebook of Criminal Justice Statistics Online. (2001). Table 1.84.
   http://www.albany.edu/sourcebook/1995/pdf/t184.pdf

TURNBO, C. (1993). Differences that make a difference: Managing a women's correctional institution. In *Female offenders: Meeting the needs of an neglected population* (pp. 12–16). Laurel, MD: American Correctional Association.

WARD, D. A., & KASSEBAUM, G. G. (1965). *Women's prison: Sex and social structure.* Chicago: Aldine.

WICKS, R. J. (1980). *Guard! Society's professional prisoner.* Houston, TX: Gulf Publishing.

WINES, E. C., & DWIGHT, T. W. (1867). *Report on the prisons and reformatories of the United States and Canada.* Albany, NY: Van Benthuysen and Sons Steam Printing House. Reprinted by AMS Press, New York, 1973.

SECTION VII

Women and Crime

29

Women's Training for Organized Crime

Sex and Sexuality

Sue Mahan

An explanation of gang membership has to be based on the overwhelming impact of racism, sexism, poverty and limited opportunity structures. (Chesney-Lind & Shelden, 1998, p. 50)

A collection of published materials about organized criminal groups was the basis for an examination of the participation of females. Not confined to U.S. groups, this comparative approach examined ten groups other than the U.S. mafia. Criminal groups from other cultures and other historical periods in the Americas were considered. From this broad perspective, available information suggested that the current role of women in organized crime is less significant than at other times. Investigation showed that women's involvement in organized crime is limited by gender expectations as well as by their use as sexual commodities. Important questions were raised about opportunities for women in organized crime, which are also related to those in legitimate enterprise.

Throughout history, in studies of organized crime (OC) the idea of opportunity appears as an important explanatory factor. As with other kinds of careers, opportunities to be a gangster are not equally distributed. Some people have many opportunities to get involved; others have few or no opportunities to join a criminal gang. It is significant to examine situations that provide more or fewer opportunities, and to study the ways that OC opportunities are structured (Cloward & Ohlin, 1960). In this chapter we examine the ways in which opportunities in OC are structured by history, ethnicity, and poverty as each relates to women. It is a review of published materials about ten different OC groups with regard to gender and sex.

Issues of poverty and racism limit both legitimate and illegitimate opportunities for men and women. But from this review it was noted that there are sex and gender issues that are additional barriers to female involvement in OC. First, strong sexual double standards limit expectations for females. Second, women are involved as commodities, not traders, in the sex market. This survey points out the ways in which gender roles and sexual exploitation limit opportunities for women.

WHAT IS ORGANIZED CRIME?

OC is a crime of enterprise. That basic assumption follows from the work of Chambliss and Block and others who do not believe that OC is run and controlled by a national syndicate. "It is a mistake to look for a godfather in every crime network" (Chambliss, 1988, p. 9). OC consists of a coalition of politicians, law-enforcement personnel, businessmen, labor leaders, and (in some ways least important of all) gangsters. The tendency to engage in systematic criminal behavior exists because criminal behavior is good business, makes sense, and is by far the most efficient and profitable way to organize the operations of political offices, businesses, law enforcement agencies, and trade unions in a capitalist democracy.

Block and Chambliss (1981) described OC as the sum of innumerable conspiracies, most often local in scope, which are part of the social and political fabric of everyday life. Crime enterprises pose a threat not to the political structure of society, but on a more subtle level to basic values and morals (Van Duyne, 1996). Traditional studies of OC in the United States have examined the ethnic families originating in New York and Chicago who gained national power from crime during the era of Prohibition. For a new perspective, the present study did not include the American Mafia but focused on other U.S. and international OC groups.

Most writers would agree with Lavey (1990), who described OC as synonymous with corruption, murder, extortion, error, manipulation, and guile involved in conscious, willful, and long-term illegal activities. In addition, it is generally assumed that OC practices a division of labor and has as its aim the realization of large financial profits as quickly as possible.

Beyond this general level of agreement, though, there are differences in definitions of what is and what is not OC. Although debating the definitions of OC preoccupies many scholars, contradictions and controversy make agreement unlikely. To avoid conflict or ambiguity, in this review the term *organized crime* is used for a criminal group with the following characteristics, supplied by Abadinsky (1994, p. 6):

- *Nonideological*. The primary motivating force for OC is profit.
- *Hierarchical*. There is a pyramid organization with a few elites and many operatives.
- *Limited membership*. The group must maintain secrecy and ensure loyalty.
- *Perpetuates itself*. There must be recruitment and training.
- *Violence and corruption*. Corruption is essential and violence is a resource.
- *Specialization*. OC groups form "task forces" to achieve organizational goals.
- *Monopolistic*. Maximizing profits means minimizing competition.
- *Explicit rules and regulations*. Members of OC groups have codes of honor.

Of course, having their own rules does not mean that gangsters always follow them. A code of behavior is also not to be confused with an ideology. Pursuit of profit is considered a driving force rather than a world view.

LITERATURE REVIEW

An extensive literature review was carried out for ten different OC groups.[1] The reference section includes the bibliographic information for the review with numerous sources about each of the 10 groups. These groups were chosen because they were exemplars of different forms of OC, with a body of literature describing them. For each, there was a fascinating account that brought the group to life. These intimate accounts for each of the 10 groups are included as an appendix. There may be an unlimited number of OC groups that would be useful for studies regarding sex and gender. This work may inspire more investigation—not just literature reviews, but social scientific research of all types.

Table 1 lists the OC groups that were included. It indicates whether roles of women have been reported, if there are legendary women members, and if women's roles have been the subject of research. The table shows graphically how little is known about women's roles in OC.

The following examination of the ten exemplar groups focuses on three issues that are significant to OC and opportunities: poverty and economics, ethnicity and racism, and violence and sexism. Two groups, street gangs and outlaw motorcycle gangs, have been best described by social scientists. These descriptions provide pertinent information concerning the barriers to opportunities for women developed from gender roles and sexism.

Historical Opportunities

It is likely that women's roles in OC have diminished with the contemporary trend toward rationality and internationality. Historical analysis provides more examples than contemporary studies do of female ringleaders and gangsters. Block (1980, 1981) studied the role of women in big-city OC at the turn of the century and found women in control of brothels,

TABLE 1   The Place of Women in 10 OC Groups

	Mentioned in Description of Decisions or Control	Legendary Women	Research
1. Pirates	Yes	Yes	
2. Moonshiners	Yes	Yes	
3. Corporate crime	No	No	
4. Russian *Organizatsiya*	No	No	
5. Chinese triads	No	Yes	
6. Japanese *Yakuza*	No	No	
7. Medellin cartel	No	No	
8. Street gangs	Yes	Yes	Yes
9. Prison gangs	No	No	
10. Outlaw motorcycle gangs	Yes	No	Yes

saloons, and other OC enterprises. These women were members of crime families and had opportunities in OC because of their connections. Potter and Gaines (1992) also described the significant roles of women in gambling and brothels run by organized gangs in southern U.S. river ports during the nineteenth century.

1. Pirates.   Piracy flourishes where elites promote smuggled traffic in plunder and stolen goods (Kenney & Finkenauer, 1995). In the early eighteenth century there were famous pirates who were women. They were known for their eagerness to plunder and their zeal in battle. The saga of female pirate Anne Bonney suggests that like other pirates operating off the east coast of the United States, she had friends in high places in Charleston, South Carolina, in 1720. In the pamphlets and journals of their day, Anne Bonney and her sometime companion, Mary Read, took on heroic grandeur. Together they plundered the seas, and together they were eventually captured by an armed sloop belonging to the governor of Jamaica. When Mary Read was sentenced to hang, she reportedly told the court: "[A]s to hanging, I think it no great hardship, for, were it not for that, every cowardly fellow would turn pyrate and so infest the seas, that men of courage must starve" (Browning & Gerassi, 1980, p. 60).

2. Moonshiners.   In moonshining organizations, women's roles were more diversified, as the operation was usually located at or near the home, and the entire family was likely to be involved in production and marketing. Women in the mountain South in the latter part of the nineteenth century aided and protected the men in the moonshine business. They had the important task of lookout, who delayed revenue officers with warrants to search for stills. They gave wholly unreliable information in answer to officers's questions and reportedly even pummeled officers with fists and occasionally fired at them. For example, Mollie Miller of Tennessee was first noticed during a raid on her father's still in which three revenuers were killed and the rest retreated under heavy fire. She went on to become a leader of Polk County moonshiners, credited with the deaths of three revenuers and four or five informers. Another Tennessee moonshiner named Bettie Smith wrote a book about her life: *The Blue Headed Sapsucker, or the Rock Where the Juice Ran Out.* Her testimony at a trial in which she was asked to explain how and to whom she sold her whisky, is part of moonshine lore. "A hunting party of gentlemen came out my way, and got out of whiskey, but found it difficult to buy any. After a while I told a man if he would put his jug down on a dollar and go away, he might when he came back, find the jug full of whiskey." The judge asked: "Would you know the man?" "Oh yes, sir," she responded, " I recognized him in a moment. You are the man, judge" (Miller, 1991, pp. 37, 38). Potter and others described a leadership role for women in rural OC that continues because of its roots in agriculture and home production (Potter & Gaines, 1992).

Modern Crimes of Enterprise

3. Corporate Crime.   In the study of enterprise it is noteworthy that women are very seldom active in the highest levels of sophisticated corporate crime (Albanese, 1993). Although Heidi Fleiss may have organized Hollywood prostitution at a corporate level, and Leona Helmsley was convicted for criminal international hotel deals, these female-headed criminal corporations involved smaller capital and less impact than the multinational-level corporate corruption that has been responsible for the rape of the third world (Clinard, 1990; Lyman and Potter, 1997). For example, compare a female's responsibility for crimes of enterprise with the chairman of Union Carbide Corporation, Warren Anderson's, responsibility for the world's worst industrial accident in Bhopal, India, in 1984. More than 3000 people died and 200,000 were injured. Union Carbide is the third-largest chemical producer in the United States and one of the fifty largest industrial corporations. It operates more than 700 facilities in more than thirty-five countries. Five years after it happened, Union Carbide paid a settlement of $470 million to the Indian government for the accident at Bhopal (Clinard, 1990, p. 139).

In transnational crime, women's involvement has been called *pink collar*, as women involved in corporate crime are seen at clerical or administrative levels rather than making decisions or taking control (Daly, 1989). Just as women find that traditional institutions exclude them from the top levels, careers in crime for women at the top are also exceptional. Some writers see increasingly more participation by women in upper world crime. They assume that female participation in highly lucrative OC is a demand to be respected and acknowledged (Taylor, 1993, p. 198). Despite such assumptions, OC opportunities for women seldom afford them respect. The importance of females to crimes of enterprise has almost never been acknowledged. Steffensmeier (1983) pointed out that crime, in its more organized and lucrative dimensions, is virtually a male phenomenon. OC usually operates in ways that emphasize secrecy, trust, reliability, sophistication, and muscle. Compared to their male counterparts, potential female offenders are at a disadvantage in selection and recruitment into secret criminal groups. They are less likely to have access to crime skills and relationships of tutelage. OC as a career path is closed to most females, and the huge profits from illicit enterprise do not usually go to women. Where the stakes are high and the risk is great, OC is highly sexually segregated. The greater the profit, planning, monopoly, and stability of a criminal organization, the less likely are women to be in positions of power within it (Steffensmeir, 1983, p. 1026).

4. Russian Organizatsiya.　　The Russian criminal Organizatsiya comes from a white-collar background. Its members have been linked to credit-card, IRS, and utilities frauds in the United States. The first known criminal enterprise of the Organizatsiya was a very large scale fuel tax scam that made millions in the northeastern United States during the 1980s (Kleinknecht, 1996). As with other rational, sophisticated criminal organizations, no women are known to be involved in the Mafiya.

Racism and Ethnicity

Connections between the issues of poverty and racism and the development of OC have been discussed widely. Some authors have presumed that OC develops because of ethnic or racial characteristics that facilitate it. However, efforts to show the causal links between OC and particular groups or social classes have proved fruitless. OC is not limited to ethnic enclaves or caused by desperate poverty (Albanese, 1989). Outside the law, demands of secrecy and loyalty, needs for recruitment, and long-term associations are related to neighborhoods and communities and ties of kinship and culture (MacKenzie, 1967). For this reason, ethnicity cannot be ignored, even though it cannot be considered causal. In this regard, women are confronted by the same barriers of racism and poverty that men face. But females also face a barrier to the secrecy, recruitment, and associations that provide OC opportunities for males in their community.

5. Chinese Triads.   Women in positions of power in Chinese triads are almost unheard of. One woman known as "Big Sister Ping" was said to be the queen of "Snakeheads" or smugglers of Chinese immigrants (Kerry, 1997). But in the international drugs and arms trade, as in most other sectors of Chinese-directed OC, women are excluded. Women are asked to leave when men begin to discuss gang business.

Young women become associated with Chinese gangs through male gang members with whom they attend school. Some young women find hanging out with gang members fun; others become affiliated with gang members because they like the protection that gangs provide. Fun, excitement, and power are associated with hanging around with gang members, but so is sexual exploitation. Only those with steady boyfriends who are gang leaders are immune from rape by gang members. Gang leaders may assign females who are considered promiscuous to work in Chinatown massage parlors owned by the gang (Chin, 1996).

6. Japanese Yakuza.   In the Japanese Yakuza, there is no known woman ringleader or crime boss. Japanese gangsters are involved in the sex trade, and women are sexual commodities rather than decision makers. The trade is greatest in adolescents from Thailand and the Philippines, but there are also hundreds of young women in the United States who have been victimized by the Yakuza. They sometimes use agents who place ads for singers and dancers in entertainment presses and publications. The women who are selected are expected to act as hostesses and prostitutes in Japan, although they auditioned for a singing or dancing job. No matter what the duties of the woman, she will either not be paid or be paid far less than she was promised. Escape from Japan, and even escape from the employer, becomes nearly impossible. Women who return from what is often a hellish experience in the Yakuza clubs often seek revenge but usually get little satisfaction. Few of the agents can be located, and the victims have little in the way of legal recourse (Kaplan & Dubro, 1986, p. 251).

7. Medellin Cartel.   Contrary to the report by de Lama (1988), according to the literature, women were related to Medellin cartel membership only as romantic involvements or idolized and romanticized mother figures. According to a member of a gang of assassins on the fringes of the cartel, breaking a promise to a woman is worse than death. The assassins bring their money from murder contracts home to their mothers. The gangster becomes the provider, the surrogate father. His mother accepts his life as a sicario and, with a certain banality, she talks matter of factly about the violence. "That boy was killed by a very nice-looking kid," a mother would comment (Duzan, 1994, p. 213).

No other reports of women's involvement at the level of power or control have surfaced. Rather, reports about the cartel mention the victimization of women in both harassment and domestic violence and in political assassinations. According to one observer, "The woman's role has disintegrated into: keeping an eye on their men's weapons, serving as connections and for sexual satisfaction. Jealousy is a motive for murder. You love your girlfriend and give her a lot of presents. If she betrays you, you kill her" (Duzan, 1994, p. 214).

Poverty

8. Street Gangs.   Patterns of women members of street gangs have been studied for more than a decade in the United States and there is a significant body of criminological literature devoted to women's participation (Maher & Curtis, 1995; Moore, 1985, 1991). Current media focus has settled on girls' commission of violent crimes in youth gangs, portraying girls as "meaner now than girls in earlier generations." The gender realities of street gangs are complicated. Although the media stereotype is clear and intensely male, every so often the media discovers that there are girls in gangs and that girls can also be violent. But the notion of gang as a social concern is pretty much all male. Perhaps if the public image of gang included girls as well as boys, it would humanize it too much. The reality is that up to one-third of those involved in street gangs are likely to be females (Moore, 1991).

Women, like men, find that gangs fill a growing void created by the continued presence of homelessness and unemployment. In many inner-city neighborhoods, 80 percent of the African-American families living below the poverty level are headed by single women. The dismantling of social service programs has devastated some urban-dwelling families. The ugly reality of mothers with children moving in and out of shelters has resulted in women forming alliances to survive. According to Taylor (1993): "The difference between females and males is their method of survival. Women are more involved in the less dangerous crime; they tend to try and trick people out of their money" (p. 195).

Girls in gangs challenge the conservative view of women as "wife and mother," which is promoted in patriarchal OC groups. They are viewed as having moved outside the realm of traditional values. Being marginal, girl gangsters may substitute strong ties to other outlaws for weak ties to their conventional families. Toughness, meanness, and aggression are highly valued for all gang members. Respect means a lot to both boys and girls. The streets may be dominated by young men, but girls and young women do not necessarily avoid the streets. They are involved in "hanging out," "partying," and the occasional fight. During the 1990s, research on girl gangs moved beyond simple, stereotypical notions about these groups as auxiliaries of male gangs to a more careful assessment of girls' lives (Chesney-Lind & Shelden, 1998).

According to Campbell's (1984) examination of the roles for females in street gangs, there are some essential patterns in girls' gang membership. It was clear that the girls' heterosexuality is crucial to their membership because it perpetuates male control. "Dykes" are scorned and abused. The separate nature of men and women is an explicit part of gang philosophy. Women's sexuality can be controlled by being labeled "cheap" and receiving abuse if they dispense sexual favors too freely. Reproductive functions also are a matter of male decision but women's responsibility. An important female role is that of the mother figure, offering advice and counsel on personal matters. The mother figure plays the role of social and emotional leader. A woman is afforded respect as a maternal figure. There are also aggressive girls in gangs who try to succeed on male terms. They are accepted with the same indulgence accorded to junior males. "The tomboy will grow out of it, have children, and a decent male will provide for her, keep her at home, and save her from the streets," according to the fundamentally conservative philosophy of gangs (Campbell, 1984, p. 246).

Males control gangs and continue to live out the male roles they grew up with, casting girls in all too recognizable complementary positions to themselves. In street gangs, girls find not a new sense of self, nor a new set of values, but the old ones disguised in a new way (Campbell, 1984, p. 257). For girl gangsters, as for their mothers, the most enduring bond in their lives is with their children. Children represent an escape from the abiding sense of isolation, the possibility of continuity and loyalty, and unconditional acceptance. Campbell provides the "new" woman's dream, the "new" agenda that she found among the gang girls she studied: "No more suffering or poverty. No more lonely, forced 'independence,' living alone on welfare in a shabby apartment. First, a good husband, strong but not violent, faithful but manly. Second, well-dressed children. Third, a beautiful suburban apartment. Later for the revolution" (p. 267).

9. Prison Gangs.   The links between street gangs and prison gangs in the United States have been well established (Jacobs, 1974; Moore, 1978). There is a growing body of research and literature on prison gangs. The authors depict a world that is strongly male dominated. Prison gangs may be the epitome of machismo; there are no "broads," according to Davidson (1974). Gang "ethics" prohibit feminine sexual practices. Prisoners who play the female sexual role are known as "punks." According to prison gangsters, "there is a certain weakness in 'punks'." As described in the literature about prison gangs, extreme negative treatment of punks implies negative feelings about women, for whom they are surrogates in this violent subculture (p. 83).

There are no studies of female prison gangs per se. Studies have examined cliques and pseudofamilies and have often focused on homosexuality or gender issues rather than on criminal organizations of incarcerated women (Pollock-Byrne, 1990). There is no real evidence to determine how female street gang members are involved when they are incarcerated (Davidson, 1974).

Sexism

10. Outlaw Motorcycle Gangs.   There have been several studies of outlaw bikers that examined the participation of women. It is the second pattern in OC about which there is substantial social sciences literature. In 1966, Hunter S. Thompson studied the Hell's Angels from a journalistic perspective. Although Thompson did not take into account views of the women involved, his description of degradation and sexual perversion was intensely personal. He carefully described one scene, which he labeled "somewhere between a friendly sex orgy and an all-out gang rape" (p. 247). Thompson explained the contradiction when he wrote: "So the Hell's Angels are working rapists . . . and in this downhill half of our 20th century, they are not so different from the rest of us as they sometimes seem. They are only more obvious" (p. 249). Thompson saw the relationship between OC patterns and roles and the patterns and roles in legitimate society.

The role of women in outlaw biker gangs is illustrative of the role of women in other OC enterprises (Hopper & Moore, 1990). Although women have a more or less active role in the various organizations, sexuality is a factor that separates and defines women's membership. The sex trade itself is often run by OC groups, including bikers. Since women may be commodities on the sex market, their care and control are important to the group's income. Control is a major factor if humans are to be sold and used as objects. The most effective form of control is voluntary. Outlaw bikers are able to control women to some extent based on a philosophy about appropriate male dominance and female submission. To some extent the control exerted on female gang participants is also based on fear. The threat of punishment and the arbitrary nature of rules for which punishments are attached leave women who are involved with outlaw bikers feeling insecure and powerless (Wolf, 1991).

The exclusion of women from formal participation and the pervasive attitude of chauvinism does not meant that females have no importance or influence. Women who participate in the outlaw subculture fall into one of three major categories: "broads," who drift in and out of the subculture in a casual and temporary status; "mamas," who maintain social–sexual interaction with the club as a whole on an informal or economic basis; and "ol' ladies," who have a long-standing personal relationship with a single member (Wolf, 1991, p. 133).

Many women who participate in the outlaw biker gang lifestyle had a history of involvement in prostitution and other sex-related services before they became part of the group (Quinn, 1987). For them, affiliation with outlaw bikers may offer social status and a sense of physical security from abuse by customers and pimps. Many veteran biker women see their male companions as somewhat interchangeable agents of status and protection.

Jackson and Wilson (1993) found that motorcycle gang members in Great Britain were all male, tough, aggressive, dogmatic, hedonistic, sensation seeking, impulsive, risk taking, irresponsible, and lacking in self-esteem and ambition. They were also significantly anxious and depressed. Despite these self-destructive tendencies, it appeared from other sources that outlaw bikers were taking increasing control of importation, distribution, and sales of illicit drugs, contraband alcohol, and the black-market tobacco trade throughout North America. The British Columbia Hell's Angels were regarded as one of the wealthiest outlaw motorcycle gangs in the world in 1996 (Criminal Intelligence Service Canada, 1996).

The outlaw biker gangs' public image contrasts with their private OC role. Their nature as hedonistic and thrill seeking on the one hand, and rational profit motivated on the other, puts women at a double disadvantage in these gangs. Female members' role as obedient followers and their status as objects have led women into roles increasingly defined by sexuality and made outlaw biker gangs extremely gender segregated. With opportunities for females structured by their value as sexual commodities, the status of women in OC is necessarily controlled by the men who run the market and who are the buyers.

DISCUSSION

From this review it is clear that knowledge about women's place in present-day OC is limited. Since there are more known historical OC figures who were women than there are modern women gangsters, it appears unlikely that today's women are becoming more important in the world of OC.

In the two OC groups about which there is a body of literature concerning female membership (street gangs and motorcycle gangs), two different patterns for women emerge. In street gangs, females participate at all levels, yet are still limited by the expectations for females held by the group. Very traditional gender roles were apparent in the expectations for female gangsters to be nurturing and supporting and in the girls' own desires to be provided for in a conventional family manner.

In outlaw motorcycle gangs, gender inequality was apparent in the expectations for female bikers to handle all domestic chores and to provide sexual favors on demand, as well as to remain silent and subservient. The double standard was made even more extreme by the sex trade carried on by outlaw motorcycle gangs. Their exploitation as commodities in the sex market presented barriers to decision-making levels of the gang. Sexual exploitation also determined the female's personal importance to the gang.

Two issues, gender and sexuality, stand between women and opportunities in OC. Historical literature about OC shows that gender roles and expectations can and do change with the passing of time. The literature also shows that in some contexts women have been able to take control of the market for sexual services. However, today in the structure of OC and the climate of violence in which it exists in the Americas, the sex trade has increasingly grown more oppressive and exploitative of women. It is an interesting parallel to the position for women and opportunities in legitimate enterprise. Women face barriers to opportunity because of expectations for females and exploitation for their sexuality in both the legitimate and criminal worlds.

NOTE

1. This review is part of a larger work entitled *Beyond the Mafia* by Sue Mahan (Newbury Park, CA: Sage Publications, 1998).

REFERENCES AND BIBLIOGRAPHY

ABADINSKY, H. (1994). *Organized crime* (4th ed.). Chicago: Nelson-Hall.

ALBANESE, J. (1989). *Organized crime in America* (2nd ed.). Cincinnati, OH: Anderson Publishing.

ALBANESE, J. (1993). Women and the newest profession: Females as white collar criminals. In C. Culliver (Ed.), *Female criminality: the state of the art*. New York: Garland Publishing.

ALBANESE, J. (1996). *Organized crime in America* (3rd ed.). Cincinnati, OH: Anderson Publishing.

ALLSOP, K. (1961). *The bootleggers and their era*. Garden City, NY: Doubleday.

BAKER, M. (1996). *Badguys*. New York: Simon & Schuster.

BARLEYCORN, M. (1975). *Moon-shiners manual*. Willits, CA: Oliver Press.

BLOCK, A. (1980). Searching for women in organized crime. In S. K. Datesman & F. R. Scarpitti (Eds.), *Women, crime and justice*. New York: Oxford University Press.

BLOCK, A. (1981). Aw! Your mother's in the Mafia: Women criminals in progressive New York. In L. H. Bowker (Ed.), *Women and crime in America*. New York: Macmillan.

BLOCK, A. (1994). *Space, time, and organized crime* (2nd ed.). New Brunswick, NJ: Transaction Books.

BLOCK, A., & CHAMBLISS, W. J. (1981). *Organizing crime*. New York: Elsevier/North-Holland.

BOOTH, M. (1990). *The triads: The growing global threat from the Chinese criminal societies*. New York: St. Martin's Press.

BOWKER, L. H. (ED.). (1981). *Women and crime in America*. New York: Macmillan Publishing.

BROOKHISER, R. (1965, June). Patriots, rebels and founding fathers: Analysis of Shays' rebellion and the whiskey rebellion. *New York Times, 144*, 15–27.

BROWNING, F., & GERASSI, J. (1980). *The American way of crime*. New York: G.P. Putnam's Sons.

BUCKWALTER, J. R. (ED.). (1990). *International perspectives on organized crime*. Chicago: Office of International Criminal Justice, University of Illinois at Chicago.

BURNEY, J. (1912). *History of the buccaneers of America*. London: Allen & Unwin.

BUTTERFIELD, F. (1997, August 17). Study: Cohesion in community lowers violence. *Daytona Beach Sunday News Journal*, p. 3A.

CALIFORNIA DEPARTMENT OF JUSTICE, BUREAU OF INVESTIGATION. (1996). *Russian organized crime: California's newest threat.* Sacramento, CA: CDJ.

CAMPBELL, A. (1984). *The girls in the gang: A report from New York City.* New York: Blackwell.

CARSE, R. (1965). *The age of piracy.* New York: Grosset & Dunlap.

CHAMBLISS, W. (1988). *On the take: From petty crooks to presidents* (2nd ed.). Bloomington, IN: Indiana University Press.

CHAMBLISS, W. J. (1995). State organized crime: The American society of criminology. In N. Passas (Ed.), *Organized crime* (pp. 183–280). Aldershot, Hants, England: Dartmouth Publishing.

CHANG, D. H. (1995). A new form of international crime: The human organ trade. *International Journal of Comparative and Applied Criminal Justice, 19*(1), 1–18.

CHESNEY-LIND, M., & SHELDEN, R. G. (1998). *Girls, delinquency, and juvenile justice* (2nd ed.). Belmont, CA: Wadsworth Publishing.

CHIN, K. (1990). *Chinese subculture and criminality: Non-traditional crime groups in America.* Westport, CT: Greenwood Press.

CHIN, K. (1995). Triad societies in Hong Kong. *Transnational Organized Crime, 1*(1), 47–64.

CHIN, K. (1996). *Chinatown gangs: Extortion, enterprise, and ethnicity.* New York: Oxford University Press.

CHU, Y. (1996). Triad societies and the business community in Hong Kong. *International Journal of Risk, Security and Crime Prevention, 1*(1), 33–40.

CLINARD, M. B. (1990). *Corporate corruption: The abuse of power.* New York: Praeger.

CLOWARD, R., & OHLIN, L. (1960). *Delinquency and opportunity.* New York: Free Press.

COURTWRIGHT, D. T. (1986). *Violent land: Single men and social disorder from the frontier to the inner city.* Cambridge, MA: Harvard University Press.

CRESSY, D. R. (1995). Methodological problems in the study of organized crime as a social problem. In N. Passas (Ed.), *Organized crime* (pp. 3–14). Aldershot, Hants, England: Dartmouth Publishing.

CRIMINAL INTELLIGENCE SERVICE CANADA. (1996). *Annual report on organized crime in Canada* (revised August 27).

CROWGEY, H. G. (1971). *Kentucky bourbon: The early years of whiskey making.* Lexington, KY: University Press of Kentucky.

CUMMINS, E. (1995). *California prison gang project* (final report). EDRS 387 616, CE 069 978. Chicago: Spencer Foundation.

DALY, K. (1989) Gender and varieties of white collar crime. *Criminology, 27*(4), 769–794.

DATESMAN, S. K., & SCARPITTI, F. R. (EDS.). (1980). *Women, crime, and justice.* New York: Oxford University Press.

DAVIDSON, R. T. (1974). *Chicano prisoners: The key to San Quentin.* Prospect Heights, IL: Waveland Press.

DAWLEY, D. (1992). *A nation of lords: The autobiography of the Vice Lords* (2nd ed.). Prospect Heights, IL: Waveland Press.

DEBNAM, B. (1997, August 19). The most famous pirate of all: Blackbeard the feared. *Daytona Beach News Journal,* p. 2C.

DE LAMA, G. (1988, November 20). Colombia becomes the Lebanon of Latin America. *Chicago Tribune,* p. 5.

DEMONT, J. (1996). Moonshine revival: History and hard times mean more illegal booze. *Maclean's, 109*(37), 18(1).

DOBNIK, V. (1997, January 25). Report: Chinese being paid slave wage. *Daytona Beach News Journal,* p. 12A.

DUZAN, M. J. (1994). *Death beat: A Colombian journalist's life inside the cocaine wars* (P. Eisner, Trans.). New York: HarperCollins (original work published 1992).

ESQUEMELING, J. *The buccaneers of America.* London: George Routledge & Sons (reprint of the manuscript originally produced in 1684–1685).

FENNELL, T. (1994). Risky business: Tax weary Canadians help support a boom in smuggled alcohol. *Maclean's, 107*(28), 14(3).

FONG, R. S., & BUENTELLO, S. (1991). The detection of prison gang development: An empirical assessment. *Federal Probation, 55*(1), 66–69.

FREEMANTLE, B. (1995). *The Octopus: Europe in the grip of organized crime*. London: Orion.

GIBBS, N. R. (1995, September 19). Yummy. *Time, 144*, 55–59.

GILBERT, J. N. (1996). Organized crime on the western frontier. *Journal of Criminal Organizations, 10*(2), 7–13.

GOODSON, R., & OLSON, W. (1995, January–February). International organized crime. *Society*, pp. 18–29.

GRASSI, A. (1990). The role of the courts in combating international crime. In J. R. Buckwalter (Ed.), *International perspectives on organized crime* (pp. 37–47). Chicago: Office of International Criminal Justice, University of Illinois at Chicago.

HANDELMAN, S. (1994). The Russian mafya. *Foreign Affairs, 73*(2), 83–96.

HANDELMAN, S. (1995). *Comrade criminal: Russia's new mafya*. New Haven, CT: Yale University Press.

HOPPER, C., & MOORE, J. (1990). Women in outlaw motorcycle gangs. *Journal of Contemporary Ethnography, 18*(4).

Huey, L. S., Hurysz, J., & Hurysz, L. M. (1995). Victimization patterns of Asian gangs in the United States. *Journal of Gang Research, 3*(1), 41–49.

HUFF, C. R. (ED.). (1996). *Gangs in America* (2nd ed.). Thousand Oaks, CA: Sage Publications.

JACKSON, C., & WILSON, G. D. (1993). Mad, bad or sad? The personality of bikers. *Personality and Individual Differences, 14*(1), 241–242.

JACOBS, J. B. (1974). Street gangs behind bars. *Social Problems, 21*(3), 395–409.

JAMIESON, A. (1995). Transnational dimensions of Italian organized crime. *Transnational Organized Crime, 1*(2), 151–172.

JANKOWSKI, M. S. (1991). *Islands in the street: Gangs and American urban society*. Berkeley, CA: University of California Press.

JONES, L., & NEWMAN, L., with ISAY, D. (1997). *Our America: Life and death on the south side of Chicago*. New York: Scribner.

KAPLAN, D. E., & DUBRO, A. (1986). *Yakuza: The explosive account of Japan's criminal underworld*. Menlo Park, CA: Addison-Wesley.

KEISER, R. L. (1979). *The Vice Lords: Warriors of the streets* (Fieldwork ed.). New York: Holt, Rinehart & Winston.

KELLNER, E. (1971). *Moonshine: Its history and folklore*. Indianapolis, IN: Bobbs-Merrill.

KENNEY, D. J., & FINCKENAUER, J. O. (1995). *Organized crime in America*. Belmont, CA: Wadsworth Publishing.

KERRY, J. (1997). *The new war*. New York: Simon & Schuster.

KINNEAR, K. L. (1996). *Gangs: A reference handbook*. Santa Barbara, CA: ABC-CLIO.

KLEINKNECHT, W. (1996). *The new ethnic mobs: The changing face of organized crime in America*. New York: Free Press.

KNOX, G. W. (1994a). *National gangs resource handbook: An encyclopedic reference*. Chicago: National Gang Crime Resource Center, Chicago State University. Wyndham Hall Press.

KNOX, G. W. (1994b). *An introduction to gangs* (new rev. ed.). Chicago: Wyndham Hall Press.

KOTLOWITZ, A. (1991). *There are no children here*. New York: Doubleday, Anchor Books.

LAMOTT, K. (1963). *Chronicles of San Quentin: The biography of a prison*. London: John Long.

LANG, A. (1684). Adventures of buccaneers. In J. Esquemeling (Ed.), *The buccaneers of America* (pp. xiii–xix). New York: E.P. Dutton.

LAVEY, D. (1990). Interpol's role in combating organized crime. In J. R. Buckwalter (Ed.), *International perspectives on organized crime* (pp. 87–93). Chicago: Office of International Criminal Justice, University of Illinois at Chicago.

LEE, R. W., III. (1995). Colombia's cocaine syndicate. In N. Passas (Ed.), *Organized crime* (pp. 281–317). Aldershot, Hants., England: Dartmouth Publishing.

LICENSED BEVERAGE INDUSTRIES. (1974, January). *Moonshine: Formula for fraud and slow death.* New York: LBI.

LICENSED BEVERAGE INDUSTRIES. (1966, October). *Moonshine merchants: A study and report.* New York: LBI.

LOMBARDO, R. M. (1990). Asset forfeiture: Civil remedies against organized crime. In J. R. Buckwalter (Ed.), *International perspectives on organized crime* (pp. 49–62). Chicago: Office of International Criminal Justice, University of Illinois at Chicago.

LUPSHA, P. A. (1995). Individual choice, material culture and organized crime. In N. Passas (Ed.), *Organized crime* (pp. 105–125). Aldershot, Hants., England: Dartmouth Publishing.

LYMAN, M., & POTTER, G. W. (1997). *Organized crime,* Upper Saddle River, NJ: Prentice Hall.

MA, Y. (1995). Crime in China: Characteristics, causes and control strategies. *International Journal of Comparative and Applied Criminal Justice, 19*(2), 247–256.

MACDONALD, S. B. (1988). *Dancing on a volcano: The Latin American drug trade.* New York: Praeger.

MACKENZIE, N. (Ed.). (1967). *Secret societies.* New York: Holt, Rinehart & Winston.

MAHER, L., & CURTIS, R. (1995). In search of the female urban gansta. In B. R. Price and N. J. Sokoloff (Eds.), *The criminal justice system and women* (2nd ed.). New York: McGraw-Hill.

MALTZ, M. D. (1990). *Measuring the effectiveness of organized crime control efforts* (Monograph 9). Chicago: Office of International Criminal Justice, University of Illinois at Chicago.

MARTENS, F. T. (1990). African-American organized crime. In J. R. Buckwalter (Ed.), *International perspectives on organized crime*. Chicago: Office of International Criminal Justice, University of Illinois at Chicago.

MARTIN J. M., & ROMANO, A. T. (1992). *Multinational crime: Terrorism, espionage, drugs and arms trafficking.* Menlo Park, CA: Sage Publications.

MARTINEZ, R., JR. (1996). Latinos and lethal violence: The impact of poverty and inequality. *Social Problems, 43*(2), 131–146.

MARX, G., & PARSONS, C. (1996, November 11). *Chicago Tribune*, pp. 1–8.

MCCORMACK, R. J. (1996). *Organized crime: A north American perspective.* Trenton, NJ: College of New Jersey Department of Law and Justice.

MCDONALD, W. F. (1995). The globalization of criminology: The new frontier is the frontier. *Transnational Organized Crime, 1*(1), 1–12.

MCDONALD, W. F. (1997). Crime and illegal immigration: Emerging local, state, and federal partnerships. *National Institute of Justice Journal, 232*, 2–10.

MILLER, W. R. (1991). *Revenuers and moonshiners.* Chapel Hill, NC: University of North Carolina Press.

MONTI, D. J. (1994). *Wannabe gangs in suburbs and schools.* Cambridge, MA: Blackwell.

MOORE, J. W. (1978). *Homeboys: Gangs, drugs, and prisons in the barrios of Los Angeles.* Philadelphia: Temple University Press.

MOORE, J. (1985). Isolation and stigmatization in the development of the underclass: The case of Chicano gangs in east Los Angeles. *Social Problems, 33*(1), 1–10.

MOORE, J. (1994). The chola life course: Chicana heroin users and the barrio gang. *International Journal of the Addictions, 29*(9), 1115–1126.

MOORE, J. W. (1991). *Going down to the barrio.* Philadelphia: Temple University Press.

MYERS, W. H., II. (1996). ORB weavers: The global webs, the structure and activities of transnational ethnic Chinese criminal groups. *Transnational Organized Crime, 1*(4), 1–36.

NAYLON, R. T. (1996). From underworld to underground enterprise crime, informal sector business and public policy response. *Crime, Law and Social Change, 24*(2), 79–150.

NEAPOLITAN, J. (1996). Cross national crime data: Some unaddressed problems. *Journal of Crime and Justice, 19*(1), 95–112.

New York State Organized Crime Task Force, New York State Commission of Investigations, New Jersey Commission, and others. (1996). *An analysis of Russian-émigré crime in the tri-state region*. Albany, NY: Tri-state Joint Soviet-Émigré Organized Crime Project.

Pace, D. F. (1991). *Concepts of vice, narcotics, and organized crime* (3rd ed.). Englewood Cliffs, NJ: Prentice Hall.

Paris-Steffens, S. (1990). The role of the United Nations in combating organized crime. In J. R. Buckwalter (Ed.), *International perspectives on organized crime* (pp. 13–17). Chicago: Office of International Criminal Justice, University of Illinois at Chicago.

Parsels, E. (1996). Capitalism fosters gang behavior. In C. P. Cozic (Ed.), *Gangs: Opposing viewpoints*. San Diego, CA: Greenhaven Press.

Passas, N. (Ed.). (1995). *Organized crime*. Philadelphia: Temple University Press.

Patrick, J. (1973). *A Glasgow gang observed*. London: Eyre Methuen.

Pollock-Byrne, J. M. (1990). *Women, prison and crime*. Pacific Grove, CA: Brooks/Cole.

Posner, G. L. (1988). *Warlords of crime: Chinese secret societies: The new Mafia*. New York: McGraw-Hill.

Potter, G. W. (1994). *Criminal organizations: Vice, racketeering, and politics in an American city*. Prospect Heights, IL: Waveland Press.

Potter, G. W., & Gaines, L. (1992). Country comfort: Vice and corruption in the rural south. *Journal of Contemporary Criminal Justice, 8*(1), 36–81.

Quinn, J. F. (1987). Sex roles and hedonism among members of outlaw motorcycle clubs. *Deviant Behavior, 8*(1), 47–63.

Rankin, H. (1969). *The golden age of piracy*. New York: Holt, Rinehart & Winston.

Renard, R. D. (1996). *The Burmese connection: Illegal drugs and the making of the golden triangle*. Boulder, CO: Lynne Rienner.

Rhodes, R. P. (1984). *Organized crime: Crime control vs. civil liberties*. New York: Random House.

Romo, R. (1983). *East Los Angeles: History of a barrio*. Austin, TX: University of Texas Press.

Royal Canadian Mounted Police Training and Development Branch. (1994). Outlaw motorcycle gangs. *Royal Canadian Mounted Police Gazette, 56*(3–4), 1–39. Project Focus, Canada.

Ruggiero, V. (1996). War markets: Corporate and organized criminals in Europe. *Social and Legal Studies, 5*(1), 5–20.

Ruth, D. E. (1996). *Inventing the public enemy: The gangster in American culture*. Chicago: University of Chicago Press.

Ryan, P. J. (1995). *Organized crime: A reference handbook*. Santa Barbara, CA: ABC–CLIO.

Saga, J. (1991). *Confessions of a Yakuza: A life in Japan's underworld*. Tokyo: Kodansha.

Sale, R. T. (1971). *The Blackstone Rangers: A reporter's account of time spent with the street gang on Chicago's south side*. New York: Random House.

Salzano, J. (1994). It's a dirty business: Organized crime in deep sludge. *Criminal Organizations, 8*(3–4), 17–20.

Sanders, W. B. (1994). *Gangbangs and drive-bys: Grounded culture and juvenile gang violence*. Hawthorne, NY: Aldine de Gruyter.

Sanz, K., & Silverman, I. (1996). The evolution and future direction of southeast Asian criminal organizations. *Journal of Contemporary Criminal Justice, 12*(4), 285–294.

Sato, I. (1991). *Kamikaze biker: Parody and anomie in affluent Japan*. Chicago: University of Chicago Press.

Scarpitti, F. R., & Block, A. A. (1987). America's toxic waste racket: Dimensions of the environmental crisis. In T. S. Bynum (Ed.), *Organized crime in America: Concepts and controversies*. Monsey, NY: Willow Tree Press.

Schatzberg, R., & Kelly, R. J. (1996). *African-American organized crime: A social history*. New York: Garland Publishing.

SEIBEL, G., & PINCOMB, R. A. (1994). From the Black P Stone Nation to the El Rukns. *Criminal Organizations, 8*(3–4), 3–9.

SEYMOUR, C. (1996). *Yakuza diary: Doing time in the Japanese underworld.* New York: Atlantic Monthly Press.

SHELLEY, L. I., SABERSCHINSKI, H., SINURAJA, T., ET AL. (1995). East meets West in crime. *European Journal on Criminal Policy and Research, 3*(4), 7–107.

SILBERMAN, M. (1995). *A world of violence.* Belmont, CA: Wadsworth Publishing.

SLAUGHTER, T. P. (1986). *The whiskey rebellion: Frontier epilogue to the American Revolution.* New York: Oxford University Press.

SMALL, G. (1995). *Ruthless: The global rise of the Yardies.* London: Warner.

STEFFENSMEIER, D. J. (1983). Organizational properties and sex segregation in the underworld: Building a sociological theory of sex differences in crime. *Social Forces, 61*(4), 1010–1032.

SUTHERLAND, E. H. (1949). *White collar crime.* New York: Holt, Rinehart & Winston.

TAYLOR, C. S. (1993). *Girls, gangs, women and drugs.* East Lansing, MI: Michigan State University Press.

THOMPSON, H. S. (1966). *Hell's Angels: A strange and terrible saga.* New York: Ballantine Books.

United States Code. Title 15. Criminal street gangs. Section 150001.

U.S. CONGRESS SENATE COMMITTEE ON GOVERNMENTAL AFFAIRS PERMANENT SUBCOMMITTEE ON INVESTIGATIONS. (1993). *The new international criminal and Asian organized crime: Report* (Report Item 1037-CMF). Washington, DC: U.S. Government Printing Office.

U.S. DEPARTMENT OF HEALTH AND HUMAN SERVICES. (1992). Elevated blood lead levels associated with illicitly distilled alcohol: Alabama, 1990–1991. *Morbidity and Mortality Weekly Report, 41*(17), 294(2).

U.S. DEPARTMENT OF JUSTICE. (1985). Prison gangs: Their extent, nature and impact on prisons (Grant 84-NI-AX-0001). Washington, DC: U.S. Government Printing Office.

U.S. GENERAL ACCOUNTING OFFICE. (1996). *Drug control: U.S. heroin program encounters many obstacles in southeast Asia* (Report to congressional requesters). Washington, DC: U.S. GAO.

VAKSBERG, A. (1991). *The Soviet Mafia* (J. & E. Roberts, Trans.). New York: St. Martin's Press.

VAN DUYNE, P. C. (1996). The phantom and threat of organized crime. *Crime, Law and Social Change, 24*(4), 341–377.

VARESE, F. (1994). Is Sicily the future of Russia? Private protection and the rise of the Russian Mafia. *Archives of European Sociology, 35*, 224–258.

VIGIL, J. D. (1994). *Barrio gangs: Street life and identity in southern California.* Arlington, TX: University of Texas Press.

VIGIL, J. D. (1997). *Learning from gangs: The Mexican American experience* (Report RC 020 943). Los Angeles, CA: University of California at Los Angeles. (ERIC Clearinghouse on Rural Education and Small Schools Temporary Accession RC 020 943)

VOLOBUEV, A. (1990). Combating organized crime in the U.S.S.R.: Problems and perspectives. In J. R. Buckwalter (Ed.), *International perspectives on organized crime* (pp. 75–82). Chicago: Office of International Criminal Justice, University of Illinois at Chicago.

WALTHER, S. (1994). Forfeiture and money laundering laws in the United States. *Crime, Law and Social Change, 21*(1), 1–13.

WESSELL, N. H. (Ed.). (1995). Special issues on crime in Russia. *Russian Politics and Law, 33*(4), 3–72.

WILKINSON, A. (1985). *Moonshine: A life in pursuit of white liquor.* New York: Alfred A. Knopf.

WILLIAMS, P., & SAVONA, E. (1995). The United Nations and transnational organized crime. *Transnational Organized Crime, 1*(3), 1–194.

WOLF, D. R. (1991). *The Rebels: A brotherhood of outlaw bikers.* Toronto, Ontario, Canada: University of Toronto Press.

WOODIWISS, M. (1988). *Crime, crusades and corruption: Prohibition in the United States, 1900–1987.* Totowa, NJ: Barnes & Noble Books.

ZHANG, S. X., & GAYLORD, M. S. (1996). Bound for the golden mountain: The social organization of Chinese alien smuggling. *Crime, Law and Social Change, 25*(1), 1–16.

APPENDIX: EXEMPLARS FOR TEN OC GROUPS

1. *Corporate corruption: The abuse of power*, by Marshall B. Clinard. New York: Praeger, 1980.

2. *The new ethnic mobs: The changing face of organized crime in America*, by W. Kleinknecht. The Organizatsiya (Chap.11). New York: Free Press, 1996.

3. *The American way of crime*, by Frank Browning and John Gerassi, Pirates and profiteers (Chap. 4). New York: G.P. Putnam's Sons, 1980.

4. *Revenuers and moonshiners: Enforcing federal liquor law in the mountain South, 1865–1900*, by Wilbur R. Miller. Chapel Hill, NC: University of North Carolina Press, 1991.

5. *Chinatown gangs: Extortion, enterprise and ethnicity*, by Ko-lin Chin. New York: Oxford University Press, 1996.

6. *Yakuza: The explosive account of Japan's criminal underworld*, by David E. Kaplan and Alex Dubro. Reading, MA: Addison-Wesley, 1986.

7. *Death beat: A Colombian journalist's life inside the cocaine wars*, by Maria Jimena Duzan (translated and edited by Peter Eisner). New York: HarperCollins, 1992.

8. *There are no children here*, by Alex Kotlowitz. New York: Doubleday, Anchor Books, 1991.

9. *Chicano prisoners: The key to San Quentin*, by R. Theodore Davidson. Prospect Heights, IL: Waveland Press, 1974.

10. *The rebels: A brotherhood of outlaw bikers*, by Daniel R. Wolf. Toronto, Ontario, Canada: University of Toronto Press, 1991.

30

Classifying Female Serial Killers

An Application of Prominent Typologies

Laura J. Moriarty and Kimberly L. Freiberger

Several typologies have been created to categorize serial murder, although none have been tested for their usefulness in classifying a sample of serial murders. The present study tests two typologies, one developed by Dietz (1986) and the other by Holmes and DeBurger (1985), to classify incidents of female serial murder. No other research has examined the utility of current typologies to classify female serial murder. The study hypothesis is that the current typologies will not accurately classify female serial killers. Using content analysis, three sources were examined to collect the data: *Women Serial and Mass Murderers: A Worldwide Reference, 1580 through 1990* (Segrave, 1992), *Hunting Humans: An Encyclopedia of Modern Serial Killers* (Newton, 1990), and *Serial Murderers and Their Victims* (Hickey, 1997). The population consists of sixty female serial killers who have killed three or more people over time. The results indicate moderate support for the hypothesis. While 65 percent of the cases can be classified when the typologies are combined, about 1 in 3 (35 percent) cannot be classified using the current schemes. For these cases, motive was found to include attention, jealousy, frustration, cult, and revenge. It is recommended that the current typologies be combined with the additional categories of motive to better explain female serial murder.

There is no universally accepted definition of serial murder; therefore, it is important to begin our chapter with a discussion of serial murder as distinguished from other types of multiple homicides. Rappaport (1988, p. 39) indicates the importance in clarifying mass murder, spree killing, and serial murder. He states that "differentiating the types of murder enables us to gain perspective on the overall phenomenon, recognize how one type of offender compares with other types, and enables us to gain understanding and insight into the psychopathology of each type, since they differ so."

The most significant factor in defining categories of murder is the time frame between killings. Jenkins (1994, p. 21) concurs and defines *mass murder* as "murders committed in a brief period in one place" and *spree killing* as "those carried out over a few days or a week." Law enforcement defines *serial murder* as "the sexual attack and murder of young women, men and children by a male who follows a pattern, physical or psychological" (Hickey, 1991, p. 7). A problem with such a specific definition (i.e., sexual attack and male offender) is that many cases of serial murder will not be classified as such because a sexual attack may not be part of the crime and/or the offender may not be a male.

Academic researchers have proposed simple and elaborate definitions of serial murder. For example, Hickey defines a *serial killer* as "any offender who killed three or more victims over time (Hickey, 1991, p. 6). Keeney and Heide (1994) provide a more detailed definition of *serial murder* as "the premeditated murder of three or more victims, committed over time in separate incidents, in a civilian context, with the murder activity being chosen by the offender" (p. 384). Either of these approaches is valid, for our purposes, because both capture all offenders, whether male or female, who have killed over a period of time, whether or not a sexual act was part of the crime.

Contrary to popular belief, serial murder is not a recent or an exclusively male phenomenon (Egger, 1990; Leyton, 1986). A historical analysis of serial murder conducted by Eric Hickey refutes these beliefs. Hickey's research identified over 300 serial killers, with 117 dating back to the early nineteenth century and 62 being female.

Serial murder is believed to represent a relatively small proportion of all homicides in the United States (Hickey, 1997, p. 13); however, researchers have developed typologies to assist with classifying such behavior. These researchers typically focus on male offenders when developing such typologies. Historically, women who commit serial murder are labeled as "black widows" or "angels of death" and are summarily dismissed (Keeney & Heide, 1993, p. 4). Recent research, however, indicates that women are active in the crime of serial murder and should be part of academic discussions and research pursuits (Fox & Levin, 1993; Hickey, 1991, 1997; Keeney & Heide, 1994; Skrapec, 1994). U.S. homicide rates indicate that females account for roughly 12 to 15 percent of all murders. Ironically, women represent the same percentage of serial murderers (Hickey, 1991, 1997; Keeney & Heide, 1993, 1994; Skrapec, 1994). Conservative estimates attribute between 400 and 600 victims to female serial killers (Hickey, 1997, p. 205).

Dangerous females take the lives of innocent people every year. Segrave (1992, p. 6) lists 12 women who killed among them a total of 71 people, including 18 husbands, 29 of their own children, seven other children (e.g., stepchildren), four mothers, one father, four cousins, five in-laws, one brother, one aunt, and one uncle.

Serial killer Aileen Wuornos, the "Spiderwoman," is one of the most notorious female serial killers. Upon interrogation, Wuornos confessed to killing seven men by shooting each one multiple times. On January 30, 1992, a jury of five men and seven women took less than two hours to deliberate and return a guilty verdict, imposing the death penalty against Wuornos. During her trial in early 1992, television and newspaper accounts referred to her as "America's first female serial killer" and suggested that the presence of Aileen Wuornos marked the incipient stage of a trend toward growing numbers of women who commit serial murder (Fox & Levin, 1994, p. 259). Although Wuornos is often referred to as "America's first female serial killer," she is not the first, and undoubtedly will not be the last.

This raises the concern of how to study female serial killers. Can the same strategies used to understand serial killing in general be applied specifically to female serial killers? At present we do not know because there is a dearth of literature on female serial killers in comparison to males. In this chapter we explore the application of a useful tool, typologies, to the study of female serial murder.

TYPOLOGIES OF SERIAL MURDER

Typologies are a tool for organizing and classifying large amounts of data into mutually exclusive and mutually exhausting categories in order to better understand, predict, and prevent criminal behavior. Most serial murder typologies describe the act, the motive(s), or the personalities of the offenders and their mobility pattern. The FBI, for example, uses profiling techniques to identify characteristics of "organized" and "disorganized" murder crime scenes. Ressler, Burgess, and Douglas (1989) describe organized sexual murder offenders as more likely to plan the crime, use restraints, commit sexual acts with live victims, show or display control over the victim (e.g., manipulate or threaten victim), and use a vehicle in the commission of the crime. Disorganized offenders are more likely to leave a weapon at the scene, position the corpse, perform sexual acts on the corpse, keep the corpse, try to depersonalize the corpse, and are less likely to use a vehicle in the commission of the crime.

Holmes and DeBurger (1985) characterize serial murder by examining offender motive and propose four categories:

1. *Visionary.* The offender is psychotic, often hearing voices or seeing visions or both. In each incidence, the person believes that the voices or visions are instructing the offender to kill. In some cases the offender says "God" told him to kill; in other cases it is the "devil" or demons providing the instruction.

2. *Mission-oriented type.* The offender is attempting to correct a situation deemed inappropriate by the offender. His mission or purpose is to rectify the situation by getting rid of (killing) the undesirables or those unworthy to live with other humans. An example is a serial killer who kills only prostitutes.

3. *Hedonistic type.* The offender is motivated to kill for pure pleasure. The offender likes the way it feels when he kills. Holmes and DeBurger identify subcategories of the hedonistic type, offering the following reasons for such pleasure:

    a. Lust-oriented. Sexual gratification is derived from the killings.

    b. Thrill-oriented. Thrills or excitement are derived from the killings.

    c. Comfort-oriented. Enjoyment of life is derived from the killings.

4. *Power/control oriented.* The offender is driven primarily by the need to exert power or control over others. Gratification is achieved by total submission of the victim. The offender often has a self-inflated sense of importance and power.

Dietz (1986, as cited in Lester, 1995, p. 71) developed five categories of serial killers. His classifications are somewhat different than those of Holmes and DeBurger:

1. *Psychopathic sexual sadists.* These offenders have an antisocial (psychopathic) personality disorder and reflect sexually sadistic tendencies.
2. *Crime spree killers.* These offenders are motivated by the search for excitement, money, and valuables.
3. *Functionaries of organized criminal operations.* This category of offenders includes ethnic gangs, street gangs, members of organized crime, contract killers, illegal mercenaries, and terrorists.
4. *Custodial prisoners and asphyxiators.* These offenders include caretakers of the ill or of children and cases involving physicians and nurses.
5. *Supposed psychotics.* These offenders claim to be acting under the influence of hallucinatory voices or delusions.

Ronald Holmes (1989) developed a typology based on spatial mobility of an offender, which he labels as geographically stable serial killers or geographically transient serial killers. Those serial killers who live in one area and murder in that same area or nearby are labeled *geographically stable*, while those who travel about to kill are *geographically transient*.

Holmes, Hickey, and Holmes (1991) present a female serial killer typology based on behavioral patterns. They identify five categories:

1. *Visionary.* The offender is committing the crimes because of a break with reality. Their definition of visionary is very similar to that of Holmes and DeBurger's visionary and Dietz's supposed psychotics.
2. *Comfort.* The offender is motivated to kill for material gain, typically insurance benefits or acquisition of business interests or real estate.
3. *Hedonistic.* The offender is motivated to kill for the pure pleasure of it.
4. *Discipline.* The offender is under the influence of a charismatic leader. The motive to kill is psychological in that the woman desires acceptance by her "idol."
5. *Power.* The offender is motivated by power. She desires ultimate domination of her victims.

Although several typologies have been created to categorize serial murder, none have been tested for their usefulness in classifying a sample of serial killers. Further, no research has examined the utility of current typologies to classify female serial murder. Researchers have focused primarily on male offenders, resulting in a void in the literature. In the present chapter we examine female serial killers, attempting to apply the male-dominate serial killer typologies to this group. Our purpose is to determine if these typologies explain female serial killing or if other typologies must be developed.

METHODOLOGY

The population studied is 60 female serial killers who have murdered three or more people over a period of time. The names of the 60 female serial killers studied are found in the Appendix. Only these cases where the motive is clearly specified are included. Secondary data sources include Kerry Segrave's (1992) *Women Serial and Mass Murderers: A Worldwide Reference, 1580 through 1990*, Michael Newton's (1991) *Hunting Humans: An*

Encyclopedia of Modern Serial Killers, and Eric Hickey's (1997) *Serial Murderers and Their Victims*. These sources provided information on sixty-two female serial killers; however, motive could be discerned in sixty. Therefore, two cases were dropped from the analysis.

The population was divided into two groups: group 1, consisting of early or pre–World War II cases of serial murder ranging from 1800 to 1945; and group 2, consisting of recent or post–World War II cases ranging from 1946 to 1996. We compiled these two groups to manage the data better. Within these two groups, motive was examined using a combination of manifest and latent content analysis. Once motive was identified in each case, open coding was used to analyze and code the motive by reviewing each case for a specific and consistent set of variables.

Motive was conceptualized as the reasons or incidents causing one to act or the impulses behind the act to commit murder. Further, motive was operationalized according to the specific categories proposed by Dietz (1986) and Holmes and DeBurger (1985). Since all serial killings are not sexual murders, we exclude Ressler et al.'s organized and disorganized classification scheme. We also do not use Holmes, Hickey, and Holmes' female typology because this classification outline includes three of the same elements (visionary, hedonistic, power) found in the Holmes and DeBurger typology. We believe that the two typologies used in this research have the greatest potential for classifying female serial killers.

Therefore, using the Dietz typology, the attributes of motive are psychopathic sexual sadists, crime spree killers, functionaries of organized criminal activities, custodial prisoners and asphyxiators, supposed psychotics, unclassifiable, and mixed. Using the Holmes and DeBurger typology, the motive attributes are visionary, mission-oriented type, hedonistic type (including the subcategories of lust oriented, thrill oriented, and comfort oriented), power/control, unclassifiable, and mixed (see Table 1 for the conceptualization of each attribute).

Our primary interest is to test whether the typologies described above are applicable to female serial killers. We do so by focusing on the following questions:

- Does the Dietz or Holmes and DeBurger typology best describe early cases (1800–1945) of female serial killing?
- Does the Dietz or Holmes and DeBurger typology best describe later cases (1946–1996) of female serial killing?
- When the cases are combined, which typology best describes all the cases?
- What percentage of all the cases cannot be classified using the Dietz and Holmes and DeBurger typologies?
- What percentage of all the cases are mixed or overlap categories found within the typologies?
- Do the typologies need to be expanded to include categories specific to female serial killers to better classify these offenders?

RESULTS

Table 2 represents the percentage of cases conforming to Dietz's typology from the period 1800–1945. As indicated, twenty-five of the sixty cases examined occurred during this period. The percentages indicate that 16 percent are unable to be classified using this

TABLE 1   **Conceptualization of the Attributes of Each Typology**

Typology	Attribute	Operationalization
Dietz	Psychopathic sexual sadists	Antisocial personalities, sexually sadistic tendencies
	Crime spree killers	Excitement, money, and valuables are the motive for killing.
	Functionaries of organized criminal activities	Ethnic gangs, street gangs, members of organized crime, contract killers, illegal mercenaries, terrorists
	Custodial poisoners and asphyxiators	Caretakers who kill
	Supposed psychotics	Delusional killers
	Unclassifiable[a]	Motive is not represented by any category in the typology.
	Mixed*	Motive reflects two or more categories listed above.
Holmes and DeBurger	Visionary	Delusional killers
	Mission-oriented type	Motive to kill is to eliminate "undesirables."
	Hedonistic type, including subcategories of lust oriented, thrill oriented, and comfort oriented	Killing is pleasurable. Pleasure is derived from sexual gratification (lust), the thrill of killing (thrill), or enjoying life (comfort).
	Power/control	Motive is to have ultimate control over victims.
	Unclassifiable[a]	Motive is not represented by any category in the typology.
	Mixed[a]	Motive reflects two or more categories listed above.

[a]We added these categories to the original typologies.

typology, 12 percent are mixed, and the remaining 72 percent can be classified into the specific categories of crime spree killer (64 percent), custodial prisoners and asphyxiators (4 percent), and supposed psychotics (4 percent). No cases are categorized as psychopathic sexual sadists or functionaries of organized crime.

Table 3 reports the percentage of female serial killings conforming to Dietz's typology from 1946 to 1996. There are thirty-five such cases. As documented, 26 percent cannot be classified using Dietz's typology, 34 percent are mixed, and the remaining 40 percent classify into the specific categories of crime spree killers (31 percent), custodial prisoners and asphyxiators (6 percent), and supposed psychotics (3 percent). Again, no cases are categorized as psychopathic sexual sadists or functionaries of organized crime.

TABLE 2   Percent of Cases Conforming to Dietz's Typology, 1800–1945

Type	Frequency	Percent
Psychopathic sexual sadists	0	0
Crime spree killers	16	64
Functionaries of organized crime	0	0
Custodial prisoners and asphyxiators	1	4
Supposed psychotics	1	4
Unable to classify	4	16
Mixed cases	3	12
	25	100

Table 4 provides the percentage of cases conforming to Holmes and DeBurger's typology from 1800 to 1945. Of the 25 cases, 16 percent are unable to be classified, 12 percent are mixed, and the remaining 72 percent are classified as hedonistic type (68 percent) and visionary type (4 percent). No cases are categorized as mission oriented or power/control oriented.

Table 5 displays the percentage of cases conforming to Holmes and DeBurger's typology from 1946 to 1996. Here 17 percent of the cases are unable to be classified, 40 percent are mixed, and the remaining 43 percent fall into the specific categories of hedonistic (34 percent), visionary (6 percent), and power/control oriented (3 percent). No cases are categorized as mission oriented.

Table 6 contains the percentage of cases conforming to Dietz's typology for the entire time period, 1800 to 1996. A high percentage (45 percent) is classified as crime spree killers, while a considerable number of cases are unable to be categorized (22 percent). An additional 25 percent are mixed. As mentioned previously, no cases are psychopathic sexual sadists or functionaries of organized crime.

TABLE 3   Percent of Cases Conforming to Dietz's Typology, 1945–1996

Type	Frequency	Percent
Psychopathic sexual sadists	0	0
Crime spree killers	11	31
Functionaries of organized crime	0	0
Custodial prisoners and asphyxiators	2	6
Supposed psychotics	1	3
Unable to classify	9	26
Mixed cases	12	34
	35	100

TABLE 4   Percent of Cases Conforming to Holmes and DeBurger's Typology, 1800–1945

Type	Frequency	Percent
Visionary type	1	4
Mission-oriented type	0	0
Hedonistic type	17	68
Power/control type	0	0
Not able to classify	4	16
Mixed cases	3	12
	25	100

Table 7 represents the percentage of cases conforming to Holmes and DeBurger's typology for the entire time frame. Here 17 percent of the cases are unable to be classified, 28 percent are mixed, 48 percent are hedonistic offenders, 5 percent are visionary, and 2 percent are power/control oriented. Again, none are mission oriented.

The hedonistic offender as proposed by Holmes and DeBurger contains three subcategories: thrill oriented, lust oriented, and comfort oriented. Table 8 represents the percentage of cases conforming to the subcategories of the hedonistic type of female serial offender. Twenty-nine cases are classified as hedonistic. The largest percentage (79 percent) is subclassified as comfort oriented, 14 percent thrill oriented, and 7 percent lust-oriented offenders.

There are 21 cases or 35 percent of the sample that cannot be classified when combining the Dietz and Holmes and DeBurger typologies. They were further analyzed recording specific motive. The categories of motive not found in the Dietz or Holmes and DeBurger typologies but clearly the motive for some female serial killers include:

TABLE 5   Percent of Cases Conforming to Holmes and DeBurger's Typology, 1946–1996

Type	Frequency	Percent
Visionary type	2	6
Mission-oriented type	0	0
Hedonistic type	12	34
Power/control type	1	3
Not able to classify	6	17
Mixed cases	14	40
	35	100

TABLE 6   Percent of Cases Conforming to Dietz's Typology, 1800–1996

Type	Frequency	Percent
Psychopathic sexual sadists	0	0
Crime spree killers	27	45
Functionaries of organized crime	0	0
Custodial prisoners and asphyxiators	3	5
Supposed psychotics	2	3
Unable to classify	13	22
Mixed cases	15	25
	60	100

TABLE 7   Percent of Cases Conforming to Holmes and DeBurger's Typology for the Entire Time Frame, 1800–1996

Type	Frequency	Percent
Visionary type	3	5
Mission-oriented type	0	0
Hedonistic type	29	48
Power/control type	1	2
Not able to classify	10	17
Mixed cases	17	28
	60	100

TABLE 8   Percent of Cases Conforming to Holmes and DeBurger's Subcategories of Hedonistic Type, 1800–1996 ($n = 29$)

Type	Frequency	Percent
Thrill oriented	4	14
Lust oriented	2	7
Comfort oriented	23	79
	29	100

- *Attention.* Motive for the killing is to gain attention (i.e., notice).
- *Frustration.* Stressful situations compel the woman to kill as an alternative way to solve the situation.
- *Jealousy.* The woman kills because she feels she will be supplanted in a relationship by someone else. She is afraid she will lose the affection of a significant other.
- *Cult.* Killings are part of the cult's behavior. The female is part of a cult where obsessive devotion leads to murder.
- *Revenge.* Motive for the killing is to inflict pain in return for injury or insult. The woman retaliates.

Table 9 reports the distribution of cases into these new categories. Of the 21 cases, 33 percent are classified as attention killings, 29 percent as frustration killings, 19 percent as revenge killings, and 10 percent each as jealousy and cult killings.

DISCUSSION

Our findings are generally consistent with previous research regarding the motives of female serial killers. We found that by using the Dietz typology, 45 percent of the cases are classified as crime spree killings. When using the Holmes and DeBurger model, 48 percent are classified as hedonistic murders. Crime spree killers commit murder for the excitement of the act or monetary benefit, while hedonistic killers do so for the pure pleasure of the act. These findings are consistent with the literature in general. For example, Holmes and Holmes (1994) explain that female serial killers murder for "comfort" purposes, which include money, insurance benefits, or business interests. Lester (1995, p. 57) proposes that "the most common motive for female killers [is] monetary gain, closely followed by enjoyment." And Newton (1990, p. 2) indicates that 31 percent of female serial killers have murdered for gain, compared to 3 percent of their male counterparts.

TABLE 9   Percent of Cases (Not Classified Using the Dietz or Holmes and DeBurger Typologies) Conforming to the New Categories of Motive ($n = 21$)

Motive Type	Frequency	Percent
Attention	7	33
Jealousy	2	10
Frustration	6	29
Cult	2	10
Revenge	4	19
	21	100

Even though the present findings are consistent with the literature, the results are problematic. There are 21 or 35 percent of the cases that cannot be classified using the current typologies. This amounts to slightly more than one in three female serial killers not being classified when combining the Dietz and Holmes and DeBurger classification schemes. To classify female serial killers more accurately, we added specific categories to the typologies. We discovered that to better explain female serial killing, categories such as attention, jealousy, frustration, cult killings, and revenge must be incorporated into the typologies. Of the 21 cases not classified, 7 or 33 percent are determined to have attention as the motive for the killings.

CONCLUSIONS

Although the crime of serial killing is a relatively rare event, it is much more infrequent for the offender to be female. However, female murder and female serial murder occur at comparable rates. Therefore, both should be the focus of academic scholarly pursuits.

With most of the research on serial murder focusing on males, we were interested in finding out if the male serial murder typologies explained female serial murder. In the majority of these cases (65 percent), the typologies proposed by Dietz and Holmes and DeBurger explained the motive of the female serial killers.

A concern, however, is the realization that about one in three cases cannot be classified using these typologies. The motives for these cases are attention, jealousy, frustration, cult, and revenge and are not included in the typologies listed above. Therefore, to better comprehend female serial murder, we suggest adding the categories listed above to the two male serial murder typologies. The combination of the Dietz, Holmes, DeBurger and current research findings will provide a more complete understanding of female serial murder.

REFERENCES

DIETZ, P. E. (1986). Mass, serial and sensational homicides. *Bulletin of the New York Academy of Medicine, 62,* 447–491. As cited in Lester, D. (1995). *Serial killers: The insatiable passion.* Philadelphia: Charles Press.

EGGER, S. (1990). *Serial murder: An elusive phenomenon.* New York: Praeger.

FOX, J. A., & LEVIN, J. (1994). *Overkill: Mass murder and serial killing exposed.* New York: Plenum Press.

HICKEY, E. W. (1991). *Serial murderers and their victims.* Pacific Grove, CA: Brooks/Cole.

HICKEY, E. W. (1997). *Serial murderers and their victims* (2nd ed.). Belmont, CA: Wadsworth Publishing.

HOLMES, R. (1989). *Profiling violent crimes.* Newbury Park, CA: Sage Publications.

HOLMES, R., & DEBURGER, J. (1985). Profiles in terror: The serial murderer. *Federal Probation, 49,* 29–34.

HOLMES, S., HICKEY, E., & HOLMES, R. (1991). Female serial murderesses: Constructing differentiating typologies. *Journal of Contemporary Criminal Justice, 7,* 245–256.

HOLMES, R., & HOLMES, S. (1994). *Murder in America.* Thousand Oaks, CA: Sage Publications.

JENKINS, P. (1994). *Using murder: The social construction of serial homicide.* New York: Aldine de Gruyter.

KEENEY, B. T., & HEIDE, K. M. (1993). The latest on serial murderers. *Violence Update, 4,* 1–10.

KEENEY, B. T., & HEIDE, K. M. (1994). Gender differences in serial murder: A preliminary analysis. *Journal of Interpersonal Violence, 9*, 383–398.

LESTER, D. (1995). *Serial killers: The insatiable passion*. Philadelphia: Charles Press.

LEYTON, E. (1986). *Compulsive killers*. New York: University Press.

NEWTON, M. (1990). *Hunting humans: An encyclopedia of modern serial killers*. Port Townsend, WA: Loompanics Unlimited.

RAPPAPORT, R. (1988). The serial and mass murderer: Patterns, differentiation, pathology. *American Journal of Psychiatry, 146*(7), 887–891.

RESSLER, R., BURGESS, A., & DOUGLAS, J. (1988). *Sexual homicide: Patterns and motives*. Lexington, MA: D.C. Heath.

SEGRAVE, K. (1992). *Women serial and mass murderers: A worldwide reference, 1580 through 1990*. Jefferson, NC: McFarland.

SKRAPEC, C. (1994). The female serial killer: An evolving criminality. In Birch, H. (Ed.), *Moving targets: Women, murder and representation* (pp. 241–268). Los Angeles, CA: University of California Press.

APPENDIX: CASES OF FEMALE SERIAL KILLERS USED IN THIS STUDY

Amy Archer-Gilligan	Anjette Donovan Lyles
Susan Atkins	Rhonda Bell Martin
Margie Velma Barfield	Blanche Taylor Moore
Martha Beck	Robin Murphy
Kate Bender	Judith Neeley
Debra Denise Brown	Ruby C. Padgett
Carol Bundy	Bonnie Parker
Patty Cannon	Lofie "Louise" Peete
Faye Copeland	Dorthea Montavo Puente
Anna Cunningham	Jane Quinn
Nannie Hazel Doss	Terri Rachels
Ellen Etheridge	Mary Rose Robaczynski
Christine Falling	Sarah Jane Robinson
Carino Favato	Lydia Sherman
Tille Gburek	Sally Skull
Janie Lou Gibbs	Mary Eleanor Smith
Amy Gillgan	Della Sorenson
Gwendolyn Graham	Gloria Tannenbaum
Belle Gunness	Bobbie Sue Terrell
Anna Marie Hahn	Marybeth Tinning
Marie Hilley	Jane Toppan
Waneta Hoyt	Lydia Trueblood
Mary Jane Jackson	Leslie Van Houten
Dorothy Jean Jatajke	Louise Vermilyea
Martha A. Johnson	Annette Washington
Genene Jones	Charlene Williams
Sharon Kinne	Martha Hasel Wise
Tillie Klimek	Catherine Wood
Patricia Krevwinkle	Martha Woods
Diana Lumbrera	Aileen Wuornos

31

Listening to Women's Voices

Considering Why Mothers Kill Their Children

Cheryl L. Meyer and Cindy E. Weisbart

❖

There is a morbid curiosity related to mothers who kill their children. One need only observe the fascination of cases such as Andrea Yates, Susan Smith, and Melissa Drexler (a.k.a. the "prom Mom") to view the level of public interest. Not only does the topic fascinate us, but it produces strong reactions that range from empathy, to disgust, to horror. These reactions often become the basis of vehement opinions regarding the women involved and what should happen to them.

However, it is not as if mothers killing their children is a new phenomenon. In fact, "there is every reason to believe that infanticide is as old as human society itself, and that no culture has been immune. Throughout history, the crime of infanticide has reflected specific cultural norms and imperatives. Historians of infanticide cite a host of factors associated with the incidence of this crime: poverty, over-population, laws governing inheritance, customs relating to non-marital children, religious and/or superstitious beliefs regarding disability, eugenics, and maternal madness" (Meyer & Oberman, 2001, p. 1).

Given the pervasiveness and longevity of the crime of infanticide, there is little research, particularly focused on mothers who kill their children. These mothers are generally referred to as a homogeneous group with little differentiation among them. However, even in a cursory review of cases it is clear that there are at least two types which can quickly be distinguished from each other, mothers who kill their newborns, and mothers who commit other forms of infanticide. For example, Melissa Drexler, a teenage mother who disposed of her newborn baby in a rest room at her high school prom, is very different from Susan Smith, who drowned her 14-month-old and 2-year-old by submerging her car in a lake. In obvious ways, their actions, demographics, and reactions were very different. Prevention and intervention strategies should also differ.

Meyer and Oberman (2001) developed a typology to aid in understanding why mothers kill their children. They have five categories of mothers who kill their children; filicide related to an ignored pregnancy, abuse-related filicide, filicide due to neglect, assisted or coerced filicide, and purposeful filicide and the mother acted alone. Their typology addresses the unique interaction of social, environmental, cultural, and individual variables within each of these categories of filicidal mothers, to provide some insight into the factors that come together and result in these acts. Although other typologies have been formulated, only one included any U.S. cases (for an extensive discussion of other typologies, see Meyer and Oberman, pp. 20–31). Meyer and Oberman's typology is based solely on U.S. cases and is current. In this chapter we discuss Meyer and Oberman's types and provide an illustrative case study for each one. The case studies we include were generated through our interviews with mothers who were convicted of killing their children. Both methodologies are outlined below.

Oberman's (1996) research provided the impetus for Meyer and Oberman's typology. Oberman had searched NEXIS, a news database that provides full text articles and publications from news magazines, regional and national newspapers, newsletters, trade magazines, and abstracts for cases of infanticide and accumulated 96 cases. From these cases Meyer and Oberman formulated a draft typology and began new searches of NEXIS to gather all cases reported from January 1990 through December 1999.

Three independent reviewers from their research team read every case. The cases were assigned to one of the categories based on the reviews. When the cases had been separated into categories, the researcher for that category then followed up all their cases in regional databases. For example, if a case occurred in New York, the researcher for that case would access the NEXIS regional databases and local news resources (e.g., *The New York Times*) for the years following the initial report to determine the disposition of the case and access further details. Cases that could not be followed up extensively through further searching were deleted from the sample. These included cases where the mother was never located or the name of the mother was not released because she was a juvenile. More details regarding case selection and exclusion are included in Meyer and Oberman (2001, p. 33). Meyer and Oberman's data set included 219 cases.

To determine patterns, Meyer and Oberman recorded available information for each case related to the age of the mother, age and gender of child, method of death, marital status, number of children in the family and in the home, geographical location, date of crime, charge/conviction, mother's behavioral response after death, history of domestic violence, mental health and substance abuse history, socioeconomic status, the need for public assistance, children's protective service involvement, frequency of weapon use, any motive mentioned, and birth order of child. Furthermore, the researcher for each category also tracked characteristics that were specific to her category.

As noted previously, the case studies included in this chapter were generated from our individual interviews conducted with mothers convicted of killing their children. The interviewer was always accompanied by a trained notetaker since audio or video recording is ill advised within the prison setting (given the previous negative association that taping has for these women with the courts, media, etc.). Care was taken to train each notetaker to provide as much word-for-word transcription of each interview as possible, thus preserving the verbalized meaning that each women gave to her story. The interviews were guided by several semistructured questions that were driven by the overall research question: What is it like to be a woman who has killed her children? Each woman who was interviewed could answer any or all of the following eight questions:

1. Tell me about what your life has been like, growing up as a youngster, up until now.
2. What was going on in your life at the time your child died (precipitating events, increased stress)?
3. Did anyone know you were going through a difficult time? Who were the people you confided in, and what help did they offer?
4. In your own words, tell me about what happened.
5. How do you think this could have been prevented?
6. How do you feel you have been treated by the system (the police, the courts, etc.)?
7. What changes would you make to the "system" in general?
8. If you had three wishes for the future, what would they be?

Each interview lasted approximately two hours. Seventeen interviews were conducted. The case studies provided in this chapter *paraphrase* portions of the interviews. The essence of the interview remains the same, but the mother's words and/or details of the crime have been changed to protect confidentiality. Some cases represent an amalgam of two cases.

THE TYPOLOGY

Meyer and Oberman (2001) provide five main types.

Filicide Related to an Ignored Pregnancy

At the time of her conviction, Mary was a young woman in her early 20s with three young children. Mary was living with relatives at the time she became pregnant with her fourth child. This pregnancy was the result of a rape by a "friend" of the family. Mary gave birth to her baby alone in the bathroom of her house. She describes feeling terrible pain and believed that she was physically ill. Instead, she was undergoing labor and when she realized this, she became very scared and describes blacking out and then later burying her daughter in the backyard. Mary is not sure how the baby died. According to the coroner's report, Mary's newborn died from suffocation. Mary was convicted of first-degree murder and received a sentence of 15 years to life.

Mary was obviously very young when she had her first three children. As Mary looks back at the time of the death of her fourth child, she notes that she had support from her family. However, at the time Mary states she felt "scared," worrying "they'll think less of you or that it was your fault." Mary concealed her pregnancy by wearing oversized clothes and by denying she was pregnant to anyone who asked. She did not get any medical care and, despite desperately wanting to share the burden of her secret with close family members, she did not.

Mary states: "After my daughter died, it's like a piece of my life died. Several times I have thought to myself . . . you should have died instead of your daughter. I hid the pregnancy from everyone . . . that was the hardest part—ignoring my pregnancy. It was so hard to deny and hide knowing that there is a life inside you. I had no medical care . . . I didn't even see a doctor. I kept thinking, 'it can't be true . . . this isn't happening to you.' Several times I wanted to talk with my family but I was too scared . . . several times I wanted to sit down and tell them but I thought 'they'll think less of you or that it was your fault.' It was not that way at all. Now they tell me: You should have come to us and we would have helped you any way we could. . . .

It's hard being in here [prison] knowing that I am convicted of killing my child—the hardest thing is knowing that I am convicted of killing my child. People turn up their nose up at you and treat you differently. Some don't care and treat you human but a lot don't. I don't even talk to people about my case. I just want to be treated like a human. We are all here and we all made mistakes."

Meyer and Oberman (2001) found mothers in this category committed neonaticide after either denying or concealing their pregnancy. Resnick (1970) created the term *neonaticide* to refer to killing a child within the first 24 hours of life.

Meyer and Oberman analyzed 37 cases of neonaticide. Mary's story is very typical of the patterns they found in other cases. The mothers in their sample ranged in age from 15 to 39, but the average age was 19.3 years old. Clearly, these women were young. It appears most of these women did not receive prenatal care, which is consistent with the fact that they were denying or concealing their pregnancy. All but one of the women was single. Sometimes the fathers were not aware of the pregnancy, other times they were but rejected the mother and her pregnancy, or as in Mary's case, the pregnancy was the result of a rape. Approximately one-third of these women had other children prior to committing the neonaticide.

Whether it was self-imposed or real, most of these women felt they would receive little or no support relating to the pregnancy, and in fact might be ostracized or physically punished. In general, they were overwhelmed by feelings of shame, guilt and/or fear. Due to this fact, some, like Mary, actively concealed their pregnancy, while others denied it even to themselves. This was not difficult to do given that some of these women continued to menstruate and gained minimal weight. When they began to experience the abdominal cramps and indigestion that often comes with labor, many thought they needed to defecate and, like Mary, completely dissociated with what happened during the birth. They were later horrified to learn what had become of their infants. Approximately 80 percent of the women were at home when labor began with 38 percent of those women giving birth in the bathroom. In 70 percent of the cases, the child died from being smothered.

The reaction of the criminal justice system to mothers who commit neonaticide is quite varied. Like Mary, a very few women are charged with first-degree murder. However, some are charged with no crime at all. Similarly, when charges are filed, the outcome varies from acquittal to life imprisonment. Compounding this is the question of whether the women should be tried as adults if they are minors.

Not surprisingly, there is a link between neonaticide and abortion. Meyer and Oberman point out that regions with limited abortion access have higher rates of neonaticide. Since many of these women are under 18 years old and afraid of the consequences of revealing their pregnancy, parental notification laws may also effectively eliminate this option for them. However, this is not to suggest that abortion and neonaticide are completely intertwined. Recall that many of the women who eventually commit neonaticide deny their pregnancy and would therefore have no reason to seek abortion services.

There is some societal recognition that neonaticide is becoming a widespread problem. Individual citizens and communities have begun to create initiatives such as anonymous dropoff ordinances. These ordinances allow mothers to drop off their newborns at designated locations with no legal repercussions. There is also a 24-hour hotline available for mothers who do not want their newborns. Although it is admirable to see the heightened attention and concern given to neonaticide, these initiatives fail to take into account that neonaticide is rarely a premeditated act, so it is unlikely that a mother will consider these options. In addition, for a mother to use the drop-off initiative, she would often have to sneak her newborn to a drop-off center, risking detection.

It may be more successful to place emphasis on intervention and prevention. This could be accomplished by educating the women themselves, and those who often spend the most time with teens, their peers. It would be relatively inexpensive to place information and resources related to neonaticide into high school sex education curriculum. In addition, teachers and school counselors could also be provided with seminars to aid them in assisting girls who may be struggling with an unplanned pregnancy.

Greater emphasis on education could assist physicians as well. Although most of the women did not seek prenatal care, when they did, physicians failed to detect the pregnancy or asked the teen about her sexual activity with her mother present. If a teen is concealing a pregnancy, it is unlikely that she will admit her sexual activity in front of her mother. These neonaticides might have been prevented if the physician were better educated on the topic, which might have led to more direct examination and certainly, interviews without the mother present.

In the United States, a person must be 18 to vote and 21 to consume alcohol legally. We have also carved out exceptions for juveniles in our criminal justice system. These restrictions and exceptions are in place to protect juveniles and society from the errors of immature judgments. Most of the women who commit neonaticide are teens who made bad judgments in bad circumstances. Their actions cause pain on numerous levels, marring many lives, including their own. Surely, we can create safety nets to catch these women before it becomes too late.

Abuse-Related Filicide

Felicia is a young African-American woman who was incarcerated in her early 20s for involuntary manslaughter and child endangerment. She was sentenced to up to 25 years for hitting her 4-year-old child so hard she died. Felicia readily admitted that she had a history of abusing her daughter and that Felicia herself was the victim of extensive and severe physical and psychological abuse and neglect by her stepfather. She also observed incessant violence against her mother by her stepfather, which, she noted, led to her mother abusing drugs heavily. In addition to abuse that she experienced and witnessed at home, Felicia was later assaulted by her baby's father, who beat and raped her. This rape resulted in the conception of her daughter.

Felicia has spent much of her time behind bars thinking about why she hurt her daughter and has finally concluded that she learned her behaviors from her parents' modeling. While Felicia, arguably, had a choice as to whether she decided to act on such learning, there were many factors that predisposed her to make the wrong choice for herself and her child.

Felicia states: "My mother and stepfather are both recovering addicts. The abuse came at the hand of my stepfather. I recall my stepfather hitting me . . . and he also hit my mother. He threatened me with a knife several times if I didn't do exactly what he said. I tried to commit suicide three times when I was a kid. I was tired of being hit on—you know what I mean?

When I finally saw a counselor, she told me about the cycle of abuse and the 'generational curse.' I feel like the system failed me until I was sent to her. She really helped me to understand myself. In my case, my daughter was just doing something she knew she wasn't supposed to do. . . . I never had any patience and I slapped her real hard in the face. She fell, hitting the corner of the wall and she died two days later in the hospital.

My whole thing is to get to the core of it and try to prevent it. I feel like in my situation had that been done, I wouldn't be here."

Mothers who abuse their children or who kill their children through abuse have received scant research attention. In part, this may be due to definitional issues. For example, a fine line often distinguishes abuse from neglect. In addition, there are clear ethnic and cultural variations in what constitutes acceptable discipline practices and what is abusive. Generally only extreme cases come to the attention of the public.

Meyer and Oberman's (2001) abuse-related filicide category is comprised of mothers whose purposeful physical assault unintentionally led to the child's death. Like Felicia, most of these women had previously assaulted their child or children. However, none of these mothers purposely killed their child, and even the courts recognized this fact since many were charged with involuntary manslaughter instead of voluntary manslaughter or murder. This category can be distinguished from the assisted/coerced category because the mother either acted alone or was primarily responsible for the death.

Meyer and Oberman researched 15 cases in this category, but there was very little information available on three of those cases. The children killed ranged in age from 6 weeks to 6 years. However, only two were under a year old. The women had an average of four children, but ten of the women had four or more children. One woman had only one child, but none of the remaining 14 women killed her firstborn child. There were approximately equal numbers of male and female victims. All of the children but one, who drowned, died as a result of beatings. Almost half of the fatal assaults involved a blow to the head. Although the mothers seemed to abuse all their children, several cases mentioned that the victim seemed to be a target of violence more often than the other children.

Child welfare had previously been involved with 12 of the women and was probably involved with two more, although that was not clear. In two-thirds of the cases the mother had previously lost custody and killed the child after reunification. Although it was unclear how long the mother and child had been reunited, in at least five cases it had been less than six months. Of the five cases that were not reunifications, three of the mothers had previously been reported to child welfare. No one in our sample of mothers was an adolescent, although many were adolescent when they first bore a child. The average age was 27, with a range of 21 to 39 years old. Substance use was clearly a factor in eight of the cases and at least a third of the victims had been born addicted to substances, but information was not available on the other cases. At least two of the women were pregnant at the time of the killing. Information about the mother's childhood could only be found on two women, and they had both been exposed to childhood violence. What was also glaringly absent from most of the cases was any discussion of the fathers and their level of involvement with the children. Most of the fathers did not appear to reside with the mother.

A few factors have been identified which may indicate that a mother is at risk for abusing her child. Clearly, the factor that has received the most attention as it relates to both parents is the Intergenerational Transmission Hypothesis (Milner, Robertson & Rogers,

1990). Quite simply, this theory suggests that being abused as a child, or observing abuse as a child, is related to abusing as a parent. Felicia referred to this theory when she talked about the generational curse and the cycle of abuse. The transactional model (Cicchetti, 1989) augments this approach, suggesting that although prior abuse may predispose someone to abuse, the actual occurrence would depend on a host of mitigating and aggravating circumstances. Aggravating factors include poverty, adolescent parenting, drug use, lack of emotional support, poor social skills, domestic violence, and depression. Mitigating factors would reflect the opposite of these.

When examining these findings, several issues emerge as potential areas of reform to assist in prevention and intervention. Given that most of Meyer and Oberman's sample had previous contact with the child welfare system, that would be one place to begin.

In general, there are both procedural and policy criticisms leveled at many child welfare systems. The procedural criticisms include the following: (1) the caseloads are too high and there is a lack of lack of supervision; (2) the record-keeping systems are outdated and records are lost or destroyed; (3) case workers are trained inadequately; (4) services are not provided or not provided long enough; and (5) case workers are inadequately paid, resulting in high turnover. All of these stem from inadequate funding. After a particularly tragic death in New York, funding was increased, which resulted in numerous reforms in the child welfare system. As New York increased funding, their child welfare system became more efficient and less criticized. However, it is difficult to convince legislators to address economic needs until such tragedies occur. Although most people would probably agree that those who abuse their children need services, very few people want to fund such services.

In addition to procedural concerns, policies have also recently been challenged. For example, child welfare systems have been accused of placing too much emphasis on family reunification/preservation and the corresponding argument that parent's rights should be terminated more quickly (for a full discussion of this issue, see Meyer and Oberman, 2001). This emphasis seems to be shifting, although calling for a quick termination of parental rights is shortsighted. The majority of children (up to 90 percent) are not removed from parental homes because of abuse but because of neglect. The neglect is usually the result of poverty. Terminating parental rights more quickly would adversely affect these families without addressing the real problem–poverty. Since a disproportionate number of families involved with the child welfare system are families of color, terminating parental rights more quickly would result in destabilizing homes that are already affected by racism on other levels. In addition, some families of color probably became involved in the child welfare system because of discriminatory practices. This could be due to racial biases of child welfare workers and/or the difficulties and ambiguities inherent in defining abuse and neglect. This is further exaggerated by a general lack of ethnocultural understanding and training on the part of child welfare workers.

Moreover, a quicker termination may not benefit children. After termination, children simply end up in an overburdened foster care system with no links to anyone, and now, no family name. This is not to say that parents' rights should not be terminated. However, in general, there is a scarcity of adoptive parents, and once it is clear that the family cannot be reunited, unless relatives or foster parents are petitioning for adoption, all too often children end up remaining in foster care whether or not the parents' rights are terminated. The focus should be on increasing adoption options before severing family ties so that a new link is readily available for children when family ties are severed.

Further compounding these concerns with the child welfare system are abuses within the foster care system. In November 2000, the lead article on the cover of *Time* was entitled "The Shame of Foster Care." The article begins with numerous stories of child abuse in the foster care system, generally by *foster* parents or families. The authors argue the foster care system is in a crisis nationwide, with lawyers threatening class action suits in 20 states. They report that the number of children in foster care has doubled in the last five years, from approximately one-fourth of a million to half a million. Agencies are plagued with poor and outdated record-keeping, inadequate case monitoring, bad decisions, high turnover (as much as 70 percent), poorly trained staff, low accountability, and unwieldy bureaucracies which are often created when agencies contract with private facilities to aid them in providing services.

Perhaps the best prevention and intervention for mothers who abuse their children will come from grassroots community involvement. These would include neighborhood-based services such as citizen watches or volunteer advocates. Certainly, schools could hire a counselor or redefine the responsibilities of a counselor to act as more of a liaison with child protective services. The goal of all of these programs is to allocate more responsibilities to inner systems, including schools, families, and communities, making the village more responsible for raising the child. However, in the end it is not the innovativeness of the program as much as the commitment of the community and individuals within the community which ensures programs are implemented and monitored, thus facilitating success.

Filicide Due to Neglect

Linda was the victim of physical and sexual abuse at the hands of her uncle from age 2 to age 11. At the age of 13, she was raped. As an adolescent, she received some counseling because she was acting out in school, but Linda doesn't feel that this was very helpful for her. At the age of 18, she became pregnant as a result of a relationship with a man she eventually married. They had another child together. However, Linda describes the relationship as troubled. They eventually divorced and Linda moved into her own apartment in the same neighborhood. Her ex-husband began stalking her and making threatening phone calls to her. She was forced to move to a different town in order to get away from him. The apartment into which she moved was where the incident occurred in which both of her children were killed.

Linda had been living at the new apartment for over a year and had begun dating a young man who lived in a nearby house. On the evening of the incident, Linda put her two children down to sleep and decided to go visit her new boyfriend, ostensibly for just a short time. She left her apartment, leaving a space heater on in the master bedroom where her children were asleep. While she was gone, the space heater somehow caught the bedding on fire and both children died. Linda was charged with two counts of involuntary manslaughter and received a prison term of ten years.

Linda talks about her circumstances in the following excerpts: "A lot of people here call me "baby-killer" and it bothers me. People say I'm a violent killer. It's not that I purposefully did anything to them. . . . I am not a violent person. When they call me baby-killer, it is really painful. I don't think I killed my children . . . its hard to deal with being in here . . . and its hard to understand how my family can stick by me . . . because I have a lot of guilt and I started hating myself and I am thinking, 'how can they not hate me'?"

Meyer and Oberman (2001) found that like Linda, mothers in this category did not kill their child purposely but either failed to attend to the child's basic needs or were irresponsible in their reaction to the child's behavior. Therefore, they subdivided their cases into neglect-omission and neglect-commission cases, respectively. *Neglect-omission cases* included instances where the mother did not attend to health, nutrition, or safety needs of the child, often by not providing adequate supervision. There were six predominant ways that children died; fire, automobile suffocation, bathtub drowning, layover suffocation, nutrition, and inattention to safety needs. Some fires were the result of children playing with matches, while others were the result of structural issues such as faulty wiring. However, as in the case of Linda, the children were generally alone in the house when fire broke out. Automobile suffocation resulted when the children were left in a car that eventually grew too hot. The bathtub drownings resulted from inadequate supervision while the child was in the tub. Layover suffocation occurred when the mother or other children suffocated the child by rolling over on her during sleep. A child whose nutritional needs were not being met generally died of dehydration or starvation. Finally, inattention to safety needs involved cases where a child died because a mother did not fully consider her safety. For example, one child choked to death on cigarette butts when a mother did not remove them from the ashtray.

In *neglect-commission cases*, an irresponsible action of the mother caused the death, such as shaking the baby too hard or placing something over the child's head to stop the child from crying. As with the omission cases, the mother did not kill the child purposely.

Meyer and Oberman studied a total of 76 cases of neglect. The average age of mothers at the time the filicide occurred was 25.46 years. Most mothers were 20 years old when their child(ren) died. The average age the women in this category became mothers was 22.05 years, and the majority became mothers between the ages of 17 and 20 years. The fact that these mothers were relatively young may underscore other concerns. For example, a young mother may not have had the opportunity to complete her education. This has tremendous implications for her ability to earn money and her ability to secure other resources. In addition, the overwhelming majority (85 percent) of mothers in this category were single parents, which probably further compounded their economic situation and available resources. There was no second income in the home or second pair of hands to help with the multitude of tasks. Moreover, among the cases reviewed, 41 percent of the families had three or more children. Not surprisingly, 90 percent of the cases in this category involved mothers living in poverty. Mothers could afford only the basic needs. There were no extra funds to pay to have homes exterminated when it was needed or for a babysitter to provide a respite. Since these mothers generally had weak social support systems, they rarely had any breaks from their children. Finally, in at least 41 percent of the cases there were mental health issues, including mood disorders, such as depression, or chemical dependency.

In short, mothers who commit fatal child neglect are often in need of extensive assistance in numerous areas encompassing both global and specific domains. It is imperative that professionals provide a continuum of care for neglectful mothers. One way to accomplish this is by establishing comprehensive pediatric health centers, specifically targeting the zero-to-3 population, as most neglected children fall into this age range. Neglectful mothers must typically travel from agency to agency and town to town as they seek services such as public assistance benefits, prenatal care, medical and dental care, mental health intervention, and parenting skills training. The creation of full-service pediatric community health care centers would allow for a facility where the needs of both parents and children can be fulfilled. Support for this type of model has already been seen in one innovative program that is dedicated to health-care delivery to children in the first three years of life.[1] Toward this end, close partnerships are created between mothers and healthcare professionals to address not only the physical needs of the child, but also to address emotional and intellectual growth as well as healthy child development. In addition to physicians and nurses, the model utilizes specialists who have specific training in child development and focus their services on behavioral and developmental issues for children. The specialists have many roles within the program, including conducting home visits to support and enhance interactions between the parent and infant, conducting ongoing checkups that assess both child development and family factors, helping mothers manage common behavioral concerns, such as fussiness, sleep, or discipline problems, facilitating parent education groups, and staffing a telephone information line to answer questions about child development. Essentially, this holistic approach views the promotion of children's development and assistance to parents as primary goals when treating a child's physical illnesses. Certainly, a key feature to each center should be the incorporation of parent education into every single visit.

Although such a program may assist with the stresses that neglectful mothers face, the real problem is poverty. It is beyond the scope of this chapter to address poverty in the United States. However, we can better understand mothers who kill their children through neglect if we begin to recognize the impact of a lack of power and privilege on disenfranchised groups within U.S. society, such as those living in poverty.

Assisted or Coerced Filicide

Renee had her first child at the age of 13 and by the age of 20 she had four children (two boys and two girls). Renee was convicted of killing her youngest boy in conjunction with her boyfriend. Renee's boyfriend was known for his impatience with Renee's children (none were his biological child) and he had a history of acting out his impatience with them and Renee with an explosive and often violent temper. Renee's youngest child died when he did not obey the boyfriend precisely and the boyfriend struck the child, sending him flying across the room. After the child died, Renee helped dispose of the body. The autopsy revealed the little boy died from an acute trauma to the head. Renee and the boyfriend were each charged and convicted of murder and abuse of a corpse. Renee is currently serving a sentence of 15 years to life.

Renee was molested as a very young child. She describes her childhood as "absolute chaos" with "constant fighting and brawling" among family members. She has a history of drug and alcohol abuse and has attempted suicide several times. She describes her circumstances as follows: "I turned into a revengeful drinker; I was real passive and I couldn't say no when family came over with friends and they wanted to drink and party. At the time I was caring for the kids and then I got frustrated and said to hell with it and I started using alcohol.

My kids were very rowdy but I made them that way because I didn't want them pushed around. Child protective services was called on me and my boyfriend all the time. They would come and investigate and would see that my kids were fed and clean—no bruises. I just said to hell with the rest of the world . . . we made it together as a family."

Meyer and Oberman (2001) researched 12 cases in the assisted/coerced category. In assisted/coerced filicide, mothers kill their child purposely while acting in conjunction with a partner—generally, a romantic partner—who contributes in some manner to the death. This is a unique category in that most women who kill their children act alone, and the majority of filicide research focuses on women who act alone. Meyer and Oberman subdivided their cases in this category into two subcategories: active and passive. In the active subcategory, the women were involved directly in their children's death. In the passive category, the women were charged with their children's deaths, due to their inability to protect their children.

The characteristics of women in this category are unlike that of women in other categories. Most notably, during the time period in which they kill their children, these women are involved with a partner who has the tendency to be abusive and violent. The nature of the violence within these relationships is crucial to understanding the circumstances of the children's death. The violence perpetrated by the women's partners is generally not comprised of isolated, aggressive events but includes multiple types of abuse (i.e., physical, psychological, sexual, destruction of property) occurring in a cycle that often increases in frequency and intensity. The abuse is always intended to control and to invoke fear in the victims (Meyer & Oberman, 2001). One possible consequence of domestic violence is increased aggressiveness on the part of the victim.

This risk is increased by the fact that women in the partner-involved infanticide category, like Renee, were often involved with partners who were not the biological parent of the child killed. Meyer and Oberman discuss the literature which suggests that children are more at risk of being harmed by caretakers who are not related biologically.

The majority of women in this sample were experiencing multiple social stressors, including poverty and the presence of multiple children in the home. In the active subcategory, the deaths of children typically resulted from discipline-related abuse that escalated into death. All the children in this sample had been abused physically. Numerous women reported that the death occurred during their attempts to discipline. Their purpose had not been to kill the child, as the use of a gun or more lethal method of killing (i.e., hanging, fire) might suggest. Instead, the majority of the deaths resulted from beatings. These incidents appear to have occurred during times that are typically stressful for parents, such as toilet training. There are similarities between passive and active partner-assisted women; however, women in the passive category did not kill their children. Rather, as in Renee's case, they were unable to prevent their partner from harming the child and/or may not have reported the death accurately to authorities.

One has only to look at the conviction and sentencing data for women from the partner-involved category to see the criminal justice system's bias against women and lack of understanding about the nature of domestic violence. This bias is most striking in cases from the passive partner-assisted category, because these involve women who did not abuse their children. Rather, these women were held responsible for their child's death because they were expected to be able to prevent their partner from killing their child. Two of the four women in Meyer and Oberman's sample were not even present when their child was killed, yet were blamed for not preventing the death.

Clearly, this category illustrates that merely blaming and punishing women cannot solve the complex problem of partner-involved filicide. Rather, professionals and community members must work together to build resources to address the larger problem of domestic violence, in addition to working to reduce the isolation of mothers and children who are vulnerable to such violence.

Purposeful Filicide and the Mother Acted Alone

Catherine, a Caucasian woman, was approximately 25 years old at the time she committed her crime. Catherine laid out the facts of the case, taking responsibility for every action she made. Catherine killed all 4 of her children, one after another over the period of one day. She received 4 charges of murder and 4 consecutive life terms.

Like several of the other women described in this chapter, Catherine had a chaotic and unpredictable young life. She characterizes her early adolescence as "quiet and rebellious." She became sexually active around age 13. At the age of about 14, she ran away with her boyfriend; she later married this man when she became pregnant by him. This man was extremely physically, sexually, and psychologically abusive of Catherine. At one point he attempted to have her involuntarily committed to a psychiatric hospital. They had several separations, the final of which occurred when she was pregnant with their last child. Although their relationship had ended, custody had not yet been decided and a bitter custody battle began. At a time when Catherine was trying to get back on her feet, attending school, living with her parents, and holding down a job, she was raped by an unknown assailant. This assault seems to have triggered a sense of hopelessness and Catherine resolved to kill her children and herself. The latter never occurred and she is currently serving out her sentence.

She described her relationship with her children as follows: "They always came first. They were more of an appendage. I loved them very much. Killing them was not out of hate. It was a suicide. I could never envision them without me. I could not accept that my ex-husband could raise them better than me. I wanted to die and I wanted the kids with me in death. Everything I valued was my kids and if I had them with me in death then there was nothing holding me back and the thought that I could kill them—I was totally worthless and once I started thinking that and felt that way about myself I couldn't stop myself."

Overall, the purposeful filicide cases, as with Catherine's case, are perhaps the most difficult to comprehend. *Although we may not condone it*, it seems somehow easier to understand how a neonaticide could occur or a mother could kill through neglect or abuse. However, it is seemingly incomprehensible how a mother could, acting alone, kill her child on purpose. Although arguably the neonaticides are committed on purpose, there is a host of other factors that set them apart from the purposeful category. For example, in the present category the mothers are older, often kill more than one child, and the children are generally not neonates. To explain these mothers, generally, two lay theories are proposed; the mother must be "mad or bad."

Women portrayed as *mad* have been characterized as "good mothers" who by all accounts have conformed to traditional gender roles and whose crimes seem to be the result of mental illness. In contrast, women characterized as *bad* do not seem to suffer from mental illness and are labeled as cold, callous, evil mothers who have often been neglectful of their children or their domestic responsibilities. This dichotomy is easily seen in one woman, Andrea Yates. Yates was convicted of murder but was not given the death penalty. The prosecutor sought the death penalty suggesting Yates was "bad" or purposely killed her children and it was not the result of a mental illness. Of course, the defense claimed the opposite, that she is "mad" and the deaths were the result of mental illness. Unfortunately, this dichotomy is woefully inadequate and begs the question, just what is a mental illness?

In the legal arena, when the mental status of a defendant comes into question, it generally relates to either the issue of competence to stand trial or to the defendant's mental state at the time of the offense. In general, the standard for competence to stand trial is whether the defendant understands the charges against her, and the proceedings, so as to be able to aid her attorney in her defense. After much deliberation, Andrea Yates was found competent to stand trial. Although competency issues arise in the purposeful filicide cases, more often, mental status issues are at stake.

Mental status at the time of the offense relates to the plea that a defendant makes regarding her mental capacities when she committed the offense. The most commonly used plea relating to mental status at the time of the offense is, of course, the insanity defense.

Each state fashions its own definition or test for insanity. However, a common test for insanity is some variant of the *M'Naghten test*, which states, in part: "To establish a defense on the ground of insanity, it must be clearly proved that, at the time of the committing of the act, the party accused was laboring under such a defect of reason, from disease of the mind, as not to know the nature and quality of the act he was doing; or, if he did know it, that he did not know what he was doing was wrong" [10 Cl.&F. 200, 8 Eng. Rep 718 (H.L. 1843)].

Arguably, even the most psychotic person knows that what he or she is doing is wrong. Andrea Yates called her husband and 911 to report her crimes. The pivotal terms, then, involve interpreting what it means to know the "nature and quality" of one's actions. Wisconsin used a variant of the M'Naghten test and found Jeffrey Dahmer, a man who killed numerous victims and then consumed some of their body parts, to be sane.

To aid jurors in better understanding the mental capacities of the defendant and the insanity test used by the state, both prosecution and defense attorneys usually hire mental health experts. This brings definitions of mental illness used by mental health professionals into the legal arena. Unlike the dichotomous legal system where a person is sane or insane, using the *Diagnostic and Statistical Manual of Mental Disorders, Fourth Edition (DSM-IV*, American Psychiatric Association, 1994), the mental health professions outline an array of illnesses with specific diagnostic criteria for each one, many of which could apply to mothers who purposely kill their children.

Would Andrea Yates have had a mental illness according to the *DSM-IV*? We did not interview Andrea Yates but read numerous accounts of her behavior. Clearly, she was and had been depressed and suicidal. She was probably grappling with depression the day she killed her children and has continued to grapple with it in prison following the murders. Although Andrea Yates may meet the psychological criteria for mental illness, and in fact was hospitalized for her mental illness, that obviously may not satisfy legal standards for insanity and seems to have had little bearing on her competence to stand trial.

Meyer and Oberman struggled with these definitional issues as well. They originally divided this category into purposeful filicide with mental illness and purposeful without mental illness. However, as the discussion above illustrates, there was no way to create exact definitions of purposeful filicide with mental illness and purposeful filicide without mental illness. In fact, they came to view it as a continuum, not a dichotomy, with many exceptions and no rules. For example, if the mother demonstrated signs of mental illness in the past but not at the time of the murder, would she represent purposeful filicide with or without mental illness? Or if the mother had no history of mental illness but attempted or successfully committed murder–suicide, would it be considered purposeful filicide with or without mental illness? What if the suicide was because of cultural issues or for altruistic reasons such as to spare the child what she believed would be a life of abuse? What if the woman was suffering from a disorder, such as postpartum psychosis, which is not a recognized mental disorder in the *DSM-IV*? They finally decided not to try to separate out cases into subcategories of with or without mental illness but to include them all under a category known as purposeful filicide.

Despite the level of diversity between the cases and the paucity of available information in some instances, striking and clear patterns emerged among the 79 cases that Meyer and Oberman reviewed. For example, unlike mothers in other categories, nearly 39 percent of mothers within this category killed more than one child, and when examining only cases of murder–suicide, the number jumped to 68 percent. Additionally, 16 percent of the cases involved serial deaths, where the mother killed multiple children over an extended period. Over one-half (57 percent) of the multiple deaths involved attempted or successful murder–suicides. This large percentage suggests that mothers who commit infanticide and then attempt suicide pose a greater risk to kill all or the majority of their offspring. Although one cannot definitively state why these mothers killed multiple children, Catherine identified one reason—that she did not want someone else to raise her children. Other reasons include sparing children the pain of growing up without a mother or overwhelming financial pressures.

These numbers are alarming and highlight the need among the general public for education and awareness regarding mental illness. With education and awareness, the stigma of mental illness may be reduced, and seeking treatment for mental illness may increase. Generally, the last person to seek help when mental illness strikes is the person with the mental illness. That places the responsibility on her loved ones to be aware of signs of mental illness and act to help her.

In 37 percent of the cases involving multiple killings, mothers chose fire as the primary mode of death. In these instances, mothers set fire to their homes or cars, and in a few cases, killed their children by some other means, such as a gunshot wound or drowning, and then in a final act, set fire to their homes. This phenomenon is unique to the mothers within the purposeful filicide category. Again, it is difficult to determine why these mothers chose fire. Many of these mothers may have felt their lives were spiraling out of control, and in their minds, the fire may have been a final attempt to exert a sense of control over what had been an otherwise powerless existence. Additionally, a fire is a far more passive method of killing.

Close to 42 percent of women in this category experienced a recent failed relationship, separation, or divorce prior to the murders. This number increases if expanded to include the death of a loved one. For example, Andrea Yates lost her father shortly before killing her five children. The loss of a relationship should be taken seriously and monitored closely by family member and friends. Clearly, with these mothers, it is a warning sign.

Although mothers within this category seem like premeditated murderers who killed their children violently, upon deeper examination, one of the most distinctive features of these women's stories was their devotion to their children. Catherine describes herself as a loving mother and devoted to her children. Although it may seem like an oxymoron to describe women who kill their children as loving mothers, by all accounts that is exactly what most of them were. The overwhelming majority of them had no history of abuse or neglect toward their children, and most people who knew them spoke of their undying love for their kids.

Issues of culture and ethnicity played a significant role within this category, particularly as they related to immigrant women. A large number of immigrant women were represented in comparison to the other subtypes. Many immigrants face unique challenges when they move to the United States. Issues of acculturation and assimilation, as well as language barriers, often make the adjustment to American life a difficult one. In seeking prevention and intervention strategies, greater multicultural education for professionals and laypersons could help identify and alleviate any number of travails for new immigrants.

A very small percentage of mothers within this category suffered from postpartum disorders (8 percent). Since Andrea Yates's case, this issue has received more media attention. The National Organization for Women passed a national resolution to increase attention to postpartum disorders, and legislation has been introduced into Congress to increase funding for research. Still, no funding has been approved and this continues to be an area in need of research, education, and outreach. Simple interventions could save numerous lives. For example, it could be quite effective and cost-efficient to have pediatricians ask and provide education about postpartum syndromes at well baby checks.

Like most women in this category, Andrea Yates gave many warning signs, but they were either ignored entirely or minimized. Friends, family, and the health care system need to understand these signs and learn to take appropriate action to help prevent these tragedies.

CONCLUSIONS

In this chapter we have provided an overview of five different types of mothers who kill their children. Within each type we have provided some suggestions for changes in policy or prevention and intervention strategies based on the specific circumstances of those mothers. However, there were other important issues and observations that we have not addressed which emerged throughout all the categories. The most salient of these relates to the social construction of motherhood and is revealed in the following anecdote.

Once while being interviewed by the media, the first author for this chapter was asked: "Don't you think a mother has a duty to protect her children?" My response was: "I think that every parent has a duty to protect their children." This exchange really embodies the social construction of motherhood. Simply put, on the whole, societal expectations for mothers are different than expectations for fathers. It is beyond the scope of this chapter to argue the value or origins of such expectations, but in our research, they often played a part in the tragic circumstances and outcomes. For example, sometimes this related not to fears and self-doubt that a mother harbored related to her parenting ability but her reluctance to discuss these concerns so as not to appear to be a "bad" mother or a failure at what everyone termed the *mothering instinct*. Although we expect new mothers to be facile at these tasks, we laugh at the inexperience of new fathers, holding fathers to separate unrealistic expectations. The social construction of motherhood is also evidenced in the fact that although many of these mothers were single parenting, the absence of the father or the father's contribution to the crime is rarely addressed in these cases. For example, in many of these cases, the father clearly failed to protect the child but was never charged.

Not surprisingly, a mother's feelings of fear and self-doubt are often aggravated by the social expectation that she should be feeling unadulterated joy about being a mother. Frequently, the result of such an expectation is depression, which becomes compounded as the woman withdraws from friends and family. In fact, our research revealed that isolation was a warning sign across all categories, from the teen who commits neonaticide to the mothers who experience postpartum syndromes. Although isolation is self-imposed in some women's circumstances, such as in the case of neonaticide, or imposed by others in different circumstances, such as in the case of domestic violence, the end result was the same—devastating isolation. To really consider the impact of such isolation, imagine the number of times each day we ask for social validation from our peers or family. How often do we ask for opinions such as "How did I do?" or "How do I look?" Now imagine that it was impossible to obtain that feedback, especially while you were engaging in a new, unfamiliar, and exhausting endeavor that you had never done before (yet everyone expected you to know how to do it). One of the most frequent comments we heard in our interviews of mothers was that the one thing they had learned in prison was to reach out for help when they needed it, despite their prior socialization experiences, which kept them from doing so before. While saying this, they also recognized the danger in reaching out; the social construction of mother-hood is institutionalized. Admitting that you need help to social services agencies, or that you feel unsure about your ability to raise your child, creates the very real danger that you may lose your children through these same agencies. This creates a catch-22 situation: reach out and put oneself at risk or remain isolated and at risk. Fathers who reach out for help may not suffer the same scrutiny. Consider the response when a father is widowed versus when a mother is widowed. When a father is left to raise children through widowhood, there is an outpouring of parenting support we rarely see for mothers in the same circumstances.

Although it would be grandiose to believe that societal expectations will change with any rapidity, we could increase other support for mothers quite easily. We have identified several ways to do this throughout the chapter. However, the obstacle does not seem to be the venue in which to increase support, but the desire. Our personal commitment to such endeavors seems lacking. When our attention is focused on the issue of mothers who kill their children, there is little exploration into understanding why such an act occurred and much more discussion about what the consequences of her actions should be. For example, the emphasis on Andrea Yates was really not on what led her to kill her children but rather, whether she should receive the death penalty. Little progress will be made toward prevention if we do not try to understand causes. And we need to focus on prevention. We found over 1000 reported cases of mothers who killed their children in the 1990s alone. That averages to one case every three days, and these were just *reported* cases. Many children were never found, or the child was found and the mother could not be identified, or the mother was a juve-nile and the case was never reported. We can no longer continue to ignore these tragedies.

What was perhaps the most disturbing observation for all the researchers involved in both the construction of the typology and the interviews was that *on the whole*, these mothers were not atypical prior to the deaths of their children. In the last paragraph of their book, Meyer and Oberman (2001) stated: "If there is one central point to this book, it is this: To the extent that we conceive of the crime of infanticide as a rare and exceptional act committed by a deranged or evil woman, we are dangerously wrong" (p. 177). This sentiment was reiterated in numerous interviews. One mother stated: "People have to stop thinking we are cruel and hard, we just went through an emotional battle. I've had girls tell me that they went through what I went through but they had their husbands and mothers to help them through it. The family has to get involved. People are so closed that they don't want to see anything. They see everything in black and white, but they really need to see color."

Another mother said, "I love all my children just like everyone else . . . it devastated me . . . it could have happened to any woman. . . . I was wanting to be a mother—something all women want . . . and to be doing something that you never thought about doing or being. . . . it's not like taking drugs or becoming an alcoholic and getting behind the wheel of a car and knowing the consequences . . . but having a baby which everyone does. . . . What kind of mother do people think I am? I have this black stain on me."

Few people want to consider themselves capable of unacceptable acts. This is why Milgram's (1965) findings in the early 1960s—that "good" people would obey an authority even though it meant harming an innocent person—shocked both his research participants and himself. It is why the My Lai massacre and the acts of Hitler's army shocked us. It is why Rodney King shocked us. Still all of these examples highlight the fact that given the right set of circumstances, average people can do heinous things. Most of the mothers in our research were ordinary women who had dealt with extraordinary circumstances during the course of their lives and just prior to their crimes.

Nothing in this chapter is meant to create an excuse for these mothers or their acts. The intent of this chapter is to increase understanding of these mothers and the circumstances that are involved in their crimes. In doing so there is an inherent challenge to all of us to become more attentive to and involved in the lives of other human beings.

NOTE

1. A full history, mission, and philosophy of the Healthy Steps model can be obtained at www.healthysteps.org.

REFERENCES

AMERICAN PSYCHIATRIC ASSOCIATION. (1994). *Diagnostic and statistical manual of mental disorders.* Washington, DC: American Psychiatric Association.

CICCHETTI, D. (1989). How research on child maltreatment has informed the study of child development: Perspectives from developmental psychopathology. In D. Cicchetti & V. Carlson (Eds.), *Child maltreatment: Theory and research on the causes and consequences of child abuse and neglect* (pp. 377–431). New York: Cambridge University Press.

MEYER, C. L., OBERMAN, M. (with WHITE, K., RONE, M., BATRA, P. & PROANO, T.). (2001). *Mothers who kill their children: Understanding the acts of moms from Susan Smith to the "prom mom."* New York: New York University Press.

MILGRAM, S. (1965). Some conditions of obedience and disobedience to authority. *Human Relations, 18*, 57–76.

MILNER, J. S., ROBERTSON, K. R., & ROGERS, D. L. (1990). Childhood history of abuse and adult child abuse potential. *Journal of Family Violence, 5*, 15–34.

OBERMAN, M. (1996). Mothers who kill: Coming to terms with modern American infanticide. *American Criminal Law Review, 34*, 1–110.

RESNICK, P. J. (1970). Murder of the newborn: A psychiatric review of neonaticide. *American Journal of Psychiatry, 126*, 1414–1420.

SECTION VIII
Girls and Delinquency

32

Developing Gender-Specific Services for Delinquency Prevention

Understanding Risk and Resiliency

Barbara Bloom, Barbara Owen, Elizabeth Piper Deschenes, and Jill Rosenbaum

INTRODUCTION

Within the last few years the proportion of female youthful offenders has increased, while there has been a decrease in crime among male juvenile delinquents (Acoca, 1999). Despite the increase in the number of girls and young women arrested and placed within the juvenile justice system over the last several decades, female youthful offenders remain a small proportion of the juvenile justice population (Belknap, 1996; Chesney-Lind & Shelden, 1998). The nature of female delinquency is generally less threatening to the public order than that of male juveniles, who are more likely to be arrested for violent crimes and serious property crimes (Chesney-Lind & Shelden, 1998). Consequently, girls and young women have been relatively invisible in the juvenile justice system. This invisibility affects every aspect of the juvenile justice system and results in a lack of attention to girls in juvenile justice research and theory and a lack of programs and services for female youthful offenders (Belknap, 1996).

Until recently, few resources within the juvenile justice system have been directed toward the needs of at-risk girls, despite their unique situation. For example, a report issued by the Law Enforcement Assistance Administration in 1975 indicated that only 5 percent of federally funded juvenile delinquency projects and only 6 percent of all local funds were directed toward girls (Chesney-Lind & Shelden, 1998). More recently, a meta-analysis of program evaluations conducted since 1950 on 443 delinquency programs reported that 34.8 percent were exclusively for males and an additional 42.4 percent served mostly males; only 2.3 percent served girls exclusively, and only 5.9 percent served a majority of females (Lipsey, 1990). Within the last few years the Office of Juvenile Justice and Delinquency Prevention (OJJDP) launched a multilevel approach, which has resulted in publication of an inventory of state efforts (Community Research Associates, 1998), an inventory of best practices and training curricula (Greene, Peters & Associates, 1997), and a variety of program development activities (Budnick & Shields-Fletcher, 1998).

Although social scientists have studied delinquency and other high-risk behaviors of male adolescents for decades, most research has not focused specifically on high-risk girls. This has resulted in little insight into the reasons for their involvement in the juvenile justice system (Belknap, 1996; Chesney-Lind & Shelden, 1992; Leonard, 1982; Naffine, 1987; Smart, 1976). Many studies of delinquency included few girls and young women in their samples, and this has set a precedent for most of the research on juvenile delinquency (Calhoun, Jurgens, & Chen, 1993; Miller, Traponi, Fejes-Mendoza, Eggleston, & Dwiggins, 1995; Minnesota Advisory Task Force on the Female Offender in Corrections, 1994). Belknap (1997) describes the lack of research related to females as a telling indicator of "girls' and women's invisibility in theories [which] has doggedly followed them in every way imaginable" (p. 2). This is also true of policy research and development, as well as institutional and programmatic responses. When the major sociological theories of delinquency focus almost exclusively on males, it raises a concern as to whether these theories should be used to explain girls' delinquent behavior as well.

Feminist theorists suggest that the focus on gender goes beyond simply adding another variable to the study of female crime and delinquency (e.g., "add women and stir"). Contemporary feminist research has contributed to our understanding of the female experience in a way that does not simply contrast it to that of men. Feminist criminology, particularly when informed by concern for sexual victimization, offers a great deal to the study of female crime and delinquency (Chesney-Lind, 1992; Owen & Bloom, 1995). From this perspective, exploitation by men acts as a trigger for behavior by females, causing them to run away or begin abusing drugs at an early age. These behaviors are often referred to as *survival strategies* that ultimately result in girls' involvement in the juvenile justice system (Chesney-Lind, 1992). However, even feminist criminology has failed to fully explore the intersection of race, class, and gender in girls' and women's offending until recently (Bloom, 1996).

Interest has begun to shift to the unique issues of female delinquency, the nature and causes of girls' involvement in crime, and the biological and developmental issues that are particular to girls and young women. The ways in which girls develop their identity and relationships with others have begun to influence theory and research about female crime and delinquency. According to Gilligan (1982), boys develop their identity in relation to the world, while girls develop their identity in relation to others. For girls, moral decisions are based on specific personal situations, in contrast with the more common male focus on assertive decision making and exercising judgments based on absolutes. Gilligan asserts that in women's lives, attachment, interdependence, and connectedness are critical issues that form the foundation of their identity; and female moral development is often based on personal views and a commitment to others. Often, this commitment involves giving up or sacrificing one's own well-being for the benefit of others.

Professionals working with women and girls are articulating the need to recognize the centrality of relationships as a central tenet in the female's psychological life (Covington, 1998; Gilligan, 1982; Pipher, 1994). This approach recognizes that women's and girls' psychological profile differs from that of men, including the accumulated effects of exposure to abuse and trauma, battering, and an overemphasis on gender-based expectations such as care-taking and docility. Further, female behaviors are seen as reactions to multiple sources of marginalization and as expressions of resistance. This shift has profound implications for treatment and services for those who work with girls and women in the criminal justice system (Bloom, 1997).

Developing gender-specific programs for females requires a better understanding of the unique situation of girls and the risk factors relating to juvenile delinquency and their involvement in the juvenile or criminal justice system, but to date there have been relatively few studies. Risk and resiliency factors are associated with various spheres of influence, such as family, peer, and individual characteristics, school and social environments, and community status. How, and to what extent, these factors are present and interact can significantly increase the likelihood of involvement in delinquency and subsequent treatment by the juvenile justice system. Traditionally, researchers have focused on risk factors that are likely to result in negative or self-destructive behaviors among youth. More recently, experts have also endeavored to identify resiliency or protective factors described by Scott (1994) as "those characteristics or circumstances which enable individuals to grow, thrive, and succeed in spite of what appear to be insurmountable odds" (p. 5).

Through a review of the literature, in this chapter we discuss various factors within the following domains for risk and resiliency in relationship to girls' delinquent behavior: community, school, family, individual and peers. The review of the existing research on girls in the juvenile justice system identified the following themes: (1) the increased involvement of girls in the juvenile justice system; (2) risk factors for their involvement in the juvenile justice system; and (3) differential treatment of girls once they are in the system (Girls Inc., 1996). These findings are summarized to provide suggestions for gender-specific programming for the prevention of female delinquency.

PROFILE OF AT-RISK ADOLESCENT FEMALES

Female adolescents at risk or involved in the juvenile justice system often come from impoverished, urban, inner-city environments; have been reared in female-headed, single-parent households; or have experienced foster care placement. They have a higher likelihood than their male counterparts of being channeled into the juvenile justice system as a result of fleeing physically and/or sexually abusive home environments, and they are more likely to have abused drugs and/or alcohol than adolescent girls in the general population (Washington, 1997). Several studies have identified the following common characteristics of at-risk adolescent females [American Correctional Association (ACA), 1990; Chesney-Lind & Shelden, 1998; Girls Inc., 1996; Greene, Peters & Associates, 1997; Minnesota Advisory Task Force on the Female Offender in Corrections, 1994]:

- Age 13 to 18 years
- History of victimization, especially physical, sexual, and emotional abuse
- School failure, truancy, and drop-out
- Repeated status offenses, especially running away
- Unstable family life, including family involvement in the criminal justice system,

lack of connectedness, and social isolation

- History of unhealthy dependent relationships, especially with older males
- Mental health issues, including history of substance abuse
- Overrepresentation among communities of color
- Economically marginalized populations

COMMUNITY RISK AND RESILIENCY FACTORS

Community risk factors include social and structural factors that influence the environment in which girls are raised. The literature has focused on racial or ethnic background, socioeconomic status, and issues of immigration or acculturation. Research also suggests that communities that provide extracurricular and social activities can foster resiliency for young women. To this end, communities need to provide a continuum of opportunities for drug and alcohol education, abuse and sex education, nontraditional job training, social skills development, places to go (e.g., safe havens), and mentoring opportunities.

Race and Ethnicity

Girls from racial/ethnic minority groups are caught in the double bind of the gender and racial expectations of their communities of origin and those of the dominant culture. Moreover, racial and ethnic minority girls have different experiences with the dominant institutions in this society (West, 1994). Although it is essential to identify and correct gender bias in the juvenile justice system, attending to gender alone is not an adequate response for girls of color in detention.

Even though arrest and incarceration rates have increased for girls in general during the past decade, girls of color are overrepresented in the juvenile justice population. Girls of color constitute the largest and fastest-growing segment of female adolescents in secure detention, and race and class play as significant a role as gender in girls' development and life choices, as well as in their treatment (Amaro, 1995; Anderson, 1996; LaFramboise & Howard-Pitney, 1995; Martin, 1993; Nelson, 1997; Orenstein, 1994; Washington, 1997). Using data collected in 29 states, the National Council on Crime and Delinquency reported that African-Americans comprise nearly 50 percent of all girls in secure detention, Hispanics 13 percent, and Caucasians 34 percent.

There are disparities in the treatment of girls involved in the juvenile justice system. Minority families are viewed as "less interested in their children" than are white families (Frazier & Bishop, 1995, p. 43). This may result in a style of response that reflects stereotypes of the dominant culture when dealing with minority families (Washington, 1997). For example, Miller (1994) found that African-American and Latina girls were 70 to 80 percent more likely than white girls to be recommended for detention-oriented placement. The behavior of African-American girls was often typified as being the result of inappropriate lifestyle choices, whereas the behavior of white girls was framed in terms of self-image problems, peer pressure, and abandonment issues (p. 20). Girls of color are at particular risk for inadequate treatment of prior sexual abuse (Washington, 1997).

Socioeconomic Status

Socioeconomic background is a strong predictor of female, as well as male, adolescents' risk for involvement in the juvenile justice system (Washington, 1997). Poor youth are more likely to be processed through the official criminal justice system, while their more affluent counterparts are more likely to be diverted into private treatment programs (Belknap, 1996; Frazier & Bishop, 1995; Girls Inc., 1996; La Free, 1989, in Washington, 1997).

The proportion of U.S. children living in poverty varies significantly by race and ethnicity: 12 percent white; 30 percent African-American; 27 percent Latino/Hispanic; 20 percent Asian/Pacific Islander; 26 percent Native American (Brindis, Peterson, & Brown, 1997) as well as geography. At 25 percent, California has the tenth highest proportion in the nation of children and youth living in poverty (California Department of Finance, 1993).

To a large extent, socioeconomic status is a factor in girls' committing certain types of crimes (e.g., girls steal things they need or think they need but cannot afford). Girls and young women are particularly susceptible to these temptations because they believe that their popularity is linked to physical appearance and fashion during adolescence. Once arrested, socioeconomic status also limits their ability to post bond or pay for a private attorney, as well as the types of services they receive (Belknap, 1996). On the other hand, if a delinquent girl's family has money or insurance, she may be diverted out of the juvenile justice system and placed in a private facility for services such as a drug treatment or mental health counseling or therapy. If a girl or young woman comes from a low-income family, these options may not exist. As a result, there is more of a chance that delinquent girls from low-income families will end up in the juvenile justice system and may not receive the services that they need (Girls Inc., 1996).

SCHOOL RISK AND RESILIENCY FACTORS

Studies of school performance of girls and boys suggest that the marginalization and stereotyping of women in popular culture are unintentionally reinforced in schools [American Association of University Women (AAUW) 1992]. Shortchanging girls of classroom attention, the emphasis on competitive (rather than cooperative) learning, a shortage of the use of women as role models in texts and lesson plans, sexual harassment by fellow students, and reinforcing gender stereotypes of abilities all have a negative impact on girls' aspirations. Declining school performance is related to a decrease in self-esteem among preadolescent and adolescent girls (AAUW, 1992). Although girls begin their school years with skills and ambitions comparable to those of boys, by the time they are in high school, "most have suffered a disproportionate loss of confidence in their academic abilities" (p. 5). Even though there is no strong evidence that single-sex education is better for girls than coeducation, some of the positive results are a heightened regard by girls for math and science, an increase in girls' risk taking, and a gain in girls' confidence from academic competence (AAUW, 1998).

Despite the unintentional negative effect of the school environment on many girls, studies have shown that school performance continues to be important to them, and school failure can contribute to their delinquency (Adler, 1987; Cernkovich & Giordano, 1979b). Other studies found that a positive outlook and performance in school-related activities, and an emphasis on the importance of math, science, and computer skills were strong correlates for academic success and a reduction in delinquent behavior for girls (AAUW, 1992; Chesney-Lind & Shelden, 1998).

Truancy contributes to delinquency, drug use, and dropout (Garry, 1996). A recent report from the Los Angeles County Office of Education concluded that "chronic absenteeism is the most powerful predictor of delinquent behavior—(for) behavior involving drugs, alcohol, or violence" (Shuster, 1995, p. 1). In California, approximately 15 percent of all students drop out during their four years of high school (Rothenbaum, 1998). Girls and young women who drop out are less likely than boys to return to school or to obtain a GED (Posner, 1990).

The educational system seldom takes into account the psychosocial construction of girls' lives, especially during middle adolescence. Evidence points to the difference in school cultures between girls (adult and teacher oriented) and boys (group and peer oriented), and the importance of designing school programs that take these differences into account (Block, 1984, in Chesney-Lind & Shelden, 1998).

School environments that recognize the unique learning styles of girls (e.g., cooperative learning and group problem solving versus individual competitiveness) and have high expectations for academic performance, especially in the math and sciences, are especially able to provide for resiliency in young women. These schools foster community partnerships and provide extracurricular activities not only to the student but to the entire family, including education on issues of abuse, sexuality, drug and alcohol use, and job training. Gender-specific nontraditional vocational job training for girls is also an important school component.

FAMILY RISK AND RESILIENCY FACTORS

The family environment of many at-risk or delinquent girls includes parental substance abuse and violence as well as physical, sexual, and emotional abuse. Additional characteristics of family dysfunction, which place girls at risk for future delinquency, include parental rejection and/or abandonment (e.g., experiencing little love, affection, or warmth), inadequate supervision, witnessing or experiencing conflict, marital discord, and violence in the home. Studies indicated that the majority of California Youth Authority (CYA) female wards came from single-parent and multiproblem families (Owen & Bloom, 1997; Rosenbaum, 1989). Both parents had deserted one out of every 10 CYA wards in the 1960s. Even fewer girls in the 1990s grew up in two-parent families than in the 1960s (25 percent versus 15 percent). Windle (1997) focused on the adverse effects of parental drinking on adolescents, including the contribution made by disruptive, alcohol-influenced parenting behaviors to internalizing (e.g., depression, anxiety) and externalizing problems (e.g., delinquency) by their children.

Family Criminality

Familial involvement in crime is another correlate for delinquency. Family characteristics, which appear to have more of an impact on girls than on boys, include the involvement of a family member in the criminal justice system (Dembo et al., 1998). An ACA (1990) study indicated that 64 percent of juvenile girls in detention had a family member who was or had been incarcerated.

Two studies of girls incarcerated in the California Youth Authority indicated that the vast majority came from families where criminality was common. Seventy-six percent of female CYA wards in the 1960s (Rosenbaum, 1989) and 89 percent of female CYA wards in the 1990s (Owen & Bloom, 1997) had family members who had been arrested. Owen and Bloom (1997) indicated that nearly one-half of the respondents reported that their father had been incarcerated and one-fourth reported that their mother had been incarcerated. About three-fourths of the girls in the 1960s had at least one family member with a criminal record, and half of the time it was the girls' mothers who had felony arrest records. The girls reported that 71 percent of their parents fought regularly with the children. Family conflict over alcohol was noted in 81 percent of the families; 34 percent of the fathers were known alcoholics, as were 31 percent of the mothers. Owen and Bloom note that although records were not kept on domestic violence unless a specific charge was filed, in the 1960s " a number of the known fathers had spent time in jail for fighting with their wife." Nearly one-third of parents of the CYA wards in the 1960s had histories of mental illness.

Foster Care and Out-of-Home Placement

An examination of the living situations of incarcerated girls prior to detention provides additional insight into another dimension of their family situations. In a study of girls' living situations prior to incarceration in the California Youth Authority, Owen and Bloom (1997) found that 40.6 percent lived with a parent or guardian, 12.3 percent with a spouse or partner, 11.8 percent with a grandparent or other relative, and 9.9 percent with a friend or roommate. An additional 9.8 percent reported living alone or in a program, and 9.9 percent reported having no permanent address or being homeless.

Statistics of public juvenile facilities indicate that 69,075 juveniles were in residential custody in 1995. California had the highest number, 19,567, 28 percent of the nation's total (Poe-Yamagata & Butts, 1996). A study by the ACA (1990) indicated that over half (54 percent) of juvenile females in detention indicated that they lived with parents or grandparents prior to their incarceration.

The increase in the number of juvenile girls committing certain categories of delinquent acts has resulted in more out-of-home placements. On the national level, the increase in the number of girls and young women involved in person offenses (e.g., homicide, robbery, aggravated assault, simple assault), which resulted in out-of-home placement, is nearly twice that of boys (Poe-Yamagata & Butts, 1996). The California Department of Social Services (1998) reports that approximately 5 percent of the 100,000 youth in out-of-home placement are referrals from probation.

Data from the California Department of Social Services (1998) also provides information on the numbers and reasons for removal from the home for girls and boys ages 10 through18 during 1997. In 1997, 26,004 boys and 25,038 girls were removed from their homes. The vast majority of both boys and girls were removed for neglect (boys 36 percent; girls 39 percent) and physical/sexual abuse (boys 13 percent; girls 20 percent). Only 4 percent of the girls and 17 percent of the boys were removed for law violations.

Family Dysfunction, Substance Abuse, Physical and Sexual Abuse

Research has consistently shown childhood abuse and neglect and family disruption to be significant factors related to female delinquency (ACA, 1990; Calhoun et al., 1993; Chesney-Lind, 1995; Daniel, 1994; Minnesota Advisory Task Force on the Female Offender in Corrections, 1994; Robinson, 1994; Schwartz, Willis, & Battle, 1991). Childhood abuse and family dysfunction manifest themselves in a variety of ways, including physical and sexual abuse, physical neglect, lack of supervision, and emotional maltreatment. In addition, there may be negative role modeling by one or both substance-abusing parents, with the presence of drugs within the home contributing to an unsafe environment from which girls attempt to escape by running away.

Family dysfunction is another characteristic in the lives of female delinquents. Parenting styles tended to be chaotic and inconsistent, and youths were victims of abuse and neglect. Positive feedback and nurturance from parents were noticeably lacking. Nearly 40 percent of the mothers of the CYA wards in the 1960s had been charged with child abuse and/or neglect, some within the first six months of their daughter's life (Rosenbaum, 1989). This proportion was even higher by the 1990s, when two-thirds of the wards interviewed reported that they were victims of child abuse or emotional abuse by a family member (Owen & Bloom, 1997). Nearly one-half reported that they were victims of sexual abuse, and over one-third had experienced sexual assault by peers or a stranger. Over half of the wards in the 1960s were mothers themselves by the time they left CYA. For the most part, they lacked the supports and resources needed to raise children and cope with their environment.

Research has shown that girls respond differently than boys to family dysfunction. For example, Dornfeld and Kruttschnitt (1992) found that marital discord, marital stability, and change influence the lives of boys and girls differently. These responses were not limited to gender stereotypes, however. The study found only minimal support for a commonly held hypothesis that in response to a given stressful event, boys act out and girls internalize their feelings. Girls and young women residing with an unmarried parent for a prolonged period of time were more likely than boys to report having used alcohol. Males were more likely than females to appear depressed and anxious as a result of divorce. The study results suggest that marital dissolution places boys at risk for depression and girls for delinquency.

Childhood abuse and neglect play a significant role in girls' involvement in the juvenile justice system, especially if the abuse occurs within the family (Dembo, Schmeidler, Sue, Bordon, & Manning, 1995; Dembo, Williams & Schmeidler, 1993). The resulting problem behaviors are often related to these traumatic home events and can include sexual acting out, often in defiance of parents and guardians. Dembo et al. (1995) describe this as a representation of "culturally conditioned expression of aggression against society" (p. 88). The interpersonal problems and corresponding coping behaviors (e.g., running away, sexual promiscuity) of girls result in status offenses and adjustment problems (e.g., dropping out of school) rather than delinquent behavior.

According to Kelley, Thornberry, and Smith (1997), childhood maltreatment is a significant, high predictor of all types of delinquent behavior; and the seriousness or violence level of delinquency increases with the severity of maltreatment experienced. Official records of delinquent behavior show a 13 percent higher rate for maltreated youth than for those without such a history (Kelley et al., 1997). In addition to serious delinquent behavior and violence, childhood maltreatment was found to be strongly correlated with teen pregnancy, drug use, lower school performance, and mental health problems.

Research data consistently point to a strong link between abuse and juvenile female delinquency (ACA, 1990; Culross, 1997; Girls Inc., 1996; Miller et al., 1995). Although boys have a greater risk of emotional neglect and serious physical injury from abuse, girls are sexually abused three to four times more often than boys but have a lower risk of emotional neglect and serious physical injury than boys (Kilpatrick & Saunders, 1997; Sedlak & Broadhurst, 1996). Victimization starts at an early age. For girls, sexual abuse starts earlier and lasts longer than abuse of boys and is more likely to be perpetrated by a family member.

As many as two-thirds to three-fourths of delinquent girls report a history of sexual abuse, and 60 percent of young women involved in the juvenile justice system report physical abuse (ACA, 1990; Chesney-Lind, 1989; Chesney-Lind & Shelden, 1992). Owen and Bloom's 1997 study of girls in the California Youth Authority found that 85 percent indicated abuse of some type during their lives. Another study by the ACA (1990) found that 47 percent of girls reporting physical abuse indicated that they were abused ten or more times. Over half (54 percent) of girls who told someone that they were being abused indicated that reporting it made things worse, or at best, the abuse continued with no change. Only 25 percent of girls who reported abuse to someone indicated that the abuse stopped (ACA, 1990).

Often, abuse in the home prompts adolescent girls to run away, which is one of the most prevalent risk factors for girls' involvement in the juvenile justice system. The high incidence of runaway incidents bears a closer look, as this survival strategy may lead to incarceration (Calhoun et al., 1993; Chesney-Lind, 1995). Girls and young women often run away, not only to escape abuse but also to protect family relationships. Often, they believe that they somehow deserved, encouraged, or invited abuse; and running away and the subsequent delinquent survival behaviors are easier to deal with than feelings of complicity in their own abuse.

Actual arrest rates show that girls and boys run away from home in about equal numbers, but parents and police may respond differently to the same behavior. Parents may be more likely to call the police when their daughters do not come home, and police may be more likely to arrest a female than a male runaway (Chesney-Lind, 1997).

Chesney-Lind (1997) describes the situation of girls who repeatedly run away to escape physical or sexual abuse, and subsequently engaging in street crime to survive. "Some girls resort to panhandling and shoplifting, other theft for money, food, and clothes. Some exchange sex for these necessities and become involved in prostitution and drug abuse. Girls' situations often are worsened by patriarchal law enforcement and justice systems that require girls to obey parents and stay at home. In many cases girls are sent back to their victimizers. Even when taken out of their homes, courts have few placement alternatives for girls and sometimes are left only with returning them home" (p. 5).

Once a girl is on the street, her exposure to other risk factors is increased. A study by Iwamoto, Kameoka, and Brasseur (1990) of homeless youth in Waikiki, about half of whom were girls, revealed that their most urgent needs are housing, jobs, and medical services. Exposure to violence is greatly increased for homeless adolescents, who are also more likely to suffer from poor nutrition, sexual exploitation, and exposure to human immunodeficiency virus (HIV) infection and sexually transmitted diseases (Deisher & Rogers, 1991). Because runaways are out of school, they are also at risk for arrest for truancy, and their educational advancement opportunities are affected.

Many abused girls who are picked up for status offenses such as running away or being truant are returned to the abusive home environment—the runaway girl is seen as the problem; while the parents' problems, including physical and sexual abuse, are not discovered. For many years these girls' accounts of abuse were ignored, and they were institutionalized in detention centers and training schools inappropriately as delinquents. If group homes or other out-of-home placement options are lacking or full, judges have no alternative but to keep girls in secure facilities until placement becomes available. Placement in secure detention facilities may be inappropriate given the circumstances that led to their running away (Anderson, 1994). Furthermore, research indicates that many workers in the juvenile justice system lack experience with and knowledge about sexual abuse (Baines & Alder, 1996). Thus, even though it is widely recognized that most girls entering the juvenile justice system have been sexually abused, the workers in the system may be ill prepared to respond appropriately to this issue.

Resiliency Factors

Grossman, Beinashowitz, and Anderson (1992) noted that cohesion and communication with a mother were important predictors of resiliency and delinquency avoidance for both boys and girls. Collectively, the findings of these authors concluded that although girls and boys respond differently to family events, the responses couldn't be predicted along gender lines.

Ideally, youth would acquire resiliency traits at home. However, they can also be learned and reinforced outside the home. Other external factors, besides the involvement of a caring adult, can help youth to increase their resiliency. Benard (1991) cited positive and high expectations of the youth from adults and others around them, and opportunities for meaningful involvement within the school, family, or community as important factors. Brooks (1994) believes that it is important for adults to help children build on their current skills and abilities, or *islands of competence* (i.e., areas that are, or could be, sources of pride and accomplishment), as a way of helping them to take pride in themselves, thereby increasing their resiliency. By taking a strength-based perspective of youth, the focus becomes one of assisting youth in developing support systems and skills that will help them meet their needs and overcome difficulties (Brendtro & Ness, 1995).

Specific resiliency factors in any given case often depend on the particular context of the person's life and are related to other factors. For young people, a key factor is the presence of a caring adult with whom the youth has developed a significant relationship based on trust and mutual respect. Such persons could be a parent or primary caregiver, but other family members, teachers, and members of the community can also fill this role.

Families that encourage connectedness and child centeredness provide positive role models and social messages regarding risky behaviors such as drug and alcohol abstinence. Access to services such as drug and alcohol treatment, and parenting and family management skills, can positively affect the nurturance factor within troubled families.

INDIVIDUAL AND PEER RISK AND RESILIENCY FACTORS

Hawkins, Catalano, and Miller (1992) have identified two categories of risk factors for adolescents: broad societal, cultural, and contextual factors, which provide legal and normative expectations for behaviors, and factors found within the individuals and their interpersonal environments (e.g., families, schools, and peer groups). Contextual factors include laws and norms favorable to the availability of drugs and alcohol, and extreme economic deprivation and neighborhood disorganization. Individual and interpersonal factors include physiological factors, family alcohol and drug behavior and attitudes, poor or inconsistent family management, family conflict, low bonding to the family, early and persistent problem behaviors, academic failure and poor school commitment, peer rejection in elementary grades, association with drug-using peers, alienation and rebelliousness, attitudes favorable to drug use, and early onset of drug use (Hawkins et al., 1992).

Substance Abuse

Studies of juveniles in the criminal justice system reveal higher rates of illicit drug use than that of adolescents among the general population (Rolf, Nanda, Baldwin, Chandra, & Thompson, 1990; Sigda & Martin, 1996, in Monahan, 1997). Substance abuse plays a role in how girls engage in delinquent behavior in two ways. First, if a girl comes from a family in which one or both parents are substance abusers, she may feel the need to run away from a home in which substance abuse is prevalent. Alternatively, she may stay in the home and take advantage of the lack of parental supervision due to substance abuse by violating curfews or skipping school. Second, girls who have been victims of physical and/or sexual abuse may turn to drugs or alcohol as a way to "self-medicate" and block out the trauma of the abuse. By turning to drugs and alcohol, girls put themselves at risk for arrest (Dembo, Williams & Fagan, 1994).

The vast majority of runaway and homeless youth in Los Angeles reported substance use during the preceding month (Young, Gardner, & Lopez, 1997). In a study of San Francisco teenagers, Shorter, Schaffner, Shick, and Frappier (1997) identify ways in which older drug dealers recruit runaway girls to handle street sales. Young girls, often girlfriends of older dealers, are convinced to take the risks of dealing because they will probably face lighter consequences if caught. Drug use, especially crack cocaine, affects girls who become prostitutes by increasing their risk of contracting sexually transmitted diseases and HIV, and, if they are mothers, losing their children to the foster care system.

Some of the risk factors for adolescent females' involvement in alcohol and drug use identified by Bodinger-de Uriarte, Austin, and Thomas (1991, p. 29) are early alcohol and drug use; parents, especially mothers, are alcohol and drug abusers; victims of physical and/or sexual abuse; poor family and school bonds; unconcerned with traditional feminine norms; numerous social opportunities for alcohol and drug use; poor self-concept, especially with physical appearance; difficulties coping with stress and life events, especially in the areas of dating and sexual activity; and involvement in other problem behaviors. Childhood exposure to violence, sexual abuse, and physical maltreatment lead to an increased likelihood of drug and alcohol problems for girls later in life (Rosenbaum & Murphy 1995).

The ACA (1990) study of female juveniles in detention reported the types of substances abused included alcohol (59 percent), marijuana (50 percent), and cocaine (20 percent). Over half reported abusing more than one type of substance. A recent study of 668 adolescents detained in juvenile facilities in 13 California counties found that of the 78 females in the study, 69 percent reported alcohol use and 70 percent reported tobacco use in the 30 days prior to the interview (Monahan, Gil-Rivas, Danila, & Anglin, submitted). Thirty-one percent of the 67 females who agreed to be tested for illicit drugs were positive for at least one drug (marijuana, amphetamines, and cocaine), and 10.4 percent tested positive for two or more drugs (Monahan et al., submitted). Owen and Bloom's study (1997) of 162 female CYA wards found evidence of significant, widespread drug use among this population. The study found the mean age for first use of alcohol was 11 years old. Eighty-three percent of the respondents indicated drug use at age 14 or younger, with half using before they were 12, and 70 percent by age 13. About 15 percent reported use of three or more illegal substances during their youth.

Victimization

A history of victimization is often a precursor to involvement in the juvenile justice system. According to data from the National Crime Victimization Survey and the Federal Bureau of Investigation, females 12 to19 years old have higher rates of violent victimization (murder, sexual and physical assault, robbery) than do females in any other age group (Craven, 1997). Homicide is the second-leading cause of death for females 15 to 19 years old (Anderson, Kochinek & Murphy, 1996). A study of intentional injury in a primary care pediatric setting found that 10 percent of injuries to adolescent females resulted from violence in dating relationships and 45 percent were inflicted by other adolescent girls (Sege, Stigol, Perry, Goldstein, & Spivak, 1996). Another study found that 31 percent of girls interviewed had been in a physical fight in the past 12 months (Kann et al., 1996). National data indicate that adolescents are nearly three times as likely as adults to be victims of violent crimes (Sickmund, Snyder, & Poe-Yamagata, 1997).

Delinquent Peer Factors and Gangs

The significance of peer influence cannot be underestimated. A socialization process centered on peer relationships and experimentation, generally through joining and participating in groups, characterizes adolescence. The role of delinquent peer relationships in encouraging delinquency and how a young person associates or avoids association with delinquent peers has been examined (Agnew, 1993; Snyder, Dishion, and Patterson, 1986; Thornberry, Krohn, Lizotte, & Chard-Wierschem, 1993; Warr, 1993).

Association with delinquent peers often leads to gang membership or association that puts youth at risk for engaging in criminal activities. Little is known about whether gangs attract adolescents who are already highly delinquent or whether they create highly delinquent adolescents as a part of the gang process (Thornberry et al., 1993). The fact remains that gang members are significantly more likely to engage in delinquent behaviors than are nongang members (Esbensen, Huizinga, & Wieher, 1993). Thornberry et al. (1993) agree and add that gang participation is a more important factor in predicting delinquency than is the type of person who is being recruited into the gang.

There is little research on the role of delinquent peers that is specific to girls and young women. Female gangs are typically viewed as extensions of male gang membership. However, studies have found that between 10 and 46 percent of gang members are female (Campbell, 1991; Esbensen et al., 1993; Esbensen & Winfree, 1996; Fagan, 1990; Moore, 1991). Esbensen and Deschenes (1997) attribute the wide range of estimates to the fact that most studies have been ethnographic rather than quantitative in design and have tended to focus on adult women rather than adolescent girls.

Several studies suggest that females join gangs in an attempt to escape the reality of being victims of poverty (Fagan, 1996; Hagedorn, 1988; Vigil, 1988; Wilson, 1987). Thus the potential for gang involvement is heightened for marginalized girls, where lack of education, employment opportunities, and lives of poverty leave them with few resources or alternatives. These studies describe the lives of these girls as characterized by instability, exposure to violence in the home and community, fear of abuse, and the experience of watching other family members, especially their mothers, being victimized. These multiple factors heighten the need for attachment and a sense of belonging for marginalized girls and young women that can lead to gang involvement. At-risk young women tend to be isolated from society and alienated from social institutions (Felkenes & Becker, 1995). Consequently, they drop out of school at an early age and engage in violent or other criminal behavior, including gang membership.

Esbensen and Deschenes (1997) have identified other differences between female gang and nongang members. Compared to other girls, the female gang members are less committed to school, more inclined to report limited opportunities, more socially isolated, and less likely to disapprove of and feel guilty for violent behavior. Girls in gangs who engage in violent crime appear to have low social control and to learn the criminal behavior from their peers. They are more likely than nongang girls to have lower self-esteem and higher levels of risk seeking and impulsivity.

Sexual Activity and Maturity

Traditionally, female delinquency has been equated with female sexuality. Patriarchal society has made a concerned effort to control female sexuality, both socially and legally. This has fostered a double standard: boys are expected to explore and "sow wild oats," while girls are expected to remain chaste (Belknap, 1996; Girls Inc., 1996).

Young women are not only monitored and controlled vis-à-vis their sexuality but also by their physical appearance. A study by Rosenbaum and Chesney-Lind (1994) found that male intake personnel at the California Youth Authority noted physical appearance in terms of cultural standards. This was particularly the case if the girl had a charge of "immorality" on her record. Physical attractiveness was least likely to be noted for girls detained for serious offenses.

Early physical development may be linked to engagement in delinquency among some girls (Caspi, Lyman, & Moffit 1993). Girls who mature early may be more vulnerable to peer pressure because others attribute greater social maturity to them than is warranted by their chronological age. Thus these girls tend to associate with older peer groups. Furthermore, the onset of puberty adds pressures for entering into relationships with boys. As a result, girls who mature early may feel the need to engage in delinquent acts to impress boys, or alternatively, they may join delinquent peer groups, such as gangs, to have greater access to boys. Also, girls who have been physically or sexually abused have earlier and higher rates of sexual activity and are more likely to have multiple partners and engage in a wider range of sexual behaviors (Levitt, 1994).

Teen Pregnancy and Parenting

During the past two decades the United States experienced a dramatic increase in the number of teenagers becoming pregnant (Rosenberg, Ventura, & Maurer, 1996). Levitt (1994) found that over 1 million of the estimated 11 million sexually active teenage girls in the United States will become pregnant every year. Teen mothers are disproportionately poor young women of color. Black and Latina teenagers are 67 percent more likely to get pregnant than are white teens (Levitt, 1994). Teen pregnancy and related child care responsibilities account for approximately 47 percent of girls who drop out of school. Dropouts who do not receive a high school diploma lack many of the necessary life skills to survive in the world (Chesney-Lind & Shelden, 1992). Davidson's (1983) survey of teenage mothers found that approximately 90 percent receive no financial aid from the fathers of their children.

Unintentional pregnancy is a major risk factor for juvenile female offenders (Monahan, (1997). Data from a survey of 430 juvenile facilities found that 68 percent had one to four pregnant teens among their correctional population at any time, despite the fact that they could not provide adequate prenatal care services for high-risk pregnancies (Breuner & Farrow, 1995).

Health

According to Monahan (1997), the physical and mental health needs of adolescents have only recently been a source of concern within the juvenile justice system. Historically, resources were used primarily to support the health needs of males, who constitute the majority of the juvenile offender population. As a result, little information is available regarding the physical and mental health needs of female delinquents, a small but growing and important subpopulation of juveniles at risk for serious health-related problems. The lack of access to health care is a significant risk factor for marginalized girls and young women.

A study of 156 randomly selected juvenile offenders in the King County Youth Facility in Seattle, Washington identified the following acute and chronic health problems among them: asthma and other respiratory illnesses, seizure disorders, allergies, diabetes, sexually transmitted diseases, conditions associated with stress and trauma, poor nutritional status and obesity, dermatological problems, and dental cavities (Farrow, 1991). "Chronic health conditions are common and have often gone untreated prior to entry in the juvenile justice system" (Owens, 1991, in Monahan, 1997, p. 3). Few had received a physical or dental examination within the past two years and a majority (83 percent) had a lifetime history of treatment in an emergency room for a traumatic injury (Farrow, 1991).

Monahan (1997) found that the majority of girls in correctional settings have gone without primary health care during their lifetime and suffer from preventable and/or treatable health problems (e.g., inadequate nutrition, dental caries, and asthma). As stated elsewhere, many female offenders come from low-income urban communities. Young female offenders are also exposed to high levels of violence associated with gang involvement, weapons possession, and other delinquent activities prevalent in their communities (Ash, Kellermann, Fuqua-Whitley, & Johnson, 1996; Rhodes & Fischer, 1993).

Numerous studies have documented higher-than-average risk behaviors and levels of sexually transmitted diseases (STDs) among incarcerated youth and a correlation between the level of substance abuse and these behaviors (Alexander-Rodriguez & Vermund, 1987; Boudov, 1997; Canterbury et al., 1995; McCabe, Jaffe, & Diaz, 1993; Morris, Baker, & Huscroft, 1992; Rolf, Nanda, Baldwin, Chandra, & Thompson, 1990; Shew & Fortenberry, 1992; Wood & Shoroye, 1993).

Monahan et al. (submitted) asked 78 adolescent female arrestees for information related to sexual activity for the 30 days prior to their interviews. About half of the females indicated that they had sex while under the influence of drugs or alcohol. The majority of respondents (86 percent) had been sexually active and had used condoms inconsistently or not at all (73 percent), with over half of females reporting that they had two or more sexual partners, and 14 percent having contracted a sexually transmitted disease at some time in the past.

With a higher-than-average risk for HIV infection, another study of 113 incarcerated males and females revealed that they had less knowledge of preventive strategies for HIV and reported high rates of HIV risk behaviors than did a comparison group of students attending a public high school (DiClemente, Lanier, Horan, & Lodico, 1991). Despite the elevated risk for HIV and STDs among juveniles in detention, HIV has not yet become as widespread as other STDs among this population. A review of available information on results of HIV testing of confined juveniles resulted in less than 1 percent testing positive (Widom & Hammett, 1996).

Mental Health

The developmental tasks faced by females during puberty, including understanding and coping with menarche, adjusting to ongoing physical, psychological, and social changes, and exploring their sexual identity contribute to the risk for mental health disorders (Woods, 1995). Juvenile female offenders are exposed to additional levels of stress and other threats to their ability to cope with and meet the tasks associated with normal psychological and social development, including childhood abuse (Hutchinson, 1992). Early sexual exploitation is associated with disturbances in self-esteem and self-concept, the development of high-risk behaviors, academic failure, and the inability to establish and maintain healthy relationships in adulthood (Hutchinson, 1992). In addition to abuse and neglect, many adolescents have been exposed to physical violence, such as witnessing assaults against their mothers, other family members, or other people within their surrounding communities (Dembo, Williams, Wothke, Schmeidler, & Brown, 1992; Lake, 1993).

Psychopathology, particularly depression, among female juvenile offenders has been reported by numerous researchers (Armistead, Wierson, Forehand, & Frame, 1992; Milin, Halikas, Meller, & Morse, 1991). Unlike males, who tend to express depression externally by aggression or other forms of acting-out behaviors, females are more likely to become socially isolated or engage in self-destructive behaviors (Dembo et al., 1993).

Several studies have documented mental health disorders are more common in juvenile justice facilities than among the general population (Greenbaum, Foster-Johnson, & Petrila, 1996; Melton & Pagliocca, 1992; Myers, Burket, Lyles, Stone & Kemph, 1990; Otto, Greenstein, Johnson, & Friedman, 1992; Rottenberg, 1996, 1997). Mental health problems are present for between 10 percent and 60 percent of the referrals. Among incarcerated adolescents there is a high incidence of conduct disorder, but more females than males diagnosed with both antisocial and borderline personality disorders (Eppright, Kashani, Robinson, & Reid, 1993).

Trauma.   As a result of abuse, neglect, and exposure to violence, research has indicated that many juvenile female offenders suffer from undiagnosed and untreated posttraumatic stress disorder (PTSD), which, without treatment, may have long-term adverse effects (Steiner, Garcia, & Matthews, 1997; Vermund, Alexander-Rodriguez, Macleod, & Kelley, 1990). Posttraumatic stress disorder has been linked to maladaptive behaviors such as delinquency, drug use, and increased sexual activity. A study by Waterman (1997) of 42 girls and young women in the California Youth Authority found that 52 percent suffered from PTSD secondary to some form of abuse; a greater rate than those of girls from other environments and boys from the same environment. Many of the subjects had been exposed to family and community violence.

Suicide.   Contributors to adolescent suicide include feelings of helplessness and hopelessness, loneliness, impulsivity, the lack of a stable environment, and increased external and internal stressors. Davis, Bean, Schumacher, and Stringer (1991) found that 13.5 percent of adolescents had a history of suicide attempts and 21.3 percent had made threats, indicating high rates of suicidal risk factors among adolescent detention populations.

A national study by the ACA (1989) found 57 percent of female juveniles in detention had attempted suicide, the majority of whom exhibited symptoms of depression. Only 22 percent indicated that they had received mental health services. Mental health problems can be exacerbated by the social isolation associated with incarceration (Hutchinson, 1992; Mitchell & Varley, 1990; Parent et al., 1994). When girls and young women are confined in detention facilities, detention staff often lack the experience and training needed to provide appropriate services for the mental health needs of this population (Baines & Alder, 1996). The ACA (1989) found only 355 juvenile facilities contracted for psychological services for detainees. Thirty percent of juvenile detention facilities reported the need for substance abuse treatment for detainees, indicating that between 60 and 80 percent of juvenile females required substance abuse treatment at intake. The ACA study also found that 41 percent of juvenile detainees indicated that the type of help they felt they needed most during their first detention was psychological counseling, followed by drug counseling (19 percent). Of those who received program services during detention, 35 percent indicated that the program that helped them most was mental health counseling.

National correctional and public health associations have recently recognized the need for reform within the juvenile health services system (ACA, 1989; American Medical Association, 1984; Child Welfare League of America and the American Academy of Pediatrics, 1988; Dubler, 1986; National Commission on Correctional Health Care, 1992). Although improved health care standards are widely supported, inadequate resources frequently inhibit or delay their implementation (Owens, 1991). A national study of juvenile detention facilities by the Office of Juvenile Justice and Delinquency Prevention reported that (1) the majority of adolescents were not receiving a full assessment within one hour of admission as set forth in national standards, (2) fewer than one-fifth of the adolescents had such an assessment within one week, (3) one-third of the adolescents were screened by unqualified staff, (4) approximately one-fourth had no access to tuberculosis screening, (5) fewer than half had access to screening for sexually transmitted diseases, and (6) many institutions did not provide sufficient staff to monitor suicidal youth adequately (Parent et al., 1994). Notification of medical staff prior to release of juveniles can assure that necessary treatment has been provided or arrangements are made for follow-up in the community. However, in many facilities, adolescents are frequently discharged without this being done (Thompson, 1992).

Juvenile facility health services have been described as deficient in many areas (American Medical Association, 1990; Anno, 1984; Bazemore & McKean, 1992; Brown, 1993; Farrow, 1991; Office of Juvenile Justice and Delinquency Prevention, 1996). Monahan (1997) found that the health care services provided to adolescent and young adult women in detention settings is episodic and often does not include health promotion or prevention. The American Academy of Pediatrics (1989) conducted a study of medical services in 79 juvenile facilities and found that the majority were below community standards in health assessment, physical examinations, care provided by staff during "sick calls," and screening for mental health problems. The study noted that many correctional health professionals held low opinions of the adolescents under their care, sometimes violating patients' rights to privacy during examinations and treatments, or interpreted complaints as manipulative or malingering behaviors, which could result in unnecessary delays in providing care.

The deficiencies found in juvenile health services may be related to the fact that facility staff are often not adequately trained to intervene in the multiple and complex risk behaviors commonly found among the youth in their care (Alexander-Rodriguez & Vermund, 1987; Dembo, 1996). Professional staff training and support within juvenile health services has been described as below standard and in need of reform (Feinstein, 1992; Jameson, 1989).

Although deficiencies in the quality of care provided to adolescent females and inadequate training of correctional staff to intervene on their behalf can unintentionally cause harm, some correctional policies and procedures perpetrate harm directly. These include the use of social isolation as a sanction, which can exacerbate stress and anxiety and contribute to self-destructive behaviors; and the danger of sexual assault by staff or other detainees (Chesney-Lind & Rodriguez, 1983; Faith, 1993). Excessive and improper use of physical restraints while in custody is another harmful practice that can result in psychological trauma and physical injury (Mitchell & Varley, 1990). Other potentially harmful medical practices include standing orders for delousing, body cavity searches for drugs or other prohibited items, and the use of sedatives for behavior control and exposure to communicable diseases such as tuberculosis (American Academy of Pediatrics, 1989; Owens, 1992).

Resiliency Factors

Aspects of a person's personality can make them more resilient to stressors and better able to avoid participation in delinquent behaviors. For instance, resilient people "see obstacles as something that can be overcome, endured, or changed; persevere in finding ways to improve situations; develop a range of strategies and skills to address a situation; and have a broad range of interest and goals" (Scott, 1994, p. 5). Benard (1991) identified resiliency factors that include social competence, problem-solving ability, autonomy, and a sense of purpose and belief in the future. Certain community and individual factors can protect against the adverse effects of exposure to violence (Osofsky, 1996). These include access to a supportive adult, having a safe place in the neighborhood that is protected from violence, and having the individual resources to find alternatives to violence.

With a focus on youth development, individual resilience/protective factors incorporate positive self-concept and gender identification with feelings of competency, spirituality, healthy risk taking, and adaptability. Girls with strong verbal skills, who are willing to articulate and discuss issues and explore creative solutions, including developing their own support systems, are especially resilient. As their own self-concept grows, these young women are more able to incorporate an awareness of social norms and their intuitive ability to "read the scene" into their repertoire of survival skills. Their ability to explore multiple options, make plans, and accept responsibility for the outcome of those plans is enhanced.

PROMISING PROGRAM COMPONENTS

Programming for girls and young women needs to be shaped by their unique situations. In other words, programs and services should be gender-specific. Girls Inc. (1996) describes gender-specific services for young women as those designed "to meet the unique needs of female offenders; that value the female perspective; that celebrate and honor the female experience; that respect and take into account female development; and that empower young women to reach their full potential" (p. 24). However, Bloom (1997) notes that specific direction on how to achieve these objectives is not readily apparent from the existing literature. Historically, research, programs, and treatment have been based on the male experience, and often neglect women's needs. Effective programming for girls and women should be shaped by and tailored to their unique situations and problems. To do this, there is a need to develop a theoretical approach to treatment that is gender sensitive and addresses the realities of girls' and young women's lives (Bloom, 1997).

Austin, Bloom, and Donahue (1992) identified promising programs and intervention strategies for supervising female offenders in the community. Austin et al. (1992) found that "promising community programs combined supervision and services to address the specialized needs of female offenders in highly structured, safe environments where accountability is stressed" (p. 21). Austin et al. stated that promising programs often use an *empowerment model*, in which skills are developed to allow women to gain independence and multidimensional strategies that address specific women's needs (e.g., substance abuse, parenting, relationships, gender bias, domestic violence, and sexual abuse).

Bloom (1997) argues for rigorous evaluation to measure the effectiveness of gender-specific interventions in terms of client outcomes, given the fact that information on the long-term effectiveness of these gender-specific strategies is nonexistent. This would allow researchers to move away from impressionistic data and toward empirically based documentation of program effectiveness.

Appropriate services for girls and young women must have multiple components that address the complex issues that adolescent females face. They consist of educational opportunities, employment and vocational training, placement options, and mental and physical health services, all of which must be delivered in a culturally sensitive manner. Bloom (1997) discusses the need to incorporate the idea of females' sense of self, which manifests and develops differently in female-specific groups as opposed to coed groups; and how the unique needs and issues (e.g., physical/sexual emotional victimization, trauma, pregnancy and parenting) of women and girls can be addressed in a safe, trusting, and supportive female-focused environment.

Covington (1998) argues for a holistic approach to develop gender-specific services for this population. An approach based on relational theory would incorporate "physical, psychological, emotional, spiritual, and sociopolitical issues" (p. 18), including theories of treatment of addiction and trauma. A holistic model of treatment should include a comprehensive case management approach along a continuum of care, ranging from community-based prevention, intervention, and treatment to aftercare. This continuum could include residential and day treatment as well as other female-focused inpatient or outpatient services.

Girls Inc. (1996) describes essential elements for effective prevention programs for juvenile females. First, juvenile females should have employment and vocational training that presents a wide array of career opportunities and is not constrained by gender stereotypes. In addition, girls should be provided with adequate and appropriate physical and mental health care, accurate information about sex, eating disorders, HIV and acquired immunodeficiency syndrome (AIDS), and strategies on how to protect themselves from sexual, physical, and substance abuse. Finally, girls and young women need access to opportunities where they can feel safe to explore and learn from each other about the issues they face as young women.

The Girls Inc. (1996) study also stresses that early intervention programs could help girls resolve many of the problems that place them at risk for engaging in delinquent behavior. The study suggests that almost every girl would benefit from good prevention programs that help them acquire the skills, knowledge, and values that promote health, happiness, and productivity. Furthermore, early intervention programs could address risk factors for juvenile delinquency, such as alcohol and drug use, school problems, abuse, and association with delinquent peers.

Belknap, Holsinger, and Dunn (1997) describe key issues from a series of focus groups with delinquent girl detainees, which are important to consider when identifying components for promising gender-specific interventions. For these girls and young women, the important issues are gaining and keeping respect and counseling to address traumatic experiences. Many express concerns on how they will "make it" once they were released.

Researchers agree that the most effective approaches should be holistic, client-centered, and empowering (Austin et al., 1992; Chesney-Lind & Shelden, 1992; Greene, Peters & Associates, 1997; Mayer, 1995). Responses should employ a strengths-based approach rather than attempting to "cure" the client of pathology.

Bloom (1997) argues that treatment should be based on a theory of female psychological development emphasizing the centrality of relationships, connectedness, and mutuality as fundamental aspects of healthy, growth-promoting relationships. Treatment and services should build on girls' and women's strengths/competencies and avoid focusing on their deficiencies. Cultural awareness and sensitivity should be promoted, and the cultural resources and strengths in various communities should be utilized. Female development should be addressed within a context of race, class, gender, and sexual orientation. Female physical and mental health and wellness should be promoted, including raising awareness about HIV/AIDS, STDs, eating disorders, family planning, nutrition, relaxation, and exercise. Educational and vocational training opportunities should be commensurate with girls' and women's interests and abilities so as to garner their potential (including traditional and nontraditional career options). Program staff should be representative in terms of gender, race/ethnicity, and sexual orientation. She suggests that girls and women can benefit from mentors from their particular communities who exemplify survival and growth, as well as resistance and change.

As the information above indicates, there is a growing body of research and program information available that speaks to the issues and situation of at-risk girls and young women. Program developers and service providers should consider the multidimensional issues faced by girls and young women and develop a multidisciplinary response. To do this, policymakers must take into consideration the need to bridge systems and coordinate a variety of public- and private-sector resources.

ACKNOWLEDGMENTS

This research was supported by Grant 96-JF-FX-0006 from the California Office of Criminal Justice Planning (OCJP). The opinions, findings, and conclusions in this report are those of the authors and not necessarily those of OCJP.

REFERENCES AND BIBLIOGRAPHY

ACOCA, L. (1999, October). Investing in girls: A 21st century strategy. *Juvenile Justice, 6*(1).

ADLER, F. (1975). *Sisters in crime: The rise of the new female criminal*. New York: McGraw-Hill.

AGNEW, R. (1993). Why do they do it? An examination of the intervening mechanisms between social control variables and delinquency. *Journal of Research in Crime and Delinquency, 30*, 245–266.

ALEXANDER-RODRIGUEZ, T., & VERMUND, S. H. (1987). Gonorrhea and syphilis in incarcerated urban adolescents: Prevalence and physical signs. *Pediatrics, 80*, 561–564.

AMARO, H. (1995). Love, sex and power: Considering women's realities in HIV prevention. *American Psychologist, 50*(6), 437–447.

AMERICAN ACADEMY OF PEDIATRICS. (1989). Health care for children and adolescents in detention centers, jails, lock-ups, and other court-sponsored residential facilities. *Pediatrics, 84*, 1118–1120.

AMERICAN ASSOCIATION OF UNIVERSITY WOMEN. (1992). *How schools shortchange girls*. Washington, DC: AAUW.

AMERICAN ASSOCIATION OF UNIVERSITY WOMEN. (1998). *Separated by sex: A critical look at single-sex education for girls*. Washington, DC: AAUW.

AMERICAN CORRECTIONAL ASSOCIATION. (1989). *Certification standards for health care programs*. Laurel, MD: ACA.

AMERICAN CORRECTIONAL ASSOCIATION. (1990). *The female offender: What does the future hold?* Washington, DC: St. Mary's Press.

AMERICAN MEDICAL ASSOCIATION. (1984). *Standards for health services in juvenile correctional facilities*. Chicago: AMA.

AMERICAN MEDICAL ASSOCIATION. (1990). Health status of detained and incarcerated youths. *Journal of the American Medical Association, 263*, 987–991.

ANDERSON, G. (1994). Juvenile justice and the double standard. *America, 170*, 13–15.

ANDERSON, M. (1996) *Race, class and gender: Common bonds, different voices*. Thousand Oaks, CA: Sage Publications.

ANDERSON, R. N., KOCHINEK, K. D., & MURPHY, S. L. (1996). *Report of final mortality statistics, 1995*. Hyattsville, MD: National Center for Health Statistics.

ANNO, B. J. (1984). *The availability of health services for juvenile offenders: Preliminary results of a national survey*. Chicago: National Commission on Correctional Health Care.

ARMISTEAD, L., WIERSON, M., FOREHAND, R., & FRAME, C. (1992). Psychopathology in incarcerated juvenile delinquents: Does it extend beyond externalizing problems? *Adolescence, 27*, 309–314.

ASH, P., KELLERMANN, A. L., FUQUA-WHITLEY, D., & JOHNSON, A. (1996). Gun acquisition and use by juvenile offenders. *Journal of the American Medical Association, 275*, 1754–1758.

AUSTIN, J., BLOOM, B., & DONAHUE, T. (1992). *Female offenders in the community: An analysis of innovative strategies and programs*. Washington, DC: National Institute of Corrections.

BAINES, M., & ALDER, C. (1996). Are girls more difficult to work with? Youth workers perspectives in juvenile justice and related areas. *Crime and Delinquency, 42*, 467–485.

BAZEMORE, G., & MCKEAN, J. (1992). Minority overrepresentation. In L. S. Thompson & Farrow, J. A. (Eds.), *Hard time, healing hands: Developing primary health care services for incarcerated youth* (pp. 99–119). Arlington, VA: National Center for Education in Maternal and Child Health.

BELKNAP, J. (1996). *The invisible woman: Gender, crime, and justice.* Cincinnati, OH: Wadsworth Publishing.

BELKNAP, J. (1997). *Gender specific services workshop: A report to the governor.* Cincinnati, OH: University of Cincinnati.

BELKNAP, J., HOLSINGER, K., & DUNN, M. (1997). Understanding incarcerated girls: The results of a focus group study. *Prison Journal, 77,* 381–404.

BERNARD, B. (1991). *Fostering resiliency in kids: Protective factors in the family, school, and community.* San Francisco: Far West Laboratory for Educational Research and Development.

BLOOM, B. (1996). Triple jeopardy: Race, class, and gender as factors in women's imprisonment. Unpublished doctoral dissertation. University of California–Riverside.

BLOOM, B. (1997). Defining "gender-specific": What does it mean and why is it important? Paper presented at the National Institute of Corrections' Intermediate Sanctions for Women Offenders National Project Meeting, September 1997, Longmont, CO.

BODINGER-DE URIARTE, C., AUSTIN, G., & THOMAS, C. (1991). *Substance abuse among adolescent females.* Portland, WA: Western Regional Center for Drug-Free Schools and Communities, pp. 1–29.

BOUDOV, M. (1997). *Juvenile hall STD prevalence monitoring project: Progress report.* Los Angeles: Los Angeles County STD Program.

BRENDTRO, L., & NESS, A. (1996). Fixing flaws or building strengths? *National Educational Service Newsletter, 4.*

BREUNER, C. C., & FARROW, J. A. (1995). Pregnant teens in prison: Prevalence, management, and consequences. *Western Journal of Medicine, 162,* 328–330.

BRINDIS, C., PETERSON, S., & BROWN, S. (1997). *Complex terrain: Charting a course of action to prevent adolescent pregnancy: An analysis of California's policy landscape.* San Francisco: UCSF Center for Reproductive Health Policy Research.

BROOKS, R. B. (1994). Children at risk: Fostering resiliency and hope. *American Journal of Orthopsychiatry, 64,* 545–553.

BROWN, R. T. (1993). Health needs of incarcerated youth. *Bulletin of the New York Academy of Medicine, 70,* 208–218.

BUDNICK, K. J., & SHIELDS-FLETCHER, E. (1998). OJJDP Fact Sheet #84: What about girls? Washington, DC: U.S. Department of Justice.

CALHOUN, G., JURGENS, J., & CHEN, F. (1993). The neophyte female delinquent: A review of the literature. *Adolescence, 28,* 461–472.

CALIFORNIA DEPARTMENT OF FINANCE. (1993). *County population projections for 1996.* Sacramento, CA: CDF.

CALIFORNIA DEPARTMENT OF JUSTICE. (2001). *Adult and juvenile arrests reported, sex and law enforcement disposition by specific offense statewide: January through December 1999.* Sacramento, CA: California Department of Justice, Division of Law Enforcement, Law Enforcement Information Center.

CALIFORNIA DEPARTMENT OF SOCIAL SERVICES. (1998). *Foster care information system.* Sacramento, CA: Information Services Bureau.

CAMPBELL, A. (1991). *The girls in the gang* (2nd ed.). Cambridge, MA: Basil Blackwell.

CANTERBURY, R. J., McGARVEY, E. L., SHELDON-KELLER, A. E., WAITE, D., REAMS, P., & KOOPMAN, C. (1995). Prevalence of HIV-related risk behaviors and STDs among incarcerated adolescents. *Journal of Adolescent Health, 17,* 173–177.

CASPI, A., LYNAM, D., & MOFFITT, T. (1993). Unraveling girls' delinquency: Biological, dispositional and contextual contributions to adolescent misbehavior. *Developmental Psychology, 29,* 19–30.

CERNKOVICH, S., & GIORDANO, P. (1979a). Delinquency, opportunity and gender. *Journal of Criminal Law and Criminology, 70,* 141–151.

CERNKOVICH, S. & GIORDANO, P. (1979b). A comparative analysis of male and female delinquency. *Sociological Quarterly, 20,* 131–145.

CHESNEY-LIND, M. (1989). Girl's crime and women's place: Toward a feminist model of female delinquency. *Crime and Delinquency, 35*, 5–29.

CHESNEY-LIND, M. (1992). *Rethinking women's imprisonment: A critical examination of trends in female incarceration.* Unpublished manuscript. University of Hawaii at Manoa.

CHESNEY-LIND, M. (1995). Girls, delinquency, and juvenile justice: Towards a feminist theory of young women's crime. In B. Price & N. Sokoloff (Eds.), *The criminal justice system and women* (2nd ed., pp. 71–88). New York: McGraw-Hill.

CHESNEY-LIND, M. (1997). *Female offenders: girls, women and crime.* Thousand Oaks, CA: Sage Publications.

CHESNEY-LIND, M., & RODRIGUEZ, N. (1983). Women under lock and key. *Prison Journal, 63,* 47–65.

CHESNEY-LIND, M., & SHELDEN, R. (1992). *Girls, delinquency and juvenile justice.* Pacific Grove, CA: Brooks/Cole.

CHESNEY-LIND, M., & SHELDEN, R. (1998). *Girls, delinquency and juvenile justice* (2nd ed.). Belmont, CA: Wadsworth Publishing.

CHILD WELFARE LEAGUE OF AMERICA AND THE AMERICAN ACADEMY OF PEDIATRICS. (1988). *Standards for health care services for children in out-of-home care.* Washington, DC: Authors.

COMMUNITY RESEARCH ASSOCIATES. (1998). *Juvenile female offenders: A status of the states report.* Washington, DC: Office of Juvenile Justice and Delinquency Prevention.

COVINGTON, S. (1998). The relational theory of women's psychological development: Implications for the criminal justice system. In R. Zaplin (Ed.), *Female offenders: Critical issues and effective interventions* (pp. 113–131). Gaithersburg, MD: Aspen Publishers.

CRAVEN, D. (1997). *Sex differences in violent victimization* (NCJ-164508). Washington, DC: Bureau of Justice Statistics.

CULROSS, P. (1997). Relationships between victimization and offending among female adolescents. Background paper for OCJP Modeling Gender-Specific Services in Juvenile Justice: Policy and Program Recommendations Project.

DANIEL, M. (1994). *Models for change: National juvenile female offenders conference.* Laurel, MD: American Correctional Association, pp. 106–109.

DAVIDSON, S. (1983). *The second mile: Contemporary approaches to counseling young women.* Tucson, AZ: New Directions for Young Women.

DAVIS, D. L., BEAN, G. J., SCHUMACHER, J. E., & STRINGER, T. L. (1991). Prevalence of emotional disorders in a juvenile justice institutional population. *American Journal of Forensic Psychology, 9*, 1–13.

DEISHER, R. W., & ROGERS, W. M. (1991). The medical care of street youth. *Journal of Adolescent Health, 12*(7), 500–503.

DEMBO, R. (1996). Problems among youth entering the juvenile justice system: Their service needs and innovative approaches to address them. *Substance Use and Misuse, 31*, 81–94.

DEMBO, R., PACHECO, K., RAMIREZ-GARMICA, G., SCHMEIDLER, J., GUIDA, J., & RAHMAN, A. (1998). A further study of gender differences in service needs among youth entering a juvenile assessment center. *Journal of Child and Adolescent Substance Abuse, 7*(4), 49–77.

DEMBO, R., SCHMEIDLER, J., SUE, C., BORDEN, P., & MANNING, D. (1995). Gender differences in service needs among youth entering a juvenile assessment center: A replication study. *Journal of Correctional Health Care, 2*, 191–216.

DEMBO, R., WILLIAMS, L., & FAGON, J. (1994). Development and assessment of a classification of high risk youths. *Journal of Drug Issues, 24*, 25–53.

DEMBO, R., WILLIAMS, L., & SCHMEIDLER, J. (1993). Gender differences in mental health service needs among youths entering a juvenile detention center. *Journal of Prison and Jail Health, 12*, 73–101.

DEMBO, R., WILLIAMS, L., WOTHKE, W., SCHMEIDLER, J., & BROWN, C. H. (1992). The role of family factors, physical abuse, and sex victimization experiences in high-risk youths' alcohol and other drug use and delinquency: A longitudinal model. *Violence and Victims, 7*, 245–246.

DiCLEMENTE, R. J., LANIER, M. M., HORAN, P. F. & LODICO, M. (1991). Comparison of AIDS knowledge, attitudes, and behaviors among incarcerated adolescents and a public school sample in San Francisco. *American Journal of Public Health, 81*, 628–630.

DORNFELD, M., & KRUTTSCHNITT, C. (1992). Do the stereotypes fit? Mapping gender-specific outcomes and risk factors. *Criminology, 30*, 397–419.

DUBLER, N. N. (1986). *Standards for health services in correctional institutions* (2nd ed.). Washington, DC: American Public Health Association.

EPPRIGHT, T. D., KASHANI, J. H., ROBINSON, B. D., & REID, J. C. (1993). Co-morbidity of conduct disorder and personality disorders in an incarcerated juvenile population. *American Journal of Psychiatry, 150*, 1233–1236.

ESBENSEN, F., & DESCHENES, E. (1997). *Boys and girls in gangs: Are there gender differences in behavior and attitudes?* (Grant 94-IJ-CX-0058). Washington, DC: National Institute of Justice.

ESBENSEN, F., DESCHENES, E., & WINFREE, L. T., JR. (1998, March). Differences between gang girls and gang boys: Results of a multi-site survey. Paper presented at the annual meeting of the Academy of Criminal Justice Sciences, Alberquerque, NM.

ESBENSEN, F., & HUIZINGA, D. (1993). Gangs, drugs, and delinquency in a survey of urban youth. *Criminology, 3*, 565–589.

ESBENSEN, F., HUIZINGA, D., & WIEHER, A. (1993). Gang and non-gang youth: Differences in explanatory factors. *Journal of Contemporary Criminal Justice, 9*(2), 94–116.

ESBENSEN, F., & WINFREE, L. (1996). *Race and gender differences between gang and non-gang youth: Results from a national survey*. Paper presented at the annual meeting of the Academy of Criminal Justice Sciences.

EVALUATION AND TRAINING INSTITUTE. (1996). *Study of gender specific services: Initial review of the literature*. Sacramento, CA: Office of Criminal Justice Planning.

FAGAN, J. (1990). Social processes of delinquency and drug use among urban gangs. In C. R. Huff (Ed.), *Gangs in America* (pp. 183–219). Newbury Park, CA: Sage Publications.

FAGAN, J. (1996). Gangs, drugs and neighborhood change. In R. Huff (Ed.), *Gangs in America* (2nd ed., pp. 39–74). Thousand Oaks, CA: Sage Publications.

FAITH, K. (1993). *Unruly women: The politics of confinement and resistance*. Vancouver, Canada: Press Gang.

FARROW, J. A. (1991). Health issues among juvenile delinquents. In L. S. Thompson (Ed.), *The forgotten child in health care: Children in the juvenile justice system* (pp. 21–33). Washington, DC: National Center for Education in Maternal and Child Health.

FEINSTEIN, R. A. (1992). Training. In L. S. Thomspon & J. A. Farrow (Eds.), *Hard time, healing hands: Developing primary health care services for incarcerated youth* (pp. 37–47). Arlington, VA: National Center for Education in Maternal and Child Health.

FELKENES, G., & BECKER, H. (1995). Female gang members: A growing issue for policy makers. *Journal of Gang Research, 2*, 1–10.

FRAZIER, C., & BISHOP, D. (1995) Reflections on race effects in juvenile justice. In K. Leonard, C. Pope, & W. Feyerherm (Eds.), *Minorities in juvenile justice* (pp. 16–46). Thousand Oaks, CA: Sage Publications.

GARRY, E. (1996, October). Truancy: First step to a lifetime of problems. *Juvenile Justice Bulletin*. Washington, DC: Office of Juvenile Justice and Delinquency Prevention.

GILLIGAN, C. (1982). *In a different voice: Psychological theory and women's development*. Cambridge, MA: Harvard University Press.

GILLIGAN, C. (1992). *Meeting at the crossroads*. New York: Ballantine.

GIRLS INCORPORATED NATIONAL RESOURCE CENTER. (1996). *Prevention and parity: Girls in juvenile justice*. Indianapolis, IN: Girls Inc.

GREENE, PETERS & ASSOCIATES. (1997). Materials presented at annual meeting of American Society of Criminology, San Diego, CA.

GREENBAUM, P. E., FOSTER-JOHNSON, L., & PETRILA, A. (1996). Co-occurring addictive and mental disorders among adolescents: Prevalence research and future directions. *American Journal of Orthopsychiatry*, 52–60.

GROSSMAN, F. K., BEINASHOWITZ, J., & ANDERSON, L. (1992). Risk and resilience in young adolescents. *Journal of Youth and Adolescence, 21*, 529–550.

HAGEDORN, J. M. (1988). *People and folks: Gangs, crime, and the underclass in a rustbelt city.* Chicago: Lake View Press.

HAWKINS, J. D., CATALANO, R. F., & MILLER, J. Y. (1992). Risk and protective factors for alcohol and other drug problems in adolescence and early adulthood: Implications for substance abuse prevention. *Psychological Bulletin, 112*, 64–105.

HUTCHINSON, J. (1992). Mental health. In L. S. Thompson, & J. A. Farrow (Eds.), *Hard time, healing hands: Developing primary health care services for incarcerated youth* (pp. 121–133). Arlington, VA: National Center for Education in Maternal and Child Health.

IWAMOTO, J. J., KAMEOKA, K., & BRASSEUR, Y. C. (1990). *Waikiki homeless youth project: A report.* Honolulu, HI: Catholic Services to Families.

JAMESON, E. J. (1989). Incarcerated adolescents. The need for the development of professional ethical standards for institutional health care providers. *Journal of Adolescent Health Care, 10*, 490–499.

KANN, L., WARREN, C. W., HARRIS, W. A., COLLINS, J. L., WILLIAMS, B. I., ROSS, J. G., & KOLBE, L. J. (1996). Youth risk behavior surveillance: United States, 1995. *Morbidity and Mortality Weekly Report, 45* (SS-4), 1–83.

KELLEY, B. T., THORNBERRY, T. P., & SMITH, C. A. (1997). *In the wake of childhood maltreatment.* Washington, DC: Office of Juvenile Justice and Delinquency Prevention.

KILPATRICK, D., & SAUNDERS, B. (1997). *The prevalence and consequences of child victimization.* Washington, DC: National Institute of Justice.

LAFRAMBOISE, T., & HOWARD-PITNEY, B. (1995). Suicidal behavior in American Indian female adolescents. In S. Canetto & D. Lester (Eds.), *Women and suicidal behavior* (pp. 157–173). New York: Springer.

LA FREE, G. (1989). *Rape and criminal justice: The social construction of sexual assault.* Belmont, CA: Wadsworth Publishing.

LAKE, E. S. (1993). An exploration of the violent victim experiences of female offenders. *Violence and Victims, 8*, 41–51.

LEONARD, E. B. (1982). *Women, crime, and society.* New York: Longman.

LEVITT, D. (1994). *Teen families and welfare dependency in California* (ISBN 0-929722-83-3). Sacramento, CA: California Family Impact Services.

LINDGREN, S. (1996). Gender specific programming for female adolescents. Unpublished master's thesis. Augsberg College, Minneapolis, MN.

LIPSEY, M. (1990). *Juvenile delinquency treatment: A meta-analytic inquiry into the variability of effects.* New York: Russell Sage.

MARTIN, T. (1993). From slavery to Rodney King: Continuity and change. In H. Madhubuti (Ed.), *Why L.A. happened: Implications of the 1992 Los Angeles rebellion* (pp. 27–40). Chicago: Third World Press.

MAYER, J. (1995). *Taking girls into account: Changing a juvenile services agency from within.* Baltimore: Maryland Department of Juvenile Services.

McCABE, E., JAFFE, L. R., & DIAZ, A. (1993). Human immunodeficiency virus positivity in adolescents with syphilis. *Pediatrics, 92*, 695–698.

MELTON, G. B., & PAGLIOCCA, P. M. (1992). Treatment in the juvenile justice system: Directions for policy and practice. In J. J. Cocozza (Ed.), *Responding to the mental health needs of youth in the juvenile justice system.* Seattle, WA: National Coalition for the Mentally Ill in the Criminal Justice System.

MILIN, R., HALIKAS, J. A., MELLER, J. E., & MORSE, C. (1991). Psychopathology among substance-abusing juvenile offenders. *Journal of the American Academy of Child and Adolescent Psychiatry, 30*, 569–574.

MILLER, J. (1994) Race, gender and juvenile justice: An examination of disposition decision-making for delinquent girls. In M. Schwartz & D. Milovanovic (Eds.), *The intersection of race, gender and class in criminology* (pp. 219–246). New York: Garland Publishing.

MILLER, D., TRAPANI, C., FEJES-MENDOZA, K., EGGLESTON, C., & DWIGGINS, D. (1995). Adolescent female offenders: Unique considerations. *Adolescence, 30*, 429–435.

MINNESOTA ADVISORY TASK FORCE ON THE FEMALE OFFENDER IN CORRECTIONS. (1994). *Needs assessment and recommendations for adolescent females in Minnesota.* St. Paul, MN: Minnesota Department of Corrections.

MITCHELL, J., & VARLEY, C. (1990). Isolation and restraint in juvenile correctional facilities. *Journal of the American Academy of Child and Adolescent Psychiatry, 2*, 251–255.

MONAHAN, G. (1997). *The physical and mental health needs of female adolescents at risk or involved in the juvenile justice system.* Los Angeles: UCLA Drug Abuse Research Center.

MONAHAN, G., GIL-RIVAS, V., DANILA, B., & ANGLIN, D. A. (submitted). *Health-risk behaviors of adolescents in the juvenile justice system.*

MOORE, J. (1991). What leads sexually abused juveniles to delinquency. *Corrections Today, 42.*

MORRIS, R. E., BAKER, C. J., & HUSCROFT, S. (1992). Incarcerated youth at risk for HIV infection. In R. DiClemente (Ed.), *Adolescents and AIDS: A generation in jeopardy* (pp. 52–70). Newbury Park, CA: Sage Publications.

MYERS, W. C., BURKET, R. C., LYLES, B., STONE, L., & KEMPH, J. P. (1990). DSM-III diagnoses and offenses in committed female juvenile delinquents. *Bulletin of the American Academy of Psychiatry and the Law, 18*, 14–54

NAFFINE, N. (1987). *Female crime: The construction of women in criminology.* Sydney, Australia: Allen & Unwin.

NATIONAL COMMISSION ON CORRECTIONAL HEALTH CARE. (1992). *Standards for health services in juvenile confinement facilities.* Chicago: NCCHC.

NELSON, J. (1997). *Straight, no chaser.* New York: G.P. Putnam.

OFFICE OF JUVENILE JUSTICE AND DELINQUENCY PREVENTION. (1993). *Juvenile justice and delinquency prevention act of 1974.* Washington, DC: OJJDP.

OFFICE OF JUVENILE JUSTICE AND DELINQUENCY PREVENTION. (1996). *Prevention and parity: Girls in juvenile justice.* Washington, DC: OJJDP.

ORENSTEIN, P. (1994). *School girls.* Garden City, NJ: Doubleday.

OSOFSKY, J. D. (1995). The effects of exposure to violence in young children. *American Psychologist, 50*(9), 782–788.

OTTO, R. K., GREENSTEIN, J. J., JOHNSON, M. K., & FRIEDMAN, R. M. (1992). Prevalence of mental disorders in the juvenile justice system. In J. J. Cocozza (Ed.), *Responding to the mental health needs of youth in the juvenile justice system.* Seattle, WA: National Coalition for the Mentally Ill in the Criminal Justice System.

OWEN, B., & BLOOM, B. (1995). Profiling women prisoners. *Prison Journal, 75*, 165–185.

OWEN, B., & BLOOM, B. (1997). Profiling the needs of young female offenders: Final report to executive staff of the California Youth Authority (Grant 95-IJ-CX-0098). Washington, DC: National Institute of Justice.

OWENS, J. W. (1991). The importance of standards in providing health care for incarcerated youth. In L. S. Thompson (Ed.), *The forgotten child in health care: Children in the juvenile justice system* (pp. 49–53). Washington, DC: National Center for Education in Maternal and Child Health.

PARENT, D., LEITER, V., LIVENS, L., WENTWORTH, D., WILCOX, S., & STEPHEN, K. (1994). *Conditions of confinement: Juvenile detention and corrections facilities.* Washington, DC: Office of Juvenile Justice and Delinquency Prevention.

PIPHER, M. (1994). *Reviving Ophelia*. New York: Ballantine Books.

POE-YAMAGATA, E., & BUTTS, J. A. (1996). *Female offenders in the juvenile justice system: Statistics summary*. Washington, DC: Office of Juvenile Justice and Delinquency Prevention, pp. 1–6.

POSNER, M. (1990, March). *Female dropouts: The challenge. Women's Educational Equity Act Digest*.

RHODES, J., & FISCHER, K. (1993). Spanning the gender gap: Gender differences in delinquency among inner-city adolescents. *Adolescence, 28*, 879–890.

ROBINSON, R. A. (1994). Private pain and public behaviors: Sexual abuse and delinquent girls. In C. K. Riessman (Ed.), *Qualitative studies in social work research*. Thousand Oaks, CA: Sage Publications.

ROLF, J., NANDA, J., BALDWIN, J., CHANDRA, A., & THOMPSON, L. (1991). Substance misuse and HIV/AIDS risks among delinquents: A prevention challenge. *International Journal of Addiction, 25*, 533–559.

ROSENBAUM, J. (1989). Family dysfunction and female delinquency. *Crime and Delinquency, 35*, 31–44.

ROSENBAUM, J. (1993). The female delinquent: Another look at the family's influence on female offending. In R. Muraskin & T. Alleman (Eds.), *It's a crime: Women and justice* (pp. 399–416). Upper Saddle River, NJ: Prentice Hall.

ROSENBAUM, J., & CHESNEY-LIND, M. (1994). Appearance and delinquency: A research note. *Crime and Delinquency, 40*, 250–261.

ROSENBAUM, M., & MURPHY, S. (1995). *An ethnographic study of pregnancy and drug use*. Final Report to the National Institute on Drug Abuse (Grant RO1-DA 06832).

ROTHENBAUM, D. (1998). Phone interview. Sacramento, CA: Educational Demographics Unit, California Department of Education.

SCHWARTZ, I. M. WILLIS, D. A., & BATTLE, J. (1991). *Juvenile arrest, detention, and incarceration trends 1979–1989*. Ann Arbor, MI: University of Michigan's Center for the Study of Youth Policy.

SCOTT, J. L. (1994). The victor's crown of resiliency. In C. M. Todd (Ed.). *Child care center connections* (pp. 5–7). Urbana, IL: University of Illinois Cooperative Extension Service.

SEDLAK, A. J., & BROADHURST, D. D. (1996). *Executive summary of the third national incidence study of child abuse and neglect*. Washington, DC: Administration for Children and Families, U.S. Department of Health and Human Services.

SEGE, R., STIGOL, L. C., PERRY, C., GOLDSTEIN, R., & SPIVAK, H. (1996). Intentional injury surveillance in a primary care setting. *Archives of Pediatrics and Adolescent Medicine, 150*, 277–283.

SHEW, M. L., & FORTENBERRY, J. D. (1992). Syphilis screening in adolescents. *Journal of Adolescent Health, 13*, 303–305.

SHORTER, A. D., SCHAFFNER, L., SHICK, S., & FRAPPIER, N. S. (1996). *Out of sight, out of mind: The plight of adolescent girls in the San Francisco Juvenile Justice System*. San Francisco, CA: Center on Juvenile and Criminal Justice.

SHUSTER, B. (1995, June 28). L.A. school truancy exacts a growing social price. *Los Angeles Times*, p.12.

SICKMUND, M., SNYDER, H. N., & POE-YAMAGATA, E. (1997). *Juvenile offenders and victims: 1997 update on violence*. Washington, DC: Office of Juvenile Justice and Delinquency Prevention.

SIGDA, K. B., & MARTIN, S. L. (1996). Substance use among incarcerated adolescents: Associates with peer, parent, and community use of substances. *Substance Use and Misuse, 31*, 1433–1445.

SMART, C. (1976). *Women, crime, and criminology: A feminist critique*. London: Routledge & Kegan Paul.

SNYDER, J., DISHION, T.J., & PATTERSON, G. R. (1986). Determinants and consequences of associating with deviant peers during preadolescence and adolescence. *Journal of Early Adolescence, 6*, 29–43.

STEINER, H., GARCIA, I. G., & MATTHEWS, Z. (1997). Post-traumatic stress disorder in incarcerated juvenile delinquents. *Journal of the American Academy of Child and Adolescent Psychiatry, 36*, 357–365.

THOMPSON, L. S. (1992). Health status and health care issues. In L. S. Thomspon, & J.A. Farrow (Eds.), *Hard time, healing hands: Developing primary health care services for incarcerated youth* (pp. 21–36). Arlington, VA: National Center for Education in Maternal and Child Health.

THORNBERRY, T. P., KROHN, M., LIZOTTE, A., & CHARD-WIERSCHEM, D. (1993). The role of juvenile gangs in facilitating delinquent behavior. *Journal of Research in Crime and Delinquency, 30*, 55–87.

VERMUND, S. H., ALEXANDER-RODRIGUEZ, T., MACLEOD, S., & KELLEY, K. F. (1990). History of sexual abuse in incarcerated adolescents with gonorrhea or syphilis. *Journal of Adolescent Health Care, 11*, 449–452.

VIGIL, J. D. (1988). *Barrio gangs: Street life and identity in southern California.* Austin, TX: University of Texas Press.

WARR, M. (1993). Parents, peers, and delinquency. *Social Forces, 72*, 247–264.

WARREN, M. (1982). Delinquency causation in female offenders. In N. Hahn-Rafter & E. Stanko (Eds.), *Judge, lawyer, victim, thief.* Boston: Northeastern University Press.

WASHINGTON, P. (1997). Policy and program considerations for racial-ethnic minority girls at risk or involved in the juvenile justice system. Background paper for OCJP Modeling Gender-Specific Services in Juvenile Justice, Policy and Program Recommendations Project.

WATERMAN, J. D. (1997). *Post-traumatic stress disorder and incarcerated female juvenile delinquents.* Unpublished doctoral dissertation.

WEST, C. (1994). *Race matters.* New York: Vintage Books.

WIDOM, R., & HAMMETT, T. (1996, April). HIV/AIDS and STDs in juvenile facilities. *Research in Brief.*

WILSON, W. J. (1987). *The truly disadvantaged: Inner city, the underclass, and public policy.* Chicago: University of Chicago Press.

WINDLE, M. (1997). Effect of parental drinking on adolescents. *Research in Brief, 97.*

WOOD, V., & SHOROYE, A. (1993). Sexually transmitted disease among adolescents in the juvenile justice system of the District of Columbia. *Journal of the National Medical Association, 85*, 435–439.

WOODS, N. F. (1995). Young women's health. In C. I. Fogel & N. F. Woods (Eds.), *Women's health care: A comprehensive handbook.* Thousand Oaks, CA: Sage Publications.

YOUNG, N. K., GARDNER, S. L., & LOPEZ, J. (1997). *Alcohol and other drug use among California's adolescent population and the current systems' responses.* Fullerton, CA: California State University, Department of Alcohol and Drug Programs, pp. 6–20.

33

Gender Differences in Delinquency Career Types and the Transition to Adult Crime

Kimberly Kempf-Leonard and Paul E. Tracy

There are few topics that rival the research and policy attention currently bestowed on serious, violent, and chronic juvenile offenders. Major efforts are under way to identify these threatening offenders, develop effective intervention strategies to stop their criminality, and initiate prevention programs that will assure that subsequent youth do not follow in such delinquency career paths. Unfortunately, little attention has been devoted to females in this important policy arena. In this chapter we examine gender differences in serious, violent, and chronic offending among the 1958 Philadelphia birth cohort. With a large number of subjects and extensive criminal history information through age 26, these data enable us to make gender comparisons across delinquent and criminal careers that are unavailable in many other investigations. Based on our findings, we offer suggestions on how knowledge about gender differences might affect future research and policy efforts.

PRIOR RESEARCH

Serious, violent, chronic juvenile offenders first gained notice in the 1970s with the publication of *Delinquency in a Birth Cohort* (Wolfgang, Figlio, & Sellin, 1972), *The Violent Few* (Hamparian, Schuster, Dinitz, & Conrad, 1978), and Shannon's (1978, 1980) research on three cohorts in Racine, Wisconsin. These studies identified a very small proportion of juvenile offenders that were responsible for the majority of juvenile crime, including the most serious acts of delinquency. More recently, Tracy, Wolfgang, and Figlio (1990) reported an even greater involvement by chronic offenders in the 1958 Philadelphia birth cohort, and Tracy and Kempf-Leonard (1996) extended the research on the 1958 cohort to include the transition from delinquency career to adult crime. These studies have provided significant descriptions of juvenile careers, and according to Walker (1985), *Delinquency in a Birth Cohort*, in particular, is "the single most important piece of criminal justice research in the last 25 years and a major influence on crime control thinking" (p. 39).

The widespread interest in the topic of career criminals and criminal careers led the National Academy of Sciences to convene a Panel on Research on Criminal Careers in 1983 to assess the evidence and recommend directions for future research. According to panel chairperson Al Blumstein, "members were in general agreement about the findings and conclusions of the scientific evidence on criminal careers, but there were divergent views on the ethics of how such information should be used in dealing with offenders." Views among panelists ranged from objections to any criminal justice action based on anticipated future offending to a desire to see even weak results put to use as quickly as possible (Blumstein, Cohen, Roth, & Visher, 1986, p. x). A better understanding of the ethical issues associated with measurement difficulties and various intervention ideas may be the major legacy of the panel's two published volumes.

Of relevance here is the fact that females were included in fewer studies reviewed by the panel. Based on those studies and concerning gender differences in criminal careers, it was reported that "[I]n general, patterns of participation among females parallel those among males: higher estimates for broad crime domains and low thresholds of involvement. The most consistent pattern with respect to gender is the extent to which male criminal participation in serious crimes at any age greatly exceeds that of females, regardless of source of data, crime type, level of involvement, or measure of participation" (Blumstein et al., 1986, p. 40). There was reportedly "substantial debate" over causes of the strong empirical associations between demographic variables and aggregate arrest rates, but "the panel did not attempt to resolve those theoretical debates" (p. 26). Concluding comments about gender differences included: "much ambiguity surrounds the underlying theoretical meaning of differences," and "these differentials reflect relationships with other variables that are not yet well understood" (pp. 24–25).

More recently, the Office of Juvenile Justice and Delinquency Prevention initiated a Comprehensive Strategy for Serious, Violent, and Chronic Juvenile Offenders (Howell, 1995; Wilson & Howell, 1993), and established a study group on serious and violent juvenile offenders. In a volume published in 1998, this study group reviewed knowledge about serious, violent, and chronic juvenile offenders and the types of interventions that can reduce their level of offending (Loeber & Farrington, 1998).

Perceptions of gender differences in offending are clearly evident among members of the study group. One chapter begins with the contention that "in any birth cohort, the incidence and prevalence of violent and serious delinquency are more frequent among males than females" (Lipsey & Derzon, 1998, p. 86). The only chapter devoted to demographic descriptions of serious juvenile offenders is based on data for which information on females are available, and therefore it includes discussion only on issues pertaining to race and ethnic differences in offending. In a footnote, the authors comment that gender differences are beyond the scope of their paper and refer to a study based solely on young black women (Hawkins, Laub, & Lauritsen, 1998, p. 46).

A few descriptive findings of similar gender patterns are reported. For example, among the 524 females and 580 males in the Denver Youth Study, problem use of both alcohol and marijuana was higher among both male and female serious offenders than among other delinquents. (Huizinga & Jakob-Chien, 1998, pp. 50–51). The finding of higher rates of violence among male adolescents with histories of abuse and neglect compared to other males in the Rochester Youth Study also held for females (Smith & Thornberry, 1995). Prevalence of serious offending across multiple years for females in the National Youth Survey data was 3.8 percent for late-onset females versus 15.4 percent for early-onset females and 2.5 percent for late-onset males versus 12.7 percent for early-onset males (Tolan & Gorman-Smith, 1998, p. 76).

Among efforts to identify different pathways of development, a primary focus of the study group, findings based on females have either not been reported or have been discounted. For example, Loeber and Hay (1994) reported that their conceptual model of three pathways based on 1500 males in the Pittsburgh Youth Study can account for most delinquency career patterns. There has been, however, only one subsequent test of this model using data from the National Youth Survey and 1102 boys in the Chicago Youth Development Study, and no gender comparisons were made (Tolan & Gorman-Smith, 1998, pp. 80–84).

In reporting on relationships between predictor variables and outcome measures for serious or violent offending among the prospective longitudinal studies in their meta-analysis, Lipsey and Derzon (1998) identify that most of the studies include samples that are primarily male (p. 89). It is interesting that they still identify gender as a significant predictor of subsequent violent and/or serious delinquency, more than any other personal characteristics examined (pp. 96–98). In their assessment of potential targets for preventative intervention, they note that although gender and race are not "malleable," the prediction models suggest that male gender is "not a feasible target" among the 6 to 11 and 12 to 14 age groups (p. 100).

The link between early aggression and conviction and subsequent behavior is cited as "among the most stable characteristics, when measured for populations" (Tolan & Gorman-Smith, 1998, p. 73). The correlations for this relationship, however, are identified as "0.25 to 0.40 for males and lower for females" in two studies (i.e., Cairns, Cairns, Neckerman, Geist, & Gariepy, 1988; Coie & Dodge, 1983) and as "nonsignificant for females" in one other (i.e., Huesmann, Eron, Lefkowitz, & Walder, 1984; Tolan & Gorman-Smith, 1998, p. 73). Violence at age 15 predicted violence in later years among the 205 males, but less consistently and strongly among the 219 females in the Rutgers Health and Human Development Project (White, 1992). Similar findings from the Seattle Social Development Project show that gender is significantly able to predict self-reported violent behavior at age 18, with the likelihood of violence among males double that of females (Hawkins et al., 1998, p. 144). Other gender differences were reported for the Seattle Social Development Project. Inverse relationships between violent behavior and both parent–child communication and school bonding were weak for females, but strong for males (Williams, 1994, pp. 136, 138). The influence of delinquent siblings, however, was stronger for girls than for boys (p. 140).

Among other findings reviewed by the study group, Denno (1990) reported an inverse relationship between academic achievement and subsequent violent offending for both males and females, and the relationship was strongest for females. For both males and females, leaving home before age 16 was linked to increased levels of violence in McCord and Ensminger's Woodlawn Study of African American Children in Chicago (Hawkins et al., 1998, pp. 137–138). Finally, in the only report on gender differences among factors associated with gang membership, Thornberry (1998) provided the following account for the 250 females and 750 males in the Rochester Youth Study: "On the one hand, school variables, access to and values about drugs, and prior delinquency operate in generally similar ways for males and females. On the other hand, neighborhood characteristics appear to be much more important in increasing the likelihood of gang membership for the females than for the males. In contrast, family, peer, and psychological states (depression, stress, and self-esteem) are more potent predictors of gang membership for the males than the females" (p. 156).

Apart from the relatively small number of comparisons identified here, no other gender-based predictions of behavior are reported in the OJJDP study group volume. We do not posit that gender bias is responsible for the omission of gender differences in this research, as measurement difficulties associated with observing the low-base-rate phenomena of serious, violent, and chronic juvenile offenders in general, and for females in particular, are clearly noted. For example, Huizinga & Jakob-Chien (1998) contend that "because statistical significance is dependent on sample sizes, some differences that appear to be substantively significant are not statistically different, especially for girls" (p. 53). It also is reported that "estimates for females are less stable," but there is some suggestion of (a) a lower propor-tion of high aggression but (b) a higher proportion of serious criminal behavior among the more aggressive (Tolan & Gorman-Smith, 1998, p. 74). These authors conclude that because most studies have focused on males, there are substantial limitations in applying knowledge based only on males, and much of what can be concluded about serious, violent, and chronic juvenile offenders may apply only to males (p. 70).

The notable exception to research based on small numbers of subjects is analysis of 151,209 juvenile court careers by Howard Snyder. He provides interesting evidence that the large majority of youth handled by the juvenile court were referred only once. Most of the delinquents were never charged with a serious offense. Delinquents born later were not more frequent, more serious, or more violent than their earlier counterparts. Most chronic offenders did not commit violence, although most violent delinquents were also chronic offenders. Further, the majority of chronic and violent offenders also were involved in serious but nonviolent offending. In these findings, Snyder (1998) finds "comfort in the fact that the juvenile justice system is largely achieving its goal of successfully intervening in the lives of delinquent youth" (p. 442). He also contends, however, that "the juvenile justice system may be spreading its net wider, bringing in more juveniles, not more serious juvenile offenders because much of the recent growth in referrals was due to nonserious offenses" (p. 443). Regrettably absent in this interesting work is an indication of gender differences, although females presumably are included among the large number of cases spread across 15 cohorts that Snyder examined.

Of course, it is nothing new to ignore gender differences. Omission of how males and females differ actually is more the routine than the exception (Bergsmann, 1989; Chesney-Lind, 1997, pp. 17–21). A recent reminder of this situation appears in the aptly named book, *The Invisible Woman*, in which Belknap (1996) comments: "[I] found it frustrating to search through mainstream journals (and some books) to find out if women and/or girls were included in the research questions or samples. For example, studies with male-only samples rarely identified this in the title, while studies with female-only or female and male samples almost consistently reflected this in their titles. If women were excluded from the study, then most authors perceived no need to include 'male' in the title" (p. 4).

Although seldom questioned, the justification usually offered for not conducting gender-specific analyses is that too few females are available for observation. Indeed, a plethora of convincing evidence exists that both the male prevalence and incidence of offending far exceed that of females. But beyond these two basic parameters of offending, the knowledge base is more limited about the nature of other aspects of offending that might be characterized by gender differences. In fact, we know little about female offending in general. The irony, of course, is that by ignoring gender differences in offending, prior research may be failing to focus on the demographic factor that may actually have the greatest ability to distinguish crime; it is at least better than age, race, or social class, which are far more common in scientific inquiries about offending (Hagan, Gillis, & Simpson, 1985; Leonard, 1982).

Another problem with the lack of attention paid to female offending is that considerable unfounded speculation exists in place of accumulated research. Both historically and today, there is a tendency to view female offenders and offending as aberrations, abnormal even among society's deviants, and certainly not feminine. For example, Lombroso's beliefs in the late nineteenth century that females are less developed on the evolutionary scale and that female criminals exhibit male characteristics are no longer appreciated, but support for his contention that female delinquency is linked to biological traits can certainly still found today. Similarly, Pollack's contention in 1950 that the onset of menstruation, pregnancy, and menopause are linked to criminality has been widely cast aside, but his idea that females use their sexuality to obtain deferential treatment reappears today as the chivalry hypothesis in some explanations of differential treatment. Freud's concept of penis envy has been strongly questioned, but the influence of his views is evident in psychological theories that trace gender differences in personality development and adaptations.

The influence of these early theorists is evident among the criminal career panel debates on explanations based on "biological differences, differences in moral training, differences in socialization experiences, and fewer criminal opportunities for girls because they are more closely supervised" (Blumstein et al., 1986, p. 25). Although there is no consensus on the relative influence of nature or nurture, and most explanations integrate popular elements, prevailing theories include themes that gender differences in offending can be explained by corresponding gender differences in socialization, cognitive abilities, personality adaptations, neurological functioning, and hormonal and biochemical composition (Weisheit & Mahan, 1988). The most common diminished views of female offending continue to relegate it to a symptom of moral, emotional, or family problems and not "real" [male] delinquency and crime (Caine, 1989; Chesney-Lind, 1997; Naffine, 1987).

More important than presumptions about the inherent causes of crime, however, is the lack of attention and the misguided responses that females receive from criminal justice agencies. The range of behavior generally considered acceptable is narrower for females (Chesney-Lind, 1973, 1995; Dembo, Williams, & Schmeidler, 1993; Kempf-Leonard & Sample, 1998), and different factors appear to affect how females are processed (Chesney-Lind & Shelden, 1992; Gelsthorpe, 1989; Krohn, Curry, & Nelson-Kilger, 1983; Rosenbaum & Chesney-Lind, 1994; Visher, 1983). Females may receive from police more restrictive, harsher, and longer interventions than do comparable males (Visher, 1983), courts, and correctional facilities (Bishop & Frazer, 1992; Chesney-Lind, 1973; Krisberg, Schwartz, Fishman, Eisikovits, & Guttman, 1986; Rhodes & Fischer, 1993). Females are also sent for treatment to mental hospitals in lieu of traditional juvenile justice facilities more often than males (Chesney-Lind, 1995; Miller, 1994; Weithorn, 1988). Further, some female-specific treatment programs dictate stereotypical feminine behavior (Chesney-Lind & Shelden, 1992; Gelsthorpe, 1989; Kersten, 1989), and even new reform efforts in this area may be problematic (Kempf-Leonard & Sample, 1998).

Some of these situations no doubt exist because inadequate resources are allocated and too few programs attend to the prevention and treatment of girls and women who offend (Chesney-Lind, 1997, p. 90; Lipsey, 1992, p. 106; Valentine Foundation, 1990, p. 5). Even among those criminal justice agencies that do try to respond to females, there are many inappropriate services, interventions, and sanctions. According to Chesney-Lind (1997), "there have been major changes in the way that the United States has handled girls' and women's crime in recent decades that do not necessarily bode well for the girls and women who enter the criminal justice system" (p. 3). In placing blame, Chesney-Lind says, "[the silence about females] has hidden key information from public view and allowed major shifts in the treatment of women and girls—many on the economic margins—to occur without discussion and debate."

The "forgotten few" female offenders (Bergsmann, 1989) may be small in number, but their ability to help us understand wider behaviors should not be discounted. Even differential treatment by juvenile and criminal justice has been attributed to paternalism prevalent in general society (Chesney-Lind, 1995; Odem, 1995; Price & Sokoloff, 1995), which itself merits better understanding. Indeed, our understanding of crime and criminal justice would be much less, and criminology might not have become the large and growing field it now has if its "parent disciplines" had forestalled attention to deviants among investigations of routine behaviors. It is for these reasons that we believe it is important to examine gender differences among serious, violent, and chronic juvenile offenders and their transition to adult crime.

DATA

In this chapter we utilize the data files from the 1958 Philadelphia Birth Cohort Study. Records from all public and private schools in Philadelphia were used to identify the population of 27,160 males and females born in 1958 who resided in Philadelphia at least from ages 10 through 17. Together with the criminal history data that were collected for the cohort through age 26, these data are superior to those on which many previous investigations have been based. The present data permit the systematic structuring of the longitudinal sequence of police contacts and thereby help to facilitate the identification of youths, both delinquents and nondelinquents, who are most likely to proceed to adult crime.

The 1958 Philadelphia birth cohort comprises a population and, as such, is not vulnerable to the usual threats of external validity posed by sampling procedures because every available subject is included regardless of their delinquency or adult crime status. This cohort of 13,160 males and 14,000 females is the largest of its kind and includes detailed information drawn from several sources able to identify characteristics of its members. Further, the requirement of Philadelphia residence between ages 10 and 18 for defining the cohort provides a uniform time frame and setting within which cohort members were at risk of offending. Sample mortality is not problematic in this longitudinal investigation because the retrospective data collection involved unobtrusive archival examination of records that are maintained routinely by the Philadelphia Police Department and area schools.

The crime measures are drawn from police rap sheets and the associated investigation reports that were provided by the Juvenile Aid Division of the Philadelphia Police Department. These records were used to characterize police encounters that the cohort experienced before age 18. In addition to official arrests, the rap sheet data also contain "police contact" information. The police maintain records of these contacts that result in "remedial," or informal, handling of the youth by an officer whereby youth are generally remanded to the custody of their parents. Thus the juvenile delinquency data contain both official arrests and informal contacts that did not result in an arrest, thus representing a total record of official delinquency, and further, representing a much better record of delinquency than data that were based solely on arrest information. The police investigation reports were used to supplement information provided in the rap sheets with detailed descriptions of the criminal event in which the subject was involved. The Municipal and Court of Common Pleas of Philadelphia served as data sources for offenses committed by the cohort after reaching the legislatively imposed adult status of age 18. Adult criminal history data are available through December 31, 1984, or through age 26 for all cohort members. The 1958 Philadelphia Birth Cohort Study is rich in the criminal history and offense data available to assess important criminological issues. Further description of the 1958 Philadelphia Birth Cohort Study data collection procedures and the results of a comparison study of the juvenile delinquency careers for males in the 1958 and 1945 Philadelphia cohorts may be found in Tracy and Kempf-Leonard (1996) and Tracy et al. (1985, 1990).

It is important to note that an assumption was made that the residential status of subjects remained stable after age 17. FBI rap sheets on adult offending were obtained to capture even migratory adult crime, but those data were not used because it was too difficult to identify subjects accurately. Married females with new surnames were lost because the distinct federal numbering system necessitated identification based on the subject's name.

RESULTS

Delinquency

Female subjects ($n = 14,000$) comprise 51.5 percent of the 27,160 persons in the 1958 Philadelphia birth cohort. Yet they comprise just 14.1 percent of the 6287 delinquents, and 14.9 percent of the cohort members who committed offenses as adults. Collectively, these females were responsible for 3897 juvenile offenses and 909 adult crimes. In this chapter we investigate gender differences and similarities in the nature and distribution of these offenders and offenses. We first examine the prevalence of delinquency, which refers to the proportion of a subject group that has been recorded officially as delinquent.

Table 1 shows 4315 males and 1972 females were officially recorded as delinquent; thus the prevalence of delinquency is 32.8 percent for males and 14.1 percent for females in the 1958 cohort. Given the smaller number of females, a gender comparison based merely on frequencies or counts would be inappropriate—the males would predominate and comparisons would be misleading. However, the percentage of delinquents adjusts for the population size at risk. Thus, in calculating the ratio of males to females, we rely on the percentage rather than the frequency. The ratio of the percentage of male delinquents to that of female delinquents indicates that for each female delinquent, there were about 2.3 male delinquents. As would be expected from prior research, males are much more likely than their female peers to become officially involved with the juvenile justice system.

Gender differences in the frequency, or incidence, of delinquency are shown in Table 2. We first provide data for all officially recorded delinquent acts, followed by only those delinquent acts that were law violations or crimes (i.e., status offenses were excluded). The

TABLE 1   Frequency and Percentage of Delinquents by Gender

	Males		Females		M / F
	Number	Percent	Number	Percent	Ratio
Nondelinquents	8,845	67.2	12,028	85.9	0.78 : 1
Delinquents	4,315	32.8	1,972	14.1	2.33 : 1
Total	13,160	100.0	14,000	100.00	

largest proportion of both male delinquents (41.8 percent) and female delinquents (59.9 percent) had only one officially recorded delinquent offense of any kind. Roughly one-third each of the males and females exhibited moderate recidivism and had from two to four delinquent offenses. High recidivism, five through nine offenses, were observed for 15.2 percent of the males and 6.2 percent of the females. The smallest proportion of both males (7.6 percent) and females (1.2 percent) had very high recidivism and accumulated ten or more official contacts with police.

The male/female ratios for these percentages indicates a distinct gender effect. That is, as delinquency becomes more frequent, or more chronic, each female offender has a much higher percentage of male counterparts. The ratios start at 0.69 : 1 at the level of one-time

TABLE 2   Number and Percentage of Delinquent Offense Groups by Gender

	Males		Females		M / F
	Number	Percent	Number	Percent	Ratio
Nondelinquents					
All offenses					
(including status)					
1	1804	41.8	1182	59.9	0.69 : 1
2–4	1529	35.4	643	32.6	1.09 : 1
5–9	654	15.2	123	6.2	2.45 : 1
10+	328	7.6	24	1.2	6.33 : 1
Total	4315	100.0	1972	99.9	
Criminal law violations					
0	504	11.7	876	44.7	0.26 : 1
1	1697	39.3	794	40.3	0.98 : 1
2–4	1383	32.1	274	13.9	2.31 : 1
5–9	515	11.9	24	1.2	9.92 : 1
10+	216	5.0	4	0.2	25.0 : 1
Total	4315	100.0	1,972	100.3	

offender, then increase consistently as we move to two to four offenses (1.09 : 1), and then five to nine offenses (2.45 : 1). Among the group responsible for the highest incidence of delinquency—ten or more offenses—there were 6.3 male delinquents for each female.

When delinquents who committed only status offenses are excluded and only criminal law violations are considered, the pattern shown above becomes even more pronounced. The group with no law violations, or status offenders only, includes just 11.7 percent of the male delinquents compared to 44.7 percent of the female delinquents. Similarly, the offender group with but one single crime encounter includes 40.3 percent of the females and 39.3 percent of the males. Thus, taken together, a substantial proportion of females, 85 percent, committed either no crimes or at most one crime in their delinquency career as compared to 51 percent of male delinquents.

When we examine recidivists, we see that at the level of two through four criminal law violations, only 13.9 percent of the females compared to 32.1 percent of the males were so classified. At the level of high criminal violations, five through nine offenses, this group included 11.9 percent of the males but only 1.2 percent of the females. Finally, at the highest recidivism level of criminal violations, ten or more offenses, we find 5 percent of the male delinquents but less than 1 percent of the females (0.2 percent).

The ratio of these percentages indicate that about four female delinquents for each male delinquents with no law violation and approximately one-to-one among the group with a single crime. However, there were 2.3 males per female among delinquents with two to four offenses, 9.9 males per female for five to nine offenses, and 25 males per female for 10 or more offenses. These ratios clearly indicate that as the levels of crime-related delinquency (as opposed to any type of offending, which includes status offenses) increase, fewer and fewer females are found compared to males.

In Table 3 we turn to data concerning gender differences in the probabilities of recidivism at each offense rank in the delinquency career, from the first to the nth offense. The probability estimate for male delinquents making the transition from a single offense to a second one is 0.58, compared to 0.40 for female delinquents, or looked at another way, about 42 percent of males compared to 60 percent of females commit only one delinquent offense. Male delinquents have a higher probability of recidivism than do female delinquents at each offense rank. The exception to this pattern occurs for the transition between 19 and 20 offenses for which the probability for females stays at 1.0 until the twenty-fourth offense. But these higher scores are unreliable, as they are based on only one female delinquent.

Although Table 3 confirms the greater involvement of males in delinquent recidivism, and that the distribution of career totals is smaller and more constrained for the females, these results also indicate that female recidivists, like males, exhibit a pattern of escalating recidivism probabilities as offense rank increases. That is, while far fewer female delinquents recidivate at each offense rank, the pattern of such recidivism follows a probabilistic process that is very similar to that for males, thus suggesting a difference of degree rather than of kind.

Of the 19,145 officially recorded offenses, male delinquents were responsible for 15,248 (79.6 percent) and female delinquents for 3897 (20.4 percent). The distribution of these offenses across specific offense categories is shown in Table 4. The most common offense categories among male delinquents were truancy (13 percent), disorderly conduct (12 percent), burglary (11 percent), theft (11 percent), drugs (5 percent), and simple assault (5 percent). By comparison, female delinquents were most actively involved in runaway

TABLE 3   Juvenile Recidivism Probabilities: All Delinquent Acts

	Males			Females		
Offense Rank	Career Frequency	Total Frequency	Probability	Career Frequency	Total Frequency	Probability
1	1804	4315	1.0000	1182	1972	1.0000
2	705	2511	0.5819	379	90	0.4006
3	502	1806	0.7192	163	411	0.5203
4	322	1304	0.7220	101	248	0.6034
5	212	982	0.7531	51	147	0.5927
6	174	770	0.7841	32	96	0.6531
7	119	596	0.7740	18	64	0.6667
8	74	477	0.8003	13	46	0.7188
9	75	403	0.8449	9	33	0.7174
10	56	328	0.8139	6	24	0.7273
11	46	272	0.8293	6	18	0.7500
12	40	226	0.8309	3	12	0.6667
13	37	186	0.8230	2	9	0.7500
14	25	149	0.8011	2	7	0.7778
15	16	124	0.8322	1	5	0.7143
16	10	108	0.8710	1	4	0.8000
17	12	98	0.9074	1	3	0.7500
18	13	86	0.8776	1	2	0.6667
19	16	73	0.8488		1	0.5000
20	11	57	0.7808		1	1.0000
21	8	46	0.8070		1	1.0000
22	2	38	0.8261		1	1.0000
23	2	36	0.9474		1	1.0000
24	6	34	0.9444	1	1	0.0000
25	3	28	0.8235			
26	4	25	0.8929			
27	1	21	0.8400			
28	2	20	0.9524			
29	3	18	0.9000			
30	3	15	0.8333			
31	1	12	0.8000			
32	2	11	0.9167			
33		9	0.8182			
34	3	9	1.0000			

TABLE 3   *(continued)*

Offense Rank	Males			Females		
	Career Frequency	Total Frequency	Probability	Career Frequency	Total Frequency	Probability
35		6	0.6667			
36		6	1.0000			
37	1	6	1.0000			
38		5	0.8333			
39	1	5	1.0000			
40		4	0.8000			
41	2	4	1.0000			
42		2	0.5000			
43		2	1.0000			
44		2	1.0000			
45		2	1.0000			
46		2	1.0000			
47		2	1.0000			
48	1	2	1.0000			
49		1	0.5000			
50		1	1.0000			
51		1	1.0000			
52		1	1.0000			
53	1	1	1.0000			

(39 percent), theft (13 percent), truancy (9 percent), disorderly conduct (8 percent), and simple assault (5 percent). As would be expected from prior research, males predominate significantly among index crimes for which the male/female ratios are quite substantial. Further, the gender ratios show similarities for the offenses of runaway, forgery, fraud, investigation of person, and incorrigibility, while the biggest differences occur for rape, drunk driving, auto theft, burglary, robbery, and weapon offenses, for which the male/female ratios are substantial.

The overall estimate for male/female percent ratio based on total number of offenses indicates that over four male delinquents were apprehended for every female delinquent. Similarly, the offense rate for males, 1.158.66, is about four times higher (4.16) than the rate, 278.36, for females. Clearly, these offense data demonstrate, as expected, that delinquency of males far exceeds that of females when frequency of violations is the operative measure.

In Table 5 we examine gender differences among delinquents who could be classified as serious, violent, and/or chronic offenders. Violent offenders had delinquency records that included homicide, rape, robbery, aggravated assault, or aggravated sexual intercourse.

TABLE 4   Number, Percent, and Rate (per 1,000) of All Delinquent Acts by Gender

	Males			Females			M / F
	Number	Percent	Rate	Number	Percent	Rate	Ratio
Index offenses							
Homicide	55	0.4	4.18	5	0.1	0.36	11.61 : 1
Rape	101	0.7	7.67	2	0.1	0.14	54.79 : 1
Robbery	1,290	8.5	98.02	43	1.1	3.07	31.93 : 1
Aggravated assault	561	3.7	42.63	107	2.7	7.64	5.58 : 1
Burglary	1,673	11.0	127.13	52	1.3	3.71	34.27 : 1
Theft	1,671	11.0	126.98	500	12.8	35.71	3.56 : 1
Vehicle theft	640	4.2	48.63	18	0.5	1.29	37.70 : 1
Nonindex offenses							
Males predominate							
Simple assault	698	4.6	53.04	209	5.4	14.93	3.55 : 1
Arson	42	0.3	3.19	7	0.2	0.50	6.38 : 1
Receive stolen goods	69	0.5	5.24	7	0.2	0.50	10.48 : 1
Weapons	457	3.0	34.73	23	0.6	1.64	21.18 : 1
Vandalism	813	5.3	61.78	63	1.6	4.50	13.73 : 1
Drugs	714	4.7	54.26	100	2.6	7.14	7.60 : 1
Drunk driving	40	0.3	3.04	1	0.0	0.07	43.43 : 1
Liquor laws	211	1.4	16.03	43	1.1	3.07	5.22 : 1
Truancy	1,987	13.0	150.99	347	8.9	24.79	6.09 : 1
Disorderly	1,837	12.0	139.59	319	8.2	22.79	6.13 : 1
Trespass	603	4.0	45.82	93	2.4	6.64	6.90 : 1
City ordinance	534	3.5	40.58	82	2.1	5.86	6.92 : 1
Sex offenses	66	0.4	5.02	9	0.2	0.64	7.84 : 1
Gambling	8	0.1	0.61	1	0.0	0.07	8.71 : 1
Vagrancy	35	0.2	2.66	4	0.1	0.29	9.17 : 1
Drunkenness	166	1.1	12.61	17	0.4	1.21	10.42 : 1
Prostitution	11	0.1	0.84	1	0.0	0.07	12.00 : 1
Escape	205	1.3	15.58	14	0.4	1.00	15.58 : 1
Conspiracy	31	0.2	2.36	2	0.1	0.14	16.86 : 1
Incorrigible	6	0.0	0.46	4	0.1	0.29	1.59 : 1
Explosives	8	0.1	0.61	n/a			
Disturbance	5	0.0	0.38	n/a			
Fraud	6	0.0	0.46	6	0.2	0.43	1.07 : 1
Females predominate							
Runaway	467	3.1	35.49	1,518	39.0	108.43	0.33 : 1
Invest. person	235	1.5	17.86	296	7.6	21.14	0.84 : 1
Forgery	3	0.0	0.23	4	0.1	0.29	0.79 : 1
Total	15,248	100	1158.6	3,897	100.0	278.36	4.16 : 1

TABLE 5   Number and Percent of Offenders by Delinquency Career Type

| | Males | | Females | | M / F |
	Number	Percent	Number	Percent	Ratio
Violent offender	1128	26.1	140	7.1	3.68 : 1
Serious offender	2182	50.6	326	16.5	3.07 : 1
Serious specialist	112	2.6	3	0.2	13.0 : 1
Chronic offender	982	22.8	147	7.5	3.04 : 1

These violent delinquents included 1128 males, or 26 percent of the 4315 male delinquents, and 140 females, or 14 percent of the 1972 female delinquents. Thus for every violent female delinquent there were nearly four males who could be classified as violent.

The serious offenders include all violent offenders, plus those with burglary, theft, vehicle theft, arson, and vandalism in excess of $500. In this category there were 2182 males (50.6 percent) and 326 females (16.5 percent). The male/female ratio is about 3 : 1. Serious crime specialists committed over half of their total career offenses in that category. There were 112 male specialists in serious crime (2.6 percent) but only 3 females, for a male/female ratio of 13 : 1.

The familiar classification of chronic offenders is those with a career total of five or more offenses. There were 982 chronic male delinquents (22.8 percent) and 147 chronic female delinquents (7.5 percent) for a male/female ratio of 3 : 1.

Adult Crime

It is important to move beyond the delinquency dimension and examine the transition to the adult sphere of criminality. Whatever may be the differences in youthful misbehavior, it is instructive to investigate the nature of the relationship between delinquency career types and adult crime by gender. Do males and females make the transition in the same way? Do the same delinquency factors put females and males at risk for adult crime, or is there a gender interaction with delinquency patterns? These issues need to be addressed.

The intersection among serious, violent, and chronic juvenile offenders, and the proportion of each that subsequently became adult offenders is depicted in Tables 6 and 7 and in Figure 1. In Table 6 we note that there were 895 males who were classified as both serious and chronic offenders. Although comprising only one-fifth of all male delinquents, this group represents 91.1 percent of the total chronic subset and 41.0 percent of the serious male delinquents. In contrast, the 69 serious and chronic female delinquents comprised less than 4 percent of the total, 46.9 percent of the chronic group, and 21.2 percent of the serious female delinquents. For each such female delinquent, there were approximately two male delinquents. Delinquents who were both violent and chronic offenders included 612 males, or 14 percent, and 39 females, or 2 percent. This career type represented two-thirds of the male chronic offenders, one-fourth of the female chronic offenders, just over half of the violent males, and just over one-fourth of violent females. The male/female percent ratio was again 2 : 1.

TABLE 6   Number and Percent of Career Types by Gender[a]

Career Type	Males Number	Males Percent of Delinquents	Females Number	Females Percent of Delinquents	M / F Ratio
Total delinquents	4315	100.0	1972	100.0	n/a
Serious delinquents	2182	50.6	326	16.5	3.07 : 1
Violent delinquents	1128	26.1	140	7.1	3.68 : 1
Chronic delinquents	982	22.8	147	7.5	3.04 : 1
Serious and chronic	895	20.7	69	3.5	5.91 : 1
Percent of serious		41.0		21.2	1.93 : 1
Percent of chronic		91.1		46.9	1.94 : 1
Violent and chronic	612	14.2	39	2.0	7.10 : 1
Percent of violent	54.2		27.9		1.94 : 1
Percent of chronic		62.3		26.5	2.35 : 1
Not delinquents	8845	67.2[b]	12,028	85.9[b]	0.78 : 1

[a]There is no consensus on the optimal cutoff to define chronic offenders, or whether the same definition should apply to males and females. One argument offered against a gender-neutral definition is that it is likely to capture a much smaller proportion of female offenders than male offenders, who also would "probably represent a more extreme group" (Blumstein et al., 1986; Loeber, Farrington, & Waschbusch, 1998, pp. 15–16). Having already addressed high incidence separately, however, the traditional definition of five or more offenses is adopted here.

[b]Rather than all delinquents, this percentage is based on the population total of 13,160 males and 14,000 females.

The prevalence of subsequent adult offending through age 26 is shown in Table 7 separately by gender for each delinquency career type. Among both males and females, adult offending was least prevalent among nondelinquents (14 percent males, 3 percent females) and most prevalent among chronic offenders who also had records of either violent or serious crimes (64 percent males, 44 percent females). Although parallel patterns of adult prevalence exist among the delinquency career types for males and females, the lower prevalence among females is very clearly evident. The male/female ratio of nearly 6 : 1 suggests the most variation among virgin adult offenders, those with no juvenile record. The ratio for overall delinquents is 3.5 : 1, and for each of the serious, violent, and chronic delinquency careers the adult offending ratios identify males/females 2 : 1.

Figure 1 provides a useful display of the information given in Tables 6 and 7, using the familiar Venn diagram approach with intersecting circles to represent the proportion of delinquents in each of the significant delinquency career types. All delinquents are encompassed within the outer circle. Those delinquents who had no record of any serious offense, and fewer than five official encounters with the police, are included in the proportion of the larger circle outside the other circles. Overlapping areas between the circles represent delinquency careers with attributes from two or more groups. The shaded portion of each circle represents the percentage of each delinquency career subgroup that also committed adult crime.

TABLE 7   Number and Percentage of Career Types by Gender[a]

Career Type	Males			Females			M / F Ratio
	Number of Delin-quents	Number Adult Crimes	Percent of Row	Number of Delin-quents	Number Adult Crimes	Percent of Row	
Total delinquents	4315	1805	41.8	1972	236	12.0	3.48 : 1
Serious delinquents	2182	1123	51.5	326	81	24.8	2.08 : 1
Violent delinquents	1128	634	56.2	140	36	25.7	2.19 : 1
Chronic delinquents	982	619	63.0	147	42	28.5	2.21 : 1
Serious and chronic	895	571	63.8	69	30	43.5	1.47 : 1
Violent and chronic	612	394	64.4	39	17	43.6	1.48 : 1
Not delinquents	8845	1273	14.4	12,028	304	2.5	5.76 : 1

[a]There is no consensus on the optimal cutoff to define chronic offenders, or whether the same definition should apply to males and females. One argument offered against a gender-neutral definition is that it is likely to capture a much smaller proportion of female offenders than male offenders, who also would "probably represent a more extreme group" (Blumstein et al., 1986; Loeber et al., 1998, pp. 15–16). Having already addressed high incidence separately, however, the traditional definition of five or more offenses is adopted here.

In comparison to Snyder's analysis of multiple court cohorts, we use a more conservative definition of chronic offending, the traditional five or more police contact, whereas he relied on a cutoff of four or more delinquency referrals to court (Snyder, 1998, p. 437). We had no cases of kidnapping and include rape as a violent offense. We also include vandalism of property in excess of $500 as a serious offense, which Snyder does not, and he includes drug trafficking and weapons as serious nonviolent offenses (p. 429). Despite these differences, there is value in comparing our findings of the intersecting career paths of delinquents.

In Snyder's career paths, 33.6 percent were serious delinquents, 14.5 percent were chronic delinquents, 8.1 percent were violent, 12.1 percent were serious and chronic, and 1 percent was violent and chronic. Although based on a single earlier cohort and in some cases a more conservative definition, each significant career path included a higher proportion of delinquents in our study. For example, in comparison to Snyder's 33.6 percent, we had 50.6 percent of the males and 16.5 percent of the females identified as serious delinquents. In comparison to his 14.5 percent, we found chronic delinquents among 22.8 percent of the males and 7.5 percent of the females. In comparison to his 8.1 percent, 26.1 percent of the males and 7.1 of the females in our cohort were violent delinquents. Similarly, his finding of 12.1 percent as serious and chronic delinquents corresponded to our finding of 20.7 percent of the males and 3.5 percent of the females. Finally, 1 percent violent and chronic delinquents for him, compared to 14.2 of the males and 2 percent of the males for us. Although variation in delinquent behavior across geographic locations or birth year may yield some answers to these difference in delinquency career paths, it is also likely that Snyder's failure to control for gender differences provides at least a partial explanation. Our ability to control for adult offending illustrates further the extent to which observations of gender differences are important.

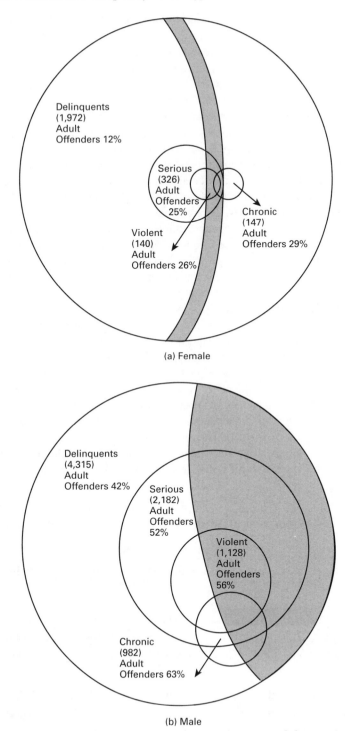

FIGURE 1   Venn diagram showing intersection between delinquency career types: (a) female; (b) male.

Ultimately, there is value in specifying the statistical strength and significance of the connection between delinquency career types and making the transition to adult crime. Thus in Table 8 we provide the results from a logistic regression model that predicts adult crime status on the basis of the three delinquency career types. These multivariate results present the highly interesting finding that the type of career a delinquent had as a juvenile is highly predictive of adult status for both males and females and in almost exactly the same way. That is, a violent delinquency career is not significant for females and does not quite reach significance for males. Yet, for both males and females having been either a serious delinquent or a chronic delinquent is highly predictive of adult status. Each of the effects was significant for males and females and produced substantial odds ratios. However, the odds ratios observed were strongest for females. If a female delinquent was a serious offender, she was 2.7 times more likely than nonserious females to move on to adult crime. The corresponding score was 1.5 among males. Similarly, among females, chronics were 2.4 times more likely to have a record of adult crime than nonchronic offenders, while the odds were slightly less among males (2.3 : 1). Of importance here is the fact that although females are less likely to become serious delinquent or chronic juvenile offenders, when they do reflect these career types, these effects are more pronounced in producing adult crime status among females than among males.

In Table 9 we present a few details on the gender differences in the type of adult criminals in the cohort just to highlight the fruitful lines of research that can be conducted on male and female offending across the life course. We focus on offenders rather than offenses because we want to highlight the qualitative dimension rather than the mere quantitative extent of the adult criminality. It is readily apparent that there are more similarities than differences in the adult offending careers. Females and males have similar percentages for index crimes, theft offenses, and offenses involving weapons. Yes, males predominate, but not as substantially as is the case for other crimes, such as robbery, drugs, and alcohol. These results surely indicate that females are almost as likely as males to become certain types of adult criminals. We would expect, however, that the frequency with which males commit these acts would be far greater than for females. Yet it is the propensity itself that holds almost equal interest to the more usual inquiry surrounding the frequency of offending.

TABLE 8   Prediction of Adult Status by Juvenile Career Types and Gender

Juvenile Career Types	Coefficient	Standard Error	p-Value	Odds Ratio
Females				
Violent delinquent	-0.034	0.264	0.898	0.967
Serious delinquent	1.012	0.195	0.000	2.750
Chronic delinquent	0.888	0.210	0.000	2.430
Males				
Violent delinquent	0.176	0.090	0.052	1.192
Serious delinquent	0.424	0.080	0.000	1.528
Chronic delinquent	0.834	0.086	0.000	2.302

TABLE 9   Number and Percent of Adult Offender Types by Gender

Offender Type	Females		Males	
	Number	Percent	Number	Percent
Any type	236	100.0	1805	100.0
Index	51	63.9	1364	75.6
Violence	96	40.7	854	47.3
Robbery	21	8.8	515	28.5
Theft	81	34.3	916	50.7
Weapon	58	24.6	661	36.6
Drugs	37	15.7	534	29.6
Alcohol	13	5.5	221	12.2

SUMMARY AND IMPLICATIONS

We have investigated a number of topics surrounding gender differences in delinquency. The following summarize the major findings with respect to the topic areas of interest: prevalence, incidence, and juvenile delinquent subgroups.

The prevalence data clearly indicated that the phenomenon of delinquency is very different among girls than among boys. Of the 14,000 girls in the 1958 cohort, 1,972, or about 14 percent, had at least one delinquent offense before reaching age 18. The boys were almost two and one-half times more likely to be delinquent than were their female counterparts. When prevalence was broken down by level of delinquency status, the gender differences were pronounced. Among females, 60 percent of the delinquents were one-time offenders, whereas only 7 percent were chronic recidivists. Thus the girls were about one and one-half times more likely to be delinquents with but one delinquent offense, while boys were about three times more likely to have been a chronic offender with five or more offenses. In particular, therefore, chronic delinquency was a very different phenomenon among girls than among boys in the 1958 cohort. Of the 1972 female delinquents, 147 were classified as chronic offenders. These chronic females represented just 1.4 percent of the girls at risk, 7.5 percent of the delinquent subset, and 18.5 percent of the recidivists. The proportion of male chronics exceeded that of females by factors of 7.5 : 1 among subjects, 3 : 1 among delinquents, and 2 : 1 among recidivists.

The 1972 female delinquents were responsible for a total of 3897 delinquent acts. The offense rate (per 1000 cohort members) was 278.36. Seven hundred and twenty-seven, or 18 percent of the female offenses, were UCR Index offenses, with a rate of 52.0 per 1000 cohort girls. One hundred and fifty-seven of the female offenses were violent index offenses (4 percent of the total delinquent acts and 22 percent of the index crimes) with a rate of 11 per 1000 girls in the cohort.

The gender effects shown among these data were quite pronounced. The offense rate for boys was four times greater than that for girls. The gender disparity increased to a factor of almost 9 : 1 for UCR Index offenses. The male/female ratio increased even further, to

14: 1 for violent offenses. The most glaring differences occurred for the following serious offenses: 14: 1 for homicide, 33: 1 for robbery, 10: 1 for aggravated assault, 34: 1 for burglary, and 37: 1 for vehicle theft.

We also examined the intersection among various classifications of delinquency to determine the extent to which the categories of the serious offender, the violent offender, and the chronic offender were capturing the same group of delinquents. We found that males were much more likely than females to be serious and chronic (about six times more likely), and violent and chronic (about seven times more likely).

Finally, however, we also examined the prevalence of adult crime in association with the various offender classifications in order to detect the extent to which a history of a particular type and/or frequency of juvenile delinquency was predictive of adult crime status. We found first that females had comparatively low adult crime status compared to males. That is, 236 (12 percent) of the 1972 female delinquents and 304 (2.5 percent) of the females at risk went on to commit a crime as an adult. These findings were overshadowed by the male results, which showed that 1805 (41.8 percent) of the 4315 male delinquents and 1273 (14.4 percent) of the males at risk had records of adult crime. However, we also found that when we examined the intersection of the offender classifications and their association with adult crime, the gender disparity diminished. That is, male delinquents were about 3.4 times as likely as female delinquents and male subjects were 5.76 times as likely as female subjects to go on to adult crime, but the results for serious, violent, and chronic offenders were generally in the range of twice as likely. More interestingly, when we examined the intersections, we found that the male predominance declined even further, to about 1. 5: 1 for both the serious and chronic and violent and chronic intersections. Clearly, these findings indicate that a combined history of frequent and serious, or frequent and violent, places a female a substantial risk of adult crime that is closer to her male counterpart than when such combined traits are missing from the juvenile career. Thus, a female who uncharacteristically has a delinquency career that is similar to her male counterpart rather than her female peers (who generally have a limited involvement in delinquency) exhibits a substantially higher risk of continuing the offense career as she becomes an adult, just like her chronic male counterpart. In fact, our multivariate model indicated that the connection between delinquency career type and adult crime was strongest for females.

Overall, our results produce the finding that males are far more involved in offending than females. However, when analysis of recidivism and seriousness of offending are extended to females, the findings show that females are indeed found among the small group of offenders present at the limited end of the continuum of those who behave most badly.

Our findings have highlighted many differences; still others remain to be examined. For gender differences to be understood, research must attend to offending over the criminal career, or life course, and focus on crime-specific modeling. For example, a better understanding of the links between crime and responses to victimization, including how juvenile justice processing serves to label the responses of female victims as offenses, would help illuminate the criminal career pathways that flow from such victimization. Important contextual differences across age, race, social class, and geographic location also merit a lot more attention (Chesney-Lind, 1997; Simpson, 1991). We must examine gender similarities to understand better the differences. We will, and we urge other researchers, to take seriously Chesney-Lind's contention that "[g]irls' pathways into crime, even into violence, are affected by the gendered nature of their environments and particularly their experiences as marginalized girls in communities racked by poverty" (p. 176).

While Feld (1997, p. 132) argues that juvenile courts go to great lengths to evade the unpleasant topic of punishment and its "disagreeable qualities," it is the contention of Chesney-Lind (1997) that such feelings of avoidance and discomfort are directed even more acutely at females. Meanwhile, disproportionate media accounts of serious juvenile crime approaching epidemic proportions (Blumstein, 1995; DiIullio, 1996; Fox, 1996) have given rise to the notion of the "superpredator" (DiIullio, 1996), including the liberated "female gangsta" (Chesney-Lind, 1997, pp. 34–37; Maher & Curtis, 1995). Such media portrayals have affected public perception of juvenile offenders and the corresponding "feeding frenzy" of policy responses (Howell, 1998; see also Doi, 1998; Zimring, 1996).

Issues about the social construction of childhood and adolescence have been raised (Bernard, 1992; Feld, 1997). It has also been argued that teenagers, in general, tend to be demonized in contemporary American society, and that serious, violent, and chronic juvenile offenders exist because society has not acted responsibly toward youth in other important arenas (Males, 1996). Concerning females, criticism has been advanced that "those who tout these 'crime waves' use a crude form of equity feminism to explain the trends observed and, in the process, contribute to a 'backlash' against the women's movement" (Chesney-Lind, 1997, p. 56; Faludi, 1991).

The policy debate and legislative action has resulted in harsher, more restrictive codes and procedures for processing juvenile offenders, especially serious, violent, and chronic delinquents, in nearly every state (Torbet et al., 1996; Walker, 1995). Some policy initiatives aim to limit discretion, standardize court decisions, and classify offenders for correctional supervision and treatment (Weibush, Baird, Krisberg, & Onek, 1995; Wilson & Howell, 1993). Other changes couple juvenile justice with criminal justice, typically through greater use of juvenile transfer to criminal court (Fagan, 1995; Howell, 1997; Singer, 1996; Tracy & Kempf-Leonard, 1998). Accountability is a recurrent theme, with changes aimed at holding juvenile offenders—and sometimes also their parents—responsible for their actions (Albert, 1998). In some areas, the accountability objective links with treatment (Bazemore & Day, 1996; Bazemore & Umbreit, 1995; Wilson & Howell, 1993), but more often the focus is on punishment and retribution (Feld, 1997). According to Feld, "[t]hese recent changes signal a fundamental inversion in juvenile court jurisprudence from treatment to punishment, from rehabilitation to retribution, from immature child to responsible criminal. . . . The common over-arching legislative strategy reflects a jurisprudential shift from the *principle of individualized justice* to the *principle of offense*, from rehabilitation to retribution, and an emphasis on the seriousness of the offenses rather than judges' clinical assessments of offenders' 'amenability to treatment'" (p. 79). Feld subsequently advocates abolition of the juvenile court in favor of a single explicitly punitive criminal justice process in which culpability and sanctions are discounted for youth (Feld, 1997). Although Feld might appear the lone advocate of this position, it is clearly implicit in much of the public and policy debate.

In terms of effectiveness, it is important to note that a purely punitive response to serious juvenile offenders discounts advances made in the area of treatment. According to Lipsey (1992), "It is no longer constructive for researchers, practitioners, and policy-makers to argue about whether delinquency treatment and related rehabilitative approaches work. As a generality, treatment clearly works. We must get on with the business of developing and identifying the treatment models that will be most effective and providing them to the juveniles they will benefit" (p. 85). In their review of programs, Lipsey and Wilson (1998) identify reductions in recidivism as high as 40 percent among the best programs for serious juvenile offenders, a larger effect than shown for delinquents in general. They conclude: "If anything, then, it would appear that the typical intervention in these studies is *more* effective with serious offenders than with less serious offenders" (p. 23). Characteristics of the most effective treatment programs were intensive services, more contact hours, longer stays, multiple services, consistent implementation, and external evaluation teams. Most important, not only has treatment been found far more effective in reducing recidivism than punishment (Gendreau, 1996), but it is also clearly more cost-effective (Greenwood, Model, Rydell, & Chisea, 1996).

We know that effective treatment can be administered by the juvenile courts. Rates of recidivism tend to be lower in juvenile courts than in criminal courts (Howell, 1997, p. 3). Moreover, our own research shows that early routine probation intervention is effective, even for serious chronic juvenile delinquents, whereas the same may not be true of routine commitment to correctional facilities (Tracy & Kempf-Leonard, 1996, pp. 109–142). Similarly, Dean, Brame, and Piquero (1996) attributed lower recidivism to early probation intervention among several hundred North Carolina youth they followed for six years. Howell (1997, p. 5) also reports on a 12-month follow-up evaluation, in which reductions as high as 50 percent in arrests, court petitions, probation violations, and new facility commitments were attributed to an early intervention program in a California probation department.

Of course, as might be expected, attention to females is noticeably absent among the policy discussion and most of the policy initiatives. Two notable exceptions appear under provisions of the JJDP Act of 1974, as reauthorized in 1992:

1. To be eligible for federal funding, each state must provide "an analysis of gender-specific services for the prevention and treatment of juvenile delinquency, including the types of such services available and the need for such services for females and a plan for providing the needed gender-specific services" (Public Law 102-586, 1992).

2. As part of the challenge grant program for state advisory groups, additional funds are available to examine policies for gender bias and to develop female-specific programs. Based on the number of responses from states, the gender area has been the most popular among those available in the challenge grant program (Girls Inc., 1996, p. 26).

In the larger policy arena, however, these two initiatives make barely a mark.

In light of our observations that policy responses to serious, violent, and chronic juvenile offenders have not attended to gender differences although our research findings suggest that they should, we offer four recommendations. First, most policy reforms are predicated on notions of individual responsibility and accountability, which should require that we know more about the high incidence of delinquency that involves adolescents' miscalculation of risk (Bernard, 1992; Feld, 1997; Matza, 1964). Zimring, 1996 (pp. 90–99) equates the "self-autonomy" of adolescence with a "learner's permit" that provides youth with the opportunity to make choices and learn responsibility, yet "preserves the life chances for those who make serious mistakes." Although gender is not mentioned, Feld (1997, p. 121) acknowledges that "youthful development is highly variable." It is age which explains his view that "the ability to make responsible choices is learned behavior, and the dependent status of youth systematically deprives them of chances to learn to be responsible" (p. 114). Given prevailing arguments that girls are more sheltered and closely supervised than boys, yet their prevalence also is lower, gender differences in response to independence and in learning responsibility could prove very valuable in the policy arena. Fortunately, many scholars research gender differences in development (e.g., Bem, 1993; Chesney-Lind & Shelden, 1992; Messerschmidt, 1993, Orenstein, 1994; Osgood, Wilson, O'Malley, Bachman, & Johnson, 1996; Sadker & Sadker, 1994), and their contributions need to be targeted appropriately and included in the policy responses to juvenile offenders.

Second, Feld (1997) relies on knowledge gleaned from delinquency career research that desistance, maturation, or "aging out" typically occur, which he interprets as a natural phenomenon, to justify the feasibility of his system as follows: "Unlike a rehabilitative system inclined to extend its benevolent reach, an explicitly punitive process would opt to introduce fewer and more criminally 'deserving' youths into the system. . . . In allocating scarce resources, [this system] would use seriousness of the offense to rationalize charging decisions and 'divert' or 'decriminalize' most of the 'kids' stuff' that provides the grist of the juvenile court mill until it became chronic or escalated in severity" (pp. 128–129). This stance in favor of ignoring problem juvenile behavior until it reaches an intolerable level, however, also ignores research findings showing success associated with early intervention. Further, it creates a system in which the needs of economically and culturally outcast populations are conveniently ignored. Not only does this omission seem contrary to Feld's own concern for social justice (pp. 72, 132–136), but it is likely to adversely affect females, who are disproportionately represented among the socially marginalized populations (Chesney-Lind, 1997, p. 115). Thus we recommend rejection of Feld's abolition idea.

Third, although we strongly advocate a better understanding and more awareness of gender similarities and differences in delivering services, we currently find ourselves in opposition to gender-specific policy developments. Because justice should equate to equity, female-specific services seem likely to perpetuate stereotype and diminished aid to girls and women (Chesney-Lind, 1997, p. 162). In this area, we agree with Feld (1997, p. 121) that fairness and the objectivity of law are sacrificed when dispositions reflect subjective explanations of behavior and personal responsibility. Indications to this effect in the form of well-intentioned but premature or poorly conceived programming efforts, already exist among the new policy initiatives (Kempf-Leonard & Sample, 1998).

Our findings indicate gender differences in degree of serious, violent, and chronic offending, but gender similarities in general career patterns of interest. These findings lend support to suggestions that status offenders should be reintegrated as a feasible target of mainstream juvenile justice (Krisberg & Austin, 1993). Gender similarities in behavior, coupled with evidence of gender bias or differential processing, serve to remind us of the warning that criminal justice functions to maintain the modern patriarchy (Chesney-Lind, 1997, p. 4). How this occurs would be the important first step in helping to abolish it. Of course, obstacles to equity presented by the greater social stratification of rights and privileges remain (Simpson, 1991). Fortunately, the progressive ideas found within the new strategy for a comprehensive juvenile justice system are consistent with our findings and with other research on gender differences, and on male serious, violent, and chronic juvenile offenders (Howell, 1995, 1997; Wilson & Howell, 1993). Thus we support a balanced approach of prevention, early intervention, and graduated sanctions that provides for treatment, just as it aims to strengthen the family, support core institutions in their supporting roles of youth development, and identify and control the small group of serious, violent, and chronic juvenile offenders.

Criminology must confront the fact that both theory and research have not fully appreciated the full range of issues surrounding male and female involvement in delinquency and crime. The offending behavior of females cannot be dismissed as merely a less frequent or less serious analog to that of males. Such a dismissal has two noteworthy consequences. First, it precludes the development of common explanations, where they are appropriate, but more important, it prevents the conceptualization and investigation of gender-specific perspectives where they are warranted and very necessary. Second, it precludes the investigation of the differential processing that females receive in the juvenile and criminal justice systems and the effects of such processing on subsequent offending. Criminologists must therefore heed the caution expressed by Chesney-Lind and Shelden (1992) that girls experience a childhood and adolescence heavily colored by their gender, and it is simply not possible to discuss their problems, their delinquency, and what they encounter in the juvenile justice system without considering gender in all its dimensions (p. 212).

REFERENCES

ALBERT, R. L. (1998). *Juvenile accountability incentive block grants program.* OJJDP Fact Sheet 76. Washington, DC: Office of Juvenile Justice and Delinquency Prevention.

BAZEMORE, G., & DAY, S. E. (1996). Restoring the balance: Juvenile and community justice. *Juvenile Justice, 3*(1), 3–14.

BAZEMORE, G., & UMBREIT, M. (1995). Rethinking the sanctioning function in juvenile court: Retributive or restorative responses to youth crime. *Crime and Delinquency, 49*, 296–316.

BELKNAP, J. (1996). *The invisible woman.* Belmont, CA: Wadsworth Publishing.

BEM, S. (1993). *The lenses of gender.* New Haven, CT: Yale University Press.

BERGSMANN, I. (1989). The forgotten few: Juvenile female offenders. *Federal Probation, 53*, 73–78.

BERNARD, T.J. (1992). *The cycle of juvenile justice.* New York: Oxford University Press.

BISHOP, D., & FRAZER, C. (1992). Gender bias in the juvenile justice system: Implications of the JJDP Act. *Journal of Criminal Law and Criminology, 82*(4), 1162–1186.

BLUMSTEIN, A. (1995, August). Violence by young people: Why the deadly nexus? *NIJ Journal,* pp. 1–9.

BLUMSTEIN, A., COHEN, J., ROTH, J. A., & VISHER, C. A. (1986). *Criminal careers and "career criminals."* Washington, DC: National Academy Press.

CAINE, M. (ED.). (1989). *Growing up good: Policing the behavior of girls in Europe.* Newbury Park, CA: Sage Publications.

CAIRNS, R. B., CAIRNS, B. D., NECKERMAN, H. J., GEIST, S. D., & GARIEPY, J. L. (1988). Social networks and aggressive behavior: Peer support or peer rejection? *Developmental Psychology, 24*, 815–823.

CHESNEY-LIND, M. (1973). Judicial enforcement of the female sex role. *Issues in Criminology, 8*, 51–71.

CHESNEY-LIND, M. (1995). Girls, delinquency, and juvenile justice: Toward a feminist theory of young women's crime. In B. R. Price & N. J. Sokoloff (Eds.), *The criminal justice system and women* (2nd ed., pp. 71–88). New York: McGraw-Hill.

CHESNEY-LIND, M. (1997). *The female offender: Girls, women, and crime.* Thousand Oaks, CA: Sage Publications.

CHESNEY-LIND, M., & SHELDEN, R. (1992). *Girls delinquency and juvenile justice.* Pacific Grove, CA: Brooks/Cole.

COIE, J. D., & DODGE, K. A. (1983). Communities and changes in children's socioeconomic status: A five-year longitudinal study. *Merrill-Palmer Quarterly, 29*, 261–282.

DEAN, C. W., BRAME, R., & PIQUERO, A. R. (1996). Criminal propensities, discrete groups of offenders, and persistence in crime. *Criminology, 34*, 547–574.

DEMBO, R., WILLIAMS, L., & SCHMEIDLER, J. (1993). Gender differences in mental health service needs among youths entering a juvenile detention center. *Journal of Prison and Jail Health, 12*, 73–101.

DENNO, D. (1990). *Biology and violence: From birth to adulthood.* Cambridge: Cambridge University Press.

DiIULLIO, J. J. (1996, Spring). They're coming: Florida's youth crime bomb. *Impact*, pp. 25–27.

DOI, D. J. (1998, April). The MYTH of teen violence. *State Government News*, pp. 17–19.

FAGAN, J. (1995). Separating the men from the boys. In R. Howell, R. Hawkins, B. Krisberg, & J. Wilson (Eds.), *Sourcebook on serious violent juvenile offenders* (pp. 238–257). Thousand Oaks, CA: Sage Publications.

FALUDI, S. (1991). *Backlash: The undeclared war against American women.* New York: Anchor Books.

FELD, B. C. (1997). Abolish the juvenile court: Youthfulness, criminal responsibility, and sentencing policy. *Journal of Criminal Law and Criminology, 88*(1), 68–136.

FOX, J. A. (1996). *Trends in juvenile violence: A report to the U.S. attorney general on current and future rates of juvenile offending.* Boston: Northeastern University.

GELSTHORPE, L. (1989). *Sexism and the female offenders: An organizational analysis.* Aldershot, Hants. England: Gower Publishing.

GENDREAU, P. (1996). The principles of effective interventions with offenders. In A. T. Harland (Ed.), *Choosing correctional options that work* (pp. 117–130). Thousand Oaks, CA: Sage Publications.

GIRLS INCORPORATED NATIONAL RESOURCE CENTER. (1996). *Prevention and parity: Girls in juvenile justice.* Indianapolis, IN: Girls Inc.

GREENWOOD, P. W., MODEL, K. E., RYDELL, C. P., & CHIESA, J. (1996). *Diverting children from a life of crime: Measuring costs and benefits.* Santa Monica, CA: RAND Corporation.

HAGAN, J., GILLIS, A. R., & SIMPSON, J. (1985). The class structure of gender and delinquency: Toward a power-control theory of common delinquent behavior. *American Journal of Sociology, 90*, 1151–1178.

HAMPARIAN D. M., SCHUSTER, R., DINITZ, S., & CONRAD, J. (1978). *The violent few.* Lexington, MA: Lexington Books.

HAWKINS, J. D., HERRENKOHL, T., FARRINGTON, D. P., BREWER, D., CATALANO, R. F., & HARACHI, T. W. (1998). A review of predictors of youth violence. In R. Loeber & D. P. Farrington (Eds.), *Serious and violent juvenile offenders* (pp. 106–146). Thousand Oaks, CA: Sage Publications.

HAWKINS, D. F., LAUB, J. H., & LAURITSEN, J. L. (1998). Race, ethnicity, and serious juvenile offending. In R. Loeber & D. P. Farrington (Eds.), *Serious and violent juvenile offenders* (pp. 30–46). Thousand Oaks, CA: Sage Publications.

HOWELL, J. C. (ED.). (1995). *Guide for implementing the comprehensive strategy for serious, violent, and chronic juvenile offenders.* Washington, DC: Office of Juvenile Justice and Delinquency Prevention.

HOWELL, J. C. (1996). Juvenile transfer to the criminal justice system: State of the art. *Law and Policy, 18*, 17–60.

HOWELL, J. C. (1997). *Juvenile justice and youth violence.* Thousand Oaks, CA: Sage Publications.

HOWELL, J. C. (1998). *Juvenile justice and youth violence.* Thousand Oaks, CA: Sage Publications.

HUESMAN, L. R., ERON, L. D., LEFKOWITZ, M. M., & WALDER, L. O. (1984). Stability of aggression over time and generations. *Developmental Psychology, 20*, 1120–1134.

HUIZINGA, D., & JAKOB-CHIEN, C. (1998). The contemporaneous co-occurrence of serious and violent juvenile offending and other problem behaviors. In R. Loeber & D. P. Farrington (Eds.), *Serious and violent juvenile offenders* (pp. 47–67). Thousand Oaks, CA: Sage Publications.

KEMPF-LEONARD, K., & SAMPLE, L. (1998). Disparity based on sex: Is gender-specific treatment warranted? Paper presented at the annual meetings of the Academy of Criminal Justice Sciences.

KERSTEN, J. (1989). The institutional control of girls and boys: An attempt at a gender-specific approach. In M. Caine (Ed.), *Growing up good: Policing the behavior of girls in Europe* (pp. 129–144). Newbury Park, CA: Sage Publications.

KRISBERG, B., & AUSTIN, J. F. (1993). *Reinventing juvenile justice.* Newbury Park, CA: Sage Publications.

KRISBERG, B., SCHWARTZ, I. M., FISHMAN, G., EISIKOVITS, Z., & GUTTMAN, E. (1986). *The incarceration of minority youth.* Minneapolis, MN: Hubert Humphrey Institute of Public Affairs.

KROHN, M., CURRY, J., & NELSON-KILGER, S. (1983). Is chivalry dead? *Criminology, 21*, 417–439.

LEONARD, E. (1982). *Women, crime, and society*. New York: Longman.

LIPSEY, M. W. (1992). Juvenile delinquency treatment: A meta-analytic inquiry into the variability of effects. In T. D. Cook, H. Cooper, D. S. Cordray, H. Hartman, L. V. Hedges, R. J. Knight, T. A. Louis, & F. Mosteller (Eds.), *Meta-analysis for explanation* (pp. 83–127). New York: Russell Sage.

LIPSEY, M. W., & DERZON, J. H. (1998). Predictors of violent or serious delinquency in adolescence and early adulthood: A synthesis of longitudinal research. In R. Loeber & D. P. Farrington (Eds.), *Serious and violent juvenile offenders* (pp. 86–105). Thousand Oaks, CA: Sage Publications.

LIPSEY, M. W., AND WILSON, D. B. (1998). Effective intervention for serious juvenile offenders: A synthesis of research. In R. Loeber & D. P. Farrington (Eds.), *Serious and violent juvenile offenders* (pp. 315–335). Thousand Oaks, CA: Sage Publications.

LOEBER, R., & FARRINGTON, D. P. (EDS.). (1998). *Serious and violent juvenile offenders* (pp. 106–146). Thousand Oaks, CA: Sage Publications.

LOEBER, R., FARRINGTON, D. P., & WASCHBUSCH, D.A. (1998). In R. Loeber & D. P. Farrington (Eds.), *Serious and violent juvenile offenders* (pp. 13–29). Thousand Oaks, CA: Sage Publications.

LOEBER, R., & HAY, D. F. (1994). Developmental approaches to aggression and conduct problems. In M. Rutter & D. F. Hay (Eds.), *Development Through Life: A Handbook for Clinicians* (pp. 488–516). Oxford: Blackwell.

MAHER, L., & CURTIS, R. (1995). In search of the female urban "gangsta": Change, culture, and crack cocaine. In B. R. Price & N. J. Sokoloff (Eds.), *The criminal justice system and women* (2nd ed., pp. 148–166). NewYork: McGraw-Hill.

MALES, M. A. (1996). *The scapegoat generation: America's war on adolescents*. Monroe, ME: Common Courage Press.

MATZA, D. (1964). *Delinquency and drift*. New York: Wiley.

MESSERSCHMIDT, J. (1993). *Masculinities and crime: Critique and reconceptualization*. Lanham, MD: Rowman & Littlefield.

MILLER, J. (1994). Race, gender and juvenile justice: An examination of disposition decision-making for delinquent girls. In M.D. Schwartz & D. Milovanovic (Eds.), *The intersection of race, gender and class in criminology* (pp. 219–246). New York: Garland Publishing.

NAFFINE, N. (1987). *Female crime: The construction of women in criminology*. Sydney, Australia: Allen & Unwin.

ODEM, M. E. (1995). *Delinquent daughters*. Chapel Hill, NC: University of North Carolina Press.

ORENSTEIN, P. (1994). *School girls*. New York: Doubleday.

OSGOOD, W., WILSON, J., O'MALLEY, P., BACHMAN, G., & JOHNSON, L. (1996). Routine activities and individual deviant behavior. *American Sociological Review, 61*, 635–655.

PRICE, B. R. & SOKOLOFF, N. J. (EDS.). (1995). *The criminal justice system and women* (2nd ed.). New York: McGraw-Hill.

PUBLIC LAW 102-586. (1992, November 4). Juvenile justice and delinquency prevention, fiscal years 1993–96. 106 Stat. 4982.

RHODES, J., & FISCHER, K. (1993). Spanning the gender gap: Gender differences in delinquency among inner city adolescents. *Adolescence, 28*, pp. 880–889.

ROSENBAUM, J., & CHESNEY-LIND, M. (1994). Appearance and delinquency: A research note. *Crime and Delinquency, 40*, 250–261.

SADKER, M., & SADKER, D. (1994). *Failing at fairness: How America's schools cheat girls*. New York: Charles Scribner's Sons.

SHANNON, L. (1978). A longitudinal study of delinquency and crime. In C. Wellford (Ed.), *Quantitative studies in criminology*. Beverly Hills, CA: Sage Publications.

SHANNON, L. (1980). *Assessing the relationship of adult criminal careers to juvenile careers*. Washington, DC: U.S. Government Printing Office.

SIMPSON, S. (1991). Caste, class, and violent crime: Explaining difference in female offending. *Criminology, 29*(1), 115–135.

SINGER, S. (1996). *Recriminalizing delinquency*. Cambridge: Cambridge University Press.

SMITH, C., & THORNBERRY, T. P. (1995). The relationship between childhood maltreatment and adolescent involvement in delinquency. *Criminology, 33*, 451–481.

SNYDER, H. N. (1998). Serious, violent, and chronic juvenile offenders: An assessment of the extent of and trends in officially recognized serious criminal behavior in a delinquent population. In R. Loeber & D. P. Farrington (Eds.), *Serious and violent juvenile offenders* (pp.428–444). Thousand Oaks, CA: Sage Publications.

THORNBERRY, T. (1998). Membership in youth gangs and involvement in serious and violent offending. In R. Loeber & D. P. Farrington (Eds.), *Serious and violent juvenile offenders* (pp. 147–166). Thousand Oaks, CA: Sage Publications.

TOLAN, P. H., & GORMAN-SMITH, D. (1998). Development of serious and violent offending careers. In R. Loeber & D. P. Farrington (Eds.), *Serious and violent juvenile offenders* (pp. 68–85). Thousand Oaks, CA: Sage Publications.

TORBET, P., GABLE, R., HURST, H., MONTGOMERY, I., SZYMANSKI, L., & THOMAS, D. (1996). *State reponses to serious and violent juvenile crime*. Washington, DC: Office of Juvenile Justice and Delinquency Prevention.

TRACY, P. E. & KEMPF-LEONARD, K. (1996). *Continuity and discontinuity in criminal careers*. New York: Plenum.

TRACY, P. E., & KEMPF-LEONARD, K. (1998). Sanctioning serious juvenile offenders: A review of alternative models. *Advances in Criminological Theory, 8*, 135–171.

TRACY, P. E., WOLFGANG, M. E., & FIGLIO, R. M. (1985). *Delinquency in two birth cohorts: Executive summary*. Washington, DC: U.S. Government Printing Office.

TRACY, P. E., WOLFGANG, M. E., & FIGLIO, R. M. (1990). *Delinquency careers in two birth cohorts*. New York: Plenum.

VALENTINE FOUNDATION. (1990). *A conversation about girls*. Bryn Mawr, PA: The Foundation.

VISHER, C. (1983). Gender, police arrest decisions, and notions of chivalry. *Criminology, 21*, 5–28.

WALKER, S. (1985). *Sense and nonsense about crime: A policy guide*. Monterey, CA: Brooks/Cole.

WALKER, S. (1995). *Sense and nonsense about crime: A policy guide* (2nd ed.). Monterey, CA: Brooks/Cole.

WEIBUSH, R. G., BAIRD, C., KRISBERG, B., & ONEK, D. (1995). Risk assessment and classification for serious, violent, and chronic juvenile offenders. In J. C. Howell, B. Krisberg, J. D. Hawkins, & J. J. Wilson (Eds.). *A sourcebook: Serious, violent, and chronic juvenile offenders* (pp. 171–212). Thousand Oaks, CA: Sage Publications.

WEISHEIT, R., & MAHAN, S. (1988). *Women, crime and criminal justice*. Cincinnati, OH: Anderson Publishing.

WEITHORN, L. A. (1988). Mental hospitalization of troublesome youth: An analysis of skyrocketing admission rates. *Stanford Law Review, 40*, 773–838.

WHITE, H. R. (1992). Early problem behavior and later drug problems. *Journal of Research in Crime and Delinquency, 29*, 412–429.

WILLIAMS, J. H. (1994). Understanding substance use, delinquency involvement, and juvenile justice system involvement among African American and European-American adolescents. Unpublished dissertation. University of Washington–Seattle.

WILSON, J. J., & HOWELL, J. C. (1993). *A comprehensive strategy for serious, violent, and chronic juvenile offenders*. Washington, DC: Office of Juvenile Justice and Delinquency Prevention.

WOLFGANG, M. E., FIGLIO, R. M., & SELLIN, T. (1972). *Delinquency in a birth cohort*. Chicago: University of Chicago Press.

ZIMRING, F. E. (1996, August 19). Crying wolf over teen demons. *Los Angeles Times*, p. B5.

ZIMRING, F. E. (1996). *American youth violence*. New York: Oxford University Press.

34

Film Portrayals of Female Delinquents

Realistic or Stereotypical?

Laura L. Finley and Peter S. Finley

INTRODUCTION

Most Americans agree that the media have at least some influence on people. As such, they help shape our understanding of society. As Richard Quinney says, "social reality begins in the imagination" (Bailey & Hale, 1998, p. 2). Not all types of media appear to be equally interesting to Americans, though. Many historical reviews of the popular arts in the Western world reveal a culture persistently fascinated with crime (Lovell, 2001). Although it could possibly affect viewers or readers in positive ways, most research addresses the potential negative effects of media. Twenty-one percent of adults polled in 1995 blamed television more than any other factor for teen sex and violence (Bok, 1998). Fewer data exist regarding the effects of viewing film, but a logical assumption is that similar rates of concern would be noted, especially as increasing numbers of adolescents have access to VCRs and cable television that show films (Snyder, 1991).

It is also known that much media is intentionally marketed to young people. A study released in September 2000 found that "the entertainment industry routinely markets to young people violent movies, video games and music, ignoring its own rating guidelines for age-sensitive material" (Srinivasan, 2000, p. 1). The report included a survey of marketing practices and found that most R-rated films had at least some promotional efforts targeted at underaged viewers. Sissela Bok, in *Mayhem*, explains that previous generations of kids had virtually no money to spend. In 1997 it was estimated that those under 14 would spend $20 billion directly and influence another $200 billion (Bok, 1998). With this kind of discretionary income it is obvious why advertisers and media moguls focus their attention on adolescents.

Although it is clear that the media have some effect on teens, exactly what kinds of effects these are is still an area of much contention. It also depends on what aspect of the media is being viewed. For example, many people argue that seeing violence and sex has an impact on viewers. Others also maintain that the media portray many groups in a stereotypical fashion, which affects the viewer in a different way. The combination of effects is also important.

Research already exists in all these areas. Much of it has, however, focused on the effects of violent viewing or stereotypes of particular minority groups. As Paul Kooistra and John Mahoney, Jr. note in *Making Trouble*: "[C]rimes, (some) shows may seem to imply, are desperate acts of irrational evil committed by dark-skinned males and sexually depraved females. These deviants are a breed of humans different from 'us'; they reject many of 'our' goals and values" (Ferrell & Websdale, 1999, p. 48). Most of the research to date has also focused on males. When females are depicted in crime films it tends to be as victims, where the ideal "innocent victim is either white and upper class or a member of a minority group acting in distinctly non-stereotypical ways (a Latina honor student and class valedictorian who is killed by a mugger)" (p. 131). One area that has not been well researched is how female criminals are portrayed in the media. As Chesney-Lind points out, "women's everyday violence and aggression, and its social context, have been ignored or trivialized. Instead we witness the sporadic 'discovery' of rather heinous female offenders" (p. 133).

This research, a content analysis, analyzes 13 current films marketed to teens that depict female delinquents. It describes how female delinquents in each film are portrayed and analyzes the results compared to real figures and characteristics of female delinquency. Inferences about the implications of the findings on viewers and those involved with the criminal justice system were also explored. This research is important because it is a relatively new area of exploration. Further, as our perceptions about criminality invariably shape our responses to it, it is critical to look at how these perceptions are formed. As Mark Costanzo wrote in *Just Revenge*, "as fear and anxiety grow, the public becomes increasingly receptive to any policy that has even a remote chance of pushing back the perceived tidal wave of violence." He also quotes Glenn Pierce and Michael Radelet as saying, "[I]n terms of political strategy, media-promoted stereotypes of criminals and crime are invaluable vehicles for politicians advocating capital punishment" (Costanzo, 1997, p. 162). Even police officers and judges may be adopting certain techniques in order to maximize media attention. For example, Aaron Doyle noted in *Entertaining Crime* that some judges will "pass spectacular individualized sentences apparently targeted to achieve media attention." Doyle also cites examples of officers who "parade suspects in handcuffs in strategic locations so they can be photographed by the news media" (Fishman & Cavender, 1998, p. 110). Thus we may be using inappropriate punishments for female delinquents based on a faulty, media-promoted perception, rather than reality.

One limitation of this study is the methodology. Content analysis can be criticized for being too susceptible to researcher bias. When dealing with something as subjective as film depictions there is an increased concern that the researcher may "find what he or she is looking for." This was controlled for in that both researchers viewed the films and coded the portrayals using the same scale, which served to triangulate the results. Another limitation is that most of the data regarding true female delinquency is from the mid-to-late 1990s. Although it is likely that trends are similar, it would clearly be best to have the most up-to-date data.

Due to the length of time it takes to analyze a film, typically two hours in length, one delimitation of this study is that it covers only 13 films. Another delimitation is that all of these films had to be accessible at the local video store, due to time constraints. Further, films chosen focus on females who commit felonies, which may exclude other films that depict only misdemeanors, such as those that depict underage drinking. Most films viewed for this study, however, seemed to incorporate both types of offenses.

Several operational definitions are necessary to ensure clarity of the research. *Film* refers to any movie made for theater distribution; made-for-television specials were purposely excluded, due to lack of easy access. Films were chosen for several reasons. First, both researchers' high school students recommended them. As the goal was to analyze films marketed to teens, this was helpful information. Second, Blockbuster Video's "Video Guide" indicated that these films were about female delinquency. Finally, time was spent perusing the racks at Blockbuster for plot descriptions that sounded relevant. Criteria used for selection of films that depict female delinquents include: (1) the film's main character(s) are females; (2) the female(s) commit at least one felony; and (3) the felony committed was central to the plot. *Current* film was defined as those being released between the later 1980s and the year 2000. *Teen-marketed* refers to films that were intended for, although not necessarily exclusively, an audience aged 13 to 20. Most of the films in this genre are rated "R," which indicates that they are only to be viewed by those above 17 unless a parent or guardian is present. However, it was already noted that many makers of "R"-rated movies do indeed market their films to younger people. Finally, a working hypothesis that guided the research was developed. It was posited that current films depicting female delinquents do so in predominantly stereotypical ways that do not accurately reflect reality regarding female delinquency.

LITERATURE REVIEW

The relevant literature for this content analysis comes from three main areas; research regarding media effects on viewers, data and theory regarding female criminality, and existing content analyses that pose similar questions.

Media Effects

Although this research is not specifically focused on analyzing violence, the literature about violent media can help provide guidelines for the content analysis. Further, most depictions of crime and criminals include violence, which makes this information relevant. The types of affects involved in watching violent media are categorized differently by different researchers. For the purposes of this research they are lumped into three categories. *Direct behavioral effects* are those arguments which claim that viewing violent media entices or prompts people to be aggressive or violent. *Desensitization* refers to the reduced empathy for crime or violence victims as a result of viewing violent media. The *mean world syndrome*, a name coined by George Gerbner, refers to the perception that viewers of violent media may have that the world is a dangerous place. This is an exaggerated fear or concern. All three of these typically include stereotypical portrayals of the groups involved. For example, one content analysis of films about prisons found that guards are most often depicted as "smug hacks" (Bailey & Hale, 1998). Although all three types of effects are both interesting and important, the third is the most applicable to this study.

The impressions about criminality and overall safety that Americans hold are often not based on actual experience but on media coverage. In *The Mythology of Crime and Criminal Justice*, Kappeler, Blumberg, and Potter say that "media are mythmakers." This causes concern in that media may offer us "distorted images of crime, criminals and law enforcers" (Bailey & Hale, 1998, p. 2). For example, Costanzo notes that most Americans overestimate murder rates. This effect occurs even more for those dubbed "heavy viewers" (Costanzo, 1997). This is what George Gerbner refers to as the mean world syndrome. He says: "Our analysis has found that exposure to violence-laden television activates an exaggerated sense of insecurity and mistrust and anxiety about the mean world seen on television" (Bok, 1998, p. 62). Researchers are not entirely positive how the mean world syndrome occurs, but many subscribe to the cultivation theory, which holds that repeated patterns of portrayals found throughout the media shape viewers perceptions about the real world (Fishman & Cavender, 1998). A criticism of existing work in this area, however, is that it has been conducted largely regarding males and applied to males. If the same principles hold true for the depiction of female criminals, however, people may be more fearful and more concerned about a perceived increase in female criminality than they realistically need to be.

Research indicates that media coverage consistently overrepresents certain types of crime. For example, violent, random crimes are frequently covered, even though 55 percent of all murders occur between acquaintances. An especially disturbing content analysis of the frequency of media violence, conducted by the National Coalition on Television Violence, reported that "by age 16, the typical U.S. child will view an average of approximately 500,000 murders on television" (Fishman & Cavender, 1998, p. 21). Ninety-three percent of all crime is property crime, although this is not clear from media representations either. In a content analysis of the television program *Cops*, Aaron Doyle found that the shows "over-represent both violent crime and the proportion of crime solved by police" (Fishman & Cavender, 1998, p. 104). Typically, white-collar crime is ignored completely. This type of depiction gives viewers the perception that violent crime rates are out of control, when actually they are relatively stable or decreasing. "As a result, researchers conclude that crime in the media 'bears little resemblance' to reality" (Bailey & Hale, 1998, p. 111).

Beyond finding distorted images of crime in the United States researchers have found relationships between viewing television crime stories and ideologies of crime and criminals. For example, viewers believe that criminals are psychological and social deviants, formal punishment deters crime, capital punishment is appropriate, prisons are rather lenient places, and the U.S criminal justice system is becoming softer. Such characterizations of crime and criminals increase the public's fear of crime, do not depict those populations most victimized, and focus on psychological rather than social explanations of crime (Bailey & Hale, 1998, p. 112). For example, a 1996 survey found that regular viewers of *Cops* and three other "reality television" programs were "significantly more fearful than infrequent viewers of being sexually assaulted, beaten up, knifed, shot or killed" (Fishman & Cavender, 1998, p. 107). In another analysis of *Cops*, Kooistra, Mahoney, and Westervelt found that African-Americans are underrepresented as victims. While content analyses indicate that fictional programs tend to underrepresent African-Americans as criminal suspects, nonfiction or more reality-based programs such as *Cops* overrepresent them (Fishman & Cavender, 1998). Once again, these data seem to be focused on males. Further, few content analyses focus on the portrayals of delinquents, despite the fact that this group has received some of the most negative press in recent years. *Superpredators* is a term that has been used to describe the perceived growth and brutality of teen crime. This research will apply the extant literature on media analyses to the relatively new area of female delinquency. We turn next to the literature regarding actual rates of female delinquency, which provide a basis for comparison.

Female Delinquency

There are numerous theories today of why females become delinquent, despite the fact that until recent decades few criminologists really considered women as criminals or delinquents. In the 1970s the notion that the women's liberation movement caused increased rates of female crime, promoted by Adler and Simon, was introduced. Although never proven to be true in any way, this theory has maintained extensive press coverage and is still popular. Another common theme among early criminological work regarding female delinquents is a heavy emphasis on their sexuality. Most useful for comparison, however, are real statistics and descriptions of female delinquency in recent decades. Chesney-Lind notes that as of 1995, females represented only 25 percent of all arrests of young people. Of those youths arrested in 1994, only 5.8 percent were for serious violent offenses (Chesney-Lind, 1997). Of these, only 3.2 percent were girls (Ferrell & Websdale, 1999). Between 1992 and 1996 the rate of female arrests for violent crimes did increase 25 percent with no increase in male arrests, but this could be due to a number of factors, including relabeling of offenses and increased police attention (CSPV Fact Sheet, 2000). Arrests and charges of females for "other assaults" skyrocketed between 1986 and 1996, resulting in an increase of 142.6 percent. Girls are, however, more likely to be arrested for noninjury assaults or as bystanders and/or male companions in fighting (Polakow, 2000). In a study of the Maryland juvenile justice system, Mayer found that 97.9 percent of person-to-person offenses involved assault, with half of these a fight with a family member, most often a parent (Polakow, 2000).

Among females arrested, the most common reason is for status offenses, those violations that are criminal only because of the perpetrator's age. In 1994, 23 percent of all girls arrested were due to status offenses, compared to only 8.6 percent of boys (Chesney-Lind, 1997). Twenty-five percent of all girls' delinquency is due to shoplifting. There are significant differences between characteristically male shoplifting and female shoplifting, though. Females tend to shoplift fewer, less costly items and are less sophisticated in the way that they do it. Self-reports actually indicate that males shoplift more, but for a variety of reasons, females are more frequently detected (Chesney-Lind, 1997).

Chesney-Lind also found that a major reason for the presence of girls in the juvenile justice system was because their own parents had insisted on their arrest (Chesney-Lind, 1997). Another major factor related to why females become delinquent is sexual abuse. Finkelhor and Baron found in 1986 that roughly 70 percent of victims of sex abuse are girls. In girls the abuse typically starts earlier, is more likely to be at the hands of a family member, and tends to last longer than abuse of boys (Chesney-Lind, 1997). Research also shows that delinquent families have more mother–daughter conflicts and more neurotic fathers (Snyder, 1995, p. 55).

In regard to more serious or violent offenses, girls who have killed are more likely to use a knife and to kill as a result of a conflict. This is quite different from boys, who more often kill during the commission of another crime. Females are also more likely to murder a family member of someone very young (Chesney-Lind, 1997). Further, girls are most likely to kill alone when they do kill; boys typically kill as part of a group. Thus "the stereotype of girls becoming gun-toting robbers was not supported" (Ferrell & Websdale, 1999, p. 125).

African-American females are the most rapidly increasing group in prisons today. From 1986 to 1991 the percentage of African-American women in prisons skyrocketed by 828 percent, due largely to the War on Drugs (Chesney-Lind, 1997). This is a rate two times larger than that of black males (Miller, 1998). In actual fact, black women are more likely to engage in personal crimes; white women in drugs, alcohol, and status offenses (Chesney-Lind, 1997). Further, although many more African-American women are arrested and convicted for drug-related offenses, "treatment slots remain disproportionally filled by white female substance abusers" (Miller, 1998, p. xvi).

Punishment efforts are also telling. Of females in any facility, 62 percent are in private facilities; 85 percent of these are for nondelinquent offenses, including status offenses, neglect, or voluntary admissions. White women are more likely than black women to be incarcerated in private facilities (Chesney-Lind, 1997). An analysis of 14 state and federal institutions revealed that the typical incarcerated female is black (over 50 percent), unmarried (80 percent), the mother of at least one child (75 percent), and on welfare (over 50 percent) (Miller, 1998). In general, a disproportionate number of juveniles confined to detention centers are male, black, and/or Hispanic. Another trend is incarcerating psychiatrically ill adolescents; according to Maccoby and Martin, in 1983 over 25 percent of those institutionalized for some delinquent offense were mentally ill (Snyder, 1995a).

Women's criminality also differs from men's in that their delinquent careers tend to be much shorter and less serious. Females typically desist after one referral (Chesney-Lind, 1997). Interview data from Chesney-Lind indicates that despite popular opinion, female delinquents have highly traditional ideas regarding gender roles. Most aspire to stay at home and be mothers (Chesney-Lind & Shelden, 1998).

Although not specific to females, much evidence suggests that problems in school are tied closely to delinquency rates. Various theories have been put forth to explain this relationship, including the idea that schools are coming to resemble prisons. Other studies suggest that those most at risk for school problems are the same groups that are most at risk for delinquency: those from a lower socioeconomic status (Cox & Conrad, 1996).

In sum, although the media has portrayed a rise in frequency and brutality of female delinquency, this seems to be at least partially untrue. These descriptions of actual female crime trends will be invaluable in providing a means of comparison. A final area that informs this project is data regarding how to conduct content analyses dealing with the criminal justice system.

Existing Content Analyses Regarding Criminality

A critical concept in analyzing crime and/or violence is first to decide what definition of violence will be used. Graeme Newman proposes this one: "Violence is a series of events, the cause of which, or the outcomes of which, cause injury or damage to persons or property" (Bailey & Hale, 1998, p. 42). From there he differentiates between two types of violence: instrumental and expressive. *Instrumental violence* refers to those acts that are used as a means of achieving a particular end. *Expressive violence* is more explosive; it is a way to show emotions. Newman says that both are used extensively in the movies (Bailey & Hale, 1998). He next describes the various ways that each is portrayed in film and provides examples. Instrumental violence can be in ten different forms. It may be a "rebellion against justice," as depicted in *Star Wars*; an act of vengeance, as per *Death Wish*; a rebellion against bureaucracy, like those in the "Dirty Harry" movies; a method of problem solving, such as those depicted in private investigator films or the James Bond series; a means of extracting confessions, as seen also in James Bond; a way to demonstrate authority (typically of an "evil" person, such as a corrupt sheriff); a method of exposing corruption, as in the Harrison Ford film *Witness*; a method of establishing order, as per *Batman*; a view of higher morality, such as *The Untouchables*; or a means of conflict resolution, as seen in *The Godfather, Boyz N' the Hood*, and *Colors*.

Expressive violence is portrayed in 12 ways, according to Newman. These include stereotyping ethnic groups, such as in *Lawrence of Arabia*; teen rebellion, like that in *Rebel without a Cause* and *The Outsiders*; a natural act, like *Twister*; an act by a beast, like *Godzilla* or *Jaws*; "Going one better," as seen in any James Bond movie or the *Die Hard* trilogy; any war scene; fun, usually incorporated in cartoons, like *Who Framed Roger Rabbit?*; mysticism, like that of the *Friday the 13th* series; "the madman," exemplified by Hannibal Lecter in *The Silence of the Lambs*; vengeance; and sex, as seen in more recent films depicting female criminals, such as *Sleeping with the Enemy* and *Basic Instinct* (Ferrell & Websdale, 1999). Although most of the characteristics seem to be describing males, Newman's categorization of the types of violence will be used to analyze female acts as well. Therefore problems or insufficiencies with Newman's classification for this particular application can be noted.

Newman also described the various ways that these acts are "enplotted" into films. He describes 16 enplotting techniques that will guide this analysis. According to Newman, violence can be simultaneous, or a mounting up of problems that the hero must solve; can be shown for shock value; can be in the form of a torture scene; can be used to reveal a bloody or otherwise mangled body; is often used as a "hook" early in a film to grab the viewer's attention; can take the form of some innovative or technological means of destruction; can be displayed through a violent chase scene; can be seen through the destructive effects of fire; can simply be tied in with blood; can be used as a means of contrasting opposites; can be accompanied by contrasting music; can be used in a comedy; can be a way to have the "loser" or "underdog" win; can be a scene of absolute injustice, such as when the hero's family is killed in *Gladiator*; can be a "board game plot," where the "good guy" and the "bad guy" take turns acting violent; and can be as a means of ritual predictability, meaning that the viewer knows the type of movie and expects a certain amount and type of violence from it (Ferrell & Websdale, 1999).

Snyder identifies four important subgroups of criminals that can be contrasted with the media depictions outlined by Newman. The first group he calls *undersocialized–aggressive delinquents*. These adolescents are disobedient, disloyal, destructive, and have a general lack of concern for others. They are often depicted in movies about true stories, such as *Badlands*, which portrayed the killing spree of Charles Starkweather and Carol Fugate in 1958. The second group Snyder dubs *socialized–aggressive delinquents*. These youths typically commit crimes in groups and tend to commit less severe crimes. This is also the profile of gang members. 1971's *A Clockwork Orange* and 1988's *Colors* are good examples. *Attention deficit* describes the third group. These kids are preoccupied dreamers; they are often sluggish and impulsive. Probably the best known depiction of this group is in 1955's *Rebel without a Cause*. Finally, some juvenile delinquents display what Snyder calls *anxiety–withdrawal–dysphonia*. These kids are shy, hypersensitive, socially withdrawn, anxious, and sad. School problems are also common. Possibly as many as 38 to 58 percent of all juvenile delinquents fall in this category, which can also be seen in *Rebel without a Cause* (Snyder, 1995b). Neuman and Snyder's ideas will be incorporated into the coding of each film and the subsequent analysis.

METHODOLOGY

This content analysis began with an initial viewing of the films for plot familiarity. Several of the films have already been viewed, so this step was abbreviated. The next step involved a second viewing of each film with note-taking about the following areas. These areas were developed based on the literature noted above.

1. Perceived socioeconomic status of the offender(s)
2. Perceived educational level of the offender(s)
3. Perceived family background of the offender(s)
4. Physical appearance of the offender(s)
5. Crime(s) committed
6. Context of crime(s) committed
7. Perceived attitude of the offender(s)
8. Perceived attitude of the victim(s)
9. Perceived attitude(s) of others involved
10. Consequences of the crime(s)

Additional areas to be noted include:

1. Degree of violence and type, as outlined by Neuman (expressive versus instrumental)
2. How the violence is portrayed (Neuman's 10 forms for instrumental violence or 12 forms for expressive violence)
3. How the violence is enplotted (Neuman's 16 ways)
4. Which of Snyder's four delinquent types each film character fits into (undersocialized–aggressive, socialized–aggressive, attention-deficit, or anxiety–withdrawal–dysphonia)

This method was chosen simply because no better way has been identified in the literature to date that allows researchers to analyze the role that film may play in the creation or perpetuation of stereotypes about female delinquency. Content analysis is an increasingly accepted means of studying popular culture, as indicated by the proliferation of texts dealing with this in recent years, including Ferrell and Websdale's and Bailey and Hale's. It produces in-depth qualitative data that truly probes the topic. Similarly, the study of the role of popular culture in the study of criminology, often called *cultural criminology*, has been gaining acceptance among those in criminology and other fields. These criminologists have "begun to widen the notion of 'criminalization' to include more than the simple creation and application of criminal law" (Ferrell & Websdale, 1999, p. 10).

In addition, the current atmosphere, which can be traced to the early 1980s, presents an approach to crime that can be labeled "get tough." Although there are many factors associated with this view, anxieties about stagnant wages, downsizing, and an uncertain future clearly contribute (Fishman & Cavender, 1998). As Aaron Doyle says, "this punitiveness involves the displacement of anxieties and angers from other sources" (Fishman & Cavender, 1998). This philosophy, which has been reflected through various forms of mass media, is finally starting to be challenged. Similarly, the role of the media, especially that on the screen, is now being linked to perpetuating the "hegemony of masculinity," as described by Gray Cavender in Ferrell and Websdale's text. Cavender says that certain films "traffic in ideology, which includes beliefs about fear of crime and other social concerns. They also depict images of masculinity and femininity, in their hegemonic forms, and in alternative forms as well" (Ferrell & Websdale, 1999, p. 172). John Braithwaite and Kathleen Daly sum it up well when they say, "violence is gendered: it is a problem and consequence of masculinity" (Miller, 1998, p. 151). These data make this particular study especially timely and important; not only does it look at how a specific realm of crime is presented, but it looks at how females may be further subordinated through popular culture and the potential implications of it.

Film Descriptions

Foxfire, a 1996 film starring Angelina Jolie, was dubbed a female-bonding movie in Blockbuster's "Video Guide." The story begins with a female student, Rita, being verbally harassed by her science teacher because she is squeamish about frog dissection. A mysterious stranger, Legs (Jolie), emerges through the classroom window to "save the day." After class, Rita, Legs, and three other girls, Goldie, Maddie, and Violet, meet and discover that the same teacher has been sexually harassing both Rita and Violet. The girls plot their revenge, which involves setting the teacher up to start harassing Rita while the others witness it, then beating him up. All are suspended for several weeks, during which time they bond as friends. Some jocks are very upset that their teacher/coach may be fired for the harassment, so they threaten the girls and eventually set it up to rape Maddie. Again, Legs saves the day by pulling a knife on the boys, and the group of girls steal their car. They end up crashing after a police chase. All of the girls except Legs are remanded to their parents' care; since she has a record, she is sentenced to six months to a year. The group drifts apart some during this time, and Goldie becomes a heroin addict. Cindy, the girlfriend of the head jock, feels bad and admits to the judge what really happened, so Legs is released. The girls demand $10,000 from Goldie's father to put her through rehab, but he refuses. Legs turns a gun on him and they kidnap him. In the course of some confusion, he is shot accidentally by Rita.

The violence portrayed in *Foxfire* is expressive, as it is seen as a way for the girls to get even with those people (males) who have wronged them. It is an example of teen rebellion, although since it seems somewhat justified, it is not a clear-cut example of rebellion. It could also be included under the headings of "vengeance" and "sex," as the act that spawned the car chase was an attempted sexual act against Maddie. None of the enplotting techniques described by Newman fit clearly; the closest is the loser/underdog idea. Of Snyder's four types of delinquents these girls may fit into two. On one hand they may be dubbed socialized–aggressive, as the crimes they committed were not especially brutal and they worked in a group, but two of the girls, Rita and Goldie, appear to be reserved and have some emotional issues, thus making them fit more closely in the anxiety–withdrawal–dysphonia subgroup.

Natural Born Killers, starring Woody Harrelson and Juliette Lewis, is the story of Mickey and Mallory Knox, two so-called "natural-born killers" who go on a killing spree. The spree begins when they kill Mallory's abusive dad and oblivious mother and run off together. They seem to enjoy the killing as well as the media attention; they become cult idols. When they are finally caught and are isolated from one another in jail, a prison riot ensues, kicked off by an interview with Mickey to be aired as Superbowl half-time entertainment. During the riot, Mickey and Mallory escape.

Mallory's violence is also of an expressive nature; she grows to enjoy it for its own sake. This depiction is most like the "madman" category, as it is so brutal that the average viewer is supposed to be appalled. It is clearly enplotted as a means of shock value. The movie did indeed have that effect; many groups protested its release, and at least one lawsuit was filed as a result of actions taken after viewing the film. Both Mickey and Mallory would be included in the undersocialized–aggressive subgroup.

Girls' Town does not star any major pop-culture icons. It depicts four middle- to lower-class high school seniors in a ghettolike area. Nicki, a pretty black girl, is very smart, reserved, and is headed for Princeton. Emma also seems to be smart; she is a Caucasian girl going to Columbia for some type of art. Angela is a beautiful black girl whose main personality characteristic seems to be angst. Patty, a Hispanic girl, has a baby by an abusive man, Eddie, who appears much older and is not married to her. She is not very bright; she has been held back in school a number of times. The action begins early, when Nicki commits suicide. After reading her journal the girls discover that she had been raped. Emma announces that she was also raped, and the girls start seeking revenge against the males they perceive as having wronged them. First they vandalize the car of the boy who raped Emma, then they break into Eddie's apartment and steal some things, which they pawn. They all seem to enjoy the feeling of revenge. The final crime is a confrontation with the man who raped Nicki. The girls end up beating him up.

The acts perpetrated by the *Girls' Town* characters are expressive; they are both acts of vengeance as well as tied to sex. All the crimes they committed, at least in their eyes, were the result of harmful sex acts committed by men. Again it is difficult to identify the enplotting technique used when applying Newman's rubric; the closest is probably the loser/underdog technique, as in *Foxfire*. These girls probably fall into the subgroup of socialized–aggressive, since they committed less serious crimes as a part of a group.

Wild Things, a 1997 film starring Neve Campbell, Denise Richards, Matt Dillon, and Kevin Bacon, is the story of a twisted sex and extortion plot. Matt Dillon plays Mr. Lombardo, a popular high school counselor and ladies man. He has numerous affairs and flirts with the students. One particular girl, Kelly (Richards), has a serious crush on him. She is wealthy, beautiful, and smart. Lombardo has also had an affair with her mother, who is one of the most influential people in town. Kelly claims that Mr. Lombardo raped her and is supported in this story by Susie (Campbell), who is a pretty, smart girl from the "wrong side of the tracks." During the trial, however, Susie recants and says it was all a scam. Lombardo then sues Kelly's mom and makes a lot of money. We next see Lombardo and the two girls celebrating, so clearly the entire thing was concocted to steal money. Susie become paranoid, though, and Lombardo and Kelly allegedly kill her. The investigator, Duquet (Bacon), senses that something is shaky and confronts Kelly. In the course of a scuffle, she is killed. The scene then flashes to a beautiful island, where we see Lombardo meeting with Duquet, yet another plot twist. Lombardo kills him on a boat, where Susie is also riding along, clearly not dead. She then kills Lombardo and sails off alone.

The violence in *Wild Things* is instrumental; all actors commit their crimes with the hopes of becoming rich. None of the types of instrumental violence identified by Newman seem to fit well in this case. It could be argued that "rebellion against bureaucracy" is the main theme, as Kelly's mother seems to control most of what occurs in the town via her wealth, yet the viewer gets the feeling that Lombardo and crew do not pick her because of her influence, merely her money. None of Newman's enplotting techniques work here; surprisingly, he does not identify any that address violence perpetrated for money. Kelly and Susie most closely fit into the category of undersocialized–aggressive, as both have a general lack of concern for others.

The In Crowd was made in 2000 and does not feature any big names. It tells the story of Adrian, a poor but pretty girl who is institutionalized because she vandalized the vehicle of a man with whom she became obsessed. A helpful doctor arranges for her to have a job at a country club for rich, beautiful kids. Most of them have drinking and/or drug problems. She is befriended by Brittany, the "leader" of the crew. Brittany becomes jealous of Adrian, though, when Adrian is accepted by the others and when it appears that she was flirting with Brittanny's lover. She kills another friend who knows her "secret," which is revealed later, and beats to death the doctor for refusing to sleep with her again. This is blamed on Adrian, who is sent to jail. During the course of this we discover Brittany's secret—she killed her own sister several years ago because she was more popular than Brittany. Her body is buried at the club. A friend breaks Adrian out of jail, and she and Britanny chase one another around for a while before Brittany is caught. She ends up cracking up and is institutionalized, where she promptly begins charming the orderlies.

Brittany and Adrian's violence are both acts of expression; Adrian seems to be mostly acting out of teen rebellion, whereas Brittany acts out of vengeance. Sexuality is closely tied to both girls' actions. The violent acts are enplotted as a means of contrasting opposites: Brittany as evil and Adrian as good but misunderstood. Brittany would be considered undersocialized–aggressive, as she disregards the welfare of anyone but herself.

Teaching Mrs. Tingle stars Katie Holmes, of *Dawson's Creek* fame. Holmes plays LeeAnn, a great student with scruples. She is also very pretty. She is vying for valedictorian honors with Trudy, who is very nasty. History class will determine who wins and is taught by the notoriously mean Mrs. Tingle, who seems to hate LeeAnn. LeeAnn hangs around with her friend, Jolene, and Luke, a cute but unmotivated student who steals Mrs. Tingle's final exam answer key. Although she has no intention of using it, LeeAnn gets caught with the key and Mrs. Tingle is planning to have her expelled. The three go to her home to reason with her, which does not work, and they end up tying her up. They also try to blackmail her by staging some dirty pictures of her and the coach from the school. The movie ends with Mrs. Tingle being killed as a result of a struggle.

The kidnapping and subsequent violence committed by LeeAnn, Jolene, and Luke is instrumental; none of these teenagers appears to be a major delinquent—they are simply trying to get Mrs. Tingle to listen to them. "Exposing corruption" may fit here, as Mrs. Tingle seems to abuse her authority as a teacher. "Violence as a means of conflict resolution" also works; since Mrs. Tingle was not cooperative with them when they spoke to her, they felt they needed to resort to violence. It is enplotted in a somewhat amusing way so may fall under the category of "violence as comedy." It also depicts a "contrast of opposites," as LeeAnn, Jolene, and Mrs. Tingle are all juxtaposed against one another. None of Snyder's subgroups are applicable here.

Manny and Lo, a 1988 film, is quite different from the others. Lo is the older sister to Manny. Both girls were orphaned when their mother died and they ran away from foster care. They travel around, sleeping at various places, and seem to have money, although it is not clear where it comes from. Lo discovers that she is pregnant and it is too late for an abortion. They find a vacant home to stay in and discover that they know nothing about having a baby. They kidnap a nice, motherly lady, Elaine, who is working at a baby store. Initially, Elaine resists, but eventually they set up a somewhat happy home. Lo gets upset with Elaine at one point and they leave her somewhere in the country. She goes into labor, though, so they find Elaine again and she has the baby. She says she wants to give it to Elaine, but it appears that they all stay together.

Although no serious violence occurs in this film, kidnapping can be considered a form of violence. As such, this film depicts instrumental violence. Manny and Lo use the kidnapping as a means of solving their problem: specifically, dealing with Lo's pregnancy. None of Snyder's subgroups really fit this film.

1993's *The Crush* stars Alicia Silverstone and Cary Elwes. Silverstone plays Darian, a 14-year-old beautiful rich girl with an incredibly high IQ. She is very spoiled and very manipulative. She develops a crush on Nick (Elwes), who is renting a guest house from her parents. She becomes obsessed with him and jealous of his girlfriend or anyone she perceives as a threat. She vandalizes Nick's car, sabotages her friend's horse so that she breaks her arm, and locks Nick's girlfriend in a room with a bee's nest, to which she is allergic. She then claims that Nick assaulted her sexually. He is arrested. The movie ends with them fighting and her being institutionalized. The viewer sees that she is developing a crush on a young, good-looking doctor there.

Darian's violent acts are all expressive and committed as acts of rebellion. They are also tied to her sexuality. The "board game" enplotting technique is used here; Nick counters each of Darian's acts, culminating in a "showdown" at the end. Of the subgroups, Darian would best fit into undersocialized–aggressive, as she is incredibly narcissistic.

Jawbreaker depicts four beautiful rich girls who "rule the school." Because they are jealous that she is popular as well as nice, three of them kidnap the fourth to play a joke on her. They tie her up and stuff a jawbreaker in her mouth, then put her in their trunk. She dies, however, and two of the girls, led by the manipulative Courtney, spend the rest of the movie covering up for the crime. The third, Julie, feels bad, and eventually finds evidence to prove what happened. None of the girls are punished legally, but the film ends with the public shaming of Courtney.

The kidnapping and death of Elizabeth in *Jawbreaker* is accidental and committed out of jealousy; it is therefore an expressive act of violence. It is enplotted through a strange sense of humor. These girls would be categorized as socialized–aggressives due to their group actions.

2000's *Crime and Punishment in Suburbia*, a modern-day remake of *Crime and Punishment*, is the story of RoseAnn, a pretty, wealthy, and smart girl. She is emotionally abused by her drunkard stepfather, Fred, as is her mother. Her mother has an affair, which further disturbs RoseAnn's world. Fred gets drunk one night and rapes RoseAnn, which is the last straw. She talks her boyfriend, Jimmy, into helping her kill him. Since it was obvious they did not get along, however, her mother is implicated in the murder. RoseAnn begins hanging out with Vincent, a high school "outsider." Eventually, the true story comes out, and RoseAnn goes to jail, which she actually prefers to her previous life.

The violence in this film could fit into both categories; it is instrumental in that RoseAnn acts out of concern for her own safety, but the way that she and Jimmy kill Fred also seems to be an expressive act of vengeance. Further, RoseAnn's life appears as an example of "absolute injustice" because of the abuse she suffers at the hands of Fred. She might be considered an example of anxiety–withdrawal–dysphonia because she clearly is anxious, withdrawn, and sad.

Christina Ricci and Lisa Kudrow star in 1998's *The Opposite of Sex*. Ricci plays Dee Dee, a lower-class girl who is manipulative and immoral. She runs away from her home with her mother and stays with her much older gay brother, Tom. Once there she seduces his boyfriend, claims that she is pregnant by him, and steals money from her brother. They run away, but she continues to try to get money from Tom, using blackmail. Dee Dee ends up shooting an old boyfriend, who was probably the baby's father, and flees the scene. She serves six months for this.

All of Dee Dee's actions are instrumental; she needs money, and above all, she wants to rebel against authority. Although the film is not focused on violence, it clearly seeks to shock the viewer through the way that Dee Dee is portrayed as unscrupulous and uncaring. She would be considered undersocialized–aggressive, as she does not commit serious, violent crimes.

Cruel Intentions stars teen sex symbols Sarah Michelle Gellar, Ryan Philippe, and Reese Witherspoon. Sebastian and Katherine (Philippe and Gellar), are rich, beautiful, and spoiled stepsiblings. Their parents are never present. Katherine, a cocaine addict, is upset that she was dumped for a new girl, Cecille, so she makes a deal with Sebastian, well known as a ladies' man, to seduce her and ruin her reputation. If he does it, she will have sex with him. Meanwhile, Sebastian needs a new challenge, which comes in the form of his efforts to sleep with Annette (Witherspoon), another new girl and avowed virgin. Sebastian does what Katherine wants but has also fallen in love with Annette. Katherine sees this as another slight and arranges to have Annette find out the truth and to have Sebastian beat up. He dies and Katherine ends up humiliated when his diary is made public, but no legal consequences are shown.

Katherine and Sebastian's actions are a combination of instrumental and expressive; both use sex as a means of achieving what they want and both simply enjoy manipulating others. Neither fits into any of Snyder's four subgroups.

1996's *Set It Off* is a different type of female delinquency film. First, it depicts four African-American females. Second, these women are considerably more aggressive than all of the others, with the exception of Mallory in *Natural Born Killers*. It relies heavily on negative stereotypes of African-American criminality. The film begins with a violent bank robbery committed at a bank where one of the main characters, Frankie, is employed. The police feel that she was somehow involved because she knew the assailants and did not follow proper procedure. She is angered at this accusation as well as the fact that the bank fires her. "Stony," another friend from the projects, has been working hard to help send her brother to college in the absence of her parents, who were both killed in a car accident. He is mistaken as one of the bank robbers and killed by the police, which provides Stony with the motivation to commit crime. Cleo (Queen Latifah) is simply a poor girl from the projects who is full of angst. The fourth girl, referred to as T.T., has a young child and never has enough money to support them. The four girls regularly drink and get high together; they also discuss robbing a bank several times. They finally decide to act on this when T.T. brings her son to the janitorial company they all work at and he gets into some chemicals; at the hospital, Social Services is called and he is taken from her. The girls obtain weapons from a local thug and make off with $12,000 from their first robbery. The second robbery is not as smooth; the cops have tentatively identified them and they almost get caught. This time they get $75,000 each. They hide it at work, however, and the boss runs off with it. While trying to get it back from him, a struggle occurs and T.T. shoots and kills him. They decide to commit one last robbery, at the biggest bank and the place where Stony's boyfriend works. The police show up and, after some car chases, all but Stony are killed.

The violent acts depicted in this film could be considered both expressive and instrumental. It is expressive for Cleo, as she is motivated by angst. It also becomes a way for Frankie and Stony to express their antipolice feelings. It is instrumental for T.T., who only agrees to commit the robbery so that she can make money to support her son. The violence begins as a "hook," then continues as a mounting of problems for our vigilante females to solve. The girls would be considered undersocialized–aggressives, as they work in a group. However, their crimes are quite serious, and they end up disregarding the safety of anyone else involved, so they could be dubbed socialized–aggressives.

ANALYSIS

One obvious commonality among virtually all the movies is the portrayal of the delinquent or delinquents as beautiful, perhaps even sexy, girls. The only film that does not rely on this type of portrayal completely is *Manny and Lo*, although neither of the girls would really be considered ugly. Although clearly some of this can be attributed to Hollywood's drive for ticket sales, it would seem to viewers who did not know otherwise that all female delinquents are good looking. Further, male delinquents are not always depicted as being good-looking, nor can we describe the general population this way, so this was an important feature. Although obviously many girls who do commit crimes may be beautiful or sexy, the nearly complete lack of showing anything different is disturbing because it ignores the fact that most delinquent girls come from backgrounds where they would not have the resources to "primp themselves." Further, it serves to reinforce the idea that any female who may possibly be considered "strong" must also be beautiful and sexual. It perpetuates the hegemony of masculinity, as described by Davis in Ferrell and Websdale (1999).

A second but related commonality is the focus on sex or sexual acts. In *Cruel Intentions, The Opposite of Sex, Teaching Mrs. Tingle, Jawbreaker, The Crush, The In Crowd*, and *Wild Things* the girls use sexuality to achieve what they want. For example, Katherine offers Sebastian sex in order to help her in *Cruel Intentions*, and Dee Dee uses sex to extort money from her kind brother in *The Opposite of Sex*. Several other films also involve sex, but in a different way. These films portray a female's sexuality as a way that she is vulnerable. For example, Manny and Lo probably never would have kidnapped anyone if she had not been pregnant. Similarly, RoseAnn's crime was a direct result of her rape by her stepfather in *Crime and Punishment in Suburbia*. Although problematic, this link between female delinquency and sexuality has been a theme among criminologists since they began to consider female crime. The problem is that, especially in the first type of portrayal, it tends to allow all women to be viewed as sexually manipulated. Then when some are taken advantage of sexually, as in the second portrayal, some viewers have less sympathy. On the other hand, some, predominantly women, may see their actions as justified because of the sexual abuse, which sends the message that it is appropriate to seek violent revenge if this occurs.

Although overdone, there is some truth to this depiction. A large percentage of those females who do commit crimes have been abused. As noted earlier, 70 percent of female delinquents have suffered some form of abuse, typically at the hands of a family member. Therefore, the movies that utilized this type of depiction did so realistically. A related issue is that of mother–daughter conflict. The literature shows that delinquent females endure more difficult mother–daughter relationships than the general population. The movie portrayals, however, did not depict this. In only one case, *Girls' Town*, was there a visible mother–daughter conflict. That was between Angela and her mother and did not appear to be a significant part of her delinquency. In addition, female delinquents tend to have more neurotic fathers, as noted by Snyder (1995b). Although *neurotic* is a vague term, RoseAnn's stepfather probably fits. Interestingly, few of the films even depicted fathers or father figures.

Another common theme is the depiction of the delinquent acts as justifiable. Six of the films very clearly depict the perpetrators' actions as justified. For example, even though her actions are horrendous, Mallory's killing of her abusive father and oblivious mother in *Natural Born Killers* seems, if not justified, at least understandable. All the crimes committed by the girls in *Girls Town* are depicted as being a result of abusive actions by males. Although very extreme, the girls' decision to rob a bank in *Set It Off* is portrayed as the only way that they can all get out of the projects. Even *Teaching Mrs. Tingle* depicts the kidnapping and abuse of Mrs. Tingle as rightful action against an authoritarian teacher. *Manny and Lo* and *Crime and Punishment in Suburbia* also feature justified crimes. Other films made it less clear, but implied the same. For instance, throughout *The Opposite of Sex* the viewer wonders whether Dee Dee was abused by her stepfather. One problem with this type of depiction, as noted above, is that it sends a message to viewers that taking the law into your own hands is sometimes the best response. As Pamela Donovan notes in *Entertaining Crime*, this type of film allows the viewer to "stand up and be counted, uncontroversially and without much effort" (Fishman & Cavender, 1998, p. 132). Female viewers who have experienced similar types of abuse may find this message especially strong. Further, there is concern that when teachers or others in authority positions are portrayed in negative ways, students may feel increased hostility toward their real teachers and administration.

Another commonality between most of the films is the depiction of the "spoiled rich girl." Half of the films portray the delinquents in this way. Although it is probably true that a larger portion of females who commit crimes belong to this group than we really know about, as a result of criminal justice practices that "weed out the rich," as Jeffrey Rieman says, the reality is that the females who are in jail are typically poor and minorities (Rieman, 2000). Interestingly enough, only three movies showed any minority delinquents: *Girls' Town, Set It Off*, and *Foxfire*. As we know that more of this group is actually arrested than any other, this underrepresentation serves to defocus attention on discriminatory policies that are placing African-American girls and poor white girls in the criminal justice system. Since we cannot argue against what we are unaware of, the American public may feel that there is no race-related problem associated with American criminal justice.

One more commonality is the depiction of the female delinquents as being very smart. Three-fourths of the films relied on this depiction. It seems to send a message to the viewer that smart girls can outwit the system, as only one film that featured this portrayal also showed a significant punishment. Even in this film, *Crime and Punishment in Suburbia*, RoseAnn doesn't appear to be in a horrendous situation; she even claims she likes her life in the jail. Once again, this depiction may or may not be like reality, but it is definitely not like the figures we know of women and girls who are actually incarcerated. Although not always an indication of someone's intelligence, we do know that most incarcerated people, male or female, are less educated than the general population.

An additional point of analysis made is the lack of accuracy the movies had in regard to the types of offenses portrayed. True to existing content analyses, serious and violent crimes are significantly overrepresented, with all of the films except *Manny and Lo* focusing on this. According to the literature, status offenses are the most frequently occurring acts of female delinquency. These were very rarely portrayed in the movies. Legs, in *Foxfire*, was obviously a runaway and Goldie, in the same movie, also runs away. The only other depiction of this is Dee Dee, in *The Opposite of Sex*. Many of the movies, however, did depict the specific status offense of underage drinking. For example, the girls in *Girls' Town, Set It Off*, and *Foxfire* drank frequently, as did Dee Dee in *The Opposite of Sex*, RoseAnn in *Crime and Punishment in Suburbia*, all of the kids in *The In Crowd*, Mickey and Mallory in *Natural Born Killers*, Susie and Kelly in *Wild Things*, and LeeAnn's friends in *Teaching Mrs. Tingle*. Finally, although the literature says that females are often turned in to the police by their parents, this did not hold true for the movie depictions. In fact, the opposite was more likely. For example, Goldie's dad refused to help the other girls find her when she runs off and shoots up with heroin, then refuses to help her pay for rehab.

We know from the literature that when females kill someone it is typically done alone, as a result of a conflict, and with a weapon other than a gun. Although the last two characteristics generally held true, the females in these films typically acted in groups. For example, the girls worked together in *Foxfire*, RoseAnn had her boyfriend help her kill Fred in *Crime and Punishment in Suburbia*, the girls in *Jawbreaker* worked together, and Mallory killed when she was accompanied by Mickey in *Natural Born Killers*. Aside from Mallory, who killed because she enjoyed it, all other killings were the result of a conflict. *Jawbreaker* was a different kind of conflict, though: a conflict based on jealousy. Mallory, in *Natural Born Killers*, did use a gun, as did the girls in *Set It Off*. The armed robberies and murders depicted in this film were not at all consistent with the literature on how women kill and under what circumstances.

Finally, less than half of the films depict any form of legal consequence for the girl's actions. Those spending time in jail include RoseAnn from *Crime and Punishment in Suburbia*, Legs in *Foxfire*, Dee Dee in *The Opposite of Sex*, and Mallory in *Natural Born Killers*. However, only RoseAnn serves a lengthy term; Legs is released fairly quickly, Dee Dee serves only a six-month sentence, and Mallory escapes after a relatively short time. Two others are depicted as spending time in mental institutions: Darian in *The Crush* and Brittany in *The In Crowd*. Clearly, the lack of consequence for serious crimes can have several effects. First, it may present young viewers with the misconception that "crime pays." Second, it may reinforce fear of female crime in viewers, as it appears that girls are simply "getting away with it." Finally, it may further a law-and-order mentality that deceives viewers into thinking that crime is rampant and nothing is being done about it.

CONCLUSIONS

In sum, although the films studied did include some realistic components, they rely on stereotypical portrayals much of the time. These include stereotypes about female delinquent's sexuality, an overemphasis on serious and violent crimes, a lack of legal consequence for the offender(s), and an image of the female delinquent as a spoiled but smart rich girl. The lack of focus on poor and minority delinquents is definitely not consistent with reality. As Rieman notes, for the same behavior, poor and minority defendants are more likely to be arrested, charged, convicted, sentenced, and sentenced longer than are middle- or upper-class offenders (Rieman, 2000).

It also appears that, while partially applicable, existing content analysis techniques for addressing violent or crime genre films need some revision in order to better apply to female aggressors. Female criminality tends to be enplotted differently than male criminality. Further, Snyder's delinquent subgroups would also need to be redefined or expanded to better cover female delinquency.

As more and more films, television, and advertisements are marketed to teens, America will continue to see an increase in the call for and perceived need for immediate gratification. As Snyder says, "Our present broad socialization encourages youth to follow their impulses—to do whatever attracts them or feels good" (Snyder, 1995b). Movies merely reinforce this, as we've seen here, and may influence other social institutions as well, including families, legal practices, and schools. As Stuart Hall says: "There is no escape from the politics of representation" (Ferrell & Websdale, 1999, introductory page). In sum, "children and adolescents with limited ability to think in the abstract may come away (from movies) with the wrong message" (Snyder, 1995b, p. 336). Wright (1995) has implied that "popular movies describe personalities and promote ways of behaving that are models for what we are supposed to be and the ways we should act" (Snyder, 1995a, p. 55). As Gray Cavender notes: "Movies are entertainment. However, like other aspects of popular culture, movies, especially crime films, do more than entertain. They circulate ideologies—about good and evil, order and disorder—and images of masculinity and femininity" (Ferrell & Websdale, 1999, p. 172). At this point it seems as though these films are indeed promoting ways of behaving for young girls, some of which have some disturbing implications for young viewers as well as for the public at large.

Clearly, learning more about how particular groups are depicted in the media is important on a number of fronts. As most of the existing literature of this nature describes males, work analyzing females can broaden the knowledge in many fields, including criminology, sociology, women's studies, and communications. This type of work can also help create more informed viewers. A final direction that this research supports is a move toward what Barak calls *newsmaking criminology*, where "criminologists integrate themselves into the ongoing mediated construction of crime, develop as part of their role in this process alternative images and understandings of crime issues" (Ferrell & Websdale, 1999, p. 13).

REFERENCES AND BIBLIOGRAPHY

BAILEY, F., & HALE, D. (ED.). (1998). *Popular culture, crime and justice.* Belmont, CA: Wadsworth Publishing.

BOK, S. (1998). *Mayhem.* Reading, PA: Addison-Wesley.

CHESNEY-LIND, M. (1997). *The female offender: Girls, women and crime.* Thousand Oaks, CA: Sage Publications.

CHESNEY-LIND, M., & SHELDEN, R. (1998). *Girls, delinquency and juvenile justice.* Belmont, CA: Wadsworth Publishing.

COSTANZO, M. (1997). *Just revenge.* New York: St. Martin's Press.

COX, S., & CONRAD, J. (1996). *Juvenile justice: A guide to practice and theory* (4th ed.). Madison, WI: Brown & Benchmark.

CSPV fact sheet: Female juvenile delinquency. (2000). *Center for Study and Prevention of Violence.* Accessed September 25, 2000.
www.colorado.edu/UCB/Research/cspv/factsheets/femalejuvenileviolence.html

FERRELL, J., & WEBSDALE, N. (EDS.). (1999). *Making trouble: Cultural constructions of crime, deviance, and control.* New York: Aldine de Gruyter.

FISHMAN, M., & CAVENDER, G. (EDS.). (1998). *Entertaining crime.* New York: Aldine de Gruyter.

LAWRENCE, R. (1998). *School crime and juvenile justice.* New York: Oxford University Press.

LOVELL, J. (2001). Crime and popular culture in the classroom: Approaches and resources for interrogating the obvious. *Journal of Criminal Justice Education, 12*(1), 229–244.

MILLER, S. (ED.). (1998). *Crime control and women.* Thousand Oaks, CA: Sage Publications.

POLAKOW, V. (ED.). (2000). *The public assault on America's children.* New York: Teacher's College.

RIEMAN, J. (2000). *The rich get richer and the poor get prison.* Boston: Allyn & Bacon.

SNYDER, S. (1995a). Movie portrayals of juvenile delinquency: Part 1. Epidemiology and criminology. *Adolescence, 30*(117), 53–64.

SNYDER, S. (1995b). Movie portrayals of juvenile delinquency: Part 2. Sociology and psychology. *Adolescence, 30*(118), 327–337.

SNYDER, S. (1991). Movies and juvenile delinquency: An overview. *Adolescence, 26*(101), 121–132.

SRINIVASAN, K. (2000). Shame on you. ABCNEWS.com. Accessed February 23, 2001
www.abcnews.go.com/sections/entertainment/DailyNews/mediaviolence000910.html

SECTION IX
Conclusions

Conclusions

Roslyn Muraskin

The frequent feeling that women commit only minor crimes masks the trend occurring in today's world: that is, that women are committing more crimes and have become the focus of many studies with regard to women and crime. As described in this book, the pace at which women are being convicted of serious crimes shows that there is a faster pace than in previous years. According to Catherine MacKinnon, " [e]quality in human societies is commonly affirmed but rarely practiced. As a principle, it can be fiercely loved, passionately sought, highly vaunted, sentimentally assumed, complacently taken for granted, and legally guaranteed. Its open detractors are few. Yet despite general consensus on equality as a value, no society is organized on equality principles. Few lives are lived in equality, even in democracies. As a fact, social equality is hard to find anywhere" (2001, p. 2).

In the words of Justice Ruth Bader Ginsburg, "[t]he classification man/dependent woman is the prototypical sex line in the law and has all the earmarks of self-fulfilling prophecy." That discrimination against women is of a long tradition is for us an under-statement. Have we remembered the ladies? Are women not deserving of the same rights and privileges as men?

> Words are more than a collective art; they are simultaneously a collective cage. Unconscious and unquestioned obedience to established meanings binds humankind with steel bands to both the good and the bad of yesterday. Law is called upon to serve goals other than predictability and certainty, which, logic being what it is, walk backwards. The paramount obligation of law is to secure, to make safe, equal rights and justice under the law. This is the daunting task of the remarkably few words which comprise the United States Constitution. (Thomas, 1991, p. xx)

We have come a long way since the days of Rousseau (1906) when he wrote that "[t]he whole education of women ought to be relative to men. To please them, to be useful to them, to make themselves loved and honored by them, to educate them when young, to care for them when grown, to counsel them, to console them, and to make his life sweet and agreeable to them—these are the duties at all times, and what should be taught them from their infancy."

As we have learned throughout this book, women have had to struggle to be considered persons under the law and to be afforded the same opportunities as men before the law. The struggle continues. Man may have been considered to be the protector of woman, but in the world in which we live today, every woman and man deserves to be given the same chance to succeed. History has taught us that women have suffered as much and perhaps more than men. As confirmed in the Declaration of Seneca Falls in 1848: "[T]he history of mankind is a history of repeated injuries and usurpations on the part of man toward woman, having in direct object the establishment of an absolute tyranny over her."

The Fourteenth Amendment to the Constitution of the United States declares that "no state . . . shall . . . deny to any person within its jurisdiction the equal protection of the laws." That amendment is to be applied equally to women and men. Hopefully in today's world, we no longer adhere to the tenets of the words of Justice Brenner as he delivered the majority opinion in the case of *Muller* v. *Oregon* (1908):

> That woman's physical structure and the performance of maternal functions place her at a disadvantage in the struggle for subsistence is obvious. This is especially true when the burdens of motherhood are upon her. . . .
>
> [H]istory discloses the fact that woman has always been dependent upon man. He established his control at the outset by superior physical strength, and the control in various forms. . . . She is properly placed in a class by herself, and legislation designed for her protection may be sustained, even when like legislation is not necessary for men, and could not be sustained.

Admittedly, laws can discriminate, but such discrimination becomes unconstitutional when it is judged to be arbitrary and serves no legitimate purpose. *Frontiero* v. *Richardson* (1973) needed one more vote to declare that *sex was a suspect classification*, although it did concede that differential treatment accorded men and women serves no practical purpose. Women and men are equal before the law—that is sound judicial practice. Today, the attitude of the criminal justice system seems to have changed. We recognize that women are victims of crime and that they, too, perpetuate crime. We recognize that equal treatment is demanded and is an absolute necessity. Having moved from traditional homebound social roles into positions of power and influence, women have become more assertive and aggressive while being capable of competing with men in all realms of life. As noted, litigation, changes in laws, and constitutional amendments have held our criminal justice system to task in demanding that women are properly defined as people and are deserving of all the rights and privileges of men. To do otherwise would make our system of law a public disgrace.

After the impeachment trial of former President Clinton, in which he was acquitted on all charges, it was suggested that sexual matters were now so central to modern life that the courts could not avoid getting more deeply involved in such issues. Others, including some feminists' reaction to the impeachment trial, felt that the concentration on sexual interaction was hurtful to women, having diverted attention from women's rights. Two schools of thought have emerged: Expand the definition of rape, for example, to include other forms of intimidation beyond violence, such as the coercion of women to have sex with men who have power over them—professors, therapists, or lawyers, for example—while others argue that there is too much preoccupation with sexual matters. Regardless of the impact of this historical case, women's rights and privacy continue to be a focal point for discussion.

In the words of MacKinnon (2001), "[u]nless something is done, even if recent rates of measurable progress for elite women continue, no American now alive will live in a society of sex equality, nor will their children or their children's children" (p. 2). She continues, "[s]ex is often guaranteed by law, including where sex inequality is pervasive in society. More imagined than real in life, sex equality in law tends to be more formal or hypothetical than substantive and delivered. In legal application, the meaningfulness of sex equality guarantees varies dramatically, its observance ranging from obvious to anathema. Around the world and throughout history, in settings from the institutional to the intimate, sex equality remains more promise than fact" (p. 3).

In the words of philosopher Richard Rorty, to be a woman "is not yet the name of a way of being human." [Richard Rorty, "Feminism and Pragmatism," in *The Tanner Lectures on Human Values, 1992*(1) 7 (Grethe B. Peterson ed., 1992) (describing MacKinnon's theory)]. His formulation at once recognized that woman's lives would not be "human" by the standards set by men, and that women's reality has not been reflected in the standard for what "human" is. It invites redefinition of the human standard in the image of women's realities and unrealized possibilities, as well as proposes change in women's situation to meet the existing standard of a "human" life. Can one challenge the validity of a standard and assert a right to the benefits of its application to it at the same time? Are women "human"? (p. 3)

Although litigation provides an opportunity for all persons to have a role in altering their conditions of life, a judicial opinion requiring such comprehensive changes does not necessarily bring about such change. We have found that litigation is but a catalyst for change rather than an automatic mechanism for ending wrongs found. We know that within the criminal law, litigation indicates that disparate treatment of any kind is not permissible absent meaningful and objective justification. From Lombroso to the present, "criminological thought has been wrought with the sexism inherent in assuming that there exist two distinct classes of women—those on pedestals and those in the gutter" (Muraskin, 1989).

Throughout history, we have lived with a double standard. Disparate treatment can no longer exist, for it is all about women and men, justice and fairness. And we must never forget the ladies, for then *it will be a crime.*

REFERENCES

MacKinnon, C. A. (2001). *Sex equality*. New York: Foundation Press.
Muraskin, R. (1989). Disparity of correctional treatment: Development of a measurement instrument. Unpublished doctoral dissertation, City University of New York.

Rousseau, J. J. (1906). *Emile, or a treatise on education* (W. H. Payne, Ed.). As found in Cynthia Ozick "Women and Creativity," in Vivian Gornick and Barbara Moran, eds., *Woman in Sexist Society.* New York: Signet 1971.

Thomas, C. S. (1991). *Sex discrimination in a nutshell* (2nd ed.). St. Paul, MN: West Publishing.

CASES

Frontiero v. *Richardson*, 411 U.S. 677 (1973).

Muller v. *Oregon*, 208 U.S. 412 (1908).

Index

❖